1863

JOSEPH E. STEVENS

BANTAM BOOKS

NEW YORK   LONDON   TORONTO
SYDNEY   AUCKLAND

1863

THE REBIRTH OF
A NATION

1863: THE REBIRTH OF A NATION

A Bantam Book / April 1999

Library of Congress Cataloging-in-Publication Data
Stevens, Joseph E. (Joseph Edward), 1956–
1863 : the rebirth of a nation / Joseph E. Stevens.
p.   cm.
Includes bibliographical references and index.
ISBN 0-553-10314-8
1. United States—History—Civil War, 1861–1865. I. Title.
E468.9.S87   1999   98-42414
973.7—dc21   CIP

Published simultaneously in the United States and Canada

PRINTED IN THE UNITED STATES OF AMERICA
BVG   10 9 8 7 6 5 4 3 2 1

Book design by Jennifer Ann Daddio.
Maps by Bette Brodsky.

CONTENTS

Part Four: Fall

For Anastasia and Aaron

The fiery trial through which we pass will light us down, in honor or dishonor, to the latest generation.

—ABRAHAM LINCOLN

Power unanointed may come—
Dominion (unsought by the free)
And the Iron Dome,
Stronger for stress and strain,
Fling her huge shadow athwart the main;
But the Founders' dream shall flee.

—HERMAN MELVILLE

Will the America of the future—will this vast, rich Union ever realize what itself cost back there, after all?

—WALT WHITMAN

America at War

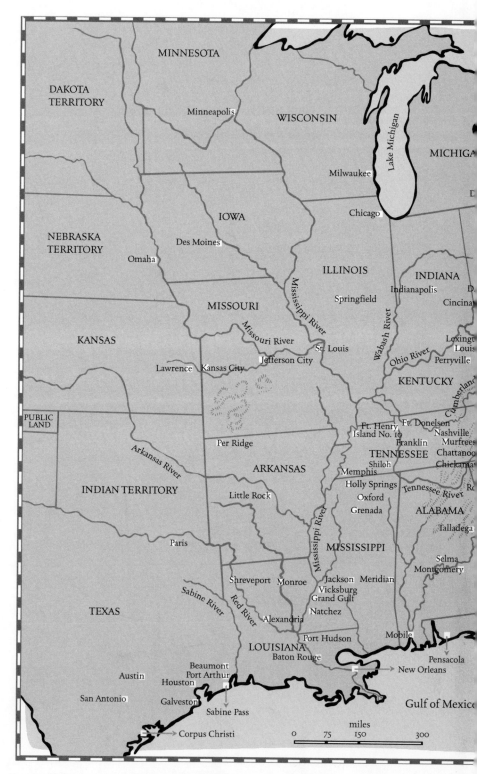

MINNESOTA

DAKOTA
TERRITORY

Minneapolis

WISCONSIN

MICHIGA

Lake Michigan

Milwaukee

IOWA

Chicago

NEBRASKA
TERRITORY

Des Moines

Omaha

ILLINOIS

INDIANA

Springfield

Indianapolis

D.

Cincina

MISSOURI

Mississippi River

Wabash River

Lexingt
Louis

KANSAS

Missouri River

Ohio River

St. Louis

Perryville

Lawrence   Kansas City

Jefferson City

KENTUCKY

PUBLIC
LAND

Cumberland

Per Ridge

Ft. Henry   Ft. Donelson
Island No. 10   Nashville
Franklin   Murfrees
TENNESSEE   Chattanoo

Arkansas River

ARKANSAS

Shiloh   Chickama

Memphis

INDIAN TERRITORY

Little Rock

Holly Springs
Oxford

Tennessee River

Grenada

ALABAMA

Mississippi River

Talladega

Paris

MISSISSIPPI

Selma
Montgomery

Shreveport   Monroe

Jackson   Meridian
Vicksburg
Grand Gulf

Red River

TEXAS

Sabine River

Natchez

Alexandria

Port Hudson

Mobile

LOUISIANA

Baton Rouge

Pensacola

Austin
Port Arthur
Houston
Beaumont

New Orleans

San Antonio

Galveston

Sabine Pass

Gulf of Mexico

Corpus Christi

miles

0   75   150   300

1863

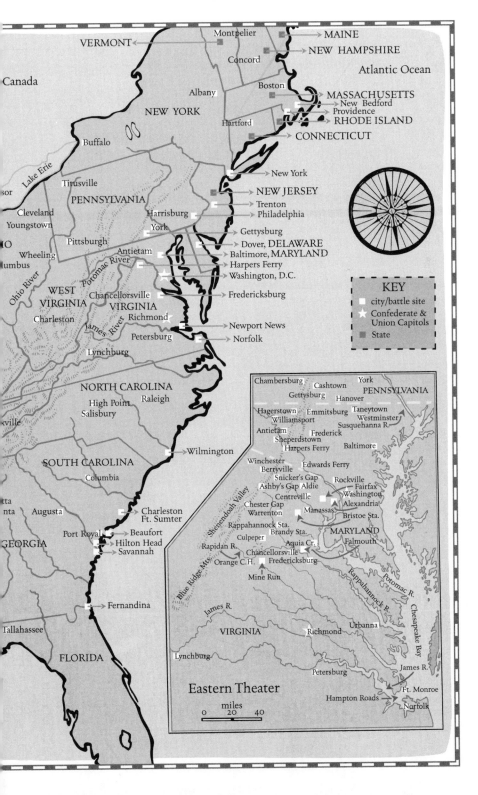

Canada

VERMONT
Montpelier
MAINE
NEW HAMPSHIRE
Concord
Atlantic Ocean
Boston
Albany
MASSACHUSETTS
New Bedford
NEW YORK
Providence
RHODE ISLAND
Hartford
CONNECTICUT
Buffalo
Lake Erie
New York
Titusville
NEW JERSEY
sor
PENNSYLVANIA
Trenton
Cleveland
Harrisburg
Philadelphia
Youngstown
York
IO
Pittsburgh
Gettysburg
Wheeling
Antietam
Dover, DELAWARE
umbus
Potomac River
Baltimore, MARYLAND
Ohio River
Harpers Ferry
WEST
Washington, D.C.
VIRGINIA
Chancellorsville
VIRGINIA
Fredericksburg
Charleston
James River
Richmond
Petersburg
Newport News
Lynchburg
Norfolk

NORTH CAROLINA
Raleigh
High Point
Salisbury
ville

SOUTH CAROLINA
Wilmington
Columbia

tta
Augusta
Charleston
nta
Ft. Sumter
GEORGIA
Port Royal
Beaufort
Hilton Head
Savannah

Fernandina

Tallahassee

FLORIDA

KEY
■ city/battle site
★ Confederate &
Union Capitols
■ State

Eastern Theater

Chambersburg
Cashtown
York
Gettysburg
Hanover
PENNSYLVANIA
Hagerstown
Emmitsburg
Taneytown
Williamsport
Westminster
Susquehanna R.
Antietam
Frederick
Sheperdstown
Baltimore
Harpers Ferry
Winchester
Edwards Ferry
Berryville
Snicker's Gap
Rockville
Ashby's Gap Aldie
Fairfax
Centreville
Washington
Chester Gap
Alexandria
Warrenton
Manassas
Bristoe Sta.
Shenandoah Valley
Rappahannock Sta.
Culpeper
Brandy Sta.
MARYLAND
Rapidan R.
Aquia Cr.
Falmouth
Blue Ridge Mts.
Chancellorsville
Orange C.H.
Fredericksburg
Rappahannock R.
Mine Run
Potomac R.
James R.
Urbanna
VIRGINIA
Richmond
Chesapeake Bay
Lynchburg
Petersburg
James R.
Ft. Monroe
Hampton Roads
Norfolk

miles
0   20   40

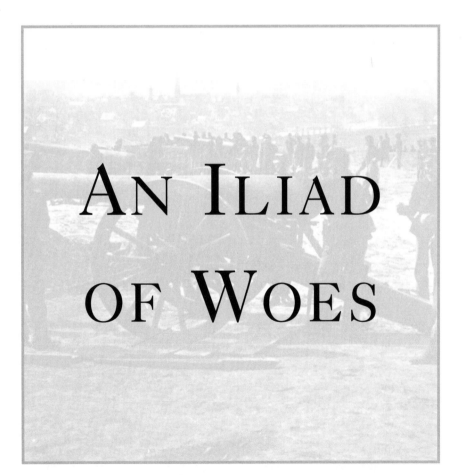

AN ILIAD
OF WOES

WE CANNOT
ESCAPE HISTORY

Dusk of a damp, dreary day in late November 1862. Abraham Lincoln slipped out of the White House and hurried toward the War Department building at the corner of Seventeenth Street and Pennsylvania Avenue. Dressed in an ill-fitting black broadcloth suit and a shabby gray-plaid shawl, he looked like a ghostly undertaker as he glided through the ashen twilight. Arriving at the War Department, he loped up a dimly lit flight of stairs, entered the second-floor telegraph office, and made directly for the cipher desk, where copies of the latest military dispatches were filed in the upper-right-hand drawer awaiting his inspection.

The operator on duty jumped from his chair, saluted smartly, and stepped to one side so the president could more easily get at the thick stack of carbons. Unannounced visits like this were nothing new. Lincoln came at least once, and sometimes two or three times a day, to find out what was happening with the Union armies at the front and to escape the petitioners, office-seekers, and cranks who pestered him incessantly in the White House.

Acknowledging the cipher operator's salute with a nod, he began flipping through the bundle of dispatches, reading the most recent messages. "Well, I guess I have got down to the raisins," he said, as he rearranged the flimsy sheets and returned them to their place in the drawer. Like so many of the odd expressions that spiced his speech, this one came from a humorous story, an anecdote about a little girl who had overeaten, beginning with a bag of raisins. She brought up the contents of her stomach until at last, with a pathetic cry of relief, she announced that her ordeal was almost over, for she had got down to the raisins. "So," Lincoln explained with a wry smile, "when I come to the message in this pile that I saw on my last visit, I know that my troubles are just about through, for I too am down to the raisins."

That there was no fresh intelligence in the stack of telegrams did not surprise him. During the past year and a half, he had spent countless hours in this office awaiting military news, and if the experience had taught him anything, it was that the Union's generals disliked having the commander in chief looking over their shoulders via the telegraph as they fought their battles.

Not that any battles were presently in progress—a fact that troubled Lincoln deeply. For weeks he had been trying without success to spur the Federal armies into action. East to west along a thousand-mile line running from Virginia to the Mississippi River, almost a quarter of a million Union troops were sitting idle while their commanders stockpiled supplies, clamored for reinforcements, and stubbornly refused to come to grips with the enemy.

Vexing as this inactivity was, Lincoln had come to the War Department today not to fret about balky generals but to do some writing. He moved to his accustomed spot, the desk of telegraph-office superintendent Major Thomas Eckert, pulled a sheaf of scribbled-on papers from his coat pocket, and began reading and marking changes in a spiky, slanting scrawl.

The manuscript was a draft of his Annual Message to Congress, which was scheduled to reconvene on December 1. Like his recalcitrant generals, the returning legislators were a chronic source of worry and irritation to Lincoln. Early in his presidency, when the war was just beginning, he had hoped that they might suspend their partisan bickering and close ranks behind him. But the eruption of finger-pointing and second-guessing that accompanied the outbreak of hostilities had quickly dispelled that notion. Nowadays it seemed to him that all that the senators and representatives really cared about was making his life miserable. He would have been hard-pressed to say which faction was worse: the antiwar Democrats, called "Copperheads" after a particularly vi-

Abraham Lincoln and his private secretaries, John G. Nicolay (left) and John Hay (right). (Courtesy U.S. Army Military History Institute)

cious species of poisonous snake, or the radical Republicans, dubbed the "Jacobins" by his private secretary John Hay, who thought they resembled the bloodthirsty fanatics who had perpetrated the Reign of Terror during the French Revolution.

So scathing had congressional criticism of Lincoln's administration become that even he, with skin thickened by thirty years in Illinois state politics, had to wince sometimes in pained astonishment. The Copperheads accused him of being an iron-fisted despot intent on using the war to establish a dictatorship. They wanted to bring about an immediate, unconditional cease-fire and negotiate a peace settlement favorable to the South. The Republican radicals, on the other hand, charged that he was an irresolute good-for-nothing unwilling to prosecute the war harshly enough. Stern, self-righteous, and itching for power, they were hell-bent on usurping his executive authority.

Lincoln told a group of White House visitors that he felt like the celebrated tightrope walker Blondin trying to carry a sack of gold across Niagara Falls. "Would you shake the cable," he asked his callers, "or keep shouting out to him 'Blondin, stand up a little straighter!' 'Blondin, stoop a little more!' 'Go a little faster'; 'Lean a little more to the north'; 'Lean a little more to the south'? No. You would hold your breath as well as your tongue and keep your hands off until he was safe over."

He knew his scolding would have little effect. The congressmen coming back from recess would be eager to find fault and offer unwanted advice. It was his duty to listen patiently, and then try to steer them and the country in the direction he wanted to go, beginning with the document he was working on today.

The Annual Message (which in later years would be known as the State of the Union Address) consisted of a detailed account of the nation's affairs during the twelve months past. It was also an important political vehicle, a once-a-year opportunity for the president to spell out his legislative program, plead for congressional support, and try to rally public opinion to his side.

There was great need for rallying, of that Lincoln was sure. After twenty months of war, the South remained defiant. It was, if anything, stronger than it had been when hostilities began. Northerners now realized that even if victory were achieved, it would not bring the hoped-for result: reestablishment of the antebellum status quo. Instead of restoring the past, the war was inexorably destroying it.

Lincoln understood the public's fear of the unknown. He too shrank from the unwanted, unfathomable consequences of so cataclysmic an upheaval. Yet he believed there could be no turning back. At stake was nothing less than the success or failure of the American experiment in self-government. If the vision of America's Founding Fathers was to be vindicated, if the transcendent idea of government of, by, and for the people was to survive and flourish, then the principle of majority rule and the Union that embodied it had to be saved. "The central idea," he had written early in the war, "is the necessity of proving that popular government is not an absurdity. We must settle this question now, whether in a free government the minority have the right to break up the government whenever they choose."

If the people of the South were allowed to repudiate the results of the 1860 presidential election and set up a separate country because they did not wish to abide by the will of the majority, it would mean the end of democracy in America. Secession, if countenanced, would lead to unchecked subdividing along regional and political lines. It would result in anarchy and, he feared, a return to autocratic rule. In 1776 Americans had shrugged off the autocrat's yoke and begun the work of creating a new nation founded on the principles of liberty and equality and dedicated to the idea that men should be masters of their own destiny. Now the future of that nation was in doubt. Lincoln was convinced that the coming year would be decisive—as pivotal in the life of the nation as 1776 had been. In 1863 the North would either move resolutely to put down the rebellion, restore the Union, and bring about a national rebirth, or the Confederacy would triumph and the Founders' dream would die.

With a weary sigh he rocked back in his chair, hoisted his feet onto Major Eckert's desk, and ran his fingers through his bristly black hair. "The will of God prevails," he had written in September as he pondered the ramifications of a war without limits and admitted to himself that he was no longer controlling events. It was a frightening, yet strangely comforting thought. He was not a religious man in the churchgoing sense. He had, in fact, been accused of being a closet skeptic. But he sincerely believed in an overruling Providence, a Supreme Being who endowed people with individual destinies and impelled them to action by His influence on their minds.

What, he wondered, was Providence's design for him and for the country? "In great contests each party claims to act in accordance with the will of God," he had written as he groped toward an answer. "Both *may* be, and one *must* be wrong. God cannot be *for,* and *against* the same thing at the same time. In the present civil war it is quite possible that God's purpose is something different from the purpose of either party—and yet the human instrumentalities, working just as they do, are of the best adaptation to effect His purpose. I am almost ready to say this is probably true—that God wills this contest, and wills that it shall not end yet."

The contest had been proceeding since the winter of 1860–61, when three decades of strife between North and South over the future of slavery and the nature of federalism had finally exploded into open conflict. Convinced that Lincoln's election meant the loss of their liberty, property, and honor — South Carolina, Mississippi, Florida, Alabama, Georgia, Louisiana, and Texas seceded from the Union and formed a new nation, the Confederate States of America, headed by Jefferson Davis.

Lincoln responded by branding secession illegal and vowing to defend United States military installations located on Southern soil. This pledge made an armed showdown inevitable. It came on April 12, 1861, when Confederate forces fired on Fort Sumter in Charleston Harbor. After Sumter fell, Lincoln called on the Northern states to furnish the national government with 75,000 troops to assist the 16,000-man regular army in putting down the insurrection. This in turn led Virginia, Tennessee, Arkansas, and North Carolina to cast their lot with the Confederacy. Anticipating a short, splendid war, tens of thousands of eager volunteers rushed to the colors, fired by romantic visions of adventure and glory.

The war turned out to be neither short nor glorious. A series of battles fought in 1861 and 1862 produced horrifying casualty lists but not decisive results. The "great eagle-scream" of patriotism that had greeted the call to arms in the spring of 1861 trailed off into a croaking squawk of protest in the fall of 1862. This was especially true in the North, where it had been widely assumed that the Union's overwhelming preponderance in men and matériel would lead to an easy victory. As it became clear that there would be no walkover, grumbling increased, enlistment declined, and sullen voters delivered a stinging rebuke to the Lincoln administration in the 1862 congressional elections. "The people have furnished men and means in abundance for all purposes to conquer the enemy, but after a year and a half of trial . . . we have made no sensible progress," an embittered Union supporter wrote.

Lincoln could readily sympathize with this sentiment. He was by temperament and training a lawyer and a politician, not a warlord. His firsthand experience of soldiering had been limited to a six-week stint as a captain of volunteers in the Black Hawk Indian War of 1832. Yet more than any of the West Pointers who presumed to instruct him on strategic matters, he possessed the instincts of a warrior: the urge to move fast, hit hard, and not let up until the enemy was crushed. He knew there had been too much hesitating at the highest levels of Union command, too much concern for planning and preparation and not enough for marching and fighting. As 1862 drew to a close, he began discarding the worst of the laggards.

First to go was Major General Don Carlos Buell, who had been appointed commander of the Army of the Ohio back in November 1861. Again and again Buell had been directed to advance into east Tennessee and rescue the pro-Union population there from rebel oppression. Each time he had refused, citing muddy roads and insurmountable logistical problems. Finally, after a ten-month delay, he had begun to advance toward Chattanooga, only to retreat when a small force of Confederates moved to oppose him. At the Battle of Perryville, fought on October 8, 1862, he had blocked a rebel thrust into Kentucky, but then declined to pursue his retiring foe. Two weeks later Lincoln fired him and gave his command to a more aggressive officer, Major General William S. Rosecrans.

The man who had been Rosecrans's superior, Major General Ulysses S. Grant, was another hard fighter. In February 1862 he had captured Fort Henry on the Tennessee River and Fort Donelson on the Cumberland. Then he had moved south to Shiloh near the Tennessee-Mississippi border and slugged it out with the rebels for two gore-drenched days in April. In the wake of this bloodbath, horrified critics accused him of being a drunken butcher. Lincoln thought otherwise; he rebuffed calls for the general's scalp with the stark observation: "I can't spare this man. He fights."

Now Grant was readying his Army of the Tennessee for a campaign against Vicksburg, the Confederate citadel on the Mississippi River. The president meant to stick with him, although he intended to hedge his bet in case the persistent rumors about Grant's addiction to alcohol proved true. The capture of Vicksburg, which would give the Union undisputed control of the Mississippi and cut the Confederacy in half, was too important an objective to be entrusted entirely to a man whose sobriety was suspect, so Lincoln approved two additional plans for seizing the strategically vital stronghold. The first involved a thrust upriver from New Orleans, to be led by Major General Nathaniel P. Banks, former member of the House of Representatives and former governor of Massachusetts. The second would be a downriver foray directed by another ex-congressman, Major General John McClernand of Illinois. Satisfied that this trio of expeditions would take Vicksburg, Lincoln turned his attention eastward, where the preeminent source of his displeasure with army leadership—Major General George Brinton McClellan—lay, or to be more accurate, sat, while the fall campaign season slipped away.

On September 17, 1862, McClellan had vanquished a Confederate army at Antietam in west-central Maryland. But then, instead of moving swiftly to smash the reeling rebels, he had bivouacked near the battlefield, offering one excuse after another why he and his soldiers could not ad-

vance into Virginia and force a final, decisive battle. When the president finally decreed a southward movement, McClellan complied so slowly that
the Confederates had ample time to place their by-now rejuvenated divisions squarely in his path. Disgusted, Lincoln cashiered McClellan on November 7. Command of the Army of the Potomac passed to Major
General Ambrose E. Burnside.

The president hoped that a tough, realistic strategy for winning the war
would emerge now that the high priests of procrastination were gone. Simultaneous assaults against the rebel armies guarding Richmond, Chattanooga, and Vicksburg were what he had in mind. It was an exhilarating
prospect, and his mood brightened considerably. He was even able to
chuckle when he read about the acid-tongued Washingtonian who remarked that the shake-up in the Union high command was long overdue—that the North might now hope to defeat the Confederacy "some
time within the present century."

Lincoln's high hopes were soon dashed. Instead of burning hot, fast, and
true, the fuse he had lit flickered weakly, then fizzled and died. The
concerted triple attack against the three Confederate armies failed to materialize. As the final weeks of 1862 rolled by, he watched with disbelief,
dissolving into dismay, as one after another the generals he had selected for
their energy and aggressiveness let him down.

The first to fail was Nathaniel Banks. After receiving his orders from
the War Department on November 8, he announced that he was embarking at once for Louisiana, where he would lose no time advancing up the
Mississippi toward Vicksburg. Two weeks later Lincoln was shocked to see
a requisition that Banks—in New York City, not New Orleans—had submitted to Quartermaster General Montgomery Meigs. He was asking for a
vast quantity of supplies as well as a giant herd of horses and mules to haul
it all. It was an outrageous request, and the president dashed off a letter to
Banks telling him so. The general replied that the requisition was a mistake
and repeated his promise to depart at once. But he did not set sail for another two weeks. It was nearly Christmas before he reached New Orleans
and took command of his expeditionary force.

By then Lincoln's attention had been diverted to another mess caused
by his own misguided attempt to mix politics and military strategy in the
western theater. In late September John McClernand had taken a leave of
absence from the Army of the Tennessee and come east to confer with the
president and Secretary of War Edwin Stanton. A crisis was brewing in the
farm country of Indiana, Iowa, and his native Illinois, he told the two men.

Because the Mississippi River was closed to commercial navigation, western farmers had to rely on railroads to move their agricultural products to eastern ports for shipment to overseas markets. Greedy rail magnates had taken advantage of the situation by raising freight rates sky high, hurting the West's economy and provoking a powerful upsurge of peace-at-any-price sentiment. McClernand complained that Grant was moving too slowly to dislodge the rebels and get river traffic flowing normally again. He wanted the president's permission to raise an army among his Democratic supporters in Illinois. With this force he would break the Confederate stranglehold on the lower Mississippi and deliver the farmers of his native section from the clutches of the eastern railroad barons, thus saving the West for the Union and hastening the end of the war.

Lincoln was well aware of McClernand's political ambition. He suspected that the ex-congressman's scheme was inspired by his desire to be the next Democratic presidential nominee rather than by genuine concern for the welfare of his former constituents. He approved the plan, however, reasoning that if western Democrats were busy fighting Confederates, they would have little energy left for attacking his administration.

Grant, meanwhile, was getting ready to embark on his own campaign against Vicksburg. He intended to take the bulk of the Army of the Tennessee into central Mississippi, then wheel west toward his objective. At the same time a corps commanded by his trusted subordinate, William T. Sherman, would float downriver from Memphis, land just above Vicksburg, and assault the rebel stronghold from that direction. If all went according to plan, Grant's thrust would draw the Confederates out of their fortifications, allowing Sherman to slice through and take the city.

Preparations for the offensive were almost complete in early November when Grant learned that dozens of new regiments claiming to be under the command of John McClernand were arriving in Memphis. Upset by this challenge to his authority, Grant wired Washington for an explanation. Union general in chief Henry Halleck assured Grant that he was still in charge and urged him to use the fresh troops as he saw fit. Grant promptly ordered Sherman to round up all of McClernand's regiments and set out for Vicksburg as soon as he could assemble a fleet of transports. Then he put his own army in motion, marching to the town of Oxford in the north-central portion of the Magnolia State.

Now it was McClernand's turn to be upset: his Praetorian Guard was advancing to battle under someone else's banner. His army had been stolen, he raged. He wanted it back, and he also wanted his status as an independent commander spelled out unequivocally to Halleck and Grant. This outburst made it clear to Lincoln that he had blundered when he gave his blessing to McClernand's self-serving scheme. He informed the apoplectic

Illinoisan that he was to head a corps rather than an autonomous army, and that instead of operating independently, he was to take orders from Grant.

The other generals Lincoln had recently promoted were having problems as well. In the east Ambrose Burnside was telling anyone who would listen that he was not qualified to command the Army of the Potomac. Many of his subordinates agreed with him, and on Capitol Hill there was talk of bringing McClellan back. Lincoln had to admit that Burnside was off to an inauspicious start, but at least he meant well and was, in sharp contrast to his sluggish predecessor, trying to execute a prompt, vigorous offensive against the rebels in Virginia.

The same could not be said of William Rosecrans in Tennessee. Instead of attacking the enemy as Lincoln had ordered, he had moved the Army of the Ohio, now redesignated the Army of the Cumberland, to Nashville and begun amassing supplies. The White House and the War Department pleaded and threatened, to no avail: Rosecrans insisted that he would not advance until he was ready.

That was where matters stood as the old year drew to a close and the new one approached. A repeat of 1862, with its dreadful casualties and ruinous military failures, would give rise to a burgeoning peace movement at home and to a push abroad for diplomatic recognition of the Confederacy. Lincoln had tried to forestall these developments by appealing to the public for faith in the prowess of Union arms and by issuing a preliminary Emancipation Proclamation, aimed in part at keeping England and France from siding with the South and slavery. Neither effort appeared to have been successful. The results of the fall elections showed that voters were losing confidence in the North's ability to win the war. As for the preliminary proclamation, it had been greeted with hoots of derision in the capitals of Europe. Battlefield victories—real ones, not glorified standoffs like Antietam and Perryville—were needed to turn things around. But so far not one of the three major offensives the president had envisioned when he reshuffled his high command had come to pass, and like King Sisyphus, condemned for eternity to roll a heavy boulder uphill without ever reaching the top, Lincoln was sensing that all his labors might prove in vain. "I certainly have been dissatisfied with the slowness of Buell and McClellan," he wrote on November 24, "but before I relieved them I had great fears I should not find successors to them who would do better; and I am sorry to add that I have seen little since to relieve these fears."

These words were calm and measured, but the anguish and exhaustion they concealed were clearly etched on the face of their author. "His hair is grizzled, his gait more stooping, his countenance sallow, and there is a sunken, deathly look about the large, cavernous eyes," wrote newspaperman Noah Brooks. And yet Lincoln refused to quit. "I know very well that many others might . . . do better than I can," he told his cabinet, "and if I were satisfied that the public confidence was more fully possessed by any one of them than by me, and knew of any Constitutional way in which he could be put in my place, he should have it. I would gladly yield it to him. But . . . there is no way in which I can have any other man put where I am. I am here. I must do the best I can, and bear the responsibility of taking the course which I feel I ought to take."

The first step was to issue the Emancipation Proclamation in its final form on January 1, 1863. By freeing slaves in the rebellious states, Lincoln would not only be weakening the Confederate war effort, he would be unleashing the moral force of an idea so powerful that, four score and seven years earlier, it had driven the world's mightiest empire to its knees. He would make the idea of freedom—not the finite, conditional freedom of the Constitution, but the sweeping, unlimited freedom of the Declaration of Independence—the Union's sword and buckler. In so doing, he would turn the war into a revolutionary struggle, one that would not end until the South had been "destroyed and replaced by new propositions and ideas."

There was still a chance that slave-owning Southerners might heed the warning implicit in the preliminary proclamation, accept Lincoln's long-standing offer of gradual, compensated emancipation, and end the rebellion before January 1, 1863. He intended to make this offer one last time in his December message to Congress. But the likelihood of its being seriously considered, much less embraced, was extremely remote. He expected to sign the final Emancipation Proclamation on New Year's Day, and he harbored no illusions about the profound consequences this action would have. It was a radical step requiring explanation and justification, both to the present and future generations, and he was determined not to shirk that responsibility. Hence the hours he spent toiling in the telegraph office or in his White House "workshop," composing the Annual Message, which would be read to Congress on December 1.

The printed text was almost twenty pages long, a fact that bothered Lincoln. He tried hard to avoid prolix speeches, preferring to cut to the heart of an issue whenever possible. Once, when asked to give a patriotic address on the occasion of a flag raising, he had stunned the assembly by uttering exactly one sentence: "The part assigned to me is to raise the flag, which, if there be no fault in the machinery, I will do, and when up, it will be for the people to keep it up."

Pithiness of that sort was not possible in a hybrid document like the Annual Message, which lumped together formal reports on the activities of the executive branch with the discretionary remarks of the president. It was a cumbersome combination, but custom and the dictates of the Constitution required it; hence the manuscript's length.

The message began with an excruciatingly dry discussion of foreign relations, followed by an equally dull report on the state of the national finances. It continued in this vein, turgid and tiresome, until suddenly at midpoint its tone shifted and its pace quickened. " 'One generation passeth away, and another generation cometh, but the earth abideth forever,' " Lincoln declaimed, or rather the House and Senate clerks did, for in keeping with a tradition established by Thomas Jefferson, the president did not deliver the message in person. "That portion of the earth's surface which is owned and inhabited by the people of the United States is well adapted to be the home of one national family; and it is not well adapted for two, or more." This was the geographical argument for union, and Lincoln buttressed it by quoting a passage from his inaugural address. " 'Physically speaking we cannot separate. We cannot remove our respective sections from each other, nor build an impassable wall between them.' "

He then spelled out his plan for gradual emancipation, proposing that the Constitution be amended to provide that every state that abolished slavery before January 1, 1900, be compensated for each slave counted in the eighth national census. He knew this program would be abhorrent to the advocates of perpetual slavery, but, he argued, "the length of time [to implement it fully] should greatly mitigate their dissatisfaction. The time spares both races from the evils of sudden derangement—in fact, from the necessity of any derangement."

Having extended an olive branch, he now brandished the sword, lest his talk of an accommodation be misconstrued as an admission of weakness. The war would continue and the Emancipation Proclamation would take effect, unless the South agreed to his plan and returned to the Union.

The message was at last drawing to a close, and so too, Lincoln suspected, was a long chapter in the life of the nation. He had tried to effect a reconciliation, but all his instincts told him the effort was in vain. Ahead lay total war, and beyond that a perilous, inscrutable future.

"The dogmas of the quiet past are inadequate to the stormy present," he observed, half in sorrow, half in defiance. "The occasion is piled high with difficulty, and we must rise with the occasion. As our case is new, so we must think anew and act anew. We must disenthrall ourselves, and then we shall save our country."

The speech was over, or so it seemed, and a smattering of applause spilled from the packed galleries. But the noise died down abruptly when the clerk took a deep breath, adjusted the pages he held in front of him, and read on.

And now in stark, stately phrases, following one on the other in a powerful, almost scriptural rhythm, came the great trumpet call summoning the nation to its rendezvous with destiny in 1863: "Fellow-citizens, we cannot escape history. We of this Congress and this administration, will be re-membered in spite of ourselves. No personal significance, or insignificance, can spare one or another of us. The fiery trial through which we pass will light us down, in honor or dishonor, to the latest generation. We say we are for the Union. The world will not forget that we say this. We know how to save the Union. The world knows we do know how to save it. We—even we here—hold the power and bear the responsibility. In giving free-dom to the slave, we assure freedom to the free—honorable alike in what we give and what we preserve. We shall nobly save or meanly lose the last, best hope of earth."

A FAITHFUL SENTINEL

The Honorable Jefferson Davis, president and commander in chief of the army and navy of the Confederate States of America, stood at the podium in the representatives' hall of the Mississippi state capital. It was Friday, December 26, 1862, and a pale winter sun hovered over the city of Jackson. Its cool light streamed through the chamber's high windows, reflected off the lofty ceiling, and bathed the speakers' platform with a wan, milky glow.

The audience—state legislators, government officials, distinguished citizens of Jackson—filled the rows of desks stretching back from the rostrum and packed the lobby and overhanging gallery until there was scarcely room to move. There was none of the shifting, rustling, and whispering that usually attended a speech in the chamber. All eyes were on the tall, gaunt man who stood before them, elegant in a black broadcloth suit, gray satin vest, and black silk scarf knotted loosely around a stiff white collar. They searched anxiously for telltale marks of strain and weariness in the familiar face. The strong, handsome line of the jaw was unchanged, as were the high cheekbones, aquiline nose, and prominent forehead; but the thin, tightly drawn lips and the dark eyes, one clouded and sightless, the other sunken and haunted, were those of a death's-head.

"After an absence of nearly two years, I again find myself among those who, from the

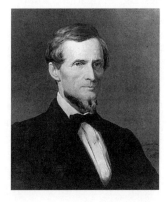

Jefferson Davis.
(Courtesy The Museum of the
Confederacy, Richmond, Virginia)

days of my childhood, have ever been the trusted objects of my affection," Davis began, slowly swiveling his head from left to right so his good eye could make contact with each of his listeners. "The responsibilities of [the presidency] have occupied all my time and have left me no opportunity for mingling with my friends in Mississippi or for sharing in the dangers which have menaced them. But wherever duty may have called me, my heart has been with you, and the success of the cause in which we are all engaged has been first in my thoughts and prayers."

In fact, it was the failure, not the success, of that cause that had brought him on the twelve-hundred-mile rail journey from the capital at Richmond to his war-torn home state. The Confederacy's strategy for winning independence—defending Southern soil from Yankee incursions, counterattacking when the opportunity arose, baffling and bleeding Union forces in an effort to wear down the North's resolve—was working in the East, where Robert E. Lee and his hard-fighting Army of Northern Virginia had confounded all of the enemy's attempts to capture Richmond. But here, in the region Davis referred to as "the further West," the military situation was deteriorating rapidly.

It was an alarming, and to Davis, intensely frustrating state of affairs. At the war's outbreak he had hoped to lead Mississippians in the field, the task for which his West Point training and distinguished service in the Mexican War had prepared him. Instead he had been elected president of the newly formed Confederate government, and now he was stuck discharging the difficult and often distasteful duties of the chief executive while others conducted the defense of his beloved Magnolia State.

"I was called to another sphere of action," he told his listeners by way of explanation and apology. "How, in that sphere, I have discharged the duties and obligations imposed on me, it does not become me to constitute myself the judge. But . . . I can say with my hand upon my heart that whatever I have done has been done with the sincere purpose of promoting the noble cause in which we are engaged. The period which has elapsed since I left you is short. . . . And in that short period remarkable changes have been wrought in all the circumstances by which we are surrounded."

Here he paused, as though to give his listeners a chance to hark back to the spring of 1861, the season that had seen the birth of the new nation and the onset of war, events less than two years old but already so distant that they seemed to belong to a different epoch. The high hopes and fervid emotions of those days had been twisted and battered by developments few could have foreseen. And now Mississippi itself was in mortal danger, facing subjugation at the hands of a Yankee horde, and its people were looking to Davis for deliverance.

At this critical juncture could you not visit the army of the West?" Mississippi governor J. J. Pettus had telegraphed the president in early December. His appeal was quickly followed by an importunate letter from Mississippi senator James Phelan. "The present alarming crisis in this state, so far from arousing the people, seems to have sunk them in listless despondency," Phelan wrote. "The spirit of enlistment is thrice dead. Enthusiasm has expired to a cold pile of damp ashes. . . . If ever your presence was needed as a last refuge from an 'Iliad of woes,' this is the hour."

Davis decided to heed Phelan's plea and embark on a tour of the western theater, boosting civilian morale and inspiriting the two main armies assigned to defend this part of the Confederacy. The first of these, the Army of Tennessee commanded by Braxton Bragg, was encamped around Murfreesboro, near the geographic center of the Volunteer State. The second, the Army of Mississippi under John C. Pemberton, was entrenched some 250 miles to the southwest along the Yalobusha River, near the town of Grenada in north-central Mississippi. Both armies were outnumbered, and both were bedeviled by dissension and disarray.

Back in November Davis had tried to remedy the problem of insufficient manpower by appointing an overall theater commander to coordinate the activities of the two forces. He hoped this officer would take advantage of interior lines to shift troops between threatened points in Tennessee and Mississippi. His choice for the post was Major General Joseph E. Johnston, who was now almost entirely recovered from a shoulder wound received six months earlier at the Battle of Seven Pines. Johnston had accepted the appointment as commander of the newly formed Department of the West with reluctance. He did not think the president's idea of shuttling troops back and forth between Bragg's and Pemberton's armies would work, and when he arrived in Chattanooga, where his headquarters was to be located, he complained that his position was nominal and useless.

Johnston's balkiness disappointed Davis. Instead of working to solve the problems in his department, he seemed intent on compounding them, making direct presidential intervention more, not less, necessary. Davis had not wanted to leave Richmond. He was ill with dyspepsia and neuralgia brought on by tension and fatigue. He was also deeply concerned about the threat to the Confederate capital posed by the Army of the Potomac, bivouacked only fifty-five miles away at Falmouth on the Rappahannock River. He feared that his sudden departure might cause panic among Richmond's citizens. But he decided that he had no choice. Important as the capital was, the western heartland with its stocks of food, manpower, and matériel was even more indispensable.

And so on December 10 he rose from his sickbed, bade his wife and children good-bye, and sallied forth to engineer a turnaround in the West. Slipping out of Richmond in a private rail car, he rode to Lynchburg, Virginia, then southwest across the Blue Ridge Mountains into Tennessee, stopping briefly at Knoxville before traveling on to Chattanooga, where Johnston awaited him.

The short, balding general with the bristling white side whiskers and grizzled goatee greeted the president in his cramped quarters, and while his wife Lydia served coffee—"Real Rio," she proudly told a friend afterward, not the ersatz brew that had become a staple in the blockade-pinched Confederacy—he confessed to suffering from a recurrence of pain in his shoulder. Davis was genuinely sympathetic. Johnston's wound had been severe and his medical treatment, consisting of "bleedings, blisterings, and depletions of the system," long and grueling. But try as he might, he could not keep the frostiness out of his voice or bring himself to make some gesture that would lessen the antipathy that was clouding what should have been a relaxed, cordial exchange.

The two men, so similar in background and temperament, despised each other. The bad blood between them was said to date back to their cadet days at West Point, when they had vied for the favor of the same girl and Johnston had vanquished Davis in a fistfight. While the accuracy of this story was open to question, other more recent squabbles were well documented. Thus their colloquy in Chattanooga was exceedingly stiff and awkward, and Davis ended it as quickly as propriety would allow. He suggested that Johnston rest while he, Davis, went on ahead to see the Army of Tennessee for himself. They would discuss strategy when he returned in three days' time.

General Joseph E. Johnston, C.S.A. (Brady Collection, National Archives; photo courtesy of The Museum of the Confederacy, Richmond, Virginia)

The following morning, December 12, the president journeyed northwest to Murfrees-boro. Here, only thirty miles from the Union bastion at Nashville, he was pleased to find no lack of martial spirit. A boisterous crowd was on hand to greet him, and he made a rousing speech in which he promised that Tennessee would be held to the last extremity. He was further heartened the next day, when he reviewed an army corps drawn up on a parade ground on the outskirts of town. The soldiers were well dressed and well equipped, and he was deeply gratified by the way they cheered him as he rode past.

The final and most delicate part of his two-day inspection trip came that evening, when he met with his friend and fellow West Pointer, Braxton Bragg. Many in the Confederate government blamed Bragg for everything that had gone wrong militarily in the West. Davis was inclined to discount this criticism, although he did recognize that the general had faults, the worst being his extreme, almost pathological contentiousness. An apocryphal story was told about Bragg as a young officer assigned to an isolated frontier post, where because of the small size of the garrison, he was required to serve both as company commander and as quartermaster. He had submitted a request for supplies as company commander and then as quartermaster had turned himself down. "My God, Mr. Bragg," the exasperated post commandant had exclaimed, "you have quarreled with every other officer in the army, and now you are quarreling with yourself!"

But being a perfectionist in his own right, Davis was not about to condemn Bragg for insisting that regulations be followed to the letter. No Southern general was a stricter disciplinarian; no one set higher standards of performance for his junior officers or drilled his enlisted men more relentlessly than did the glowering, gray-bearded, forty-six-year-old North Carolinian. Brevetted three times for gallantry in the Mexican War, he had performed ably, if not brilliantly, at Shiloh. Following that bloody battle, he had rebuilt the shattered Army of Tennessee and led it on a bold, albeit unsuccessful, foray into Kentucky. If, as one disgruntled enlistee wrote, "not a single soldier in the whole army ever loved or respected him," that was a small price to pay in Davis's estimation for creating a tough, taut fighting force. Besides, he knew that Bragg suffered from debilitating headaches, and as a martyr to migraines himself, he was only too aware of the painful effects such a malady could have on a man's personality.

The evening conference went well. Everyone in attendance agreed that the Union army would not venture out of Nashville anytime soon. On the basis of this judgment, Davis made a snap decision. General Carter Stevenson's division—about 7,500 soldiers—would be detached from Bragg's command and sent west to reinforce Pemberton.

Bragg was distressed by the sudden weakening of his army, but his upset was minor compared with Johnston's when he learned what the president had done. This precipitous move, made without any consultation, seemed to confirm Johnston's suspicion that his new post was worthless. As if this humiliation weren't bad enough, he honestly believed that the troop transfer was a blunder. In his opinion, diminishing Bragg's already inadequate force placed middle Tennessee in jeopardy and risked the loss of the vital rail junction at Chattanooga.

Davis's mind was made up, however, and he was unapologetic about stepping on his theater commander's toes. It was precisely for the purpose of shifting forces back and forth that he had appointed Johnston, and if the stiff-necked Virginian was unwilling to shoulder the responsibility, then Davis, as commander in chief, would do it for him. In any case he had more important things to worry about than Johnston's fragile ego. Dispatches had been received from the War Department reporting that the Army of the Potomac had crossed the Rappahannock and was attacking Lee's force, which was entrenched on a low ridge just west of the town of Fredericksburg. "If the necessity demands, I will return to Richmond," Davis wrote his wife, Varina.

Necessity did not demand. A telegram arrived announcing that the Army of Northern Virginia had won a smashing victory, killing or wounding more than 10,000 Federals while suffering fewer than 5,000 casualties itself. The president was elated and deeply relieved. Johnston could summon nothing but sour grapes, however, when he read the account of Lee's lopsided triumph. "What luck some people have," he petulantly wrote. "Nobody will ever come to attack me in such a place."

Late on the afternoon of December 16, the reinvigorated president and his disgruntled theater commander departed for Mississippi. Because the Federals controlled the Memphis & Charleston line where it entered the Magnolia State at Iuka, they were obliged to take a circuitous route, traveling southeast to Atlanta, then south to Montgomery and Mobile before heading north and west to Meridian and Jackson. They finally arrived in Vicksburg on the evening of the nineteenth, having spent nearly seventy-two hours completing a trip that would have taken a single day in peacetime.

The "Queen City of the Bluffs," as Vicksburg was known to its 4,500 residents, looked more like a down-at-the-heels dowager than royalty in the dim December twilight. Perched two hundred feet above the eastern bank of the Mississippi, just downstream from a point where the river inscribed a tight horseshoe bend in the muddy bottomland, the town straggled across an unprepossessing range of gully-slashed loess hills. Founded in 1813 by Methodist minister Newet Vick, the community had few of the pretensions of its more aristocratic downstream neighbor, Natchez. It was a working city devoted to the buying and selling of cotton grown in the fertile Yazoo Delta and to the care and feeding of the boatmen who toiled on the Mississippi. Long rows of rat-infested warehouses, interspersed with dilapidated stevedores' shacks, lined the waterfront. Up the bluff, parallel to the river, ran Washington Street, the town's main thoroughfare, a slatternly strip of bars and bawdy houses rouged with red mud, powdered with yellow dust, and perfumed with the pungent scents of woodsmoke and mule dung. On the high ground above Washington Street stood the large public structures: the redbrick convent of the Sisters of Mercy, the sharp-steepled St. Paul's Catholic Church, the Gothic-towered Christ Episcopal Church, the square-belfried Methodist Church, and dominating all, the colonnaded, cupola-crowned Warren County Courthouse. Along the tree-lined lanes in this part of town were located the handful of Greek Revival mansions that gave Vicksburg what little tone it could muster and made it possible for the more well-to-do residents to say, straight-faced, that their city was "a place of education, culture, and luxury."

While Vicksburg lacked the Old World cachet of Charleston or the patrician dignity of Richmond, it was more important from a strategic standpoint than either of those places. It was, quite simply, the key to controlling the Mississippi. As long as Confederate guns frowned down from the bluffs, the great river would remain closed to commercial traffic. Holding the city also meant keeping open a 150-mile-wide corridor, extending from Vicksburg south to Port Hudson, through which the men and supplies of western Louisiana, Arkansas, and Texas could travel eastward and help sustain the rebellion. "We may take all the northern ports of the Confederacy and they can still defy us from Vicksburg," Abraham Lincoln had observed as he studied a map of the Mississippi Valley in early 1862. "It means hog and hominy without limit, fresh troops from all the states of the far South, and a cotton country where they can raise the staple without interference. . . . The war can never be brought to a close until that key is in our pocket."

The Confederate high command concurred in this judgment. In September 1862 Southern soldiers had begun constructing a chain of forts to guard the landward approaches to the city. It was this belt of earthworks that Davis and Johnston had come to see, and both men were impressed as they made their tour on the morning of December 20. The defenses looked extraordinarily formidable, and Davis was reassured that the Yankees would be repelled if they tried to attack.

Johnston was also appreciative of the engineers' industriousness, although he expressed reservations about the strategy that this long, intricate line of earthworks dictated. Better to conduct a campaign of maneuver, he argued, than to hunker down and wait for the bluecoats to strike at the time and place of their choosing.

His mood worsened on the twenty-third when he and Davis traveled from Vicksburg to Grenada, where Pemberton was digging in along the banks of the Yalobusha River. Once again Johnston was critical of the entrenchments and the passive strategy they entailed. He recommended that Pemberton withdraw to a position farther south, where he could more easily link up with the Vicksburg garrison.

Davis rejected the suggestion out of hand. He did not want another inch of Mississippi soil yielded to the invader. Nor was he about to undercut his field commander, who, like Bragg, stood accused of a variety of shortcomings, both personal and military. Thin and hawk-faced with a wiry spade beard and wispy silver hair, forty-eight-year-old John Pemberton had been a classmate of Bragg's at West Point and shared many of his more off-putting traits. The citizens of Charleston, where he had been stationed before being transferred to the West, had found him "wanting in polish" and "too positive and domineering . . . to suit the sensitive and polite people among whom he had been thrown." The populace of Mississippi, presumably less thin-skinned than the genteel folk of the South Carolina low country, had not warmed to him either. "His want of prominence . . . depresses the spirit of the people," Senator Phelan glumly opined. But what Charlestonians and now Mississippians really could not forgive him for was his place of birth. Pemberton was a Yankee, reared in Philadelphia, and despite the fact that he was a staunch states' rights man and had spent nearly all of his adult life in the South, his loyalties would always be suspect.

The president harbored no doubts about the general he had tapped to be the chief defender of his home state. Pemberton might be arrogant and inflexible, but those were precisely the qualities Davis wanted in a man whose mission it was to hold Vicksburg at all costs. He had selected the Pennsylvanian because he was convinced that he was the best officer available. He still felt that way, and after inspecting the general's defenses and doing what he could to raise the spirits of his soldiers, he returned with the brooding Johnston to the state capital and closeted himself in a hotel room to begin working on the message he would deliver to the Mississippi legislature the day after Christmas.

This address was in many ways the most important and most difficult part of the president's tour, and the one about which he felt the least sanguine. Comfortable in the role of commander in chief, he was far less certain of his abilities as a civilian leader. "He did not know the arts of the politician," his wife Varina wrote, "and would not practice them if understood." Cold and cerebral, unbendingly formal in his dealings with the public, Davis was sadly lacking in charisma, and although he could be an effective speaker, he too often couched his appeals in intellectual rather than emotional terms, disdaining as unseemly and unnecessary the sort of impassioned, podium-pounding oratory that stirred men's souls.

That his detached, distant style of leadership was demoralizing the nation and undermining the war effort had become apparent to him following the sudden decline in Southern fortunes in the spring of 1862. "Davis has fettered our people, stilled their beating pulses of patriotism, cooled their fiery ardor," one critic had complained. "He has not told the people what he needed. As a faithful sentinel, he has not told them what of the night."

This hurt, as did the charge that Davis cared more about the soldiers in Virginia than about those in Tennessee and Mississippi. It jolted him into realizing that it was imperative he get out of the capital and visit the other states of the Confederacy, showing the people that they did, in fact, have a real, live, flesh-and-blood leader. The time had come for him to articulate, clearly and forcefully, the principles for which the Confederacy was fighting, to limn the stark differences between North and South, to offer his unvarnished assessment of the military and diplomatic situation, and to sound a clarion call to duty and sacrifice in the coming year.

This, then, was his purpose as he stood on the rostrum of the Mississippi statehouse, speaking slowly and forcefully to the audience gathered before him, investing his words with all the passion and candor he could muster.

"The issue before us is one of no ordinary character," he proclaimed. "The question for you to decide is, Will you be slaves or will you be independent? Will you transmit to your children the freedom and equality which your fathers transmitted to you, or will you bow down in adoration before an idol baser than ever was worshipped by Eastern idolators?" He paused for a moment, letting his challenge ring through the chamber. Then, as if he had received an answer, he continued, his voice falling almost to a whisper as he said: "Nothing more is necessary than the mere statement of this issue."

Davis fervently believed that the Confederacy was fighting for liberty, to safeguard the rights bequeathed to it by the Founders—among them the right to own slaves and to transport them as chattel anywhere in the United States—and to defend the American proposition that government derives its legitimacy from the consent of the governed. The sovereign states had created the Federal Union and had given it all its power. Clearly it was their right to withdraw if they believed that power was being abused. Any attempt to hold them by force amounted to unconstitutional coercion. The North's attacks on slavery and its insistence that secession was tantamount to treason were part of a rhetorical smokescreen masking its real goal, which was to subjugate the South politically and economically. It was naked aggression as far as Davis was concerned. He was convinced that the South was embarked upon a righteous crusade to perpetuate republican freedoms, "a Second American Revolution, fought for principles no less high, against a tyranny no less harsh."

"I was among those who, from the beginning, predicted war," he sorrowfully told his listeners, "not because our right to secede and form a government of our own was not indisputable . . . but because I saw that the wickedness of the North would precipitate a war upon us. . . . After what has happened during the last two years, my only wonder is that we consented to live for so long a time in association with such miscreants and have loved so much a government rotten to the core. Were it ever to be proposed again to enter into a Union with such a people, I could no more consent to it than to trust myself in a den of thieves."

He moved on to contrast the character and culture of the warring sections, concentrating on the South's devotion to liberty and honor, its love of home and family, while steering clear of the issue of slavery. It might be true, as Vice President Alexander Stephens had baldly asserted, that the government of the Confederacy was founded on the "great truth, that the Negro is not equal to the white man; that slavery—subordination to the superior race—is his natural and normal condition." However, it would not do to trumpet it here in the West, where many poor farmers owned no slaves and had little use for the wealthy planters who did. Better, Davis knew, to focus on the North's baneful intentions than to dwell on the South's peculiar institution.

"These people," he continued, his words dripping with scorn, "when separated from the South and left entirely to themselves, have in six months demonstrated their incapacity for self-government. And yet these are the people who claim to be your masters. These are the people who have determined to divide out the South among their Federal troops. Mississippi they have devoted to the direst vengeance of all. 'But vengeance is the Lord's,' and beneath His banner you will meet and hurl back these worse than vandal hordes!"

A murmur rose from the audience at this, a buzz of astonishment and approval, for the orator standing before them was not the constrained, colorless Jefferson Davis they had known in years past. This was a new Davis, a hot-blooded rabble-rouser. They wanted to hear more of his fiery rhetoric, and he did not disappoint them.

"Our people have only to be true to themselves to behold the Confederate flag among the recognized nations of the earth," he cried. "The question is only one of time. . . . It is not possible that a war of the dimensions that this one has assumed, of proportions so gigantic, can be very long protracted. The combatants must soon be exhausted. But it is impossible, with a cause like ours, that we can be the first to cry, 'Hold, enough.' "

Again there was cheering, but Davis raised his hand for silence and pressed on, tersely summarizing the diplomatic and strategic challenges that faced the Confederacy in the months ahead. The enemy had two primary objectives, he declared. "One is to get possession of the Mississippi River, and to open it to navigation. . . . The other is to seize upon the capital of the Confederacy, and hold this as proof that the Confederacy has no existence." The most recent attempt to achieve the latter had been frustrated at Fredericksburg, he proudly announced. As for the former, he confessed he was deeply worried, and it was this concern that had caused him to undertake the long journey to Mississippi.

"This was the land of my affections," he declared, his voice husky with emotion. "Here were situated the little of worldly goods I possessed. . . . [I had] every confidence in the skill and energy of the officers in command. But when I received dispatches and heard rumors of alarm and trepidation and despondency among the people of Mississippi; when I heard, even, that people were fleeing to Texas in order to save themselves from the enemy; when I saw it stated by the enemy that they had handled other states with gloves, but Mississippi was to be handled without gloves—every impulse of my heart dragged me hither."

He launched into his peroration now, speaking calmly, almost serenely, letting his voice envelop the audience in its warm, reassuring folds. He believed that the war was approaching its climax; that the battles of 1863 would be decisive. And despite the crisis here in the West, he was sure that the Confederacy was going to prevail. "I can, then, say with confidence that our condition is in every respect greatly improved over what it was last year," he declared. "Our armies have been augmented; our troops have been instructed and disciplined. . . . I cannot avoid remarking with how much pleasure I have noticed the superior morality of our troops and the contrast which in this respect they present to the invader. On their valor and the assistance of God I confidently rely."

For a moment there was silence. Then came an explosion of applause, a sustained, powerful ovation that reverberated through the chamber like a clap of thunder.

PART ONE

WINTER

ONE

BLOW YE
THE TRUMPET, BLOW

January 1, 1863, was a crisp, sparkling day in Washington. A throng of holiday promenaders strolled along Pennsylvania Avenue enjoying the fresh breezes and brilliant sunshine. The air was alive with the tinkle of organ grinders playing "Ben Bolt" and "Captain Jinks," the cries of street vendors hawking rock candy and roasted chestnuts, the shouts of drivers jockeying their rigs through the crush of traffic on the muddy boulevard. Eager bootblacks scurried to and fro, polishing the shoes of sauntering swells, while on every street corner leather-lunged newsboys bawled the morning dailies. Here and there ex-soldiers with empty sleeves or trouser legs panhandled for money, but the passing pedestrians paid them little heed, ambling cheerfully down the broad sidewalks, "each and all seeming bent on the enjoyment of the festivities of the day according to their varying tastes and fancies."

For some that meant going to Gautier's, Hammack's, or Wormley's restaurant to feast on platters of pâté de foie gras, stewed terrapin, and fried Chesapeake oysters. For others it meant attending a matinee performance at Grover's National Theater, where Miss Lucille Western, the "pearl of the American stage," was appearing in "Cynthia the Gipsy, or The Flower of the Forest." For still others—off-duty army and navy officers, mostly—it meant guzzling ten-cent cocktails in the boisterous barroom at Willard's Hotel, playing faro or chuck-a-luck in one of the gambling halls on Pennsylvania Avenue's seedy south side, or dropping by one of the scores of bawdy houses located in the flourishing red-light district between Ninth and Fifteenth Streets.

The most popular destination, however, was 1600 Pennsylvania Avenue. Thousands of Washingtonians congregated there to take part in a holiday tradition almost as old as the Republic itself—shaking the hand of the pres-

Civilians in front of U.S. Christian Commission headquarters, Washington, D.C.
(Library of Congress)

ident at the annual New Year's reception. Well before noon, the hour at which the White House would be opened to the public, a great crowd had gathered in Lafayette Square to watch the cream of Washington official-dom—the members of the diplomatic corps, the justices of the Supreme Court, the generals and admirals of the armed forces—arrive to pay their respects to Mr. Lincoln.

One after another the gleaming black carriages rolled up the avenue, turned into the White House drive, rattled to a stop beside the north por-tico, and discharged their loads of ambassadors, ministers, and chargés d'affaires onto the sun-splashed gravel. They were followed by the mem-bers of the judiciary, led by tottering eighty-five-year-old Chief Justice Roger B. Taney, author of the infamous *Dred Scott* decision, which had done so much to assure the outbreak of hostilities between North and South. The heirs to those hostilities, the high-ranking officers of the army and navy, came next, strutting into the mansion in an auriferous blaze of braid and epaulets.

Finally, at twelve o'clock precisely, it was time for the ordinary citizenry to be received. The gates swung open, and the huge crowd surged forward, swamping the twenty-man detail of District police that had been posted on the White House grounds to keep order. In a welter of torn coattails and crushed bonnets, the excited mob fetched up against the north entry, where a beardless youth in an ill-fitting uniform was standing guard. This military cerberus brandished his rifle and exclaimed in a squeaky voice: "My gosh! Gentlemen, *will* you stan' back? You can't get in no faster by crowdin'!" To which appeal, an amused newspaperman reported, "the gay and festive crowd responded by flattening him against a pilaster, never letting him loose until his fresh country face was dark with an alarming symptom of suffocation."

Once inside, the visitors removed their hats and gloves, adjusted wrinkled clothing, rearranged windblown hair, and gaped with undisguised curiosity at the lavish new interior furnishings recently installed by Mrs. Lincoln. The public rooms had been completely redone. Gone were the frayed curtains, the swaybacked settees, the grimy rugs that had created an atmosphere so dingy it had reminded one guest of "the breaking up of a hard winter about a deserted homestead." In their place were plush draperies of tasseled Parisian brocatelle, ornately carved rosewood chairs upholstered in crimson satin, and exquisite Wilton weave carpets into which designs of fruit and flowers had been braided. The first lady had exceeded her $20,000 "repairs" budget by $6,700, exasperating the president, who declared it a monstrous extravagance to spend such sums on "flub dubs for that damned old house." But most in the receiving line that now extended from the entry vestibule into the main hall, to the Blue Room, and thence to the East Room, agreed that Mrs. Lincoln's interior decorating added a thrilling touch of glamour to levees such as this.

In the midst of all the splendor, the gangling, plainly dressed president looked sadly out of place. "To say he is ugly is nothing; to add that his figure is grotesque is to convey no adequate impression," marveled an English journalist. "Fancy a man about six feet high, and thin in proportion, with long bony arms and legs, which somehow seem always to be in the way; with great rugged furrowed hands, which grasp you like a vice when shaking yours; with a long scraggy neck and chest too narrow for the great arms at his side. . . . Clothe this figure then in a long, tight, badly-fitting suit of black, creased, soiled, and puckered up at every salient point of the figure (and every point of this figure is salient), put on large, ill-fitting boots, gloves too long for the bony fingers . . . and then add to all this an air of strength, physical as well as moral, and a strange look of dignity, coupled with all the grotesqueness, and you will have the impression left upon me by Abraham Lincoln."

The president stood by a small table in the center of the Blue Room, shaking hands "like a man pumping for life on a sinking vessel." He nodded and spoke as each person was introduced to him, but his eyes were restless, and he gazed over the heads of the people crowding into the small chamber as though searching for something far away.

Perhaps he was brooding about the Emancipation Proclamation, which he would sign later in the day, wondering how it would be received by a public still reeling from the Army of the Potomac's terrible defeat at Fredericksburg two weeks ago. Or perhaps he was thinking about the message received earlier that morning informing him that the Army of the Cumberland was fighting a pitched battle in middle Tennessee. He wanted to believe that Federal forces would prevail, but he feared the worst. Another bloody setback coming so soon after Fredericksburg could shatter what was left of Northern morale and bring the war to an abrupt and ignominious conclusion. With these gloomy thoughts running through his mind, he was hard-pressed to keep a smile on his face and summon a few polite words for the well-wishers who kept filing past him.

At 2 P.M. the reception finally ended. As the last batch of callers straggled out through the East Room, exiting by way of an open floor-to-ceiling window, Lincoln heaved a sigh of relief and went upstairs to his office, where a small delegation of officials, headed by Secretary of State William Seward, was waiting for him. A five-page manuscript, carefully engrossed by a State Department scrivener, had been spread on the cabinet table. With a grunt Lincoln settled into his armchair, picked up the sheets, and read: "By the President of the United States of America: A Proclamation . . . to wit: That on the first day of January, in the year of our Lord one thousand eight hundred and sixty-three . . . I do order and declare . . . that all persons held as slaves within any state or designated part of a state, the people whereof shall then be in rebellion against the United States, shall be then, thenceforward, and forever free."

As a piece of prose it was singularly uninspiring. A disenchanted historian would later say that it "had all the moral grandeur of a bill of lading." Yet it was destined to take its place beside the Declaration of Independence and the Constitution as one of the epochal documents of American history. Lincoln was keenly aware of this. "If my name ever goes into history, it will be for this act," he said to Seward as he carefully proofread the papers he held in his hands. But what, he wondered, would be posterity's verdict on the Emancipation Proclamation? Would it be remembered as the pathetic last gasp of a failed leader, or would it be celebrated as a noble edict that freed 4 million people and provided moral justification for the obscene bloodshed of this dreadful war? He did not know. But of two things he was sure: first, if slavery was not wrong, then nothing was wrong; and second, if he did not use every means at hand to save the Union, then he was unworthy of his office.

He put the proclamation back on the table and reached for his pen, savoring the moment. At long last he was going to strike in public at something he had always detested in private. He hated slavery viscerally, had done so since his youth when the sight of blacks chained together "like so many fish upon a trot-line" had sickened him. He hated it on an intellec-

Runaway slaves. (Courtesy U.S. Army Military History Institute)

tual level, too, considering it a moral abomination that deprived America's "republican example of its just influence in the world—enables the enemies of free institutions, with plausibility, to taunt us as hypocrites." Human bondage made a mockery of the Declaration of Independence, which was the wellspring of his political beliefs. It contradicted the fundamental assertion that all men are created equal, and it thwarted America from carrying out what he believed was its great historical mission—to advance the cause of liberty and democratic self-government around the globe.

As much as he loathed slavery and deplored what it had done to the country, the decision to abolish it had been a difficult one. Would emancipation lead Union soldiers to desert en masse, as many prophesied? Would it goad the slaveholding border states into casting their lot with the Confederacy? And what of the ex-slaves? Was America ready for the social convulsion that was sure to come when 4 million Negroes sought freedom's inevitable corollary, equality? Would the price of universal freedom be eternal racial strife?

Lincoln had responded to arguments for and against emancipation by bluntly restating his war aims. The paramount object was to save the Union, he insisted; his policy on slavery would be formulated with that goal in mind.

It was an inescapable fact that slaves constituted more than half the Confederacy's workforce. They raised food, manufactured munitions, hauled supplies, and dug fortifications, enabling the South to field a much larger army than would otherwise have been possible. If he took the toil of these laborers from the rebels, he would severely weaken their ability to wage war.

Equally important to Lincoln's way of thinking was the political and psychological impact of emancipation. Just as Federal armies were arrayed against Confederate forces in the field, so he was pitted against the rebel president in Richmond, engaging in a war of words, the objective of which was to seize and hold the moral high ground. The importance of this war-within-a-war could not, he believed, be underestimated. The power of public sentiment to sustain a seemingly hopeless cause had been demonstrated during the American Revolution, when the rallying cry of liberty had inspired the colonists to fight on against the stronger, better-equipped British until France entered the fray.

The analogies that could be drawn between that conflict and this one made Lincoln exceedingly uncomfortable. When Jefferson Davis trumpeted that the Confederacy stood for independence while the Union stood for tyranny, when he cast himself as Washington to Lincoln's George III, he was gaining the upper hand in the struggle of images and ideas. Lincoln knew the only way to counterattack was to raise high the banner of emancipation and transform the war from a struggle *against* secession, an undertaking that smacked of subjugation, to a crusade *for* human freedom, an endeavor consecrated by America's revolutionary heritage. By defining the enemy cause as slavery rather than independence, he would strengthen Northern resolve and make it all but impossible for the governments of Britain and France to intervene on behalf of the South. Forced to depend on its own limited resources, the Confederacy must eventually be crushed by the weight of Northern numbers.

He knew his critics would argue that emancipation by executive fiat was patently unconstitutional. They would say that by flouting that sacred document, he was, in effect, enslaving whites to free blacks. His response to the first charge was that emancipation was a military necessity essential to the preservation of the Union and therefore an action he was entitled to take as commander in chief.

As for the second accusation, he could not deny that it had a demagogic ring to it, but clearly he was not taking liberty from whites in order to give it to blacks. Rather, he was emancipating the slaves so that whites might restore the Union, thereby saving their democratic institutions and perpetuating their republican freedoms. "Must a government, of necessity, be too *strong* for the liberties of its own people, or too *weak* to maintain its own existence?" he had asked shortly after the war began. This proclamation was his answer. The struggle of today was not altogether for today. It was for a vast future also, and so extraordinary measures were necessary, including emancipation, so that America might have a chance to realize the Founders' dream of a permanent democracy based on the principles of liberty and equality.

He dipped the pen in an inkwell, but as he held it over the parchment sheets, his arm began to quiver. Grimacing, he flexed his fingers and massaged his shoulder. "I never, in my life, felt more certain that I was doing right than I do in signing this paper," he said apologetically to the small crowd of witnesses gathered about the cabinet table. "But I have been shaking hands since nine o'clock this morning 'til my arm is stiff and numb. Now this signature is one that will be closely examined, and if they find my hand trembled they will say, 'He had some compunctions.' But anyway, it is going to be done."

And with that he slowly, firmly wrote out his full name.

Abraham Lincoln.

Setting the pen down, he looked anxiously at the glistening signature. It was a little tremulous, he fretted, but then, as if a heavy weight had been lifted from his shoulders, he relaxed, settled back into his chair, and murmured in a voice just loud enough to be heard: "That will do."

A fierce blizzard ushered the new year into New England. In Boston traffic was brought to a standstill by blowing and drifting snow. Some 3,000 antislavery stalwarts ventured out nonetheless, making their way on foot to the Music Hall, where a program of speeches and music celebrating the signing of the final Emancipation Proclamation was scheduled for late afternoon.

In attendance was a pantheon of American letters: Henry Wadsworth Longfellow and John Greenleaf Whittier, Ralph Waldo Emerson and Oliver Wendell Holmes, Charles Eliot Norton and Francis Parkman. Many of the antislavery movement's leading lights were there, too, including former Boston mayor Josiah Quincy, Jr., novelist Harriet Beecher Stowe, and newspaper publisher William Lloyd Garrison.

The concert began shortly after 5 P.M., when Emerson walked out on stage and gave a dramatic reading of an ode he had composed especially for the occasion:

> *The word of the Lord by night*
> *To the watching Pilgrims came,*
> *As they sat by the seaside,*
> *And filled their hearts with flame. . . .*

My angel,—his name is Freedom,—
Choose him to be your King;
He shall cut pathways east and west
And fend you with his wing. . . .

I break your bonds and masterships,
And I unchain the slave:
Free be his heart and hand henceforth
As wind and wandering wave.

The Concord bard's passionate declamation brought the audience to its feet clapping and cheering. The rapturous mood was sustained by Oliver Wendell Holmes, who recited his poem "Army Hymn," and by conductor Carl Zerrahn, who led the Boston Philharmonic in stirring renditions of Beethoven's "Ode to Joy," Mendelssohn's "Hymn of Praise," and Handel's "Hallelujah" chorus.

The high point of the evening was to be the announcement that the president had signed the proclamation, and the anticipation in the stifling theater was palpable. But as the hours passed and no word came, the "watching pilgrims" grew anxious. Rumors that Lincoln had succumbed to political pressure and withdrawn the edict circulated through the crowd. Many people found themselves repeating the warning voiced several days earlier by abolitionist clergyman Henry Ward Beecher: "It is far easier to slide down the banisters than to go up the stairs."

Outside the Music Hall the storm had stopped, and the skies were starting to clear. The renowned black orator Frederick Douglass was walking from his lodgings near Boston Common to Tremont Temple, where he was to be the featured speaker at an emancipation celebration sponsored by the Negro-run Union Progressive Association. Douglass was in a jubilant mood as he trudged along the snow-covered streets, looking up at the stars that twinkled through breaks in the low clouds. The soft glow of the lanterns framing the Temple entrance seemed to him almost divinely radiant, and as he entered the building and took his place on the stage, he gave thanks to God that he had lived to see this day.

A line of messengers had been posted between the Temple and the city telegraph office so that news of the proclamation's signing could be rushed to the waiting audience without delay. "Eight, nine, ten o'clock came and went and still no word," Douglass wrote of the vigil. "At last, when patience was well-nigh exhausted, and suspense was becoming agony, a man advanced through the crowd, and with a face fairly illumined with the news he bore, exclaimed in tones that thrilled all hearts, 'It is coming!' 'It is on the wires!' "

There was a moment of stunned silence; then hats and bonnets were hurled into the air, and people shouted, wept, and jumped for joy. The whole audience joined in singing the jubilee song, "Blow Ye the Trumpet, Blow," after which the text of the proclamation was read aloud. Finally, when the cheering had subsided, Douglass strode to the front of the stage. He raised his arms high and led the throng in a hymn of deliverance, his organlike baritone throbbing with emotion as he sang:

> *Sound the loud timbrel o'er Egypt's dark sea,*
> *Jehovah hath triumphed, His people are free.*

At the Music Hall news of the proclamation's signing caused a commotion "such as was never before seen from such an audience in that place." Casting aside their customary reserve, the Boston abolitionists gave three thunderous cheers for Abraham Lincoln, then three more for William Lloyd Garrison. The crowd was close to hysteria when someone started a rhythmic chant for Harriet Beecher Stowe. The author of *Uncle Tom's Cabin* acknowledged the huzzahs by coming to the rail of the balcony where she had been inconspicuously seated. She was too overcome by emotion to speak. Gazing down into the sea of upturned faces, she could only wave, bow deeply, and dab at her brimming eyes.

The Music Hall celebrants eventually shouted themselves hoarse and went home. But the black revelers at Tremont Temple were too excited to disperse. At midnight they moved to the nearby Twelfth Baptist Church. There the joyful strains of "John Brown's Body," "Marching On," and "Glory Hallelujah" continued to sound until dawn, when the exhausted but still-ebullient assembly finally broke up.

Nine hundred miles southwest of Boston, in Savannah, Georgia, Colonel Charles Colcock Jones, Jr., scion of a wealthy plantation family, spent New Year's Day worrying about emancipation's effect on the Confederacy. "I look upon it as a . . . most infamous attempt to incite flight, murder, and rapine on the part of our slave population," he wrote. "The North furnishes an example of refined barbarity, moral degeneracy, religious impiety, soulless honor, and absolute degradation almost beyond belief."

The only acceptable response, he argued, was reprisal. "By the statute law of the state, anyone who attempts to incite insurrection among our slaves shall, if convicted, suffer death. Is it right, is it just to treat with milder considerations the lawless bands of armed marauders who will infest our borders to carry into practical operation the proclamation of the infamous Lincoln, subvert our entire social system, desolate our homes, and convert the quiet, ignorant, dependent black son of toil into a savage incendiary and brutal murderer?"

The answer, he concluded, was no, although he was not unmindful of the dire consequences that executing prisoners of war might have. "It does indeed appear impossible to conjecture where all this will end," he lamented.

Twenty-five miles northeast of Savannah, at Camp Saxton in the Union-controlled Sea Islands of South Carolina, the arrival of the new year and the signing of the Emancipation Proclamation were commemorated with patriotic speeches, a dress parade, and a big barbecue.

A large, predominantly black crowd began congregating for the festiv-

First South Carolina Volunteers at Camp Saxton,

ities around 10 A.M., arriving at the camp by boat and wagon from the plantations at nearby Beaufort, Port Royal, St. Helena, and Hilton Head Islands. Women wearing gingham frocks, delicately fringed shawls, white aprons, and brightly colored scarfs; men dressed in dark trousers, tightly buttoned vests, and Sunday-go-to-meeting coats, gathered about a speakers' platform that had been erected in a grove of towering live oak trees. The morning was cool and bright, and the beards of Spanish moss trailing from the branches stirred in the brine-scented breeze gusting off Port Royal Sound.

The celebration began at eleven-thirty when the soldiers of the First South Carolina Volunteers, a new all-black infantry regiment, formed into ranks behind the platform. Resplendent in their dark blue jackets and red pantaloons, the troops proudly performed the manual of arms, whipping their rifles through the movements so smartly that watching white officers whistled in amazement.

The commander of the First South Carolina, Colonel Thomas Wentworth Higginson, stepped forward and unfurled a stand of colors presented to the regiment by the Church of the Puritans in New York City. Before he could begin his prepared remarks, the blacks in the audience burst into song, their voices rising sweet and clear as they sang: "My country, 'tis of

January 1, 1863. (Library of Congress)

thee, Sweet land of liberty." The soldiers quickly joined in and did not stop until they had sung all four verses. It was a spontaneous outpouring "so simple, so touching, so utterly unexpected and startling, that I can scarcely believe it on recalling," Higginson later wrote. "It seemed the choked voice of a race at last unloosed." Deeply moved, he told the crowd that its song had expressed the true meaning of the day far more eloquently than any speech he could make. He presented the flags to the regimental color guards, who led the troops onto the adjoining parade ground, where they marched back and forth, arms swinging and bayonets flashing.

When the close-order drill was finished, the regiment was dismissed and the barbecue began. Ten steers, one for each fifty-five-man company, had been spitted and roasted over a pit of glowing coals, and ten barrels of molasses and water had been mixed and placed on long picnic tables set beneath the trees. Soldiers and spectators alike drank and feasted all afternoon, and when the sun went down, a bonfire was lit and a "grand shout"—a cross between a revival meeting and a Sunday school sing-along—commenced. The winter moon rose over the sound, its pale silver light glittering off the waves, and as the sparks from the fire floated skyward to mingle with the twinkling stars, the ex-slaves sang "some of their sweetest, wildest hymns."

That same evening, four hundred miles to the northwest, Tennessee slaveowner John Houston Bills retired to his study and breathed a sigh of relief: New Year's Day was almost over and his eighty-odd field hands had not run away. "They do not perceive that they are free by Lincoln's proclamation," he scribbled in his diary. He hoped to get several more months' work out of them before they learned of the president's action, but he knew he could not count on it. "We have anticipated trouble," he wrote, "and I think will yet have it with regard to holding them."

One hundred miles north of the Bills plantation, in the bluegrass country of central Kentucky, John Montgomery Ashley assembled his slaves in the great hall of his home and told them about the signing of the Emancipation Proclamation. Although Kentucky was a border state and thus exempt from the proclamation's provisions, Ashley had decided to give his servants the choice of continuing as his chattel or striking out on their own. He carefully explained the meaning of the document, then asked them what they wished to do.

For several minutes the blacks were silent. Then Uncle Dan, the oldest of the slaves, stepped forward. "Freedom are an unbroke filly and mighty skittish," he said, looking intently at his master. "But I are goin' to mount her just the same—rheumatiz, cane, and all. Marse Jack, you been a good master to these people, but there's nothin' like freedom—'cepting freedom."

And with that he hobbled out of the house, never to be seen by Ashley again.

Indiana private John McClure had gone to war to save the Union, not to end slavery. He felt betrayed when he learned what Lincoln had done on New Year's Day. "I used to think that we were fighting for the Union and Constitution, but we are not," he wrote with unconcealed bitterness. "We are fighting to free those colored gentlemen."

Like most of his comrades in the Union army, McClure disliked blacks and abhorred emancipation. "If I had my way about things, I would shoot ever[y] nigger I came across," he declared. As for the president's proclamation, he hoped it would fail and that "Old Abe and all the rest of his nigger lovers" would be thrown out of office in the next election.

Five blocks from the White House, in front of the offices of the Washington *Evening Star,* Henry M. Turner, the black pastor of the Israel Bethel Church, waited impatiently for word that the president had signed the Emancipation Proclamation. Although Congress had freed slaves in the District of Columbia eight months earlier, the local black community remained intensely interested in the fate of friends and loved ones still being held in bondage in Maryland and Virginia, or confined to one of the contraband camps—detention centers for runaway slaves—scattered throughout the city.

The crowd in front of the *Star* building had grown to several hundred when, shortly after 5 P.M., a man appeared at the door lugging a thick bundle of newspapers. "The first sheet . . . with the proclamation in it was grabbed for by three of us," Turner recalled years later, "but some active young man got possession of it and fled. The next sheet was grabbed for by several, and was torn into tatters. The third sheet was grabbed for by several, but I succeeded in procuring so much of it as contained the proclamation, and . . . down Pennsylvania [Avenue] I ran as for my life."

When he arrived at his church, which was nearly a mile away, he was so out of breath, he could not speak. He handed the paper to another man, who promptly read it to the assembled congregation. "They raised a shouting cheer that was almost deafening," Turner wrote. "Men squealed, women fainted, dogs barked, white and colored people shook hands . . . and cannons began to fire at the navy-yard."

At the contraband camp on North Twelfth Street, a bellman made the rounds of the living quarters, summoning the residents to the chapel. By the hundreds they poured out of the drafty barracks, which had previously housed the dragoons of General McClellan's bodyguard, and made their way across the muddy quadrangle to the meetinghouse. The camp's patriarch, a grizzled old black man known as John the Baptist, led the assembly in prayer. Then Superintendent B. D. Nichols read aloud the edict of emancipation. Ecstatic cries arose as he spoke: "I am free! I am free!" and the entire group sang "Go Down Moses" and "There's a Better Day a-Coming."

When the spirituals were finished, the former slaves took turns telling of their experiences in bondage and of the joy they felt now that the day of jubilee had finally come. "Once the time was, that I cried all night," shouted one, a man named Thornton. "What's the matter? What's the matter? Matter enough. The next morning my child was to be sold, and I never expect to see her no more 'til the day of judgment. Now, no more of that! No more of that! No more of that! They can't sell my wife and child anymore, bless the Lord! No more of that! No more of that! No more of that now!"

After dark, a torch-carrying throng gathered in front of the White House and called loudly for the president. He appeared for an instant at a second-story window. The crowd screamed and cried that "if he would come out of that palace, they would hug him to death." Reverend Turner was in the midst of the wrought-up mob, and the feeling that swept over him when Lincoln showed his face was something he would never forget. "It was indeed a time of times," he marveled; "nothing like it will ever be seen again in this life."

TWO

OLD ROSY
IS THE MAN

Later that new year's night, after the crowd outside the White House had departed, Lincoln went to the War Department to get the latest news about the battle being fought in middle Tennessee. Always anxious when Union troops were in action, he was doubly fretful now, knowing that the outcome of this particular engagement would exert a powerful influence on the way the public, North and South, perceived the just-signed Emancipation Proclamation. Victory, or at least the avoidance of defeat, was now more important than ever. If his edict freeing the slaves was to be taken seriously, it had to be backed by military success; otherwise it was like a check written on an empty bank account.

His unease stemmed in large part from his surprise that this battle was taking place at all. It was a fight he had long been agitating for, but one he had begun to think would not happen because of the recalcitrance of the Union commander in Tennessee, William S. Rosecrans.

Throughout November and the first half of December, Rosecrans had remained at Nashville, drilling his troops, piling up supplies, and rebuffing all attempts to prod him into immediate action. His plan, he informed the War Department, was to lull the rebels at Murfreesboro into a sense of complacency, then strike hard and crush them. There would be no time to stop and tinker once the offensive was under way; hence his determination to stay put until his army was completely refitted.

This emphasis on exhaustive preparation was entirely characteristic of the man the soldiers called "Old Rosy," a sobriquet that referred not only to his distinctive surname, which was Dutch in origin, but also to his bulbous red nose, which one observer had classified as "intensified Roman" in a sly double allusion to the general's fondness for whiskey and his fanatical

General William S. Rosecrans.
(Library of Congress)

devotion to the Catholic Church. Standing just under six feet tall, broad and muscular in build, with wavy chestnut-colored hair and a close-cropped beard, the Ohio-born, West Point–educated Rosecrans was an affable, outgoing officer who inspired unabashed devotion among the soldiers he led.

As fond as the Army of the Cumberland was of its new commander, it soon learned that he was not without quirks. Some of these, such as his tendency to stammer when he was excited, were of the garden variety; others, such as his requirement that all the men serving on his staff be young and blond ("sandy-haired fellows, who can drive a quill like lightning"), were decidedly eccentric. Then there was the matter of religion. Rosecrans had embraced Catholicism while at West Point, and like many converts to a new faith he was dogmatic in his adherence to its tenets and rituals. He carried a crucifix on his watch chain and a rosary in his pocket, and was accompanied everywhere by his personal priest, the Reverend Father Patrick Treacy, so that he might never miss mass. He reveled in late-night religious discussions and would keep his aides-de-camp up for hours on end "debating on such fine points as the distinction between profanity, which he freely employed, and blasphemy, which he eschewed."

Rosecrans prided himself on being a hands-on commander. "Boys, when you *drill, drill like thunder!*" he would bray, red-faced and stuttering, as the regiments paraded past him at review. If he saw a soldier who was missing a piece of equipment he would pull him out of line and loudly exhort him to "go to your captain and demand what you need! Go to him every day until you get it!" He liked to walk through the camp after taps, making sure that his men were sleeping soundly. If he saw a candle burning in a tent, he would strike at the canvas with the flat of his sword and snap, "Lights out!" This command invariably drew a profane response, which gave way to profuse apologies when the general's florid nose poked through the tent flap. He was not offended by the insults, the insincere apologies, or the snickering that followed his departure, however, and the soldiers loved him for it. "Old Rosy is the man, Old Rosy is the man!" they would bellow at the least provocation. "We'll show our deeds where'er he leads: Old Rosy is the man!"

In mid-December Rosecrans decided he was ready at last to strike out for Murfreesboro. Thanks to his hectoring of Halleck and Meigs, he had on hand all the ammunition he needed, as well as enough rations to last until February. He had also completed a reshuffling of the Army of the Cumberland's command structure. The 65,000-man force was now divided into three corps of roughly equal strength led by Major Generals Thomas L. Crittenden, George Thomas, and Alexander McCook. The advance would begin in a few days, he wired Washington on the fifteenth.

The few days stretched into a week and a half, but at last the arrangements were complete. On Christmas Day Rosecrans summoned his corps commanders and their staffs to his headquarters. The offensive was to begin on the morning of the twenty-sixth, he announced. It would be necessary to leave 20,000 men behind to garrison Nashville and guard the railroad connecting it with Louisville, but this diminution of combat strength did not worry him; the Army of the Cumberland would still outnumber the Confederate force at Murfreesboro.

At the conclusion of the conference, an orderly passed through the room handing out steaming mugs of toddy. For several minutes the officers joked and made small talk while their commander smiled benevolently at them. Then, abruptly, his smile vanished. He drained his glass, slammed his hand on a table, and shouted at the startled assembly: "We move tomorrow, gentlemen! We shall begin to skirmish, probably, as soon as we pass the outposts! Press them hard! Drive them out of their nests! Make them fight or run! Strike hard and fast! Give them no rest! *Fight them! Fight them!* Fight, I say!"

He was still sputtering and pounding his fist into his palm as the officers, some grinning with delight, others shaking their heads in consternation, took their leave and filed out into the night.

On the evening of December 26, a squad of mud-spattered Confederate cavalrymen galloped into Murfreesboro bringing news that three large Federal columns were marching southeastward from Nashville. Bragg was surprised by this sudden advance, but although his army was considerably smaller than the blue host now approaching from the northwest, he gave no thought to retreating. He ordered his cavalry to harass the Union columns while he collected his scattered infantry units. By the morning of December 28, the concentration was complete. The Army of Tennessee was deployed in an arc-shaped battle line along the banks of Stones River just west of Murfreesboro.

Cold, wet, and miserable, the Confederate soldiers waited for the Yankees to arrive. The weather was dreadful. A gusty wind whistled out of the north, driving sheets of freezing rain before it. To make matters worse, many of the men were nursing monumental Christmas hangovers. "John Barleycorn was general in chief," Private Samuel Watkins wrote. "Our [soldiers] had kissed John a little too often. They couldn't see straight."

The main body of the Union army made contact with the Confederate line on December 30. Skirmishers from both sides fanned out to pinpoint the enemy's position, a difficult and dangerous task greatly complicated by the uneven terrain and the dense stands of scrub cedar dotting it. Throughout the day, patrols blundered into each other in the dripping thickets and mist-shrouded clearings. There would be a warning shout, a spatter of gunfire, and then the combatants would fall back, circle around, and grope forward again until another chance encounter halted their progress.

After digesting the intelligence delivered by his scouts on the evening of the thirtieth, Bragg decided to attack at daybreak on the thirty-first. Even though he was outmanned, he was going to land the first blow, counting on the element of surprise to make up for any deficiency in numbers. His plan called for one division to hold the Confederate right, while the rest of the army executed a wheeling movement, jackknifing the Union right back against Stones River. If the attack succeeded, the Yankees would be cut off from Nashville and destroyed.

A mile and a half northwest of Bragg's headquarters, in a drafty log cabin beside the Nashville Turnpike, Rosecrans was planning an assault virtually identical to his Confederate counterpart's. He would hold his right with one corps and strike with the other two against the rebel right, turning it and then sweeping down on Murfreesboro from the north. The only difference between his plan and his opponent's was that he scheduled his onslaught to begin at 7 A.M., not at first light like Bragg. This one-hour discrepancy was to prove critical. It guaranteed that the Confederates would get the jump on the Federals, forcing them onto the defensive.

As night fell, the rain tapered off and the wind picked up, chilling the lightly dressed soldiers to the bone. The bulk of the Army of Tennessee was shifting southward under cover of darkness to get into position for the dawn attack. The Army of the Cumberland, meanwhile, was bedding down as best it could on the cold, muddy ground. Trying to lift the spirits of their comrades and keep warm at the same time, Union bandsmen unpacked their instruments and played "Yankee Doodle" and "Hail Columbia."

The music from the Federal camp carried to the Confederate line. Rising to the challenge, rebel bandsmen unlimbered their horns and answered the bluecoats' aural bombardment with "Dixie" and "The Bonnie Blue Flag." The ensembles continued to exchange orchestral salvos, much to the delight of the listening armies, until finally one of the bands struck up "Home Sweet Home," and as if by prearrangement, all the other musicians joined in. Thousands of voices took up the familiar refrain, swelling in a strong, sure chorus that quavered only at the song's end, when the final notes hung suspended in the icy air and the sentimental words of the last line—"Be it ever so humble, there's no place like home"—trailed away, sticking in the throats of men who knew that this might well be their last night on earth.

December 31 broke gray and dreary. A clammy mist rose from the surface of Stones River and drifted slowly to the south, mingling with the smoke of hundreds of breakfast fires. The Federals who were gathered about these blazes stamped their feet, chafed their hands, and gnawed on squares of hardtack while they waited for coffee to boil and bacon to fry. The night had passed without incident, so their rifles were stacked and their artillery pieces stood unattended. Out on the picket line, bundled-up sentries peered into the milky half light of dawn and struggled to stay awake; it was perfectly quiet and nothing was moving.

Then, at 6:22 A.M. precisely, a terrifying apparition emerged from out of the fog: two long, solid lines of rebel infantrymen advancing across the fields with their bayonets fixed. It was the vanguard of the Confederate assault—the combined divisions of Major Generals John McCown and Patrick Cleburne—approaching at the run, eerily silent save for the slapping of knapsacks, the creak of cartridge boxes, and the muffled thud of shoes. The dazed lookouts barely had time to open their mouths before the leading rank swept past them and barreled into the Federal bivouacs.

In a welter of sparks and spilled coffee, the panic-stricken breakfasters took to their heels. "Our way was through [a] cornfield," remembered Private Robert Stewart. "The stalks were yet thickly standing. The ground was frozen and rough. I could hear the bullets striking the stalks. I could hear them strike a comrade as he ran. Then there would be a groan, a stagger, and a fall. . . . I felt as though I would like to be all legs, with no other purpose in life but to run."

In a matter of minutes the rebel assault obliterated the division that had been anchoring the Union right flank. Here and there clusters of Federals bunched together and fought back, but these isolated pockets of resistance were quickly overrun by the hard-charging Confederates. Edwin Payne of the Thirty-fourth Illinois watched in horror as a Union artillery company, trying to limber up and retreat after one such abortive stand, was savaged by a point-blank volley that cut down seventy-five of its horses and nearly half its men. Moments later Payne's own regiment was engulfed by the gray tidal wave, which rolled on with scarcely a pause, sweeping everything before it.

Four miles to the north, on the Union left flank, Rosecrans was getting

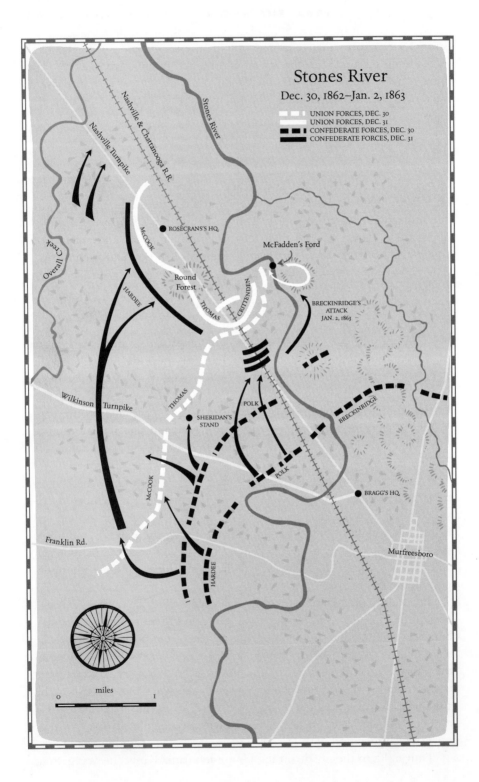

Stones River

Dec. 30, 1862–Jan. 2, 1863

UNION FORCES, DEC. 30
UNION FORCES, DEC. 31
CONFEDERATE FORCES, DEC. 30
CONFEDERATE FORCES, DEC. 31

Stones River

Nashville & Chattanooga R.R.

Nashville Turnpike

Overall Creek

McCOOK

● ROSECRANS'S HQ

HARDEE

Round Forest

THOMAS

CRITTENDEN

McFadden's Ford

BRECKINRIDGE'S ATTACK JAN. 2, 1863

Wilkinson Turnpike

THOMAS

POLK

● SHERIDAN'S STAND

BRECKINRIDGE

McCOOK

POLK

● BRAGG'S HQ

Franklin Rd.

HARDEE

Murfreesboro

miles

0   1

ready to launch his own assault, unaware of the disaster brewing to the south. He had awakened early, heard mass with Father Treacy, then ridden out to join Crittenden, whose corps was to lead the attack. The two men climbed to the top of a hill to get a better view of the impending action. It was here that they first heard the crackle of musketry coming from Mc-Cook's sector, a sharp, spasmodic popping that reminded one listener of a cane field going up in flames.

Rosecrans was unperturbed. His plan called for McCook to hold his ground while Crittenden advanced on this end of the line, and he assumed that that was what he was doing. But a few minutes later the sound of gun-fire grew louder and more ominous. It was like the rumble of heavy wag-ons rolling along a corduroy road, said one staff officer; like the rising of the wind before a summer storm, remarked another. Still Rosecrans was unmoved. McCook would hold, he insisted. His aides were not so sure. "The noise of battle was nearing too rapidly," one of them recalled. "Not only did the sound travel too rapidly, but it broke out too much to the north and curled around to our rear with infernal speed and intensity." The noise continued to draw closer, and Rosecrans, his equanimity evaporating like water sponged into a red-hot cannon bore, jumped into the saddle and spurred back to headquarters to find out what was happening.

No information had been received at the command post yet, but the earsplitting crash of artillery spoke volumes. Off to the south, in the di-rection of the Wilkinson Turnpike, stragglers began to appear. They came in driblets at first, then in streams, and finally in a churning blue torrent that filled the fields and thickets in McCook's rear.

Messages began to arrive at headquarters a few minutes later: "The right wing is heavily pressed. . . . Rebel cavalry is in our rear. . . . General Willich has been captured. . . . General Sill is dead. . . . The right wing is broken." On and on it went, each revelation more staggering than the last, the accumulated dispatches painting a picture of a battle spinning swiftly out of control.

Another general might have cracked under the strain, but not Rose-crans. He shrugged off reports of heavy losses with the curt remark: "Never mind. Brave men must die in battle." When a dispatch rider told him that McCook's corps had collapsed, he snapped: "All right—we will rectify it." His face had paled and lost its ruddy luster, an observer noted, but his eyes blazed as he barked out orders. Thomas, whose corps was holding the Union center, was to send a portion of his command to reinforce Mc-Cook. Crittenden was to cancel his attack and bring all three of his divi-sions—minus one brigade, which was to stay in place and guard the left flank—south toward the sound of the guns.

When couriers had departed with these messages, Rosecrans jammed a cigar into his mouth, growled to his assembled aides, "Mount, gentlemen!" and galloped off to try to save the day. "This battle must be won," he kept repeating, as if the words alone would make it so, but what he really needed was time—time to form his reserves into a new defensive line between the Wilkinson and Nashville Turnpikes, time to mass his remaining artillery where its fire could shatter the enemy attack.

On the Confederate side there was jubilation. The Federal flank had been turned, and now Lieutenant General Leonidas Polk's corps, its divisions led by Major Generals Jones Withers and Benjamin Cheatham, was surging forward to continue the rout started by McCown's and Cleburne's men. "We raised a whoop and yell, and swooped down on those Yankees like a whirl-a-gust of woodpeckers in a hail storm," recalled Sam Watkins. "[Our] victory was complete."

Watkins was mistaken; the rebel victory was not yet complete. A single Union division commanded by Brigadier General Philip H. Sheridan was making a stand just north of the Wilkinson Turnpike. Sheridan was a bull terrier of a man—short, square-shouldered, and bandy-legged—as stubborn a fighter as there was in the Federal army. He had placed his troops in an all-but-impenetrable tangle of rocks and cedar trees where they could withstand the attacks of a numerically superior enemy. That was precisely what they did, repulsing three separate charges, heaping the ground in front of them with rebel dead and wounded.

One of those injured was Sam Watkins, struck in the shoulder by a shell fragment. As he staggered back to a field hospital, blood soaking his uniform, he overtook another wounded man. "His left arm was entirely gone," Watkins later wrote. "His face was white as a sheet. The breast and sleeve of his coat had been torn away, and I could see the frazzled end of his shirt sleeve, which appeared to be sucked into the wound. . . . I could see his heart throb, and the respiration of his lungs. I was filled with wonder and horror at the sight. He was walking along, when all at once he dropped down and died without a struggle or a groan."

Goaded to superhuman effort by their oath-spouting commander, Sheridan's Federals fought on until they had emptied their cartridge boxes and were fending off assailants with bayonets and bare fists. Only then would the general let them retreat.

Rosecrans met the doughty five-foot five-inch brigadier as he was leading the remnants of his division north toward the Nashville Turnpike. Sheridan's face was contorted with rage, and he was railing about what a disgrace it was to have to abandon a perfectly defensible position for want of ammunition. "Watch your language," barked Rosecrans. "Remember, the first bullet may send you to eternity."

"I can't help it," Sheridan snapped back. "Unless I swear like hell the men won't take me seriously." He gestured at his powder-grimed survivors and said in a reproachful voice: "This is all that is left, General."

Rosecrans was unimpressed. "Replenish your ammunition and get your men back into the fight," he said, then galloped away, his entourage trailing behind him like the gaudy tail of a blue-and-gold kite.

A little more gratitude on Rosecrans's part would have been in order, for whether he knew it or not, Sheridan's stand had saved the day for the Army of the Cumberland. While others had succumbed to panic, lion-hearted "Little Phil" had kept his wits and handed Bragg his first setback of the day, giving his chief the time he needed to assemble his forces.

To Rosecrans's credit, he made the most of the opportunity afforded him by Sheridan's delaying action. After ordering Thomas and Crittenden to reposition their units, he rode forth to see personally to the formation of a new battle line along the Nashville Turnpike. Racing up and down, chivvying regiments, companies, and even individual platoons into position, he seemed to be everywhere at once, ignoring the storm of bullets and shells that followed him as he galloped across the field. Rosecrans's friend and fellow Catholic, Lieutenant Colonel Julius Garesche, begged him not to expose himself unnecessarily, but Rosecrans was unfazed by the danger. "Never mind me," he shouted, his voice stuttering with excitement. "Make the sign of the cross and go in!"

There was a blood price to be paid for such recklessness. Sadly it fell to Garesche, a gentle, profoundly spiritual man who had spent the night before the battle poring over his well-worn copy of Thomas à Kempis's *The Imitation of Christ,* to settle the account. Rosecrans was pounding along, roaring defiance at the enemy, when a cannonball hurtled past him and struck his friend flush in the face. Garesche's headless body rode on for almost twenty yards, fountaining gore before sliding to the ground in a ghastly heap. Horrified, Rosecrans pulled rein. But then he gathered himself, spurred his horse forward, and called over his shoulder to his aides: "I am very sorry but we cannot help it. . . . Let us push on. *This battle must be won!*"

Later, when the fighting was over, questions would be raised about Rosecrans's conduct. Sheridan and Crittenden, among others, thought that he had behaved rashly, endangering his life and the lives of his staff to supervise troop movements that should have been overseen by more junior officers. The soldiers who were in the thick of the fight were of a different mind. As far as they were concerned, Old Rosy was "the man," just like the song said, and they had nothing but praise for the way he risked his life to rally them at the moment of supreme peril.

Foolhardy or not, Rosecrans's actions on the morning of December 31 were undeniably effective. By noon he had scraped together enough fresh units, combined with the fragments of those that had been shattered earlier, to contest the Confederate onslaught in an organized and resolute fashion. The situation was still precarious; the once-straight Union line had been bent back on itself; but thanks to his determination and the stubborn ferocity of a handful of regiments, the Army of the Cumberland was intact and in position to turn defeat into victory.

The Confederate assault, which was now almost five hours old, was running out of steam. Many regiments had been bled white, and those units that had not been decimated were reeling from fatigue. Still the rebels kept pushing forward, striving to overrun the Nashville Turnpike and put the Yankees to rout.

At the apex of Rosecrans's makeshift defensive line there was a four-acre copse of oak and cedar trees known locally as the Round Forest. A brigade of Mississippians charged toward this dark glade and was ravaged by rapid-fire volleys from massed batteries of Union artillery.

As the survivors stumbled back across a bloodsoaked cotton field, a Tennessee brigade took up the attack. Once again the Union guns roared, and this second assault was repulsed with even greater slaughter than the first.

The rebel drive was now completely stalled. To get it restarted Bragg decided to hurl Major General John Breckinridge's division, which had been held in reserve all morning, into the fray. Breckinridge balked, however. He was afraid to vacate his present position on the far right flank because scouts were warning him that he was about to be assailed by a strong Union force. Bragg repeated his order, telling his subordinate that unless he was certain the enemy was upon him, he must go ahead and shift his soldiers south for an attack on the Round Forest. Breckinridge replied that he could be certain of nothing, and the two men continued to bicker back and forth until Bragg finally got word from his own scouts that the only force in Breckinridge's front was a small body of sharpshooters.

Incandescent with rage, the Confederate commander sent Breckinridge orders to march at once with the bulk of his command to reinforce Polk's corps. Polk, meanwhile, was directed to hurl all the men he could muster at the Round Forest in a last-ditch effort to crack the Union center and seize the Nashville Turnpike.

Taken together, these directives were a prescription for disaster. The slaughter of the Mississippi and Tennessee brigades had already demonstrated the futility of frontal assaults against the Round Forest, and in the hour or so since those charges had failed, the Federals had crowded even more infantry and artillery into the little patch of timber. But Bragg did not realize this. He was determined to take the Round Forest whatever the cost, and so Breckinridge's fresh brigades joined Polk's command and were flung one after another against a position that was impregnable.

As the fight roared toward its climax, Rosecrans rode along the front line shouting encouragement to his soldiers. "Be a little more deliberate and take good aim—don't fire so damned fast!" he called to an artillery captain as he passed by. To a group of frightened foot soldiers he yelled: "Men, do you wish to know how to be safe? Shoot low! Give them a blizzard at their shins!" They did as he said, and in a matter of minutes the enemy charge had been smashed.

It was now four o'clock, and dusk was gathering in the Stones River Valley. Breckinridge's last two brigades had made their way to Polk's position, and a final attempt to seize the Round Forest was about to begin. "The battle had hushed," wrote Union colonel William B. Hazen, "and the dreadful splendor of this advance can only be conceived, as every description must fall short." The rebels came forward "steadily and as it seemed to certain victory," but at that moment the artillery ranged behind Hazen's men opened with a terrific blast.

The gray wave covered several hundred more yards of ground, but the tempest of shot and shell was too much to withstand. "It got so hot for us we were ordered to lie down, with nothing to protect us but cotton stalks," remembered William McMurray of the Twentieth Tennessee. "We couldn't go forward . . . so we stayed there until it was useless to stay any longer." At last the command to withdraw was given, and "if ever you saw a lot of men get out of a place in a quick time," McMurray admitted, "the 20th Tennessee regiment did it, I being one of the foremost."

With this retreat the day's fighting was at an end. The sun slipped below the horizon, and the guns fell silent. A crepuscular glow flared briefly in the western sky, then faded into blackness, but presently the moon rose and illuminated a scene "fit for a banquet of ghouls." Soldiers from both armies left their lines to retrieve the wounded and collect and bury the dead. Some paused to rifle through discarded knapsacks, searching for sugar, hardtack, and bacon, while others cut slabs of meat from the carcasses of dead horses and lugged them back to their campsites. Scavengers, singly and in packs, skulked from body to body, harvesting weapons, ammunition, shoes, overcoats, rings, pocket watches—anything of value.

Among those prowling about the battlefield was William Hazen. He had slipped out of the Round Forest after dusk and made his way south and east along the grade of the Nashville & Chattanooga Railroad, hunting in the moonlight for the body of his friend, Julius Garesche. Not far from his starting point, he found what he was looking for. "I saw but a headless trunk," he wrote. "An eddy of crimson foam had issued where the head should be. I at once recognized his figure, it lay so naturally, his right hand across his breast. As I approached . . . and bent over him, the contraction of a muscle extended his hand slowly and slightly toward me." Hazen grasped the hand and removed his friend's West Point class ring. He also retrieved Garesche's gore-soaked copy of *The Imitation of Christ,* then called for a burial party to inter the corpse. He was watching the men hack a shallow grave in the frosty earth when a rebel deserter emerged from the shadows and wordlessly offered him a blanket. "It was stiff and glazed with blood and long use," Hazen wrote, "but it proved the most comfortable blanket I ever saw."

Night wore on, the moon set, and a frigid wind gusted out of the north. Harried surgeons plied their knives and bone saws by lantern light, performing amputations as fast as patients could be brought to them. Elsewhere the bustle of activity gradually subsided, and the soldiers, blue and gray, wrapped themselves in their overcoats, curled up on the freezing ground, and tried to doze. There would be no band concert this evening, no sentimental choruses of "Home Sweet Home." Instead, the agonized shrieks of the wounded and the moaning of the winter wind merged into a hellish lullaby, a terrible keening threnody that rose and fell but never died away.

"For a long time sleep fled my eyes," an Illinois boy recalled. "The past day seemed more like a month. . . . This was New Year's Eve, such a one as I had never before seen."

Shortly after midnight, January 1, 1863, Rosecrans convened a council of war in his log-cabin headquarters. Twenty-four hours earlier he had strutted about this same building, the cocksure superior issuing orders to an audience of submissive underlings. Now he sat haggard and bleary-eyed on a camp stool, his cigar chewed to a saliva-soaked stump, humbly asking his subordinates for advice.

McCook favored retreat, pointing out that if the Army of the Cumberland was destroyed, nothing would stand between the Confederates and the cities of Nashville, Louisville, and Cincinnati. Thomas, who had fallen asleep in his chair, jerked upright when he heard the word "retreat"; "this army doesn't retreat," he growled, then lowered his chin back onto his chest and resumed his nap. Crittenden hemmed and hawed, said his military experience was too limited for him to offer an opinion, but assured his commander that he was always ready to obey orders.

This was not helpful. Rosecrans asked the assembled officers to wait while he and McCook went out to scout possible routes of retreat. The two men mounted their horses and trotted northwest until they came to

Overall Creek, which crossed the Nashville Turnpike at right angles about a mile and a half from headquarters. On the far bank of the stream they saw a sight that startled them. Scores of shadowy figures were moving through the undergrowth, calling to one another and carrying lighted torches. The explanation for this activity was perfectly scrutable: it was freezing cold, and Union cavalrymen, ignoring orders forbidding the building of campfires, were riding along the picket lines kindling blazes for the shivering lookouts. Rosecrans could not believe that one of his directives would be disobeyed so flagrantly; he concluded that the rebels were circling around his right flank in preparation for launching a night attack. "They have got entirely in our rear and are forming a line of battle by torchlight!" he exclaimed to McCook. Jerking his horse about, he spurred back to headquarters to tell his generals that retreat was impossible. "Go to your commands," he shouted, "and prepare to fight and die right here!"

There were no such histrionics at Confederate headquarters because Bragg had gone to bed. The Army of Tennessee had suffered dreadfully in the course of pressing its daylong series of attacks, but it had inflicted extraordinarily heavy casualties, too, and Bragg was confident that January 1 would find his soldiers in sole possession of the battlefield. When scouts reported to him that a long train of Union wagons had been seen rolling northwest toward Nashville, he was sure of it. "The enemy has yielded his strong position and is falling back," he wired Richmond before retiring for the night. "We occupy the whole field and shall follow him. . . . God has granted us a happy New Year."

Daybreak brought disappointment to the Confederate commander. The Yankees had withdrawn from the Round Forest salient, deeming it too exposed to defend indefinitely, but otherwise they had not budged from the positions they held at sundown on December 31. This news baffled Bragg. He could not understand why the Union army had not admitted defeat and retreated. Perhaps they still would, he decided, and not knowing what else to do, he put his men to work picking up discarded weapons and burying the dead.

Rosecrans, like Bragg, had no plan of action beyond holding his ground, but unlike the Confederate general he kept busy New Year's Day, consolidating his forces and strengthening his lines. His most significant move was to direct the division holding the extreme left flank to cross to the east side of Stones River and occupy a hill overlooking McFadden's Ford. From this commanding position Federal soldiers could enfilade the Confederate right.

Bragg, meanwhile, was lethargic and detached, unable to exercise leadership when it was most needed. His aides sensed that victory was slipping away, and their despondency infected the rest of the army. "This gloomy

New Year's Day went by with [our] troops thus inactive," wrote Captain Ed Thompson. "As the federal army had nothing to lose but everything to gain by waiting, it waited—but meanwhile it worked. The Confederate army waited, and hoped."

The waiting and hoping continued into January 2, but still the Yankees showed no sign of falling back. Bragg, at last fathoming that Rosecrans was not going to move unless he was pushed, emerged from his headquarters to reconnoiter the field in search of a satisfactory place to resume the attack. What he saw on his far right flank alarmed him. The high ground the Federals had occupied the previous day posed a serious threat to his army. It had to be cleared. Breckinridge's division, which had been sent back to its original position on the Confederate right after its repulse at the Round Forest on New Year's Eve, was the obvious choice for the job.

The forty-two-year-old Kentuckian was flabbergasted when Bragg told him what he had in mind. He had scouted the Union-held hill earlier in the day, and in his estimation it could not be taken by the type of bayonet charge Bragg envisioned. Not only did the Yankees enjoy the advantages of high ground, good cover, and clear fields of fire, they were supported by an imposing array of cannon on the west bank of Stones River.

Bragg was not swayed by these arguments. Breckinridge's division had suffered less than any other unit in the first day's fighting, he said. It must now take its turn serving as the army's spearhead. Breckinridge continued to protest, insisting that the assault would be suicidal. Bragg cut him off. "Sir," he snapped, "my information is different. I have given the order to attack the enemy in your front and expect it to be obeyed."

Convinced that he would be dead before the afternoon was over, Breckinridge rejoined his division. "General Preston," he muttered to one of his brigade commanders, "this attack is made against my judgment, and by the special orders of General Bragg. . . . If it should result in disaster, and I be among the slain, I want you to do justice to my memory, and tell the people that I believed this attack to be very unwise, and tried to prevent it."

His subordinates were less constrained in their criticism. Colonel Robert Trabue said that the undertaking was "impractical madness." Brigadier General Roger Hanson, commander of the famous Kentucky Orphan Brigade, swore that it was "absolutely murderous" and expressed a desire to go to headquarters and kill Bragg.

Breckinridge hushed this wild talk and got on with the job of preparing for the assault. By 3:45 P.M. all was in readiness. The 4,500 Confederates who would make the attack were drawn up in two lines approximately half a mile long. Hanson, sounding far more belligerent than he felt, ordered his troops to fix bayonets. Like Breckinridge, he had been struck by a sudden premonition that he would die today.

At four o'clock a signal gun boomed, and the long lines of gray stepped off. Under heavy fire from the outset, the rebels maintained admirable order as they crossed the 600-yard-wide valley between them and their hilltop objective. Drawing to within 150 yards of the crest, they halted, triggered a volley, then leveled their bayonets and charged. This proved to be too much for the bluecoats. "Our intrepidity demoralized [them]," recalled Gervis Grainger of the Sixth Kentucky, "and they began to flee like blackbirds."

Breckinridge's victorious soldiers should have stopped where they were, brought up their artillery, and dug in for the night. But in the heat of battle all discipline was lost. Ignoring the warning shouts of their officers, they pursued the fleeing Federals, plunging down the hill's rearward slope straight into the field of fire of fifty-eight artillery pieces lined up on the opposite bank of Stones River. "Ready," the voices of Yankee gunners could be heard calling, then bright streaks of flame stabbed through the gathering dusk, and an iron blizzard howled across the river and tore into the gray ranks. It was as if the rebels had "opened the door of hell, and the devil himself was there to greet them," said a Union officer. Men and horses went down in kicking, thrashing heaps. Shrieks of pain and terror rent the air, and blood and scraps of human flesh pattered to the earth like red rain.

Dazed and reeling, scarcely comprehending what had happened to them, the survivors retreated. Officers tried to stem the tide, but it was a hopeless task. "I have never seen troops so completely broken in my military experience," declared Captain Felix Robertson. By five o'clock it was all over. The remnants of the shattered division had returned to the assault's starting point; 1,700 soldiers had fallen in barely sixty minutes of fighting.

Breckinridge rode back and forth, his face crimson with fury. "He was raging like a wounded lion as he passed the different commands from right to left," wrote one of his officers. It was the sight of his beloved Orphan Brigade that brought him up short, however; the Kentuckians had lost thirteen of twenty-three officers and 431 of 1,200 men. As Breckinridge looked at their pathetically shrunken ranks, his eyes brimmed with tears, and he cried out in an anguished voice, "My poor Orphan Brigade! They have cut it to pieces!"

Bragg, by contrast, was not unduly upset by the bloody defeat. In fact, he was able to dismiss it in two phlegmatic sentences. "The contest was short and severe," he wrote in his after-action report. "The enemy was driven back and the eminence gained, but the movement as a whole was a failure, and the position was again yielded." There was no mention of the desperate gallantry shown by the attackers or of the appalling losses they had suffered in obedience to his orders. He did make note—censoriously, of course—of their disorderly retreat, and he directed Hardee to move what was left of his corps to the right flank to shore them up. Then, with no clue as to what to do next, he dismissed his staff, crawled into bed, and went to sleep.

He was awakened at 2 A.M. by an aide bearing a message from Generals Cheatham, Withers, and Polk. The officers were worried that their troops were used up and likely to collapse if attacked. They advised an immediate retreat. Bragg peered at the note through sleep-fogged eyes, then tossed it aside and grunted at Polk's messenger: "Say to the general we shall maintain our position at every hazard."

The seeds of doubt had been planted in his mind, however, and by ten o'clock the next morning, they had sprouted and borne fruit. It was raining again, and Stones River, already swollen with runoff, was rising fast, threatening to isolate the Confederate divisions stationed on the west bank. Scouts reported that Rosecrans had been reinforced in the night. "Common prudence and the safety of my army . . . left no doubt in my mind as to the necessity of my withdrawal from so unequal a contest," Bragg later wrote.

That evening the Army of Tennessee—less 1,294 men killed, 7,945 wounded, and about 2,500 captured or missing—disengaged from the enemy and marched away to the southeast. It would not stop until it reached the Duck River Valley, some thirty miles from Murfreesboro, where Bragg hoped that rest, plentiful food, and a rigorous regimen of drill would restore it to fighting trim.

But renewing the army's faith in its commander would not be so easily accomplished, as Bragg learned firsthand on the miserable, slogging retreat from Murfreesboro. Approaching the town of Tullahoma on the afternoon of January 5, he came upon a disheveled enlisted man sitting atop a broken-down mule. "Who are you?" Bragg barked, offended by the man's slovenliness and his failure to salute.

"Nobody," came the snarling reply.

"Where did you come from?"

"Nowhere."

"Where are you going?"

"I don't know."

"Where do you belong?"

"Don't belong nowhere."

The general's face flushed with anger, and he shouted: "Don't you belong to Bragg's army?"

"Bragg's army! Bragg's army!" sneered the bedraggled soldier, his bloodshot eyes sparking with hatred. "He's got no army! He shot half of it in Kentucky, and the other half he killed up at Murfreesboro!" Then he kicked up his mule and cantered away.

It was an entirely different story for Rosecrans. His command had suffered severe losses also—1,677 men killed, 7,543 wounded, and 3,686 captured or missing—but he was hailed as a hero both by his own soldiers and
by the public at large. "God bless you, and all with you," Lincoln wired him
on January 5. Henry Halleck, who had been sorely tried by Rosecrans's interminable supply requests, grudgingly chimed in: "The victory was well
earned and one of the most brilliant of the war," he wrote. "All honor to
the Army of the Cumberland—thanks to the living, and tears for the
lamented dead."

To some it seemed like sacrilege to talk of victory when Rosecrans had
lost more than 30 percent of his army and allowed a stricken enemy to
withdraw unmolested from under his nose. But that missed the point. What
mattered most was that he had refused to be beaten at a time when the
North, dismayed by the Fredericksburg disaster and struggling to digest the
Emancipation Proclamation, could not have borne another defeat.

THREE

MIST, MUDDLE, AND FOG

It was a travel-worn Jefferson Davis who returned to Richmond late on the afternoon of January 5, having journeyed more than 2,500 miles and made better than two dozen speeches during his twenty-seven-day morale-building tour of the Confederacy. He was in high spirits, however, as he rode from the Richmond & Petersburg Railroad depot up Ninth Street, past Capitol Square, and then down Clay Street to the Executive Mansion where his wife and four children awaited him.

The trip had been a great success, in his estimation. His public appearances had done much to revive the patriotic ardor of citizens in the West, and a flood of good news seemed to lend credence to his oft-repeated claim that the condition of the Confederacy was in every respect improved over what it had been twelve months ago. He was more than ever convinced that 1863 was destined to be remembered in the same way 1781 was—as the year in which a struggling new nation defeated a military colossus and secured its independence.

As his carriage creaked up Council Chamber Hill, Davis reviewed the roll of recent successes. Here in Virginia, Lee's troops were holding fast to the heights above Fredericksburg, their guns trained out over the fields where two weeks earlier Burnside's blue-clad invaders had been repelled with terrific slaughter. The latest communiqué from Tennessee, dated January 3, claimed that Bragg had driven Rosecrans back from Murfreesboro, thwarting Union designs on the vital rail junction at Chattanooga. Farther west in the Volunteer State, cavalry commander Nathan Bedford Forrest had led four regiments of rebel horsemen on a slashing foray against Federal supply lines, inflicting 2,000 casualties, seizing a large quantity of arms and ammunition, and laying waste to a sixty-mile stretch of the Mobile & Ohio Railroad. Simultaneously, Pemberton had sent his cavalry, led by Earl Van Dorn, on a raid of the Union supply depot at Holly Springs in northeastern Mississippi. Swooping down at dawn on December 20, Van Dorn's 3,500 riders had overwhelmed the Yankee garrison and put more than a million dollars' worth of food and munitions to the torch. Grant had been forced to cancel his offensive and pull his army back into Tennessee.

This abrupt withdrawal had had the happy result of permitting Pemberton to rush reinforcements from Grenada to Vicksburg, where Sherman was getting ready to mount an attack with the troops he had brought downriver from Memphis during the third week of December. The red-bearded Ohioan had expected to find a skeleton force garrisoning the Confederate fortifications on Chickasaw Bluffs a few miles north of Vicksburg, but when he stormed the position on December 29, he ran into 14,000 dug-in defenders. After losing nearly 1,800 men without gaining an inch of ground, Sherman gave up and retreated to Milliken's Bend, a muddy stretch of bottomland on the Louisiana side of the Mississippi River fifteen miles above Vicksburg.

This catalog of triumphs delighted Davis. Holding the line in Virginia, Tennessee, and Mississippi was the key to victory for the Confederacy. But it was word of another spectacular coup scored in faraway Texas that did the most to reaffirm his faith in the resiliency and resourcefulness of Southern men-at-arms. Major General John B. Magruder—dubbed "Prince John" because of his imperious manner, flamboyant dress, and fondness for acting in Shakespearean theatricals—had humiliated the heretofore invincible Union navy in a daring New Year's Eve action at Galveston Bay. Using two shallow-draft steamboats armored with cotton bales and manned by infantry volunteers, he had sortied against a Federal fleet consisting of five ships mounting a total of twenty-eight large-caliber naval guns. The Confederate "cottonclads" *Bayou City* and *Neptune* had attacked in the dead of night and caught the Yankees dozing. One Union ship, *Westfield,* had run aground and been scuttled, while another, *Harriet Lane,* had struck its colors after being boarded by a party of saber-wielding rebels. The remaining three, *Clifton, Owasco,* and *Sachem,* had fled to the open sea, leaving the ungainly Confederate craft masters of the harbor.

While this lopsided naval battle was going on, 500 Texans had made their way across an unguarded bridge linking the mainland with the city of Galveston and stormed the wharf, which was defended by three companies of Federal infantry. At first the bluecoats had put up a hard fight, but when their supporting armada was routed, they surrendered en masse. In one fell swoop Magruder had cleared Texas soil of the last vestige of Union presence, and ruined the plans of New England textile mill owners, who had hoped to revive their cotton-starved industry with long staple from the Lone Star State.

It was a glorious victory, and taken in conjunction with Fredericksburg, Murfreesboro, Holly Springs, and Chickasaw Bluffs, it seemed to bode well for Confederate fortunes in 1863. The three cities the Federals had set out to seize—Richmond, Chattanooga, and Vicksburg—remained firmly in Southern hands, and the repulse of the invading armies had been so bloody that it seemed possible the North might soon sicken of war and sue for peace. If this came to pass, no small amount of the credit would be due Davis for his administrative acumen, strategic sagacity, and unwavering fealty to the Confederate cause. Thus it was with a warm feeling of camaraderie that he looked out at Thomas Crawford's bronze equestrian statue of Washington, hero of the first American war for independence, as his carriage rolled past it, carrying him to the handsome gray-stuccoed house at 1201 East Clay Street.

Varina Davis embraced her husband in the mansion's vestibule, and then noting how weary he looked, she pleaded with him to get some sleep. But before he could go to his bedchamber, he heard the toot of horns, the thump of drums, and the clash of cymbals drifting up from Clay Street. Looking out the window, he saw that Captain J. B. Smith's Silver Band, accompanied by a crowd of several hundred citizens, had come to serenade him on the occasion of his return from the West. The musicians played "Listen to the Mockingbird" and several other popular tunes, and the throng shouted for him to come out and speak.

The cheering redoubled when he stepped onto the portico, but it lapsed into embarrassed silence when the bandleader introduced him as "the President of the United States," before quickly correcting himself and saying "the President of the Confederate States."

"I am proud to acknowledge that title, but the other I will spurn," Davis said to the flustered musician. Then in a voice hoarse and raspy from overuse, but still possessed of what one listener described as "peculiar and startling sweetness," he spoke at length of Virginia's revolutionary heritage and compared the great deeds of bygone days with the achievements of the present generation. "You assumed to yourselves the right, as your fathers had done before you, to declare yourselves independent," he told the audience. "You have shown yourselves in no respect to be degenerate sons of your fathers."

This drew loud applause, punctuated by whoops and whistles. After the clapping had subsided, Davis continued, denouncing the motives and conduct of the Northern invaders in language that thrilled his listeners. "For what are they waging war?" he cried, striking his fist into his palm. "They say to preserve the Union. Can they preserve the Union . . . by striking at everything which is dear to man?—by showing themselves so utterly disgraced that if the question was proposed to you whether you would combine with hyenas or Yankees, I trust every Virginian would say, 'Give me the hyenas.' "

Again the crowd roared, laughing, cheering, and shouting "Good! Good!"

"My friends," Davis continued, his tone becoming softer and more intimate, "the sacrifices we have been subjected to in common, and the glory which encircles our brow has made us a band of brothers, and, I trust, we will be united forever. . . . May God prosper our cause and may we live to give to our children untarnished the rich inheritance which our fathers gave us. Good night!"

The next morning Davis received shattering news from Tennessee: Bragg had not won a great victory after all. His initial report stating that the Yankees were falling back to Nashville was false. Instead, it was the Confederates who were withdrawing.

Public reaction to this bombshell was swift and furious. "Boomerang Bragg" had done it again, raged the newspapers. His retreat from Murfreesboro had been ignominious and cowardly. His inflated claims of success—especially his premature assertion that God had granted the Southern people a Happy New Year—had been dishonest and despicable. "So far the news [from Tennessee] has come in the classical style of the Southwest," fumed the Richmond *Daily Examiner.* "When the southern army fights a battle, we first hear that it has gained one of the most stupendous victories on record; that regiments from Mississippi, Texas, Louisiana, Arkansas, et cetera have exhibited an irresistible and superhuman valor unknown in history this side of Sparta and Rome. As for their generals, they usually get all their clothes shot off, and replace them with a suit of glory. The enemy, of course, is simply annihilated. Next day more dispatches come, still very good, but not quite as good as the first. The telegrams of the third day are invariably such as make a mist, muddle, and a fog of the whole affair."

As if Bragg's belated admission that he had ceded middle Tennessee to the Yankees weren't bad enough, word soon reached Richmond that the general and his subordinates were squabbling fiercely over who was responsible for the setback. "Bragg is said to have lost the confidence of his command completely," wrote Robert G. H. Kean, head of the Confederate Bureau of War. "He is cordially hated by a large number of his officers." Confirmation of this view came on January 10 when the Chattanooga

Daily Rebel reported that unnamed Army of Tennessee staff aides were accusing Bragg of abandoning Murfreesboro against the advice of his generals and while the enemy was in full retreat. This sensational charge was reprinted by newspapers all over the South, and as a consequence the calls for Bragg's dismissal grew louder.

The last thing Davis wanted to do was fire his old friend. He hoped that the storm of criticism would soon blow over. But Bragg, chafing at the falsehoods being spread by the press, promptly made matters worse. On January 11 he sent a letter to his corps and division commanders asking them to absolve him of the *Daily Rebel's* charge. "Unanimous as you were in council in verbally advising a retrograde movement [from Murfreesboro], I cannot doubt that you will cheerfully attest the same in writing," he wrote.

If he had ended the letter there, all would have been well. But he was looking for an endorsement as well as exoneration, and so he went on, concluding his appeal with a dramatic and, as events would soon show, foolhardy promise. "I desire that you will consult your subordinate commanders and be candid with me," he huffed. "I shall retire without a regret if I find that I have lost the good opinion of my generals, upon whom I have ever relied as upon a foundation of rock."

This ill-advised declaration gave his subordinates just the opening they were looking for. Without demur they absolved Bragg of responsibility for originating the idea of retreat, then told him that he no longer possessed the army's confidence and should step down. Shocked to find that his foundation of rock was actually a pool of quicksand, Bragg told his friend, Alabama senator Clement C. Clay, that he was thinking about resigning his commission. But he soon thought better of it. His irascibility returned, and he decided that he would be damned if he would take the blame for the incompetence of others. In a letter to Louisiana senator Thomas J. Semmes, he depicted himself as a martyr betrayed by a gang of Judases. As for the circular he had written asking his corps and division commanders to critique his leadership, he insisted that it had been grossly and intentionally misrepresented. He had meant to elicit an answer to one question—had his subordinates advised him to retreat from Murfreesboro?—not to solicit their puling criticism of his abilities. His words had been twisted out of context by a cabal of hostile officers hell-bent on injuring him, he said.

General Braxton Bragg, C.S.A.
(Library of Congress; photo
courtesy of The Museum
of the Confederacy,
Richmond, Virginia)

As the torrent of letters and dispatches bearing upon the Bragg imbroglio flowed across his desk, Davis reacted with consternation and dismay. He directed Joseph Johnston to investigate the goings-on in Tullahoma and then report his findings to Richmond. The president would act after he received Johnston's recommendation.

Having dealt with the Bragg problem in this roundabout fashion, Davis was free to turn his attention to political matters and specifically to preparing a message to Congress, which would reconvene in Richmond on January 12. He did not relish the prospect of addressing that quarrelsome body, whose members seemed able to agree on only one thing: that the commander in chief was to blame for all the Confederacy's woes. In recent months they had denounced him as a despot-in-the-making for his backing of the Conscription Act; as a West Point worshiper for his insistence on appointing professionals to important military posts; and as a milksop Mars for his adoption of a defensive rather than offensive war-fighting strategy. For good measure they had attacked him personally, charging that he was aloof and arrogant, a stuffed shirt, a supercilious prig. He had tried to emulate his hero George Washington and shrug off this vituperation, writing that "revolutions develop the high qualities of the good and the great, but they cannot change the nature of the vicious and the selfish." The harsh criticism had stung him, however, and it was with a sense of trepidation bordering on dread that he set to work on his speech, knowing that he would be appealing to a suspicious, hostile audience for sympathy and support.

He began the twenty-page message with a recitation of recent Confederate triumphs, glossing over as best he could Bragg's retreat in Tennessee, moved on to a lengthy discussion of foreign relations (or the lack thereof), then launched into the centerpiece of his speech, an impassioned excoriation of the Emancipation Proclamation.

This tirade was sure to be well received by the fire-eaters in Congress and the press, but Davis knew that indignant oratory could be only a partial response to emancipation. If Lincoln's proclamation had transformed the conflict into a remorseless, revolutionary struggle, then the Confederacy had to answer with desperate measures of her own. Money, men, and supplies were urgently needed, and he therefore asked Congress to adopt a legislative program strengthening tax collection, sustaining the Conscription Act, and facilitating impressment of foodstuffs, wagons, livestock, and other items needed by Confederate forces in the field.

Davis was keenly aware of the irony inherent in his advocating such radical steps. A stalwart defender of states' rights during the antebellum years, he now was arguing that to provide for the common defense, it was necessary to concentrate power in the hands of the government at Richmond. "Our government, born of the spirit of freedom and of the equality and independence of the states, [cannot survive] a selfish or jealous disposition, making each only careful of its own interest or safety," he concluded.

This was nothing more than common sense, and the majority of the congressmen, as well as the bulk of the Southern press, accepted it as such. And yet Davis had reason to fear that many Southerners would cling to the self-destructive dogma of states' rights even if it meant throwing away the Confederacy's chance at independence. A lifetime of being in the minority, of believing that opposition was the essence of politics, had conditioned an entire generation of Southern officeholders to assail and obstruct the central government at every turn. Chief among the naysayers was Georgia governor Joseph Brown, who had denounced taxation, conscription, and impressment of private property as an assault on states' rights. Even Vice President Alexander Stephens had turned against his own administration because he thought it was becoming too powerful.

Davis was frustrated by the obtuseness of Brown and Stephens. "When everything is at stake and the united power of the South alone can save us, it is sad to know that men can deal in such paltry complaints," he wrote. He was determined to lead the Confederacy to victory even if it meant engineering unsettling changes. But he did not want to be a dictator as his enemies charged. The Confederate president, whoever he was, should possess only moral authority, he told his aide, Colonel William Preston Johnston; otherwise "the principle for which we contend is a failure."

Davis did wield arbitrary power on occasion, though not in the sinister way his critics claimed. The previous summer a South Carolina woman had asked him to intercede with army authorities and allow her fiancé to come home and marry her. "Jeems is willin', I is willin', his mammy says she is willin', but Jeems's captain, he ain't willin'," she had written. "Now when we are all willin' 'ceptin' for Jeems's captain, I think you might let up and let Jeems come. I'll make him go straight back when he's done got married and fight just as hard as ever."

The president had studied this letter with the same care he lavished on all his official correspondence, and after pondering all the possible ramifications, he had forwarded it to the secretary of war with the following notation scribbled on the back: "Let Jeems Go. Jefferson Davis."

Just before daybreak, in a cold, cramped, second-floor room in the Union Hotel Hospital in Georgetown, Louisa May Alcott of Concord, Massachusetts, was awakened by a loud knock at the door. "They've come!" a gruff voice bellowed. "They've come! Hurry up, ladies—you're wanted."

Springing from her bed, Louisa donned her uniform, threw a red scarf around her head, and rushed to the window to look out. This was the moment she had been waiting for since starting her tour of duty as an army nurse several weeks earlier. "Having a taste for 'ghastliness,' I had rather longed for the wounded to arrive," she later confessed. But when she saw the line of ambulances drawn up on the street below, her heart sank, and she briefly "indulged in a most unpatriotic wish" that she were safe at home again.

In the corridor her nose was assailed by a foul odor. The reek of stale sweat and dried blood, the stench of unemptied chamber pots and spoiled food, made her gag. She was used to sunshine and fresh air, and the dark, fetid atmosphere of this dilapidated old lodging house disgusted her. Downstairs more horrors awaited. The large room that had once served as the hotel's lobby was jammed with soldiers wounded at Fredericksburg. Some staggered in on rude crutches, while others had to be carried on canvas stretchers; exhausted and ashen-faced, they leaned against the walls or lay on the floor, shivering and moaning.

Louisa tiptoed around this human wreckage and made her way to the ballroom, which had been transformed into a forty-bed ward. Entering the dimly lit chamber with its flaking plaster and peeling paint, she beheld a heartrending sight: " 'Round the great stove was gathered the dreariest group I ever saw—ragged, gaunt and pale, mud to the knees, with bloody bandages untouched since put on days before; many bundled up in blankets, coats being lost or useless; and all wearing that disheartened look which proclaimed defeat, more plainly than any telegram."

The matron thrust a basin, sponge, towels, and a block of brown soap into Louisa's hands and told her to start washing. "If she had requested me to shave them all, or dance a hornpipe on the stove funnel, I should have been less staggered," Louisa wrote. "However, there was no time for nonsense, and, having resolved when I came to do everything I was bid, I drowned my scruples in my washbowl, clutched my soap manfully, and, assuming a businesslike air, made a dab at the first dirty specimen I saw."

The object of her attentions was a withered old Irishman who had been wounded in the head. As she pulled off his filthy boots and began bathing his feet, he rolled his eyes and blessed her, babbling in a brogue so comical that she soon found herself giggling. After that her self-consciousness disappeared, and she went from one soldier to the next, scrubbing and toweling "like any tidy parent on a Saturday night."

When the washing was done and the men had been put into bed, great platters of bread, meat, soup, and coffee were carried in, and those who could sit up and use their hands ate eagerly. After they were finished and the dishes had been cleared, the surgeons started on their rounds. Louisa ac-

Louisa May Alcott.
(Photo courtesy of the Louisa
May Alcott Association)

companied a doctor who had served with the British army in the Crimea. He was an authority on battlefield injuries and seemed to regard a shattered body "very much as I should have regarded a damaged garment . . . cutting, sawing, patching, and piecing, with the enthusiasm of an accomplished surgical seamstress." She was fascinated by the deft, nimble-fingered way he cleaned and dressed wounds, but when he took out his knives and bone saw and began performing amputations, it was all she could do to keep from being sick. No anesthetic was used, and the hapless patients thrashed in agony as their mangled limbs were resected. One or two screamed and cursed, but most suffered in silence, and the deathly hush that had fallen over the ballroom was "broken only by some quiet request for roller, instruments, or plaster, a sigh from the patient, or a sympathizing murmur from the nurse."

Miss Alcott was a budding writer of stories and poems who had recently had one of her pieces published in the *Atlantic Monthly*. She knew nothing of treating wounds and precious little about caring for the sick, but she possessed the attributes that Dorothea Dix, superintendent of female nurses, looked for in applicants to the nursing service. She was thirty and unmarried, "plain almost to repulsion in dress"—a big, rawboned woman with her hair drawn up in a severe bun, kind and gentle, yet strong enough to lift a full-grown man out of bed should the need arise. Like the other women who toiled long hours tending to the wounded soldiers, she was utterly devoted to the Union cause. "I long to be a man," she wrote in her journal, "but as I can't fight I will content myself with working for those who can." And work she did, serving and fetching, washing and feeding, flitting about the hospital "like a massive cherubim," sprinkling lavender water wherever she went in a gallant attempt to keep the bad smells at bay.

Her energy and initiative did not go unnoticed, and she was soon promoted to the position of night nurse. The soldiers in the ballroom ward learned to look forward to the late shift and the arrival of jolly Louisa, who chased away their "blue devils" by telling jokes, playing word games, and reading aloud to them from the novels of Charles Dickens. When it was time to turn the lights down, she tucked in their blankets and plumped their pillows, and as they dropped off to sleep, the last thing they saw was her stout form, wrapped in a black shawl and red muffler, settling down by the stove to begin her lonely all-night vigil.

Back in Concord Louisa had imagined that nursing would be exciting and romantic, and the squalor and tedium of hospital life came as a shock to her. Still, she thought the job had its rewards. "Though often homesick, heartsick, and worn out, I like it," she wrote. "[I] find real pleasure in comforting, tending, and cheering these poor souls who seem to love me, to feel my sympathy though unspoken, and acknowledge my hearty goodwill. . . . The men are docile, respectful, and affectionate . . . truly lovable and manly, many of them."

Her favorite was John Sulie, a tall, handsome Virginian with "a noble character, a heart as warm and tender as a woman's, a nature fresh and frank as any child's." He had been shot in the chest and was dying; on the night he perished, Louisa stayed by his bedside, holding his hand and whispering words of comfort in his ear, and at dawn when the watchman came to light the morning fire she was still there, weeping softly and struggling to free her fingers from his cold, lifeless grasp.

John Sulie's death dismayed Louisa. She tried to keep her spirits up, but found it impossible. To make matters worse, the hospital's pestilential air and bacteria-tainted water were making her sick. She was afflicted with diarrhea, nausea, and a hacking cough. During the second week of January she came down with a high fever. The doctors said she had typhoid pneumonia, and they placed her in quarantine in a tiny bedchamber on one of the hospital's upper floors.

The enforced isolation made Louisa miserable. "A pleasant prospect," she wrote, "for a lonely soul five hundred miles from home! Sit and sew on the boys' clothes, write letters, sleep, and read; try to talk and keep merry but fail decidedly, as day after day goes by, and I feel no better. Dream awfully, and wake unrefreshed, think of home and wonder if I am to die here."

The treatment for typhoid was calomel, a mercury compound administered as an emetic. It was given in huge doses that caused dreadful side effects: patients hallucinated, lost their teeth and hair, suffered from grossly swollen tongues, and exhibited other symptoms of acute mercury poisoning. If they survived this horrendous cure, they were likely to be afflicted with rheumaticlike pains and uncontrollable trembling for the rest of their lives. The doctors at the Union Hotel Hospital prescribed this therapy for Louisa, and it almost killed her.

For days on end she lay semicomatose in bed, and even when she was awake, she was far too weak to venture from her room. Dorothea Dix came to call with a basket of gifts: wine, tea, cologne, a blanket and pillow, a fan, and most precious of all, a New Testament with the initials D.D. inscribed on the flyleaf. The visit cheered Louisa briefly, but her condition continued to worsen. Finally, during the third week of January, the hospital's head nurse wired Bronson Alcott to come for his daughter lest she die alone in her dreary little cell far from home and family.

During the long journey back to Boston, Louisa slipped in and out of consciousness. In her delirium she was haunted by bizarre nightmares, the most persistent of which was "the conviction that I had married a stout, handsome Spaniard dressed in black velvet, with very soft hands and a voice that was continually saying 'Lie still, my dear!' " When her father led her from the car at North Station "all blowzed, crazy, and weak," by- standers stopped and stared. When she stumbled through the door of the house at Concord, sweating and shaking, her hair gone and her once- glowing face pale and pitifully emaciated, her mother and sister hardly recognized her.

Louisa May Alcott's great adventure was over. She had come home from the war "a ghost hidden in an old wrapper and a blanket, a soldier re- turned from her own campaign upon a field called Georgetown." For her troubles she received an envelope from Washington containing ten green- backs—the newfangled dollar bills the U.S. Treasury had recently begun printing—and a stiffly worded letter of gratitude. But the hardships she had endured, the suffering and bravery she had seen during her brief career as a nurse, meant much more to her than money or a citation. Adopting the pen name "Tribulation Periwinkle," she began writing a series of vignettes about the surgeons, soldiers, and nurses she had met, drawing from mem- ory and from the letters she had sent to her parents to re-create the strange, terrible world of the Washington hospitals.

When these articles were published in *Commonwealth* magazine in the spring of 1863, then reprinted in a slender volume titled *Hospital Sketches,* they created a sensation. Thousands of readers laughed and cried over the tales of Nurse Periwinkle, and critics hailed them as "graphically drawn" yet softened with "touches of quiet humor." Louisa, who had never ex- pected to enjoy popular success as a writer, was delighted by her newfound celebrity. She promptly put it to use recruiting other young women for the nursing service. "Let no one who sincerely desires to help the work on in this way delay going through any fear," she exhorted prospective volun- teers, adding that "I, for one, would return tomorrow, on the 'up-again- and-take-another' principle, if I could."

But privately she harbored no illusions about the grim reality of nurs- ing or about her own sad experience at the Union Hotel Hospital. "Once I went to heaven, and found it a twilight place, with people darting through the air in a queer way—all very busy, and dismal, and ordinary," she wrote in her journal. "Miss Dix . . . and other people were there; but I thought it dark and slow, and wished I hadn't come."

Louisa May Alcott's feelings of gloom and desolation were shared by many Northerners in January 1863. The war was not going well, and Lincoln's signing of the final Emancipation Proclamation had obliterated the last vestiges of political bipartisanship, pitting Democrat against Republican in a bitter clash over the nature and direction of the conflict.

The president's enemies attacked him savagely on the slavery issue, and even his closest allies wondered whether he had made a terrible mistake. Judge David Davis of Illinois, a longtime confidant, pleaded with him to alter his course on emancipation lest it tear the country apart. Old friend Orville Browning fretted that the nation was upon the brink of ruin and said that he "could see no hope of an amendment in affairs unless the president would change his policy, and withdraw or greatly modify the proclamation." But Lincoln remained resolute. While he admitted that in the short run the proclamation had done about as much harm as good, he insisted that over the long haul it would strengthen the Union cause.

Already there were indications that the edict was having the desired effect, especially abroad. Three months earlier it had seemed certain that Britain, backed by France, would recognize the Confederacy and break the Union naval blockade in order to obtain cotton for its languishing textile industry. But the signing of the proclamation had rallied the sympathies of the English working class, which bitterly opposed slavery. Mass meetings and other public demonstrations in support of the Union had helped dissuade the British government from intervening on behalf of the Confederacy. Emancipation "has done more for us here than all our former victories and all our diplomacy," exulted a member of the American delegation in London. "I never quite appreciated the 'moral influence' of American democracy, nor the cause that the privileged classes in Europe have to fear us, until I saw how directly it works."

Nor was the Union army's reaction to emancipation altogether negative, as it had first seemed. The abolitionists in the ranks—a small but vocal minority—rejoiced that the government had finally made freedom for the slaves an avowed war aim. "I do not intend to shirk now there is really something to fight for," wrote Private Uriah Parmelee of Connecticut. "I mean *Freedom*. . . . I do not expect any great success at present, but so long as I am convinced that we are on the right side I trust that no failure will dishearten me." Even more significant were the expressions of support that came from officers and enlisted men who were not abolitionists but had come to recognize that the war could no longer be fought on the old basis—that "behind the rebel army of soldiers, the black army of laborers was feeding and sustaining the rebellion and there could be no victory until its main support was taken away." Private John Burrill, a Democrat who had fulminated against abolition in the past, told his parents that he had changed his mind and was now in favor of "putting away any institution if by so doing it will help put down the rebellion, for I hold that nothing should stand in the way of the Union—niggers, nor anything else."

Lincoln was still worried about the peace movement on the home front, however. He told Massachusetts senator Charles Sumner that he feared " 'the fire in the rear'—meaning the Democracy, especially at the Northwest," more than he did the activities of the Confederate armed forces.

When the president spoke of the "Democracy at the Northwest," he was referring to the Democratic Party in Illinois, Indiana, and Ohio, states with large populations of Southern sympathizers who detested blacks and abolitionists with equal fervor and who objected to the war because it had cut off their traditional trade routes along the Mississippi, Wabash, and Ohio Rivers. Grant's failure to reopen the Mississippi, coupled with Lincoln's proclamation of emancipation, had brought the simmering antiwar passions of these negrophobic "Butternuts" to a boil. They were threatening to secede, establish a "Northwest Confederacy," and make a separate peace with the South.

The paladin of these corn-country Copperheads was a charismatic congressman from Dayton, Ohio, named Clement Laird Vallandigham. Tall and strikingly handsome, with smoky gray eyes, a large, expressive mouth, and a

smooth, sonorous voice, "Valiant Val," as his admirers called him, was an uncompromising Midwestern sectionalist. He believed the war to be a "terrible and bloody revolution" perpetrated by Lincoln and his minions for the purpose of destroying slavery, expanding the powers of the central government, and hastening the political and financial ascendancy of urban-industrial New England at the expense of the western farm country. "It is the desire of my heart to restore the Union, the Federal Union as it was forty years ago," he proclaimed, meaning the Union with slavery and states' rights intact. He worked tirelessly to accomplish that goal, condemning the conflict, castigating Lincoln, and proselytizing for peace at every turn.

Clement L. Vallandigham.
(Courtesy Ohio
Historical Society)

Not surprisingly Vallandigham's criticism of the president enraged congressional Republicans; they branded the Dayton representative a scoundrel and a traitor. But with every battlefield defeat and every new casualty list his constituency grew and his antiwar message became more alluring. "The Constitution as it is, the Union as it was," was his motto, and his program for peace, spelled out in crisp, compelling phrases, possessed a powerful demagogic appeal.

"Stop fighting," he proposed. "Make an armistice—no formal treaty. Withdraw your army from the seceded states. Reduce both armies to a fair and sufficient peace establishment. Declare absolute free trade between North and South. . . . Let slavery alone." If such a policy were embraced, he said, the warring sections would quickly reunite and all would be as it was before the conflict began. But if the struggle continued, if emancipation proceeded apace and Americans continued butchering one another, then, he warned, "I see nothing before us but universal political and social revolution, anarchy and bloodshed."

The notion that North and South would reconcile their differences and restore the old Union the moment the shooting stopped was, of course, preposterous. The Confederacy was not going to dissolve itself simply because Washington called a cease-fire. Jefferson Davis had made this clear when he told the rebel Congress on January 14 that events had rendered reunion "forever impossible." The only way the North could now make peace with the South was to recognize its independence and agree to a boundary—terms tantamount to surrender. Vallandigham ignored this, however, and went on playing to the emotions of war-weary Northerners, telling them that a quick cessation of hostilities, followed by an effortless return to the antebellum past, was possible. He was an eloquent and persuasive orator, and when he preached his gospel of peace and claimed that he possessed the "nerves of steel" and "strength of will" to bind up the nation's wounds and bring back the good old days, his listeners desperately wanted to believe him.

He, meanwhile, believed passionately in his own star. Ohio Republicans had gerrymandered him into defeat in the 1862 congressional elections, but he had no intention of returning to private life. He planned to campaign for the governorship of the Buckeye State in 1863, and if that bid went well, a run for the presidency in 1864 was a distinct possibility. He certainly acted like a national candidate as he bade farewell to Congress in February and returned to Dayton by way of Philadelphia, Newark, New York, and Hartford, addressing boisterous crowds at each stop, assailing the administration and touting himself as the Democrat who could lead the country "through the Red Sea of war and into the promised land of peace."

Lincoln knew that Vallandigham was a formidable political rival, but he was too busy grappling with other, more pressing problems to try to neutralize the Ohio demagogue now. One of his strongest supporters in the

Midwest, Indiana governor Oliver P. Morton, had sent him a telegram on January 3 saying that Peace Democrats in his state were planning a political coup d'état. "It is contemplated when the legislature meets . . . to pass a joint resolution acknowledging the Southern Confederacy and urging the states of the Northwest to dissolve all constitutional relations with the New England states," Morton wrote. "The same thing is on foot in Illinois."

On January 14 a motion was introduced in the lower house of the Indiana legislature vowing that the Hoosier State would not contribute another man or dollar to the Union war effort until the Emancipation Proclamation was rescinded. Two weeks later a second motion was brought by the insurgent representatives demanding that Lincoln call a six-month armistice, convene a national peace conference, and negotiate reunion with the South.

Adoption of these antiwar resolutions was merely a prelude to an attempt by the Democratic majority to take control of Indiana's troops away from the governor and place it in the hands of a legislative committee. If this came to pass, Morton warned, the state's volunteer regiments would be ordered to withdraw from the army and come home. The only way to head off such a catastrophe was to break up the legislature, a feat he accomplished by ordering Republican representatives to quit the statehouse, thereby depriving the body of a quorum. The trouble with this stratagem was that it left the state's coffers empty, no appropriations having been voted on before the abrupt adjournment. But Secretary of War Stanton fixed the problem by advancing Morton $250,000 from a special War Department slush fund. "If the cause fails, you and I will be covered with prosecutions, imprisoned, driven from the country," the governor wrote Stanton after receiving the six-figure Treasury warrant. The secretary was unfazed. "If the cause fails I do not wish to live," he brusquely replied.

Lincoln was troubled by this and other extralegal actions his administration had taken since being sworn into office in 1861, but he saw no alternative if the war was to be won. Military arrests, suppression of free speech, suspension of the writ of habeas corpus—all were permissible, he argued, when in case of rebellion or invasion the public safety required it.

He tried to curb the worst abuses, instructing his department commanders to exercise great caution in muzzling the opposition press, and to refrain from jailing civilians unless it was absolutely necessary. But forbearance on the part of the military was conspicuously lacking, and during the bleak winter of 1863, the dank, rat-infested cells in New York's Fort Lafayette, Boston's Fort Warren, and Washington's Old Capitol Prison filled to overflowing with political prisoners whose only crime was daring to speak out against the war.

Richard Henry Dana, Jr., author of the best-selling memoir *Two Years Before the Mast,* took the pulse of Washington in late February and concluded that the Lincoln administration was on its last legs. "The lack of respect for the president in all parties is unconcealed," he wrote in a letter to a colleague back in Massachusetts. "He has no admirers, no enthusiastic supporters, none to bet on his head. If a Republican convention were to be held tomorrow, he would not get the vote of a state. He does not act, or talk, or feel like the ruler of a great empire in a great crisis. . . . He has a kind of shrewdness and common sense, mother wit, and slipshod, low-leveled honesty, that made him a good Western jury lawyer. But he is an unutterable calamity to us where he is. Only the army can save us."

There was some truth to what Dana said. Lincoln's seat-of-the-pants administrative style was considered scandalous by much of official Washington, and his standing in the Republican Party had fallen to an all-time low. But the Massachusetts author was mistaken if he thought salvation lay with the armed forces. To the contrary, the Union's military situation, both ashore and afloat, seemed to be going from bad to worse as the winter of 1863 wore on.

The latest reversals were preponderantly maritime. This was especially discouraging, for until the New Year's Eve fiasco at Galveston Bay, Union saltwater ships had suffered nary a setback in more than twenty-one months of war. Now, in the wake of the Magruder affair, the defeats were coming thick and fast, and the coast of Texas was once again the scene of the navy's humiliation.

The most startling and costly of these incidents began late on the afternoon of January 11, when a lookout aboard the USS *Brooklyn,* flagship of the Federal squadron blockading Galveston Bay, spotted a bark-rigged vessel beating up from the southeast. Union Commodore Henry H. Bell dispatched the eight-gun side-wheeler, USS *Hatteras,* to investigate. When *Hatteras* tried to pull alongside, the mystery ship made sail and slid southward in the gathering dusk, her sharply raked prow slicing effortlessly through the Gulf swells as she led the Union gunboat farther and farther away from the rest of the fleet. Night fell, and still the two ships sailed on. Then, abruptly, the stranger slowed, allowing the Union steamer to close to within seventy-five yards.

"What ship is that?" cried *Hatteras*'s captain, Homer C. Blake.

"This is Her Majesty's ship *Petrel,*" came the prompt reply. Blake heaved a sigh of relief and put out a boat with an inspection party aboard, intending to check *Petrel's* registry. But before the launch could come along-side, another voice bellowed across the water: "This is the Confederate States ship *Alabama*. Fire!" and a heavy broadside ripped a gaping hole in *Hatteras's* side. The Union sailors tried to fight back, but their ship was sink-ing beneath them. After thirteen minutes of chaotic, one-sided combat, Blake struck his colors. One hundred six bluejackets went over the side—two had been killed by rebel fire—and six minutes later *Hatteras* slipped be-neath the waves, the thirty-fifth vessel to fall victim to the Confederate commerce raider *Alabama,* Captain Raphael Semmes commanding.

Semmes's presence in these waters, far from his favored Atlantic and Caribbean cruising grounds, was no accident. He had learned from captured Northern papers that a Union fleet was on station off Galveston and had decided to prey on it. *Hatteras's* destruction marked the first time a Confed-erate raider had vanquished a warship of the U.S. Navy, and Semmes, known as "Old Beeswax" because of the long, exquisitely groomed points of his black handlebar mustache, was exceedingly proud of the accomplishment. He was pleased, too, that he had been able to pick up all of *Hatteras's* sur-vivors and put a hundred miles between himself and the rest of the Yankee ships before Commodore Bell realized what was happening.

News of *Hatteras's* sinking shocked navy secretary Gideon Welles. "I am grieved and depressed, not so much for the loss . . . as from a conviction that there has been want of good management," he confided in his diary. But worse was yet to come. On January 15 another Confederate raider, CSS *Florida,* slipped through the cordon of Federal ships bottling up Mo-bile Bay and raced out to sea. Within three days of her breakout, she had seized and burned a trio of Union merchantmen, the first of more than thirty-five prizes she would take during a highly destructive twenty-month cruise. Nor was that all. On January 21, at Sabine Pass on the Texas-Louisiana border, a pair of Confederate cottonclads, *Josiah Bell* and *Uncle Ben,* duplicated Magruder's exploit at Galveston by attacking and captur-ing two Federal warships, *Velocity* and *Morning Light,* which had been blockading the anchorage at Port Arthur.

Despite its discomfiture at losing six ships and being outsailed and out-fought by the swashbuckling Confederate captains, the Union navy con-tinued to control the southern coast from Norfolk to New Orleans. More important than any maritime embarrassments, and far more worrisome to President Lincoln, was the precarious condition of the nation's largest ground force, the Army of the Potomac, and the shaky mental state of its beleaguered commander, Ambrose Burnside.

It was hard to see how matters could be much worse with either as the new year began. The army was in desperate shape after its mauling at Fredericksburg. Demoralized soldiers were deserting in droves; thousands of others were ill with dysentery, typhoid, and diphtheria; and the rest, unpaid, underfed, and utterly miserable, were crouching in log-and-canvas huts on the muddy plain surrounding the town of Falmouth, Virginia, sneering at patriotic pictures torn from *Harper's Weekly* or *Frank Leslie's Illustrated Newspaper,* swilling "Bust-Head" whiskey, and hoarsely chanting "Abram Lincoln, what yer 'bout? Stop this war, it's all played out!"

As for Burnside, he had lost not only the confidence of his subordinates but their loyalty and goodwill as well. His headquarters in the Phillips House, a brick mansion on the outskirts of Falmouth, had become a hotbed of jealousy and intrigue, a place where officers schemed to advance their careers and the careers of their friends at the expense of the commanding general and everyone else. A gaggle of high-ranking officers was agitating to bring McClellan back, arguing that "no human intelligence can mend matters here till that is done." Another ambitious malcontent, Major General Joseph Hooker, was angling to get the top spot for himself, casting aspersions on Burnside's character and loudly touting his own talents to anyone who would listen.

In this poisonous atmosphere Burnside felt the only person to whom he could talk freely was his valet, an ancient Negro named Robert. Every night after his paperwork was done, he would pull a chair up to the fire in the parlor of the Phillips House and unburden himself to the kindly old black man. Meanwhile, in the adjoining rooms, his smirking staff officers would wink and elbow each other and whisper that this was how the Fredericksburg battle plan had been concocted.

Despite the backstabbing, Burnside was determined to cross the Rappahannock River again. He sent a letter to the president apprising him of the proposed attack and soliciting his approval. His intention, he told Lincoln, was to bridge the stream eight miles north of Fredericksburg and fall on Lee's left with the bulk of the army, forcing the rebels to come out of their entrenchments and fight him on open ground. "There is much hazard in it," he cautioned, adding with characteristic forthrightness that his subordinates were "almost unanimously opposed" to the idea. He then offered to step down if the president wanted to appoint a new commander.

Burnside also sought guidance and encouragement from general in chief Halleck.

General Ambrose E. Burnside.
(Library of Congress)

"I do not ask you to assume any responsibility," he stated, "but it seems to me that, in making so hazardous a movement, I should receive some general directions from you."

The answers he got were far from satisfactory. Lincoln declined to accept his resignation, writing "I do not yet see how I could profit by changing the command of the Army of the Potomac." The word "yet" practically leaped off the page, clear warning to Burnside that he could be cashiered at any moment. Halleck's reply was even more disappointing—a rambling, evasive letter in which he blandly counseled the general to make a movement somewhere, as early as possible, with all or part of his army depending upon the circumstances, and to always bear in mind that "the great object is . . . to injure the [enemy] all you can with the least injury to yourself."

Burnside had asked the army's top strategist for advice and received a page and a half of twaddle; he had asked the commander in chief for a vote of confidence and been given an endorsement so lukewarm, it was more like a rebuke. Another man might have read these portents and relinquished his post without further ado. But Ambrose Burnside had shouldered the burden of high command at the president's behest, and he was not going to lay it down unless explicitly ordered to do so. In the meantime he would do his duty, and to his way of thinking that meant crossing the river and attacking Lee's Confederates.

On the morning of January 20 all was in readiness. The sullen soldiers spilled out of their huts to hear the reading of a proclamation Burnside had composed the night before. "The auspicious moment seems to have arrived to strike a great and mortal blow to the rebellion, and to gain that decisive victory which is due to the country," the broadside declared. With that the national and regimental flags were unfurled, bands struck up "Yankee Doodle," and the men shouldered their rifles and set out for Banks' Ford, eight miles up the Rappahannock.

Good progress was made at first. The sun was shining, and the roads were dry and firm. The soldiers swung along at an easy route step, enjoying the mild springlike air and the pleasant sensation of being on the march after more than a month of idleness in camp.

Around midafternoon, clouds began to arc across the sky, spreading and thickening until the last traces of blue were gone. A cold wind whistled through the trees, rattling the bare branches and whipping up little tornadoes of dust. The blue columns continued to advance at a rapid rate, snaking along narrow plantation lanes, past deserted farm fields and ramshackle barns, not stopping until they reached a gloomy pine forest that lay several miles to the rear of the fording area. Here the men fell out and pitched their shelter halves. The river crossing would be attempted the next morning after the artillery and pontoon trains had come up from Falmouth.

Just before dusk, as the soldiers were finishing their dinner of hardtack and salt pork, raindrops began to patter on the pine needles covering the forest floor. It was only a passing shower, said the veterans, glancing sagely at the steel-colored sky. But the drizzle soon became a hard rain, and as darkness fell, it turned into a driving downpour.

The deluge continued all night, and in the morning the soldiers crawled from their soaked blankets and beheld a drowned landscape. Fires were kindled to brew coffee, but the wood was too wet to burn properly. A reeking pall of smoke soon overspread the campsite, a cloud so dense and corrosive that "our eyes [were] nearly melted out of their sockets . . . and we [had] to lie on the wet ground to relieve them," recalled Sergeant Daniel Crotty of the Third Michigan.

After striking their tents and packing their knapsacks, the soldiers slogged out to the roads to resume the march to the fording site. Horse and wagon traffic had churned the tracks into shin-deep quagmires, and every step required a tremendous effort as huge clods of mud clung to shoes and trouser legs. Still the troops floundered on, lashed by the wind-driven rain, slipping, sliding, sometimes sprawling face first into the gooey sludge.

As if the rain and mud weren't bad enough, the high command had fouled up the marching orders. Two columns heading toward the river by different routes reached a crossroads at the same time, causing a traffic jam. While the officers argued over which formation had the right-of-way, hundreds of soldiers slunk off into the woods to desert; hundreds of others straggled away to relieve themselves, became separated from their units, and wandered about lost, adding to the mad, milling confusion.

As it turned out, the delay in getting down to the river did not matter, for only fifteen pontoons—not enough for one bridge, much less the five Burnside's plan called for—were at the ford ready to be hoisted into the water. The rest were stuck in the rear, their wagons mired hub-deep in the mud. Double and triple teams of horses and mules were harnessed together in a desperate attempt to get the stalled vehicles moving, but it was no use. Although the beasts labored mightily, the iron-rimmed wagon wheels refused to budge. Dozens of animals dropped dead from exhaustion, while others broke their legs and had to be shot. Their carcasses soon littered the roadside, sinking slowly into the ooze until they "were completely submerged, with ears only faintly visible."

Where mules had failed, the engineer officers thought men might succeed. Drag lines were attached to the pontoon wagons, and entire infantry companies waded into the slop, grabbed hold, and heaved for all they were worth. This produced an impressive spectacle but precious little progress.

The ponderous wheels would lurch forward for a revolution or two, then sink even deeper. Gasping for air, cursing horribly, the mud-covered soldiers pulled until their hands bled and their eyes popped, but all to no avail. "They would flounder through the mire for a few feet—the gang of Lilliputians with their huge-ribbed Gulliver—and then give up breathless," wrote the correspondent for the New York *Times*. And all the while rain poured down in torrents, prompting one observer to remark, only half in jest, that the pontoons "might as well have been unloaded and floated to their positions on the river bank."

When darkness finally put an end to this backbreaking toil, the soldiers crawled off into the bushes to rest. Some put up tents, but most were too tired to bother. They simply wrapped themselves in their sopping blankets and huddled around sputtering campfires. "Nothing was heard but the monotonous dropping of the rain and the murmurs of conversations carried on in a low voice," wrote Colonel Phillipe Regis de Trobriand. "It was a dismal night; one of those sleepless nights when everything has a funereal aspect, in which the enthusiasm is extinguished; in which courage is worn out, the will enfeebled, and the mind stupefied."

By way of raising their spirits, the men told each other that the "Mud March" would be called off the next morning and they would be sent back to their camps at Falmouth. But when the gray, drizzly dawn arrived, the original orders still stood: advance to the river, bridge it, and attack the rebels on the other side. The only concession to the appalling weather was a directive from the commanding general that a ration of whiskey be issued to all hands. Barrels of the stuff had been brought up in the night—how, nobody knew—and now it was ladled out to the incredulous soldiers, who drank it off as fast as they could and quickly lined up for seconds.

Although the decision to furnish liquor had been made with the best of intentions, the consequences were disastrous. The whiskey flowed like liquid fire into thousands of empty stomachs, and within minutes mobs of angry, frustrated men had thrown down their rifles and started fighting with one another. A Pennsylvania major pulled his revolver and threatened to shoot into the knot of flailing pugilists. Someone knocked him out with a tree branch, and the brawl continued until the whiskey was gone and the drunken combatants were utterly exhausted.

When order was finally restored, the hung-over infantrymen staggered off toward the river, but the roads were in even worse shape than the day before. "An indescribable chaos of pontoons, wagons, and artillery encumbered the road down to the river—supply wagons upset by the roadside—artillery 'stalled' in the mud—ammunition trains mired by the way," wrote the *Times* reporter. "Horses and mules dropped down dead, exhausted with the effort to move their loads through the hideous medium. One hundred and fifty dead animals, many of them buried in the liquid muck, were counted in the course of a morning's ride."

Into this mud-drenched bedlam came Ambrose Burnside, his foul-weather cape buttoned to the chin, trailed by an entourage of grim-faced staff officers. A teamster squatting in a ditch straining to move his bowels doffed his cap as the cavalcade splashed by and cried: "General, the auspicious moment has arrived!" Burnside ignored this crack, but when he arrived at Banks' Ford and looked across the rain-swollen Rappahannock, further ridicule lay in store. There, plainly visible through the lenses of his field glasses, were laughing Confederate pickets, waving to him and holding up boards on which they had scrawled with charcoal, BURNSIDE'S ARMY STUCK IN THE MUD! and ← THIS WAY TO RICHMOND!

The commanding general had endured all the taunting he could stand. A sulfurous rage was building up inside him, a wrath born of grievous frustration and profound impotence, fueled by a terrible suspicion that his plans had been thwarted not only by bad luck and wretched weather but by the perfidy of high-ranking subordinates. Hooker's conduct had been especially disgraceful. He had loudly proclaimed that Burnside was an idiot, that the president was an imbecile for keeping him on, and that nothing would go right with the army or the country "until they had a dictator, and the sooner the better."

Despite this gross insubordination and the sight of the Confederates capering on the other side of the river, Burnside kept his temper in check. He had seen on his ride to the ford that the situation was hopeless; the roads were too muddy and the water too high for the bridging operation to succeed. His only choice was to call off the crossing and tell the troops to retrace their steps. Displaying a fortitude that was heroic, although it would never be appreciated as such, he swallowed his pride and gave the order. The army obediently turned around and began crawling back the way it had come, writhing like a waterlogged earthworm as it inched its way homeward across the mist-shrouded Virginia hills. The "Mud March" was over, and so too was Burnside's career as commander of the Army of the Potomac, although he did not know it yet.

Arriving back at Falmouth on the afternoon of the twenty-third, the general closeted himself in the Phillips House, and it was there, in the privacy of the leather-and-tobacco-scented study, that the volcanic fury that had been bubbling up within him for weeks finally erupted. Taking pen in hand, he lashed out against the men who had betrayed him. "General Joseph Hooker," he scrawled, "having been guilty of unjust and unnecessary criticisms of the actions of his superior officers, and of the authorities . . . is hereby dismissed from the service of the United States as a man unfit to hold an important commission during a crisis like the present."

Composing this tirade proved so cathartic that Burnside launched into another, and then another, angry, accusatory words spewing forth like clots of white-hot lava. He rebuked five other generals for their contemptible conduct and ordered them relieved from duty, "it being evident that [they] can be of no further service to this army."

When he was done, he sent a telegram to Lincoln reading: "I have prepared some very important orders, and I want to see you before issuing them. Can I see you alone if I am at the White House after midnight?" Without waiting for a reply, he departed for Washington, determined to bring down his enemies or destroy himself trying.

Burnside had suffered enough indignities to test the mettle of the strongest man, but fate and the elements had a few nasty tricks left to play on him. It was a foggy night, and the ambulance carrying him and his companions from Falmouth to the railhead at Stoneman's Switch veered off the road, plunged over a steep embankment, and landed on its side in a ditch full of dead mules. Bruised and shaken, the general crawled from the wreck, clawed his way up to the road, and asked a passing rider for help. The man failed to recognize him. He took one suspicious sniff, told the general to go to hell, and galloped on. Outraged by this impertinence, Burnside returned to the scene of the accident and, with the aid of his fellow passengers, hauled the vehicle out of the tangle of bloated carcasses. They had gone only half a mile farther when their path was blocked by an overturned ammunition wagon. Once again everyone piled out, and after much flailing about in the mud, they managed to drag the derelict aside and continue their journey.

Arriving at Stoneman's Switch just before midnight, the disheveled travelers found that the train to the boat landing at Aquia Creek had left without them. Burnside ordered the stationmaster to call it back. The man refused, whereupon the fuming general grabbed a lantern and started down the tracks on foot. Two miles out he flagged an approaching locomotive, but before going on to Aquia and the river steamer that would take them up the Potomac to Washington, he insisted on returning to Stoneman's Switch and placing the insubordinate stationmaster under arrest.

It was eight o'clock the next morning when Burnside, his trademark side-whiskers flattened and caked with mud, his dress uniform stained and stinking of dead mule, finally stomped into the White House for his meeting with the president. He gave Lincoln the bill of indictment he had drawn up the day before and told him he could either fire the generals named in it or find himself a new commander for the Army of the Potomac.

The startled president said he needed time to discuss the matter with his advisers. One look at Burnside, however, and he knew what he had to do. When the overwrought general had departed, Lincoln prepared an order and sent it over to the War Department. It directed that Major General Ambrose E. Burnside be relieved of command "at his own request," and that Major General Joseph Hooker be appointed head of the Army of the Potomac.

FOUR

THE RIGHT ROAD

Twenty-two-year-old Kate Stone, the eldest daughter of a well-to-do Louisiana cotton planter, would always remember the winter morning in 1863 when the war arrived on her doorstep and changed her life forever. It came without warning in the guise of a wild-eyed Yankee forager, an oath-bawling hoodlum in a mud-stained blue uniform who burst out of the lilac hedge bordering the front yard, pointed a pistol at her head, shouted he would kill her if she dared defy him, then stole her pet horse Wonka.

After this snarling ruffian had left, galloping away on her beloved colt, she had run weeping and trembling to her bedroom. For the rest of the day and half the night, she had cried, great sobs of fear, rage, and grief convulsing her body. When her tears finally dried, she was a different person. The cheerful, trusting little girl who had believed she would always be safe in the sanctuary of Brokenburn, her family's sprawling 1,260-acre estate in the marshy flatlands of Madison Parish, just west of the Mississippi River, was gone. In her place was a forlorn and exceedingly vulnerable young woman who understood she could not escape the war's upheaval, even in this remote section of northeastern Louisiana, hundreds of miles away from the battlefields of Tennessee and Virginia. All at once, as if a blindfold had been lifted from her eyes, she saw that the secure, self-contained world of Brokenburn—a cosmos that had seemed as fixed and immutable to her as the blue sky and black earth of the delta country—had been shattered forever by the forces of a conflict whose magnitude and persistence, ferocity and cost, surpassed all reckoning.

The collapse of the old order had started on the spring day in 1861 when her brother William and her uncle Bo had gone off to join the Confederate army, leaving her widowed mother, Amanda Ragan Stone, to manage the plantation. At the time everyone had assumed that the men would be back in a few months, and in their absence life at Brokenburn had gone on much as always. Gangs of Negro field hands toiled from sunup to sundown, cultivating the cotton that was the basis of the Stone family's fortune, while in the rambling eight-room house set amid a picturesque grove of water oak, sweet gum, and sycamore trees, Kate, her mother, and her younger siblings entertained themselves with books, games, and other amusements. Mrs. Stone was so sure of a quick Southern victory that she began making plans for a grand tour of Europe in the summer of 1862.

But the war had not ended as expected, and instead of a homecoming there was another farewell, as two more of Kate's brothers, eighteen-year-old Coleman and seventeen-year-old Walter, left to join the army. Hard on the heels of their departure came word that William Stone had been wounded at Antietam. After that the family lived in a state of constant dread, expecting bad news at any moment. "Oh, this long, cruel suspense," Kate wrote in her diary of the nerve-racking vigil that followed each battle. "Every day adds to my conviction that my brother is desperately hurt. I cannot think of him as dead. . . . But my heart leaps to my lips and I turn sick with apprehension whenever I hear a quick step, see a stranger approaching, or note a grave look on the face of any of the boys coming in from a ride."

Other aspects of plantation life were changing as well. The ample, carefree existence the Stones had enjoyed before the war was becoming increasingly pinched and dreary as blockade-induced shortages of clothing, food, and other staples worsened. "Silk of the poorest kind is now $500 a yard and walking shoes $15 a pair and difficult to get at that," Kate noted. "It is like going back to the days of the Revolution to see the planters all setting up their looms and the ladies discussing the making of homespun dresses."

As for foodstuffs, she reported that since the spring of 1862, the family had been subsisting on a monotonous diet of milk, cornbread, and home-raised chickens. Flour, which cost fifty dollars a barrel, was hoarded like gold dust, and coffee had disappeared altogether. "After experimenting with parched potatoes, parched pindars, burned meal, [and] roasted acorns," she wrote, "all our coffee drinkers [have] decided on okra seed as the best substitute."

It was a stunning comedown for a household that had never lacked for anything before, but the Stones did not waver in their loyalty to the Confederacy, accepting privation as the price of Southern independence. "In proportion as we have been a race of haughty, indolent, waited-on people," Kate stoutly declared, "so now we [must] work and wait on ourselves. The

Southerners are a noble race, let them be reviled as they may, and I thank God that He has given me my birthplace in this fair land among these gallant people and in a time when I can show my devotion to my country."

That devotion was about to be tested, for with the fall of New Orleans and the capture of Confederate river forts in Kentucky and Tennessee, the entire Mississippi Valley lay open to Federal invasion. Union gunboats appeared on the river a few miles east of Brokenburn, churning past the levee like hulking black waterbugs. Word went out to all the planters in the region to burn their stocks of cotton lest they fall into Yankee hands. For weeks a suffocating pall of gray-brown smoke hung over the swamps and forests of Madison Parish, stinging eyes, clogging nostrils, and shrouding the sky until the sun looked like a shriveled red ball. The Stones dutifully set fire to every bale they had harvested since 1861, an act of patriotism that cost them more than $20,000 in lost earnings.

As if that sacrifice were not devastating enough, the other pillar of their prosperity—their 150 slaves—began to crumble as Union forces infiltrated the area. "In some way they have gotten a confused idea of Lincoln's Congress meeting and of the war," Kate wrote of the plantation's black workforce. "They think it is all to help them, and they expect for 'something to turn up.' " She remarked that "runaways are numerous and bold," and that "the house servants have been giving a lot of trouble lately—lazy and disobedient. . . . I suppose the excitement in the air has infected them."

The excitement rose to a fever pitch during the first week of January 1863, when a Union army bivouacked at Milliken's Bend, just fifteen miles southeast of Brokenburn. Bands of heavily armed foragers fanned out through the countryside, pillaging plantations and seizing slaves to serve as camp workers. Adding to the pandemonium was the shocking news that Abraham Lincoln had signed the Emancipation Proclamation. "What will be the result of this diabolical move?" Kate wondered; "surely not as bad for us as they intend it to be."

She was wrong. The slaves of Madison Parish were greatly emboldened. Many promptly deserted their plantations and headed for the Yankee stronghold at Milliken's Bend. Others stayed behind, but they considered themselves free and refused to obey their former owners. The Stones clung to the belief that their chattel would remain docile, but a violent outburst on the night of February 24 disabused them of that notion. Two house slaves, Jane and Aunt Lucy, got into a fight in the kitchen. Jane, who according to Kate was "nearly six feet tall and powerful . . . as black as night and with a fearful temper," hit Lucy over the head with a chair, lacerating her scalp. Then she grabbed a carving knife and threatened to cut Mrs. Stone's throat if she intervened. "How horrible," Kate wrote of the wild scene. "The quarreling and screaming, the blood streaming down Lucy's face, Jane's fiery looks and speeches, Johnny and Uncle Bob's pursuit of her as she rushed away . . . and then just as we had all quieted down, the cry of fire. The loom room had caught from some hot ashes, but we at once thought Jane was wreaking vengeance on us all by trying to burn us out. We would not have been surprised to have her slip up and stick any of us in the back."

After this ugly episode the Stones seldom ventured outside, and if their rounds took them anywhere near the slave quarters, they went armed with loaded pistols. Even in the house they felt threatened. The rumble of cannon fire from the river, where Union mortar schooners were bombarding Vicksburg, shook the floor and rattled the windows. By night the orange-red glare of burning barns and cotton gins lit up the sky, casting lurid shadows on bedroom walls and banishing restful sleep.

"The life we are leading now is a miserable, frightened one, living in constant dread of great danger, not knowing what form it may take, and utterly helpless to protect ourselves," Kate confided in her diary in mid-March. "We have been in a quiver of anxiety looking for the Yankees every minute, sitting on the front gallery with our eyes strained in the direction they will come, going to bed late and getting up early so they will not find us asleep. . . . A great many of the Negroes camped at [Milliken's Bend] have been armed by the officers, and they are a dreadful menace to the few remaining citizens. The country seems possessed by demons, black and white."

It was several days later that her own demon came crashing out of the bushes to threaten her life and steal her horse. The ordeal seared her soul. "I think I will never see lilac blooms again without recalling this sad incident," she declared. But worse was yet to come. On the afternoon of March 26 she and her sister were visiting the neighboring Hardison plantation when a gang of looters broke into the house in search of silverware and jewelry. One of them barged into the room where she was hiding, stood on the hem of her dress, brandished his pistol, and began gesturing obscenely. Kate was sure she was about to be raped. But after several minutes of taunting, her assailant snatched up his plunder and rushed out. "I was never so frightened," she shuddered afterward. "Little Sister was as still as if petrified [and] Mrs. Hardison was almost crazy [with fear]."

That evening a mob of ex-slaves gathered at the Hardison place, ransacked it, and set it on fire. Their wild shouts, the smash and tinkle of breaking glass, the rattle of gunfire, and the roar of flames were clearly audible at Brokenburn less than a mile away. For Kate's mother it was the last straw. For weeks she had been thinking about fleeing to Texas to escape the reign of terror that had descended on Madison Parish. Now she decided to depart at once, leaving everything behind in her haste to get her children to a place of safety.

The Stones hurriedly stuffed food, clothing, and a few personal me-

mentos into saddlebags. Just after midnight they set out, riding down the drive past a phalanx of silent, watchful Negroes. The former slaves "behaved well enough," Kate later wrote, "but you could see it was only because they knew we would soon be gone. We were only on sufferance." When she came to the gate at the end of the drive, she took a last look back at the house. Shadowy figures were milling around on the gallery before the bolted front door. A moment later there was a splintering crash, a gleeful yelp, and torches flared up inside as pillagers rushed from room to room, scooping up rugs, furniture, books, and anything else that appealed to them.

"So passes the glory of the family," Kate murmured as she turned away and urged her horse forward down the dark path that led westward to Texas and a life of exile. As she rode through the cold, starless night, trying to come to grips with the fact that she was now an outcast in her native land, lines from Alfred, Lord Tennyson's "The Princess" repeated over and over in her mind.

Later, she wrote down those lines, altering them slightly to reflect her circumstances:

"Tears, idle tears,
 Tears from the depth of some distant time,
 Rise in the heart and gather in the eyes,
 In gazing o'er the dreary winter fields
 And thinking of the days that are no more."

The Stones rode all night, anxious to put as much distance between themselves and Brokenburn as possible. The Yankees had ordered the parish's planters to stay put under penalty of arrest, and the Stones knew that when word of their flight reached Milliken's Bend, mounted patrols would be sent after them.

Dawn was breaking when they reached the edge of Tensas Swamp, about fifteen miles from Brokenburn. The road ended here in a little clearing, where a ramshackle wooden dock poked out into a bayou. Searching through the thicket of cattails around the dock, Kate found a pair of pirogues that had been hidden there by a family friend. These dugouts were hastily launched, and the Stones climbed in and shoved off, propelling themselves through the stagnant water with willow poles and makeshift paddles.

They had not gone fifty yards when a troop of blue-clad horsemen burst into the clearing at the head of the landing, waving carbines and shouting for them to stop. "The sight of [them] coming our way in the distance lent strength to [our] arms," Kate recalled, "and as fast as we could ply the paddles we glided through the water."

The bayou was only a few feet deep here, and the riders spurred their mounts right into it, kicking up great gouts of spray as they tried to catch the fleeing canoeists. The pirogues were faster than the floundering horses, however. They soon shot out into a deep channel where the Yankees could not follow. "Then what a shout rang out for Jeff Davis and the Confederacy!" wrote Kate. "The men could see and hear us distinctly, and we half expected a volley to come whizzing over [our heads]. But the boys would not be restrained, and their 'Farewell to the Feds!' 'Hurrah for Jeff Davis!' and 'Ho for Texas!' floated over the waters till we were out of sight."

The excitement of the chase soon wore off, and the family settled down to the task of paddling the overloaded dugouts through the maze of creeks and marshes. After an exhausting seven-hour journey, they reached the swamp's western border. From there they made their way to Delhi, a stop on the Shreveport & Vicksburg Railroad, where they hoped to book passage to Texas.

They found the little settlement seething like a kicked-over anthill. Panicky civilians were milling about the depot waiting for the next train out. On the muddy main street, horses and mules roamed unattended among piles of broken furniture, shattered packing cases, and smashed

Southern refugees. (Library of Congress; photo courtesy
of The Museum of the Confederacy, Richmond, Virginia)

steamer trunks. "It was just thrown in promiscuous heaps," Kate wrote. "Pianos, tables, chairs, rosewood sofas, wardrobes, parlor sets, with pots, kettles, stoves, beds and bedding, bowls and pitchers, and everything of the kind just thrown pell-mell here and there, with [Confederate] soldiers, drunk and sober, combing over it all, shouting and laughing. While thronging everywhere were refugees—men, women, and children—everybody and everything trying to get on the cars, all fleeing from the Yankees or worse still, the Negroes."

The Stones squeezed aboard a train that evening, but it carried them only as far as Monroe, Louisiana, forty miles farther west. They would spend the next seven weeks there, living on stale crackers and rancid salt pork, while they tried to make arrangements to continue their journey to Texas. Mrs. Stone finally purchased a wagon and a team of nags for three thousand Confederate dollars, and in early June the family started out on the 275-mile trek to Lamar County, a windswept stretch of prairie in the extreme northeastern corner of the Lone Star State.

Through it all—the hunger, the discomfort, the unrelenting hostility of the people in the countryside through which they passed—Kate managed to keep her spirits up. But when the Stones arrived in Texas and moved into their new home, a dilapidated shack on the banks of the Sulphur River some twenty-five miles from the town of Paris, the harshness of the climate and the primitiveness of the living conditions plunged her into a deep depression. Lamar County was the "dark corner of the Confederacy," she moaned, a drab, dreary place where "the earth, the air, the sky, all are a dull dead grey," and "the sun seems to emit neither heat nor light, gleaming with a dim red glare like a blood-red moon."

As the stark reality of her family's downfall sank in, the tenor of Kate's diary abruptly changed. For a time she continued to pay lip service to the Confederate cause, but reading between the lines, it was clear that she now believed that the Stones' sacrifices had been in vain—that the war was an unmitigated disaster, a catastrophe that had brought about the destruction of everything it had been supposed to save. Eventually she could no longer sustain even the pretense of patriotism. In a series of anguished entries she poured out her feelings about what the year 1863 had meant to her, her family, and the now-displaced planter aristocracy.

"*Conquered, Submission, Subjugation* are words that burn my heart, and yet I feel that we are doomed to know them in all their bitterness," she wrote. "There is a gloom over all like the shadow of Death. We have given up hope for our beloved country and all are humiliated, crushed to earth. A past of grief and hardship, a present of darkness and despair, and a future without hope. Truly our punishment is greater than we can bear."

The freebooters who had ridden roughshod over Madison Parish, loot-ing, burning, and driving the Stones into exile, belonged to Sherman's corps of the Army of the Tennessee. They were in a foul mood because their late-December assault on Vicksburg had been crushed at Chickasaw Bluffs. Now they found themselves mired in the mud on the Louisiana side of the river, unable to take another crack at the Confederate citadel be-cause flooded swamps and the rain-swollen Mississippi barred their way.

Adding to their dudgeon was the fact that Milliken's Bend was a hor-rible place, half underwater from the incessant winter downpours, awash with feces and rotting garbage, and plagued by great swarms of disease-carrying mosquitoes. There was sickness everywhere—measles, malaria, and smallpox—and the army's tiny medical department seemed helpless to do anything about it. "No proper hospital buildings have been raised," re-ported the New York *Times*. "Instead of removing the sick away or plac-ing them on hospital steamboats, or using the best houses in the vicinity for their accommodation, they have been crowded into filthy negro shanties, dank hovels located in the swamp, and pens that are not fit for swine, while the few dry and roomy houses thereabouts are assigned to officers for their use." The mortality rate was shockingly high. Scores of men died each day, and the levee, the only high ground for miles around, was honeycombed with their graves.

Aggravating the army's woes was the nagging suspicion that the man in charge, Ulysses S. Grant, was not up to the task of taking Vicksburg. Many of the soldiers had begun to question his military acumen after the defeats at Holly Springs and Chickasaw Bluffs, and when he arrived at Milliken's Bend to oversee operations there, his seedy appearance and listless de-meanor did little to reassure them. "No stranger, seeing this man in a crowd, would ever be moved to ask who he was," remarked a chaplain who had served with Grant in the Twenty-first Illinois early in the war. A reporter for the New York *World*, trying to write a profile of him, struggled to iden-tify some distinguishing characteristic and then gave up, declaring that he was "an altogether unpronounceable man," a thoroughly commonplace in-dividual "whom one would take for a country merchant or a village lawyer."

Small and slouchy, forty years old but appearing considerably older, "with rather the look of a man who did, or once did, take a little too much to drink," Grant did not conform to the popular, *Frank Leslie's Illustrated Newspaper* image of a commanding general. His leathery face, creased by

General Ulysses S. Grant.
(Library of Congress)

numerous deep wrinkles, was made even rougher looking by the prominent wart on his right cheek, the bristly brown beard sprouting from his jaws, and the thin, tightly clamped lips from which a tattered cigar stub always seemed to be protruding. Accentuating his dumpy build and coarse features was the uniform he wore, a shabby outfit consisting of badly scuffed top boots, mud-stained trousers, a common soldier's blouse, an unbuttoned blue coat "without scarf, sword, or trappings of any sort, save the double-starred shoulder straps," and a battered black Kossuth hat set "straight and very hard on his head." This sloppy rig, and the down-at-the-heels mien of its wearer, were unsettling to those who did not know him well. It caused them to question his fitness for command and lent credence to the persistent rumors that he was an alcoholic who sobered up only when his wife, Julia, was summoned from Illinois to look after him.

In fact, Grant had not touched a bottle since coming down to Milliken's Bend at the end of January, although he probably was sorely tempted after seeing how difficult it was going to be to secure a foothold on the east bank of the Mississippi from which his army could approach Vicksburg. The problem he faced was one of geography, compounded by weather. The rebel city sat on its cliff of ocher-colored loess, two hundred feet above the rain-swollen river. North of town, just beyond the vine-matted bluffs where Sherman's late-December assault had come to grief, lay the Yazoo Delta, a teardrop-shaped alluvial region bounded on the east by the Yazoo River and on the west by the Mississippi. This vast, sparsely populated lowland—170 miles long and 50 miles wide—was covered by thick forest and crisscrossed by countless creeks and sloughs, all of which had spilled over their banks because of the heavy winter storms. Traversing such a morass of mud and water with an army numbering in the tens of thousands was out of the question; Vicksburg was unassailable from that direction. An attack from the west, or river side, was likewise impossible. The bluff on which the city was situated was steep, studded with gun emplacements, and seamed with infantry trenches. Even if a landing force established a toehold along the waterfront, there was no way it could scramble up the precipitous slope under fire from the redoubts and rifle pits lining the crest. Nor

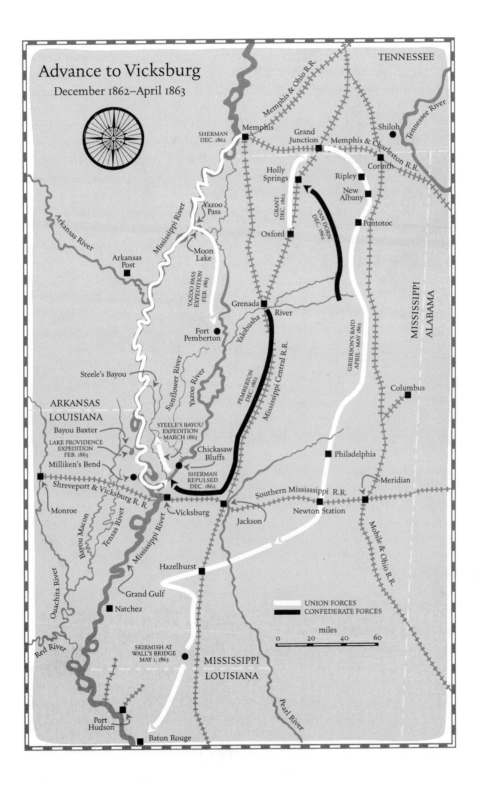

Advance to Vicksburg
December 1862–April 1863

TENNESSEE

Memphis & Ohio R.R.

Memphis & Charleston R.R.

Tennessee River

Shiloh

SHERMAN
DEC. 1862

Memphis

Grand
Junction

Corinth

Holly
Springs

Ripley

New
Albany

Pontotoc

GRANT
DEC. 1862

VAN DORN
DEC. 1862

Oxford

Arkansas River

Mississippi River

Yazoo
Pass

Moon
Lake

Arkansas
Post

YAZOO PASS
EXPEDITION
FEB. 1863

Grenada

Yalobusha   River

MISSISSIPPI

ALABAMA

Fort
Pemberton

PEMBERTON
DEC. 1862

Mississippi Central R.R.

GRIERSON'S RAID
APRIL - MAY 1863

Columbus

Steele's Bayou

Sunflower River

Yazoo River

ARKANSAS

LOUISIANA

Bayou Baxter

LAKE PROVIDENCE
EXPEDITION
FEB. 1863

Milliken's Bend

STEELE'S BAYOU
EXPEDITION
MARCH 1863

Chickasaw
Bluffs

SHERMAN
REPULSED
DEC. 1862

Philadelphia

Meridian

Shreveport & Vicksburg R. R.

Monroe

Bayou Macon

Tensas River

Mississippi River

Vicksburg

Jackson

Southern Mississippi R.R.

Newton Station

Mobile & Ohio R.R.

Ouachita River

Hazelhurst

Grand Gulf

Natchez

Red River

SKIRMISH AT
WALL'S BRIDGE
MAY 1, 1863

MISSISSIPPI

LOUISIANA

Pearl River

UNION FORCES
CONFEDERATE FORCES

miles

0   20   40   60

Port
Hudson

Baton Rouge

did a downstream crossing, requiring a dash past the batteries at Vicksburg as well as those at Grand Gulf, twenty-five miles farther south, seem feasible. Navy gunboats with their thick carapaces of oak and iron might be able to run the gauntlet, but not unarmored troop transports and supply ships.

Mulling over this array of obstacles, Grant concluded that it would be best to take the army back up the Mississippi to Memphis, establish a supply base there, then drive south along the line of the Mississippi Central Railroad before wheeling west to strike at Vicksburg from its landward side. But strategy was not the only consideration; politics had to be taken into account, too. As Grant subsequently observed, "at this time [the winter of 1863] the North had become very much discouraged. Many strong Union men believed that the war must prove a failure. . . . [To] make a backward movement as long as that from Vicksburg to Memphis would be interpreted by many . . . as a defeat, and that the draft would be resisted, desertions ensue, and the power to capture and punish deserters lost."

He did not mention that a retreat would almost certainly cost him his job, but it is likely that this also entered into his thinking. And besides, he hated the thought of retracing his steps. "One of my superstitions had always been when I started to go anywhere, or to do anything, not to turn back, or stop until the thing intended was accomplished," he wrote many years later. "I have frequently started to go to places where I had never been and to which I did not know the way, depending upon making inquiries on the road, and if I got past the place without knowing it, instead of turning back, I would go on until a road was found turning in the right direction, take that, and come in by the other side."

That was precisely what he was going to do now. He would stay at Milliken's Bend until he found the right road to Vicksburg. But the search was going to require a great deal of patience. It would be several months before the river dropped and the countryside dried out, and in the meantime his army was literally moldering away. Something had to be done at once, if for no other reason than to sustain a semblance of morale. And so he resolved to put his men to work on what he termed "a series of experiments"—a quartet of amphibious operations aimed at capturing or bypassing Vicksburg.

The first of these experiments involved excavating a canal that would permit gunboats, transports, and supply ships to steam past Vicksburg without exposing themselves to the fire of its powerful water batteries.

Just above the city the Mississippi swung through a hairpin curve, carving out a four-mile-long, one-mile-wide tongue of land called De Soto Point. The idea was to dig a big ditch across the base of this marshy peninsula, breach the levees at either end, and let the river rush through, gouging out a new channel that would, in theory, leave Vicksburg high and dry.

Grant was skeptical that the scheme would work. As planned, the canal's inlet would open on a backwater, where there was little or no current to do the work of scouring. Its outlet would disgorge boats back into the river where they would still be within range of the rebels' heavy artillery. But the project had gained a powerful sponsor in Washington. Abraham Lincoln had twice navigated the Mississippi as a young man; he had seen for himself how the stream tended to change course during the flood season, abruptly abandoning one bed for another. Now he insisted that the canal be tried. "Direct your attention particularly to [digging the ditch] across the point," Halleck instructed Grant in a telegram in late January. "The President attaches much importance to this." And so Grant went forward with the dubious venture, reckoning that even if it ended in failure, it would keep a large body of troops busy for several months.

The assignment of mucking out the mile-long watercourse was given to Sherman. Each morning a detachment of 1,000 soldiers culled from the ranks of his corps, augmented by crews of ex-slaves rounded up from neighboring plantations, shouldered picks and shovels and slogged out onto the point to do battle with the malodorous mud. The results were far from impressive. There was too much water—"water above, below, and around," Sherman glumly wrote—for the work to proceed smoothly. In February four dredges were brought in to help the struggling soldiers, but progress continued to be slow. Finally, on March 7, a torrential rainstorm sent the river boiling over the levee at the upstream end of the cut, swamping the still-unfinished canal and drowning the entire peninsula under several feet of silty water. "This little affair of ours on [De Soto] Point is labor lost," Sherman concluded after inspecting the mess. Grant agreed, and on March 27 he ordered the enterprise abandoned.

Even as Sherman and his men were digging their canal to nowhere, another of Grant's experiments was getting under way forty miles upstream at Lake Providence. Once upon a time this stagnant, mosquito-infested body of water had been an oxbow bend in the Mississippi. But the stream had shifted course during some long-ago flood and left the lake landlocked, separated from the river's present channel by a mile or so of overgrown marsh. Army engineers said the two could be reconnected "by a little digging," and they pointed out that once Union steamboats got into Lake Providence, they would be able to wend their way south through a chain of inland waterways—Bayou Baxter, Bayou Macon, the Tensas River, the Black River, and the Red River—and eventually find their way back to the

Mississippi a hundred miles south of Vicksburg. This detour was long and roundabout, but Grant was willing to try anything that might get his army safely past the Confederate stronghold. Consequently he ordered Major General James B. McPherson, the youngest and most energetic of his corps commanders, to open the Lake Providence route.

The thirty-three-year-old McPherson was an excellent choice for the job. He had taught engineering at West Point and served as supervisor on various river and harbor projects before the war. The assignment of blazing a new waterway through the wilderness of eastern Louisiana appealed to him as a grand adventure. But when he reconnoitered the first segment of the proposed route, his ardor cooled. Bayou Baxter, the main outlet out of Lake Providence, was not a stream as shown on his map, but rather a swamp full of cypress snags waiting to tear the bottom out of any boat passing by. What was more, the swamp was so shallow that even if all the underwater obstacles were removed, only the smallest, shallow-draft steamers would be able to slip through to Bayou Macon and the Tensas River.

Still, orders were orders, and in early February the general went to work clearing out the forest of sunken snags. To accomplish this his men devised an ingenious cutting tool, a large circular saw mounted on a shaft that could be raised or lowered depending on the depth of the drowned tree to be disposed of. The contraption worked well, but the process of severing and removing hundreds of submerged stumps proved so time-consuming that McPherson concluded it would be many months before a navigable pathway would be opened through Bayou Baxter, if it could be done at all. Grant came up from Milliken's Bend at the end of the month to look things over and reluctantly agreed with his subordinate's assessment. But, he later wrote, "I let the work go on, believing employment was better than idleness for the men. Then, too, it served as a cover for other efforts which gave a better prospect for success."

The effort that was now foremost in his mind was the Yazoo Pass Expedition, brainchild of his chief topographer, Lieutenant Colonel James H. Wilson. Wilson had located yet another waterway that promised to let Federal forces outflank Vicksburg. It was even longer and more convoluted than the Lake Providence route, but the youthful colonel was excited about it, and after some initial hesitation Grant became enthusiastic too.

The new route began on the Mississippi's east bank approximately 350 miles north of Vicksburg. Here the Yazoo Pass—a narrow, sluggish, silt-choked bayou—ran inland to connect with a sickle-shaped oxbow called Moon Lake. Moon Lake drained east into the Coldwater River, which flowed south into the Tallahatchie, which in turn merged with the Yalobusha to form the Yazoo, which eventually wound its way back to the Mississippi just above Vicksburg. For years shallow-draft steamers plying the big river between Memphis and New Orleans had turned off into the pass and used the network of streams to get to the delta towns of Greenwood and Yazoo City, where they delivered mail and supplies and picked up passengers and cotton. In 1857 the state of Mississippi had closed the pass by constructing a giant flood-control levee across its mouth. Colonel Wilson was sure it could be breached, however. Union boats would then ferry troops down to Haynes Bluff, fifteen miles northeast of Vicksburg. From Haynes Bluff it would be easy for the Federal infantry to march overland and assault Vicksburg from its more-vulnerable eastern side.

On the afternoon of February 3, Wilson detonated a gigantic explosive charge at the base of the levee sealing Yazoo Pass off from the Mississippi. The results were stupendous. Tons of mud erupted into the air, and the rain-gorged river, which had been rolling along at a level nine feet higher than the pass, roared through the hole gouged by the blast. Next morning the original opening, which had measured eighty feet across, was an astonishing seventy-five yards wide. The river was still pouring through, raging along, Wilson exultantly reported, "like nothing else I ever saw except Niagara Falls." It would be four days before the water levels equalized and the cataract subsided.

Ten navy warships, accompanied by twenty-two troop transports carrying 4,500 men, had gathered near the pass in anticipation of its reopening. On February 7 they steamed into the new channel and headed inland toward Moon Lake. The underpowered transports ran into trouble almost immediately. The turbulent current seized them, spun them around, slammed them hard into floating logs and piles of debris. Captain Samuel Byers remembered how the craft he was on careened through the pass "like a toy skiff in a washtub." In ten minutes, he wrote, "the rushing torrent had carried us, backward, down into the little lake. Not a soul of the 500 on board the boat in this crazy ride was lost. Once in the lake we stopped and with amazement watched other boats, crowded with soldiers, also drift into the whirl and be swept down the pass. It was luck, not management, that half the little army was not drowned."

More trouble lay in store when the fleet left the lake, heading east toward the Coldwater River. Confederate work parties had felled hundreds of trees across the waterway. To remove these obstacles the expedition's commander, Brigadier General Leonard F. Ross, had to use snatch blocks and hawsers borrowed from the navy and the muscle power of hundreds of infantrymen. "Seeing such an exhibition of strength it is easy enough to understand how the Egyptians moved the great stones, columns, and slabs from their quarry to their temples and pyramids," Colonel Wilson enthused. "I am confirmed in the opinions expressed in my previous reports concerning the practicability of this route."

Wilson's ebullience aside, it took three weeks of backbreaking labor to open a channel to the Coldwater. On February 28 the thirty-two–boat armada was finally assembled in that smooth-flowing stream, ready to steam south to the Yazoo and glory. The rebels had other ideas, however. One hundred miles downstream, near the confluence of the Tallahatchie and the Yalobusha, they had thrown together a bastion of cotton bales and sandbags, garrisoned it with 1,500 troops, and mounted thirteen big guns on its parapets. Fort Pemberton, as this redoubt was called, was not especially strong, but it was perfectly sited; the only way the Yankee ships could get past it was to move single file and at slow speed, making them sitting ducks for its artillery.

Lieutenant Commander Watson Smith, the officer in charge of the Union naval contingent, was flabbergasted when lookouts spotted the rebel fort dead ahead on the morning of March 10. Smith was a saltwater sailor, and nothing in his oceangoing experience had prepared him for a situation like this. He halted the fleet for twenty-four hours, dithering about what to do. Then he ordered the ironclads *Chillicothe* and *Baron de Kalb* to advance and test the Confederate defenses.

Fort Pemberton's guns hammered the oncoming vessels, which were unable to maneuver because of the narrowness of the channel. The Union captains frantically reversed engines, but before they could back out of range, a Confederate shell screamed through one of *Chillicothe*'s portals and

Ironclad gunboat USS Cairo. *(Library of Congress)*

exploded with an ear-splitting clang, killing two of her crew and wounding eleven. Twice more, on March 13 and March 16, the ironclads approached the fort, with the same results: they took a terrific pounding and were unable to inflict any damage in return. All of this proved too much for the high-strung Smith. He began to behave oddly, babbling to himself and shouting incomprehensible orders to his crew. On March 17 he suffered a nervous breakdown and was relieved by James P. Foster, captain of *Chillicothe*.

The navy had failed to neutralize the fort; now it was the army's turn to try. But a reconnaissance by General Ross's staff revealed not an inch of dry ground for the infantry to debark upon, only flooded swamp and oozing mud flats. The flotilla had to retrace its route back to Moon Lake.

The failure of the Yazoo Pass Expedition, coming so soon after the disappointments at De Soto Point and Lake Providence, might have dissuaded Grant from trying any more bayou experiments. But even as Ross, Wilson, Foster, and company were chugging disconsolately up the Tallahatchie, quarreling over whose fault it was that Fort Pemberton had not fallen, he was getting ready to try yet another amphibious penetration of the Yazoo Delta.

The author of this latest plan was Rear Admiral David Dixon Porter, commander of the naval squadron anchored off Milliken's Bend. Porter was an energetic, ambitious officer, who, like Grant, loathed inactivity. For some time he had been exploring the flooded country north of Vicksburg, searching for a way to get ships, men, and supplies up to Haynes Bluff on the Yazoo without having to run past the Confederate batteries atop Chickasaw Bluffs. During these excursions he had discovered that vast stretches of the delta were so deep underwater that all types of boats—even his heaviest ironclads—could abandon the river and travel safely overland. "Great forests had become channels," he wrote, "admitting the passage of large steamers between the trees, and now and then wide lanes were met with where a frigate might have passed." By using one of these forest lakes, he had determined it was possible to get from the lower Yazoo, just above its junction with the Mississippi, into a long, narrow, slow-moving body of water called Steele's Bayou. Forty miles up Steele's Bayou, Black Bayou branched off to the east and connected with Deer Creek, a meandering slough that emptied into another bayou called Rolling Fork, which led in turn to the Sunflower River. The Sunflower, a substantial deepwater stream, flowed back south and eventually emptied into the Yazoo below Fort Pemberton but above Haynes Bluff. It was a phenomenally complicated route covering two hundred winding, tree-choked miles, but Porter was sure it was navigable and would serve to outflank Chickasaw Bluffs and transport troops into Vicksburg's rear. Grant was easily convinced. He detached one of Sherman's divisions to accompany the admiral on this foray, which was dubbed the Steele's Bayou Expedition.

Porter's ships set off during the third week of March. Ironclads, mortar boats, and tugs glided along through majestic groves of oak, cypress, and cottonwood trees. Leadsmen rhythmically cast lines and sang out the soundings, while overhead flocks of ravens bobbed and flapped on their moss-festooned perches. All went well until the fleet neared the entrance to Black Bayou. There the watercourse narrowed and became so convoluted that Porter, looking back at the trailing column of vessels from the wheelhouse of his flagship, USS *Cincinnati,* saw that each one was steaming in a different direction as it tried to follow the stream's tortuous path. Stands of heavy timber blocked the way a little farther on. The ironclads had to smash their way through using brute force. Rumbling and vibrating and belching clouds of black smoke, they hurled themselves at the thick trunks, butting them aside with grinding crashes. Rats, snakes, lizards, and cockroaches that had been driven into the tree tops by the floodwaters cascaded down onto the decks as the boats plowed through their homes. Sailors grabbed brooms and frantically tried to sweep them overboard, but the creatures scuttled into every nook and cranny.

On March 19, four days after starting up Black Bayou, the battered, vermin-infested fleet finally arrived at the entrance to Rolling Fork. From this point onward, Porter hopefully wrote, "all would be plain sailing." But as he scanned the inlet ahead, he noticed something strange on its surface, "a large green patch extending all the way across." He summoned a runaway slave to the bridge and asked him what the odd-looking stuff was. "That's nothin' but willers, sir," the black man replied. "You can go through that like an eel." Thus reassured, the admiral sent *Cincinnati* forward, only to have it stick fast in the middle of the green patch, its hull gripped as if in a vise by a dense curtain of submerged willow withes.

The crew was ordered to rig scaffolding and go over the side to cut the ironclad free. But even as they set to work chopping at the tenacious saplings with knives, saws, and cutlasses, a crackle of musket fire erupted in the woods on either side. A hail of minié balls pinged off the boat's armor plates, showering the startled bluejackets with red-and-yellow sparks. This was followed by the shrill shriek of an artillery shell arcing over the trees. Two Confederate batteries were firing ranging shots preparatory to blasting Porter's hemmed-in fleet. Realizing that he was in serious trouble, the admiral hastily scribbled a note to Sherman, who was camped with his division at the lower end of Black Bayou. "Dear Sherman:" it read. "Hurry up for Heaven's sake. I never knew how helpless an ironclad could be steaming around through the forest without an army to back her."

Receiving this dispatch on the evening of the nineteenth, Sherman rounded up a couple of regiments and started off to the rescue. "The night was absolutely black, and we . . . [advanced] through the canebreak, carrying lighted candles in our hands," he wrote. "The water came above my hips. The smaller drummer boys had to carry their drums on their heads, and most of the men slung their cartridge boxes around their necks," Despite the danger of drowning, the relief column sloshed onward, skirmishing continuously with parties of wraithlike Confederates. Finally, on the afternoon of March 21, it reached the beleaguered fleet. "I doubt if [Porter] was ever more glad to meet a friend than he was to meet me," Sherman later wrote. "He informed me . . . that he had [just about] made up his mind to blow up the gunboats and to escape with his men through the swamp to the Mississippi."

Even though the graybacks had been driven off, the admiral was dead set against trying to push on to the Sunflower. "Thank you, no," he said, when Sherman offered to help get the fleet through the willows blocking the mouth of Rolling Fork. He gave the order for his ships to retreat, but even this maneuver proved extraordinarily difficult. There was no room for the vessels to turn around; they were forced to remove their rudders and drift stern first down Deer Creek and Black Bayou, careening from one tree trunk to another, much to the amusement of the watching infantrymen.

The boats were a shambles by the time they regained the big river. A few crewmembers said they had enjoyed the trip to Rolling Fork and were willing to go back, but they did so, the admiral wrote, "as people who have gone in search of the North Pole, and have fared dreadfully, wish to try it once more." As far as Porter was concerned, the Steele's Bayou Expedition had been the "hardest cruise that any Jack tar ever made," and the notion of doing it again was nonsense. He did not consider the venture a total bust, however. The experience of bushwacking through the Yazoo swamps had "inured both services to hard work which would the better enable them to overcome like obstacles in the future." And he had nothing but praise for the general who had had the courage to authorize this venture, as well as three other highly unconventional attempts to get around Vicksburg. "Some men would have given it up and said that it was not worth the loss of time," he wrote of the effort to bypass the rebel fortress; "some would have demanded half the resources of the Union; but Grant never wavered in his determination, or in his hopes of success."

Others were coming to a similar conclusion as the winter of 1863 came to a close. From the lowliest enlistee to the highest-ranking West Pointer, the soldiers of the Army of the Tennessee applauded Grant's grit and perseverance. He had won them over with his willingness to improvise, and the fact that his unorthodox amphibious operations had come to naught served only to strengthen their regard for him. "His energy and disposition to do something is what they admire," declared a reporter for the New York *World*. A correspondent for the New York *Times* concurred, writing: "The soldiers observe him coming and rising to their feet gather on each side of the way to see him pass—they do not salute him, they only watch him . . . with a certain sort of familiar reverence."

It baffled the cynical newspapermen, this bond of respect and affection that was growing between the general and his troops. They looked about and saw nothing but squalor, sickness, and defeat. Yet there was no denying that something magical was happening: frustration and failure were being transmuted into a strange kind of success. It was as if the mere act of striving—of battling the mud and water and junglelike vegetation, of being thwarted again and again but never giving up—had somehow convinced the army that it was invincible. It had a new swagger, an exhilarating feeling that no task was too big to tackle, no scheme too outlandish to try, an unshakable belief that sooner or later Vicksburg must fall.

PART TWO

SPRING

FIVE

THE DICTATES
OF WAR

Representative Albert Gallatin Riddle, Republican from Ohio, was a radical in his attitude toward slavery. He had crusaded against it his entire adult life, and Democrats considered him a dangerous fanatic for his insistence that ex-slaves ought to be armed so they could fight against their former masters. But despite his impeccable abolitionist credentials, Riddle was not one of those razor-tongued extremists who railed against the South, slavery, and Abraham Lincoln with equal vigor. Rather, he was that rarest of Washington animals, a Lincoln loyalist. Now, with the war going badly and public confidence in the administration at an all-time low, he thought it important to tell his colleagues in Congress exactly what was going to happen if they did not curtail their criticism of the chief executive and redirect their energies toward putting down the rebellion.

Speaking on the floor of the House of Representatives on the last day of February, he accused Democrats and Republicans alike of being possessed by "a morbid passion to exaggerate our misfortunes" and "gloat over the sum of our disasters, which they charge to the personal account of the president." This orgy of partisan finger-pointing had to stop, he said. A crisis as grave as any in the nation's history was at hand. It was Congress's duty to close ranks behind the president and do everything in its power to help him defeat the Confederacy.

"If we fail," the Ohio Republican said in conclusion, "it will be wholly because we are unworthy to succeed; because we will not with our whole heart and energy, might, mind, and strength, give ourselves up entirely to this war, as do the rebels; study its portents and obey its demands alone. . . . The war is greater than the president; greater than the two Houses of Congress, greater than the people . . . greater than all together; and it controls them all, and dictates its own policy; and woe to the men or party that will not heed its dictation."

Riddle did not specify what demands the war was making, nor did he speculate about the policy those demands dictated. But the portents were obvious to anyone studying the legislation that the Thirty-seventh Congress was considering as it headed toward adjournment at noon on March 4, 1863. Vast sums of money and huge numbers of men were needed to carry on a war of the magnitude and intensity that this one had attained. Only a strong central government—a government that was a major player in the national economy, a government that dominated the states and localities, a government that was capable of reaching into every city and town and compelling individual citizens to do its bidding—could marshal and wield those resources. And so with great trepidation, but also with a feeling that it was acting out of absolute necessity, Congress moved during the final days of the session to invest the federal bureaucracy with broad new powers, adopting measures that would have been unthinkable just a year before.

The first of these revolutionary measures was the National Banking Act, passed into law on February 25. This legislation had two objectives: raise money to pay for the war, which was now costing $2.5 million a day, and revamp the country's chaotic currency system, which was impeding commerce and making it difficult for the government to meet its financial obligations.

As 1863 began, the U.S. Treasury was relying on the sale of "five-twenties" (6 percent bonds, callable in five years and maturing in twenty) and the printing of greenbacks (paper money unbacked by silver or gold) to remain solvent. There were serious problems with both financing methods. The demand for war bonds was unpredictable, rising and falling with the Union's military fortunes. Government greenbacks circulated in competition with a blizzard of private banknotes issued by more than fifteen hundred different financial institutions operating under the authority of the individual states. Not only did these private notes debase the value of the Treasury's currency, they came in such a bewildering variety of sizes, styles, and denominations that even simple transactions were hard to execute.

A uniform national currency and a dependable market for government bonds were both sorely needed. The Banking Act provided for them. Under its terms five or more persons with a minimum of $50,000 in capital ($100,000 in large cities) could associate and form a bank. Upon purchasing U.S. bonds in an amount equal to one-third of the paid-in capital, they would receive a federal charter, and the Treasury would engrave money for them—National Bank Certificates—equal to 90 percent of the market value of their bonds. They would then use this money to make commercial loans and carry on other banking business, pocketing the profits just as if the certificates were of their own issue. In addition, they would receive interest payments in gold on the government bonds they had bought. This generous double return was offered in hopes of inducing state-chartered banks to obtain federal charters and withdraw their private currency from circulation, and as compensation for the fact that bank capital and banknote issues were being tied to the national debt.

Critics of the act predicted that it would lure men without means, skill, or character into banking—wildcatters who would scrape up loans to purchase the requisite number of bonds, then open fly-by-night institutions which would take business away from well-established state banks. They also assailed the act on Jacksonian grounds, accusing financiers in New York and New England of trying to create a central moneyed despotism more pernicious than the one Old Hickory had demolished thirty years earlier. But the law's proponents argued that if the United States left the power to regulate its currency to the legislation of thirty-four different states, it would be abandoning one of the most essential attributes of its sovereignty. They unabashedly appealed to Northern nationalism, pointing out that it was "the accursed heresy of state sovereignty" that had fanned the flames of Southern rebellion in the first place. Said Senate Finance Committee chairman John Sherman: "The policy of this country ought to be to make everything national as far as possible; to nationalize our country so that we shall love our country. If we are dependent on the United States for a currency and a medium of exchange, we shall have a broader and more generous nationality."

Money was one half of the war-fighting equation; manpower was the other. As the struggle between North and South entered its third spring, it was clear to Congress and the administration that there would soon be a dangerous shortage of the latter. Disease, desertion, and combat losses were not the only reasons for the deficit; 130 regiments were due to go home when their enlistment periods expired in May and June. Military planners estimated that 300,000 recruits would be needed in 1863 to make up for this attrition. Where these new soldiers were going to come from was a question no one could answer with certainty.

During the first year of the war, patriotism alone had been enough to fill the ranks. Lincoln's call for volunteers in the spring and summer of 1861 had been answered by 700,000 men. But enlistment had dropped off sharply after that initial outpouring. Even though half a million additional men eventually signed up by the end of 1862, the slowness with which they came forward and the large cash bounties they demanded as a condition of joining made it obvious that volunteering for patriotic reasons was about played out. A new, more coercive method of raising troops would have to be devised if the Union war effort was not to collapse for want of soldiers.

Tackling this politically unpalatable task during the first week of March, Congress passed the Enrollment Act of 1863, a measure authorizing the Federal government to conscript men directly into the army. Like the recently adopted National Banking Act, this legislation constituted a sharp assault on state sovereignty. In the past the job of procuring recruits, organizing them into regiments, and sending them off to war had belonged to state and local officials. Now that process was going to be controlled by Washington. When the president determined that more troops were needed, each state would be assigned a quota based on its population. If it failed to fill that quota with volunteers, a draft, organized and run by the War Department, would be held to make up the shortfall. All males between the ages of twenty and forty-five were eligible to be called. Bachelors would be the first to go, followed by married men ages twenty to thirty-five. Exemptions would be granted to draftees who had mental or physical disabilities, or who could furnish a substitute or pay a three-hundred-dollar commutation fee.

Not surprisingly, the compulsory nature of the Enrollment Act, and the wealth- and class-based inequity of its commutation clause, outraged opponents of the war. They railed that Lincoln and his abolitionist allies were trying to compel working-class white men to fight for "nigger equality" even as the "$300 exemption in the conscript law [saves] the sons of the aristocracy from the necessity of shouldering a musket." The War Department agents who would be sent into every congressional district were likened to secret police. Their real mission, it was said, was to crush civil liberties, stamp out states' rights, and make the president a dictator. The fact that Congress had authorized suspension of the writ of habeas corpus throughout the United States on March 3, the same day it passed the Enrollment Act, merely added to their paranoia.

Backers of the Enrollment Act insisted there was nothing sinister about the legislation. The president and Congress were trying to win the war, no more, no less. Conscription, like emancipation, was a matter of military necessity. But the dissidents would have none of it. As far as they were concerned, the draft was oppressive and unjust, an unconstitutional device adopted to achieve an unconstitutional end.

Clement Vallandigham was one of conscription's most vociferous critics. Barnstorming across Ohio during March and April, he urged audiences to defy Republican autocracy and repeated his call for an immediate armistice. His goal was twofold: to whip up antiwar sentiment and goad military authorities into committing a gross act of censorship that would transform his gubernatorial candidacy into a national cause célèbre.

He found a perfect foil in the person of Ambrose Burnside. The recently deposed commander of the Army of the Potomac had been sent to Cincinnati in late March to take over the Department of the Ohio, an administrative fiefdom encompassing the states of Ohio, Kentucky, Indiana, and Illinois. The department was a military dumping ground, or so the War Department thought. But Burnside had other ideas. Still smarting from Fredericksburg and the "Mud March," he established his headquarters in the Queen City and began searching for a way to rebuild his reputation. Vallandigham's rabid oratory soon came to his attention. On April 13 he published General Orders No. 38, announcing that henceforth anyone making seditious utterances in the area under his control would be subject to arrest, trial by military tribunal, and punishment by death or imprisonment.

This sweeping edict was just what Vallandigham had been hoping for. With plenty of advance notice so that Burnside would know exactly what he was up to, he addressed a Democratic rally at Mount Vernon, Ohio, on May 1. He directed his remarks not only to the assembled party faithful, many of whom were wearing copper liberty-head pennies on their lapels, but to a mufti-clad army captain who was standing at the foot of the speakers' platform scribbling notes in a little black book. For more than two hours he held forth, attacking the war and outlining his plan for peace and reunion. Then as the crowd roared its approval, he tore into Burnside's General Orders No. 38. It was a worthless scrap of paper, he sneered, a piece of rubbish that deserved to be spat upon and stamped underfoot. "The sooner the people inform the minions of usurped power that they will not submit to such restrictions upon their liberties, the better," he shouted. He concluded his speech by exhorting the throng to waste no time in toppling "King Lincoln" from his throne.

After reading Vallandigham's incendiary words, Burnside ordered his arrest. At 2 A.M. on May 5, a dozen armed soldiers broke into the candidate's Dayton house, dragged him from his bed, and hauled him off to Cincinnati, where he was formally charged with treason. The ex-congressman refused to enter a plea, claiming that the army lacked legal authority to try him or any other civilian. "I am a Democrat; for Constitution, for law, for Union, for liberty; this is my only crime," he said. The officers hearing his case were unmoved. They found him guilty and sentenced him to imprisonment for the remainder of the war. Vallandigham promptly filed for a writ of habeas corpus, but his motion was denied on the grounds that the arrest was legal and that Congress had sanctioned suspension of the writ in cases such as this.

Democrats everywhere were aghast. Martial law had been declared in an area hundreds of miles from the nearest battlefront. A candidate for high office had been locked up for making a political speech. The military dictatorship they had prophesied seemed to be materializing. With one voice they denounced Burnside's action and warned the administration that its handling of the case would "determine in the minds of more than one half of the people of the loyal states whether this war is waged to put down rebellion at the South or destroy free institutions at the North." Republicans were worried too. They feared the political damage that would result if Vallandigham won the Ohio governor's race while in jail. They waited anxiously to see what the president would do, hoping he could defuse the situation without further embarrassment to himself or the Union cause.

For two weeks Lincoln temporized. He believed he had to back Burnside, but he also wanted to avoid making Vallandigham a martyr. Finally he settled upon a shrewd solution. On May 19 he commuted Vallandigham's sentence from imprisonment to exile and ordered the army to hand him over to the rebels. Six days later a squad of Federal cavalrymen escorted the prisoner through Union lines south of Murfreesboro and delivered him, under flag of truce, to a group of startled Confederate pickets.

Southern newspaper editors were gleeful when they learned of the Ohioan's banishment to Dixie. But if they thought he was going to denounce his country and embrace the Confederate cause, they were sorely mistaken. Vallandigham insisted that he was a loyal citizen of the United States. In conversations with Confederate leaders, he reiterated his commitment to reunion through an armistice and negotiations. The Southerners replied that they would never accept peace without independence. They told their guest that an amicable settlement was impossible, and they asked him to leave Confederate soil at once. Vallandigham agreed. On June 17 he sailed from Wilmington, North Carolina, aboard the blockade-runner *Lady Davis,* bound for St. George, Bermuda. From there he booked passage to Halifax, Nova Scotia, arriving on July 5. Ten days later he was in Ontario, where he resumed his gubernatorial campaign by addressing Ohio Democrats from the Canadian side of the Niagara River. In his speech he condemned the war, blasted the president, and announced his intention to return to the Buckeye State "with my opinions and convictions . . . not only unchanged, but confirmed and strengthened."

Despite this grandstanding, which got considerable play in the Democratic press, Lincoln believed Vallandigham's banishment had served its purpose. By sending the Copperhead leader south instead of to prison, he had diminished him politically. The Ohioan was now widely perceived as a disunionist and a friend of the Confederacy rather than a champion of civil liberties. The clamor over his arrest and deportation did not die down, however, so Lincoln undertook to defend his actions in a pair of public letters published on June 12 and June 29.

In these carefully drafted documents, he stated his belief that Southern spies, aided and abetted by Northern sympathizers, were working to destroy the Constitution even as they relied upon its guarantees of freedom of speech and freedom of assembly to protect them. This was why he refused to renounce the suspension of habeas corpus or rescind martial law behind the lines. As long as subversive elements persisted in trying to assist the rebels, the entire country, not just the battlefronts, had to be treated as a war zone where civilians were subject to military arrest.

This justification of the administration's internal security measures went a long way toward laying the Vallandigham controversy to rest. But resentment of Washington's iron-fisted intrusion into state and local affairs continued to simmer, and as the spring progressed and a host of commissioners, provost marshals, and army doctors fanned out across the countryside enrolling young men and preparing for the first Federal draft, it became apparent that another, more violent outbreak of unrest was imminent.

National banking, conscription, suspension of habeas corpus, imposition of martial law in civilian areas—these rapid-fire developments heralded a revolution in the American system of government. In the span of a few months state authority had been permanently reduced and Washington's power had been hugely expanded. But as momentous as this political upheaval was, it was matched and perhaps even exceeded in importance by the startling social change that coincided with it.

Emancipation was forcing white Northerners to look at black people in an entirely new way. No longer could they be regarded as property to be returned to their owners or as bargaining chips to be used to woo the Confederate states back into the Union. Henceforward they would have to be viewed as human beings—reviled for the color of their skin perhaps, but human beings nonetheless, whose yearning for freedom, dignity, and a better life was as much a factor in the war's evolution as the actions of governments and the clash of armies.

Events were also forcing blacks to think about their place in American society and to reassess their role in the struggle that was transforming it. After two years of foot-dragging, the Lincoln administration had finally committed itself to a policy of recruiting and using colored troops. Here was the long-hoped-for chance to fight for freedom, to show whites that their assumptions about the inferiority of the colored race were wrong, to prove once and for all that people of African descent, as much as any other ethnic group, were an integral part of the American community. Frederick Douglass put it best when he wrote: "Once let the black man get upon his person the brass letters, *U.S.;* let him get an eagle on his button, and a musket on his shoulder, and bullets in his pocket, and there is no power on earth which can deny that he has earned the right to citizenship in the United States."

But the question remained: Would black men volunteer to fight for a country that had treated them so shabbily in the past?

Among the first to answer that question was James Gooding (called Henry by his family and friends), a twenty-five-year-old Negro from New Bedford, Massachusetts. On the blustery afternoon of March 4, 1863, he kissed his wife Ellen good-bye, left his lodgings near the New Bedford waterfront, and set out with fifty-three other black recruits for Camp Meigs, an army training center at Readville, a few miles south of Boston. Although he was giving up a gainful career as a sea cook to go soldiering, he was certain that he was doing the right thing. "Our people must know that if they are ever to attain to any position in the eyes of the civilized world, they must forgo comfort, home, fear, and above all, superstition, and fight for it," he wrote shortly before his departure. "They must learn that there is more dignity in carrying a musket in defense of liberty and right than there is in shaving a man's face, or waiting on somebody's table."

The unit Gooding was mustering into was a brand-new one, the Fifty-fourth Massachusetts Volunteer Infantry, the first all-black regiment raised in the North. Its sponsor was Massachusetts's Republican governor, John A. Andrew. Like Gooding, Andrew believed that blacks had to earn the respect of their white countrymen by excelling on the battlefield. Toward this end, he was determined to make the Fifty-fourth a crack outfit capable of defeating the Confederacy's best combat troops.

To make black enlistment more palatable to the Northern public and to placate racist elements within the Union army, the War Department had decreed that colored soldiers would serve in strictly segregated units under white commissioned officers. Thus the first challenge Andrew faced was finding a cadre of seasoned white commanders willing to live and work with black recruits. He feared that attracting good candidates would prove difficult. Ridicule and social ostracism awaited any officer who announced he was forsaking his old regiment to join an all-Negro outfit. He set his sights high, however, convinced that if the Fifty-fourth were to achieve the goals he had set for it, it had to be led by "gentlemen of the highest tone and honor."

He soon found a pair of infantry captains who fit the bill perfectly. Robert Gould Shaw was a twenty-five-year-old Harvard alumnus, offspring of one of Boston's leading families, and a veteran of combat with the Second Massachusetts. Norwood Penrose Hallowell was a Harvard-educated abolitionist who had fought with the Twentieth Massachusetts. Andrew offered the colonelcy of the Fifty-fourth to Shaw and the lieutenant colonelcy to Hallowell. Both men accepted. Confident that other qualified officers would sign up now that these two paragons had joined the regiment, the governor turned his attention to recruiting the enlisted men.

This turned out to be harder than he had supposed. According to the 1860 census, there were 1,973 black males of military age living in Massachusetts. If they volunteered at the same rate as whites, the Fifty-fourth could count on only 394 soldiers, about 600 short of the number needed. There was no getting around it—the regiment would have to go outside the Bay State to fill its ranks. To conduct this far-flung recruiting campaign, Andrew turned to a group of well-to-do abolitionists known as the Black Committee. Within a matter of weeks, the committee had raised $5,000 to pay for enlistment bounties, newspaper advertisements, travel expenses, and the like. It dispatched agents to the black communities in Providence, New York, Philadelphia, Cleveland, Chicago, and St. Louis and prevailed on William Lloyd Garrison, Wendell Phillips, Frederick Douglass, and other well-known antislavery orators to make public appearances on the regiment's behalf. Douglass, whose sons Lewis and Charles were among the first to join the Fifty-fourth, was an especially effective recruiter. "We can get at the throat of treason and slavery through the State of Massachusetts," he told black audiences in western New York State. "This is our golden opportunity—let us accept it and . . . win for ourselves the gratitude of our country."

Inspired by speeches like these, as well as the promise of a $50 enlistment bounty, pay of $13 a month, and $8-a-month financial aid for their families, hundreds of black enlistees were soon on their way to Camp Meigs. Public opinion in the states they hailed from was mixed as to whether their leaving was a good thing or not. "In Ohio it was considered a good joke to get the 'darkies on to Massachusetts,' " wrote Hallowell. Robert S. Corson, the Fifty-fourth's recruiting agent in Philadelphia, reported that crowds of white youths gathered at the railroad station to jeer and yell racist epithets whenever a band of Negro volunteers entrained for Boston. But in other locales there was a growing sense of unease, a feeling that Massachusetts was stealing a march on the rest of the country by tapping into the pool of black manpower. Recruiting officers were waking up to the fact that Negroes could fill enlistment quotas just as well as whites. Michigan, Illinois, Indiana, Ohio, Pennsylvania, New York, Connecticut, and Rhode Island belatedly formed their own colored units. By then Massachusetts's peripatetic recruiters had signed up enough men to fill not only the Fifty-fourth but a second all-black regiment, the Fifty-fifth Volunteer Infantry, as well.

When Henry Gooding and the New Bedford contingent marched into Camp Meigs on the drizzly evening of March 4, they were profoundly disillusioned by what they saw. The base was a collection of crudely constructed buildings sitting in a sea of icy mud. Inside the drafty, barnlike structures, tiers of coffin-shaped sleeping bunks lined windowless walls. The air was so cold, the men could see their breath. There was nothing to eat, and no one seemed to have any idea where they should go or what they should do.

It was a singularly inauspicious beginning, but in the days that followed, conditions improved and morale rebounded. The recruits were given a physical examination, sworn into the armed forces of the United States, and issued new uniforms. The barracks were scrubbed from top to bottom; food, firewood, and bedding were provided by the quartermaster; and the men began to learn the rudiments of soldiering under the tutelage of their white officers.

Infantry regiments had to be able to perform a variety of complex small- and large-unit maneuvers under fire. Only by rehearsing them over and over again could they hope to execute them properly on the battlefield. Thus the apprentice soldiers of the Fifty-fourth Massachusetts spent at least five hours a day practicing close-order drill, inside vacant buildings when the weather was bad, and outside on the rare occasions when the sun shone and the mud dried out.

At first Shaw was unhappy with the performance of the black recruits. "They are not the best class of nigs," he complained in a letter to his father. But by the end of March he had changed his mind. "I am perfectly astonished at the general intelligence these darkies display," he reported. "They learn all the details of guard duty and camp service infinitely more readily than most of the Irish I have had under my command." As his misgivings about the capacity of black men to become soldiers subsided, he stopped referring to them as "niggers" and "darkies" and started defending them against their critics in the army and the press. On April 6 he felt confident enough of their progress to invite the public to the regiment's first dress parade. The affair was a huge success, and thereafter crowds of curious onlookers were a fixture at the camp. "The skeptics need only to come out here to be converted," Shaw proudly wrote.

Despite the hard work and rigid discipline, the black volunteers adjusted well to military life. The only sore spot was money. The army paymaster had not been seen at Camp Meigs, and his absence was a source of frustration and worry to men who had left wives and children behind. Nor had the enlistment bounties or the promised state aid been paid yet. Shaw was sympathetic to the plight of his men, but he refused to tolerate any breach of discipline on account of money problems. When some members of Company B started clamoring for their enlistment bounties during a regimental review, he had them arrested and thrown in the guardhouse.

Pay protests aside, the transformation of the recruits into soldiers proceeded at a brisk pace. "Most of the companies are now quite proficient in the manual of arms," Gooding reported in one of the columns he was writing for the New Bedford *Mercury*. On May 18 several thousand spectators gathered for the presentation of the regimental, state, and national colors. This ceremony marked the end of the unit's training period and the beginning of its official army service. Governor Andrew admonished the regiment never to yield any of its banners "so long as a splinter of the staff or a thread of its web remains within your grasp." After he had inspected the troops, he handed Shaw a War Department telegram that read: "The 54th Massachusetts will report to General Hunter. Make requisitions for transportation so that they may go at once."

This was great news as far as Shaw was concerned. Major General David Hunter, head of the Department of the South, headquartered at Hilton Head, South Carolina, was an enthusiastic proponent of black combat units. Assignment to his command meant that the Fifty-fourth was likely to see action soon. The enlisted men were happy, too, not so much

Black troops. (Courtesy U.S. Army Military History Institute)

because they were being sent to South Carolina, but because their $50 enlistment bounties had finally been paid.

There was little time to enjoy the money. At 6:30 A.M. on May 28 the regiment boarded railroad cars at the Readville station for the short trip into downtown Boston. It was a beautiful spring morning, and a huge crowd had gathered to watch the Fifty-fourth march from the depot down to Battery Wharf, where the steamer *DeMolay* was waiting to transport it to the Sea Islands of South Carolina. The rattle of drums, the clatter of hooves, the rhythmic tramp of shoes on the Beacon Street cobblestones electrified the spectators. They waved flags and cheered wildly when they caught sight of the ebony-skinned soldiers striding along in their blue-and-gold uniforms.

In the midst of the enthusiastic throng was poet John Greenleaf Whittier, a committed pacifist. The sight of Negroes marching beneath the Stars and Stripes moved him to tears, and although he declined to celebrate it in verse "lest I should indirectly give a new impulse to war," he did confide to a friend that "the scene as Colonel Shaw rode at the head of his men [is one] I can never forget. The very flower of grace and chivalry, he seemed to me beautiful and awful, as an angel of God come down to lead the host of freedom to victory."

Henry Wadsworth Longfellow was likewise impressed. "Saw the first regiment of blacks march through Beacon Street," he wrote in his diary that evening. "An imposing sight, with something wild and strange about it, like a dream. At last the North consents to let the Negro fight for freedom."

The Fifty-fourth boarded *DeMolay,* and at 4 P.M. the lines were cast off, and the steamer headed out to sea. In his cabin Shaw was exuberant. "The more I think of the passage of the [regiment] through Boston, the more wonderful it seems to me," he wrote. The mood was more somber in the enlisted compartment. As the ship began to pitch and roll in the Atlantic swells, the troops found themselves thinking about the long voyage that lay ahead and the perils they would face once they reached their destination.

"There is not a man in the regiment who does not appreciate the difficulties, the dangers, and maybe ignoble death that awaits him," Henry Gooding wrote. But "when a thousand men are fighting for a very existence, who dare say [they] won't fight determinedly? The greatest difficulty will be to stop them."

While the black soldiers of the Fifty-fourth Massachusetts sailed off to war and the citizens of the North buzzed about the banishment of Clement Vallandigham, a big, bearlike man in a maroon-colored suit, black morocco boots, and gray-felt sombrero was becoming well known in the convalescent camps and hospital wards of Washington. Almost every evening around sunset he could be seen trudging down Pennsylvania Avenue on his way to either Armory Square or Judiciary Square Hospital, where he would spend four or five hours working as a volunteer nurse.

The pedestrians sharing the pavement with him were not sure what to make of his colorful clothing or of the dreamy, far-off expression on his sunburned face. Standing six feet tall and weighing 220 pounds, with a bulging haversack slung over one shoulder and a tattered notebook clutched in his huge hands, he looked immensely robust, like "some great mechanic, or stevedore, or seaman, or grand laborer of

Walt Whitman. (Library of Congress)

one kind or another." But there was something faintly effeminate about him too. A fresh lilac sprig adorned his lapel. The white linen shirt he wore was open at the collar, revealing his neck and chest. His beard was carefully brushed out, and he smelled of soap—a substance most Washingtonians used infrequently, if at all. Passersby sniffed the air and cast curious glances at him, wondering if he was someone they should recognize—an artist, say, or maybe an actor. His sweet scent and exotic appearance simultaneously attracted and repelled them, and they did not understand why.

In a city full of eccentric characters, there was no one else quite like Walt Whitman. "Old and young, of the foolish as much as the wise, regardless of others, ever regardful of others, maternal as well as paternal, a child as well as a man, stuffed with the stuff that is coarse, and stuffed with the stuff that is fine," he tramped the streets of Washington "with the sunlight and shadows falling around him." He had come down from Brooklyn in late December to search for his soldier-brother George, who had been wounded at Fredericksburg. After finding him alive and well at Falmouth, he had returned to the capital to look for work. His résumé did not inspire confidence. In the past he had been employed as a typesetter, schoolteacher, carpenter, and journalist, but he had never stuck with anything for long. He had also published a volume of unconventional verse, titled *Leaves of Grass.* It had been reviled by critics as "reckless and indecent," a "mass of stupid filth," and it had earned him only $250 in royalties.

A government clerkship was what he aspired to now, but his flamboyant garb and scandalous literary reputation scared off all the politicians he approached. "Why, how can I do this thing, or any other thing for you?" New York senator Preston King exclaimed when the forty-four-year-old poet asked him for a job. "How do I know but you are a secessionist? You look for all the world like an old southern planter—a regular Carolina or Virginia planter." Secretary of the Treasury Salmon P. Chase was even more emphatic: there was no place in his department for the man who had written that "very bad book." Whitman was a decidedly disreputable person, and that was that.

Despite these rebuffs, Walt was determined to stay on in Washington. The city's "distraction, heat, smoke, and excitement" exhilarated him. "Breaking up a few weeks since, and for good, my New York stagnation, I fetch up here in harsh and superb plight—wretchedly poor, excellent well, (my only torment, family matters)—realizing at last that it is necessary for me to fall for the time in the wise old way, to push my fortune, to be brazen, and get employment, and have an income," he wrote his friend Ralph Waldo Emerson.

While he waited for something to turn up, he explored the Capitol ("by far the richest and the gayest and most un-American and inappropriate ornamenting and finest interior workmanship I ever conceived possible"), visited the Supreme Court ("saw Chief Justice Taney and all the other black-gowned Supreme Judges—their faces old, wrinkled, heavy—a lot of old mummies"), and observed the Thirty-seventh Congress ("much gab, great fear of public opinion, plenty of low business talent, but no masterful man . . . probably best so"). And he watched Abraham Lincoln driving through the streets in an open barouche, his face like that of "a hoosier Michel Angelo, so awful ugly it becomes beautiful." The city and its denizens were fascinating: "A new world here I find," he exulted, "curious and stirring . . . never did I feel better."

He took a room in a tenement on L Street and supported himself by copying documents for the army paymaster general. Although it was tedious work, he professed not to mind. The paymaster's office was located on the fifth floor of the Corcoran Building at Fifteenth and F Streets. From its windows he could look out over the rooftops, past the truncated shaft of the Washington Monument and the reddish-brown turrets of the Smithsonian castle, to the Potomac River and Arlington Heights beyond. It was "a most noble and broad view," he remarked. But his enjoyment of it was spoiled by other, uglier sights. Day after day scores of "sick, pale, tattered soldiers," many of them missing arms or legs, hobbled up the steep flights of stairs in hopes of getting paid, only to be told that their paperwork was not in order. "This is the greatest place of delays and puttings off, and no finding any clue to anything," he complained. "The scenes of disappointment are quite affecting."

It was in January that he began visiting Washington's military hospitals. At first he went sporadically to see some Brooklyn boys he knew. Soon he was going every day, not only to cheer up his old friends but to spend time with strangers as well. Eight years earlier, in "Song of Myself," he had written:

To any one dying. . . . thither I speed and twist the knob of the door,
Turn the bedclothes toward the foot of the bed,
Let the physician and the priest go home.
I seize the descending man. . . . I raise him with resistless will.

O despairer, here is my neck,
By God! you shall not go down! Hang your whole weight upon me.

Now he found himself living those lines, roaming the whitewashed wards as sustainer of spirit and body, tending to an army of sick and wounded soldiers, many of them still in their teens. He would stop at their bedsides to talk, inquire after their needs, read aloud or write letters for them, and dispense presents of fruit, candy, and tobacco from his haversack. Other gifts he gave, too—gifts of the heart—more potent, he believed, than any medicine. "O what a sweet unwonted love (those good American boys, of good stock, decent, clean, well raised boys, so near to me)—what an attachment grows up between us, started from hospital cots, where pale young faces lie," he wrote. "I have long discarded all stiff conventions (they and I are too near to each other, there is no time to lose, and death and anguish dissipate ceremony here between my lads and me)—I pet them, some of them it does so much good, they are so faint and lonesome—at parting at night sometimes I kiss them right and left."

Not everyone approved of his ministrations. "There comes that odious Walt Whitman to talk evil and unbelief to my boys," grumbled Harriet Hawley, head nurse at Armory Square Hospital. "I think I would rather see the Evil One himself." But the poet was undeterred. The love he felt for the wounded and sick overwhelmed his own terrible doubt of appearances, made the moralizing of Nurse Hawley and others of her ilk seem blasphemous. "I know what is in their hearts—always waiting—though they may be unconscious of it themselves," he wrote of the invalids whose physical and spiritual needs had come to consume him. And he acted on that knowledge without fear or shame:

Many a soldier's arms about this neck have cross'd and rested,
Many a soldier's kiss dwells on these bearded lips.

It seemed to Whitman, as he wandered through wartime Washington, that he had stumbled upon the utopian "republic of comrades" he had fantasized about in his *Calamus* poems. Here in the nation's capital, he told his friend Emerson, was a perfect cross section of the country's "masculine young manhood . . . America, already brought to Hospital in her fair youth. . . . sailed and wagoned hither this other freight . . . genuine of the soil, of darlings and true heirs to me, the first unquestioned and convincing western crop, prophetic of the future, proofs undeniable to all men's ken of perfect beauty and tenderness and pluck that never race rivaled."

But he was mistaken. The athletic cavalrymen he admired as they paraded down Pennsylvania Avenue ("healthy, handsome, rollicking . . . all good riders, full of the devil"), the dewy-faced privates with whom he exchanged glances as he strolled the moonlit streets around the Patent Office ("O eyes wishfully turning! O silent eyes!"), the tormented boys he held hands with in the hospital wards ("I never before had my feelings so thoroughly and so far permanently absorbed, to the very roots"), were not representative of the country as a whole. In fact, only a small fraction of the North's "masculine young manhood"—about one in five—was serving in the armed forces. The rest were busy making money, something that was easier to do now than it had been in any previous period of American history.

"It may well surprise ourselves and all other nations that, during a year of the greatest civil war on record, our country has been wonderfully prosperous," the *Scientific American* declared early in 1863. The observation had a smug ring to it, but it was true. As the needs of the Union military grew, so did the industrial and agricultural output of the North. Businessmen with government contracts in hand were building factories, hiring workers, and employing new machinery and production techniques to turn out a torrent of manufactured goods. Nor had the departure of farm workers for the battlefield led to a decline in agricultural production as some had predicted. To the contrary, the introduction of commercial fertilizers and the adoption of labor-saving implements had led to a dramatic increase in farm yields. An observer traveling through Wisconsin and eastern Iowa in the spring of 1863 was astonished to see hundreds of sturdy, sun-bronzed women driving McCormick reapers through vast fields of winter wheat, bringing in a harvest so bounteous, it would feed not only the Union's soldiers and civilians but much of drought-afflicted Europe as well. "Our hired man left," one of these women said matter-of-factly. "I guess my services are just as acceptable as his."

Farther west, great wagon trains creaked across the plains carrying thousands of immigrant families (and more than a few deserters and draft dodgers) to Minnesota, Nebraska, Kansas, and the Dakotas, where they would claim free 160-acre farms courtesy of the Homestead Act. Other caravans rolled on toward the Rocky Mountains, bound for the mining districts of Colorado, Nevada, Montana, and Idaho.

The hustle and excitement of boom times were apparent everywhere, and to many Northerners it seemed as if a new nation were being born that spring, an economic colossus bursting with entrepreneurial energy and unbridled greed. For most it was a welcome development. Never had the country been so well off financially. Never had the chance to get ahead been afforded to so many people. But rampant prosperity had its drawbacks. Graft and corruption were pervasive as unscrupulous contractors took advantage of the military's sloppy procurement procedures to defraud the government of millions of dollars. "Our sailors were sent to sea in ships built of green timber, which were fitted with engines good only for the junkshop, and greased with 'sperm' oil derived from mossbunkers and the fat of dead horses," wrote War Department inspector Colonel Henry S. Olcott. "Our soldiers were given guns that would not shoot, powder that would only half explode, shoes of which the soles were filled with shavings, hats that dissolved often in a month's showers, and clothing made of old cloth, ground up and fabricated over again. . . . Every artifice that rascally ingenuity could devise, and clever men and women carry out, was resorted to."

Venality was not confined to the civilian sector. A War Department official visiting Memphis in the spring of 1863 was shocked to find Federal troops buying cotton from Southern planters for $8 a bale and selling it to Northern dealers for more than $330 a bale. "The mania for sudden fortunes made in cotton . . . has to an alarming extent corrupted and demoralized the army," he informed Secretary Stanton. "Every colonel, captain, or quartermaster is in secret partnership with some operator in cotton; every soldier dreams of adding a bale of cotton to his monthly pay." He characterized the black market as "an evil so enormous, so insidious, so full of peril to the country" that it made him sick—and he promptly invested his life savings in it.

Illicit fortunes were being made in New Orleans too. Nathaniel P. Banks was flabbergasted when, within days of his arrival in the Crescent City, he was offered $100,000 by a contract broker to look the other way while a major cotton deal was consummated. "I never despaired of my country until I came here," Banks wrote his wife a few weeks after this episode. "Everybody connected with the government has been employed in stealing other people's property. Sugar, silver plate, horses, carriages, everything they could lay their hands on. There has been open trade with the enemy. . . . We can never succeed, under such direction—our people must give up stealing or give up the country, one or the other."

Banks was not the only one appalled by the avarice afflicting much of Northern society. The New York *Herald,* in a venomous article entitled "The Age of Shoddy," took dead aim at the wheeler-dealers who had turned national tragedy to their pecuniary advantage and were now engaged in an orgy of conspicuous consumption. "This war has entirely changed the American character," the *Herald* declared. "Ideas of cheapness and economy are thrown to the winds. The individual who makes the most money—no matter how—and spends the most money—no matter for what—is considered the greatest man. To be extravagant is to be fashionable. . . . The world has seen its iron age, its silver age, its golden age. . . . This is the age of shoddy. The new brownstone palaces on Fifth Avenue, the new equipages at the Park, the new diamonds which dazzle unaccustomed eyes, the new silks and satins which rustle over loudly, as if to demand attention, the new people who live in the palaces and ride in the carriages and wear the diamonds and silks—all are shoddy."

Another example of the acquisitiveness the *Herald* deplored was the avid response of New York's nouveau riche to the major art event of the

Home, Sweet Home *by Winslow Homer. (National Gallery of Art)*

year, the National Academy of Design's thirty-eighth annual exhibition. The parvenus flocked to the grand opening on April 13, paying twenty-five cents apiece to gain admission to a gallery at 625 Broadway, where more than five hundred original works were on display. The swells came not just to look but to buy: canvases were snapped up at prices running into the hundreds of dollars.

Two pieces in particular, both by a magazine illustrator making his debut as a painter, were much coveted. *The Last Goose at Yorktown* depicted two Union soldiers stalking a wary waterfowl, while *Home, Sweet Home* showed a pair of pensive-looking infantrymen slouched in front of their tent, listening to music played by a regimental band. Of the latter a critic wrote: "There is no clap-trap about it. . . . The delicacy and strength of emotion which reign throughout this little picture are not surpassed in the whole exhibition." Said another: "It is a work of real feeling . . . as full of promise and cheer for American art as any [painting] we have ever seen." Raved a third: "If this is the work of a new beginner, where on earth will he stop?"

The answer, it turned out, was the pinnacle of his profession, for the novice painter's name was Winslow Homer.

Economic good times benefited not just the fine arts, but other forms of cultural expression as well. Opera, theater, museums, libraries, and concert halls were all well attended, and book sales boomed. Among the works being read and discussed were Victor Hugo's *Les Misérables,* Charles Dickens's *Great Expectations,* Harriet Beecher Stowe's *The Pearl of Orr's Island,* Bayard Taylor's *Hannah Thurston,* Henry Wadsworth Longfellow's *Tales of a Wayside Inn,* and Edward Everett Hale's *The Man Without a Country.* "In no period of the past . . . has the literary activity of the country been so manifest," the *American Annual Cyclopaedia* marveled. "While the price of paper has more than doubled, and the cost of printing and binding have been greatly enhanced . . . the number of new books issued surpasses that of any previous year."

The booming Northern economy was good for art, good for books, good for entertainments of all kinds, but it was extremely bad for enlistment, which declined sharply during the spring of 1863. With money-making opportunities abounding, military service was viewed as something to be avoided if at all possible. Pittsburgh lawyer Thomas Mellon made this point in a letter to his son, who was thinking about joining the army. "I had hoped my boy was going to make a smart intelligent businessman and was not such a goose as to be seduced by the declamations of buncombed speeches," he wrote. "You can learn nothing in the army. . . . There is no credit attached to going. All now stay if they can and go if they must. Those who are able to pay for substitutes do so, and no discredit attaches.

In time you will come to understand and believe that a man may be a patriot without risking his own life or sacrificing his health. There are plenty of other lives less valuable or others ready to serve for the love of serving."

Young James Mellon heeded this advice and did not enlist. Instead he hired a substitute and went to work for his father, learning the business skills that would make him one of America's most successful bankers. He was not alone in shunning military service. A veritable *Who's Who* of Gilded Age tycoons chose to stay home and devote their energies to business during 1863. Capitalizing on commercial opportunities created by the war, they laid the foundation for their careers as captains of industry and finance even as thousands of their less-fortunate contemporaries were conscripted into the Union army and sent to the Southern killing fields.

One of the draft-age businessmen taking his first steps toward great wealth that spring was twenty-three-year-old John D. Rockefeller of Cleveland. A tall, gangling youth, pallid and stoop-shouldered from long hours hunched over account books, he was a partner in the firm of Clark & Rockefeller, commission merchants in meat, grain, and hay.

Like most firms of its type, Clark & Rockefeller had profited handsomely from the war. But Rockefeller was restless. His entrepreneurial instincts told him it was time to diversify out of farm staples. The locus of agricultural activity was shifting westward. Chicago, with its sprawling stockyards, giant wheat and corn elevators, and excellent rail connections, would soon become the nation's leading grain-shipping and meat-packing center. He believed that Cleveland's commercial future lay in handling industrial raw materials: iron ore and smelted copper from the Upper Peninsula of Michigan, anthracite from Kentucky and the recently admitted state of West Virginia, and petroleum products from Pennsylvania and Ohio. The embryonic oil industry seemed the most promising, so he invested four thousand dollars in a refinery being built on Kingsbury Run, a tributary of the Cuyahoga River, about a mile and a half southeast of downtown Cleveland.

Rockefeller went into this venture, he later said, thinking it would be "a little side issue." Instead it was the produce business that became a side issue. Petroleum refining was incredibly profitable. A gallon of crude cost thirty-one cents, while a gallon of refined oil sold for as much as eighty-five cents. The potential for expansion looked limitless. Convinced that refining would become one of the nation's great industries, Rockefeller devoted himself to mastering all of its details. He pored over financial statements until he knew to a fraction of a penny what everything cost. Then he pitched in around the refinery until he had a solid understanding of the process by which crude oil was turned into kerosene, benzene, gasoline, and naphtha.

Petroleum quickly became Rockefeller's all-consuming passion. Years later his sister Mary Ann would recall that everyone in Cleveland was talking about the war that spring—everyone, that is, except her brother and his partners. "They were talking oil all the time," she wrote. "It was all foreign to me, and I got sick of it and wished morning after morning that they would talk of something else; but they didn't seem to care for anything else."

To the budding tycoon, the war was a matter of little consequence. He purchased a revolver for his brother Frank, who was serving in the Army of the Potomac, and he donated seventy dollars to the families of soldiers from Cleveland's Fourth Ward, but that was the extent of his involvement. Then, much to his disgust, the conflict intruded into his life in the form of the Enrollment Act of 1863. Realizing that he was a prime candidate for conscription, he arranged for a substitute. "I wanted to go in the army and do my part," he told an interviewer fifty-four years later. "But it was simply out of the question. . . . We were in a new business, and if I had not stayed it must have stopped—and with so many dependent on it."

So John Davison Rockefeller remained in Cleveland, working on plans to enlarge his refinery and his bank account, while a substitute whose name has been lost to history went off to war in his place.

A long with ordinary happenings, we fellows in Wall Street have the fortunes of war to speculate about and that always makes great doings on a stock exchange. It's good fishing in troubled waters." So said Daniel Drew, legendary manipulator of Erie Railroad shares and role model to a brash new breed of financial operators who were making their mark on Wall Street in 1863.

Among the shrewdest of "Uncle Dan's" disciples was twenty-six-year-old John Pierpont Morgan, eldest son of American financier Junius Spencer Morgan, managing partner in the London banking house of George Peabody & Co. A brusque, brooding young man given to icy stares and long silences, Pierpont had arrived in New York in 1857 to arrange loans for Peabody & Co., write reports on the stock market, and engage in a little commodities trading. "Do not let the desire of success or of accumulating induce you ever to do a single action which will cause you regret," Junius had lectured his son when they parted on the Liverpool docks. "Self approbation and a feeling that God approves will bring a far greater happiness than all the wealth the world can give." Pierpont disregarded his father's advice

J. Pierpont Morgan. (Courtesy Archives of The Pierpont Morgan Library, New York)

the moment he set foot in Manhattan. Soon his personal income was approaching $50,000 a year—a princely sum in the mid-nineteenth century.

Morgan's first coup came in the summer of 1861, when he was involved in a scheme to purchase 5,000 obsolete carbines from the U.S. Army, refurbish them on the cheap, then sell them back to the government at a 500 percent profit. A congressional committee that later investigated this scandalous transaction concluded that seizing upon the "pressing necessities of a nation . . . to gratify a voracious cupidity and coin money out of the common grief is a crime against the public safety." Morgan escaped censure, however, and in so doing he learned the validity of another of Daniel Drew's axioms: "The honest people of the world are a pack of fools."

By the spring of 1863, Pierpont was well launched on his career as a financial freebooter. He and his partner, Edward Ketchum, had a private telegraph wire installed in their office at 54 Exchange Place so that they could stay abreast of the war news. They used the information to anticipate moves in the stock and bond markets, reaping large profits in the process. The real action on Wall Street was in gold, however, and it was to this volatile commodity that Morgan gravitated in 1863.

Because gold was the only medium of exchange that would retain its value if the North lost the war, its price was directly linked to Union military fortunes. It rose when news from the front was bad and fell when it was good. This led to a perverse situation in which word of Union defeats sparked wild cheering on the floor of the New York Stock Exchange, while reports of Union victories drew despairing groans. Mortified by these unseemly outbursts, the board of brokers who ran the New York exchange banned the sale of bullion on the trading floor. The gold bugs were undeterred. They simply packed up and moved, establishing their own exchange in the back room of a ramshackle building located at the corner of William Street and Exchange Place. In this dingy establishment, variously described as a "rat pit" and a "den of wild beasts," the speculating never stopped. "The chaos of voices and the stamping of feet shook the building as in an earthquake, and boomed out of the open windows into the street below like the discharge of artillery," recalled trader James Medbery. "Men leapt upon chairs, waved their hands, or clenched their fists; shrieked, shouted; the bulls whistled 'Dixie,' and the bears sang 'John Brown'; the crowd swayed feverishly from door to door, and, as the fury mounted to white heat, and the tide of gold fluctuated up and down in rapid sequence, brokers seemed animated with the impulses of demons, hand-to-hand combats took place, and bystanders, peering through the smoke and dust, could liken the wild turmoil only to the revels of maniacs."

This was the money jungle that Morgan entered in 1863, slipping in silently and stealthily like a hunter in search of big game. Over a period of six weeks, he quietly bought $2 million worth of gold on margin, pushing the price up from $130 to $143 an ounce. Then with great fanfare he announced that he was sending half his stake to his father's bank in London, a ploy that drove the price even higher. When it reached $171 he sold and pocketed a profit of $160,000.

Shenanigans like these played havoc with currency values and infuriated Abraham Lincoln. "What do you think of those fellows on Wall Street who are gambling in gold at such a time as this?" he asked a White House visitor on one occasion. "For my part, I wish every one of them had his devilish head shot off."

But Morgan was unrepentant. Profits came before patriotism. As for getting his head shot off, there was no way that was going to happen. When the local enrollment board informed him that he was about to be drafted, he hastily hired a substitute—"the other Pierpont Morgan," he snidely referred to him—and thus avoided service. The rise of J. P. Morgan & Co. was not going to be interrupted by anything so dangerous and demeaning as a stint in the armed forces of the United States.

In Pittsburgh twenty-seven-year-old Andrew Carnegie was also having a busy spring. A short, sandy-haired Scotsman who had immigrated to America at the age of twelve, he was working by day as superintendent of the Pennsylvania Railroad's Western Division, and by night as a private investor, managing his holdings in a dozen Pittsburgh-area businesses, including a bank, a telegraph service, a manufacturing company, a coal mining company, four oil companies, and—most significantly in light of his future as a steel magnate—four iron mills.

Although the job of division superintendent was a prestigious one, the hard-driving Carnegie had decided to give it up as soon as the war was over. He aspired to bigger things than directing train traffic. He stayed on now only because he thought it was his patriotic duty to do so. It certainly was not the salary: although quite handsome by the standards of the day, the $2,400 a year the Pennsylvania Railroad Company paid him represented less than 6 percent of his annual income for 1863.

Carnegie's flourishing investment career had begun seven years earlier, when he bought ten shares of stock in the Adams Express Company. The day he cashed his first dividend check, he had experienced an epiphany. "I shall remember that check as long as I live," he wrote six decades later. "It gave me the first penny of revenue from capital—something that I had not worked for with the sweat of my brow. 'Eureka!' I cried. 'Here's the goose that lays the golden eggs.' " From that day forward he pursued the goose with single-minded fervor, using the information that crossed his desk in the offices of the Pennsylvania Railroad to assess the strengths and weaknesses of firms doing business with the line, and making his investment decisions accordingly.

This profitable arrangement had been disrupted by the outbreak of war. Ten days after the fall of Fort Sumter, a team of executives from the Pennsylvania Railroad was summoned to the capital to help the War Department mobilize the North's rail and telegraph system. Carnegie's assignment was twofold: link the Baltimore & Ohio and the Orange & Alexandria lines via the Long Bridge over the Potomac River, and organize a network of telegraph stations so that there could be instantaneous communication between the War Department and Union armies campaigning in Virginia.

Carnegie quickly developed a strong aversion to living and working in Washington. The heat and humidity affected his health, and the delays and

bureaucratic red tape he encountered nearly drove him mad. "Days would elapse before a decision could be obtained upon matters which required prompt action," he wrote afterward. "There was scarcely a young active officer at the head of any department—at least I cannot recall one. Long years of peace had fossilized the service." It was with a profound sense of relief that he completed his six-month tour of duty and went back to Pittsburgh in the fall of 1861.

The Iron City was thriving, and investment opportunities were plentiful. Carnegie was especially interested in the fast-growing oil industry. Not long after his return from Washington, he made the hundred-mile trip up the Allegheny River to Venango County,

Andrew Carnegie. (Courtesy Carnegie Library, Pittsburgh)

the remote area in northwestern Pennsylvania where Edwin Drake had drilled the world's first petroleum well in 1859.

The sights, sounds, and smells of the oil fields enthralled him. Wooden derricks sprouted like weeds from muddy creek bottoms, shantytowns clung precariously to steep hillsides, barrel-laden drays raced along rutted roads, and everywhere there was oil—soaking the ground, coating the trees, floating on the rivers, filling the air with its rank, primeval odor. From all sides came the scream of saws, the thump of hammers, and the hiss and chug of steam engines. Hordes of petroleum prospectors were grubbing feverishly in the glistening black muck, bidding to strike it rich or break themselves trying.

Within days of his trip Carnegie had purchased a $10,000 stake in the Columbia Oil Company, which was getting ready to drill on the Storey Farm, a promising tract located five miles south of Titusville. It proved to be a superb investment. The company tapped into a huge pool of petroleum, and before the year was out, it had paid four dividends, each totaling more than $1 million. Carnegie's cut came to $1.25 million. He used the money to buy up more of Pittsburgh's iron business—the progenitor of the hugely profitable American steel industry.

Like Rockefeller and Morgan, the enterprising young Scotsman was too busy looking after his financial affairs to pay much attention to the war. Then suddenly, and quite unfairly as it seemed to him, he was drafted. He believed that his six months at the War Department should count as military service, but Federal enrollment officials thought otherwise. Reluctantly he paid a fee to Pittsburgh's leading substitute broker, H. M. Butler, and a few days later John Lindew, a teenager recently arrived from Ireland, went off to the army in his stead.

With that problem taken care of, Carnegie got back to work, managing his businesses and making money. "I am determined," he informed his cousin in a letter written on June 21, "to expand as my means do." And like so many other Northern entrepreneurs in the boom spring of 1863, his means were expanding by leaps and bounds.

SIX

BREAD OR BLOOD

Unlike the Union, which was fighting the war with one hand and getting rich with the other, the Confederacy in the spring of 1863 was cracking under the strain of fielding and supplying its armies. Cut off from Europe by Federal blockade squadrons; lacking the population, natural resources, and industrial infrastructure that made the North's spectacular economic growth possible; saddled with a political leadership that shrank from the task of creating an efficient, centralized organization for sustaining both the armed forces and the civilian population; suffering from material shortages and hyperinflation, the South was sliding inexorably into poverty.

Consumer goods were scarce, and improvisation was the order of the day. Clothing was fashioned from worn-out sheets and old curtains. Shoes were cobbled out of canvas and wood. Blankets were obtained by cutting up carpets, while mattresses were manufactured by stuffing leaves, straw, and palmetto fronds into discarded grain sacks. Kitchen grease mixed with potash took the place of soap, cottonseed oil substituted for kerosene, and candles were molded out of suet. Ink was obtained by boiling bark and berries, goose quills replaced steel pens, and letter writers learned to shrink their script to tiny dimensions to conserve the rapidly dwindling paper supply. Coffee was brewed from parched rye, okra seed, peanuts, and sweet potato peelings, tea was made from yaupon leaves and sassafras root, and pulverized sassafras bark, mixed with chalk dust, served as tooth powder.

These ersatz domestic necessities could be tolerated for a time, but not so the growing lack of food. It had been a shibboleth among the Confederacy's founders that a nation of farmers would never go hungry. That was precisely what was happening, however. "The gaunt form of wretched famine approaches with rapid strides," a Richmond resident wrote in late

Southern farm women. (Library of Congress)

March. "Meal is now selling at $12 per bushel, and potatoes at $16. Meats have almost disappeared from the market." A Mississippian reported that "there is now much suffering amongst the poorer classes of volunteers' families—much suffering for want of *corn and salt*." A Confederate officer stationed on Alabama's Gulf Coast was appalled to see soldiers' wives foraging for grain in fields that had been harvested the year before, reduced, he wrote, to living "on the principle of 'root hog or die.'"

Like their Northern counterparts, Southern farm women had taken the place of departed husbands and sons when the war began, but without the new machinery that was revolutionizing agriculture in the North, they were unable to sustain antebellum production levels. Exacerbating the effects of the farm labor shortage was the loss of prime agricultural acreage in war-ravaged areas of Virginia, Tennessee, Mississippi, Louisiana, and Arkansas.

What little food was grown often did not make it to market because of the inadequacy of the Confederate transportation system. Most roads in the South were dirt tracks, dust-choked in summer and mud-bound in winter. They could be traversed, albeit slowly, by mule-drawn wagons, but these wagons were in short supply, having either broken down from overwork or been requisitioned for military use. Rivers that had been important avenues of commerce before the war could no longer be safely navigated because of the presence of Yankee gunboats. Nor were Southern railroads capable of carrying the logistical load for a nation at war. In the entire Confederacy there were only 9,000 miles of track (as opposed to 22,000 miles in the North). Gauges varied from three to six feet, which meant in many instances that cars could not be transferred from one line to another. At rail hubs like Richmond, Petersburg, Augusta, and Savannah, competing lines did not connect, forcing shippers to unload freight from one train, haul it crosstown, and reload it onto another train. Antiquated rolling stock caused problems too. Most of the locomotives in use had been purchased from Northern machine shops in the 1850s, and as backlogs of tools and spare parts were exhausted, it became harder and harder to maintain them. Cannibalization was resorted to, an expedient that further reduced the Confederacy's already meager inventory of railroad equipment. An adequate number of engines were kept in service this way, but they grew so decrepit that the average speed of trains traveling through the South dropped to a snail-like ten miles an hour. All of these factors added up to delays—long delays that caused foodstuffs to sit in warehouses or on rail sidings, rotting or being eaten by rats and mice, as soldiers at the front and women and children at home went hungry.

Inflation and speculation further aggravated the South's supply woes. Rapidly rising prices prompted producers and shopkeepers to hoard scarce items. When they did sell, they often refused to accept Confederate money, demanding gold or U.S. dollars instead. The "love of lucre [has] eaten like a gangrene into the very heart of the land," lamented Jefferson Davis. Proclamations denouncing profiteers, laws imposing prison terms upon persons trying to monopolize essential commodities, a widespread resort to barter—all failed to cool the speculative fever.

As the gulf between the haves and the have-nots widened, Southern opinion makers worried that class conflict was going to tear the Confederacy apart. The Rome (Georgia) *Weekly Courier,* decrying the unwillingness of wealthy slaveholders to help their less-fortunate neighbors, asked: "Can it be possible that the southern planter, the synonym of nobility and benevolence, can hear the accounts of the desperate battles, the heroic deaths of his gallant countrymen, and then turn away and ingloriously revel amidst his comfort and wealth?"

Unfortunately for the Confederacy the answer was yes. Examples of planter prodigality abounded. Catherine Cooper Hopley, a young woman hired to tutor the children of an affluent Virginia landowner, reported that her employer had bought up all the molasses, coffee, sugar, and whiskey in the neighborhood for his personal use. He continued to stack hogsheads of the stuff on the grounds of his estate until "the lawn and paths looked like a wharf covered with a ship's load." In Dallas County, Alabama, a well-to-do cotton grower did the same thing, squirreling away wholesale quantities of flour, tea, wine, spices, calico, and other hard-to-find articles. In North Carolina and Louisiana, planters made sure their womenfolk would have needles, thread, buttons, and dress materials by purchasing country stores lock, stock, and barrel and moving the contents into their homes.

Also antagonizing the poor people was the way the wealthy and well-connected avoided military service under the terms of the 1862 Conscription Act. The hiring of substitutes (cost: $1,600 and up) was permitted, and exemptions were granted to men who paid bribes or pulled strings to get government jobs or some other type of employment deemed essential by the Bureau of Conscription. Medical waivers obtained from unscrupulous doctors were also used to dodge the draft, as were fake discharge papers drawn up by enterprising forgers and sold for prices ranging from $400 to $1,000. "All shame has fled," Senator James Phelan informed Jefferson Davis after a visit to Mississippi. "It seems as if nine-tenths of the youngsters of the land whose relatives are conspicuous in society, wealthy, or influential obtain some safe perch where they can doze with their heads under their wings."

Most divisive of all was the clause in the Conscription Act that excused from service one able-bodied white man, either master or overseer, from any plantation with twenty or more slaves. The announced purpose of this provision, derisively dubbed the "twenty-nigger law," was to keep the South's black population under control. But to nonslaveholders it looked suspiciously like a loophole designed to let planters avoid army service. "Never did a law meet with more universal odium," Phelan warned Davis. "Its influence upon the poor is calamitous."

Further fueling public outrage was the cotton aristocracy's unwillingness to use its land and slaves to augment the South's food supply. Even when laws were passed limiting cotton production in favor of corn, wheat, potatoes, and beans, many planters flatly refused to change their ways. One such intransigent was Confederate congressman Robert Toombs. He demonstrated his contempt for Georgia's food-crop statute by increasing, not decreasing, the cotton acreage on his Randolph County plantation. Another maverick was Mississippi's James Alcorn. He not only continued to raise long staple at Mound Place, his Yazoo Delta estate, but sold it to Yankee agents as well. "I wish to fill my pocket," he told his wife when she pleaded with him to stop trading with the enemy. "I can in five years make a larger fortune than ever; I know how to do it, and will do it."

Such selfishness did not go unnoticed by ordinary citizens. Denunciations of the rich and demands that the government do something to help the poor poured into Richmond during the spring of 1863. The Confederate Congress was profoundly ambivalent about passing substantive legislation, fearing that any action on its part would be construed as an attempt to establish a centralized despotism. But it was obvious that steps had to be taken before a rising tide of discontent completely undermined the war effort. And so with much anguished hand-wringing and high-flown rhetoric, the senators and representatives moved to address the problems of the Southern working class.

The first issue they tackled was impressment, the bitterly resented practice of seizing private property for army use. From the beginning of the war, Confederate commissary officers had scoured the countryside in search of food, fodder, wagons, and anything else that might be of use to the military. Sometimes they paid for these items with government promissory notes. More often they took what they wanted and made no effort to compensate the farmers whose homesteads they ransacked. "We often hear persons say, 'The Yankees can not do us any more harm than our own soldiers have done,' " reported the Richmond *Enquirer.*

Congress knew that there was no alternative to impressment. It was the only way the military could feed itself. The process could be made more palatable, however, so on March 26, 1863, the Act to Regulate Impressments was passed. The bill created state boards of impressment commissioners and assigned them the task of preparing price schedules for articles desired by the army. Property that an owner needed to sustain himself and his family or to keep his business running was off limits. Disputes over which items were essential and which were not were to be settled by local arbitration.

It was a bad system. The state boards consistently set prices below market value, and commissary officers paid in depreciated currency, resulting in financial ruin for farmers whose property was requisitioned. Nor did it put an end to the worst abuses. Unruly soldiers continued to trample crops, steal livestock, wreck fences, and demolish outbuildings. But at least the Act to Regulate Impressments represented an honest attempt to grapple with an extraordinarily thorny problem, and it was generally appreciated as such.

Much less popular was a second critical piece of legislation, enacted on April 24, 1863. During the first two years of its existence, the Confederate government had relied on the printing press to finance military and civil operations, cranking out hundreds of millions of dollars unbacked by silver or gold. This flood of fiat money, combined with shortages of food and consumer goods, had produced inflation so severe that by the beginning of 1863 it took seven dollars to buy what one dollar had bought two years earlier. Now, in an effort to put the government's fiscal house in order and do something about the fast-eroding value of Confederate currency, Congress imposed an assortment of taxes. These included a 10 percent levy on profits from the sale of foodstuffs, clothing, and household goods; a graduated income tax starting at 1 percent on annual incomes less than $500 and rising to 15 percent on incomes over $10,000; and a 10 percent "tax in kind" on all agricultural products.

It was a bold bill, given the legislators' antipathy toward expanding government power, but it contained a fatal flaw: land and slaves, the real repository of wealth in the South, went virtually untouched. This concession to the politically powerful planter class cost the Treasury large amounts of revenue and outraged nonslaveholders. Why, yeoman farmers asked, should they be required to tithe the contents of their barns, smokehouses, and chicken coops when planters with money to spare paid nothing at all on their acreage and bondsmen?

Congress's clumsy handling of the despised "twenty-nigger law" further agitated the common people. Instead of repealing the provision, the legislators merely tinkered with it. The law's language was changed so that only plantations owned by a minor, a person of unsound mind, a *femme sole,* or a member of the armed forces away at the front were eligible for the exemption. A five-hundred-dollar fee for every person who avoided service in this way was also instituted. Supporters of the modification insisted that outright abrogation was impossible because unsupervised slaves posed too great a threat to white women and children. But their arguments failed to placate the ordinary folk, who felt that the planters had once again received special treatment. "For God's sake," fumed a Georgia private, "don't tell the poor soldier who now shivers in a northern wind while you snooze in a feather bed that it is just and right that the men whom Congress has exempted should enjoy ease at home, amassing untold riches, while he must fight and bleed and even die for their Negroes."

Resentment finally turned to anger in the spring of 1863. On March 18 a mob of hatchet-wielding women broke into grocers' shops in Salisbury, North Carolina, and stole flour, bacon, salt, and molasses after the proprietors refused to sell to them at heavily discounted "government prices." A similar incident occurred a few days later in High Point. At Greensboro anxious authorities arrested a group of soldiers' wives who they said were getting ready to storm the city's food markets.

But it was in Richmond during Easter week that the largest disturbance occurred, a paroxysm of looting and vandalism that shook the Confederate government and scandalized Southern society. Called the Bread Riot, the rampage had a highly unlikely figure as its instigator—a frustrated housewife named Mary Jackson.

Like many other war-dispossessed women, Mary Jackson was struggling to make ends meet by selling produce at an open-air stall in Richmond's Second Market. But bad spring weather, including a freak nine-inch snowfall on the night of March 19, and impressment of provisions by commissary officers from the Army of Northern Virginia, cut the flow of food into the capital to a trickle, putting small vendors like Jackson out of business and threatening Richmond with starvation.

By the last week of March, hunger had become so acute that the city was on the brink of an explosion. Fearing the worst, the Virginia General Assembly authorized Richmond's city council to arm its police and take whatever measures were necessary to suppress riots and unlawful assemblies. Everyone was aware that a crisis was at hand—everyone, that is, except Jefferson Davis. With timing that was atrocious even by his politically tone-deaf standards, he designated Friday, March 27 as a day of fasting and prayer. This action provoked incredulity and outrage among Richmonders. "Fasting in the midst of famine!" John B. Jones angrily wrote. "May God save this people!"

The same day that Davis called on the capital's residents to forgo food, a detailed account of the Salisbury riot appeared in the Richmond *Daily Examiner.* The account was sympathetic to the North Carolina mob and hostile to the speculators whose shops they had plundered. Whether it was this story or something else that emboldened Mary Jackson will never be known. But one thing is certain: on the afternoon of April 1 she organized a protest rally at the Belvidere Hill Baptist Church in southwestern Richmond.

At this meeting, which was attended by approximately 300 women, Jackson suggested that the city's female workers follow the lead of their Tar Heel State sisters by marching downtown and demanding food at cut-rate prices. She urged her listeners to bring along "persuaders" such as knives, hatchets, and guns, and she said that if the shopkeepers refused to sell, their goods should be taken by force.

Early the next morning—April 2, Holy Thursday—the Belvidere Hill protesters rendezvoused at the Second Market on Sixth Street between Marshall and Broad. Waving pistols and yelling "Bread or blood," they set out for Capitol Square, where they planned to present their grievances to Governor John Letcher before moving on to the business district, site of the main demonstration.

By the time the mob reached the governor's mansion, it had swelled to more than 500. Mary Jackson, the march's putative leader, had been replaced by an older, more presentable woman named Mary Johnson. It was Mary Johnson who went inside to meet with Letcher and his aides. Whatever she said was not well received, for at 9 A.M. the governor emerged from his office to warn the protesters that they would be dispersed at bayonet point if they caused any trouble.

A chorus of angry shouts greeted this threat, and in a twinkling the crowd was streaming out of Capitol Square and pouring south down

Ninth Street, heading for the provision shops on Cary Street. Hearing the commotion, John B. Jones rushed out of the War Department building at the intersection of Ninth and Bank to find out what was going on. He was told by an emaciated young woman that the demonstrators were determined to get food for themselves and their children.

As the boisterous throng approached the eight-block area where the bulk of Richmond's stores were located, another ringleader stepped forward. Minerva Meredith was a strapping butcher's assistant, "a tall, daring, Amazonian-looking woman, who had a white feather standing erect in her hat." She was carrying a navy revolver in one hand and a bowie knife in the other. Brandishing these weapons, she led the mob straight for Pollard and Walker's grocery.

The owners hurriedly bolted the front door, but to no avail; several blows from an ax shattered it. Rioters surged in and began grabbing items from the shelves. Moments later Tyler & Son, a food-and-dry goods shop, and Hicks's shoe-and-hat emporium were broken into and emptied of their contents.

When the Cary Street businesses were stripped clean, the mob headed toward Main and Franklin, its approach heralded by the crack of pistol shots and the crash of breaking glass. Hospital superintendent Henry Myers was driving a wagonload of beef down one of the boulevards when he ran head-on into a swarm of rioters. A revolver was shoved into his face, and in a twinkling 310 pounds of meat disappeared. "Bread! bread! bread!" the looters chanted, but it was clear that they wanted more than just food. Clothing, jewelry, kitchen utensils, fabric, hardware—anything portable was fair game.

Around 11 A.M. Governor Letcher and Mayor Joseph Mayo arrived on the scene, accompanied by a militia company made up of laborers from the Confederate armory and the Tredegar iron works. Letcher announced that the men would open fire if the pillaging did not stop at once. His ultimatum drew hoots of derision from the rioters. They were confident that the militia would not shoot into a crowd made up of their own wives, sisters, and daughters. The rampage was about to resume when a tall, hollow-cheeked man dressed in a well-tailored gray suit and black riding boots elbowed his way through the crowd, climbed onto the back of a dray, and began to speak. At first his words could not be heard over the booing and hissing that greeted his appearance. Then the throng hushed, and the unmistakable Mississippi intonations, mellifluous yet tinged with anger, carried up and down the length of Main Street.

"You say you are hungry and have no money," Jefferson Davis cried, his face flushed, his arms waving. "Here is all I have. It is not much but take it." He fished some coins from his pocket and flung them in the direction of the crowd. Next he pulled out his gold watch, but instead of tossing it to the rioters, he opened it, squinted at the hands, and steeled his voice: "We do not desire to injure anyone," he announced, "but this lawlessness must stop. I will give you five minutes to disperse, otherwise you will be fired on."

There was something about the jut of Davis's jaw and the fierce scowl on his face that made it clear he was not bluffing. Slowly at first, but with increasing rapidity as the deadline approached, the rioters scattered. By the time five minutes had elapsed, the street was deserted save for the distraught shop owners and the members of the Public Guard, who laughed and slapped each other on the back like condemned men who had been granted a last-second reprieve.

Davis appeared unruffled. He snapped his watchcase shut, climbed down from the dray, and strode up Tenth Street to the old U.S. Customs House, where his office was located. But despite his outward calm, he was quaking inside. He had staked the prestige of his presidency, and by extension the authority of the Confederate government, on halting the riot, and it had been a near-run thing. He was worried, too, about what officials in Washington would think when they learned there had been mob violence in Richmond. When he got back to his desk, he summoned Secretary of War James Seddon and instructed him to permit nothing about the incident to be sent over the telegraph wires. He also directed him to contact the newspapers and ask them to keep quiet about the affair.

Davis's attempt at press censorship failed. The next morning the Richmond *Whig* published a front-page editorial on the disturbance, and the following day the *Examiner* provided its readers with a detailed account of the riot, identifying its instigators as "a handful of prostitutes, professional thieves, [and] Irish and Yankee hags."

In the weeks that followed, seventeen women, including Mary Jackson, Mary Johnson, and Minerva Meredith, were arrested, tried, and sentenced to jail terms of up to three years. The harshness of the punishment reflected the official view that the Bread Riot had been wholly unjustified. But unofficially, municipal authorities recognized that people were indeed going hungry, and not long after the April 2 convulsion, free-food depots were established to help the destitute. Richmond merchants also got the message: hoarding ceased and prices fell, at least temporarily.

The Bread Riot served as a warning to the Davis administration. It showed that the Confederacy could be toppled from within as well as from without. The Southern people were approaching the limits of their endurance. What was needed, the president realized, was another confidence-boosting military success to revive civilian morale. On April 8, six days after the Bread Riot, news of such a success came, not from Mississippi, Tennessee, or Virginia, as might have been expected, but from an area that had long been considered a backwater of the war: the South Carolina coast.

Charleston, South Carolina—the "cradle of secession," one of the Confederacy's oldest and proudest cities—had her hero back. Dull, dour John C. Pemberton, cordially despised by the local gentry, had been replaced as commander of the Charleston defenses by Pierre Gustave Toutant Beauregard, the man who had driven the Yankees from Fort Sumter in April 1861.

It did not matter to Charlestonians that Beauregard arrived under a cloud, having badly mishandled Confederate forces in the fighting at Shiloh and at Corinth, Mississippi. Nor did it concern them that his flamboyant personal style, coupled with his inability to keep his mouth shut, had caused him to fall from favor with the Davis administration. The dashing, dark-complected Creole with his smoldering eyes and handsome silver-gray goatee fit their conception of a fighting general. They rejoiced at his return, feting him at picnics, parties, and dances, cheering him as he promenaded along the Battery, and applauding the fiery proclamation he issued shortly after assuming his duties: "Carolinians and Georgians! The hour is at hand to prove your devotion to your country's cause. Let all able-bodied men, from the seaboard to the mountains, rush to arms. Be not exacting in the choice of weapons; pikes and scythes will do for exterminating your enemies. . . . To arms, fellow citizens! Come to share with us our dangers, our brilliant success, or our glorious death."

Despite this bravura pronouncement, Beauregard was unhappy with his new assignment. He considered it a demotion, and he held Jefferson Davis personally responsible. "If the country be satisfied to have me laid on the shelf by a man who is either demented or a traitor to his high trust—well, let it be so," he told a friend.

His wrath subsided somewhat when he discovered that South Carolina was not as peaceful as he had supposed. Intelligence reports indicated that the Union navy, emboldened by the acquisition of nine new ironclad warships, was getting ready to strike at Charleston. Galvanized by the prospect of a career-reviving victory, Beauregard stopped sulking and started

General Pierre G. T. Beauregard, C.S.A. (Library of Congress; photo courtesy of The Museum of the Confederacy)

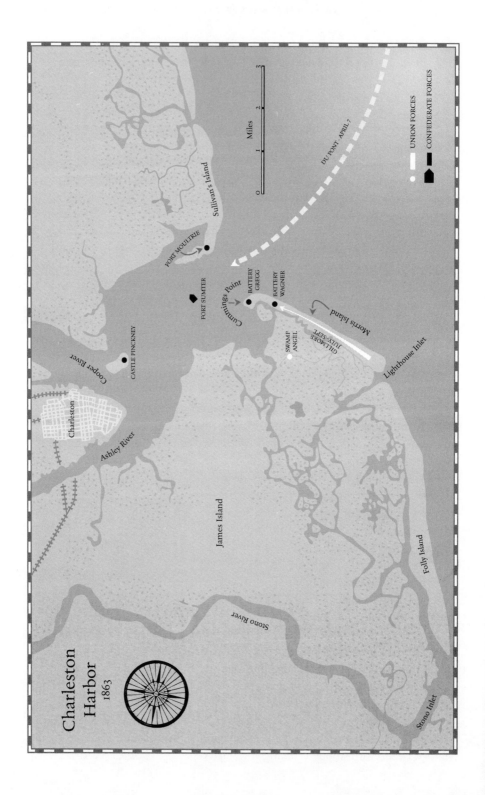

Charleston
Harbor
1863

Charleston

Ashley River

Cooper River

CASTLE PINCKNEY

FORT MOULTRIE

Sullivan's Island

FORT SUMTER

Cummings Point

BATTERY GREGG

BATTERY WAGNER

SWAMP ANGEL

GILLMORE
JULY–SEPT.

Morris Island

Lighthouse Inlet

James Island

Stono River

Folly Island

Stono Inlet

DU PONT, APRIL 7

Miles
0   1   2   3

UNION FORCES

CONFEDERATE FORCES

getting the city's defenses ready for the coming contest. At his direction the forts and batteries ringing Charleston harbor were strengthened, the main ship channel was sown with mines and other submerged obstacles, and marker buoys were anchored at various points so that Confederate artillerymen could register their guns.

The officer who would lead the Union attack on Charleston was Rear Admiral Samuel F. Du Pont, commander of the U.S. Navy's South Atlantic Blockading Squadron, headquartered at Port Royal Sound. Scion of one of America's wealthiest families (his father was a successful New York importer and his uncle was the founder of the Delaware munitions dynasty), Du Pont had joined the navy when he was only twelve years old. Now approaching sixty, he was the very picture of a seagoing admiral, broad-cheeked and ruddy, with steely blue eyes and a beard like a bull walrus.

Du Pont had planned and led the amphibious expedition that drove the rebels from Port Royal and the neighboring islands of Hilton Head and St. Helena in November 1861. He had followed that triumph four months later by capturing the port of Fernandina on Florida's Atlantic coast. Now the navy was looking to him to win more glory and make up for the recent fiascos at Galveston, Sabine Pass, and Mobile Bay, by bringing Charleston to heel.

The admiral was eager to oblige. A joint army-navy operation similar to the one that had worked so well at Port Royal was what he had in mind. He envisioned a large body of infantry, supported by the ships of his squadron, landing on one of the islands south of Charleston, marching northward to the mainland, then swinging around to attack the city from the rear. But navy secretary Gideon Welles had other ideas. Intent on impressing Congress and increasing his department's budget, he wanted the South Atlantic Squadron to capture Charleston without help from the army. Furthermore, he wanted the campaign to showcase the service's newest type of warship—the saltwater ironclad.

It had been less than a year since *Monitor*, inventor John Ericsson's revolutionary cheesebox-on-a-raft, had fought its epic duel with *Merrimack* in the waters of Hampton Roads. In that time the navy's civilian leadership had enthusiastically embraced the ironclad concept, building an entire fleet of the futuristic vessels and hatching all manner of grandiose schemes for their use. The "improved monitors," as the strange-looking craft were called, were not ships so much as they were floating batteries—self-propelled gun platforms encased in heavy armor and equipped with a pair of large-caliber naval cannon mounted in a revolving turret. Their backers boasted that they were invincible, capable of forcing their way into Southern harbors, flattening the defenses, and debouching unharmed. Secretary Welles agreed with them. He informed Du Pont that the subjugation of

Charleston was to be the first demonstration of the improved monitors' awesome power.

The admiral was skeptical. At Port Royal, New Orleans, Fort Henry, and Island No. 10, the navy had learned that nimbleness and overwhelming firepower were the keys to defeating land fortifications. These were precisely the attributes the monitors lacked. The guns they carried—an eleven-inch Dahlgren and a fifteen-inch Rodman—were bigger than anything Beauregard had in his arsenal, but it took almost eight minutes to load, aim, and fire them, meaning that they could get off only seven rounds per hour, not nearly enough to destroy forts as stoutly constructed as those in Charleston harbor. To make matters worse, the vessels were slow, unwieldy, and prone to mechanical breakdowns.

Du Pont tested the monitors by sending them to bombard Fort McAllister, a small eight-gun earthwork guarding the mouth of the Great Ogeechee River near Savannah. The results were disappointing. Despite blazing away at point-blank range, the ironclads failed to smash the Confederate position. They did demonstrate their defensive prowess, taking several direct hits from the rebel cannon with no ill effect, but as offensive weapons they were a total bust. Du Pont reported the monitors' shortcomings to his superiors in Washington and voiced his opinion that army troops were essential to the success of coastal operations.

Welles was incensed when he read this. In a blunt message delivered in mid-March, he told Du Pont to quit stalling and reiterated that the reduction of Charleston was to be an all-navy affair. The admiral did not like being bullied by a landsman who had never heard a shot fired in anger. He was convinced that an assault of the type Welles was calling for would fail. But he had to follow orders. On the afternoon of April 7 he directed the monitors *Weehawken, Passaic, Montauk, Patapsco, Catskill, Nantucket,* and *Nahant,* the experimental ironclad *Keokuk,* and the 3,500-ton armored steam frigate *New Ironsides* to sail up the Charleston ship channel and attack Fort Sumter and Fort Moultrie, the Confederate works guarding the inner harbor.

The advance of the Union flotilla was chaotic. The lead ship, *Weehawken,* was pushing a cumbersome minesweeping raft, and her wild lurching and yawing threw the entire column into disarray. Du Pont's flagship, the deep-draft *New Ironsides,* lost headway and began drifting out of control in the strong tidal current. Twice she had to drop anchor to avoid running aground. The second time she staggered to a halt, the monitors *Catskill* and *Nantucket* plowed into her side. Disgusted with the frigate's lack of maneuverability, the admiral signaled for the other vessels to move ahead on their own. *New Ironsides* was out of the fight—as useless, her surgeon later wrote, as if she had been tied up at a wharf in the Philadelphia Naval Yard.

At 3 P.M., almost two hours after starting forward, the monitors finally churned into range of Fort Sumter and Fort Moultrie. The rebel gun crews, who had been enjoying a leisurely lunch while waiting for the Yankee craft to make their way up the narrow ship channel, hoisted the Confederate and Palmetto flags and opened fire. Spouts of gray-green water erupted all around the ironclads, and then great, metallic clangs, "like a sledgehammer upon an anvil," reverberated across the harbor as rebel projectiles struck home.

The Union gunboats returned fire, but with little effect. The only damage a newspaperman could see as he scanned Fort Sumter through a spyglass was pockmarks on the walls, "as if there had been a sudden breaking out of cutaneous disease." Meanwhile Confederate shells continued to rain down on the slow-moving monitors, mangling their smokestacks, buckling their deck plating, and disabling their gun turrets. All told, the rebel batteries fired 2,206 shots and scored 316 hits; the Federal warships got off only 139 shots and struck the forts just 55 times.

At 5 P.M. Du Pont signaled for his battered flotilla to withdraw. Five of the nine ironclads were seriously damaged. The worst was *Keokuk*, which had been struck ninety times and was "riddled like a colander." She managed to limp out of the harbor and anchor in shallow water off Morris Island. Try as they might, her crewmembers could not plug the gaping holes at her waterline. She sank early the next morning, proving once and for all that monitors were not invulnerable as their advocates had claimed.

It had been Du Pont's intention to renew the attack after a brief respite, but the loss of *Keokuk* and the crippling of the other ships convinced him that it was pointless. He retired to his cabin to write a report that he knew would upset his superiors in Washington. "Charleston cannot be taken by a purely naval attack," he bluntly stated. "These monitors have admirable qualities, but they are dead failures with forts."

Not surprisingly, Secretary Welles refused to accept this conclusion. Having spent more than $5 million on the first batch of monitors and placed orders for eighteen more, he was not about to admit that he had made a mistake. As far as he was concerned, the man, not the machinery, was at fault. Even worse, Du Pont's criticism of the monitors played into the hands of the administration's congressional critics. For that transgression as much as for his supposed lack of aggressiveness, Welles relieved him of command.

If Du Pont was the scapegoat, railroaded into retirement because he refused to sacrifice the lives of his sailors on the altar of political expediency, Beauregard was the man of the hour, the hero who had once again made Sumter "a household word, like Salamis and Thermopylae." Aware that his braggadocio had gotten him into trouble in the past, he resolved to keep his after-action report low-key. But as plaudits poured in from all over the

Confederacy and the unabashed adulation of Charlestonians washed over him like warm Carolina sunshine, he forgot about self-restraint and gloated openly over his triumph. "My expectations were fully realized," he wrote in his dispatch to the War Department. "The country, as well as the State of South Carolina, may well be proud of the men who first met and vanquished the iron-mailed, terribly armed armada, so confidently prepared and sent forth by the enemy."

On April 2, the same day that Du Pont's flotilla sailed from Port Royal Sound for Charleston, and Mary Jackson and her followers rampaged through the streets of downtown Richmond, a trim, nattily dressed Englishman crossed the Rio Grande between Matamoros, Mexico, and Brownsville, Texas, and began a three-month, three-thousand-mile journey through the South. Arthur James Lyon Fremantle, a lieutenant colonel in Her Majesty's Coldstream Guards, was looking for adventure while on leave from his famous regiment. He had chosen to travel to America because it was the only place in the world where a major war was being fought. Packed in his portmanteau was a leather-bound diary in which he intended to record his impressions of the places he went, the sights he saw, and the people he met. He knew that his countrymen were intensely curious about the clash between the North and South, and he planned to publish an account of his tour when he got home.

Arthur J. L. Fremantle.
(Courtesy The Museum of the
Confederacy, Richmond, Virginia)

Like most Europeans, Fremantle had a poor grasp of Confederate geography. He was familiar with Virginia and Tennessee from the dispatches of London *Times* war correspondent William Howard Russell, and he knew where Richmond, Charleston, and New Orleans were. But of the vast expanse of territory lying west of the Mississippi River, he was woefully ignorant. The state of Texas—five times the size of England, with barely one-thirtieth of its population—came as a complete surprise to him. He could only marvel at its enormity and breathtaking emptiness as he rolled out of Brownsville in a mule-drawn wagon, sweating, swatting at flies, and trying to strike up a conversation with the driver, whose speech consisted of muttered profanity punctuated by whip cracks and the continual repetition of the sentence, " 'Get up, now, you great long-eared God-damned son of a bitch.' "

The war was not much in evidence in this part of Texas, but what little Fremantle saw of it was sickeningly barbaric. A few days after setting out he encountered a band of Confederate cavalrymen returning from a raid on a Unionist stronghold in the central part of the state. They were heavily armed with pistols and shotguns, and despite the shabbiness of their uniforms, he thought they "all looked thoroughly like business." The nature of that business became apparent a short while later. The wagon rolled past the remains of a Union sympathizer who had been lynched and dumped by the side of the road. "He had been slightly buried, but his head and arms were above the ground, his arms tied together, the rope still around his neck," Fremantle wrote. "Dogs or wolves had probably scraped the earth from the body, and there was no flesh on the bones."

Many travelers would have turned back at this point, but not the intrepid Englishman. Texas was a wilderness, he rationalized, a place where "the shooting-down and stringing-up systems are much in vogue," so it was not surprising that he should see a moldering corpse lying by the roadside. Besides, he genuinely liked the Texans, although some of their social customs were abhorrent to him. He loathed shaking hands, was disgusted by the prevalence of tobacco chewing, and found the practice of double-selling hotel beds so repulsive that he learned to sleep fully clothed, insisting that his traveling suit, no matter how badly soiled, was "a damned sight cleaner" than the bed or the person he was being asked to share it with.

Fremantle traveled north to San Antonio, east to Houston and Galveston, then north again to Navasota, Texas, where he boarded a stage bound for Shreveport, Louisiana. Riding in the stuffy, overcrowded coach proved to be an ordeal, especially when "we received an unwelcome addition to our party in the shape of three huge, long-legged, unwashed, odoriferous Texan soldiers." Meals, which consisted of rancid bacon, moldy bread, and a muddy mixture called "Confederate coffee," were also a trial.

From Shreveport, Fremantle had planned to travel to Alexandria via the Red River. But on the advice of General Edmund Kirby Smith, commander of the Trans-Mississippi Department, he decided to head for Monroe, Louisiana, instead, thereby avoiding the Union-occupied part of the state. As his coach rolled east, drawing closer to the Mississippi war zone, evidence of military activity increased. A Confederate division was encamped on the outskirts of Monroe, and the road into town was jammed with slaves being marched off to Texas.

The spectacle of blacks being herded like cattle prompted Fremantle's fellow passengers—a Louisiana state legislator, a Mississippi cotton planter, a slave buyer from Matagorda, Texas, and a Confederate captain from Missouri—to expatiate on the merits of the South's peculiar institution. "They are most anxious that I should be convinced that it is not so bad as has been represented," he recorded in his diary.

At Monroe he forsook the stagecoach and booked passage on a steamer that was going down the Ouachita River to Harrisonburg, Louisiana. From Harrisonburg he headed due east until he reached Vidalia on the west bank of the Mississippi.

Early the next morning he rowed across the big river to Natchez, a Southern city unlike any he had seen so far. Nestled on a tree-shaded bluff overlooking the Mississippi, it positively reeked of money. Palatial residences cram-full of imported furniture, fabrics, and art rose like tiered wedding cakes from lawns exquisitely landscaped with rose bushes, azaleas, and moss-draped live oaks. Sporting names like D'Evereux, Dunleith, and Magnolia Hall, these mansions testified to the stupendous wealth generated by cotton and slaves in the 1850s, an era when more than half the millionaires in the United States had lived in Natchez. Although it had fallen on hard times recently, it still retained much of its former splendor, as Fremantle discovered when he visited Longwood, the estate of Dr. Haller Nutt, one of the area's richest planters. Set deep in a forest of oak and elm trees a few miles south of town, Longwood was a four-story octagon built of brick, marble, and plaster. Containing thirty-two rooms, it was crowned by a sixteen-sided cupola topped with an onion-shaped silver dome. Fremantle believed implicitly in the superiority of all things British, but the Byzantine grandeur of this structure took his breath away. When he wrote that the "place reminded me very much of an English gentleman's country seat," he was paying it the highest compliment he could. He declined Dr. Nutt's invitation to stay as a houseguest, however, because he still had a great deal of territory to cover before his three-month leave expired.

He had reason to regret that decision a few days later, when he was arrested in Jackson on suspicion of being a Yankee spy. Hauled into the bar of a downtown hotel, he was interrogated by a group of boozy citizens, who made it clear that they would like nothing better than to hang him from the nearest lamppost. "They examined my clothes and argued as to whether they were of English manufacture," he wrote. "Some who had been to London asked me questions about the streets of the metropolis, and about my regiment. . . . I looked in vain for someone to take my part, [but] I could not even get any person to examine my papers." Finally a Confederate captain showed up, pronounced his passport genuine, and ordered him released.

Thankful to get out of Jackson alive, Fremantle next went to Canton, Mississippi, where several Confederate divisions were bivouacked. This was his first chance to inspect rebel troops in the field, and he wrote approvingly of their appearance. The officers struck him as men of talent and education, but he was critical of their refusal to crack down on straggling by the enlisted men.

After a three-day stay in Canton, he caught a train for Mobile. The two-hundred-mile journey lasted a day and a half and was interrupted by a derailment east of Jackson and a brawl at Meridian. During the latter incident the engineer shot one of the passengers, then uncoupled the locomotive, cut the telegraph wire, and bolted up the line, only to collide with another train coming in the opposite direction. "The news of this event caused really hardly any excitement amongst my fellow travelers," Fremantle marveled. "I heard one man remark that 'it was mighty mean for [the engineer] to leave . . . like that,'" but otherwise there was no complaining. He attributed this stoicism to the fact that everyone was packing a pistol, and "people are naturally careful what they say when a bullet may be the probable reply."

Mobile, which had been described to him as a cosmopolitan community attractively situated on the Gulf of Mexico, proved to be a great disappointment: "It is a regular rectangular American city," he reported, "built on a sandy flat and covering a deal of ground for its population, which is about 25,000." He became even more disillusioned when his boots were stolen while he slept at his hotel. "In consequence of [their] fabulous value . . . they must not be left outside the door of one's room," he wrote. Continuing on the next day, he passed through Montgomery, Alabama ("all state capitals appear to resemble one another, and look like bits cut off from great cities"), and Atlanta, Georgia ("war-worn, poverty-stricken, dried-up"), then changed cars for Chattanooga. From Chattanooga he headed northwest to Tullahoma, where the Army of Tennessee was headquartered. Here he hoped to see something of the "real war" as opposed to the rag-tag guerrilla operations he had witnessed in Texas.

He was destined to be frustrated, however, for although spring had arrived in the Volunteer State, the Confederate troops were still in their winter encampments, and the only fighting going on was between Braxton Bragg and his disgruntled subordinates.

Fremantle had been impressed by the intelligence and urbanity of the high-ranking Confederates he had met during the first two months of his tour. They were fine soldiers and all-round good chaps, he declared, first-class men capable of leading the South to victory. Bragg was another story, how-

ever. Not only did he fail to earn Fremantle's respect, he managed to arouse
his dislike—no mean feat, given the Englishman's unflagging amiability. "This
officer in appearance is the least prepossessing of the Confederate generals,"
he wrote after his visit to Tullahoma. "I understand he is rather unpopular on
this account, and also by reason of his occasional acerbity of manner."

That was putting it mildly. Bragg was not just unpopular, he was hated.
Back in January, Jefferson Davis had dispatched Joseph Johnston to Tullahoma to assess the situation there and tell him whether a change was called
for. Johnston discovered that Bragg's corps and division commanders were
profoundly dissatisfied with his leadership, but he declined to recommend
Bragg's ouster. He knew that if he did so, he was likely to be given command
of the Army of Tennessee himself, and while he coveted the post, he was unwilling to take it if it meant stabbing a brother officer in the back. So instead
of urging the president to replace Bragg, advice that was warranted in view
of the incipient mutiny at Tullahoma, he pressed for his retention.

Johnston's refusal to call for Bragg's dismissal caused consternation in
Richmond, where it was well known that he wanted to lead an army in the
field. The Virginian's chief congressional supporter, Senator Louis T. Wig-
fall, believed he understood the problem. "If the appointment to that command . . . without your seeking it would be agreeable to you, let me know
by telegraph and it shall be made," he wrote. "Telegraph me simply—'You
are right' or 'You understand me' or some equivalent expression and I will
understand you and act accordingly." Secretary Seddon tried a slightly different tack, suggesting to Johnston that he take charge of the Army of Tennessee by dint of his authority as theater commander, then keep Bragg on
as an organizer and administrator while he directed combat operations.
Davis also attempted to persuade Johnston, assuring him that no breach of
military etiquette would be involved in his succeeding to the command of
the Army of Tennessee.

It did no good; Johnston was adamant. Davis finally lost his temper. On
March 9 he sent Johnston a curt telegram: "Order General Bragg to report
to the War Department here for conference. Assume yourself direct charge
of the army in Middle Tennessee."

Bitter about being forced to do something he believed was wrong,
Johnston decided to thwart the president. On March 19 he learned that
Mrs. Bragg was critically ill with typhoid fever. He promptly notified the
War Department that he could not compel the general to leave his wife
when she might die at any moment. Three weeks later, when Elise Bragg
had recovered, Johnston informed the president that he had now fallen ill.
Inasmuch as he was bedridden, he deemed Bragg's continued presence at
headquarters essential.

By now it was late April, and Davis had his own health problems to deal with, namely neuralgia, an abscessed tooth, and a lingering case of the flu. He was too tired and too distracted to engage in a contest of wills with Johnston. He thought about appointing a different general to take Bragg's place, but Lee, Longstreet, and Jackson could not be spared from the Army of Northern Virginia, Pemberton was busy defending Vicksburg, and Beauregard was still needed in Charleston.

So Bragg stayed at his post, bickering with his subordinates, even as military matters languished and Rosecrans continued his threatening troop-and-supply buildup around Murfreesboro.

While their leaders quarreled, the rank-and-file of the Army of Tennessee enjoyed the longest respite from combat afforded any Confederate army in any theater of operations at any stage of the war. From the middle of January until the end of June, they remained idle in camp in the Duck River Valley. Polk's corps was bivouacked at Shelbyville and Hardee's at Wartrace, where they could defend the Nashville & Chattanooga Railroad, the Union army's likely axis of advance. They were also located where they could take maximum advantage of the well-stocked barns and smokehouses that dotted this part of south-central Tennessee. A flood of chickens, turkeys, geese, hams, and other delicacies poured into the camps, and the soldiers wasted no time in transforming their canvas tents into more substantial quarters by boarding up the sides, fashioning fireplaces out of rocks and mud, and covering the floors with leaves or straw.

Despite the abundance of good food and the construction of semipermanent housing, the first few months at Shelbyville and Wartrace were decidedly unpleasant. It was thought that the Yankees might make a sudden lunge toward Chattanooga, a threat that necessitated the building of log-and-earth breastworks. When that tiresome task was completed, a long spell of cold, wet weather made life miserable for the troops. A diarist billeted at Shelbyville described a typical week as follows:

February 15: Rained.

February 17: Still raining, which keeps us in our tents.

February 18: The same routine. No drill, no mails, idleness.

February 20: Confined to tent all day by rain and bad weather.

February 21: Raining. Still confined to tent.

The storms continued through February and most of March, turning the campsites into quagmires and keeping the men cooped up in their dingy quarters. "I don't make any more of sitting down in a crowd and pulling off my shirt and picking the lice off me than I would to sit down at a good meal at home. I have caught as many as 40 to 50 at one time," Private Sam Settles confessed in a letter to his mother. Almost everyone was afflicted with diarrhea—"my bowels has been running very bad," groaned a lieutenant in the Twenty-ninth Georgia, repeating a refrain heard hundreds of times a day—and between dashes to the latrine, there was nothing to do but sit around, whittling pipes out of corncobs, playing endless games of cards, and complaining about the mind-numbing tedium.

The rain and sleet finally tapered off at the beginning of April. The men emerged from their waterlogged huts, thrilled to be outside again after nearly ten weeks of confinement. To get them into shape and restore discipline and unit morale, the officers drilled them relentlessly, but there was still time for other, more pleasurable pursuits. "I know a good many girls here and go to see them frequently," Captain Robert Kennedy informed his sister in a cheerful letter written that spring. "Most of them are rather of the cornbread order, but there is one occasionally that possesses some attractions. We are going to have a picnic Thursday just below our camp. I am on the committee of arrangements and will go out this evening to engage the baking of some cakes."

Other soldiers found that cash worked just as well as cakes, given the plethora of prostitutes around the Shelbyville and Wartrace bivouacs. Corn whiskey was also readily available (this was Tennessee after all), and wagering on cards, dice, cockfights, footraces, and wrestling matches was immensely popular, despite efforts by army chaplains to stamp it out.

The only Confederate forces to see any significant action during this six-month holiday were the cavalry divisions of John Hunt Morgan, Joseph Wheeler, Nathan Bedford Forrest, and Earl Van Dorn. Morgan's men were posted in the vicinity of McMinnville, Wheeler's occupied an area near Liberty Gap, and Forrest's (joined in late February by a large contingent commanded by Van Dorn) were stationed at Columbia and Spring Hill. Their primary job was to keep an eye on the Union army at Murfreesboro and alert Bragg to any unusual movements that might presage an attack. They were also responsible for fending off Yankee forays into the provision-rich areas of southern Tennessee and northern Alabama and conducting raids of their own aimed at creating chaos in the enemy's rear. Not surprisingly, it was the second part of the mission that appealed most strongly to the offensive-minded cavalrymen. Picket duty, despite its critical importance to the security of the army, was too passive for their taste. Consequently they spent the bulk of their time either skirmishing with Federal patrols that probed southward from Murfreesboro, or launching slashing attacks against the enemy's lines of supply and communication around Nashville.

Joe Wheeler, a brash twenty-six-year-old Georgian, masterminded the first of these attacks, striking at the Cumberland River town of Clarksville. His troopers captured and burned three paddlewheel steamers hauling food and ammunition from Paducah, Kentucky, to Nashville, as well as a Union gunboat, *Slidell*. This rousing action won Wheeler a promotion to the rank of major general and a resolution of thanks from the Confederate Congress. It also gave him a swelled head, which led to disaster three weeks later when he ordered his division to storm the heavily fortified town of Dover, Tennessee. Forrest, who accompanied Wheeler on this expedition, argued against the attack, insisting that the risks far outweighed the rewards. Wheeler ignored his advice, however. The assault was bloodily repulsed, and a bruised and bitter Forrest (he had two horses shot from under him) swore that he would never serve with the callow major general again.

Out on the right flank, the South's most celebrated raider, John Hunt Morgan, was also having a rough time of it. Morgan was miffed that Wheeler, twelve years his junior and far less experienced, had been awarded a second star while he had only one. To make matters worse, he was not enjoying the kind of battlefield success to which he and his admirers had grown accustomed. Gossipmongers at headquarters were whispering that his December wedding to Miss Mattie Ready of Murfreesboro was to blame. He "seems to [be] losing his character for enterprise and daring," the Nashville *Daily Union* reported. "Many of his rivals . . . are unkind enough to attribute his present inefficiency to the fact that he is married. The fair Delilah, they assume, has shorn him of his locks." Morgan was stung by this jibe. Matrimony had nothing to do with his present difficulties, he grumbled; it was Bragg, not his wife, who was keeping him on a tight leash.

Morgan tried desperately to prove that he was still the hard-hitting cavalryman of old, but his efforts were unavailing. On March 20 he suffered a stinging setback when three of his regiments were mauled while attacking a force of Federal infantry at Milton. Two weeks later a Union brigade routed one of his detachments at the town of Liberty. Then, on April 19, he was utterly humiliated when a regiment of Yankee cavalry overran McMinnville, took Mattie prisoner for a few hours, and nearly captured him.

After this string of debacles, many in the upper echelons of the Army of Tennessee questioned the Kentuckian's competence. "I fear Morgan is overcome by too large a command," Bragg fretted. "With a regiment or small brigade he did more and better service than with a division." Morgan, who had never had his abilities called into question before, was mortified. He began casting about for some spectacular feat of arms that would win back the confidence of his superiors and restore his fast-fading reputation.

Another officer who was struggling to resurrect his career arrived in Tennessee at about this time. Forty-two-year-old Earl Van Dorn, known as "Buck" to his army friends, had once been considered one of the South's most promising field commanders. But after suffering horrendous defeats at the battles of Pea Ridge and Corinth, he had been relegated to a relatively minor post in charge of cavalry forces in Mississippi. In late December he had led his horsemen to victory at Holly Springs. This success had not been enough to silence his critics, however; nor did it still the controversy surrounding his private life. Slim-waisted and broad-shouldered, with long blond hair and soulful blue eyes, Van Dorn was a notorious lady-killer. He has "degraded the cause and disgusted everyone by his inattention to his duties," harrumphed a correspondent for the Nashville *Dispatch*. "He [is] never at his post when he ought to be. He [is] either tied to a woman's apron strings or heated with wine." Another journalist characterized Van Dorn as "a rake, a most wicked libertine," and Senator Phelan pleaded with Jefferson Davis to banish him from Mississippi, reporting that "the atmosphere is dense with horrid narratives of his negligence, whoring, and drunkenness."

Van Dorn felt that he was being made a scapegoat for all that had gone wrong in the western theater over the last six months. "I am weary, weary," he wrote. "I have struggled for others and they abuse me." But he continued to thirst after glory. In February, when Johnston ordered him to bring 6,000 riders north to Tennessee to bolster the cavalry screen on Bragg's left flank, he responded with alacrity.

Barely a week after his arrival in the Volunteer State, a brigade of Federal infantry moved to attack Van Dorn's headquarters at Columbia. Deploying his forces at Thompson's Station, a whistle-stop on the Nashville & Decatur Railroad, he intercepted the blue column and inflicted a crushing defeat on it. Then he went over to the offensive, capturing an enemy outpost at Brentwood, midway between Franklin and Nashville. Bragg was so impressed, he issued a congratulatory order.

Van Dorn was delighted. "I *am* a soldier," he wrote his sister, "and my soul swells up and tells me I *am* worthy to lead the armies of my country." His future looked bright, but then he ran afoul of a woman. In the town of Spring Hill, just up the road from Columbia, there lived a buxom brunette named Jessie Peters. She was the wife of George Peters, a physician who was often away from home on business. In her husband's absence Mrs. Peters was in the habit of entertaining gentlemen callers. Her principal paramour that spring was Buck Van Dorn, who made no effort to be discreet about his comings and goings, even using the doctor's own carriage to drive back and forth between Spring Hill and Columbia. When Dr. Peters found out he was being cuckolded, he flew into a rage. On the morning of May 7 he stalked into Van Dorn's headquarters, pulled out a pistol, and shot the general dead, bringing to an end one of the most colorful, albeit erratic, careers in the Confederate army.

The fourth member of Bragg's talented but troubled cavalry quartet was Nathan Bedford Forrest, better known to the newspaper-reading public as "the Wizard of the Saddle." Standing six feet two inches tall and weighing 180 pounds, with gaunt cheeks, gunmetal-gray eyes, and a grim, wolflike countenance, the forty-one-year-old Forrest was a gifted strategist and ferocious fighter. His formula for victory—attack, pursue, and annihilate—was as simple as it was effective. During the last week of April and the first week of May, he employed it in spectacular fashion, foiling a Union raid on the Army of Tennessee's supply line in northern Alabama and Georgia, and bagging 1,500 bluecoats in the bargain.

Forrest's triumph, coming a few weeks after the rout of the Federal fleet at Charleston, seemed to augur well for Confederate military fortunes in the months ahead. It also helped take people's minds off the trials of inflation, profiteering, and food shortages. Final victory appeared to be tantalizingly close. Many observers believed that if the civilian population persevered a little longer and the armed forces continued to treat the Yankee invaders as Forrest and Beauregard had done, then the struggle would be over soon.

Colonel Fremantle, for one, was convinced that Southern independence was almost at hand. "The more I think of all that I have seen in the Confederate States," he wrote, "the more I feel inclined to say . . . 'How can you subdue such a nation as this!' "

SEVEN

IN MOTION IN
ALL DIRECTIONS

Spring came suddenly to the Mississippi Valley. Overnight (or so it seemed to men accustomed to the interminable winters of the upper Midwest), the damp, gray chill of January and February vanished and was replaced by the blossom-scented warmth of March and April. Sprays of pastel color appeared against the emerald backdrop of budding leaves, and the earthy-sweet fragrance of wildflowers, pine sap, and freshly sprouted grass floated intoxicatingly on the breeze. In marshes rank with cattails and bulrushes, red-wing blackbirds swooped and sang, while on the murky, runoff-swollen Mississippi, great flocks of migratory waterfowl "arose from the water one after the other, and sailed away up the river in long, curving silver lines, bending and floating almost like clouds, and finally disappearing high up in the air above the green woods on the Mississippi shore."

For the Union army bivouacked in the fields around Milliken's Bend, it was a pleasant interlude. It was good to be young and alive in the Louisiana springtime, a fact of which the soldiers were reminded whenever they went for a walk along the levee and trod on the graves of hundreds of comrades who had succumbed to measles, malaria, or any of a dozen other lethal maladies during the winter. Those had been dark days, but now the epidemics had pretty well run their course, and the knowledge of having survived when so many others had sickened and died lay gratifyingly at the back of everybody's mind. Rumor had it that the army would be breaking camp soon, but the soldiers were too busy fishing, swimming, and frolicking in the sunshine to worry about it.

Not everyone at Milliken's Bend was having fun. In a dim, smoke-filled cabin aboard the headquarters steamer *Magnolia*, Ulysses S. Grant sat at a desk stacked high with maps and dispatches, brooding about how he was going to get his army into position for a drive against Vicksburg. All his attempts to bypass the blufftop stronghold had failed, and armchair strategists in Washington were growing impatient with the lack of progress. It appeared to them that he was floundering aimlessly in the mud, destroying his army through disease and overwork, and the old charges of drunkenness and incompetence had been resurrected, along with loud demands for his dismissal.

Even more damaging than the criticism from the nation's capital were the poisonous rumors emanating from within Grant's own headquarters. "We all knew what was notorious," Sherman wrote years later, "that General McClernand was still intriguing . . . to regain the command of the whole expedition, and that others were raising a clamor against Grant in the newspapers at the North." One of these malcontents, Brigadier General Charles S. Hamilton, had recently informed his home state senator, James Doolittle of Wisconsin, that Grant spent most of his time in a whiskey-induced stupor. "You have asked me to write you confidentially," he began, knowing full well that his words would soon be broadcast all over Washington. "I will now say what I have never breathed. *Grant is a drunkard.* His wife has been with him for months only to use her influence in keeping him sober. He tries to let liquor alone but he cannot resist the temptation." Another disgruntled brigadier general, Cadwallader Washburn, asserted in a series of letters to his congressman brother that Grant had no plans for taking Vicksburg and was frittering away time and strength to no purpose. "The truth must be told even if it hurts," Washburn wrote. "You cannot make a silk purse out of a sow's ear."

Abraham Lincoln professed to be unconcerned by all this carping. Prudence demanded that he investigate the persistent allegations of insobriety, however, so he gave his blessing to Secretary Stanton's plan to send a troubleshooter to Milliken's Bend to report on Grant's behavior. The man Stanton chose for the job was Charles A. Dana, one-time member of the transcendentalist Brook Farm colony, former managing editor of the New York *Tribune,* and now an assistant secretary of war. He set off down the Mississippi at the end of March, ostensibly to investigate the pay service of the western armies but actually to infiltrate Grant's headquarters and apprise Stanton of everything he saw and heard.

Friends in the War Department tipped Grant off to the real nature of Dana's visit, but instead of denouncing the assistant secretary as a spy, Grant welcomed him cordially, treating him like a member of his personal staff. As a result, favorable dispatches were soon on their way back to Washington. The pedantic ex-editor found a few things to harp on: the general's aides-de-camp violated the rules of grammar "at every phrase," he grumbled. But he had nothing but praise for Grant, of whom he later said: "[He] was an uncommon fellow—the most modest, the most disinterested and the most honest man I ever knew with a temper nothing could disturb and a judgment that was judicial in its comprehensiveness and wisdom. Not a great man except morally; not an original or brilliant man, but sincere, thoughtful, deep and gifted with courage that never faltered." And he was sober.

That was good enough for Stanton and Lincoln; Grant would keep his command for the time being. But the problem of getting across the river and assailing Vicksburg remained.

It was now early April, and the countryside around Milliken's Bend was coming into view as the winter floodwaters receded. Grant, still holed up in his stuffy cabin aboard *Magnolia,* decided it was time to gamble. He would march his army down the west bank of the Mississippi to a point well below Vicksburg, cross the river with the aid of Admiral Porter's fleet, then strike at the city from the south and east. It was a plan fraught with risks, but one guaranteed to break the existing stalemate, which he knew would be the ruination of the Union war effort in the West if it continued much longer.

Almost every officer on Grant's staff thought the scheme rash to the point of lunacy. It would require a large flotilla of ships to steam past the powerful Vicksburg batteries, rendezvous with the infantry, and execute an amphibious landing on an enemy-held shoreline. Once in Mississippi, the Union expeditionary force would be outnumbered. It would be operating deep in hostile territory, without a secure line of supply. And it would have nowhere to run to if it were defeated in battle.

Sherman wrote a long letter protesting vehemently against the plan. He argued that it would be better to return to Memphis and advance down the line of the Mississippi Central Railroad. But Grant was firm; under no circumstances would he confess failure and retreat to Tennessee.

Confident as he was of his ability to whip the enemy once he gained a toehold in Mississippi, Grant was not certain if Porter would be willing to risk his ships to help the army establish a bridgehead below Vicksburg. He need not have worried about the admiral's pugnacity. "I will be ready tomorrow night," Porter said when the proposal was put to him. He added that he was not too concerned about the rebel batteries, having tested their mettle twice during the winter and found it wanting both times. In February the ram *Queen of the West* and the ironclad *Indianola* had churned past Vicksburg and suffered only minor damage. Later that month a dummy gunboat that his sailors had constructed out of logs, canvas, and scrap lumber had also floated by the Confederate artillery without being sunk. If that flimsy hulk could run the gauntlet and emerge unscathed, then so too could unarmored transports, Porter said. But he cautioned Grant that it would be impossible to turn back once the expedition was begun. Steaming downstream, his ships could make it past the city, but a return trip was out of the question. Bucking the five-knot current, his vessels would be moving at a crawl, making them sitting ducks for the rebel artillerists.

The warning did not deter Grant. He would not turn back under any circumstances, he told Porter. Orders had gone out to McPherson and Sherman to be ready to march as soon as McClernand's Thirteenth Corps finished blazing a wagon road to New Carthage. He meant to be on Mississippi soil before the month of April was through.

From high atop the loess hills lining the east bank of the river, Vicksburg's defenders watched the comings and goings of the Federals with great interest but very little apprehension. The ease with which they had blocked Grant's flanking attempts at Yazoo Pass and Steele's Bayou filled them with confidence. The collapse of the De Soto Point canal project, the vicissitudes of which they had been able to observe as if from a front-row balcony seat, only added to their sense that the Yankee army was beaten and must soon withdraw. "Vicksburg is daily growing stronger," John Pemberton wired Richmond. "We intend to hold it."

He had good reason to feel pleased with himself. His successful defense of Mississippi had silenced the critics who said he was unfit to hold a post as important as the one Jefferson Davis had bestowed upon him. "In General Pemberton we have a man worthy of trust and confidence," announced the Vicksburg *Daily Whig,* which had earlier questioned his military qualifications. Not to be outdone, the Vicksburg *Daily Citizen* declared that "it is but an act of simple justice to record what seems to be a common, universal judgment . . . [that] the ceaseless, untiring personal efforts of this commander justly entitle him to the confidence and gratitude of the country."

Only one cloud marred Pemberton's sunny horizon—the transfer of Van Dorn's cavalry to Tennessee. Johnston had ordered the shift on the grounds that Chattanooga was now more gravely threatened than Vicksburg. Pemberton was distressed by the move, but he did not disagree with Johnston's strategic assessment. He, too, thought Vicksburg was secure. As April began, he concluded that Grant was about to return to Memphis. Thus when Johnston asked him to detach additional units for duty in Tennessee, he did not object.

Even as those confident words were humming along the telegraph wires, McClernand's Thirteenth Corps was moving down the west bank of the Mississippi, building a crude but serviceable road between Milliken's

Bend and New Carthage. It was a dirty, difficult job. The countryside between Milliken's Bend and New Carthage was low and soggy, dimpled
with ponds and cut up by innumerable creeks and bayous. But the soldiers
went at it with a will, chopping whole forests for corduroy, tearing apart
barns and plantation houses to get materials for bridge building, wading
through scummy, snake-infested sloughs to sink pilings and drag pontoons
into place. Lieutenant Colonel Wilson, architect of the ill-fated Yazoo Pass
Expedition, was dazzled by the energy and inventiveness of these Midwestern troops. He watched in amazement as one outfit bridged a series of
deep bayous with three three-hundred-foot spans—complex structures that
professional engineers would have taken weeks to design and erect. "Those
bridges were built by green volunteers who had never seen a bridge train
nor had an hour's drill or instruction in bridge-building," he marveled.
Grant was likewise impressed when he beheld this example of his troops'
handiwork. "[T]he ingenuity of the 'Yankee soldier' was equal to any emergency," he proudly wrote.

While McClernand's men were hacking their way through the swamps
below Milliken's Bend, Porter's sailors were readying eleven ships for the
risky nighttime run past Vicksburg. To minimize the chances of detection,
the admiral had directed that portholes be covered and navigation lights removed. Furnaces were to be banked to reduce smoke and sparks, and ex-
haust pipes, which normally vented into the stacks, were to be rerouted

*Vicksburg. (Courtesy Massachusetts Commandery Military Order
of the Loyal Legion and U.S. Army Military History Institute)*

into the closed wooden paddleboxes to muffle the hiss of escaping steam. Last but not least, all pet dogs were to be put ashore, lest a stray bark alert the rebel gunners to the presence of the passing ships.

Porter was hoping that his squadron could slip by Vicksburg unseen and unheard, but if it was spotted and fired upon, he intended to be ready. He instructed his bluejackets to stack bales of hay and cotton around the superstructures of their ships to provide protection from plunging shots. He also directed that scows full of coal and provisions be lashed to the vessels' sides. They would serve as bulwarks during the downriver run, then furnish food and fuel once the flotilla was past Vicksburg. Teams of sailors were ordered to stand by belowdecks, ready to extinguish blazes or to stuff gunnysacks full of wadded cotton into shell holes. Ammunition was served out to the portside gun crews so that they could return fire once the enemy batteries opened up.

The preparations were complete by the afternoon of April 16. As the sun dipped below the trees on the Louisiana shore and stars began to twinkle in the clear evening sky, Porter gave the signal for the squadron to cast loose its moorings. One by one the darkened ships got under way, emerging from the shelter of the riverbank like a school of giant snapping turtles. They glided out onto the broad, smooth surface of the Mississippi, which gleamed like a sheet of burnished copper in the fast-fading twilight. The gunboat *Benton* was in the lead, followed by the ironclads *Lafayette, Louisville, Mound City, Pittsburg,* and *Carondelet,* the captured Confederate ram *Price,* the supply-laden transports *Forest Queen, Silver Wave,* and *Henry Clay,* and the ironclad *Tuscumbia.*

When they reached the main channel, the vessels fell into line and reduced power until their paddlewheels were barely turning. Rounding Young's Point a little after 10 P.M., the column drew abreast of the packet *Von Phul,* which had dropped anchor at a spot providing an unobstructed view of Vicksburg. Gathered on the packet's hurricane deck, as if in the proscenium box of a theater, was a large crowd of spectators. Grant and his wife Julia were there, sitting at the starboard rail with their daughter Nellie, and their sons, Jesse, Fred, and Ulysses Jr. Staff officers, newspaper correspondents, and female guests milled about behind them, chattering and peering through field glasses at the lights of Vicksburg, which glittered brightly on the crest of the bluffs four miles to the east.

Conversation came to an abrupt halt when the Federal flotilla suddenly loomed out of the night. "A shapeless mass of what looked like a great fragment of darkness was discerned floating noiselessly down the river," wrote Franc Wilkie of the New York *Times.* "It disappeared, and then came another and another and still others—a long procession of bulky shadows, noiseless, mysterious, and drifting as if without life or volition." The spectral vessels slowly glided on, past *Von Phul,* around De Soto Point, and down the narrow straightaway that led past Vicksburg's waterfront. The observers on the hurricane deck waited anxiously for Vicksburg's artillery to open up. But nothing happened. Five minutes passed, then ten, and still it was quiet.

Benton was now under the lee of the bluffs, drifting by deserted wharves and shuttered warehouses. From his post in the pilothouse, Porter stared incredulously at the sleeping city. Turning to the ship's captain he hissed: "We will slip by unnoticed! The rebels seem to keep a very poor watch!"

At that instant the night exploded. A dazzling tongue of red-and-yellow flame shot skyward from one of the docks—a beacon alerting the gunners on the heights above. Moments later a whole series of fires blazed up along the Mississippi and Louisiana shores as Confederate sentinels ignited piles of pitch-soaked lumber. The leaping, roaring conflagration illuminated the Union warships. Muzzle flashes jetted out from the bluffs, and a deafening thunderclap rolled over the river's surface and engulfed the flotilla.

On board *Von Phul,* the rebels' opening salvo was felt before it was heard, a sudden, sharp concussion that pressed uncomfortably against the spectators' eardrums. The sound reached them then—a great shuddering boom—and as they watched transfixed, the eastern horizon began to flicker with an unearthly orange light.

"Magnificent, but terrible," were the words Grant later used to describe this pyrotechnic display. For now he sat quietly in a deck chair, puffing steadily on a cigar, holding his wife's hand, and gazing serenely skyward as if he were watching a Fourth of July fireworks show. Others found it harder to maintain their composure. Ten-year-old Ulysses Jr. was terrified by the billowing flames and the unrelenting thunder. He climbed into the lap of a startled staff officer and clung to his neck, whimpering piteously until his father ordered him to bed. Several of the civilian bystanders were almost as unnerved as the boy. They cowered at the back of the hurricane deck, cringing and covering their ears. Their frightened voices could be heard exclaiming over the crash of explosions: "Our men are all dead men! No one can live in such a rain of fire!"

Things looked and sounded worse than they really were. Steaming at the head of the column, *Benton* bore the brunt of the bombardment, but as Porter observed, "she had four inches of iron plating over forty inches of oak, so that not much impression was made upon her hull." An officer aboard *Lafayette,* which was following close behind, also remarked on the ineffectiveness of the enemy cannonade. "A perfect tornado of shot and shell continued to shriek over our deck," he wrote, "but not more than one in ten struck or did any damage." In the end, only one ship came to grief. An exploding shell ignited the cotton bales stacked on the deck of the transport *Henry Clay,* and she went up like a torch. The rest of the squadron would be ready for action as soon as the sailors made a few minor repairs, announced Porter, adding that in his opinion the threat posed by the Vicksburg batteries was more apparent than real.

Grant agreed. A week after the first run, he sent another contingent of steamers loaded with food, forage, and medical supplies downstream past the city. One vessel, *Tigress,* foundered after her stern was blown off, but the other five made it safely to New Carthage. Fifteen ships and an equal number of barges were available to ferry troops across the Mississippi to Grand Gulf, the landing site Grant had selected.

To keep Pemberton off balance, Grant now launched three diversionary actions. Two of them were designed to draw the Confederate commander's attention away from the real point of attack, while the third was aimed at disrupting his lines of communication and panicking the people of Mississippi.

The first feint involved an upriver sortie by 5,000 soldiers of Brigadier General Frederick Steele's division. These men went ashore near the town of Greenville, Mississippi, one hundred miles north of Vicksburg. From there they marched rapidly southeast, cutting a swath of destruction through the rich agricultural country bordering Deer Creek. For the better part of two weeks, they terrorized the local population, looting homes, burning corn and cotton, slaughtering livestock, and doing everything in their power to convince the rebel high command that this was the beginning of a full-fledged invasion. Then they reboarded their transports and returned to Milliken's Bend to join the rest of Sherman's corps in mounting a second, even more elaborate feint—a mock attack on the Confederate fortifications at Chickasaw Bluffs.

These demonstrations had exactly the effect Grant was hoping for. Pemberton, already flummoxed by the Union army's failure to withdraw to Memphis, was further disoriented. He began to show signs of losing his composure. "Enemy is constantly in motion in all directions," he informed Richmond as he dispatched troops first to one place and then to another in a frantic effort to counter Federal threats, real and imagined.

But it was the third diversion that created the greatest stir, both at Confederate headquarters and in the North. "The most brilliant expedition of the war," Sherman said of the operation, and Grant concurred, hailing it as a masterstroke, one of the great exploits of this or any other conflict.

History would simply record it as Grierson's Raid, in honor of the thirty-six-year-old cavalryman who led it.

Of all the heroes who emerged from the crucible of combat in 1863, none was more unlikely than Benjamin Henry Grierson of Jacksonville, Illinois. A swarthy, spade-bearded Scotsman with sunken eyes, a lopsided face, and a thick shock of coal-black hair, he was an erstwhile music teacher—a pianist, flutist, and drummer—who freely admitted that he would have been happier leading a marching band than commanding a brigade of cavalry.

As a matter of fact, he would have been happier doing almost anything besides sitting atop a horse. He had been afraid of the beasts since the age of eight, when a kick from a skittish pony had crushed one of his cheekbones. His posting to the Sixth Illinois Cavalry in the winter of 1861 had been a mistake; he had specifically asked the recruiting officer to assign him to the infantry or artillery.

For all his reluctance, however, Grierson thrived in the cavalry. He conquered his fear of horses and made himself an adequate if not spectacular equestrian. He pored over the drill manual until he was able to put his troopers through their paces without embarrassment, and he mastered the deadly art of mounted combat while skirmishing with Confederate guerrillas in the wilds of western Tennessee during the spring and summer of 1862. Promoted to colonel and given command of a brigade, he soon won the approval of Sherman, who touted his energy and aggressiveness to Grant.

Grant filed this information away, and late in February, when he began thinking about a raid through Mississippi, he fixed upon the former music teacher as the ideal man to lead it. "It seems to me that Grierson, with about five hundred picked men, might succeed in making his way south, and cut the railroad east of Jackson," he wrote. A month and a half later his instructions were more specific. Grierson's brigade was to leave La Grange, Tennessee, on April 17 and ride south into Mississippi, making all the mischief it could en route to the Southern Mississippi Railroad, which linked Vicksburg to Jackson, Montgomery, Atlanta, and points east. Severing it would snarl Pemberton's logistics and force him to detach units to repair and guard the tracks—soldiers who other-

Colonel Benjamin H. Grierson.
(Courtesy U.S. Army
Military History Institute)

wise would be available to contest the upcoming amphibious assault at Grand Gulf. Once the raiders completed their mission, they were to extricate themselves from enemy territory any way they could. One suggestion was that they return to Tennessee by way of Alabama. Another was that they swing west and link up with Grant's army in the vicinity of Vicksburg. A third was that they ride on to Baton Rouge, which was now occupied by Union forces. Whatever escape route they chose, it was essential that they move fast. If the Confederates caught them, they could expect no help from Grant, who would be busy fighting his own battles on the east bank of the Mississippi.

In all, 1,700 cavalrymen left La Grange at daybreak on April 17 and rode south toward the Mississippi state line. They had no idea where they were headed, although the orders they had received the day before—"Oats in the nosebags and five days' rations to last ten days. Double rations of salt. Forty rounds of ammunition"—led them to believe it was not too far away. Only Colonel Grierson knew that the destination was the town of Newton Station, close to two hundred miles from La Grange, and that to reach it his command would have to penetrate into the heart of Mississippi, dogged every step of the way by local militia companies and detachments of Confederate regulars. If the prospect made the ex-bandmaster nervous, he did not show it. As was his wont when he was on patrol, he pulled a Jew's harp from the breast pocket of his blouse and regaled himself with a sprightly if somewhat twangy serenade.

After a ten-hour trek through the rolling hills of northern Mississippi, the raiders halted for the night four miles northwest of the town of Ripley. Up before dawn the next morning, they wolfed down a breakfast of hardtack and raw bacon, then rode on. They passed through Ripley at 8 A.M., forded the Tallahatchie River at midday, and trotted through the town of New Albany before pitching camp for the evening on the estate of a rebel planter named Sloan.

"As usual," Grierson wrote, "we demanded the keys of smokehouses and barns, food for men and horses. Mr. Sloan wanted in a small way to resist where resistance was of course impossible; would not give up his keys until the locks were broken. When he saw his stores issued out, he was completely beside himself. . . . [He] demanded that we take him out and cut his throat and be done with it."

Grierson, who dearly loved a practical joke, decided to have some fun at the expense of the distraught planter. He turned to his orderly, winked broadly, then shouted: "Mr. Sloan is very desirous of having his throat cut. Take him out in the field and *cut his throat and be done with it!*" Without batting an eye the orderly whipped out a bowie knife, grabbed Sloan by the scruff of the neck, and started to march him away. "Now began a hubbub," wrote Grierson. "Mrs. Sloan . . . began to scream in chorus with the servants." She beseeched the Union colonel to ignore what her husband had said. Sloan also began to beg for mercy, squealing that he had changed his mind and did not want his throat cut after all. Feigning great reluctance, Grierson signaled the orderly to release the trembling prisoner. The assembled troopers roared with laughter as the chastened rebel scampered back into his house, all defiance forgotten in his haste to get away from the bowie knife.

The next day, Sunday, April 19, the raiders resumed their ride in a driving rainstorm. They sloshed southward through the hamlets of Friendship and Pontotoc, where they paused to destroy a cache of Confederate supplies, then pushed on to a sodden camp on the banks of Chiwapa Creek. Sensing that rebel forces were beginning to mobilize in his front and rear, Grierson mounted a diversion. After breakfast on the morning of the twentieth, he ordered all troopers afflicted with dysentery, fever, or incapacitating saddle sores to fall out and form an invalid's column. The Quinine Brigade, as this 175-man aggregation was called, was instructed to head back to La Grange by way of Pontotoc and New Albany, "marching by fours, obliterating our tracks, and producing the impression that we have all returned." The main body kept moving south, covering another forty miles before halting outside the hamlet of Clear Springs.

That evening Grierson detached a second party in hopes of decoying any pursuers. He ordered the Second Iowa under Colonel Edward Hatch to ride east, tear up the tracks of the Mobile & Ohio Railroad in the vicinity of West Point and Okolona, then make for La Grange, doing its best to create the impression that the entire column was returning to its base.

His instincts were sound. A regiment of Confederate cavalry—500 regulars augmented by several hundred Mississippi state militiamen—had been hot on his trail for the last two days. The commander of this mixed unit, a wily Tennessean named Clark Barteau, had not been taken in by the diversionary movement of the Quinine Brigade. He was now only thirteen miles behind the main Union force and closing fast. But when he came upon the eastward-leading tracks of Hatch's regiment, Barteau unhesitatingly ordered his column to turn and follow. His job was to protect the Mobile & Ohio from Yankee depredations. It never occurred to him that the Federals' real objective was the Southern Mississippi line a hundred miles farther south.

Grierson and his thousand-odd troopers made the most of Barteau's error. They looted the town of Starkville, then galloped on to Talking Warrior Creek, where they spent a cold, wet night huddling under their ponchos.

At dawn on the twenty-second, Grierson again sought to deceive the Confederates. He detached Company B of the Seventh Illinois and sent it to cut the telegraph wires at Macon on the Mobile & Ohio line. His instructions were simple: Do as much damage as possible while attracting the attention of the enemy, then rejoin the raiding party, which would be sweeping south through the Noxubee and Pearl River Valleys.

Drawing the rebels away from the main column was a tall order for a single company, but the Illinoisans executed it brilliantly. The Confederate brass was convinced that the M&O was about to be attacked by several thousand Yankees. All available gray troops in east-central Mississippi were rushed to its defense, leaving the roads south completely unguarded. Thus when Grierson's horsemen passed through Philadelphia, Mississippi, on the afternoon of April 23, they encountered no resistance. After resting for a few hours on a plantation north of Decatur, they pushed on toward Newton Station, confident that nothing was standing in their way.

Cloaked by a billowing cloud of dust, the column of Union riders thundered into the sleepy trackside town shortly after sunrise on April 24. They arrived just in time to capture a pair of freight trains loaded with food and ammunition destined for Vicksburg. These were quickly run off onto a siding and set ablaze. Then the work of demolition began in earnest. Squads of ax- and crowbar-toting cavalrymen fanned out to the east and west, ripping up rails, tearing down telegraph wires, and breaking apart bridges. By 2 P.M. an eight-mile stretch of track had been obliterated. Grierson was satisfied that this section of railroad would be out of operation for at least a week. He hastily reassembled his sweaty, soot-stained troopers and led them south, anxious to get away before rebel forces in the area learned of his presence and moved to surround him.

His concern was well founded. It took only a few hours for news of the Newton Station raid to reach Confederate headquarters in Jackson. The response was swift and furious. Pemberton ordered units from all over the state to converge on the shattered rail depot in an attempt to capture the blue marauders.

Realizing that a return to La Grange was out of the question, Grierson ordered his troopers to head west toward Grand Gulf. They crossed the lower Pearl River at Georgetown on April 27, transiting the rain-swollen stream on a commandeered flatboat. During this crossing the thirty-five soldiers of Company B showed up, having completed a nerve-jangling ride through countryside crawling with Confederate patrols. The reunited command entered the town of Hazelhurst on the New Orleans & Jackson Railroad an hour later. While the men tore up tracks, torched freight cars, and broke into buildings in search of food and drink, Grierson sent an unsigned telegram to Pemberton reading: "The Yankees have advanced to Pearl River, but finding the ferry destroyed they could not cross and have left, taking a northeasterly direction." Confident that this disinformation would confuse the Confederate commander, he rallied the brigade and rode southwest, setting as rapid a pace as his saddle-weary soldiers could stand.

The morning of April 28 found the column less than thirty miles from Grand Gulf. But instead of feeling relieved that the long raid was almost over, Grierson was fearful of stumbling into a trap. The countryside seemed too peaceful. There were no refugees on the road, no sign of enemy troops on the move, nothing to suggest that Grant's army had landed at Grand Gulf. Instead all was quiet, and on this sultry day, with a thick gray haze hanging low over the piney woods and the air so still and heavy it was hard to breathe, that struck him as decidedly ominous.

Heeding his instincts, he called an early afternoon halt in a field outside the hamlet of Union Church. Moments later 150 rebel horsemen burst out of the surrounding trees. A volley of carbine fire scattered them, but before the Federals could resume their westward march, a loquacious prisoner revealed that another seven companies of Confederate cavalry were waiting in ambush up ahead. That was enough for Grierson. He ordered his troopers to head in the opposite direction. "Hearing nothing of our forces at Grand Gulf, I concluded to make for Baton Rouge," he explained afterward.

The Louisiana state capital was more than a hundred miles away, a daunting distance for men who had been in the saddle for twelve consecutive days. It seemed the safest destination under the circumstances, however, so the raiders rode south and east. They stopped to burn the rail depot at Brookhaven on the afternoon of April 29, rested briefly along Bogue Chitto Creek that evening, then galloped onward to ransack the town of Summit before bivouacking at sundown on the thirtieth on Spurlark's Plantation, ten miles from the Mississippi-Louisiana border.

Grierson roused his soldiers early the next morning. "A straight line for Baton Rouge, and let speed be our safety," he told them. The sanctuary of Federal lines was little more than a day's ride away, and it seemed that the column would make it without a fight. But just before noon on May 1, the lead company ran into a Confederate detachment guarding Wall's Bridge over the Tickfaw River. The rebels opened fire, killing one bluecoat, wounding four, and capturing five others. The rest of the column came up and routed the graybacks, but the damage had been done. For the first time during the raid the brigade had been bloodied.

Although his troopers were groggy with fatigue, Grierson drove them relentlessly, afraid that if he allowed even a few minutes rest, all would be lost. The blazing hot afternoon slowly gave way to a sweltering night, and still the column rode on, across fields of sugarcane glowing silver in the pale moonlight, through tunnels formed by the moss-draped branches of live oak trees, past shuttered farm houses where dogs barked desultorily and wakeful roosters crowed in anticipation of a dawn still many hours away.

"Men by the score were riding sound asleep in their saddles," wrote Captain Henry Forbes. "The horses, excessively tired and hungry, would stray out of the road and thrust their noses to the earth in hopes of finding something to eat. The men, when addressed, would remain silent and motionless until a blow across the thigh or shoulders should awaken them, when it would be found that each supposed himself still riding with his company, which might be miles ahead. We found several men who had either fallen from their horses or dismounted and dropped on the ground, dead with sleep."

At midnight the drowsy raiders entered Louisiana. Still Grierson pressed on, unwilling to stop until he was sure the column was past the last enemy outpost and well within Union lines. A few miles northeast of Baton Rouge, he finally called a halt on the grounds of an abandoned plantation. The troopers slid from their saddles and passed out among the weeds and clumps of sedgegrass. The colonel, feeling it was his duty to stay awake, went into the deserted house to look around. In the parlor he was delighted to discover a piano; he sat down at once and began to play.

Presently one of his orderlies burst in and reported that two companies of Confederates were approaching from the west. Grierson was unperturbed. "Feeling confident that no enemy could come against us from that direction," he wrote, "I rode out alone to meet the troops without waking up my command." Just as he expected, the skirmishers turned out to be Union soldiers from Baton Rouge.

The general commanding the Baton Rouge garrison was beside himself with excitement; nothing but a welcoming parade would do. Grierson tried to beg off, pointing out that his men were utterly exhausted, but the general insisted. So later that afternoon the yawning troopers remounted and marched through the city. When the procession was over, they staggered off to a magnolia grove south of town and fell back asleep, slumbering so soundly, they could not be awakened even when cooks from the Baton Rouge garrison arrived with loaves of freshly baked bread, kettles of beef stew, and pots of hot coffee.

The raiders richly deserved their rest. They had ridden six hundred miles in sixteen days, killing and wounding about 100 of the enemy, capturing and paroling more than 500 prisoners, and destroying close to sixty miles of railroad track. More important, they had drawn Pemberton's attention away from the east bank of the Mississippi, where the Union army was about to begin its movement against Vicksburg. "The most successful thing of the kind since the breaking out of the rebellion," Grant informed

Halleck, a "brilliant cavalry exploit [that] will be handed down in history as an example to be imitated."

Even the rebel press expressed grudging admiration. "This fellow Grierson is certainly a gallant chap, and his ride will compare favorably with anything yet recorded, even in the South, where so many deeds of noble daring have been related," wrote Marmaduke Shannon. "We hope that this expedition will teach us a lesson. Bitter experience has always been our tutor in this war."

As for the self-effacing music teacher, he traveled by steamboat to New Orleans, where he received a hero's welcome. "My dear Alice," he wrote his wife from his palatial suite in the St. Charles Hotel, "I like Byron have had to wake up one morning and find myself famous." The accolades did not go to his head, however. Even when his picture appeared in *Harper's Weekly* and *Frank Leslie's Illustrated Newspaper,* he remained distinctly unaffected. Celebrity did not suit him, and after a four-day sojourn in the Crescent City, he rejoined his brigade at Baton Rouge. "I presume we will endeavor to form a junction with the forces [landing at Grand Gulf]," he wrote, his relief at getting back into action clearly palpable. "We will [try] to select the best possible route [and] to inflict the most injury to the rebels."

On April 27, the day Grierson and his raiders crossed the lower Pearl River, Grant celebrated his forty-first birthday at Perkin's Plantation, a malarial stretch of bottomland midway between New Carthage and Hard Times. Although he was keenly aware that the coming campaign would make or break Union military fortunes in the West, he showed no outward signs of apprehension as he wrote out orders to McClernand, whose four divisions would spearhead the amphibious assault on Grand Gulf. "Commence immediately the embarkation of your corps, or so much of it as there is transportation for," he directed the ex-congressman. "The plan of the attack will be for the navy to silence the batteries commanding the river. Your corps will be on the river, ready to run to and debark on the nearest eligible land. . . . The first object is to get a foothold." Entrusting this dispatch to a courier, he set out for Hard Times to observe the operation in person.

The selection of McClernand to head the landing force had been controversial. Sherman and Porter both thought it was a mistake to entrust command of the Grand Gulf assault to an amateur. Grant defended his choice by pointing out that McClernand was the army's senior corps commander and an "especial favorite of the president." He was outraged, however, when he arrived at Hard Times on the afternoon of the twenty-seventh and found that his explicit instructions were being ignored. "Not a single cannon or man had been moved," wrote a flabbergasted Charles Dana. Instead, Mc-Clernand had a brigade of troops drawn up on a makeshift parade ground listening to a campaign speech by Illinois governor Richard Yates. When this harangue was finished, "a salute of artillery was fired, notwithstanding the positive orders that had repeatedly been given to use no ammunition for any purpose except against the enemy." As if in answer to the cannons' boom, a thunderstorm began, and while lightning flashed and rain fell, McClernand retired to his tent to enjoy a connubial interlude with his wife, leaving the embarkation of his corps for later.

Grant penned a blistering letter of reprimand, but he tore it up the next morning when he saw that soldiers and supplies were at last being loaded onto the transports. Everything was set by 8 A.M. on the twenty-ninth. Porter's gunboats sallied forth to bombard the Grand Gulf batteries, while the steamers carrying McClernand's men loitered just out of range, waiting for an opportune moment to rush in and disgorge their human cargo.

Confederate shells pounded Porter's flotilla as it drew within range of the rebel-held bluffs. The ironclad *Tuscumbia* was struck eighty-one times and severely damaged, *Benton* was battered by seventy hits, and *Lafayette* and *Pittsburg* were also badly pummeled. Three other gunboats—*Carondelet, Mound City,* and *Louisville*—stayed farther back and suffered less damage, but their long-range shelling was ineffective. At 1 P.M. Porter called off the action. He had lost eighteen sailors killed and fifty-six wounded and had not silenced a single Confederate artillery piece.

Unfazed by the navy's failure, Grant quickly sketched out an alternative plan. McClernand's troops were ordered to debark and march downstream to De Shroon's Plantation, four miles southwest of Hard Times. The fleet would lie low until nightfall, then make a high-speed run past the Grand Gulf batteries. Ships and men would rendezvous at De Shroon's at dawn and proceed with the river crossing, out of range of the rebel guns. The only detail left undecided was the location of the new landing site. It had to be a place where the infantry could wade ashore unopposed, move rapidly to higher ground, then swing north and west to take Grand Gulf from the rear. No one on Grant's staff was familiar with the roads on the other side of the Mississippi, so a squad of soldiers was sent across the river in a rowboat with instructions to abduct a slave from one of the farms along the east bank. They returned just before midnight with a grizzled old black man who obligingly identified Bruinsburg as the best landing spot. From this streamside hamlet a good road led inland to the town of Port Gibson. From Port Gibson it was only a six-mile march to Grand Gulf.

Early the next morning, McClernand's four divisions and one of McPherson's landed without incident at Bruinsburg. Grant appeared almost nonchalant as he admonished the men to "push right along," but inside, he would later admit, he was brimming with emotion. "When [the crossing] was effected I felt a degree of relief scarcely ever equalled since," he wrote in his memoirs. "I was now in the enemy's country, with a vast river and the stronghold of Vicksburg between me and my base of supplies. But I was on dry ground on the same side of the river with the enemy. All the campaigns, labors, hardships and exposures from the month of December previous to this time that had been made and endured, were for the accomplishment of this one object."

Grant's relief was matched by Pemberton's frustration. The Confederate commander's strategy had begun to unravel when the first batch of Union ships made it safely past Vicksburg. It had deteriorated rapidly thereafter as Grant's troops marched unmolested down the west bank of the Mississippi while Grierson's raiders rampaged through the eastern half of the Magnolia State. Pemberton asked Johnston to return Van Dorn's horsemen to him at once, but Johnston turned him down. No reinforcements, cavalry or otherwise, would be forthcoming from Tennessee.

Next Pemberton tried to get help from the Trans-Mississippi Department, which covered western Louisiana, Arkansas, and Texas. He asked Kirby Smith to cut Grant's supply line between Milliken's Bend and New Carthage, but his appeal fell on deaf ears. Smith was preoccupied with his own problems; he even had the temerity to suggest that Pemberton send reinforcements to him.

Then, on April 28, word had come from Brigadier General John S. Bowen, commander of the Grand Gulf garrison, that the Union infantry at Hard Times was about to make a cross-river thrust. Pemberton at once alerted Carter Stevenson, the general in charge at Vicksburg, to be ready to march to Bowen's aid. Stevenson demurred. The activity at Hard Times was a feint, he argued. The real attack was going to come at Chickasaw Bluffs, where Sherman's corps was making a great show of mobilizing for an assault. Unable to track the enemy's movements because his shrunken cavalry force was off chasing Grierson, Pemberton could only wait and see what happened. News that the Federals were landing at Bruinsburg convinced him that the downriver threat was the more serious of the two. He immediately dispatched 5,000 troops from Vicksburg to aid Bowen's 6,000, but by then Grant was ashore and advancing toward Port Gibson with better than 20,000 men.

Once again Pemberton telegraphed Johnston and Jefferson Davis for reinforcements. The Confederate president was so ill, he could scarcely raise his head from his pillow; nevertheless he replied promptly to Pemberton's plea, promising to send additional troops as rapidly as possible. From Johnston there came no offer of support, however, only a curt admonition: "If Grant's army lands on [your] side of the river, the safety of Mississippi depends on beating it. For that object you should unite your whole force."

Now Pemberton faced an agonizing decision. He could follow Johnston's advice, consolidate his scattered units, and try to crush Grant before he got any farther inland. Or he could stick with his present plan of defending key points all over the state while waiting for help to arrive from the East.

His innate sense of caution inclined him toward the latter course. Stripping Port Hudson, Greenwood, Grenada, Columbus, and Jackson of their garrisons would expose them to the depredations of raiders like Grierson. Weakening Vicksburg's defenses might embolden Sherman, who was still lurking near Chickasaw Bluffs. But surrendering the initiative to Grant was even riskier, he decided. He resolved to unite his forces and move to head off the Union landing force. "Unless very large reinforcements are sent here, I think Port Hudson and Grand Gulf should be evacuated and the whole force concentrated for defense of Vicksburg and Jackson," he telegraphed his superiors on May 2. "The battle will probably be fought outside of Vicksburg."

From Tullahoma, Johnston immediately signaled his approval. "Unite all your troops," he urged. "Success will give back what was abandoned to win it." But in Richmond, Davis was appalled. He considered Port Hudson too important to be evacuated, even for a short time. He insisted that its garrison stay put and hold to the last, thereby canceling Pemberton's plan to consolidate forces.

Thus one of the pivotal strategic decisions of the war was made not by the military commander on the scene, but by a bedridden political leader a thousand miles away. Pemberton was restricted to the defensive, his army anchored to a few fortified posts, and the door to the Mississippi interior was thrown wide open to Grant.

EIGHT

HIS NAME MIGHT
BE AUDACITY

The Army of the Potomac was in terrible shape when Joseph Hooker was named its new commander on January 25, 1863. More than 85,000 men—one-third of the army's paper strength—were absent without leave, another 15,000 were on the sick list, and desertions were averaging 200 a day. The soldiers who had not yet run away or fallen victim to disease were profoundly disillusioned. Cold, dirty, and miserable, they huddled in squalid camps in the hills around Falmouth, drowning their sorrows with rotgut whiskey. "I have seen a whole regiment so drunk that they were hard put to find fifteen sober men for picket duty," wrote a soldier in the 140th Pennsylvania. "I have seen lieutenants, captains, and colonels so drunk they fell off their horses in the mud. Still the papers say this army isn't demoralized. As my messmate says, 'They don't count the drunks.' "

The situation was so bad that many in the ranks wondered if Hooker could salvage it. "All know that [he] can command and fight a division to perfection, but to take a great army like ours in hand . . . is another thing," wrote Sergeant D. G. Crotty. "[W]e all feel that General Hooker will be like the poor man that won the elephant at the raffle. After he got the animal, he did not know what to do with him."

Fortunately for all concerned, Hooker proved to be a first-rate military administrator. He improved the health of his troops by prescribing a host of long-overdue prophylactic measures. The army's medical director was called to headquarters and told that basic rules of sanitation, including proper use of latrines and burying of kitchen slops, were to be enforced in all the camps. In addition, the pestilential huts that served as living quarters were to be cleaned out, their dirt floors carpeted with fresh pine boughs, and their canvas roofs rolled back periodically so that sun and wind could purify their interiors. Soiled bedding was to be aired on a regular basis, lice- and flea-infested uniforms were to be laundered in boiling water, and last but not least, the men were to wear their hair cut short, bathe twice a week, and put on clean underclothing at least once a week. The commissary department was also ordered to make changes. Henceforward soft bread was to be issued at least four times a week, onions and potatoes twice a week, and desiccated mixed vegetables ("desecrated vegetables," the soldiers called these round, two-inch-thick cakes of compressed green matter) once a week. Not surprisingly, cleaner camps, better personal hygiene, and more nutritious food produced dramatic results. Scurvy disappeared, and the incidence of diarrhea and typhoid declined.

Having bettered the army's physical condition, Hooker turned to raising its morale. Homesickness was one of the major causes of the melancholy that had settled like a chill gray fog over the Falmouth bivouac. To combat it he established a system of regular furloughs. He also arranged to have several months' back pay distributed. ("It is wonderful how having money in the pocket improves the appearance of a soldier," wrote a member of the Nineteenth Maine. "He stands straighter, walks prouder, looks happier, acts more independent and enjoys better health.") Security was tightened to discourage desertion. And to keep the troops busy, a strenuous schedule of drill, picket duty, and dress parades was instituted. These simple steps proved wonderfully effective. Within a fortnight the army's mental outlook was much improved. Cheerfulness, good order, and discipline took the place of grumbling, slovenliness, and insubordination. Soldiers who had been so disillusioned that they wanted to lay down their arms and go home now hailed their new commander as a miracle worker.

Whenever Hooker rode through the camps, his clean-shaven face glowing with good health and high spirits, the troops would whip off their hats and cheer, and as they practiced the manual of arms or performed close-order maneuvers under his admiring gaze, they would sing:

> *For God and our country*
> *We're marching along.*
> *Joe Hooker is our leader;*
> *He takes his whiskey strong!*

This last line, bellowed out at the top of everyone's lungs, alluded to the general's well-known fondness for liquor. It was an appetite most of the enlisted men approved of, on the theory that hard drinking and hard fighting

General Joseph Hooker.
(Library of Congress)

went together hand in glove. Many of the higher-ranking officers found it worrisome, however. It was said that Hooker had been a three-bottle-a-day man in the prewar army, and although he drank less heavily (but no less regularly) now, there was still a whiff of insobriety about him, which manifested itself in his "rather too rosy face," the "nervous verve and dash in his manner," and his loud, boisterous way of conversing. Major General Carl Schurz feared that he was "a man with no firm moral force." Major General George G. Meade fretted that he was "open to temptation." And Captain Charles Francis Adams, Jr., blue-blooded son of the American ambassador to England, disparaged him as a man of "blemished character."

There was concern, too, about the discrepancy between Hooker's reputation as a top-notch combat general—gained largely through luck, favorable press coverage, and clever self-promotion—and his actual military ability. His ferocious-sounding nickname, for example, was the result of a printer's error, not any real battlefield exploit. A dispatch from the front under the heading "Fighting—Joe Hooker" had been received in the composing room of a New York newspaper, and a harried typesetter had dropped the dash, inadvertently creating the colorful cognomen. Hooker professed to hate it. "Don't call me Fighting Joe," he groaned; "it makes the public think that I am a hot-headed, furious young fellow." But the fact was, he could not have come up with a better nom de guerre if he had paid a publicity agent to coin one. It had done wonders for his career, as had his penchant for criticizing his superiors and touting himself for the top post at every turn.

Then there was the matter of Hooker's incessant blustering. "If the enemy does not run, God help them!" he would whoop to the journalists who hung around his headquarters. "I have the finest army the sun ever shone on! I can march this army to New Orleans! My plans are perfect, and when I start to carry them out, may God have mercy on General Lee, for I will have none!"

This overweening self-confidence, without much in the way of a record to back it up, led some to suspect that Hooker was a sham. No one could criticize the job he had done bringing the Army of the Potomac back from the brink of collapse, however, and even his detractors hoped that the changes he had made would enable it to live up to its vast potential, whip the enemy, and end the war.

Bad as the winter was for the Federals on Rappahannock's north bank, it was worse for the 60,000 rebels bivouacked on the other side. The pernicious consequences of the South's supply woes were painfully evident in the drawn faces and hunched postures of the Army of Northern Virginia's soldiers. There were not enough shoes, blankets, and overcoats to go around, nor was there enough food. The basic daily ration was cut and then cut again, until it consisted of four ounces of moldy bacon and eighteen ounces of weevilly flour supplemented every third day by one and a half ounces of rice and a small quantity of sugar or molasses. "The men are cheerful, and I receive but few complaints," Lee informed Seddon in late March, "still, I do not think it is enough to continue them in health and vigor . . . I fear they will be unable to endure the hardships of the approaching campaign."

He need not have worried about the latter. The soldiers' stomachs might growl and their frames grow thinner, but their spirits remained remarkably high. A healthy mix of work and play left little time for gloom and self-pity. The work consisted of light drill, guard duty, and the construction of trenches and breastworks. The play took the form of amateur talent shows, religious revival meetings, and snowball fights waged with such gusto that "tents were wrecked, bones broken, eyes blacked, and teeth knocked out—all in *fun*." These battles were especially popular with troops from the Deep South, many of whom had never seen snow before. On January 29 the Fourth Texas and Eleventh Georgia Regiments began a mammoth snowball fight that ultimately involved upward of 9,000 men and resulted in so many injuries that headquarters issued an order forbidding such skirmishes in the future.

The most important factor in sustaining morale was the soldiers' fierce pride in their combat record and their affection for, and trust in, the triumvirate of officers that led them. Commanding the First Corps was forty-two-year-old James Longstreet, called "Old Pete" by his troops. A brawny, bearlike man, stolid and slow-talking, he had been born in South Carolina, raised in Georgia, and appointed to West Point from Alabama. Not a brilliant general (he had graduated fifty-fourth in the fifty-six–man class of 1842) but a tough, unflappable one, his forte was defensive fighting of the kind that had shattered the Union army at Fredericksburg. He was convinced that good ground, stout entrenchments, and massed firepower were the ingredients for victory, and he urged his superiors to make use of them whenever possible.

The Second Corps commander was of a different mind. Thirty-nine-year-old Thomas J. "Stonewall" Jackson, known to his men as "Old Jack," believed that victory flowed from faith in God and unrelenting aggressiveness on the battlefield. Lean and ascetic-looking, his intense religiosity and peculiar habits of diet and posture (he ate plain meat and stale bread, sucked lemons, stood ramrod straight at all times, went about with his left arm raised over his head, palm facing outward, as if offering a benediction) had caused him to be branded an eccentric. But there was nothing quirky about his grasp of tactics. Swift marches and smashing blows were his specialty. His exploits in the Shenandoah Valley and at First Manassas, Antietam, and Fredericksburg had made him famous throughout the South and earned him the unabashed adoration of his troops.

Heading this martial trinity was the great idol of the Confederacy, fifty-seven-year-old Robert E. Lee. Standing five feet eleven inches tall and weighing a shade over 170 pounds, white-bearded and ruddy-complected, he was, in the opinion of one awestruck subordinate, "the best looking man in the universe." His dark brown eyes radiated authority, and his courtly demeanor—"cold and quiet and grand," wrote Richmond diarist Mary Chesnut—bespoke command even more forcefully than the three gold stars on his collar. Son of Revolutionary War hero "Light Horse" Harry Lee, linked by marriage to Virginia's first families, the Custises and the Washingtons, he was the prototypical gentleman soldier. His aristocratic deportment and sense of noblesse oblige had earned him the mocking nickname "Granny," but his superb military talents—intense combativeness and an uncanny instinct for seizing the moment—never ceased to dazzle his colleagues-in-arms. Colonel Joseph Ives put it best when he said, "If there is one man in either army, Confederate or Federal, head and shoulders above every other in audacity, it is General Lee. His *name* might be Audacity. He will take more desperate chances and take them quicker than any other general in this country, North or South."

For now Lee had to proceed with caution because his command was barely half the size of the Army of the Potomac. He implored the War Department to even the odds by sending him more troops. Instead, the Army of Northern Virginia was weakened when two divisions under Longstreet were dispatched to North Carolina to gather provisions and block Federal efforts to cut the rail lines linking Richmond to the rest of the South. They performed these tasks admirably, but their absence put Lee in a strategic bind. As spring came on, he wanted to move north, drawing Hooker and the Army of the Potomac away from Richmond. He dared not try it, however, without his entire force on hand. The scarcity of food around Fredericksburg made it necessary to keep Longstreet's divisions in North Carolina collecting supplies. Thus Lee was obliged to stay where he was and let Hooker take the lead.

During the last week of April, evidence mounted that the Army of the Potomac was preparing to embark on an offensive. Yankee observation balloons were airborne, and Yankee cavalry units—grown vastly more aggressive since Hooker had consolidated them into an autonomous corps in early February—were also active, ranging up and down the river reconnoitering the rebel defenses. Lee informed Jefferson Davis that all signs pointed to an attack. He instructed the troops guarding the Rappahannock fords above Fredericksburg to be on the lookout for an enemy crossing. Then he settled back to see what Hooker would try.

Abraham Lincoln had followed the revitalization of the Army of the Potomac with intense interest. During the first week of April, he decided to pay Hooker a visit and see for himself how the Union's largest fighting force was shaping up. Accompanied by his wife Mary, his son Tad, Attorney General Edward Bates, longtime friend Anson G. Henry, and journalistic confidant Noah Brooks, he journeyed by boat, train, and wagon to Hooker's Falmouth headquarters, arriving on the morning of April 5— Easter Sunday.

Over the next five days, he conducted military inspections, toured field hospitals, and drove from camp to camp greeting as many soldiers as he could. The high point of his visit was the "Grand Review" held on April 8. Four of the army's seven infantry corps—some 85,000 troops in all— marched past the presidential entourage. Hooker, resplendent in full dress uniform, sat tall and statuesque atop a magnificent white stallion. Lincoln wore a wrinkled black suit and was mounted on a horse that was much too small for him. He "would have presented a comical picture," recalled Private Robert G. Carter, "had it not been for those sad, anxious eyes, so full of melancholy foreboding, that peered forth from his shaggy eyebrows." Noah Brooks noticed that the president merely nodded and touched his hat when the officers saluted him, but doffed it to the enlisted soldiers as they tramped past. "What do you suppose will become of all these men when the war is over?" he asked Major General Darius Couch during the hours-long parade. Couch was startled by the question; he wondered how the commander in chief could think of peace while watching a military pageant as spectacular as this. But later he wrote that "it struck me as very pleasant that somebody had an idea that the war would sometime end."

As impressed as Lincoln was with the Army of the Potomac, he continued to have doubts about its commander. "Beware of rashness," he had cautioned Hooker when he promoted him back in January, but the bumptious general seemed not to have taken that advice to heart. He talked as though he had already won a great victory, using the phrase "When I get to Richmond" over and over again. On one occasion Lincoln cut him off, saying "*If* you get to Richmond, General—," but Hooker refused to be cowed. "Excuse me, Mr. President," he loudly retorted, "there is no 'if' in this case. I am going straight to Richmond if I live." Afterward Lincoln told Noah Brooks that Hooker's overconfidence was "about the worst thing I have seen since I have been down here." He worried, too, about the general's preoccupation with the enemy capital. When he got back to Washington, he wrote him a memorandum reminding him that "our prime object is the enemy's army in front of us, and is not with, or about, Richmond at all."

That same day Hooker sent a letter to Lincoln laying out his plan for the coming campaign. He intended to divide the Army of the Potomac into two groups and conduct a gigantic pincers movement. The first group would march twenty miles up the Rappahannock, cross at Kelly's Ford, then swing south and east to strike Lee's left flank and rear. The second would bridge the Rappahannock below Fredericksburg and come at the rebels from the opposite direction. Caught between these converging columns, the Army of Northern Virginia would be forced to abandon its fortifications and move out into open country. If it retreated south toward Richmond, both of its flanks would be exposed. If it turned east or west to fight, it could be attacked in front and rear simultaneously. Either way, it would be trapped and crushed. Lincoln telegraphed his approval, and on April 27—three months after taking command—Hooker finally put the Army of the Potomac in motion.

The Union soldiers broke camp feeling, as one New Hampshire enlisted man put it, that they at last "had got a leader who knew what to do and was going to do it." Although the day was warm and humid, they made excellent progress. The upstream attack group hiked northwest to Hartwood Church, midway between Falmouth and Kelly's Ford. The downstream contingent marched in the opposite direction to Franklin's and Fitzhugh's Crossings, a few miles below Fredericksburg.

The next day the upstream group composed of the Eleventh Corps under Major General Oliver O. Howard, the Twelfth Corps under Major General Henry W. Slocum, and the Fifth Corps under George Meade, bridged the Rappahannock at Kelly's Ford and headed south and east toward the Rapidan River. Reaching that swift, high-running stream late on the afternoon of the twenty-ninth, the Federal divisions waded across at Germanna and Ely's Fords, then bivouacked on the opposite bank.

Up at dawn on April 30, the blue column pushed eastward through a region known as the Wilderness, a jungle of scruboak and pine thickets overspread with vines, brambles, and catbriers. In this dense second-growth forest, it was impossible to see more than a few feet in any direction. The Union soldiers set as rapid a pace as possible, wanting to reach open country where they could spread out and unlimber their artillery in case they were attacked.

At about 11 A.M. the vanguard of Meade's corps emerged into a hundred-acre clearing where Orange Turnpike, the narrow dirt-and-gravel trace on which they had been marching eastward, intersected the north-south-running Orange Plank Road. This tract was called Chancellorsville after the Chancellor House, a hulking two-and-a-half-story brick-and-timber building that sat hard by the crossroads. Here, eleven miles west of Fredericksburg, Meade called a halt to give his men a breather and let the corps of Slocum and Howard catch up. The pause also gave him time to ponder Hooker's plan, the full details of which had been kept secret as a security measure. The more he thought about it, the more enthusiastic he became. By 2 P.M., when Slocum arrived, he was positively giddy. "This is splendid!" he called out as the saddle-weary general climbed down from his horse in the front yard of the Chancellor House. "Hurrah for old Joe! We're on Lee's flank, and he doesn't know it." He suggested they press their advantage immediately, but Slocum brought him up short: he had just received a dispatch from Hooker ordering that no further advance be made until the next day. Confused and a little let down, Meade busied himself setting up a picket line and getting the rest of his troops into camp. Slocum and Howard did the same, and by late afternoon the grassy clearing was covered by a sea of shelter halves.

Just before sunset a loud huzzah went up as Hooker, escorted by his staff and a gaggle of newspaper reporters, galloped into the perimeter on his white stallion. He dismounted with a flourish and entered the Chancellor House to confer with his subordinates. The Union advance along the Orange Turnpike had forced the rebels to abandon U.S. Ford on the Rappahannock, he told his subordinates. Darius Couch's Second Corps and Major General Daniel E. Sickles's Third Corps had been ordered to cross at that point and rendezvous with the Fifth, Eleventh, and Twelfth Corps at Chancellorsville. When they arrived, sometime on the morning of May 1, the upstream attack group would number close to 72,000 men.

The news from the downstream group—47,000 soldiers under the command of Major General John Sedgwick—was also good: it had successfully bridged the Rappahannock below Fredericksburg. The Army of Northern Virginia was now caught between two powerful Union forces. If all went according to plan, tomorrow would be its day of reckoning. "I have Lee in one hand, and Richmond in the other!" Hooker announced with undisguised exultation. "The rebel army is now the legitimate property of the Army of the Potomac!"

He was so sure of complete success that he drafted a congratulatory order, which was read to all the troops before they bedded down for the
night: "It is with heartfelt satisfaction the commanding general announces
to the army that the operations of the last three days have determined that
our enemy must either ingloriously fly, or come out from behind his defenses and give us battle on our own ground, where certain destruction
awaits him."

The men cheered wildly when they heard this.

Awakened by the crackle of gunfire early on the morning of April 29,
Lee hastened to join Stonewall Jackson at a blufftop observation post
a mile south of Fredericksburg. Spruce as always in a well-tailored gray
uniform, he studied Sedgwick's bridgehead through his field glasses. Federal units were spilling like a cerulean flood onto the broad plain below.
They showed no signs of girding for an immediate attack, so he told Jackson to post his four divisions on the high ground a mile back from the river
pending further orders. Returning to his headquarters, he alerted Richmond to what was happening, asked that Longstreet's divisions be recalled
(they would not arrive in time to play a part in the battle), then sat down
on a camp stool to await further developments.

A short time later a message was received from Major General J.E.B.
Stuart, head of the Confederate cavalry corps. It confirmed an earlier report
that Yankee infantry had crossed at Kelly's Ford and was marching south toward the Rapidan. The gray horsemen had been able to identify three Federal infantry corps, but could not say for certain where they were going. By
late afternoon the picture was clearer: according to the scouts, the enemy
column was now across the Rapidan and heading toward Fredericksburg. In
response, Lee ordered Major General Richard Anderson's division to march
five miles west and occupy a good defensive position straddling the road between Chancellorsville and Fredericksburg. He decided not to shift any
other troops until he was sure what Hooker was up to.

On the morning of April 30, Lee and Jackson surveyed Sedgwick's
bridgehead again with an eye toward attacking it. The terrain looked un-
favorable to Lee, but he deferred to his subordinate's judgment, telling him
to study the problem thoroughly and make a recommendation. Jackson
spent the rest of the morning and a good part of the afternoon examining
the ground the Yankees occupied. He reluctantly concluded that his superior was right—it would be too dangerous to move against the enemy here.
By then further intelligence detailing the Federal concentration at Chancellorsville had convinced Lee that Sedgwick's cross-river foray was a bluff,

and that the main enemy attack was going to come from the west. Having arrived at this conclusion, he acted. One division under Major General Jubal Early would stay behind to defend the Fredericksburg heights; Jackson would take the other three—approximately 40,000 troops—and march toward Chancellorsville at first light on May 1. "Make arrangements to repulse the enemy," Lee's orders read. To the ever-aggressive Stonewall that meant one thing: attack.

M ay 1 dawned gray and clammy. A fine mist soaked the tents in the clearing around the Orange Turnpike–Orange Plank Road intersection and dripped off the dark red bricks and white wood columns of the Chancellor House. The low-lying clouds began to lift at seven. By nine o'clock they were gone, and it had turned into a warm, dry day, perfect for fighting a battle that many in the Federal bivouac believed would result in the destruction of the Army of Northern Virginia.

The soldiers were eager to shoulder their packs and be off, but so far no word had come from headquarters, which was peculiar, because in this campaign it had been standard procedure for Hooker to issue each day's marching orders the night before. On the evening of the thirtieth he had issued his high-flown congratulatory message and nothing else. It was an omission that caused considerable head-shaking among the officers gathered in the parlor of the Chancellor House. They remarked that the commander seemed more subdued than usual. He was distracted and distant, and although his explanation for the delay was reasonable enough—he was waiting for the arrival of Sickles's corps, which was still en route from U.S. Ford—there was an unmistakable air of hesitancy about him. Some whispered that he had had too much whiskey last night and was badly hung over. Others, knowing that he had pledged to abstain from alcohol for the duration of the campaign, suspected the reverse was true: he had dried out too quickly and needed a drink to rekindle his aggressiveness.

Whatever the source of his problem, Hooker finally got the army moving at eleven o'clock. Meade, Slocum, and Howard took the lead, pushing their corps east toward the day's first objective, Tabernacle Church. When they reached it, they would be out of the Wilderness and on open ground where the enormous Federal advantage in manpower and artillery could be fully exploited. After the rest of the army came up, the entire force would roll toward Fredericksburg and smash the Army of Northern Virginia. It was a spine-tingling scenario, and the soldiers whooped and hollered as they started forward along the Turnpike, Plank, and River Roads, sure that they were going to make history today.

At almost exactly the same moment, some four miles to the east, Stonewall Jackson was ordering his troops to advance toward Chancellorsville.

The popping of musket fire, followed by the crash of bursting shells, signaled the collision of the two armies. The Federal columns recoiled in surprise, then steadied. They were preparing to push ahead and overpower the smaller Confederate force when without warning new orders arrived from Hooker: Break off the fight and retreat to Chancellorsville.

The corps commanders could not believe it. "You are a damned liar!" Henry Slocum shouted at the courier who brought him the message. "Nobody but a crazy man would give such an order when we have victory in sight!"

Darius Couch, who had ridden to the front the moment the shooting began, was sure it was a mistake. He sent an aide galloping back to headquarters to tell Hooker that the army was poised to drive the rebels all the way back to Fredericksburg. Hooker was adamant, however. The blue formations were to return to Chancellorsville and start digging in.

Baffled by this sudden about-face, the Union troops trudged back the way they had come. Jubilant but wary, the Confederates followed them, advancing cautiously lest the retreat prove to be a trick. Hooker intended no subterfuge. Jackson's approach had rattled him. He had decided that it would be wiser to fight a defensive battle than to risk an attack. "It is all right," he told his incredulous subordinates when they checked in with him at the Chancellor House later that afternoon. "I have got Lee just where I want him; he must fight me on my own ground."

His listeners were dismayed. As far as they were concerned, Hooker had lost his nerve just when resolute boldness was most called for. "[To] hear from his own lips that the advantages gained by the successful marches of his lieutenants were to culminate in fighting a defensive battle in that nest of thickets was too much," Couch wrote. "I retired from his presence with the belief that my commanding general was a whipped man."

That evening Lee and Jackson met on the Plank Road a mile southeast of Chancellorsville. As they exchanged greetings in the violet twilight, a Yankee sniper fired at them from a treetop perch. They dismounted and stepped into the woods beside the road, where they could not be so easily seen. Sitting side by side on a fallen log, they discussed the day's events and talked about what should be done tomorrow. Both men agreed that they should continue to press Hooker, but how and where was a puzzle.

The answer to their dilemma came in the form of a message from Jeb Stuart. Hooker's right flank was "in the air," the cavalryman reported; it came to an abrupt end on the Orange Turnpike about two miles east of Germanna Ford. Unprotected by any natural obstacle, it was wide open to an attack.

Lee immediately unrolled a sketch map of the region and spread it in his lap. "How can we get at those people?" he muttered as he studied it. Beside him Jackson was practically twitching with excitement. "You know best," he replied. "Show me what to do, and we will try to do it." Finally Lee's forefinger came down and touched the map, tracing a line across the front of the Federal army and around to its right rear. "General Stuart will cover your movement with his cavalry," he said matter-of-factly. Jackson jumped to his feet and saluted. "My troops will move at four o'clock," he snapped. Then he hurried off to make the necessary arrangements while Lee lay down at the foot of a tree and went to sleep.

Dawn's gray-white glow was spreading across the eastern sky when the Confederate commander awoke. He got up and joined Jackson, who was sitting on an empty hardtack box, warming his hands in front of a fire. Together they listened to the report of Major Jedediah Hotchkiss, Jackson's chief topographical engineer. Hotchkiss had spent the early morning hours gathering information about the roads running through the Wilderness.

The generals wanted to know if there was a route that would permit large numbers of troops and artillery to approach Hooker's right flank unobserved. The engineer replied that there was. From their present position a wagon trace ran southwest past an iron forge called Catharine Furnace and intersected the Brock Road. The Brock Road angled northwest until it struck the Orange Turnpike about a mile and a half beyond where the Union line ended. The twelve-mile-long route was concealed for much of its length by thick forest.

When Hotchkiss had finished, Lee spoke: "General Jackson, what do you propose to do?"

"Go around here," said Jackson, tracing the route Hotchkiss had just described on his map.

"What do you propose to make the movement with?"

"With my whole corps."

"What will you leave me?"

"The divisions of Anderson and McLaws."

There was a moment of silence while Lee digested this. The Army of Northern Virginia had been divided once. Now Jackson was suggesting that it be divided again. If Hooker discovered what was going on, he could easily use his overwhelming numerical superiority to crush the rebel detachments in turn. If, on the other hand, the strategy worked, the undermanned Confederates might surprise and destroy the Army of the Potomac. The risk was enormous, but so was the potential reward. Lee's decision was quick and unhesitating. "Well," he said, looking his lieutenant in the eye, "go on."

General Thomas J. Jackson,
C.S.A. (National Archives;
photo courtesy of The
Museum of the Confederacy,
Richmond, Virginia)

It was 7:30 A.M., three and a half hours later than promised, when Jackson's column started toward Catharine Furnace. The sun was all the way up, and the day promised to be a hot one. The troops marched four abreast along a narrow dirt path that wound through a forest of pine and blackjack oak, moving at a steady route step—about two and a half miles per hour. Many of them were hungry, having missed breakfast in their hurry to pack up and hit the road, but they were in high spirits nevertheless. They guessed what their commander was up to and approved of it wholeheartedly. "Tell Old Jack we're all a-comin'," they called out to passing officers. "Don't let him begin the fuss until we get there!"

Old Jack was riding with the vanguard, his eyes hidden beneath the bill of his pulled-down forage cap, his left arm raised in the odd gesture that was so characteristic of him. When he spoke, his words were brief and to the point: "See that the column is kept closed! Permit no straggling. Press on, press on!"

Like Lee, Hooker had risen at daybreak. He gulped a quick cup of coffee, then saddled up and set out with his staff to inspect the line his army had occupied the previous evening. It began on a wooded ridge overlooking the Rappahannock, ran southwest to Chancellorsville, then continued northwest along the Orange Turnpike until it came to an abrupt end in a tangle of underbrush a mile past Dowdall's Tavern and the Wilderness Church. Meade's corps held the left, from the river down to Chancellorsville; the corps of Couch, Slocum, and Sickles manned the horseshoe curve at the center of the line; and Howard's corps was deployed on the right, along the southern shoulder of the turnpike. It looked like an impregnable position, and Hooker told the officers accompanying him that he hoped Lee would be foolhardy enough to assault it. "How strong, how strong!" he exclaimed as he examined the trenches, rifle pits, and breastworks the troops had constructed during the night. The soldiers responded by waving their caps and cheering as he rode by.

Returning to the Chancellor House at nine o'clock, Hooker received an urgent message from a division commander in Sickles's corps. Lookouts posted in the treetops had spotted a large rebel column moving south across

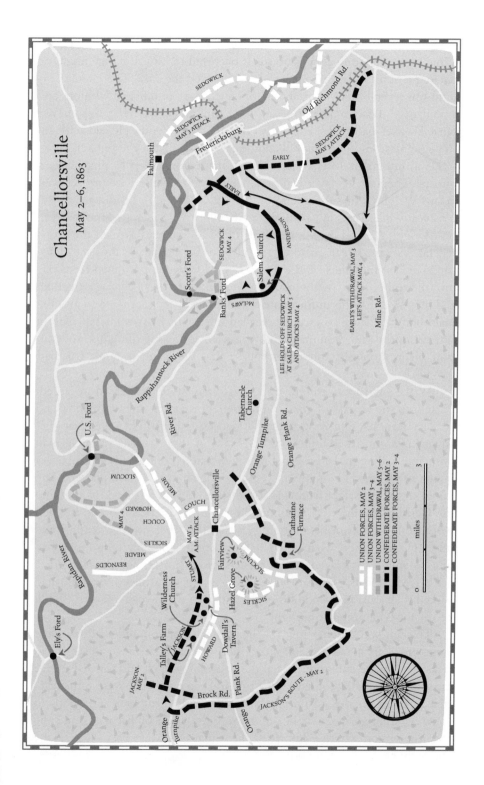

Chancellorsville
May 2–6, 1863

Falmouth

SEDGWICK

SEDGWICK
MAY 3 ATTACK

Fredericksburg

Old Richmond Rd.

SEDGWICK
MAY 3 ATTACK

EARLY

EARLY

ANDERSON

SEDGWICK
MAY 4

Salem Church

McLAWS

Banks' Ford

Scott's Ford

EARLY'S WITHDRAWAL, MAY 3
LEE'S ATTACK MAY, 4

Mine Rd.

LEE HOLDS OFF SEDGWICK
AT SALEM CHURCH MAY 3
AND ATTACKS MAY 4

Rappahannock River

River Rd.

U.S. Ford

SLOCUM

MEADE

HOWARD
MAY 4

COUCH

Tabernacle
Church

Orange Turnpike

Orange Plank Rd.

Rapidan River

REYNOLDS

MEADE

SICKLES

COUCH

STUART
MAY 3,
A.M. ATTACK

Chancellorsville

Catharine
Furnace

Ely's Ford

Wilderness
Church

Talley's Farm

JACKSON

HOWARD

Dowdall's
Tavern

Fairview

Hazel Grove

SLOCUM

SICKLES

JACKSON
MAY 2

Orange
Turnpike

Brock Rd.

Orange Plank Rd.

JACKSON'S ROUTE, MAY 2

UNION FORCES, MAY 2
UNION FORCES, MAY 3–4
UNION WITHDRAWAL, MAY 5–6
CONFEDERATE FORCES, MAY 2
CONFEDERATE FORCES, MAY 3–4

0   miles   3

the Union front. Puzzled, Hooker studied a map of the Wilderness region. What were the Confederates up to? It occurred to him that they might be circling around his right, but he soon dismissed the idea. The enemy column was several miles long, and it contained large numbers of wagons and ambulances. This could mean only one thing: Lee was retreating. It was what Hooker had expected him to do all along. Highly pleased with his strategic prescience, he ignored additional reports that suggested a flank attack was imminent. Instead he told his corps commanders to prepare for a pursuit. Then he sent word to Sedgwick to seize Fredericksburg without delay. "We know that the enemy is fleeing," he wrote in his dispatch.

Meanwhile, Jackson's men were moving ever closer to Hooker's exposed right. Around 3 P.M., elements of Sickles's corps assailed the Confederate column's rear guard in the vicinity of Catharine Furnace. They captured 300 members of the Twenty-third Georgia, but failed to recognize the real purpose of the march. "We had heard that Lee was retreating, and supposed that this unfortunate regiment had been sacrificed to give the main body a chance to escape," recalled one of Sickles's soldiers. "One of [the prisoners] said, 'You may think you have done a big thing just now, but wait till Jackson gets round on your right.' We laughed at his harmless bravado."

As the afternoon passed, other warnings were blithely disregarded. Pickets on the far end of the Union line reported that enemy infantry and artillery were massing west of the Wilderness Church. They could not get anyone in authority to listen to them. Many of these sentries were German immigrants; they spoke broken English and were considered unreliable—a bunch of damned "Dutchmen"—by the higher-ups at headquarters. The forest beyond the right flank was too thick to permit an attack of the kind the Germans thought was coming, these officers told each other. Besides, word from the Chancellor House was that the rebels were retreating, and surely Hooker knew what he was talking about. The prevailing mood was one of smug complacency. "Unharness those horses, boys, give them a good feed of oats," Howard called to a group of artillerymen who had parked their caisson outside his command post at Dowdall's Tavern. "We'll be off for Richmond at daylight."

The sun was dipping low on the western horizon and shadows were lengthening in the woods on either side of the Orange Turnpike when Jackson's Confederates completed their flanking march and formed up for the assault. They did not have to be told to keep quiet. The sounds that carried to them on the warm, pine-scented breeze—laughter and scraps of conversation, the clatter of horses' hooves, the jingle of harnesses, and the creak of wagon wheels—informed them that they were very close to the enemy line.

Jackson stood by the roadside, watching intently as his troops moved into position. He had directed them to form three lines perpendicular to the turnpike and extending a mile into the forest on either side of it. This would allow them to envelop any strongpoint they encountered without sacrificing forward momentum. Brigadier General Robert Rodes's division was in front, Brigadier General Raleigh Colston's came next, and Major General A. P. Hill's brought up the rear. Talley's farm, located on a rise overlooking the clearing where Dowdall's Tavern and the Wilderness Church were located, was the first objective. Jackson made it clear to his subordinates that they were not to stop there, however. He wanted them to keep going as hard and fast as they could, driving the Yankees all the way back to the Rappahannock. Their mission was not just to defeat Hooker's army but to annihilate it.

When he had finished going over his instructions, he pulled out his pocket watch. It was 5:15 P.M.; the sun would set at 6:48; it would be completely dark by 7:30. He did not say so, but his division commanders understood that they had been presented with a unique opportunity—the kind that professional soldiers dream of but almost never see. What they did in the next few hours could well decide the war in the Confederacy's favor.

"Are you ready, General Rodes?" Jackson asked.

"Yes sir!" Rodes replied.

"You can go forward, then."

Just ahead of the massed gray formations, screened by a tangle of underbrush, lay the Union right flank. It was anchored by two regiments of infantry numbering barely 900 men. These soldiers had stacked their muskets and were lounging about waiting to eat supper. Suddenly a herd of deer burst from the timber and bounded through their camp, followed by a flock of scampering rabbits and squirrels. Before the startled Federals could make sense of this strange animal behavior, they heard the high-pitched screech of the rebel yell and saw the lead rank of Confederates bearing down on them. A few men drew their sidearms and fired, but organized resistance was impossible: there simply was not enough time to react. "So sudden was our appearance among them that they did not even rise from over their steaming suppers," recalled one of the attackers; they "surrendered seated or half-bent, in speechless wonderment."

In a flash this first position was overrun, starting a chain reaction that rippled down the turnpike toward Chancellorsville. Companies, regiments, and entire brigades collapsed like tipped-over dominoes. By the thousands

Union infantrymen dropped their weapons and took to their heels. A few small units tried to make a stand, but it was hopeless; the Confederate onslaught was too powerful. Near Dowdall's Tavern, Howard and his staff formed a human chain across the turnpike. They brandished their pistols and swords and threatened to shoot or stab anyone who refused to stop and fight. For a moment the mob paused. But then, wrote John Collins of the Eighth Pennsylvania Cavalry, "a fresh mass of fugitives in blue filled the road," the "pressure became greater upon the line that blocked the way," and "the seething, surging sea of humanity broke over the feeble barrier."

Flushed with excitement, Jackson rode just behind the gray assault wave. A subordinate cried out: "General, they are running too fast for us. We can't keep up with them!"

Jackson was having none of it: "They never run too fast for me, sir," he shouted. "Press them, press them!"

A mile and a half to the east Hooker was chatting with his aides on the porch of the Chancellor House. He was blissfully ignorant of the cataclysm that had engulfed his right flank. Some strange acoustical effect kept the sound of battle from reaching his ears, and no courier came to tell him what was happening.

Finally the breeze shifted and the rumble of gunfire became audible. Captain Harry Russell raised his field glasses, looked up the turnpike, and jumped as if jolted by an electric shock. "My God," he shouted, "here they come!" A moment later "a confused roaring sound seemed to penetrate the air, ominous and alarming." Then "a curious sight met the eye, for all the world like a stampede of cattle, a multitude of yelling struggling [soldiers] . . . panting for breath, their faces distorted by fear."

Hooker blanched like a man who had seen a ghost. Running to his tethered horse, he vaulted into the saddle and galloped up the road to try to check the retreat. When that effort failed, he rode over to Major General Hiram Berry, commander of a division bivouacked nearby, and ordered him to throw his men into the breach. "Receive the enemy on your bayonets!" he cried, then raced away to find additional reinforcements.

It was now past seven o'clock, and the Confederate assault was running out of steam. The headlong charge through the thickets had caused the attack formations to fragment. Companies and regiments were hopelessly intermingled, and officers were having trouble maintaining tactical control. Fatigue was also a factor. The soldiers had been marching and fighting for more than twelve hours. They desperately needed water, food, and rest. Jackson had no intention of calling a halt, however. He knew the Yankee army would be finished if he could break through to the Rappahannock. He told A. P. Hill to bring up his division, which was still relatively fresh, while he rode ahead with several of his staff officers to scout the enemy position.

The woods were dark, and it was impossible to distinguish friend from foe. Small groups of men were blundering about, blazing away at any suspicious sound or unexplained movement. Union cannon at Hazel Grove and Fairview, two hilltop clearings southwest of Chancellorsville, were firing salvos down the turnpike in the direction of the Confederate advance. Shrapnel shattered branches and shredded leaves. The screams of the wounded filled the air. Fires kindled by red-hot shell fragments crackled in the underbrush.

Into this perilous no-man's-land rode Jackson and his staff, groping their way toward the Union line. "General, don't you think this is the wrong place for you?" asked a nervous adjutant.

"The danger is all over—the enemy is routed!" Jackson replied. "Go back and tell A. P. Hill to press right on!"

Moments later he and his party stumbled into a squad of North Carolina soldiers crouched in the bushes awaiting the order to attack. The North Carolinians mistook the figures on horseback for Union cavalrymen. They jumped up and unleashed a volley. "Cease firing, cease firing!" one of the staff officers frantically shouted. "You are firing into your own men!"

"Who gave that order?" a voice bawled back. "It's a lie! Pour it into them, boys!"

Another fusillade tore through the woods. This time Jackson was hit. One ball struck the palm of his right hand, another splintered his left forearm and wrist, a third smashed his left shoulder. Bleeding profusely, faint with pain, he was helped off his horse by two of his aides. A tourniquet was tied around the most serious wound, and he was half carried, half dragged to the rear. By the time he was delivered to the Confederate field hospital at Wilderness Tavern, a mile from where the bullets had struck him, he was in shock. "His hands were cold, his skin clammy, his face pale, and his lips compressed and bloodless," wrote Dr. Hunter McGuire, the corps medical director. Chloroform was administered, and the mangled left arm was amputated.

About an hour after the surgery, just as Jackson was regaining consciousness, an officer arrived from the front with urgent news: A. P. Hill, who had taken command when Jackson was carried from the field, had been struck in the leg by a shell fragment. Jeb Stuart was now in charge. He was unfamiliar with the situation around Chancellorsville and wanted Jackson to tell him what to do.

Contracting his brow, Stonewall wracked his anesthesia-fogged brain for an answer. "For a moment," Dr. McGuire wrote, "it was believed he had succeeded, for his nostrils dilated and his eye flashed its old fire, but it was only for a moment; his face relaxed again, and presently he answered very feebly and sadly, 'I don't know—I can't tell; say to General Stuart he must do what he thinks best.' "

The Union army spent the rest of the night regrouping in anticipation of renewed fighting on May 3. Slocum's and Couch's corps ringed Chancellorsville. Sickles's command defended a southwestward-jutting salient, which encompassed the high ground at Hazel Grove and Fairview. To the north the remainder of Hooker's force manned a V-shaped fallback position, with its point touching the top of the Chancellorsville line and its flanks extending back several miles to protect U.S. Ford.

Despite the debacle of the previous evening, the Federals were far from defeated. Situated squarely between the two wings of the Confederate army, with a huge numerical advantage over both, they were in an excellent position to launch a counterstroke. "It only required that Hooker should brace himself up to take a reasonable, common-sense view of the state of things," wrote Darius Couch, who was itching to make just such an attack.

But Hooker could not brace himself up. He was dazed, lethargic, demoralized. "I think that his being outgeneraled by Lee had a good deal to do with [it]," Couch observed. He also suspected that alcohol withdrawal was partly responsible for Hooker's loss of nerve. "I have always stated that he probably abstained from the use of ardent spirits when it would have been far better for him to have continued in his usual habit," he wrote.

Whatever the reason, Hooker was in a funk on the morning of May 3, and Lee was ready to take advantage. After learning that both Jackson and Hill had been knocked out of action, he sent a message to Stuart ordering him to advance at first light in an effort to unite the army and capture Chancellorsville.

Stuart sent his lead division forward at 5:30 A.M., starting a fight that veterans on both sides said was the deadliest they had ever seen. The Confederates charged, retreated, and charged again, trying desperately to break through to the Chancellorsville crossroads. The Federals stood their ground, firing from behind log barricades they had built the night before. Rookie outfits like the 123rd New York (also known as the Washington County Regiment) fought splendidly, inflicting heavy casualties on the onrushing enemy.

Stuart's troops eventually gained the upper hand thanks to an egregious tactical blunder by Hooker. A few minutes before the battle began, he ordered Sickles to evacuate Hazel Grove. The Confederates occupied the elevated clearing, wheeled thirty-six cannons to its crest, and opened fire on Fairview, twelve hundred yards to the northeast. They also bombarded the breastworks blocking Stuart's advance and the Federal wagon park in the Chancellorsville clearing.

Hooker was standing on the Chancellor House porch at 9 A.M. when a solid shot struck a pillar next to him. A heavy piece of wood crashed down on his head, knocking him unconscious. When he came to, several minutes later, he mounted his horse and tried to ride to the rear, but he was too dizzy to go far. An aide helped him from the saddle, spread a blanket for him to sit on, and gave him a stiff shot of brandy, which revived him considerably. He staggered to his feet and remounted just as a cannonball hurtled out of the sky and slammed into the blanket, turning it into a wad of smoking pulp. Other shells struck the roof of the Chancellor House just behind him, setting it on fire. The wounded men inside—amputees mostly—were dragged out and placed in rows in the yard. Many of them were subsequently killed by shrapnel as they lay helpless on the ground.

Hooker, meanwhile, had been taken to a tent half a mile north of Chancellorsville. He was suffering from a concussion (and from the mind-numbing effects of several more slugs of medicinal brandy). But he refused to turn command over to one of his subordinates. Instead he ordered the army to withdraw toward the Rappahannock. Then he passed out on a cot.

As the Union soldiers broke off the fight and retreated toward the river, the Confederates swarmed forward and captured Chancellorsville. Lee galloped into the clearing a few minutes later and was greeted with a wild ovation. It was, wrote Major Charles Marshall, one long, unbroken cheer that "rose high above the roar of battle, and hailed the presence of the victorious chief. He sat in the full realization of all that soldiers dream of—triumph; and as I looked upon him . . . I thought that it must have been from such a scene that men in ancient times rose to the dignity of gods."

Lee did not stop to savor the moment. He gave his weary regiments a few minutes' rest, then ordered them to re-form. He meant to resume the attack and hurl Hooker into the Rappahannock. Just as he was about to signal for the advance to begin, a courier galloped up with news from Fredericksburg: Sedgwick's Federals had overwhelmed Early's division and were moving west toward Chancellorsville, menacing the Confederate rear.

For the third time in as many days, Lee was forced to divide his army. He sent Lafayette McLaws and 7,000 men east to intercept Sedgwick while he and the rest of his command remained at Chancellorsville to keep an eye on Hooker. McLaws's soldiers marched rapidly down the Plank Road to Salem Church, a small, redbrick building situated on a wooded ridge four miles west of Fredericksburg. There they joined Brigadier General Cadmus Wilcox's brigade, which had been conducting an afternoon-long delaying action against Sedgwick's corps.

Shortly after 5 P.M., the head of the Yankee column struck the rebel position at Salem Church. "A tremendous roar of musketry met us from the unseen enemy posted behind a fence and a ditch," a Federal soldier wrote of this action. "Men tumbled from our ranks dead, and others fell helpless with wounds." Before a second assault could be mounted, darkness fell.

On the morning of May 4, Lee made another bold decision: he would concentrate his efforts on destroying Sedgwick's detachment, gambling that Hooker would not budge from his V-shaped defensive position. He ordered Richard Anderson to pull his division out of the Chancellorsville line and march to join McLaws at Salem Church. Jubal Early, who had rallied his troops four miles south of Fredericksburg on the afternoon of the third, was directed to retake the town, then link up with McLaws and Anderson for a combined assault on Sedgwick. Once Sedgwick's command had been crushed, the army would reunite at Chancellorsville and deliver the coup de grâce to Hooker.

The strategy was vintage Lee—a swift thrust in an unexpected direction. It might have succeeded if his soldiers had been better rested. But four days of combat had taken its toll. Officers and men were exhausted. They moved slowly, made poor decisions, got lost, failed to execute their assignments. As a result the attack began hours late, was poorly coordinated, and fizzled out after only forty-five minutes. It was enough to alarm Sedgwick, however. He ordered his troops to retreat north to Banks's and Scott's Fords on the Rappahannock, where they could make a quick getaway should the need arise. Then he sent a series of anxious messages to Hooker asking for guidance.

"Look to the safety of your corps," came the reply. At 2 A.M. on May 5, Sedgwick did exactly that, ordering his men to cross the river and pull up the pontoon bridges behind them. By 5 A.M. they were all gone. The threat to the Confederate rear had been removed. Lee could concentrate on bagging Hooker.

But Hooker was not going to stay put. At midnight he convened a council of war to discuss the subject of withdrawal. It was immediately apparent to the generals who crowded into his tent that all the aggressiveness had gone out of him. He looked pale, shrunken, and tremulous, and when he spoke, there was no doubt what was uppermost in his mind. "[He] stated that his instructions compelled him to cover Washington, not to jeopardize the army, etc.," recalled a disgusted Darius Couch. "It was seen by the most casual observer that he had made up his mind to retreat." After presenting his views, Hooker polled the corps commanders present. A majority— three out of five—wanted to go on fighting. The Federal force north of Chancellorsville still outnumbered the rebels two to one; it should attack, not fall back, they argued.

Hooker wasn't listening. When the vote was over, he announced that he was ordering the army to retire to the other side of the river. "What was the use of calling us together at this time of night when he intended to re- treat anyhow?" one of the officers snarled as he left the tent. Hooker pre- tended not to hear. He collapsed on his cot, returning to the near-comatose state he had been in ever since his close call on the Chancellor House porch. He would be among the first to cross the Rappahannock on the morning of the fifth, leaving the task of conducting the withdrawal to his disgruntled corps commanders.

They did the job professionally, if not enthusiastically, moving the army back under cover of a heavy rainstorm. By May 6 the crossing was com- plete. The weary troops plodded back to their old camps at Falmouth, wondering how a campaign that had started so well could end so igno- miniously. The answer, they decided, was a catastrophic failure of leader- ship. They had placed their trust in Joe Hooker, and he had let them down. "The commander of our army gained his position by merely brag and blow, and when the time came to show himself, he was found without the qualities necessary for a general," one soldier sadly concluded.

Noah Brooks was at the White House on May 6 when Lincoln got word that the Army of the Potomac was retreating. "Had a thunder- bolt fallen upon [him] he could not have been more overwhelmed," the correspondent wrote. "He held a telegram in his hand, and . . . his face, usually sallow, was ashen in hue. . . . Never, so long as I knew him, did he seem to be so broken, so dispirited, and so ghostlike. Clasping his hands be- hind his back, he walked up and down the room, saying, 'My God! My God! What will the country say! What will the country say!' "

In Richmond the news from Chancellorsville was cause for rejoicing. Jef- ferson Davis rose from his sickbed on May 7 to pay tribute to the Army of Northern Virginia and to give "praise to God for the success with which He has crowned our arms."

Lee was in no mood for celebrating, however. He had failed to destroy the Army of the Potomac. Worse, he had suffered grievous losses. Of the 60,892 Confederate soldiers present for duty when the fighting began, 12,821 were reported killed, wounded, or missing—22 percent of the army's strength. The Federals had suffered 17,287 casualties—13 percent of their before-battle total of 133,868. The message in these statistics was clear: a few more victories like Chancellorsville, and the Army of Northern Virginia would cease to exist as a fighting force.

Lee was also deeply concerned about the health of Stonewall Jackson. On May 4, while the battle was still raging, the wounded general had been taken by ambulance to Guiney Station, twelve miles south of Fredericksburg. It was expected he would stay there a few days regaining his strength before journeying on to Richmond for further treatment. But instead of recuperating, he had taken a turn for the worse. Now, despite heroic efforts by a team of physicians headed by Hunter McGuire, he was declining rapidly.

"Surely, General Jackson must recover," Lee said when he was told that his most trusted lieutenant was failing. "God will not take him from us."

But Jackson continued to slip, and on Sunday, May 10, McGuire told Mrs. Jackson that her husband would not live out the day. "Doctor," the mortally ill soldier said during a brief moment of lucidity, "Anna informs me that you have told her that I am to die today; is it so?" When McGuire nodded his head yes, the general meditated briefly, then said, "Very good; very good; it is all right. It is the Lord's day; my wish is fulfilled. I have always desired to die on Sunday."

Shortly after 3 P.M., with his wife and baby daughter in attendance, Jackson passed away. McGuire was also present, and he wrote of the scene: "A few moments before he died he cried out in his delirium, 'Order A. P. Hill to prepare for action! Pass the infantry to the front rapidly! Tell Major Hawks'—then stopped, leaving the sentence unfinished. Presently a smile of ineffable sweetness spread itself over his pale face, and he said quietly, and with an expression, as if of relief, 'Let us cross over the river, and rest under the shade of the trees.' "

NINE

To the Gates
of Vicksburg

Stonewall Jackson had crossed his river and Ulysses S. Grant had crossed his—calamitous events for the Confederacy, though just how calamitous would not become apparent for several months yet. Jackson's death was mourned throughout the South as a terrible tragedy, but its devastating impact on Confederate military operations would not be felt until the Army of Northern Virginia went into action again. Nor would the dire consequences of Grant's move across the Mississippi be completely understood until his campaign against Vicksburg unfolded more fully. For now they were setbacks of uncertain magnitude, and it was still possible for Southerners to minimize their importance and insist that all would be well.

Had these optimists known how disorganized and strife-torn Southern leadership was at the beginning of May, they would have felt far less secure. The trouble began in Richmond, where Jefferson Davis was desperately ill. His neuralgia had grown so bad in recent weeks that the doctors attending him feared he might lose the sight in his one good eye. Much of the time he was flat on his back in bed, barely able to move or speak. He certainly was in no condition to analyze military developments, much less devise a coherent strategy for dealing with them. Yet he refused to delegate authority to his aides and continued to make all the key decisions himself, single-handedly running the war from his darkened sickroom.

As for the Confederacy's top generals, they seemed more interested in quarreling with one another than fighting the enemy. In the East, Lee and Longstreet were at odds over how the Army of Northern Virginia should be deployed in the aftermath of Chancellorsville. Longstreet believed the Rappahannock line was secure for the time being, and he proposed detaching two divisions (his own) and sending them to Tullahoma to reinforce Bragg for an attack against Rosecrans. Lee objected strongly to this plan. Hooker could resume his offensive at any time, he pointed out, and while it was true he had whipped the Army of the Potomac without Longstreet's divisions, he needed them now to ensure Richmond's safety.

In Tennessee the long-simmering paper war between Bragg and his subordinates had boiled over once again. Bragg had sent out a circular letter in mid-April charging one of his corps commanders with disobedience and demanding to know which of his other generals supported him. Most of the addressees had refused to answer, a disobedient act in itself. Several had openly backed the accused, maintaining that he could destroy Bragg if push came to shove. Cooler heads called for an end to this quarrel, but the principals refused to back down, and the upshot was that nearly every high-ranking officer in the Army of Tennessee was busy accumulating evidence in anticipation of a court-martial, even as military matters languished and Rosecrans continued his threatening troop-and-supply buildup around Murfreesboro.

Disgraceful as this bickering was, it paled in comparison to the mess in Mississippi, where friction between Johnston and Pemberton was placing Vicksburg, and by extension the entire western half of the Confederacy, in peril. Johnston "receives no intelligence from General Pemberton, who ignores his authority, is mortified at his command over him, and receives his suggestions with coldness or opposition," a War Department inspector wrote. That discouraging report had been submitted in April, before the crisis brought on by the Union landing at Bruinsburg. Now with Johnston pressing Pemberton to move out of Vicksburg, and Davis telling him that he must hold the place at all hazards, the paralysis of Confederate command in the West was nearly complete.

While Pemberton was being tugged back and forth by the conflicting dispatches from Johnston and Davis, Grant was wasting no time. Within hours of getting his army ashore at Bruinsburg, he was pushing inland. He defeated Bowen's Confederates in a short, sharp battle at Port Gibson on May 1, then advanced rapidly to the northeast, expanding and consolidating his beachhead. Two days after the Port Gibson victory, he sent a message to Sherman at Milliken's Bend, ordering him to bring two of his three divisions and 120 wagons filled with bacon, coffee, and hardtack across the river to join the main body. "The enemy is badly beaten, greatly demoralized, and exhausted of ammunition," his letter read. "The road to Vicksburg is open. All we want now are men, ammunition, and hard bread. We can subsist our horses on the country, and obtain considerable supplies for our troops."

This last statement signaled an abrupt change of plan. For weeks Washington had been urging Grant to cooperate with Nathaniel Banks's Army of the Gulf, which had moved upriver from New Orleans to Baton Rouge in early March. Deferring to this advice, Grant had resolved to send a corps downstream to help Banks capture Port Hudson, the complex of redoubts, trenches, and rifle pits that formed the southern anchor of the Confederates' Mississippi River defenses. Once that strongpoint had been captured and a supply line established between New Orleans and Grand Gulf, the campaign against Vicksburg would proceed.

But on May 3 Grant learned that the Army of the Gulf had embarked on an expedition up Louisiana's Red River and would not return to the Port Hudson area for several weeks. He immediately decided to forget about Banks and strike out on his own. "To wait for his cooperation would have detained me at least a month," he later explained. Under present circumstances a delay of even a few days was unacceptable to him. His soldier's intuition told him that this was the decisive moment. In the wake of the Grierson Raid, Sherman's Chickasaw Bluffs feint, and his own cross-river lunge, Pemberton's Confederates were off balance and vulnerable. He did not want to give them time to regroup or receive reinforcements. Nor did he wish to relinquish field command to Banks who, despite (or perhaps because of) his political background, was senior to him in rank. He was well aware that his decision to operate independently would alarm War Department officials, but he also knew there was no way they could stop him if he acted quickly enough.

He did receive some resistance from an unexpected source. Sherman had disapproved of the campaign from the outset; now he protested that the muddy track running from Milliken's Bend to Hard Times was inadequate to serve as a supply line for the whole army. "Stop all troops," he advised his superior, "for this road will be jammed sure as life." He was flabbergasted when Grant replied that the road's condition did not matter. With the exception of hardtack, coffee, and salt, he was counting on the farms of Mississippi to provide his soldiers with all the provisions they needed. What was more, the advancing blue columns were not going to be accompanied by a wagon train, at least not in the formal sense. Immediately after the Bruinsburg landing he had directed his soldiers to start confiscating vehicles from nearby plantations, as well as the horses, mules, and oxen to pull them. This motley collection of carts, carriages, buckboards, and buggies would suffice to haul the army's ammunition and medical supplies, he insisted. He wanted to press onward as swiftly as possible, and he exhorted Sherman to stop fretting and hurry up.

The strategy Grant had settled on was daring, but not without precedent. In 1847, as a youthful second lieutenant, he had accompanied Win-

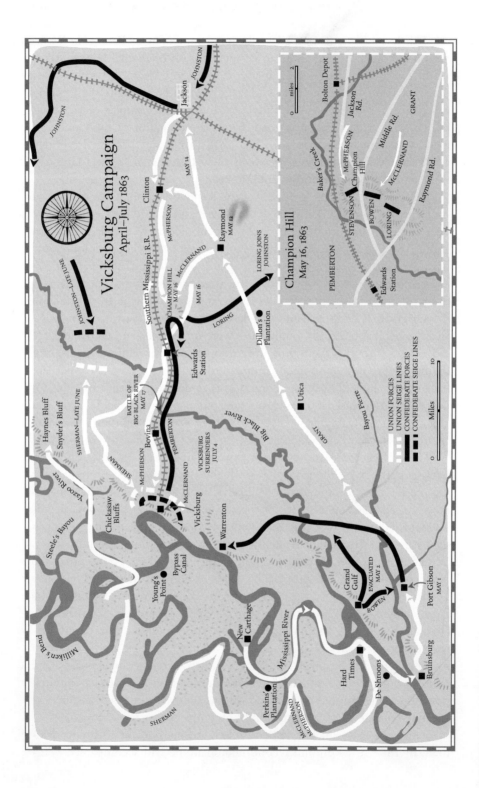

Vicksburg Campaign
April–July 1863

Champion Hill
May 16, 1863

field Scott's army as it penetrated 260 miles into the highlands of Central Mexico, defeating in detail a numerically superior enemy force and capturing the fortress of Chapultepec on the outskirts of Mexico City. No less a military authority than the Duke of Wellington had praised that campaign as the most brilliant in modern warfare. Sixteen years later Grant intended to duplicate it in Mississippi. Grand Gulf would be his Vera Cruz, Jackson his Puebla, and Vicksburg his Chapultepec. Just as speed and surprise had sparked Scott's victory over the Mexicans, so mobility and unpredictability would key his triumph over the rebels.

As the first week of May drew to a close, Union patrols reported that approximately 20,000 of Pemberton's troops were digging in behind the Big Black River, a sluggish, silt-laden stream that lay between the Federals and Vicksburg. They obviously thought that Grant was going to drive straight toward the city. He made several feints to keep them thinking that way. His real target, however, was the Southern Mississippi Railroad linking Jackson and Vicksburg. By obstructing this line he would prevent Pemberton from receiving supplies or reinforcements via Jackson. The Confederate general would have to fight where he was or fall back into Vicksburg, where he could be bottled up and destroyed.

McClernand was ordered to advance up the Big Black River toward the railroad hamlet of Edwards Station while McPherson and Sherman, whose soldiers had arrived from Milliken's Bend on May 7, swung eastward and headed for the same point by way of Utica and Raymond. The three corps would operate independently and thus be susceptible to envelopment should the rebels go over to the offensive. Grant doubted that this would happen, however. He did not think Pemberton was particularly aggressive, and he had the utmost confidence in his men. "Since leaving Milliken's they have marched by night as by day, through mud and rain, without tents or much other baggage, and on irregular rations without a complaint, and with less straggling than I have ever before witnessed," he wrote. "[I]f all promises as favorable hereafter as it does now, [we will] not stop until Vicksburg is in our possession."

On May 12 Pemberton transferred his headquarters to the town of Bovina on the west bank of the Big Black River between Jackson and Vicksburg. He hoped that by situating himself closer to the front, he would be able to get a better feel for what his opponent was doing. The failure of Confederate intelligence to provide him with information about the enemy's movements proved a bitter disappointment, however. Even though the Union army had been in Mississippi for two weeks, no one on

General John C. Pemberton, C.S.A. (Eastern National Parks and Monuments Association)

his staff could pinpoint its exact location or say anything definitive about its plans. As a result he felt compelled to place troops all along the Big Black lest Grant find an unguarded bridge or ford and make a sudden lunge toward Vicksburg.

Pemberton's subordinates could see that he was tired, jittery, and unsure of himself. One of them, Major General William Wing Loring, tried to tell his superior what to do. "Is it not, then, our policy to take the offensive before [the Yankees] can make themselves secure and move either way as it may suit them?" he wrote on May 9. "I believe if a well-concerted plan be adopted we can drive the enemy into the Mississippi if it is done in time. They don't expect anything of the kind; they think we are on the defensive."

Pemberton refused to consider Loring's proposal. "I must stand on the defensive at all events until reinforcements reach me," he declared. He did make one moderately aggressive move, ordering a 3,000-man brigade commanded by Brigadier General John Gregg to march from Jackson to Raymond, where it would be in position to strike Grant's flank and rear should he try to seize the Big Black railroad bridge between Bovina and Edwards Station. But that was the extent of his maneuvering; otherwise he sat tight and waited for the enemy to come to him.

Grant was about to oblige, but not at the Big Black as Pemberton had anticipated. It was Gregg's understrength brigade arrayed on the outskirts of Raymond that was going to bear the brunt of the first Federal assault. Shortly after 10 A.M. on May 12, skirmishers from McPherson's Seventeenth Corps, moving along the Utica-Raymond Road, made contact with Gregg's men on the banks of Fourteen Mile Creek just south of the village. The Yankee soldiers were feeling their oats, having spent the last week ransacking plantation houses, gorging on plundered provisions, and dallying with Mississippi girls "plump, rosy, engaging, and delicious." Now they were ready to show the graybacks how well they could fight.

Much to their surprise, Gregg's Confederates did not slink away the moment the first shots were fired. Instead they raised the rebel yell and charged. McPherson's men were stunned by the ferocity of this attack. They began to fall back, grudgingly at first, but then faster and faster. The retreat was about to turn into a rout when Major General John A. Logan, commander of the Union Third Division, arrived on the field.

The thirty-six-year-old Logan was an anomaly in the Union army: a political general who was a hard fighter. Called "Black Jack" by his troops because of his swarthy complexion and drooping coal-colored mustache, the former Illinois congressman was utterly fearless. He rushed into the melee along Fourteen Mile Creek, rallied the faltering bluecoats, and led them on a desperate counterattack.

For two and a half hours the fighting seesawed back and forth, but eventually the weight of Union numbers told. The Confederates disengaged and fell back toward Jackson. The Federals advanced into Raymond and tore the town apart. "I prayed most earnestly for protection," Raymond resident Anne Martin wrote her sister Emma three days later. "[Our] doors were locked but they broke them open and took everything. . . . If you are ever invaded, Emmie, don't bury anything. Hearing that Mrs. Robinson had buried her silverware, they dug up every foot of her garden until they found it. . . . Martha Durden's baby was buried in the yard and would you believe it: that child's remains were dug [up] no less than three different times."

When news of the Raymond battle reached Grant on the evening of the twelfth, he promptly discarded his plan for severing the railroad and decided to attack Jackson instead. It would be foolhardy to face Pemberton's army with Gregg's brigade loose in his rear, and besides, seizing the state capital would accomplish the same goal as occupying Edwards Station. "All the enemy's . . . men and stores would come by [way of Jackson]," he wrote, and "as I hoped in the end to besiege Vicksburg, I must first destroy all possibilities of aid."

New orders went out. On the morning of May 13 McPherson's soldiers marched to Clinton, nine miles west of Jackson, while Sherman's men advanced to the town of Mississippi Springs, eleven miles southwest of the capital. The two commanders were told to make a coordinated assault on the fourteenth. McClernand's corps was posted in the vicinity of Raymond, where it could block Pemberton if he moved eastward or go to the aid of McPherson and Sherman should they run into trouble. It was a dazzling bit of strategic improvisation, a placement of forces "as nearly perfect as the human mind and hard marching could make it," an admiring military historian later wrote. Grant was confident that it would result in the crushing of Gregg's contingent and the swift conquest of Jackson. Once that was out of the way, he would be able to give his undivided attention to Pemberton.

Unbeknownst to Grant, he was facing a new opponent at Jackson. On May 9 a telegram from the Confederate War Department had been delivered to Johnston at his Tullahoma headquarters. "Proceed at once to Mississippi and take chief command of the forces there," it read. Johnston did not wish to assume responsibility for a campaign he considered as good as lost, but the order from Richmond left him no choice. Arriving at Jackson on May 13, he found the rain-shrouded Mississippi capital abuzz with rumors. The bluecoats who had mauled Gregg's brigade at Raymond were said to be advancing rapidly from the west. Another Union column was reportedly slicing up from the south. Alarmed, Johnston went to the Bowman House Hotel to confer with Gregg about his plans for defending the city. What he learned appalled him. Trenches had been dug a week earlier, but only 6,000 men were available to hold them against an estimated 25,000 enemy troops. No help could be expected from Pemberton, either. His army was still on the far side of the Big Black, cut off from Jackson by McClernand's well-positioned blocking force. "I am too late," Johnston telegraphed Richmond at the conclusion of the conference. At 3 A.M. he ordered a withdrawal to Canton, twenty miles to the northeast.

When the soldiers of McPherson's and Sherman's corps stormed the Jackson earthworks just before noon on May 14, all they encountered was a small rear guard. Brushing aside this force, they entered the city, eager to raise the Stars and Stripes above the Mississippi statehouse. The streets were crawling with looters, and many of the Yankees broke ranks and joined in the pillaging. As the afternoon wore on and large quantities of whiskey were consumed, the orgy of destruction grew wilder and wilder. "Foundries, machine-shops, warehouses, factories, arsenals and public stores were fired as fast as flames could be kindled," wrote newspaperman Sylvanus Cadwallader.

Grant celebrated victory by sleeping in the same Bowman House suite that Johnston had occupied the night before. He did not intend to tarry long, however. Just before retiring he had been handed a copy of a message from Johnston to Pemberton, obtained earlier in the day by a Union spy. It instructed Pemberton to strike the Union rear at Clinton. Johnston's 6,000-man detachment would cooperate.

Armed with this intelligence Grant ordered McPherson to leave Jackson at daybreak and march west to join McClernand, whose corps was in the process of shifting from Raymond to Bolton Depot, twelve miles east of the Big Black. Once at Bolton Depot, the two corps would commence a westward sweep aimed at intercepting Pemberton and preventing him from joining Johnston. Sherman's divisions would stay behind in Jackson completing the destruction of roads and bridges, then proceed to Bolton to reinforce McClernand and McPherson for what promised to be the climactic battle of the campaign.

Prodded by Johnston's dispatch, Pemberton was moving at last, but not with all of his strength and not in the direction specified. After consulting with his division commanders, he had decided to march southeast in an attempt to interdict Grant's supply line. Leaving 10,000 men to garrison Vicksburg and guard the Big Black River crossings, he set out with

23,000 troops on the afternoon of May 15, advancing toward Dillon's Plantation, a settlement on the Raymond–Port Gibson Road. "The object is to cut the enemy's communications and to force him to attack me," he explained in a note to his superior.

Johnston was irate when he received this message. It was bad enough that a direct order was being disobeyed. Much worse was the fact that the two Confederate armies were drifting apart just when it was vital that they link up. Fuming, he dictated a brusque response to Pemberton, telling him to march to Clinton immediately.

It was Pemberton's turn to bridle when he read this directive early on the morning of May 16. Johnston had been in Mississippi less than seventy-two hours, yet he was dictating strategy to an officer who had been on the scene for more than seven months. Pemberton's choice was compliance or court-martial, however, so he instructed his troops to head toward Clinton. "The order of countermarch has been issued," he informed Johnston. He gave his army's location—approximately seven miles southeast of Edwards Station—described the route he intended to follow, and added almost as an afterthought: "Heavy skirmishing is now going on to my front."

The musketry Pemberton could hear as he scribbled his message to Johnston was the sound of his pickets firing at a vedette of blue cavalry. These outriders were the vanguard of McClernand's and McPherson's corps advancing west via the Raymond, Middle, and Jackson Roads.

Pemberton was startled by the sudden appearance of enemy troops. For a few minutes he did nothing, hoping they would withdraw so he could continue his march to Clinton. When the sound of small-arms fire swelled, however, and was augmented by the thud of exploding artillery rounds, he realized that a full-scale battle was in the offing. The crisis momentarily discombobulated him. "He looked as if he was confused—and he gave orders in that uncertain manner that implied to me that he had no matured plans," wrote staff officer William Drennan.

Pemberton rapidly regained his composure when he saw that the surrounding countryside was well suited for defensive fighting. From the Raymond Road a mile east of Baker's Creek, a wooded ridge ran northeast for three miles, ending at a 140-foot-high knoll situated on the farm of Sid and Matilda Champion. Pemberton hurriedly deployed his three divisions on this high ground. Loring's was on the right astride the Raymond Road, Bowen's was in the center, and Stevenson's was on the left where the Jackson Road crossed Champion Hill and intersected the Middle Road.

Alerted that his army had found the rebels, Grant arrived at the front at 10 A.M. A quick perusal of the terrain told him that Champion Hill was the key to the battlefield. Capturing it was going to be difficult. Stevenson's infantry was thickly posted in the timber on its lower slopes, and his artillery was sited at various spots on its bald crest. Even as Grant watched, Confederate gun crews unlimbered their pieces and began lobbing long-range shots at the bluecoats of Brigadier General Alvin P. Hovey's division, who were standing in a meadow at the hill's base. Hovey wanted to advance and silence the enemy guns, but Grant told him to hold off until Logan's division, which was approaching rapidly along the Jackson Road, had deployed on his right flank.

The wait was hard on Hovey's men. They were in what Samuel Byers termed "that most trying position of soldiers . . . being fired on without permission to return the shots." Sergeant Charles Longley observed his comrades laughing and joking as Confederate shells fell around them, but he was not fooled by their show of insouciance. Silent prayers were being offered up, he wrote—"mental promises of amendment"—and many of the soldiers were scrawling "little notes or memoranda," farewells to loved ones couched "in pathetically covert terms, so that, if possible they might be saved from the ridiculous in case the future did not permit them to be tragic."

Logan's troops were in place by ten thirty. Grant signaled for the assault to begin, and with what one soldier described as "an absolute sense of relief," the long blue line advanced toward the north slope of Champion Hill.

"On and upward you go," wrote Sergeant Longley. "Thicker and faster falls the hissing hail. At last the timber grows larger and you begin to locate the flaming line whence the trouble comes. . . . The more accustomed

A Union regiment in battle formation. (Courtesy Behringer-Crawford Museum)

eye now detects here and there a gray-clad enemy. . . . You note one, perhaps striving to find shelter behind a slender tree. . . . Instantly you aim and
fire, and when he falls backward . . . you scream aloud in the very frenzy of
self-congratulation. At this very moment, while every human instinct is
carried away by a torrent of passion, while kill, *kill,* KILL, seems to fill your
heart and be written over the face of all nature—at this instant you hear a
command (it may have come from the clouds above, you know not) to 'Fix
bayonets, forward charge!' and away you go with a wild yell in which all
mouths join."

Straight up the hillside the blue soldiers went, driving Carter Stevenson's defenders before them. The cost was high. Hundreds of men were cut
down by canister and minié balls. The Union thrust never lost momentum,
however, and the rebels, intimidated by the reckless bravery of their assailants, broke and ran. "Their backs are toward you," wrote Longley. "They
fly—the line becomes a crowd—you pause only to fire. You see them
plunging down in all directions. . . . A full artillery team catches the eye
just long enough to see a leader fall and the six horses almost stand on end
as they go over and down in struggling confusion—now the battery itself
is ours, and fairly won, and cheer follows cheer!"

More cannons were captured as the blue line swept over the hill's crest
and down the other side. "Tell General Grant that my division cannot be
whipped by all the rebels this side of hell!" Logan bawled at a staff officer
sent to inquire how his command was doing. "We are going ahead, and
won't stop until we get orders!" Thrilled by this message, the usually phlegmatic Grant told the same courier to go to Logan and "tell him he is making history today." He also sent word to McClernand, who had been
dawdling on the Middle Road all morning, to join the fight.

Grant was not the only one wondering what had happened to Mc-
Clernand. For the last four hours, Pemberton had been expecting the Illinois general to make a flanking attack somewhere south of the Raymond
Road. He was so sure this was where the main Union thrust was going to
come that he declined to shore up his left, even as it was crumbling under
the sledgehammer blows of Hovey and Logan. By 1 P.M. he could no
longer ignore what was happening on Champion Hill. The disintegration
of Stevenson's division spelled disaster for his entire command. He called
on Bowen and Loring to rush their units north to contain the Union onslaught. Incredibly, both generals refused. They said they dared not weaken
their present positions when so many Federal troops were massed in their
front. Frantically, Pemberton reiterated the order, and this time Bowen
obeyed, telling his men to march toward the sound of the guns. Loring still
would not budge, however. His decision to stay put was based on a sincere
conviction that the Confederate right was in grave danger, but animosity

against Pemberton played a large part, too. He had long harbored a grudge toward his superior, a "degree of hatred," wrote an officer who knew both men well, that made him "willing for Pemberton to lose a battle provided that he would be displaced." He had been overheard making "ill-tempered jests" at Pemberton's expense earlier that morning, and when the order to reinforce Stevenson came, "the courier who brought it was not out of hearing, before he made light of it and ridiculed the plan [Pemberton] proposed."

For a time it seemed as if Loring's insubordination would not matter. Bowen's division marched swiftly to the Middle Road–Jackson Road intersection and launched a ferocious counterattack. "We ran, and ran manfully," one of the Union soldiers recalled. "It was terribly hot, a hot afternoon under a Mississippi sun, and an enemy on flank and rear, shouting and firing. The grass, the stones, the bushes, seemed melting under the shower of bullets that was following us to the rear. We tried to halt, and tried to form. It was no use."

Bowen's men pushed the Federals back three-quarters of a mile and recaptured Champion Hill. But just as panic was spreading through the blue ranks, a fresh Union division entered the fray, halting the Confederate assault in its tracks. The battle now became a bloody free-for-all in which "each side took their turn in driving and being driven." For over an hour the fighting raged, with neither army able to gain the upper hand. Then another wave of Federals went into action, and the rebels started to waver. At almost the same moment, McClernand's corps began to advance along the Middle Road. Suddenly Bowen's and Stevenson's divisions found themselves being crushed between powerful Yankee columns converging from the north and east.

Pemberton desperately needed reinforcements, but none were to be had. "Where is Loring?" he cried in an agony of frustration. When no one on his staff could answer, he mounted his horse and galloped off to find out for himself.

The Confederates who had been holding Champion Hill and the Middle Road–Jackson Road crossroads were now in full flight. Colonel Edward Goodwin of the Thirty-fifth Alabama ordered his troops to use their bayonets to halt the running men, but "even this could not check them," he later wrote. "The colors of three regiments passed through. We collared them, begged them and abused them in vain."

Pemberton returned empty-handed a few minutes later. He was told that the Yankees had cut the Jackson Road where it crossed Baker's Creek, sealing off one of the two escape routes open to the west. Realizing that his army would be trapped and annihilated if he did not act at once, he passed the word for his troops to retire toward the Raymond Road bridge, the only other span over Baker's Creek. It was at this inopportune moment that Loring finally appeared, having marched his division north along a cart path none of the other Confederate generals knew about. Pemberton was heartsick. "Had the movement [by Loring] been promptly made when first ordered, it is not improbable that I might have maintained my position," he stated in his after-action report. But the situation was beyond salvaging now, and the withdrawal continued. The gray troops hurried south across Baker's Creek, heading for Big Black Bridge ten miles away. During the retreat, Loring's division vanished again. It would be three days before Pemberton learned that his mulish subordinate had gone south instead of west, become lost in the marshy bottoms along Baker's Creek, abandoned all of his artillery and most of his supplies, and finally limped off to join Johnston near Jackson.

As the firing died down and the haze of powder smoke shrouding Champion Hill began to lift, the slanting rays of the late-afternoon sun illuminated a scene of shocking carnage. Three thousand six hundred fifty-three men had been shot, most within an area measuring less than a square mile. "All around us lay the dead and dying, amid the groans and cries of the wounded," wrote Private Wilbur Crummer. "Our surgeons came up quickly, and taking possession of a farmhouse, converted it into a hospital."

Charles Dana was riding across the battlefield with Colonel John Rawlins of Grant's staff "when suddenly a man, perhaps forty-five or fifty years old, who had a Confederate uniform on, lifted himself up on his elbow and said: 'For God's sake, gentlemen, is there a Mason among you?' 'Yes,' said Rawlins, 'I am a Mason.' He got off his horse and kneeled by the dying man, who gave him some letters out of his pocket. When he came back Rawlins had tears on his cheeks. The man, he told us, wanted him to convey some souvenir—a miniature or a ring, I do not remember what—to his wife, who was in Alabama."

Returning to headquarters, Dana encountered another wounded Confederate who "stood up suddenly and said: 'Kill me! Will someone kill me? I am in such anguish that it will be mercy to do it—I have got to die. Kill me—don't let me suffer!' We sent for a surgeon, who examined his case but said it was hopeless. He had been shot through the head so that it had cut off the optic nerve of both eyes. . . . Before morning he died."

Even the usually imperturbable Grant was shaken by what he saw and heard on the night of May 16. He had a job to do, however, and so with a steely self-discipline that astounded his more emotional subordinates, he ignored the gore, blocked out the screams, and concentrated on the matter at hand. After conferring with his staff, he ordered McClernand and Sherman to pursue Pemberton's army at first light. Then he tried to get some rest.

While Grant was dozing, the bedraggled remnants of the Confederate army were stumbling into the earthworks guarding the eastern approaches to Big Black Bridge. Carter Stevenson's troops were so worn out, they were deemed unfit for further service and sent across the river to Bovina. Bowen's men were in slightly better shape, so it fell to them to keep the bridgehead open until Loring's division, which Pemberton was still expecting to turn up, had passed through to safety. Bowen's soldiers filed into the entrenchments at midnight, flopped to the ground, and were instantly insensible, oblivious to hunger, mud, and aching muscles—everything but their overwhelming need for sleep.

Loring did not appear the next morning, but Grant did. Locating Pemberton's rear guard just after daybreak on May 17, he pushed McClernand's corps forward, intending to attack at once. He quickly changed his mind after examining the terrain and the enemy's defenses. Where the railroad crossed the Big Black, the river looped west, carving out a U-shaped bulge of bottomland. The rebel breastworks ran across the mile-wide neck of this bulge and were fronted by a waist-deep bayou into which a large number of trees had been felled to form an abatis. Smashing head-on into this position looked to be too risky. Grant decided to wait for Sherman's corps, which was fording the Big Black at a point five miles upstream, to march down the west bank and strike it from the rear.

He was being overly cautious as it turned out. Fatigue, losses, and lack of ammunition had made cowards of the Confederate soldiers. Instead of girding for battle, they were fretting about how they were going to get away if the Yankees breached their line. Reports that the bridge had been doused with turpentine so it could be set ablaze at a moment's notice only increased their alarm. Many of them chose to desert rather than be caught in what they were convinced was a death trap.

The Federals, on the other hand, were itching for a fight. After Raymond, Jackson, and Champion Hill, they believed they were invincible. As if to prove it, they kept inching forward, especially the Iowans and Wisconsans of General Michael Lawler's brigade, who had occupied a swale only three hundred yards from the enemy fortifications.

It was a warm morning, and Lawler, a huge, hot-tempered Irishman, was in his shirt sleeves, sweating profusely and growing angrier by the minute as snipers' bullets forced his men to crouch low in their muddy covert. Finally he could stand it no longer. Massing his regiments into a tightly packed column, he led them forward at the dead run, brandishing his sword and bellowing like a bull.

The rebel defenders were dumbfounded when they saw this formation racing toward them. They got off a ragged volley, then bolted for the rear, frantic to reach the bridge before it was set on fire. They were still stampeding across when its timbers were lit. The crackling wall of flames halted the attackers in their tracks, but it also consigned many Confederates to capture. Before the morning was over, 1,751 of them would be taken prisoner. Union casualties—almost all from Lawler's brigade—came to just 39 killed and 237 wounded.

Pemberton watched this disaster unfold from the western side of the Big Black. He was at a loss to explain what had happened. Bowen's division should have been able to repel Lawler's charge with ease. How, he wondered, could it have collapsed so abruptly and ignominiously? The answer came quickly in the form of hundreds of panicky stragglers surging down the road to Vicksburg. They pushed past him with no sign of recognition, faces haggard, eyes bloodshot, voices harsh and grating as they exclaimed over and over again: "We are sold! We are sold! All Pem's fault! We are sold!"

Devastated, he mounted his horse and let himself be swept along by the retreat. For several miles he rode in silence, listening to the soldiers' bitter recriminations. Then he turned to Major Samuel Lockett and said: "Just thirty years ago I began my military career by receiving my appointment to a cadetship at the U.S. Military Academy, and today—the same date—that career is ended in disaster and disgrace."

Like a wolf pack pursuing a wounded animal, the Union army swarmed across the Big Black River in the predawn hours of May 18, passing over bridges constructed of cotton bales and scrap lumber. By midmorning it was racing west, gobbling up isolated Confederate outposts as it went. Before sundown it had reached the outskirts of Vicksburg. Sherman's corps was on the right, where Graveyard Road entered the town from the northeast, McPherson's was in the center, straddling the Jackson Road, and McClernand's was on the left, athwart the Southern Mississippi Railroad tracks.

The following day, May 19, Grant ordered an assault by the entire army. He believed the enemy was demoralized and would not put up much of a struggle. The first part of this formulation was correct. Pemberton's troops were in desperate shape after their drubbings at Champion Hill and the Big Black. But the second part was dead wrong. Now that they had no place left to run, the rebels were determined to fight and fight hard. Further bolstering their resolve was the phenomenal strength of the defensive position they occupied.

The belt of fieldworks began at Fort Hill, a promontory overlooking the Mississippi one and a half miles north of Vicksburg, then ran east and south in a sinuous D-shaped curve, following the spine of a high ridge until it zigzagged back to the river bank at South Fort, three miles below town. At salient points on this ridge, and at places where roads and railroad tracks ran into Vicksburg, massive earthen fortresses had been built. They had parapets twenty feet thick and dry moats in front so would-be attackers would have to climb high, nearly vertical precipices to gain entrance. The forts were carefully sited so that their big guns could lay down a deadly crossfire, and they were interconnected by an elaborate network of mutually supporting trenches and rifle pits.

As if these man-made barriers were not daunting enough, the area's topography strongly favored the defense. Over the centuries heavy rains had eroded the soft loess soil, carving out a tortuous maze of sheer-sided ravines. These gulches were "so steep that their ascent was difficult to a footman unless he aided himself with his hands," reported a Union engineer who had explored them. They were also choked with dense mats of foliage—entanglements of brush, cane, and vines, "which under fire were absolutely impassible."

Grant's troops plunged into this labyrinth at 2 P.M. on May 19, advancing toward strongpoints 500 to 1,500 yards distant. Almost immediately their assault formations fell apart as men got hung up in the undergrowth or were shunted off in the wrong direction by the meandering gullies. Numerous halts had to be called to regroup, and when at last the lead companies approached the enemy parapets, they were struck by a hail of bullets. The survivors dived for cover, and there they lay until darkness allowed them to withdraw unseen. The assault had cost 942 casualties and accomplished nothing.

Following this failure, Grant was faced with a difficult decision. He could either concede that Vicksburg's defenses were impregnable and settle down to a siege or he could call for another attack, knowing that his army would suffer extremely heavy losses. After agonizing for twenty-four hours, he chose the latter course. He still thought the city could be taken by storm, and he was convinced that a successful assault, no matter how bloody, would be less expensive in the long run than a protracted siege. Consequently he ordered his corps commanders to make a second thrust on the morning of May 22, utilizing every man and gun at their disposal.

His plan for this operation foreshadowed tactics that would be used half a century later on the battlefields of World War I. Rather than assaulting the entire Confederate perimeter, the Union forces were to concentrate on a three-and-a-half-mile segment, massing their offensive power in hopes of scoring a quick breakthrough. Before the attack began, the army's entire inventory of artillery, augmented by all the naval firepower Admiral Porter could bring to bear, would conduct a five-hour preliminary bombardment. To prevent Pemberton from shifting troops once the onslaught was under way, all three corps were to advance in unison, jumping off at precisely 10 A.M., as indicated by watches synchronized the night before.

The soldiers who had not participated in the first assault were all in favor of this aggressive strategy. The men who had made the May 19 effort were far less enthusiastic. They knew what they were up against, and as the artillery thundered during the early-morning hours of the twenty-second, they wandered around their bivouacs preparing for the worst. Sergeant Osborn Oldroyd reported that members of his regiment "were busy divesting themselves of watches, rings, pictures, and their keepsakes, which were being placed in the custody of the cooks, who were not expected to go into action."

At the appointed hour the barrage lifted, and the bluecoats started forward, dragging scaling ladders behind them. Just as it had three days earlier, the rugged terrain and thick vegetation slowed the attack to a crawl. Soldiers who had set out at a dead run, determined to sprint across no-man's-land before enemy fire could hit them, were staggering and gasping for breath after the first hundred yards. "Up the hill we pressed, through the brambles and brush, over the dead and dying," wrote Lieutenant Colonel Lysander Webb. "Up we struggled, over logs, into ditches, clinging here to a bush to keep from falling backwards, and there to a thorny bramble—oh! that was a half hour which may God grant we shall never be called upon to experience again."

It was much the same along the rest of the line. Unit after unit slogged forward, only to be shot to pieces when it finally drew near its objective. A few soldiers managed to claw their way into the deep ditches fronting the rebel forts, but they could advance no farther and ended up being slaughtered when the defenders rolled fused artillery shells down into their midst. Only on McClernand's front was a shallow penetration made—a minor success that the overeager general, still dreaming of becoming one of the war's great heroes, promptly parlayed into a major tragedy. Glimpsing the flag of one of his regiments flying over an enemy parapet, McClernand concluded that the fort had fallen. He sent word to Grant that his corps had punched a hole in the Confederate line and would pour through and take Vicksburg if it were properly supported. Grant was incredulous. "I don't believe a word of it," he snapped after reading the message. But he went ahead and ordered Sherman and McPherson to renew their assaults as a diversion in McClernand's favor, reasoning that the Illinoisan's note was official and had to be credited.

It was a costly decision. McClernand was mistaken about what he had seen. A handful of men from the Twenty-second Iowa had secured a lodgment inside one of the rebel redoubts, but there was no breakthrough. When the rest of the army charged at 3 P.M., trying to exploit an opening that didn't exist, wholesale slaughter resulted. Grant was disgusted: "General McClernand's dispatches misled me as to the real state of facts," he declared afterward. They "resulted in the increase of our mortality list fully fifty percent, without advancing our position or giving us any other advantages." Federal losses for the day topped 3,000. The Confederates had suffered fewer than 500 casualties.

As afternoon passed into evening, a mauve-colored dusk gathered in the trees lining the Mississippi River bluffs. The sun's afterglow illuminated swelling masses of cumulus clouds on the western horizon, painting them gold, lavender, and vermilion. On a rise beside the Graveyard Road, Grant sat atop his horse, puffing a cigar and watching the wounded limp in from the battlefield. He regretted that so many men had been killed or injured, but he was not discouraged. Casting aside the smoldering cigar stump, he jerked his horse about and headed back to his tent.

"We'll have to dig our way in," a newspaper reporter heard him say as he disappeared into the fast-fading twilight.

PART THREE

SUMMER

TEN

INVASION

On May 15, the day Stonewall Jackson was laid to rest in a Shenandoah Valley graveyard, Robert E. Lee was summoned to Richmond for a strategy conference with President Davis and Secretary of War Seddon. The two officials were deeply concerned about the situation in Mississippi, where Grant was poised to overwhelm Pemberton and capture Vicksburg. They wanted to ask their leading general how to avert this catastrophe.

Lee had already pondered the problem and concluded that "it becomes a question between Virginia and Mississippi." If a large part of his command were detached and sent to Vicksburg, as several of the president's advisers were suggesting, he feared that the Army of the Potomac, now in camp recuperating from its Chancellorsville drubbing, would lunge south and take Richmond. The thought of Hooker's horde overrunning the Confederate capital while his divisions were off fighting in Mississippi was more than Lee could bear. And so he proposed an alternative strategy—an invasion of the North.

Standing before a large wall map in Davis's office, he outlined his plan: he would march his army north through the Shenandoah Valley, cross the Potomac into Maryland, then move rapidly into southern Pennsylvania, where he would be in position to menace Washington, Baltimore, and Philadelphia. With three of their biggest cities in danger, the Yankees would in all likelihood recall troops from the West, thus easing the pressure on Vicksburg. They would certainly have to pull the Army of the Potomac out of Virginia, thereby eliminating the long-standing threat to Richmond. An invasion offered other advantages as well. It would allow Lee's soldiers to obtain food, clothing, and remounts in the enemy's country while giving the war-weary residents of the Old Dominion a chance to tend their farms and stockpile supplies without interference from either side. It would also strengthen the hand of the Peace Democrats and perhaps even compel the Lincoln administration to sue for peace.

Davis and Seddon were enthralled, and so was the rest of the Confederate cabinet when Lee briefed it the next day. Only one member voiced doubts. Postmaster General John H. Reagan thought that the defense of Vicksburg should be the top priority. He disputed Lee's contention that an invasion of Pennsylvania would change the situation in Mississippi. The only way to halt Grant's rampage, he insisted, was to destroy him. To do that massive reinforcements had to be sent to the Magnolia State, including 30,000 troops drawn from the Army of Northern Virginia. If this placed Richmond in danger, so be it; holding Vicksburg and preserving communications with Louisiana, Arkansas, and his home state of Texas was more important than safeguarding the capital.

Davis was sympathetic to Reagan's point of view, but he was not about to veto Lee's plan. The aristocratic Virginian was the Confederacy's best general, and after his masterful performance at Chancellorsville, he seemed infallible. Who in this group could presume to question his military judgment or argue with his ability to defeat the enemy on the field of his

General Robert E. Lee, C.S.A.
(Courtesy Cook Collection, Valentine Museum)

choosing? Even the strong-willed Reagan realized that he had to defer to Lee's strategic thinking, and so it was agreed that the invasion of the North would begin as soon as the necessary preparations could be made.

Lee returned to Fredericksburg on May 18 and set about restructuring his command for the upcoming campaign. For the past year the Army of Northern Virginia had been organized into two infantry corps, one led by Jackson, the other by Longstreet. Each corps contained four divisions—too many, Lee thought, for one general to manage effectively. Jackson's death allowed him to discard this cumbersome arrangement and divide the army into three three-division corps.

Longstreet, who had recently

returned from his extended supply-gathering expedition, would remain at the helm of the First Corps. The Second Corps, Jackson's old command, would go to Major General Richard S. Ewell. Affectionately known as "Old Bald Head" for his egg-smooth pate, the forty-six-year-old Ewell had served with distinction in the Shenandoah Valley and at Second Manassas, where he had lost a leg to a Yankee minié ball. He was just now returning to active duty after a nine-month convalescence. Major General Ambrose Powell Hill, considered by many to be the best division commander in the Army of Northern Virginia, would head up the newly created Third Corps. Jeb Stuart would continue to lead the Confederate cavalry.

Lee announced his reorganization on May 30. Four days later he put the army in motion, sending the lead units up the Rappahannock to Culpeper. Altogether he had 75,000 troops at his disposal—60,000 infantry, 10,000 cavalry, 5,000 artillery. It was a small force for so bold an undertaking, but one in which he had absolute confidence. "There never were such men in an army before," he declared as he prepared to break camp. "They will go anywhere and do anything if properly led."

While Lee was preparing for a new campaign, the North was coming to terms with the Chancellorsville debacle. Fearing a firestorm of protest, War Department censors had withheld news of the defeat as long as possible. When the story finally broke, antiwar Democrats went into paroxysms of self-righteous rage. Even staunch defenders of the president's war policy were aghast. "It is horrible—horrible!" exclaimed Horace Greeley, editor of the New York *Tribune*. "And to think of it, 130,000 magnificent soldiers cut to pieces by less than 60,000 half-starved ragamuffins!"

But much to the politicians' and pundits' surprise, the public seemed relatively unfazed by the defeat. The black despondency that had gripped the nation after Fredericksburg did not reappear. Some observers attributed this calm to the booming war economy. Others speculated that people were numb, their capacity for grief and outrage diminished by all the bloodshed of the past year. But the most likely explanation was that a majority of Northerners had accepted the fact that this was going to be a long struggle with many ups and downs, and that a single setback was not going to determine the outcome. As correspondent Charles Carleton Coffin put it in the Boston *Journal*: "The country is not lost—or endangered even—by this failure. There is no reason why men should lose heart or allow their hopes to go down. The [war] will not probably be decided by a single great victory—one grand triumph of arms, the annihilation of an army—but by the powers of endurance. The party which can stand the pounding longest will win."

While civilians could shrug off Chancellorsville and go on about their business, it was not so easy for the soldiers who had borne the brunt of the fighting and dying. Around campfires at Falmouth, they reviewed the battle and concluded that it was the commanding general, not the rank and file, who had been beaten. "Hooker's career is well exemplified by that of a rocket," one of them scornfully wrote. "He went up like one and came down like a stick."

The statements Fighting Joe made immediately after the battle did not help matters. Once he was safely back across the Rappahannock, he issued a proclamation declaring that "the events of the last week may swell with pride the heart of every officer and soldier of this army. We have added new luster to its former renown." As if this preposterous claim weren't bad enough, he sent a letter to the president insisting that the Army of the Potomac had not been beaten at Chancellorsville. Although disgusted by this piece of self-serving drivel, Lincoln made no move to replace the man who had written it. He was not disposed to throw away a gun because it had misfired once, he told a White House visitor; Hooker would keep his post for the time being. He did caution the general against attempting another offensive, however. "I shall not complain if you do no more for a time than to keep the enemy at bay," he wrote.

That was not going to be easy. On May 27 the Army of the Potomac's intelligence chief reported that Lee's troops were preparing for action. Six days later balloon-borne observers confirmed that long files of gray infantry were trudging northwest toward Culpeper. A small detachment had been left behind to guard Fredericksburg, but otherwise the entire rebel army was on the move.

Hooker digested this information and concluded that Maryland was Lee's likely target. His response showed just how badly Chancellorsville had rattled him. Instead of pursuing his opponent and bringing him to battle, he announced that he was going to head in the opposite direction, cross the Rappahannock, and capture Fredericksburg. Lincoln was flabbergasted. The plan was a recipe for disaster, he wired Hooker. It would result in the Army of the Potomac becoming "entangled upon the river, like an ox jumped half over a fence and liable to be torn by dogs front and rear, without a fair chance to gore one way or kick the other."

Hooker received this message on June 5. The next day he learned that the vanguard of the Confederate army—Stuart's cavalry—was camped near Brandy Station, some thirty miles northwest of Fredericksburg. Hungry for additional information and hopeful that a hit-and-run attack might disrupt Lee's invasion timetable, he ordered his cavalry corps to ride to Brandy Station and "disperse and destroy" Stuart's horsemen.

Brigadier General Alfred Pleasonton, the thirty-eight-year-old commander of the Army of the Potomac's mounted wing, was delighted with this assignment. It would give him a chance to show Hooker and the rest of the Union brass what the "new" Federal cavalry was capable of. The "old" cavalry had been the laughingstock of the army. Parceled out among the infantry divisions, it had been used almost exclusively for escort and messenger service. "Whoever saw a dead cavalryman?" Union foot soldiers hooted whenever a squad of blue-clad riders clattered by, and indeed, the cavalry had compiled such a poor record during the first two years of the war that it was seldom called on to participate in any real fighting. But now all that had changed. Consoli-

General J.E.B. Stuart, C.S.A.
(Courtesy The Museum of the
Confederacy, Richmond, Virginia)

dated into three 3,000-man divisions, heavily armed with Colt revolvers and Sharps breech-loading carbines, the Federal cavalry corps was a force to be reckoned with, and it was looking for a place to prove it.

James Ewell Brown Stuart, famous throughout the Army of Northern Virginia for his flamboyant sense of style, had outdone himself on the occasion of Robert E. Lee's June 8 visit to Brandy Station. Decked out in knee-high boots, elbow-length gauntlets, and a smart new uniform complete with yellow sash, scarlet-lined cape, and an oversize hat to which a long ostrich plume was attached with a golden clasp, he looked as if he had just stepped from the pages of a novel by Sir Walter Scott. The normally reserved Lee could barely contain himself when he beheld this gaudy getup, and a grin creased his face when he caught sight of the garlands of flowers hanging from the withers of Jeb's horse.

Stuart could be forgiven such foppery because he was a superb cavalry commander, equally adept at raiding and reconnoitering. It was the latter that Lee was concerned with as he prepared to launch his invasion. It would be up to Stuart's riders to screen the infantry while it was on the march, and to keep headquarters constantly apprised of the enemy's position and movements. This was the critical task Lee wanted to discuss with his subordinate. But first he would review the cavalry corps, which had been assembled on a broad, dusty plain midway between Brandy Station and the Rappahannock River.

The 10,000 mounted troopers had formed two lines, each one three miles long. It took Lee nearly twenty minutes to gallop past the front rank, turn, and gallop back along the rear rank, hat raised in salute. He then ascended a grassy hillock and watched as all five brigades wheeled into column and paraded past him. Stuart led the way on his flower-draped charger, saber held at tierce point, face beaming with pride. An infantry officer observing this display was stricken with envy. "Wouldn't we clean 'em out," he grumbled loud enough for everyone in the reviewing party to hear. But Lee, who had been a cavalryman before the war, thoroughly approved of the show. "It was a splendid sight," he wrote his wife. "The men and horses looked well. . . . [and] Stuart was in all his glory." When the pageant was over, he pulled his drama-loving subordinate aside and told him that he and his command were to move out the following morning, June 9, to cover the northward advance of Ewell's infantry.

One of the things that had been neglected amid all the pomp and festivities was patrolling. The Confederates were completely unaware that while they had been parading for Lee, the Union cavalry had approached to within two miles of their bivouac.

L ate on the afternoon of June 8, Alfred Pleasonton divided his command into two wings. Brigadier General John Buford's division was ordered to advance to Beverly Ford on the Rappahannock, four miles northeast of Brandy Station, while the divisions of Brigadier General David M. Gregg and Colonel Alfred Duffie rode to Kelly's Ford, five miles downstream. At daybreak on June 9 the two forces would cross the river and converge on Brandy Station. To preserve the element of surprise, Pleasonton forbade the lighting of fires that evening. The troopers ate a cold supper, then went to sleep with their carbines close at hand and the reins of their still-bridled horses looped around their wrists.

The eastern sky was brightening and a cool white mist was rising from the surface of the Rappahannock when Buford's soldiers splashed across Beverly Ford at 4 A.M. on June 9, swept aside a handful of startled rebel pickets, and galloped four abreast down the narrow country lane that led to Brandy Station.

Awakened by the crack of pistol shots, the Confederates who were camped closest to the river rolled out of their blankets, grabbed their weapons, and ran coatless and bootless for their horses. Major Cabell E. Flournoy quickly formed them into a column and charged straight at the oncoming Yankees. Colonel Benjamin F. Davis, commander of the brigade spear-heading the Union attack, was one of the first to fall. He was urging his men forward when a Confederate spurred up behind him. Davis turned and slashed with his saber, but the rebel ducked out of the way, leveled his revolver, and fired a bullet into Davis's head, killing him instantly. A few minutes later Flournoy's outnumbered horsemen were forced to retreat, but they had delayed the Federals long enough to let the rest of the Confed-erate cavalry deploy into a defensive line two miles northeast of Brandy Station.

Buford's division smashed into this line but failed to crack it. Then it was the rebels' turn to counterattack. Led by Brigadier General William E. Jones, they drove the Yankees back toward Beverly Ford. A Confederate victory seemed certain until a scout rode up with the news that another column of bluecoats had been spotted heading from Kelly's Ford toward Brandy Station. Jones immediately relayed the report to Stuart, who scoffed at it: "Tell General Jones to attend to the Yankees in his front, and I'll watch the flanks!" he barked. A short while later a second courier galloped up and confirmed the message delivered by the first. Still Stuart remained skepti-cal. "Ride back there and see what this foolishness is about," he told a staff officer. At that moment the sound of carbine fire rolled up from the south, leaving no doubt that trouble was coming from that direction.

This time Stuart responded with alacrity. He ordered two regiments to break off their attack on Buford's division, reverse field, and ride as fast as they could to meet the approaching Federal horsemen. The opposing ranks plowed into each other on an eminence called Fleetwood Hill. A chaotic fight full of furious charges, countercharges, and desperate close-quarters combat ensued.

Finally, around 4:30 P.M., the approach of Confederate infantry forced Pleasonton to pull his command back across the Rappahannock. Although he had suffered heavy losses, he was pleased with the day's work. His troop-ers had more than held their own against the vaunted rebel riders, gaining a sense of confidence in themselves that would prove invaluable in the weeks ahead. As another officer later put it, Brandy Station "*made* the fed-eral cavalry."

For his part Jeb Stuart was mortified. He tried to put the best face on things, claiming that he had won a glorious victory. No one believed it, and for the first time in his career he found himself subject to biting criticism. The "puffed-up" cavalry commander had been so busy "rollicking, frolick-ing, and running after girls" that he had neglected to take the most basic precautions to guard against a surprise attack, the Richmond newspapers reported. He should grow up, stop treating the war as if it were "a tournament invented and supported for the pleasure of a few vain and weak-headed officers," and start exercising "vigilance, vigilance, [and] more vigilance."

Stuart was stung by this rebuke, but instead of taking a more serious approach to his job, he became even more reckless, convinced that the best way to silence his critics was to perform another headline-grabbing exploit of the kind that had made him famous in the first place.

It would be several weeks before he had an opportunity to strike out on his own, however. The Army of Northern Virginia had begun its advance toward the Potomac.

Ewell's corps led the way, pouring into the Shenandoah Valley by way of Chester Gap. As it did so, the Southern military establishment held its breath, waiting to see how Old Bald Head would fare in his first campaign as Stonewall Jackson's successor. The one-legged general rode in a buggy, a pair of crutches at his side. He looked frail and sick, and observers wondered if he would be able to endure the rigors of a hard march. The hollow cheeks, sallow complexion, and bloodshot eyes were misleading, however. After his lengthy rehabilitation Ewell was spoiling for a fight. He set a blistering pace, moving his men smartly through the valley toward Winchester, a strategic railroad junction guarded by a 5,100-man Federal garrison under the command of Major General Robert H. Milroy.

For the past week the Union War Department had been pleading with Milroy to abandon this outpost and fall back to Harpers Ferry. He had stubbornly refused, insisting that he could hold Winchester against any force the rebels might send against it. Now he was going to pay for his overconfidence. On the afternoon of June 14, Ewell ordered Jubal Early's division to attack Milroy's fortified position northwest of Winchester. It did so, spearheaded by Brigadier General Alexander Hays's Louisiana Brigade, one of the best combat units in the army.

Ewell was perilously close to the front, cheering on the attackers. "Hurrah for the Louisiana boys!" he shouted, tears streaming down his face. "There's Early! I hope the old fellow won't be hurt!" At that instant there was a loud thud, and Ewell staggered backward. He had been hit in the chest by a spent minié ball. Bruised but otherwise unharmed, he lurched back to his observation post just in time to see the bluecoats retreat pellmell in the direction of Harpers Ferry. He immediately ordered Edward Johnson to take his division and cut off the fleeing Federals. It was exactly what the departed Stonewall would have done, excited staff officers agreed. The results were everything they and their chief could have hoped for: Johnson's men caught Milroy's column and smashed it in the early morning hours of June 15, clinching a victory that was as complete as any Jackson had won during his storied Valley Campaign.

It was an auspicious start to Ewell's career as corps commander, but he did not linger at Winchester celebrating. Lee had told him to get his troops to Maryland as rapidly as possible, and that was exactly what he intended to do. On June 16 Robert Rodes's division forded the Potomac at Williamsport, and two days later Early's and Johnson's men splashed across at Shepherdstown. June 19 found the Second Corps at Hagerstown, poised to plunge into Pennsylvania. Lee signaled for it to go ahead, instructing Ewell to march toward the Susquehanna River, gathering supplies as he went. "Your progress and direction will, of course, depend upon the development of circumstances," he wrote; however, if the Pennsylvania capital of Harrisburg "comes within your means, capture it."

At the same time, Lee threw his other two corps into motion. Longstreet's troops left Culpeper on June 15, transited the Blue Ridge via Ashby's and Snicker's Gaps, and entered the Shenandoah Valley near Berryville on June 19. A. P. Hill's men came after them, following Ewell's route of march through Chester Gap. Lee himself headed northward on June 17, moving his headquarters from Culpeper to Berryville, where he could better oversee the advance of the army, which was now strung out over sixty miles, its head near the Pennsylvania border, its tail in the vicinity of Front Royal, Virginia.

While this maneuvering was going on, Stuart's cavalry was fighting a series of skirmishes in the Loudoun Valley east of the Blue Ridge. At Aldie, Middleburg, and Upperville, gray troopers clashed with Union horsemen trying to force their way through Ashby's Gap. The Federals attacked with great vigor, but failed to get into the Shenandoah. Predictably, Stuart proclaimed the screening operation a brilliant success. It was not brilliant enough to make up for the humiliation of Brandy Station, however, and he asked Lee's permission to take three brigades and slash at the flanks of the Army of the Potomac as it followed the rebel forces northward. Lee consented, with the proviso that as soon as Hooker crossed the Potomac, Stuart was to rejoin the rest of the Confederate army. Providing headquarters with intelligence about the enemy's movements was the cavalry's top priority; harassing Hooker and terrorizing Yankee civilians was secondary.

Stuart had other ideas. He had been in touch with John Singleton Mosby, the famous Confederate guerrilla leader. Mosby had suggested that the cavalry ride completely around the Army of the Potomac, severing its communications and creating panic in Washington and Baltimore. Here was an adventure worthy of a Southern Lochinvar, an exploit that would expunge the stain of Brandy Station. Stuart embraced it with unbridled enthusiasm. Detaching his three most experienced brigades, he led them out of Salem Depot, Virginia, at 1 A.M. on June 25. His superior had cautioned him to be watchful and circumspect, but prudence was the furthest thing from his mind. Glory was what he was after—glory and redemption—and Lee, Longstreet, Ewell, and Hill would have to look out for themselves while he went hunting for it.

Two years and two months into the war, the Union cavalry had yet to produce a character as colorful and charismatic as Jeb Stuart. Benjamin Grierson had flirted with fame in early May, but his bashful personality and the fact that he had performed his exploits in Mississippi, far from the newsrooms of Washington and New York City, had prevented him from becoming a public idol. Southern reporters had swashbucklers like Stuart and John Hunt Morgan to write about, while their Northern counterparts were stuck with a shy ex-schoolteacher who hated horses. But all that changed in June when a dashing young cavalryman from Michigan charged hell-for-leather into the national limelight.

Twenty-three-year-old George Armstrong Custer was a war correspondent's dream. He was boyishly handsome, with sparkling blue eyes, a drooping blond mustache, and golden shoulder-length ringlets perfumed with cinnamon-scented hair oil. He regularly sought out hand-to-hand combat, which he called "the most exciting sport I ever engaged in." He

Captain George Armstrong Custer and General Alfred Pleasonton. (Library of Congress)

was a superb equestrian who delighted in galloping toward the enemy, hat in one hand and saber in the other, holding the reins to his plunging horse in his teeth. His superiors could not say enough about his energy, enterprise, and tactical acumen, and to top it off he was unabashedly ambitious. He considered the war a heaven-sent opportunity to rise above his small-town roots, and he made no bones about the fact that he meant to be a general someday. All he needed was a chance to show the army hierarchy what he could do. When Alfred Pleasonton invited him to join his staff in the spring of 1863, he jumped at the chance, knowing that as a general's aide he would have ample opportunity to showcase his talents before an influential audience.

On May 21 Pleasonton sent the young captain on a raid deep into rebel territory. The goal of the expedition was to capture a packet of dispatches and a large quantity of Confederate currency being carried by boat from Richmond to Urbanna, on the lower Rappahannock River. Custer completed the mission with flair. He seized the boat with the documents and cash, burned a bridge and a pair of rebel schooners, took a dozen enemy soldiers prisoner, ransacked a Confederate warehouse in Urbanna, and made it back to Union lines without losing a man.

Two weeks later he was in action again, riding with the lead Union brigade as it charged toward Brandy Station on the morning of June 9. When the brigade's colonel was slain, he took over as acting commander and led the three regiments for the rest of the day. Pleasonton was so impressed by his aide's initiative that he mentioned him by name in his dispatches and gave him the honor of presenting a captured Confederate battle flag to General Hooker.

The press began to take notice of Captain Custer after the Battle of Brandy Station, but it was a dramatic incident in the Loudoun Valley that propelled his name into the headlines. Custer was accompanying Brigadier General Judson Kilpatrick's command on the afternoon of June 17 when it encountered a Confederate brigade outside the town of Aldie. Kilpatrick, a hyperaggressive Irishman known to his men as "Kill-Cavalry," ordered an immediate attack, which he led personally, along with Colonel Calvin S. Douty and Custer. As the three officers raced toward the rebels, a bullet struck Douty in the head, killing him instantly. A moment later Kilpatrick's mount was shot from under him. Custer rode on alone, yelling and waving his saber, leading a column of blue troopers toward the center of the enemy line.

After a brief melee the Federals retreated. Custer's overwrought horse bolted in the wrong direction and carried him deep into the Confederate rear. "I was surrounded by rebels and cut off from my own men," he later recounted, "but I made my way out safely, all owing to my *hat,* which is a large broad brim, exactly like that worn by the rebels. Everyone tells me that I look more like a rebel than my own men." He neglected to mention that he had cut down three Confederates with his saber and taken another one prisoner during his mad dash back toward the Union line—an astounding feat witnessed by several hundred cheering soldiers, all of whom had given him up for dead.

The reporters attached to the cavalry corps were agog. Custer's gallant charge, his hairbreadth escape, and the floppy felt sombrero provided material for a slew of exciting stories. But what really made the young Michigander a national celebrity was a widely distributed engraving showing him with his curls spilling from beneath his rakish hat and his uniform jacket unbuttoned and blowing open in the breeze, looking every inch the "golden-haired apotheosis of war."

Custer was delighted with his sudden notoriety but disappointed that it had not resulted in higher rank. While he remained shackled to Pleasonton's staff, other cavalry captains with combat records less distinguished than his were being awarded regimental commands. Despite his accomplishments his career seemed to be stalled, and the toast he offered at every mess—"To promotion or death"—was starting to stick in his craw.

Custer was not the only disgruntled officer in the Army of the Potomac during the latter part of June. At headquarters there was intense frustration as the Confederate offensive gathered steam and Hooker did nothing. "He acts like a man without a plan, and is entirely at a loss what to do," fumed Brigadier General Marsena Patrick. "He knows that Lee is his master, and is afraid to meet him in fair battle."

Prodded by Lincoln, Hooker finally pulled his army out of the Falmouth cantonment and moved it north parallel to Lee's line of march. His heart wasn't in it, however. When Brigadier General Herman Haupt asked him what his plans were now that the troops were on the march, he said he didn't know or care; henceforward he would simply do what he was told, no more, no less, and if disaster resulted, it would be someone else's fault, not his.

On June 17, four days after starting out, the Army of the Potomac reached the Fairfax-Centreville area twenty miles west of Washington. Here the soldiers rested while Hooker engaged in a contentious telegraphic exchange with the War Department. He wanted all available troops in the Washington area assigned to his command. To get his way, he grossly exaggerated the size of the Army of Northern Virginia. "He has declared that the enemy are over 100,000 strong," one of his staff officers wrote. "It is his only salvation to make it appear that the enemy's forces are larger than his own, which is all false, and he knows it." Stanton and Halleck knew it too. They declined to strip the capital's defenses. Hooker felt betrayed. He complained bitterly that lack of support made it impossible for him to conduct successful operations—an obvious attempt to shift blame for any future battlefield failures away from himself.

On June 23 Hooker traveled to Washington to meet with the president and his military advisers. One of the items discussed was the status of the 10,000-man garrison at Harpers Ferry. Hooker thought it should be attached to his army, while Halleck favored leaving it where it was. Lincoln sided with Halleck, reinforcing Hooker's belief that the administration lacked confidence in him. He left the meeting in a black mood, convinced that his days as army commander were numbered. It was reported that he was drunk when he returned to his headquarters later that evening, and drunk again the next day. Alarmed by this rumor, Lincoln telegraphed Hooker, asking if it were true. Hooker denied that he had lost control. He angrily inquired if the president believed every story he read in the press. "It did not come from the newspapers," Lincoln shot back, "nor did I believe it; but I wished to be entirely sure it was a falsehood."

While this wrangling was going on, Confederate columns continued to snake through Maryland into Pennsylvania. For the past fortnight, Hooker had denied that an invasion of the North was in the offing. Now the evidence was overwhelming. On June 25 he finally reacted. He ordered his army to cross the Potomac at Edwards Ferry and march to Frederick, Maryland.

Lincoln was encouraged by these developments. Where others saw peril, he glimpsed opportunity. By leaving its Virginia base and entering Union territory, the rebel army was exposing itself to total destruction. Federal forces had the advantage in numbers, and if they maneuvered aggressively, they should be able to cut off and annihilate the invaders. "We cannot help beating them, if we have the man," the president said to Gideon Welles.

But Hooker was not the man. Demoralized by his dealings with the War Department, unsure of his ability to handle the army ("I don't know whether I am standing on my head or feet," he plaintively wrote), daunted by the prospect of facing Lee again, he was looking for a way out. On June 27 he found one. After losing another argument with Halleck over the disposition of the Harpers Ferry garrison, he sent a telegram to Washington asking to be relieved of command.

His request was promptly granted, and the search for a successor began.

Pennsylvania looked like paradise to the invading Confederates. Its lush fields of wheat, oats, and corn; its well-tended orchards of apple, peach, and cherry trees; and its tidy split-rail fences and big whitewashed barns ("positively more tastily built than two-thirds of the houses in Waco," exclaimed an awestruck Texas private) were in stark contrast to the desolate landscapes they had left behind in Virginia. The farther north the gray columns went, the larger and more prosperous the farms became. On all sides, henhouses, milk parlors, and vegetable gardens beckoned irresistibly. With eyes as big as saucers and stomachs growling like exploding artillery rounds, the soldiers broke ranks and helped themselves.

This fertile countryside was populated by the Pennsylvania Dutch, a thrifty, hardworking people whose ancestors had immigrated to America from southwestern Germany in the early 1700s. They wanted nothing to do with the war, and when the hungry Confederates descended on their farms, they offered no resistance beyond angry looks and sharp words. What upset them most, wrote Colonel E. Porter Alexander, was not the loss of foodstuffs, which they could easily replace, but the mess the soldiers made. Dirt and disarray offended their sense of order, something he discovered when he stopped at a farmhouse one hot afternoon to ask for a drink of water. The farm's owner was standing in the front yard, so distraught he could barely speak. He pointed to mud tracked onto his porch and to a path beaten through his wheat field and sputtered: "Dere ain't no water! De well is done pump dry! And just look at dis porch vere dey been! And see dere ver dey tramples down dat wheat! Mein Gott! Mein Gott! I'se heard of de horrors of war before but I never see what dey was till now!"

Alexander felt sorry for the man and rode on without bothering him any further, but most of the Confederates were not so considerate. Recalling the shattered farmsteads of Virginia and figuring that turnabout was fair play, they foraged with a heavy hand. "Here's your played-out rebellion!" they called to the unhappy householders as they ripped apart barns and rifled root cellars.

The passivity of Pennsylvania's civilians greatly encouraged the Southerners. It supported their theory that the North would sue for peace if it suffered one more major defeat. "We might get to Philadelphia without a fight, I believe, if we should desire to go," one of them declared. Ewell, who was now at Chambersburg, was eager to capitalize on the situation. On June 25 he divided his corps into two detachments, the better to exploit the bounty of the Pennsylvania countryside. He ordered Early's division to march to York by way of Gettysburg, while he accompanied the divisions of Rodes and Johnson as they made their way down the Cumberland Valley to Carlisle.

Early's men departed at daybreak on June 26, heading across South Mountain, a two-thousand-foot-high ridge that lay between Chambersburg and Gettysburg. At the foot of the escarpment, about two miles east of Greenwood, they came upon the Caledonia iron works, a business belonging to Congressman Thaddeus Stevens. Stevens was a fire-breathing Republican radical; he had exhorted Federal soldiers to "Free every slave—slay every traitor—burn every rebel mansion." Thus when the order was given to demolish his furnace, forge, and rolling mill, the Confederates were only too happy to obey. Continuing on their way after this enjoyable diversion, they scaled the mountain and advanced down the eastern slope toward Cashtown and Mummasburg. Although it was a steamy day, with intermittent rain showers dampening the road, the hike was not unpleasant. "The cherry crop was immense," one of the soldiers recalled, "and the great trees often overhung the highway laden with ripe fruit. The infantry would break off great branches and devour the cherries as they marched along. Regiments thus equipped reminded me of the scene in *Macbeth* where 'Birnam's wood do come to Dunsinane.' "

Approaching Gettysburg late that afternoon, the division ran into the Twenty-sixth Pennsylvania Militia, a home-defense unit that had been mustered into government service four days earlier. The "band-box boys," as the rebels called these amateurs, fired a few wild shots and then took to their heels, which was a good thing, Early sarcastically wrote, as otherwise some of them might have been hurt.

On June 28 the Southern soldiers ransacked York. They also wrecked a ten-mile section of the Northern Central Railroad before moving on to Wrightsville on the Susquehanna River. Early hoped to cross the Wrightsville-Columbia bridge, cut the Pennsylvania Railroad at Lancaster, then attack Harrisburg from the east. His plan was frustrated, however, when pickets guarding the bridge set it afire. The Susquehanna was too deep to be forded at Wrightsville; he was forced to take his division back to York and await further orders from Ewell.

Old Bald Head was in Carlisle, having arrived there on the afternoon of June 27. His detachment had seized 3,000 head of cattle, 5,000 barrels of flour, and $50,000 worth of miscellaneous supplies during its trek through the Cumberland Valley. Its lead elements were now camped on the outskirts of Harrisburg, and the city looked ripe for the taking. Scouts reported that bridges over the Susquehanna were intact and that the breastworks on the east bank were only lightly defended. Ewell knew that the capture of the Pennsylvania state capital would send shock waves through the North. He ordered General Rodes to prepare his division for a cross-river assault.

The attack never took place. On the afternoon of June 29, a courier arrived at his headquarters with an urgent dispatch from Lee: Ewell's corps was to drop whatever it was doing and hurry south to rejoin the rest of the Army of Northern Virginia, which was concentrating for battle in the vicinity of Cashtown.

S hortly after midnight on June 28, a U.S. government locomotive ground to a halt at the train station in Frederick, Maryland. Colonel James Hardie, aide-de-camp to Secretary of War Stanton, climbed down from the cab. Drunken enlisted men "ripe for rudeness or mischief" filled the depot's waiting room, and Hardie bitterly regretted that he was not wearing his uniform. He was even sorrier when he stepped outside and tried to commandeer a vehicle to take him to the Army of the Potomac's encampment on the edge of town. No one believed him when he said he was a colonel traveling on official business. Only after he flashed a wad of greenbacks was he able to obtain a horse and buggy. The driver demanded an exorbitant sum, but Hardie did not haggle; he had to get to the army as quickly as possible and find Major General George Gordon Meade.

Several hours earlier Hardie had been summoned to the War Department, where a meeting between Stanton and Lincoln was just breaking up. The two men had been discussing who should succeed Hooker. It was imperative that a selection be made immediately, but the list of candidates left much to be desired. Stanton had gone over each general's qualifications, finding much to criticize and little to praise. Finally, after considerable hemming and hawing, he had recommended Meade as the best of a mediocre lot. As a corps commander Meade had shown that he was a competent handler of troops; he had kept his nose out of politics; and he was from Pennsylvania. This last credential seemed to impress the president. "He will fight well on his own dunghill," Lincoln muttered. Halleck hastily drafted the necessary orders, and Hardie was dispatched to Maryland to deliver them.

Now the colonel was driving through the rain-soaked countryside south of Frederick, searching for Meade's bivouac. At 3 A.M. he found it. Talking his way past a suspicious sentry, he entered Meade's tent. "I'm afraid I've come to give you some trouble, General," he announced as he shook the sleeping officer awake. Meade bolted upright on his cot, certain, he later wrote, that he was about to be arrested for criticizing Hooker. When

Hardie explained that he was being placed in command of the army, Meade protested that he didn't want the job. Hardie told him he had no choice, whereupon the general snatched the order from his hands and studied it intently. He was silent for a moment as he digested its contents; then he stood up. "Well," he sighed, hitching up his sagging long underwear, "I've been tried and condemned without a hearing, and I suppose I shall have to go to the execution."

A short while later Meade and Hardie arrived at Army of the Potomac headquarters to effect the change of command. Hooker took the news gracefully. He ushered his successor into his tent and briefed him on the current situation. The two generals shook hands at the conclusion of the meeting, and it was only then that Hooker's composure slipped. His face wrinkled up and his eyes teared as he confessed to Meade that he was glad to be rid of the responsibility of command. He had "had enough," he said, "and almost wished he had never been born."

On June 10, the day that the Confederate army set out for Pennsylvania, Lee had written an unusual letter to President Davis. In it he had taken note of the growing antiwar movement in Indiana and Ohio, discussed its potential for "dividing and weakening our enemies," and suggested to the president that he consider making overtures to the "friends of peace at the North."

The idea intrigued Davis, and now that the Army of Northern Virginia was rampaging through Pennsylvania, he thought it was time to act on it. Vice President Stephens was of a like mind. From his home in Crawfordville, Georgia, he proposed that he contact his old friend Abraham Lincoln (the two had served in Congress together in the late 1840s) to discuss the issue of prisoner-of-war exchanges. Once he was in conference with Lincoln on this point, he wrote, "I am not without hopes, that indirectly, I could turn attention to a general adjustment, upon such a basis as might ultimately be acceptable to both parties and stop the further effusion of blood."

Davis promptly called Stephens to Richmond. On June 26 the two men met and talked over the details of the proposed diplomatic mission. The vice president would travel to the U.S. capital and enter into negotiations with Lincoln. Although Davis did not say so, he hoped that Stephens would arrive in Washington from the south at the same time that Confederate troops, fresh from a smashing victory in Pennsylvania, were marching toward it from the north.

George Armstrong Custer was in a foul mood on the night of June 28. It was pouring rain, and he had been assigned the tedious chore of inspecting pickets. Hunching his shoulders in a vain effort to keep water from running under his collar, he splashed from one outpost to the next, checking that the vedettes were awake and properly posted. It took several hours for him to make the circuit, and by the time he returned to General Pleasonton's command post, he was drenched, exhausted, and thoroughly dejected.

Sliding off his horse, he tramped through the mud to the big tent he shared with the other members of Pleasonton's staff. As he threw back the flap and stepped inside, a mocking voice intoned: "Gentlemen, General Custer!" There was a roar of laughter, and then someone else called out, "How are you, General? You're looking well, General!"

Under ordinary circumstances Custer would have ignored the teasing, but not tonight; he was too wet and too tired. When another joker shouted, "Hello, General!" he swore loudly and balled up his fists. Before he could lunge at his tormentor, his good friend, Lieutenant George W. Yates, pinned his arms and whispered, "Look on the table."

Turning around, he saw an official War Department envelope addressed to BRIGADIER GENERAL GEORGE A. CUSTER, U.S. VOLS. sitting on his camp desk. Thinking it was part of the joke, he angrily tore it open. Out fell his commission as brigadier general and orders for him to assume command of the Second Brigade of the Third Cavalry Division. With trembling hands he examined the documents to see if they were genuine; they were. In an attempt to inject more aggressiveness into the Union cavalry corps, Alfred Pleasonton had recommended his hard-charging aide for a brigadier's star. Custer had been jumped three grades—major, lieutenant colonel, and colonel—and made a general. He was a general at the age of twenty-three, the youngest in the army by more than two years.

He mumbled his thanks as the other staff officers crowded around to offer their congratulations. Tears of joy filled his eyes, and it was all he could do to keep from breaking down completely.

Later that same evening, at the Army of Northern Virginia's headquarters in Shetter's Woods east of Chambersburg, Lee was awakened by a loud rapping on his tent pole. It was Major John W. Fairfax of Longstreet's staff. He told the general that a Southern spy (or "scout," as they were euphemistically called) had just come through the picket line with startling news. The Union army was not in Virginia, as the Confederate high command had assumed; it had crossed the Potomac and was camped at Frederick, only thirty-five miles from Chambersburg.

Lee rose from his cot and began to pace around the tent, frowning and pulling at his beard. As a rule, he distrusted spies. But it had been four days since he had heard anything from Jeb Stuart, and he was starved for intelligence about the enemy's movements.

"I don't know what to do," he finally said to Fairfax. "I have no confidence in any scout. What do you make of this fellow?"

The major had no opinion, but he allowed that Longstreet thought highly of the man. With a sigh Lee agreed to see him. A moment later a short, stoop-shouldered individual with a matted brown beard and darting hazel-colored eyes stepped into the tent.

His name was Harrison, he said, and he had spent the past two weeks hanging around the bars and brothels of Washington, gathering information about the Army of the Potomac. On June 26 a garrulous Union officer had told him that Federal formations were advancing into Maryland. He had immediately set out to find and tally them, traveling by night and making his observations by day. As of this morning, he told Lee, five corps of Yankee infantry were located within a ten-mile radius of Frederick. He had also heard a rumor that Hooker had been fired and replaced by a general named Meade.

Lee listened impassively, betraying neither surprise nor concern, but after Harrison left, he sprang into action. The enemy army was perilously close. He had to concentrate his divided forces before they were defeated in detail. Orders flew fast and furious. A courier galloped off to Carlisle to recall Ewell. Another headed for Fayetteville, where Hill's corps was bivouacked. A third raced into Chambersburg to alert Longstreet. Harrisburg was no longer the Confederate objective, Lee informed his lieutenants; instead, the Army of Northern Virginia would converge on Cashtown, where it would be in position to intercept the bluecoats as they advanced into Pennsylvania.

The absence of Stuart's cavalry made Lee extremely anxious. He sought to disguise his unease by bantering with his subordinates, but when they began to disparage the Army of the Potomac's new commander, saying he was bound to be another bungler like Burnside and Hooker, he brought them up short. He had served with Meade before the war, he said, and knew him to be a solid professional. "General Meade will commit no blunder on my front," he lectured his staff, "and if I make one he will make haste to take advantage of it."

The young officers piped down out of deference to their chief, but they were far from chastened. To a man they believed that the Yankees were going to be routed in the coming battle, regardless of who was leading them. "[We] scare them so badly they will be half whipped before they commence to fight," one of them crowed in a letter to his wife. "I wish we could meet and have the matter settled at once."

That wish was about to be granted.

Forty-seven-year-old George Gordon Meade was a singularly unattractive soldier. Tall, scrawny, and balding, with scaly skin, a beaklike nose, and a cold myopic stare, he looked, in the words of one of his subordinates, like "a damned old goggle-eyed snapping turtle." A scowl seemed permanently etched on his face. His voice was pinched and querulous, and he was always on the brink of losing his temper. His long-suffering adjutant, Colonel Theodore Lyman, likened him to a firecracker with a fuse that was permanently lit; an explosion was never far off.

Meade was a West Point graduate and Mexican War veteran who had spent the bulk of his military career working as a topographer at various backwater posts. When the South seceded, he had made use of his wife's political connections (she came from a prominent Philadelphia family) to trade his surveyor's transit for a general's sword, then methodically worked his way up the Army of the Potomac's chain of command. He had performed well enough to merit steady advancement, but not so brilliantly as to draw undue attention to himself. His colleagues in the Union officer corps considered him a "smooth bore, [not] a rifle," and they were surprised that he had been chosen to succeed Hooker. Most of the enlisted men had never heard of him. "What has Meade ever done?" they asked when his promotion was announced. The best thing anyone could say about him was that he had never made any ruinous mistakes. Of course he had never had any great successes either. The army would have to "take him on trial," one man glumly wrote, and pray that he was up to the task.

Meade was under pressure from the moment he took the helm on June 28. He had to figure out where his forces were, familiarize himself with his predecessor's plans, study intelligence reports on the Confederate army, determine what his course of action was going to be, and communicate it to the War Department, which was already pressing him for details of his strategy. Hooker had intended to strike westward into the Cumberland Valley, severing Lee's communications with Virginia and forcing him to fall back toward the Potomac. Meade thought this was a poor idea. He did not believe there were any communications to be cut, and after consulting with Major General John Reynolds, the army's senior corps commander, he rejected Hooker's scheme in favor of a march on Harrisburg, which seemed to be the Confederates' main target. "I must move toward the Susquehanna," he wired Halleck late on the afternoon of June 28, "keeping Washington and Baltimore well covered, and if the enemy is checked in his attempt to cross the Susquehanna, or if he turns toward Baltimore, give him battle."

In conformance to this strategy, the army set out at daybreak on June 29. The cavalry led the way, followed closely by the infantry and artillery. North toward Emmitsburg, Taneytown, and Westminster the blue soldiers went, digging hard for the Pennsylvania line. As they passed through villages where cheering citizens waved flags, threw flowers, and pressed forward to offer them food and drink, their spirits rose and their determination to expel the invaders hardened.

As the sun was setting on June 29, a flaxen-haired horseman with a shiny new brigadier's star sewn on the crown of his hat galloped into the bivouac of the Second Brigade, Third Division, Army of the Potomac Cavalry Corps, at Littlestown, Pennsylvania. He was wearing a black velveteen jacket adorned with thick loops of gold braid, breeches of the same material stuffed into glossy Philadelphia top boots, a blue flannel sailor shirt with white stars embroidered on the collar tips, and a long, loosely knotted cravat of bloodred silk. As he dismounted, troopers came running from all over the encampment to get a closer look at him. After he strode into the headquarters tent, there was an explosion of whistles and profane exclamations. Nonregulation uniforms were fairly common in the cavalry, but this outfit was so gaudy, it left the onlookers dumbfounded.

George Armstrong Custer was five months shy of his twenty-fourth birthday, but he had some very definite ideas about how a general should dress. His mentor, Alfred Pleasonton, had told him that a successful commander was like a stage actor: he had to hold the undivided attention of his men, make them feel they were participants in a rousing drama, inspire them to forget their fears and plunge headlong into combat. It was with that advice in mind that Custer had contrived his garish costume. He wanted to make himself as conspicuous as possible so that in battle his soldiers (and any newspapermen who might be about) would always know where he was. He also wanted to give his brigade a sense of identity. He hoped the troopers would emulate him by sporting oversize hats and bright red neckerchiefs of their own. Of such things was esprit de corps born.

For now he was an outsider, and the greeting he received inside the headquarters tent was far from cordial. The Second Brigade's colonels were all older than Custer, and they all thought they were more deserving of a general's star than he. Their sullen expressions and sloppy salutes conveyed their envy and resentment more powerfully than words.

The young brigadier knew that he had to take control of the situation at once. Any sign of doubt or hesitation on his part, any attempt to be conciliatory or ingratiating, and all would be lost. Puffing out his chest and slapping his riding crop against his boots, he tongue-lashed the assembled officers. They were to obey his every order, instantly and to the letter, or he would run them out of the army, he said. Then he went on an inspection tour of the camp and found fault with everything. He berated the regimental commanders in front of their men and threatened severe punishment if corrective action was not taken immediately.

By the time Custer retired for the evening, his subordinates were livid. Captain Frederick Whitaker heard them raging about "having this 'boy,' this 'popinjay,' this 'affected dandy,' with his 'girl's hair,' his 'swagger,' and 'West Point conceit,' put 'over *men,* sir, men old enough to be his father.' " Custer heard them, too, but he did not flinch. He had to show that he was the boss. He had antagonized the brigade's officers tonight, but he was sure they would have a change of heart after they had seen him in action. One rousing saber charge, and there would be no more questions about his fitness to lead; one glorious victory, and they would gladly accept his strict discipline. The Second Brigade was going to be the best outfit in the cavalry, and he was going to win a second star or die trying.

The first Confederate unit to reach Cashtown was Major General Henry Heth's division of Hill's corps. It arrived on the afternoon of June 29 and went into camp to wait for the rest of the army to show up. One of Heth's aides had picked up a copy of the Gettysburg *Compiler* that morning and spotted an advertisement for R. F. McIlheny's dry-goods store. The notice read: "1863 Spring Styles, splendid assortment of . . . boots and shoes, comprising men's fine calf boots, men's balmorals, men's congress gaiters . . . all of which will be sold as cheap as the cheapest. Let all who wish to supply themselves with good and substantial work call and examine our stock." The aide knew that the division desperately needed footwear. He showed the ad to Heth, who smiled and immediately sent for one of his brigadiers, James Johnston Pettigrew.

Pettigrew was to take his troops over to Gettysburg first thing tomorrow, Heth announced, and pay a visit to merchant McIlheny's store.

It was hot and muggy on the morning of June 30 when the North Carolinians of Pettigrew's brigade started out on their foraging expedition. Normally they would have griped about the sultry weather and the superfluousness of the mission, but not today: they wanted new shoes as badly as their generals did. They made good time as they tramped eastward along the Chambersburg Pike, and by 11 A.M. they could see the rooftops of Gettysburg on the horizon.

Pettigrew rode ahead to reconnoiter. He scanned the hazy landscape and satisfied himself that no enemy troops were in the vicinity. He was about to tell his men to move forward when out of the corner of his eye he spotted a dust plume spiraling into the air south of town. Peering through his binoculars, he saw that it was being kicked up by a column of Federal cavalry cantering up the Emmitsburg Road. He quickly wheeled his mount around and galloped back to his command, swearing loudly as he went. Before leaving Cashtown, he had been told to avoid getting into a fight; Lee didn't want to start a battle until the entire Confederate army was at hand. Pettigrew knew that his infantrymen could easily brush aside this party of blue riders, but orders were orders. He directed his brigade to withdraw to a point four miles west of Gettysburg, then headed back to Cashtown to tell Generals Heth and Hill what he had seen.

When Heth heard that Pettigrew had returned empty-handed, he was bitterly disappointed. He conceded that the North Carolina brigadier had followed Lee's instructions to the letter, but he made it clear that he didn't think much of such extreme punctiliousness. Hill was sure that the force Pettigrew had spotted was a scouting party, nothing more. He had it on good authority that the Army of the Potomac was still in Maryland.

Heth perked up when he heard this. "If there is no objection, General," he said, "I will take my division tomorrow and go to Gettysburg and get those shoes."

"None in the world," Hill cheerfully replied.

ELEVEN

SIEGE

The clink and scrape of thousands of picks and shovels rose from the ridgetops east of Vicksburg as Grant's soldiers spaded their way through the sandy soil of the Mississippi River bluffs, laying out a line of entrenchments parallel to those of Pemberton's Confederates. It was hard work in the steamy summer heat, but there was very little complaining. After storming the city's defenses twice and being bloodily repulsed both times, the Federals were willing to give siege warfare a try. "Out-camping" the enemy, their commander called it, explaining that as long as the rebels were hemmed in by land and water, they would have to subsist on the supplies they had on hand, and "these could not last always." In other words, empty stomachs would accomplish what bullets could not.

It sounded simple enough, but the Union soldiers soon discovered that laying siege was a complex and tedious business. First the Confederate perimeter had to be encircled by fortifications. Then came the time-consuming task of digging zigzag approach trenches, called "saps," toward the main enemy strongpoints. Firing steps, artillery emplacements, and timbered dugouts where men could eat and sleep had to be constructed, and a network of "parallels"—trenches branching off perpendicular to the main approaches—had to be laid out to facilitate the movement of troops and allow for storage of food, ammunition, and other gear.

Grant's biggest concern, as he began investing Vicksburg, was the size of his army. Its smallness had worked to his advantage during the May campaign, when the premium was on speed and maneuverability. Now that there were siege works to dig, entrenchments to garrison, and a complicated logistical network to manage, a force of 50,000 was not sufficient. Although Pemberton was unaware of it, Union troops were spread so thin during the last week of May that two of the eight roads leading out of town were virtually unguarded. Grant needed reinforcements, and fast.

In the past the War Department had always treated the Army of the Tennessee like an unwanted stepchild when it came to allotting troops and equipment; but now that it had won a string of spectacular victories and was poised to take Vicksburg, nothing was too good for it. By the second week of June, five additional divisions were on their way to Mississippi from Tennessee, Kentucky, and Missouri. The knowledge that he would soon enjoy decisive numerical superiority did wonders for Grant's confidence. "The enemy are now undoubtedly in our grasp," he assured the authorities in Washington. "The fall of Vicksburg and the capture of most of the garrison can only be a question of time."

Inside the beleaguered city Pemberton insisted that he had made the right decision when he elected to stand and fight. He knew that his army was in dire straits, however; unless help arrived soon, the supply situation would become critical. Thanks to his foresight in ordering the troops to gather up everything edible on the retreat from the Big Black River, there were enough provisions to feed the army and the civilian population for approximately six weeks. But of ammunition—percussion caps in particular—there was an alarming shortage. "An army will be necessary to relieve Vicksburg," he informed his superiors in a dispatch smuggled through the Union lines. "Will it not be sent? Please let me hear from you, if possible."

Vicksburg's citizens were also looking for deliverance, and there was no doubt in their minds where it would come from. Johnston, they told each other, was getting ready to march to their rescue. Once his plans were perfected, he would fall on Grant's rear, and the siege would be lifted. This rosy scenario was repeated so often and with such conviction that it became an article of faith among civilians and soldiers alike. "The utmost confidence is felt that we can maintain our position until succor comes from the outside," declared *Daily Citizen* editor J. M. Swords in an edition shrunk by a shortage of newsprint to a size of six by eighteen inches.

What the townspeople did not know, and would not have believed if they had been told, was that the man they were counting on to act as their savior was loath to mount a rescue mission. "Vicksburg is of no value," Johnston had written Pemberton on May 17. "If it is not too late, evacuate." Pemberton had rejected this counsel, and now Johnston was inclined to let him suffer the consequences. A visitor to the Virginian's camp at Canton, twenty miles northeast of Jackson, was dismayed by the petulant, pessimistic mood prevailing there. Everyone denigrated Pemberton as a coward and traitor and spoke of the fall of Vicksburg as if it were a foregone conclusion.

Even though he planned no action now or at any time in the foreseeable future, Johnston deemed it prudent to string Pemberton along rather than tell him the unpleasant truth. "I am trying to gather a force which may relieve you," he advised his subordinate in a note dated May 19. "Hold out." Several days later he sent an even more encouraging message: "Bragg is sending a division. When it comes, I will move to you. Which do you think is the best route? How and where is the enemy encamped? What is your force?"

Pemberton's hopes soared when he received this communiqué. He immediately penned a response answering all of Johnston's questions. When a week passed with no reply, he followed up with a second, more urgent message: "When may I expect you to move, and in what direction? My subsistence may be put down for about twenty days."

There was no reply.

While Pemberton waited and Johnston prevaricated, the Union besiegers tightened their stranglehold on Vicksburg. On May 27, at the behest of General Sherman, Admiral Porter sent one of his biggest ironclads, the fourteen-gun *Cincinnati,* to blast the Confederate batteries on Fort Hill, a bluff overlooking the Mississippi three-quarters of a mile north of the city. The idea was to neutralize the rebel bastion so that Sherman's infantry could smash through and take the town.

Cincinnati quickly ran into trouble. Her crewmembers could not elevate their guns high enough to hit the batteries on the steep hill, and the current was so swift that the bow had to be pointed upstream to hold position, thereby exposing the unarmored stern to enemy fire. The Confederate artillerists took advantage, riddling the ironclad's vulnerable aftersection with eight- and ten-inch shells. The magazine was destroyed, the hull holed, and twenty sailors killed or wounded. With his vessel sinking beneath him, *Cincinnati*'s commander steered toward the Louisiana shore and ordered the crew to abandon ship. Moments later the gunboat went down in three fathoms of water, drowning fifteen men who were trapped belowdecks. The mission had failed miserably, but Sherman and Porter were unfazed. Later that night they sent a salvage team to recover *Cincinnati*'s guns. Within a few days these pieces had been refurbished and mounted in a ridgetop battery that was bombarding Fort Hill.

On the landward side Grant's foot soldiers were rapidly mastering the fine points of siege warfare. "Whether a battery was to be constructed by men who had never built one before, a sap roller made by those who had never heard the name, or a ship's gun carriage to be built, it was done, and after a few trials, well done," wrote the army's chief engineer. By the end of May, a twelve-mile-long chain of forts, artillery emplacements, and rifle pits ringed the rebel defenses, and the bluecoats had begun to burrow their way toward the enemy earthworks.

To shield themselves while they worked in the approach trenches, the Federals fabricated protective devices called "sap rollers"—large, earth-filled baskets that could be trundled forward as the excavation progressed. These mobile barricades were impervious to bullets, so the Confederates used homemade incendiary projectiles—minié balls stuffed with turpentine-soaked cotton—to set them ablaze. The Union soldiers countered by posting sniper teams all along the line. Whenever they saw movement behind the rebel breastworks, they opened fire, forcing the enemy to take cover. The acknowledged ace among the Yankee sharpshooters was Lieutenant Henry C. Foster. Called "Coonskin" in recognition of his hunting skills, he would hole up in a camouflaged burrow for days at a time, waiting to pick off any grayback who was careless enough to expose himself.

The Confederates had their snipers too. They turned parts of the front line into free-fire zones that Union soldiers ventured into only at great peril. One such place was a gully not far from Grant's headquarters. The road crossing it had been declared off limits to pedestrian and wagon traffic because so many men and animals had been killed there. However, reported Sylvanus Cadwallader, horsemen would occasionally ride to the edge of the timber cover and then, putting spurs to their animals, dash across the open ravine. He was watching one afternoon when a dispatch rider was hit while running the gauntlet. The bullets came "whizzing and zipping," Cadwallader wrote; one of them nicked the courier's bladder. Although the wound was oozing blood and urine, the man insisted he was not seriously hurt and rode on to headquarters with his satchel full of messages. He was dead by morning.

Rebel harassing fire slowed but did not stop the advance of the Union sappers. Artillery barrages, which would have brought their digging to an abrupt halt, could not be resorted to because the ammunition supply was so low. Federal batteries suffered no such shortage. They were in action from dawn to dusk, flinging shells at the rebel defensive works and at Vicksburg itself. By the second week of June, Grant had more than 200 land-based guns at his disposal. The firepower of this massive arsenal was augmented by the mortars and naval cannon of Porter's fleet.

By and large the targets selected were military, but the Union gunners—particularly those manning the mortar schooners tied up along the Louisiana shore—were not averse to dropping ordnance into the town. "Rats, into your ratholes!" they jeered as their shells exploded over the rooftops.

A Union artillery emplacement. (Courtesy U.S. Army Military History Institute)

The fiery stream of projectiles was terrifying to Vicksburg's residents. Although the toll in dead and wounded was relatively light, horror stories abounded. People talked of the two men who had been shaking hands when a shell burst left one of them holding the severed fingers of the other; of the baby boy torn from his mother's arms and pinned to the nursery wall by an iron splinter; of the amputees killed in bed when a mortar round leveled their hospital ward. Almost as bad for morale were the near misses. A man chopping firewood in the yard of his Washington Street home was called away for a moment; when he returned, he found that a bombshell had finished the job for him, pulverizing his sawbuck and smashing the logs into kindling. Nine-year-old Willie Lord barely escaped being cut in two when a projectile passed so close to him that it scorched his jacket. Dora Miller was in her second-story bedchamber when an explosion outside riddled the room with shrapnel, tearing huge chunks of plaster from the ceiling and covering her with dust and debris. "I snatched up my comb and brush and ran down [to the cellar]," she wrote in her journal. "It has taken all the afternoon to get the plaster out of my hair, for my hands [are] rather shaky."

After enduring a few days of shelling, many Vicksburgers chose to abandon their homes and move into caves quarried out of the loess hills. These bomb shelters came in a wide variety of shapes and sizes. Some were like animal burrows, tiny grottoes that could be entered only on hands and knees. Others were spacious, multiroom affairs furnished with tables, chairs, lamps, and rugs. But whether large or small, lavishly appointed or bare, the musty, mosquito-infested caves were wretched places to live. Emma Balfour felt a sense of suffocation from being underground, an incipient panic stemming from claustrophobia, and nightmare visions of being buried alive. Willie Lord tried to pretend that he had been transported to the magical world of the *Arabian Nights*, but "squalling infants, family quarrels, and the noise of general discord" always brought him crashing back to reality. His sister, Lida, was more succinct in her description of the cramped conditions: we were packed together "like sardines in a box," she wrote.

For the cave dwellers the timetable for eating and bathing was dictated by the rhythms of the shelling. When the Yankee guns fell silent, the people scurried from their holes to empty chamber pots, light cooking fires, wash themselves, and bolt down unappetizing meals. Always they kept their eyes and ears open. The warble of an incoming Parrott shell or the telltale smoke trail of a smoldering mortar fuse would send them scuttling back into their subterranean shelter—rodentlike behavior that prompted Union artillerists to rename Vicksburg "Prairie Dog Village."

During the first week of June a petition was circulated among the townspeople calling on Pemberton to arrange a cease-fire so that noncombatants could be evacuated from the city. Only four signatures were obtained, clear indication that the Vicksburgers were determined to stick it out despite the danger and discomfort. "Not the slightest fear was expressed of the city ever falling into the hands of the enemy," wrote a reporter for the *Daily Whig.* "Not a man, woman, or child believed such an event at all likely to occur."

Between June 8 and June 14, four fresh Federal divisions arrived by riverboat from Memphis, giving Grant a total of 77,000 men. "Our situation is for the first time, during the entire western campaign, what it should be," he announced, secure in the knowledge that once he got these reinforcements deployed, there was no way the Vicksburg garrison could escape. By the end of the month, Union saps would be butting up against the base of the enemy's parapets. Then if hunger and lack of ammunition had not already forced them to capitulate, the Confederates would be overwhelmed by breaching operations, followed by a massive assault. Nor was he worried about Johnston leading a relief column into Vicksburg. "You say he has 30,000 men with him?" Grant said to an apprehensive staff officer. "That will give us 30,000 more prisoners than we now have."

As certain as he was of final victory, Grant was an unhappy man during the first two weeks of June. His wife had gone home to Illinois, and he sorely missed her companionship. To make matters worse, the plodding pace of the siege left him bored and restless. He tried to keep busy supervising the work of the sappers, but there were many days when time hung heavy on his hands. To satisfy his need for physical activity, he would saddle up his favorite horse, a jet-black steed named Jeff Davis, and gallop full speed across the fields in the rear of the Union batteries. When his craving for excitement became more than he could stand, he would head for the front lines and deliberately expose himself to enemy fire. "You God-damn idiot, get down!" an irate Minnesota private yelled on one of these occasions, unaware of whom he was addressing. When he was told that he had just cursed at the commanding general, he snarled: "I don't care who he is! What's he fooling around here for anyway? We're shot at enough without taking any chances with him."

It was around this time that Grant's appetite for alcohol got the better of him. He had kept his drinking under control for the past six months, taking an occasional nip but not overindulging as he had done in the past. It was characteristic of him to turn to the bottle whenever he was bored or depressed, however, and that was exactly what he did during the third week of the siege.

The trouble started on the evening of June 5, when John Rawlins, Grant's chief of staff, noticed a crate of champagne sitting beside Grant's tent. Rawlins, the son of an alcoholic, was a rabid teetotaler. He considered it his sworn duty to keep the general sober at all times. He ordered the offending case removed, then confronted Grant about it. Grant said he was saving the champagne to celebrate the fall of Vicksburg, but Rawlins wasn't fooled. Empty bottles scattered around the tent made it clear that the festivities had started early. Stalking off to his own quarters, Rawlins composed a reproachful letter to his superior. "Tonight when you should . . . have been in bed, I find you where the wine bottle has just been emptied in company with those who drink and urge you to do likewise," he wrote. Such dissolution was intolerable in an officer who had been entrusted with the lives of thousands of men, he declared. He threatened to resign his post unless the general pledged to leave liquor alone.

Grant slipped out of camp before Rawlins could deliver his letter. Accompanied by several members of his staff, he rode to the boat landing at Chickasaw Bayou and embarked on a steamer that was heading up the Yazoo River to the town of Satartia. The announced purpose of this trip was

General Ulysses S. Grant and Colonel John A. Rawlins.
(Courtesy Chicago Historical Society)

to inspect Union troops based at Satartia, but it soon became clear that Grant had other activities in mind. "He made several trips to the barroom of the boat in a short time and became stupid in speech and staggering in gait," wrote Sylvanus Cadwallader, who happened to be a passenger on the craft the general had commandeered.

Cadwallader admired Grant and did not want to see him jeopardize his career. He decided to intervene before things got completely out of hand. "I enticed him into his stateroom," he later wrote, "locked myself in with him (having the key in my pocket), and commenced throwing bottles of whiskey which stood on the table, through the windows, over the guards, into the river. Grant soon ordered me out, but I refused to go. . . . As it was a very hot day and the stateroom almost suffocating, I insisted on his taking off his coat, vest, and boots, and lying down in one of the berths. After much resistance I succeeded, and soon fanned him to sleep."

When the steamer reached Satartia several hours later, Grant was still in a stupor. His aides agreed that the inspection tour should be canceled. The boat turned around and headed back downriver with the general snoring loudly in his bunk. To the immense relief of his entourage, he emerged from his cabin the next morning "fresh as a rose, clean shirt and all, and quite himself." But within the hour he was drunk again and demanding to be taken to Chickasaw Bayou.

Cadwallader knew this would never do. "If we had started then we would have arrived at the Bayou about the middle of the afternoon, when the landing would have been alive with officers, men, and trains from all parts of the army," he wrote. Determined to keep Grant from disgracing himself in public, he connived with the captain to run the steamer onto a mudbank and keep it there until after sunset.

The docks at Chickasaw Bayou were dark and deserted when the vessel tied up later that evening. Cadwallader ordered the horses unloaded at once, hoping to make a quick getaway. When he went to Grant's stateroom, the general was nowhere to be found. Acting on a hunch, he headed for a nearby sutler's boat. There he discovered Grant sitting at a table covered with whiskey and champagne bottles. Cadwallader begged him to return to Vicksburg at once, an admonition Grant obeyed with startling alacrity. Rushing down the gangplank, he leaped onto his horse, dug in his spurs, and rocketed off into the night.

"The road was crooked and tortuous, following the firmest ground between sloughs and bayous, and was bridged over these in several places," recounted Cadwallader. "Each bridge had one or more guards stationed at it to prevent fast riding or driving over it, but Grant paid no attention to roads or sentries. He went at full speed through camps and corrals . . . and literally tore through and over everything in his way."

Grant was soon lost from sight, but Cadwallader refused to give up the chase. He galloped on, and after crossing the last bayou bridge, three-quarters of a mile from the landing, he overtook his quarry. By now Grant had abandoned his reckless gait and was riding at a slow walk. Cadwallader steered him into a roadside thicket, helped him dismount, and coaxed him into lying down and going to sleep. Then he accosted one of the general's aides and asked him to ride to army headquarters and tell Rawlins that an ambulance was needed immediately. The vehicle arrived an hour and a half later, and after some wrangling Grant climbed in and let himself be carried back to camp.

"We reached headquarters about midnight," Cadwallader recalled. "I stepped out of the ambulance first, and was followed promptly by Grant. He shrugged his shoulders, pulled down his vest . . . and started to his tent as steadily as he ever walked in his life."

The correspondent was dumbfounded; he could not believe Grant had sobered up so quickly. "I turned to Rawlins," he wrote, "and said I was afraid he would think I was the man who had been drunk." Rawlins scowled fiercely. "No," he muttered. "I know him. I want you to tell me the exact facts—and all of them—without any concealment."

He listened to Cadwallader's tale from start to finish, shaking his head and growling in disgust. But he never reported the incident to anyone; nor did he resign from his post as he had threatened to do. He knew that if the story got out, Halleck would sack Grant and replace him with McClernand, a general he considered incompetent. Besides, Grant's binge had done no harm to himself or the army. Rawlins decided to keep it that way. He swore Cadwallader to silence, and Washington never learned of the episode. The newspaperman worried that he would be banished from the department, but when he ran into Grant twenty-four hours later, the general acted as if nothing had happened. To Cadwallader's intense relief, no mention of the incident was made, then or ever afterward.

While the Union commander wrestled with his personal demons, his army continued to tighten its grip on Vicksburg. Artillery pounded the Confederate fortifications around the clock, giving the defenders no chance to rest or make repairs. Sappers worked ceaselessly, pushing their approach trenches closer to the rebel ramparts. Sharpshooters sniped without letup, and cavalry patrolled relentlessly, hunting down Confederate couriers trying to slip back and forth between Vicksburg and Johnston's camp at Canton.

The pressure took its toll. Pemberton reported losing 1,000 men during the last week of May, most to desertion. In early June he was forced to put his army on reduced rations. Each soldier was to be issued four ounces of bacon, four ounces of cornmeal, and six ounces of dried peas per day— less than half the amount they were accustomed to receiving. Dysentery was widespread due to poor hygiene and dirty drinking water, and mosquito-borne diseases also became increasingly prevalent.

As disturbing as these developments were, it was Johnston's failure to mount a rescue mission that upset Pemberton the most. "I have sent couriers to you almost daily," he wrote on June 7. "When may I expect you?" Receiving no reply, he dashed off another note on June 10: "I am waiting most anxiously to know your intentions. . . . Can you not send me a message . . . ?" On June 14 he pleaded: "No information as to your position or movements. . . . The enemy has run his saps to within twenty-five yards of our works." On June 15: "I think your movement should be made as soon as possible." On June 19: "My men have been thirty-four days and nights in trenches, without relief, and the enemy within conversation distance. We are living on very reduced rations, and, as you know, are entirely isolated. What aid am I to expect from you?"

Johnston did not respond.

Unaware of the Virginia general's reluctance to come to their rescue, the citizens of Vicksburg continued to anticipate his arrival. Every time there was a loud cannonade, they would perk up, believing that he was approaching at last. Rumors regarding his whereabouts, the size of his relief force, and his plans for lifting the siege were a staple of conversation. J. M. Swords did his best to breathe life into these reports and to keep spirits high. HO! FOR JOHNSTON! he headlined the June 18 edition of the *Daily Citizen*. "We have nothing to record of his movements," but nevertheless, "we may repose the utmost confidence in his appearance within a very few days. . . . Hold out a few days longer, and our lines will be opened, the enemy driven away, the siege raised, and Vicksburg again in communication with the balance of the Confederacy." It was flimsy stuff, but the people accepted it as gospel, reading it aloud to each other as they huddled in their caves, and copying it into their diaries as though the act of writing it down would somehow make it real.

The sad truth was that Johnston had no intention of trying to save Vicksburg or its defenders. As of June 1, his command numbered approximately 24,000 men—not enough, in his estimation, to drive off the Federals or to engineer a breakout by Pemberton's force. He informed Richmond that he would not go to the city's aid until he received "such reinforcements as will give guarantee of success." The president was angered by the tone of this dispatch. Preventing Vicksburg's fall was of paramount importance, so crucial to the Southern war effort that bold, even desperate measures were called for. And yet here was Johnston declining to risk his reputation unless victory was certain. "We cannot hope for numerical equality, and time will probably increase the disparity," Davis testily wired. Johnston continued to stall, and when the president suggested that he transfer troops to himself from Bragg's army, he claimed that he did not have the authority to do so, as the orders sending him to Mississippi superseded the orders that had made him commander of the Department of the West. Davis assured him that he did indeed have the authority to draw reinforcements from Tennessee, but Johnston disagreed. A long exchange of telegrams ensued, with the two men quibbling over the wording of various orders, each asserting that the other was in error and attempting to prove it with citations to various official documents. While this argument dragged on, Secretary Seddon was monitoring the progress of the siege and becoming more and more worried: "You must rely on what you have," he telegraphed Johnston on June 5; "to relieve Vicksburg, speedy action is essential."

Still Johnston refused to move. In a message to Richmond dated June

15, he dropped all pretense of aggressiveness and flatly stated that Pemberton could not be saved. His defeatism appalled the administration. "Vicksburg must not be lost without a desperate struggle," Seddon wired on the sixteenth. "The interest and the honor of the Confederacy forbid it."

Johnston took three days to respond. When he did, it was to complain that the War Department did not understand the difficulties he was facing. Disgusted, Seddon tried to shame him into action: "The eyes and the hopes of the whole Confederacy are upon you," he wrote. "[I]t is better to fail nobly daring, than, through prudence even, to be inactive." The stratagem did not work. Johnston remained adamant: he would not budge from his base at Canton.

Desperate to loosen the enemy's grip on Vicksburg, the government asked Kirby Smith, commander of the Trans-Mississippi Department, to strike at Union supply depots on the Louisiana side of the river. Smith agreed. He ordered his chief subordinate, Major General Richard Taylor, to undertake the operation. Taylor thought it was a bad idea, but he grudgingly obeyed. At dawn on June 7, he sent a brigade of Texans to attack Milliken's Bend, which was defended by a battalion of recently recruited black soldiers. Although they had received virtually no training and were armed with antiquated muskets, the former slaves fought fiercely. With the help of two of Porter's gunboats, which steamed in close to the levee to provide artillery support, they repulsed the Confederates. That was enough for Taylor; he ordered his force to retreat. "As foreseen, our movement resulted, and could result in nothing," he grumbled. Kirby Smith apparently agreed, for he made no further attempt to aid Pemberton, despite repeated entreaties from Richmond.

With his drinking spree behind him and Vicksburg firmly in his grasp, Grant was feeling his oats. "All is going on here now just right," he wrote a friend on June 15. "We have our trenches pushed up so close to the enemy that we can throw hand grenades over into their forts." Pemberton was not much of an opponent, he averred, nor was Johnston.

Bolstering Grant's confidence were the plaudits he was receiving from Washington. The president himself had called the Vicksburg campaign "one of the most brilliant in the world." Assured that he was in good standing with Lincoln and the War Department, Grant did something he had been wanting to do for months: fire his longtime nemesis, John McClernand.

Unceremoniously relieved of his corps command, McClernand went home to Illinois, where he commenced writing letters to Stanton and Lincoln demanding that he be reinstated. He was the victim of "an atrocious act of usurpation, oppression, and injustice," he claimed, perpetrated by a bungler who had settled on him as a scapegoat for his own failings.

McClernand thought his political connections were strong enough to trump Grant, but he was mistaken. The president refused to intervene. "For me to force you back upon General Grant would be forcing him to resign," he wrote, adding: "I cannot give you a new command, because we have no forces except such as already have commanders."

With those words Lincoln terminated McClernand's military career and sent a clear message to the Union officer corps: henceforward battlefield performance, not political considerations, would dictate who rose and who fell. Grant—unprepossessing but indomitable—was the role model. "Why has he thus at last distanced every other general?" the New York *Times* asked. "In natural brilliancy he is probably surpassed by many of them; in science he certainly is. It all lies simply in the fact that he is *a man of success.*"

As summer settled over Mississippi like a sodden wool blanket, the Union soldiers sweated, slapped mosquitoes, and fought a losing battle against boredom. Shirking was raised to an art form. "Without the stimulus of danger or pecuniary reward, the troops will not work," an officer complained.

One soldier who did not succumb to heat-induced lethargy was Captain Andrew Hickenlooper, chief engineer of the Seventeenth Corps. During the third week of June, he asked that all the former coal miners in the corps be sent to him for a special assignment. From this pool he selected thirty-six of the strongest, most experienced men. They began excavating a tunnel from the end of Logan's Approach—a 640-yard-long trench—to a point underneath the Third Louisiana Redan, a large fort guarding the Jackson Road entrance to Vicksburg. Each six-man team worked for an hour at a time, "two picking, two shoveling, and two handing back the grain sacks filled with earth." Digging through the soft loess, they finished the fifty-foot-long main gallery in two days, then completed two smaller side tunnels radiating out at forty-five-degree angles. On the morning of June 25 they packed 2,200 pounds of gunpowder into the side tunnels, laid down double strands of safety fuse, then sealed off the main gallery with dirt and timbers.

At 3:30 P.M. on June 25 the fuses were lit. Moments later the ground heaved, there was a subterranean rumble, and an immense fountain of earth shot skyward.

Volunteers from the Thirty-first and Forty-fifth Illinois Regiments rushed forward, expecting to encounter no resistance. The Confederates had heard the sounds of digging beneath them, however, and withdrawn to a trench at the rear of the redan. From this sheltered position they savaged the attackers with musketry and artillery fire. Nearly 200 Illinoisans were killed or wounded.

Hickenlooper refused to give up. He had his diggers back at work excavating a new tunnel as soon as the smoke from the first explosion cleared. Six days later, a second, larger one was detonated, inflicting 120 casualties on the Confederates.

As spectacular as Hickenlooper's mines were, starvation was a far more potent weapon. By the end of June, its effect on the rebel troops was becoming apparent to officers on both sides. A Texas colonel reported that his men had "swollen ankles and symptoms of incipient scurvy." A Union officer wrote that the rebels' "indifference to our approach became at some points ludicrous." He offered as an example an incident in which a Federal detachment working to connect two approach trenches discovered that the junction point lay inside the enemy picket line. Their miscalculation was brought to the attention of the rebels, who agreed to withdraw a short distance so that construction could proceed without unnecessary bloodshed. The Union sappers apologized for the inconvenience, but the Confederates were unconcerned: "Oh, that don't make any difference," one of them said. "You Yanks will soon have the place anyway."

Spirits were flagging in Vicksburg as well. Many of the townspeople had abandoned hope of relief and were simply waiting for the end to come. Their city was in ruins. The stench of rotting animal carcasses and unburied human excrement permeated the air. Hunger was a remorseless, gnawing presence that humbled even the most fastidious of appetites. Individuals who had sworn they would never touch mule meat now counted themselves lucky to get a piece of it. Nor did they turn up their noses at other, even more distasteful repasts. "It is a difficult matter for persons surrounded with abundance to realize the feeling produced by extreme hunger," wrote a civilian who lived through the siege. "It must be felt to be realized; and if once felt, the idea of eating dogs, cats, rats, or even human flesh would contain nothing repulsive or repugnant to the feelings."

In Richmond the president and secretary of war were trying everything they could think of to goad Johnston into moving. Davis even floated the idea of going to Mississippi and taking command himself, but his aides talked him out of it, arguing that the duties of his office would not permit him to leave the capital.

Pemberton continued to beseech Johnston to act. A chilling note of desperation had crept into his dispatches. "If I cut my way out, this important position is lost, and many of my men, too," he wrote on June 23. "Can we afford that?" He proposed that Johnston approach Grant and try to strike a deal: Union forces would occupy Vicksburg in exchange for letting Pemberton's army march out with all its arms and equipment. Such an overture "would come with greater prospects of success and better grace from you, while it necessarily could not come at all from me," Pemberton concluded.

It was a preposterous idea. As far as Grant was concerned, Vicksburg and its garrison were already his; he would never agree to such an arrangement. The mere suggestion of it jolted Johnston, however. Suddenly it dawned on him that he was about to be party to an appalling humiliation. This notion was reinforced by a letter he received from his wife, Lydia, who voiced the fear that public opinion would hold him, not Pemberton, responsible for losing Vicksburg. "Don't be uneasy on that subject," Johnston reassured her. "One who discharges his duty manfully and unselfishly will always be respected, although he may not be thought a great man, and I assure you that to be the object of popular clamor is no wish of mine." But he was uneasy on the subject. "Negotiations with Grant for the relief of the garrison, should they become necessary, must be made by you," he wrote Pemberton on June 27. "It would be a confession of weakness on my part, which I ought not to make, to propose them."

He also decided that he had better mount a relief expedition. He still thought it folly to sacrifice two armies for an illusory hope of saving one, but with his reputation on the line, he realized that some sort of face-saving action was necessary. Reluctantly he ordered his troops to prepare for action. On July 3 he informed Pemberton of his plans: he would create a diversion, he wrote, "and thus enable you to cut your way out. . . . I hope to attack the enemy on your front about the 7th. . . . Our firing will show you where we are engaged. If Vicksburg cannot be saved, the garrison must."

It was too late. Pemberton had already begun surrender talks with Grant.

On the morning of July 3, Union soldiers lounging near the Shirley House, 350 yards east of the Third Louisiana Redan, were startled to see a white pennant appear on the parapet of the rebel works. Soon another appeared, and another. The sputter of sniper fire ceased, and all was still. Two Confederate officers emerged and made their way across no-man's-land under a flag of truce. A Union officer went out to meet them and receive Pemberton's written message. "I have the honor to propose an armistice for several hours, with the view to arranging terms for the capitulation of Vicksburg," it read. "I make this proposition to save the further effusion of blood, which must otherwise be shed to a frightful extent, feeling myself fully able to maintain my position for a yet indefinite period."

Grant's reply was uncompromising: "The useless effusion of blood . . . can be ended at any time you may choose, by an unconditional surrender of the city and garrison," he wrote. However, if Pemberton wanted to talk, he was willing to meet him later that afternoon.

The Confederate commander was stung by this curt note, but thinking that Grant might prove more tractable in person, he donned a clean uniform and, at the appointed hour of 3 P.M., rode out to rendezvous with him. As hundreds of curious soldiers looked on, the two commanders shook hands under a little oak tree two hundred feet from the Confederate earthworks, then sat down to negotiate.

The parley got off to an uncomfortable start. After a long, embarrassing silence, Pemberton abruptly asked Grant what terms he was willing to offer. "Those terms stated in my letter of this morning," Grant replied. Pemberton reddened. "The conference might as well end!" he snapped. "I can assure you, sir, you will bury many more of your men before you will enter Vicksburg!" Then he got to his feet as if to leave.

"Very well," Grant muttered, but before the situation could deteriorate further, one of Pemberton's aides intervened. He suggested that the staff officers retire and talk the matter over informally. The two commanders assented, and while they squatted in the shade of the scrubby oak, their subordinates haggled over the conditions of surrender.

The Confederates argued that the garrison should be allowed to keep its arms. This proposal was unceremoniously rejected by the Federal officers. After fifteen minutes of further discussion, it was agreed that Grant would send his final terms to Pemberton by ten o'clock that evening. The Confederate general was to answer promptly. In the meantime all hostilities would be suspended.

When he got back to his headquarters, Grant called his corps and division commanders together. Despite his tough talk about unconditional surrender, he was prepared to offer Pemberton generous terms. Instead of being held as prisoners of war, the rebel soldiers would be paroled—that is, released on their own recognizance after signing an oath not to fight again until they had been exchanged for Federal captives. Officers would be allowed to keep their sidearms, uniforms, and one horse apiece. Thirty wagons would be provided to carry the Confederate force's rations, cooking utensils, and other miscellaneous items. Grant's reasons for advancing this proposal were purely pragmatic. "Had I insisted upon an unconditional surrender there would have been over 30,000 men to transport to Cairo, very much to the inconvenience of [my] army," he wrote. "Then again Pemberton's army was largely composed of men whose homes were in the southwest; I knew many of them were tired of the war and would get home just as soon as they could."

Pemberton's reply was received after midnight. He accepted Grant's terms "in the main" but asked that his troops be permitted to march out of their works and stack arms in the area between the lines, thereby avoiding the humiliation of being present when the Yankees paraded into Vicksburg.

Grant responded that the Confederate soldiers could stack their arms wherever they wanted so long as they signed their parole papers.

The Confederate commander answered within the hour: "The terms proposed by you are accepted." Vicksburg had surrendered.

TWELVE

THE LAST
FULL MEASURE
OF DEVOTION

At five o'clock on the morning of July 1, the 7,500 Confederates of Henry Heth's division broke camp at Cashtown, Pennsylvania, and set out for Gettysburg, eight miles to the east. Although the sun had just risen, the air was already stifling. The macadamized surface of Chambersburg Pike felt hot to the men marching barefoot on it. Doing something about those unshod feet was the reason for this expedition. There were shoes in Gettysburg, and Heth wanted his soldiers to have them. There were also Federals, but according to Confederate intelligence they were mounted troops and should be no match for a large body of infantry. A minor skirmish was the most that Heth expected. He certainly had no inkling that he was about to trigger the greatest battle of the war.

On another day against a different opponent, a minor skirmish was probably all Heth would have gotten. But he and his troops were about to collide with elements of the Union First Cavalry Division commanded by Brigadier General John Buford, a hard-bitten regular with some unconventional ideas about how horse soldiers should be used in combat. The mass saber charge beloved by such would-be Murats as Jeb Stuart and George Armstrong Custer was an anachronism as far as Buford was concerned. He believed that cavalry should fight on foot, taking advantage of favorable terrain and the superior firepower of their breech-loading carbines. Now he was about to test his tactical theories against Heth's oncoming Confederates.

The engagement began at 8 A.M., when the lead Confederate brigades ran into Buford's troopers about a mile west of Gettysburg. The Federals had dismounted and spread out along McPherson Ridge and its northern extension, Oak Ridge. They were heavily outnumbered, but by fighting the way

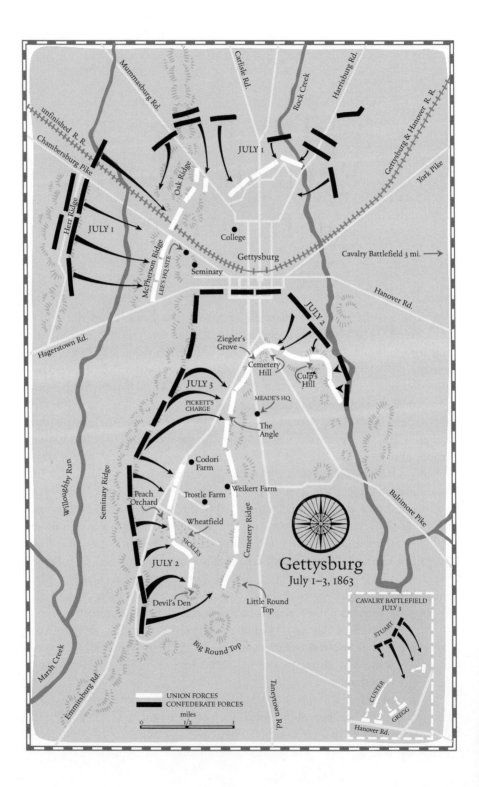

unfinished R. R.

Chambersburg Pike

Mummasburg Rd.

Carlisle Rd.

Rock Creek

Harrisburg Rd.

Gettysburg & Hanover R. R.

York Pike

JULY 1

Oak Ridge

Herr Ridge

JULY 1

McPherson Ridge

LEE'S HQ SITE

College

Seminary

Gettysburg

Cavalry Battlefield 3 mi. →

Hanover Rd.

JULY 2

Ziegler's Grove

Cemetery Hill

Culp's Hill

MEADE'S HQ

JULY 3

PICKETT'S CHARGE

The Angle

Hagerstown Rd.

Willoughby Run

Seminary Ridge

Codori Farm

Trostle Farm

Weikert Farm

Peach Orchard

Wheatfield

SICKLES

Cemetery Ridge

Baltimore Pike

JULY 2

Devil's Den

Little Round Top

Gettysburg
July 1–3, 1863

Marsh Creek

Emmitsburg Rd.

Big Round Top

Taneytown Rd.

UNION FORCES
CONFEDERATE FORCES

miles

0   1/2   1

CAVALRY BATTLEFIELD
JULY 3

STUART

CUSTER

GREGG

Hanover Rd.

their commander had taught them—kneeling behind fences and trees, waiting for the enemy to draw close, then using their carbines to put an immense volume of lead on target—they were able to repel the first rebel charge.

Buford was watching the action from the cupola of the Lutheran Theological Seminary, which sat atop a ridge several hundred yards to the rear of his division's position. Although he was delighted with the stand the blue cavalrymen were making, he knew they could not keep it up indefinitely. The enemy force was growing stronger by the minute. Unless help arrived soon, he would have to cede Gettysburg to the Confederates. He sent an urgent message to John Reynolds, commander of the nearest Union infantry corps, asking him to bring troops up as rapidly as possible. Then he returned to his observation post to watch the gray formations prepare for a second assault.

Reynolds reached the battlefield around 9 A.M. He saw that the contest was lopsided and that withdrawing to a better position was the prudent thing to do. But like Buford, he hated the idea of surrendering Gettysburg. The town was an important road center, and the hills and ridges flanking it looked ideal for fighting a defensive battle. Calling for a message pad, he hastily scribbled a note to Meade, who was headquartered at Taneytown, Maryland, fourteen miles south of Gettysburg: "The enemy is advancing in strong force, and I fear he will get to the heights beyond the town before I can. I will fight him inch by inch, and if driven into the town, I will barricade the streets and hold him back as long as possible." He also dashed off a dispatch to Oliver O. Howard telling him to hurry his corps forward from Emmitsburg. Then he spurred back to his own command to guide it cross-country to the scene of the fighting.

Buford's troopers were about to give way when 3,500 Federal infantrymen swarmed up the back side of McPherson Ridge to reinforce them. Reynolds, riding out in front, saw that the key to the position was a triangle-shaped copse of trees just south of where Chambersburg Pike crossed the rise. A brigade of Tennesseans led by General James J. Archer had entered these woods and was threatening to breach the Union line. Reynolds galloped straight for the stand of timber. "Forward, men, forward! for God's sake, and drive those fellows out of the woods!" he shouted. At that instant a minié ball struck him behind the right ear, and he tumbled from the saddle, dead.

The unit Reynolds had ordered to charge was the "Iron Brigade," the First Brigade of the First Division of the First Corps. It was a crack western outfit, famous throughout the army for its ferocity in combat. Its men all wore black-felt slouch hats with the brim pinned up on the left side to distinguish themselves from the rest of the Union troops, who were required to wear regulation blue kepis. Now they ran past Reynolds's body, into the grove of trees, and fired point-blank at Archer's soldiers. The Tennesseans responded in kind. The struggle continued until the Confederates recognized the distinctive headgear of their opponents and began to quail. "There are those damned black-hatted fellers again!" one of them cried as he broke for the rear. "'Tain't no militia! It's the Army of the Potomac!" His comrades followed him, and the retreat became a rout. Several hundred rebels were taken prisoner, including the slow-footed Archer, who was tackled to the ground by Private Patrick Maloney of the Second Wisconsin.

The charge of the Iron Brigade relieved the pressure on the Union front south of the Chambersburg Pike. But north of the road the situation was still desperate. Confederate troops commanded by Brigadier General Joseph R. Davis had broken through the blue line. They were about to exploit the penetration when they were struck in the right flank by three Union regiments rushing up from the south.

Raked by deadly enfilading fire, Davis's soldiers sought cover. Many of them scrambled into a railroad cut running parallel to the Chambersburg Pike. Laying their muskets on the rim of this ready-made trench, they picked off hundreds of their exposed assailants. The Federals refused to retreat. Forming into a V-shaped wedge, they charged and drove the Confederates down the twenty-foot-high embankment to the railroad bed below. It looked as though the cut would become a slaughter pen. But instead of shooting into the mob milling at their feet, the bluecoats shouted: "Throw down your muskets! Down with your muskets!" Hundreds of Southerners did exactly that. Davis managed to escape, but his command was decimated. Of the 2,300 men he had led into action an hour earlier, more than half had been killed, wounded, or taken prisoner.

With the mass surrender at the railway cut, the opening phase of the battle came to an end. Both sides caught their breath, adjusted their lines, and waited for reinforcements. No thought was given to backing down. The Confederates intended to renew the attack on a much larger scale. The Federals, now commanded by Major General Abner Doubleday, were determined to hold the McPherson Ridge line. Thus the stage was set for a bigger, more important battle. Bitter as the morning's fighting had been, it was only a harbinger of the fury to come. Subordinate field commanders had selected the ground and precipitated the combat. Now their superiors were frantically pouring in troops, feeding a chain reaction that was about to race out of control.

The explosion occurred shortly after 2 P.M. when Rodes's division of Ewell's corps, marching south from Carlisle, smashed into the Federal right flank on Oak Ridge, a half mile north of the Chambersburg Pike. Two blue divisions from Howard's corps, just arrived from Emmitsburg, moved up to extend the Union right. As they fanned out across the open farmland north of Gettysburg, forming a mile-long line running at right angles to Doubleday's front, they were struck by yet another Confederate division—Jubal Early's—advancing westward from York.

It was at this critical juncture that Lee reached the battlefield. He was angry that an attack had been launched without his approval: "I am not prepared to bring on a general engagement today," he snapped as he studied the action through his field glasses. He also was upset by the unexplained absence of Jeb Stuart. The cavalry commander had set out to ride around the Union army a week earlier and had not been seen since. "I am in ignorance as to what we have in front of us here," Lee grumbled. "It may be the whole federal army, or it may only be a detachment." His first impulse was to stop the struggle before it escalated any further. But when he saw the northern wing of the blue line begin to buckle, he abruptly changed his mind and ordered an all-out assault by every Confederate unit on the field.

For the next two hours savage fighting raged along a three-mile semicircle north and west of Gettysburg. The battle was especially bloody on McPherson Ridge, where the rebels strove to dislodge the Iron Brigade from the grove of trees it had occupied earlier in the day. Doubleday had told the Iron Brigade to hold its position at all costs, an order the black-hatted Westerners took literally. Bolstered by a pair of Pennsylvania regiments, they slugged it out with Heth's Virginians and North Carolinians—first-class fighters themselves—who came forward in waves, bayonets fixed, battle flags flying. One of the first casualties was Heth. He was hit in the head by a spent minié ball. The blow would have killed him had it not been cushioned by a roll of wadded-up newspaper that he had stuffed into the sweatband of his oversize hat to make it fit. The Iron Brigade's commander, General Solomon Meredith, was also knocked out of action when his dying horse fell on top of him. Neither officer was awake to witness the butchery that occurred when their troops came to grips with one another.

In a forty-minute span, the 151st Pennsylvania, known as the Schoolteacher Regiment because so many of its members had taught in the Juniata County public and private schools, lost 337 out of 467 men, or 72 percent of its strength. The regiment that attacked it, the Twenty-sixth North Carolina, lost 588 out of 800 men engaged—a casualty rate of over 73 percent. The Twenty-fourth Michigan, which had started the day with 496 officers and men, ended it with 99, a loss of 80 percent. And the two rebel companies that spearheaded the assault set sanguinary records that would never be equaled: one entered the maelstrom with eighty-three soldiers and emerged with two, a casualty rate of 97 percent. The other went in with ninety and suffered the ultimate loss—100 percent.

Combat this ferocious could not continue for long. It was the outnum-

A mangled soldier. (Courtesy U.S. Army Military History Institute)

bered Iron Brigade that gave way first, retiring slowly toward Seminary Ridge. The Confederates entered the woods they had paid so dearly to capture and were sickened by what they found there. Bodies were piled three and four high; gore-soaked coats, hats, and knapsacks were strewn everywhere; tendrils of sulfurous smoke writhed obscenely among the bullet-riddled tree trunks; and piercing screams filled the air, the anguished, animal cries of men in such awful pain, they were tearing at their own wounds and "foaming at the mouth as if mad."

A mile to the northeast, in the vicinity of the Mummasburg Road, the fighting was equally vicious as elements of Rodes's division attacked down the eastern slope of Oak Ridge, striking at the apex of the jackknife-shaped Union line. To meet this thrust, Doubleday committed the last of his reserves, a division led by Brigadier General John C. Robinson. Robinson got his troops deployed behind a north-facing stone wall just in time to receive Rodes's charge. Advancing on a narrow front, the rebels made an easy target. Robinson's men mowed down close to 1,600 of them. Undeterred by this slaughter, Rodes threw more troops into the fray. The Federals began to run low on ammunition. (Robinson himself was scurrying around collecting rounds from the cartridge boxes of the dead and wounded.) Finally they relinquished the wall and pulled back to the south.

Near the Lutheran Seminary the retreating bluecoats regrouped behind a rail-and-dirt barricade, replenished their ammunition supply, and prepared to face another Confederate attack. They did not have long to wait. At approximately 4:15 P.M. William Dorsey Pender's division, augmented by the remnants of Rodes's and Heth's commands, advanced in a mile-long arc. So rapid was the firing from the Federal line, recalled a soldier, that the muskets "grew hot in our hands, and darkness [from the pall of powder smoke], as of night, settled on us."

The rebel assault stalled, paralyzed by the torrent of lead pouring down from the crest of Seminary Ridge. Then it resumed, overlapping the Union position on both the right and the left. Doubleday ordered a withdrawal. The First Corps survivors shouldered their muskets and trotted toward Gettysburg, where they found an intractable snarl of guns, wagons, ambulances, and terror-stricken troops—the wreckage of the two divisions Howard had posted on the plain north of the city. These units had been shattered by Early's flank attack, launched at the same time as Pender's Seminary Ridge assault. Now they were fleeing toward Cemetery Hill, a prominent elevation half a mile south of town.

Anarchy reigned in the streets of Gettysburg for the next half hour as mobs of confused Federals ran this way and that, getting caught in colossal traffic jams, blundering into cul-de-sacs from which there was no escape, colliding with rebel regiments pouring into town from the north. Some 1,500 bluecoats were taken prisoner. Hundreds of others hid in cellars, sheds, or woodpiles, hoping to make their way to safety when the coast was clear. The highest ranking of these fugitives was Brigadier General Alexander Schimmelfennig, one of Howard's German-born brigade commanders. Realizing that he was about to be captured, he vaulted over a fence on Baltimore Street, played dead until there were no Confederates around, then took refuge in a pigsty. He would remain there for three days, drinking from mud puddles and subsisting on the contents of the swill barrel.

It was approximately 5 P.M. when the fragments of Doubleday's and Howard's corps—some 5,000 disheveled, demoralized troops—straggled up the northern slope of Cemetery Hill and collapsed behind the stone wall ringing Evergreen Cemetery, the burial ground for which the hill was named. There they learned that they had a new commander, Major General Winfield Scott Hancock. Upon learning of Reynolds's death, Meade had ordered the thirty-nine-year-old West Pointer to ride to Gettysburg, take charge of the units there, and determine whether they should be reinforced or withdrawn.

Hancock studied the terrain and saw, as Buford and Reynolds had seen before him, that it was ideal for fighting a defensive battle. Cemetery Hill,

General Winfield Scott Hancock. (Library of Congress)

which stood eighty feet above the level of the town, was just one link in an extensive chain of heights. Half a mile to the east stood another commanding knoll, Culp's Hill. To the south, extending about a mile and a half, was a gentle swell of land called Cemetery Ridge. At its terminus loomed two steep hills—bare, boulder-strewn Little Round Top and high, thickly forested Big Round Top.

"I think this is the strongest position by nature that I ever saw," Hancock announced after completing his survey. A large number of additional troops would be required to hold it, however. The corps of Daniel Sickles and Henry Slocum were even now approaching along the Emmitsburg Road and the Baltimore Pike, but whether they would arrive in time was by no means certain. The Confederates were massing in Gettysburg, and Hancock was afraid they would storm Cemetery Hill before he could organize a battle line. Riding back and forth, he got the weary soldiers re-formed into companies, regiments, and brigades, and situated them where they could repel an enemy attack. Looking toward Culp's Hill, he decided that it should be held, too, and he ordered Doubleday to send a portion of his corps to occupy it.

With that the deployment was complete. Hancock dismounted, sat on a stone fence, and gazed through his binoculars at Gettysburg and Seminary Ridge. He was keenly aware that if the Southerners struck now, before Federal reinforcements arrived, his pitifully shrunken force might be swept from the field.

Ascending Seminary Ridge in the aftermath of Pender's attack, Lee saw the defeated Yankees streaming through Gettysburg toward their rallying point on Cemetery Hill. Studying the plateau and the dominant heights east and south of it, he realized that he had to act at once. Given even a brief respite, the bluecoats would regain their composure and dig in. To clinch today's victory and dictate the terms of tomorrow's contest, the Confederates had to seize the high ground south of Gettysburg this evening.

Lee hunted up A. P. Hill and asked him if his corps could make the attack. Hill replied that it could not. If anyone was to resume the offensive, it would have to be Ewell. Lee immediately sent his aide-de-camp to tell the Second Corps commander to carry Cemetery Hill, if practicable.

Ewell did not find it practicable. His corps had lost close to 3,000 men. Units had become scattered, and discipline had been lost. Many soldiers were wandering around Gettysburg celebrating their victory rather than getting ready for further action. Federal snipers posted in buildings at the southern end of town added to the confusion by taking potshots at the milling gray throng. Among those hit was Ewell. A bullet struck his artificial limb with a resounding thwack, but Old Bald Head was unfazed: "You see how much better fixed for a fight I am than you are," he grunted to the officer riding next to him. "It don't hurt a bit to be shot in a wooden leg." His phlegmatic response was reflective of his overall frame of mind. He was tired and apathetic—not inclined to round up his battered divisions and hurl them against a position as formidable as Cemetery Hill.

Back on Seminary Ridge, Lee was waiting impatiently for the sound of Ewell's guns. Although he had added a discretionary clause to his instructions, he expected the heights to be stormed. In dealing with Stonewall Jackson, it had never been necessary for him to dictate; he could couch his orders in deferential terms and still count on them being executed. It had not occurred to him that Ewell, accustomed to direct, unambiguous commands, might take the phrase "if practicable" at face value and fail to launch the desired attack. He grew more and more concerned as the minutes dragged by and the silence continued. Finally, around six o'clock, he set out for Gettysburg to find out what was wrong.

The evening shadows were lengthening when Lee pulled up in front of the house Ewell had taken as his headquarters. The corps commander and General Rodes were in the backyard, sitting in the shade of a grape arbor. One look at their drawn faces and slumped shoulders, and Lee understood why no assault had been made. It was too late to rectify the situation, so he sat down beside the two officers and began thinking about tomorrow. What was the condition of the troops? he asked Rodes. Worn out, the normally combative Virginian replied. He did not think they could be counted on to conduct further offensive operations.

Lee did not like this answer. Turning to Ewell, he asked: "Can't you, with your corps, attack on this flank at daylight tomorrow?" Ewell stared straight ahead. His bulbous eyes were unfocused, his hands folded in his lap, his splintered prosthesis propped at a grotesque angle in front of him. His lips moved, but no words came out. After an awkward pause Jubal Early, who had just joined the group, spoke for him. An assault on Cemetery Hill was likely to fail, he said; the slope was too steep, the Yankee entrenchments too extensive. It would be wiser, in his opinion, to strike the southern end of Cemetery Ridge.

Rodes and Ewell seconded this suggestion, plainly relieved at the thought of somebody else bearing the brunt of the battle. "Then perhaps

I had better draw you around toward my right, as the line will be very long and thin if you remain here, and the enemy may come down and break through it," Lee said.

No, Early quickly replied, the Second Corps could hold the ground it had captured today. It was attacking that was problematic. Once again Ewell and Rodes hastened to agree.

Lee was taken aback by this timidity. Under Jackson, the Second Corps had been his premier striking force. But Jackson was gone, and the unquenchable offensive spark that had animated him was absent in his successor.

"Well," Lee said, distressed by Ewell's diffidence, "Longstreet will have to make the attack. Longstreet is a very good fighter when he gets in position and gets everything ready, but he is so slow."

Old Bald Head made no response. Sighing in frustration, Lee took his leave and rode back through the deepening dusk to his headquarters on Seminary Ridge.

For the citizens of Gettysburg, it had been a day unlike any they had known or ever dreamed of knowing, a day of harrowing experiences and wrenching emotions they would remember for the rest of their lives.

What remained fixed in fifteen-year-old Tillie Pierce's mind was the horror that overwhelmed her when she saw the hideous things that razor-sharp shrapnel and soft lead slugs can do to the human body.

Around 1 P.M., when the fighting resumed northwest of Gettysburg, Tillie's mother had sent her to the Jacob Weikert farm on Cemetery Ridge, thinking that she would be safer there. The Weikert place turned out to be no sanctuary. It was a hotbed of Union military activity—a transit point for reinforcements marching north along the Taneytown Road, and a field hospital for casualties being evacuated from McPherson Ridge.

Not long after Tillie's arrival, an artillery battery careened past. Suddenly one of the caissons exploded. The driver flew through the air, tumbling end over end like a rag doll. A pair of stretcher bearers rushed over, picked him up, and carried him toward the Weikert house. Tillie could not tear her eyes away. The man's clothing had been blown off. His body was a black, misshapen mass. There were nothing but bloody sockets where his eyes had been. "Oh, my God," she heard him say as the stretcher bearers hustled him past, "I forgot to read my Bible today. What will my poor wife and children say?"

A group of wounded soldiers wandered up a short while later. One of them was missing his right thumb. "That's dreadful," Tillie gasped, staring at the oozing red stump.

"This is nothing," the man replied, eyeing his mangled hand the way a butcher would size up a cut of meat. "You'll see worse than this before long."

True to his word, ambulances full of human wreckage soon began to arrive. The broken bodies were lifted out and laid in long rows on the ground. As darkness fell, surgeons moved among them performing operations by lantern light. Tillie had taken refuge in the Weikerts' kitchen, but curiosity eventually got the better of her. She ventured out to the barn, where the worst cases had been brought. A putrid stench, powerful as a punch to the solar plexus, assaulted her the moment she stepped through the door. The straw underfoot was black with blood, and a ghastly chorus of shrieks and groans rose from the structure's shadowy recesses: "Help me, doctor, don't leave. . . . Oh, please! . . . Shoot me, somebody, please be kind, shoot me. . . . Doctor! . . . Somebody, somebody get this dead man off me! . . . Water! . . . Doctor! . . . Water! . . . Oh, God! Please give me some water!"

Tillie Pierce. (Courtesy Adams County Historical Society)

Heart pounding and head reeling, Tillie staggered to the well and filled two buckets. She could not bring herself to go back inside the barn, however. She shoved the pails through the door, then fell to her hands and knees, vomiting so violently, she thought she would tear apart.

Twelve-year-old Albertus McCreary remembered the fear that gripped him as he huddled in the hot, airless basement of his family's house at the corner of Baltimore and High Streets, listening to the sounds of the battle raging outside.

At first the rumbles, thumps, and cracks were muffled and distant. Then like a fast-approaching thunderstorm, they grew louder and more distinct. The walls shook, and dust sifted down from the ceiling. Suddenly the trapdoor flew open, and five Confederates came pounding down the steps.

"We thought our last day had come," Albertus wrote forty-three years later. "Father stepped forward and asked them what they wanted. One fellow . . . with a red face covered with freckles, and very red hair, dirty and sweaty, with his gun in his hand, said 'We are looking for Union soldiers.'"

Herded back upstairs by the rebels, the McCrearys were astonished to see that no fewer than thirteen Federals had been found hiding in the house. After a brief interrogation by a Confederate officer, who sat at the head of the dining room table as if he were waiting to be served Sunday dinner, the prisoners were marched away. Albertus followed them out to the street and was startled to see a large group of Negroes—the entire colored population of Gettysburg—stumble past, prodded along at bayonet point by a squad of boisterous Southerners.

At first he didn't understand what was happening. Then he heard the anguished voice of one of the black women calling out: "Goodbye! Goodbye! We are going back to slavery."

Thirteen-year-old Billy Bayley remembered being wakened in the middle of the night by a loud knock on the door. Fearing the worst, he jumped out of bed and followed his mother downstairs to see who it was. Standing on the stoop was a boy not much older than Billy, dressed in a tattered gray uniform. His hair was plastered down on his head, his redrimmed eyes were wide with fright, and sweat and tears had cut tracks through the powder grime covering his cheeks. He was from North Carolina, he said in a trembling voice. He had been in the thick of the fighting today, seen hundreds of men killed, and was deathly afraid it would be his turn tomorrow. Could he please hide here until the battle was over?

Harriet Bayley did not hesitate. Grabbing the terrified boy by the arm, she pulled him inside and shut the door. Lighting a taper, she led him up to the attic where the featherbedding was stored for the summer. Crawl under the comforters where no one can see you, she told him.

Weeping with relief and gratitude, the little North Carolinian burrowed into the nest of bedding. He would stay there for the next three days, not emerging until the danger was past.

Twenty-seven thousand other men and boys would not be so lucky.

Lee awoke from a fitful sleep at 3:30 A.M., dressed and breakfasted by firelight, then trudged up to the crest of Seminary Ridge as dawn was breaking. Sweeping his binoculars from left to right, he studied the Yankee line, searching for weak spots. The heights overlooking Gettysburg were crawling with troops and guns. Cemetery Ridge was more lightly defended, and he sent several staff officers to reconnoiter in that direction and determine if an attack was feasible.

Despite his misgivings about the capabilities of his corps commanders—Ewell and Longstreet in particular—Lee had made up his mind to continue the offensive. The Army of Northern Virginia could not stay where it was for long because it would run out of food and forage; nor could it maneuver in the presence of the enemy without a cavalry screen to shield its flanks. Stuart's horsemen had finally been located, but they would not arrive until tomorrow at the earliest. The only choice, Lee was convinced, was to strike now, employing a series of well-timed attacks to dislodge the Federals from the high ground. When the scouting party returned and reported that the Union left was vulnerable, he quickly sketched out a battle plan. Longstreet's corps (minus Major General George E. Pickett's division, which was still a day's march away from the battlefield) would hit the enemy's left flank. Once this attack was under way, Hill's corps would smash the Union center. Ewell, meanwhile, would demonstrate against the right, and when the Yankees shifted troops from that sector to reinforce their threatened left, launch an all-out assault on the hill he had failed to take the night before. The annihilation of the Army of the Potomac would swiftly follow.

There was just one problem with this strategy: Longstreet was bitterly opposed to it. The idea of attacking a numerically superior enemy dug in on high ground struck him as madness. He urged his chief to disengage, find a favorable position south of Gettysburg, and fight a defensive battle along the lines of Fredericksburg. "No," Lee said, gesturing toward Cemetery Ridge. "The enemy is there, and I am going to attack him there."

Longstreet continued to argue. "If he is there, it will be because he is anxious that we should attack him—a good reason, in my judgment, for not doing so."

"No," Lee repeated, his face reddening with impatience. "They are there in position, and I am going to whip them, or they are going to whip me."

Longstreet said no more, but he was convinced that Lee was committing a terrible blunder. He delayed putting his divisions in motion as long as possible, hoping his superior might change his mind. When he finally did get them moving, he set a painfully slow pace. As a result his men did not reach the designated jump-off point until three thirty in the afternoon, a full seven hours after Lee had ordered them to get into position for the attack.

The line the Federals held on the morning of July 2 was approximately three miles long. It began on the forested slopes of Culp's Hill, ran west to Cemetery Hill, made an abrupt left turn at a patch of trees called Ziegler's Grove, then extended south for a mile and a half along Cemetery Ridge, stopping just short of Little Round Top.

The right portion of this line, from Culp's Hill over to Cemetery Hill, was defended by three corps—the Twelfth under Major General Henry W.

Slocum, the First under Major General John Newton (Doubleday had been summarily relieved), and the Eleventh under Howard. The center, which encompassed Ziegler's Grove and the northern half of Cemetery Ridge, was occupied by Hancock's Second Corps. The left, which included the southern half of the ridge down to the Round Tops, was the responsibility of the Third Corps under Sickles. The Fifth Corps, led by Major General George Sykes, had been placed in reserve. It would be joined later in the afternoon by Major General John Sedgwick's Sixth Corps, which was marching up from Manchester, Maryland, thirty miles to the southeast.

It was a very strong position, but Dan Sickles, a lawyer and ex-congressman from New York City, was dissatisfied with it. He did not like the looks of the ground his men had been asked to defend. Cemetery Ridge lost altitude the farther south it went, sloping steadily downward until finally it was no longer a ridge at all, but rather an expanse of low, marshy ground. Half a mile west there was higher ground—a broad, flat knoll crowned by a peach orchard. Sickles fretted about the rebels placing artillery there. Nor was that all. Southeast of the Peach Orchard there was a large, tree-ringed wheatfield that also dominated his position. Southeast of that, in the direction of the Round Tops, was an area local residents called the Devil's Den, a ten-acre maze of boulders, hillocks, and rocky ravines that provided a covered approach to his left flank. The more Sickles studied these terrain features, the more apprehensive he became. He decided that he should advance and occupy them before the enemy did. Around 10 A.M. he rode over to army headquarters to ask permission to do so.

Meade had reached the battlefield ten hours earlier and set up shop in the Leister farmhouse, a small white-frame structure beside the Taneytown Road, half a mile south of Cemetery Hill. He was tired and cranky after a sleepless night, and he dismissed Sickles's request with the condescending remark: "Oh, generals are all apt to look for the attack to be made where they are." Sickles would not be put off. The position assigned to his corps was a poor one, he insisted. He asked the army commander to come see for himself. Meade flatly refused. Other, more pressing matters required his attention. He was anticipating a Confederate attack from the north, not the west, and he did not want to waste time inspecting a portion of the line he believed was in no danger. He told Sickles to leave his troops where they were and stop worrying. Still Sickles persisted: Was he or was he not authorized to use his own best judgment in posting his corps? "Certainly, within the limits of the general instructions I have given you," answered Meade, his patience wearing thin. "Any ground within those limits you choose to occupy, I leave to you."

That was good enough for Sickles. Returning to his command, he ordered it to advance to the west and form a new, mile-and-a-half-long defensive line extending down the Emmitsburg Road from the Codori farm to the Peach Orchard, then doglegging southeast through the Wheatfield to Devil's Den at the foot of Little Round Top. Flags fluttering and drums rattling, the 10,000 soldiers of the Third Corps obeyed. It was a splendid sight, and all eyes on the Union front were riveted to it—all eyes, that is, except for those of Meade, who was still holed up in the Leister house. The movement looked so deliberate and purposeful that John Gibbon, a division commander in the Second Corps, wondered if he had missed an order for a general advance. His superior, Winfield Scott Hancock, assured him he had not: "Wait a moment," he said, his voice dripping with scorn; "you will see them [come] tumbling back."

Many of Sickles's soldiers agreed with Hancock's assessment, once they got a good look at their new position. The left was in the air, the right was half a mile ahead of the Second Corps on Cemetery Ridge, and the center was vulnerable to attack from three directions. As one of Sickles's subordinates later put it: we "stuck out like a sore thumb."

The Confederates thought so too. Around 3:30 P.M. they began shelling the Peach Orchard from a plateau six hundred yards to the west. It was the sound of this bombardment that alerted Meade to the fact that trouble was brewing on the left. Abruptly adjourning a council of war he had just called, he ordered Sykes to bring the Fifth Corps up to support Sickles. Then he rode toward the sound of the guns, accompanied by half a dozen staff officers, including Brigadier General Gouverneur K. Warren, the army's chief topographer.

As the entourage pounded down Cemetery Ridge, the crackle of musketry became audible, and puffs of cottony white smoke could be seen curling up from the dark woods at the base of the Round Tops. Meade had a sudden premonition of disaster: "Warren!" he shouted. "I hear a little peppering going on in the direction of that hill off yonder. Ride over, and if anything serious is going on, attend to it." Warren waved in acknowledgment, jerked his horse's head in the direction of Little Round Top, and sped off while the rest of the party continued on toward Sickles's command post.

When Meade saw where the Third Corps was situated, he was aghast. His carefully drawn defensive line had been ruptured by the impetuous action of a headline-hungry politician. "General!" he roared when he found Sickles in the Peach Orchard, "you are too far out!" Sickles politely disagreed, explaining that he had gained the advantage of higher ground by moving his men to this position. "This is higher ground," Meade spluttered, "but there is still higher in front of you, and if you keep on advancing you will find constantly higher ground all the way to the mountains!"

"I will withdraw if you wish, sir," huffed Sickles.

"I wish to God you could," shouted the army commander, "but the enemy won't let you!" At that instant a shell exploded overhead. Meade's horse reared in terror, then rocketed off to the east, carrying the general back toward Cemetery Ridge.

Moments later the Confederate attack smashed into Sickles's left flank, and the second day's battle was joined.

His beard dripping sweat, his face wreathed in smiles, Jeb Stuart galloped up to Lee's headquarters late on the afternoon of July 2. Although exhausted by twelve hours in the saddle, he was in high spirits, eager to brag about his latest exploit. After setting out from Salem, Virginia, on June 25, he and his cavalrymen had galloped east around Manassas Junction, then north past Fairfax Court House to Rowser's Ford on the Potomac, a scant fifteen miles from Washington. At Rockville, Maryland, they had attacked a Federal wagon train, capturing 900 mules, 400 prisoners, and 125 vehicles loaded with food and supplies. From Rockville they had continued northward into Pennsylvania, cutting telegraph lines, ripping up railroad tracks, and fighting skirmishes with Federal detachments at Hanover and Carlisle. It was at the latter place that Jeb had finally gotten word of the Army of Northern Virginia's whereabouts. Leaving his men to follow in his path, he had ridden through the night to get to Gettysburg.

Stuart strode up to his chief, expecting to be congratulated. Instead Lee stiffened and raised his hand as if to slap his subordinate. "General, where have you been? I have not heard a word from you for days, and you the eyes and ears of my army."

Stuart blinked, took a step backward, stammered: "I have brought you 125 wagons and their teams, General."

"Yes, but they are an impediment to me now."

The exchange was "painful beyond description," an eyewitness wrote. Lee was white-lipped with fury; Stuart was close to tears. Then as quickly as it had flared, the commanding general's temper subsided. "Let me ask your help now," he said to Stuart in a gentle voice. "We will not discuss this matter further. Help me fight these people."

Gettysburg was barely recognizable to its residents on the afternoon of July 2. Once-tidy streets were littered with debris. Dead horses, abdomens ballooning in the summer heat, lay in the gutters. Bands of Confederates prowled from building to building hunting for food and drink.

Wagons rattled back and forth in a steady stream. Shells whistled overhead, and the ground shuddered from explosions.

At the south end of town, rebel sharpshooters dueled with their Union counterparts on Cemetery Hill. A block of row houses had been commandeered and subjected to a unique form of interior renovation: the south wall of each building, except for the last one facing Cemetery Hill, had been demolished so that Confederate marksmen could move back and forth without exposing themselves to enemy fire. The arrangement worked well until a well-aimed Federal shell struck the upper floor of the southernmost house, obliterating the snipers' perch.

Sallie and Joseph Broadhead lived on Chambersburg Street, less than half a mile from Seminary Ridge. When Confederate artillery roared into action around 10 A.M., the couple scooped up their four-year-old daughter and rushed down into the cellar. The noise was terrifying—"as though heaven and earth were being rolled together," Sallie wrote in her diary—and the brick-and-stone walls quivered with each salvo.

The bombardment subsided during the early afternoon, and the Broadheads decided it was safe to come up into the daylight. "My husband went to the garden and picked a mess of beans, though stray firing was going on all the time," recalled Sallie. "He persevered until he picked all, for he declared the rebels should not have one. I baked a pan of shortcake and boiled a piece of ham, the last we had in the house . . . and we had the first quiet meal since the contest began."

Tillie Pierce was resting after a long bout of water carrying, when a wagon piled high with coffins pulled up next to the Weikert house. A work party unloaded it, stacking the crude pine boxes beside a badly wounded soldier. "We'll be putting you in one of these soon," the driver said to the man, smirking and gesturing at the coffins.

"Go to hell," groaned the soldier. "I'll consider myself lucky if I *get* one."

The Confederate attack began shortly after 4 P.M., launched *en echelon* from south to north by Longstreet's two divisions commanded by Major Generals John Bell Hood and Lafayette McLaws.

Hood's soldiers stepped off first, heading not northeast along the Emmitsburg Road as Lee had ordered, but due east toward the Round Tops, the Devil's Den, and the southern edge of the Wheatfield. This change was necessitated by the presence of Sickles's corps. To attack obliquely, as called for by Lee's plan, would result in the division being enfiladed from the right and rear. Better, Hood thought, to push straight ahead, smash Sickles's left flank, then pivot northward and advance up Cemetery Ridge toward Gettysburg. He knew it would be a costly undertaking, but he had complete confidence in the ability of his Alabama, Georgia, and Texas troops to pull it off. Standing up in his stirrups, he bellowed, "Fix bayonets . . . forward and take those heights!" and led the division straight into the Devil's Den.

A plume of smoke boiled from the maze of granite boulders, and minié balls thrummed through the air "with the noise of partridges in flight." The Confederates did not hesitate. They rushed forward, each regiment vying to be the first to reach the objective. Casualties were heavy. Among those hit was Hood, his left arm torn from biceps to wrist by a splinter of hot iron. He was carried from the field, bleeding profusely, but his absence had little effect. "By this time order and discipline were gone," recalled Sergeant Valerius C. Giles. "Every fellow was his own general. Private soldiers gave commands as loud as the officers. Nobody paid any attention to either."

As the Devil's Den melee roared toward its climax, the Fifteenth and Forty-seventh Alabama infantry came under fire from a band of Union sharpshooters posted behind a stone wall on the lower slope of Big Round Top. With an angry yell the rebel regiments wheeled around and charged toward the waist-high barricade. Wanting no part of so unequal a contest, the sharpshooters fled uphill. The Alabamians followed, legs pumping and chests heaving, until they reached the summit of Big Round Top. There they flopped down, gasping for air.

Colonel William C. Oates, the commander of the two regiments, let his soldiers rest while he tried to figure out what to do next. Looking north he saw the rooftops of Gettysburg, the crests of Cemetery and Culp's Hills, the green spine of Cemetery Ridge, and to his immediate front the bald, rock-encrusted dome of Little Round Top. He realized with a start that the promontory his men had scaled dominated the entire battlefield. If he could get a battery of rifled artillery onto it and clear a firing lane through the trees, every inch of the Union line would be in range. He was pondering this electrifying prospect when a member of Brigadier General Evander M. Law's staff rode up. Law, who had become division commander when Hood was wounded, wanted the Alabama regiments to push ahead and capture Little Round Top. Oates protested that Big Round Top was too valuable to abandon, but the staff officer was adamant: General Law's orders must be carried out at once.

With a deep sense of foreboding, the Alabama colonel told his men to get up. He was sure that a glorious opportunity was being squandered. A few cannons firing from this eminence would do untold damage to the bluecoats. There was nothing he could do, however. His job was to obey, not to argue points of strategy.

He waited for the troops to stagger to their feet, then led them down the mountainside toward the saddle that connected the two Round Tops.

Six hundred yards to the northeast, Gouverneur K. Warren was on the verge of panic. He had arrived at the summit of Little Round Top a short while ago and found it almost deserted. The discovery horrified him. Although not as high as neighboring Big Round Top, the craggy knob commanded the entire Union line. He ordered the handful of signalmen occupying the hill to wigwag their flags so that the enemy would think it was strongly garrisoned. Then he sent his aides for help.

The first officer to respond to Warren's call was Colonel Strong Vincent. He double-timed his brigade up Little Round Top and deployed it among the granite slabs and oak and maple thickets on the hill's southwestern slope. Moments later Oates's two regiments, supported by the Fourth Alabama and the Fourth and Fifth Texas, came charging out of the trees.

The fighting was especially furious on the far left, where the Twentieth Maine, led by Colonel Joshua Lawrence Chamberlain, dueled with Oates's Alabamians. The combat was hand to hand: Oates saw a Confederate sergeant bayonet a Yankee through the head; Chamberlain heard bones snapping and cracking as his men wielded their muskets like axes, felling rebels with chopping blows to the head and arms.

Afraid that his regiment was about to be swamped, the Maine colonel ordered his soldiers to fix bayonets and charge. The Alabamians were thrown off balance by the momentum of this downhill rush. They reeled backward, braced momentarily, reeled backward again, then broke and ran, not stopping until they had reached the safety of Big Round Top.

At the right end of Colonel Vincent's line, the Sixteenth Michigan was being hard pressed by a pair of Texas regiments. Desperate to rally the troops, Vincent plunged into the fray. A bullet struck his chest, and he fell mortally wounded. The Michiganders gave way, and for a moment it looked as though Little Round Top would fall to the Confederates. But once again Warren came to the rescue. Seeing what was happening, he raced down the hillside in search of reinforcements. The first unit he found was the 140th New York, commanded by Colonel Patrick O'Rorke.

O'Rorke responded immediately to Warren's frantic appeal; wheeling his mount around, he led his 500 soldiers upward at a dead run. "As we reached the crest a never-to-be-forgotten scene burst upon us," remembered Lieutenant Porter Farley. "A great basin lay before us full of smoke and fire, and literally swarming with riderless horses and fighting, fleeing, and pursuing men. . . . [It was] a scene very like hell itself—as terrific as the warring of Milton's fiends in pandemonium."

The violence galvanized O'Rorke. He leaped from the saddle, yanked out his sword, and plunged down the hill's western face, straight into the teeth of the charging Texans. "Here they are men, commence firing!" he roared, then toppled over dead as a bullet ripped through his neck. His regiment plowed into the Confederates and hurled them back. "In less time than it takes to write it, the onslaught of the rebels was fairly checked," wrote Farley. "In a few minutes the woods in front of us were cleared except for the dead and wounded."

The Army of the Potomac had held Little Round Top by the narrowest of margins.

While Hood's soldiers were battling for control of the Devil's Den, Little Round Top, and the southern end of the Wheatfield, McLaws's division was waiting impatiently for the signal to join the attack. Longstreet finally gave the go-ahead at 5:30 P.M., and the four brigades surged toward the Peach Orchard, the Emmitsburg Road, and the northwestern edge of the Wheatfield.

Struck by this fast-moving juggernaut, Sickles's salient crumbled. Meade fed in reinforcements, and for a few minutes the situation stabilized. But then the Peach Orchard was overrun, Sickles was borne off the field on a stretcher, his right leg mashed to a pulp by a cannonball, and the Union position collapsed.

McLaws's victorious division, joined on its left by elements of A. P. Hill's corps, pressed ahead toward Cemetery Ridge, aiming for the hole Sickles had left when he moved his corps earlier in the day. Federal gun crews fought desperate delaying actions in the vicinity of the Trostle farm, firing canister charges as fast as they could ram them into the gun tubes. Still the gray wave swept forward, making straight for the mile-wide gap.

For the second time in as many days, it fell to Hancock to save the Army of the Potomac. Eyes ablaze, face flushed, he rapidly shifted units to meet the Confederate threat. He personally led Colonel George Willard's New York brigade to a point just north of the Weikert house and ordered it to pitch into an oncoming rebel formation. The New Yorkers leaped forward with a shout. Willard was killed instantly, decapitated by a shell fragment, but his men drove the enemy back at bayonet point.

The crisis was not over yet. Riding north, Hancock spied another column of butternut infantry moving unopposed toward the crest of Cemetery Ridge. "I saw that in some way five minutes must be gained or we would be lost," he later wrote. Just then a lone Federal regiment marched up from the rear. It was pitifully small—eight companies, just 262 soldiers. "My God!" Hancock exclaimed. "Are these all the men we have here? What regiment is this?"

"First Minnesota," answered the unit's commander, Colonel William Colvill.

"Colonel, do you see those colors?" Hancock shouted, pointing to the battle flags carried by the Confederates. Colvill nodded yes. "Then take them!"

A tremor ran through the ranks of Minnesotans. "Every man realized in an instant what that order meant," recalled Lieutenant William Lochren; "death or wounds to us all." But there was no hesitating. Down the front of the ridge they ran, lowering their bayonets at the last instant. The rebels recoiled in shock, then regained their composure and savaged the undersize blue regiment. In less than fifteen minutes, 215 of the First Minnesota's 262 officers and men were hit. They accomplished their mission, however. Hancock was given the time he needed to find additional troops. Unable to advance any farther, the gray column withdrew.

That left one Confederate formation, Brigadier General Ambrose R. Wright's Georgia brigade, still trying to break through into the Union rear. Shrugging off the effects of Federal artillery fire, it reached the crest of Cemetery Ridge and captured several batteries. For a brief, thrilling moment, Wright believed that victory was in his grasp. Straight ahead was Taneytown Road, awash with fleeing men and stampeding animals, and just beyond it stood Meade's headquarters.

The Georgia general's feeling of elation was short-lived. Blue troops by the thousands were converging on his command from the right and left. When he looked over his shoulder, expecting to catch sight of gray units coming to his support, he saw that the field was empty save for the dead and wounded. His men were all alone a mile out in front of the rest of the Confederate army. Reluctantly he gave the order to withdraw, and like a spent wave washing back to the sea, the brigade streamed across the shallow valley toward Seminary Ridge.

With the retreat of Wright's command, the assault on the Union left was at an end. More than 6,000 Southerners had fallen, and all that had been gained was the Devil's Den, the Peach Orchard, and the blood-soaked real estate in between. "We have not been so successful as we wished," Longstreet announced. Other officers were even blunter in their assessment, blaming poor planning, bad staff work, and inadequate tactical supervision for the costly repulse.

The second-guessing was just beginning. The argument over who or what was to blame for the failure of the July 2 attack would rage for years to come. But as the sun set, its dying rays struggling to penetrate the smoke that shrouded the battlefield, Confederate victory still seemed a distinct possibility. Ewell's corps was assailing the Union right, which had been weakened by the subtraction of units sent to plug holes in other parts of the line. A victory there would redeem the setbacks at Little Round Top and Cemetery Ridge and render moot all the recriminations about flawed strategy and ineffective generalship.

At 6:30 P.M., following a two-and-a-half-hour cannonade, the divisions of Edward Johnson and Jubal Early charged up the wooded slopes of Culp's Hill and Cemetery Hill. In the dusk the muzzle flashes of thousands of discharging muskets looked like lightning zigzagging around the hill-tops. The sound, wrote a Federal soldier, "was one solid crash, like a million trees falling at once."

Johnson's men carried a line of Union trenches on the southern spur of Culp's Hill but could advance no farther. Early's attack came closer to scoring a breakthrough. His division bulled its way past three successive lines of bluecoats, got in among the batteries sited on the brow of Cemetery Hill, and fought hand to hand with the artillerymen, who had nothing but rammers, sponge staffs, and handspikes with which to defend themselves. Once again lack of support and the timely arrival of Federal reinforcements (sent by the ubiquitous Hancock) blunted the rebel thrust. For several minutes shadowy masses of troops surged back and forth. Then the outnumbered Confederates fled, tumbling and rolling down the steep slope until they were back where they had started.

Except for a few skirmishes between groups of edgy pickets, the day's fighting was over. The din that had been unabating for six hours died away. Moonlight illuminated torn thickets and trampled meadows where stretcher bearers wandered among thousands of bodies. Private soldiers prowled the battlefield also, hunting for missing comrades or stripping corpses of clothing and valuables. Others searched for drinking water, a precious commodity in the July heat. Still others lay down and tried to sleep—a difficult task given the unceasing cries of the wounded.

At midnight Meade summoned his corps commanders to a council of war. Although outwardly calm, he was inwardly agitated, deeply unsettled by the events of the past forty-eight hours. The Army of the Potomac had been pushed to the limit by the rebel attacks. It had lost close to 20,000 men and stood to lose a great many more if the struggle resumed in the morning. He wanted to ask his principal subordinates what they thought should be done next.

The generals crowded into the parlor of the Leister house, puffing on cigars, drinking from the water bucket an orderly had placed on the table at the room's center, and talking desultorily about the day's fighting. A flickering candle, stuck to the tabletop with its own wax, provided the only light. Meade, stoop-shouldered and gaunt-faced, slumped in a rickety cane-bottomed chair. His spectacles were halfway down his nose, and beads of perspiration stood out on his balding forehead. The other officers sat on a rope bed that had been shoved into a corner or lounged against the wall. The reek of gunpowder, horses, and stale sweat was overpowering.

Meade quickly got to the point. He wanted each general to state for the record whether he thought the army should withdraw, remain where it was, or attack. The response was unanimous: Stay and fight on the defensive. Meade nodded curtly. "Such then is the decision," he said, and the meeting broke up.

As the officers filed out into the night, Meade pulled aside John Gibbon, whose division was posted near the center of the Cemetery Ridge line. "If Lee attacks tomorrow, it will be in *your* front," he told the young general. Startled, Gibbon asked why he thought so. "Because he has made attacks on both our flanks and failed," Meade replied. "If he concludes to try it again, it will be on our center."

Even as this prediction was being made, the Confederate commander was pacing around his headquarters tent, pondering what his next move should be. He was disappointed that Longstreet's and Ewell's assaults had fallen short, but he was not discouraged. Twice his troops had come within an eyelash of breaching the Union line. He was convinced that with better coordination and more effective artillery support, success could be achieved. It was risky to keep storming a well-defended ridge, but aggressiveness was the sine qua non of his generalship. He had invaded the North in pursuit of a decisive victory, and he was determined not to leave until he had won it. He resolved to strike at the heart of Meade's position with all the power he could muster.

Dawn, Friday, July 3. The sound of cannon fire reverberating off the southeastern slope of Culp's Hill jolted both armies awake. Federal artillery was bombarding the trenches the Confederates had captured the previous night.

Riding down Seminary Ridge toward Longstreet's bivouac, Lee heard the cannonade begin and correctly surmised that Ewell's corps was about to be attacked. The knowledge did not alter his plan. He still intended to pierce the Union center, using Pickett's fresh division as the spearhead. Heth's and Pender's divisions, now commanded by Generals James Pettigrew and Isaac Trimble, would provide support. The total number of troops involved would be approximately 12,000. Their advance was to be preceded by a massive artillery bombardment aimed at paralyzing the enemy at the point of attack.

Longstreet was still hoping Lee would adopt a defensive strategy. When he saw him ride up to his command post, he called out: "General, I have had my scouts out all night, and I find that you still have an excellent opportunity to move around to the right of Meade's army and maneuver him into attacking us."

Lee cut him off. "No," he said, gesturing toward the northeast. "I am going to take them where they are." Longstreet's disappointment turned to dismay when his chief outlined the battle plan. The objective was a small grove of trees three-quarters of a mile distant on the otherwise bare crest of Cemetery Ridge. Troops approaching it would be exposed to the fire of nearly every musket and cannon on the Federal line. "General," Longstreet said to Lee, "it is my opinion that no 15,000 men ever arrayed for battle can take that position." The Confederate commander was not dissuaded. He told Longstreet to assemble the assault force. Then he set out to supervise the placement of the army's artillery.

For the next three hours, Lee rode along the Confederate front, positioning batteries and mentally mapping the routes he wanted the attack units to follow. During the course of this reconnaissance, he saw for himself what poor condition many of the troops were in. "[T]hese poor boys should go to the rear; they are not able for duty," he exclaimed as he inspected the walking wounded in one of Trimble's brigades. But if he had second thoughts about proceeding with his plan, he kept them to himself. "The attack must succeed," he said. "The attack must succeed."

Longstreet's heart sank into his boots when he heard this. "With my knowledge of the situation, I could see the desperate and hopeless nature of the charge and the cruel slaughter it would cause," he wrote years later. "Never was I so depressed as on that day."

Two miles from where Lee was mustering his legions, in the kitchen of a modest brick house at the southern end of Baltimore Street, twenty-year-old Jennie Wade was kneading bread dough. A sturdy, plain-faced woman with dark eyes, full lips, and long black hair coiled into a thick braid on top of her head, she bent to her work, doing her best to ignore the battle noise that drifted in from outside. The growl of gunfire from nearby Culp's Hill was punctuated by the thud of snipers' bullets striking the exterior of the house. Jennie did not flinch; she was sure the brick walls would keep her safe.

Shaping the dough into a loaf, she placed it in a tray to rise, then straightened up and wiped her hands on her apron, inhaling the rich, yeasty scent. In the adjoining room her mother and sister Georgina were busy tending to Georgina's five-day-old son. The baby's father was away in the Union army. Jennie's fiancé, Johnston "Jack" Skelly, was in the army, too, a corporal in the Eighty-seventh Pennsylvania. She pulled his daguerreotype from her dress pocket and studied it. Jack was seated in the photographer's chair, stiff and uncomfortable-looking in his new uniform, a musket in his lap, his face deadly serious. They planned to marry as soon as the war was over, and she smiled at the thought of him cradling an infant in his arms instead of a weapon.

The crash behind her sounded like an ax splintering a pile of dry boards; the whack of the bullet severing her spine was like a cleaver cutting through a shank of meat.

In the other room the baby let out a high-pitched wail. Mrs. Wade screamed and rushed into the kitchen. Jennie lay facedown on the floor, a crimson pool spreading beneath her body. The minié ball had drilled through two wooden doors before burying itself in her back.

Jack Skelly's blood-spattered picture rested a few inches from Jennie's lifeless hand. The battle had claimed its first—and only—civilian casualty.

One hundred seventy-five miles south of Gettysburg, at Rocketts Landing in Richmond, Confederate vice president Alexander Stephens boarded the packet

Jennie Wade. (Courtesy U.S. Army Military History Institute)

steamer CSS *Torpedo*. The boat would carry him down the James River under flag of truce to the Union naval base at Newport News. Once there he would contact the commander of the North Atlantic Blockading Squadron and ask for permission to proceed up the Potomac to Washington.

In his coat pocket Stephens was carrying a letter from Jefferson Davis to Abraham Lincoln. It spoke of the need to establish a prisoner-exchange cartel and hinted that other topics, including a peace settlement, were open for discussion.

The letter was highly unusual in that Davis had identified himself not as President of the Confederate States of America but as "Commander-in-Chief of the land and naval forces now waging war against the United States." It was common knowledge that Lincoln refused to recognize the existence of the Confederate government and would accept no communications from it. By omitting any reference to the CSA, Davis was making it possible for Lincoln to respond to his letter without compromising his principles. It was a rare display of flexibility on the Confederate president's part, and it showed how hopeful he was that this diplomatic initiative would bear fruit.

Stephens was less optimistic. He did not think Lincoln would agree to negotiate as long as Lee's army was on Northern soil. But in the interest of ending the war, he was willing to act as Davis's emissary. And so with the stricken expression of someone suffering from seasickness, he curled up in the cramped cabin of *Torpedo* and endured as best he could the packet's pitching and rolling as it chugged downstream toward Hampton Roads.

Artillery crashed and small arms crackled as the early-morning struggle on Culp's Hill continued. Johnson's Confederates, realizing they would be pulverized by Union cannon fire if they stayed in the trenches at the base of the slope, had elected to attack rather than retreat. They scrambled up the hillside toward the Yankee breastworks, only to be driven back by blistering volleys. During this contest many Federal defenders expended more than 160 rounds of ammunition; for decades thereafter a ghostly stand of dead oak trees, some with upward of 200 bullets embedded in their trunks, offered mute testimony to the intensity of their fire.

At the Leister house, 1,400 yards west of Culp's Hill, Meade bent over his maps, trying to figure out what Lee was up to. Last night he had predicted that the Confederates would strike the Union center. Now he was not so sure. He suspected that the action at Culp's Hill was intended to draw his attention to the right flank, while the main blow fell on his left. He decided to shift units accordingly, and by midmorning the area around the Round Tops was bristling with men and guns. The center, by contrast, was lightly defended; fewer than 6,000 soldiers were spread across the half-mile-long front that was to be the target of Lee's final assault.

Meade was writing dispatches when a stout, red-faced farmer burst into his headquarters. Shaking his fist, the man shouted in a thick German accent that his house was being used as a hospital. Dead men had been buried in his garden. Amputated arms and legs were scattered all over his yard. He had a claim against the government. He intended to hold the general accountable.

Meade's temper snapped. He leaped to his feet, thrust his face to within inches of the farmer's, and roared: "You craven fool! Until this battle is decided, you don't know, and neither do I, if you will have a government to apply to! If I hear any more from you, I will give you a gun and send you to the front line!"

Two orderlies seized the man by the arms and hustled him out before he could say anything else. Meade, still trembling with fury, sat down and resumed writing.

Jeb Stuart had been cut to the quick by Lee's rebuke on the afternoon of July 2. He realized, belatedly, that his absence during the opening phase of the battle had severely limited the army's strategic options. Now he was anxious to make amends and get back into his chief's good graces.

After familiarizing himself with the terrain around Gettysburg, he devised a plan for supporting the upcoming infantry assault. He and his horsemen would swing wide around Ewell's left, get into the Union rear, and pounce on units retreating from Cemetery Ridge.

Lee approved, and late on the morning of the third, Stuart and 6,300 troopers trotted three miles east along the York Pike, then veered south to a wooded elevation known as Cress Ridge. The plan called for the Confederate cavalry to remain hidden until it was time to swoop down on the fleeing Yankees. But as usual Stuart had bigger ideas. He wanted to engage the enemy cavalry, then charge west toward Cemetery Ridge at the same time Pickett's men approached it from the front. Thus when his command arrived at Cress Ridge, Stuart ordered an artillery officer to unlimber a howitzer and fire a series of random shots in all directions. His subordinates supposed that this salvo was a prearranged signal to notify Lee that the cavalry was in place. But in actuality it was Jeb Stuart throwing down the gauntlet, daring the Union mounted wing to come out and fight.

The challenge would soon be accepted. The Federal Second Cavalry Division under Brigadier General David McMurtrie Gregg was approaching Cress Ridge from the south. Right behind it was the Michigan Brigade of Judson Kilpatrick's division led by a very excited, very determined George Armstrong Custer.

When Stuart saw the blue riders forming a battle line along the Hanover and Low Dutch Roads, a thousand yards southeast of his position, he was delighted. He ordered 1,500 of his troopers to dismount and move forward to test the Yankees' resolve. He anticipated a brief fight, culminating in a rout. It would, he thought, be an ideal warm-up for the main event: the hell-for-leather charge into Meade's rear.

Shortly after 11 A.M., the shooting on the eastern flank of Culp's Hill subsided, and an uneasy hush descended over the battlefield. The air was oppressively hot and humid, with only a slight westerly breeze to stir it. On Cemetery Ridge, Union soldiers checked and rechecked their muskets, fingered the blades of their bayonets, and waited for something to happen. It was "as still as the Sabbath day," one of them recalled. Another remembered it growing so quiet that he could hear the hum of honeybees working.

Brigadier General Henry J. Hunt, the Army of the Potomac's chief of artillery, made sure that his gun crews were ready. Across the way on Seminary Ridge, Colonel E. Porter Alexander, the best artillerist in the Army of Northern Virginia, was doing the same thing. Lee and Longstreet were looking to him to silence the Union batteries and demoralize the Union infantry so that it would be in no condition to resist the rebel attack when it came. One hundred seventy-eight guns of various types and calibers, each one furnished with 130 to 150 rounds of ammunition, were aimed at Cemetery Ridge. Longstreet would signal for the cannonade to begin when the assault columns were in position. It would be up to Alexander to gauge the effectiveness of the fire and tell Pickett when the infantry should advance.

By noon everything was ready, but Longstreet declined to initiate the action. For over an hour he stalled, hoping Lee would change his mind and cancel the assault. Finally he could delay no longer. With a heavy heart he gave the order for the bombardment to begin. At precisely 1:07 P.M. the sweltering stillness was broken by two cannons firing in quick succession. Moments later the rest of the Confederate guns cut loose with an earth-jarring roar.

Hunt's artillerymen held their fire until they could identify the rebel batteries that were doing the most damage. Then they went into action, adding to the earsplitting din. Smoke billowed across the field, obscuring everything except the flash of bursting shells. The thunder was like nothing ever heard on the American continent; it was audible in Pittsburgh, more than 150 miles away.

The Federal infantrymen on Cemetery Ridge's forward slope hugged the ground as shot and shell screamed overhead. The Confederate gunners were firing high, and as a result casualties were relatively light. "All we had to do was flatten out a little thinner," explained a Maine soldier, adding that "our empty stomachs did not prevent that." The Union artillerists were less fortunate. Posted on the exposed crown of the ridge, they took a terrible beating.

The devastation was even worse on the ridge's reverse slope. Meade's headquarters was struck repeatedly. A direct hit destroyed the front steps, another shattered the columns supporting the porch roof, and a third ripped through the second-story garret, filling the lower rooms with dirt and debris. Sixteen horses hitched to the fence enclosing the yard were torn limb from limb. A shell fragment hit Major General Daniel Butterfield in the neck. Another carried away two legs of a table at which Brigadier General Seth Williams was sitting, barely missing his knees. Colonel Joseph Dickinson went down, blood trickling from a wound in his side. But despite the mortal danger, Meade refused to leave, arguing that dispatch riders would expect to find him here. Only after a solid shot smashed into a doorjamb inches from his head did he agree to move to a safer location a mile to the southeast.

As the artillery duel intensified, Hunt moved among his batteries, checking their condition. He worried that the caissons were being emptied too quickly. It was imperative that enough ammunition be left to contest the infantry assault he was sure was coming. At 2:45 P.M. he issued a fateful order: cease firing. One by one the Federal cannons fell silent. A pair of badly shot-up batteries in the vicinity of Ziegler's Grove was given permission to withdraw.

From his vantage point on Seminary Ridge, Alexander noted the sudden slackening of Union fire, saw the two batteries pulling back, and concluded that it was time for the Confederate attack to begin. "For God's sake come quick," he scrawled in a hasty note to Pickett. "Come quick or my ammunition will not let me support you properly."

After reading the message, Pickett rode up to Longstreet and asked, "General, shall I advance?"

Longstreet, choked with emotion, merely nodded in the affirmative. "My feelings had so overcome me that I could not speak, for fear of betraying my want of confidence," he later wrote.

"I shall lead my division forward, sir," Pickett said, then galloped back to his command.

Three miles east of Gettysburg, Stuart's skirmish line was clashing with elements of Custer's brigade in open pastureland between the Rummel and Lott farms, just north of the Hanover Road.

Eager to wrest the initiative from his opponent, Custer ordered the Fifth Michigan Cavalry to advance and greet the approaching rebels with a series of rapid volleys from its Spencer seven-shot repeating rifles. Astounded by the Spencers' awesome firepower ("You'ns load in the morning and fire all day!" exclaimed a Confederate prisoner), Stuart's troopers fell back. But their leader, unwilling to be stymied by a single regiment regardless of its armament, fed more men into the fray. The Fifth Michigan, fast running out of bullets, was forced to retire.

As the Yankees retreated with whooping graybacks in hot pursuit, observers on both sides concluded that the engagement was over. Custer refused to give up, however. Abandoning his command post on the Hanover Road, he galloped to the front. Picking up the Seventh Michigan Cavalry as he went, he charged to the Fifth's rescue. A tremendous fight erupted along a fence row on the Rummel farm. Stuart committed several more regiments but was unable to dislodge the Seventh Michigan, which clung to the post-and-rail barrier with bulldog tenacity. After an hour of pitched combat, both sides withdrew to regroup and tend to their wounded.

The respite was brief. Stuart was desperate to break through the Union line so he could assault Meade's rear. He had held eight of his best regiments in reserve; now he ordered them forward. As the rebel horsemen advanced across the field, accelerating to a trot and then to a full gallop, the Michigan Brigade began to waver. There was only one fresh regiment left, the First Michigan Cavalry; for it to try to stop the oncoming gray host by itself looked suicidal. "Great heavens!" gasped one of its officers when the order to charge was given. "We will all be swallowed up!"

General George Armstrong Custer.
(Courtesy Little Bighorn Battlefield National Monument)

It was a moment made for Custer. Doffing his hat so his long blond hair could flow free, he screamed "Come on, you Wolverines!" and spurred his horse straight toward the enemy. With a wild shout, the First Michigan followed, trying to catch up to the young brigadier, who was already four lengths ahead, the point of his saber leveled at the breast of the lead Confederate rider.

"The two columns drew nearer and nearer," recalled one of the participants; "the speed increased, every horse on the jump, every man yelling like a demon." Then the detachments collided head-on. The tremendous impact sent horses tumbling end over end. The clash of steel on steel, the crack of pistol shots, and the screams of the combatants filled the air.

In the first five minutes, the Michigan regiment lost eighty-six men. But inspired by its intrepid leader, it sliced like a wedge deep into the rebel formation, splitting it in two. "For a moment, but only for a moment," Custer wrote in his official report, "that long, heavy column stood its ground; then, unable to withstand the impetuosity of our attack, it gave way in a disorderly rout, leaving vast numbers of dead in our possession. . . . I challenge the annals of warfare to produce a more brilliant or successful charge."

He had good reason to be exuberant. A general for less than a week, he had whipped the legendary Jeb Stuart and covered himself with glory. More important, he had held the rebel cavalry at bay so that the Union infantry could concentrate on repulsing Pickett's attack without worrying about the security of its flanks and rear.

In the woods behind Seminary Ridge, the Confederates who would make the climactic assault nervously awaited the order to start forward. Their officers moved among them, dressing their ranks and shouting last-minute instructions: "Advance slowly, with arms at will. No cheering, no firing, no breaking to quick step. Dress on the center." As was customary at times like this, generals gave little speeches. "Don't forget today that you are from old Virginia!" Pickett exhorted his division. Brigadier General Lewis Armistead appealed to the troops to "remember your wives, your mothers, your sisters, and your sweethearts." Then it was time to go. The command rang out: *"Forward! Guide center! March!"* The first line moved ahead at route step—110 strides per minute.

As they cleared the trees and emerged into sunlit fields, the rebel infantrymen realized just how perilous their assignment was. "A passage to the valley of death" was the way a staff major described the long, gently ascending approach to the enemy line. Some men prayed or sang hymns; others talked incessantly, trying to screw up their courage. "June Kimball, are you going to do your duty today?" one Tennessean asked himself as he gazed at the ground on which, in all likelihood, he would soon be wounded or killed. "I'll do it, so help me God," he answered.

By now the smoke from the bombardment had lifted, and the long lines of Confederates could be seen clearly from Cemetery Ridge. First came a wave of skirmishers, widely spaced, weaving left and right like bird dogs sniffing for game. A hundred yards behind was a second wave of skirmishers. Another hundred yards back were the main assault columns—nine brigades in three solid ranks, each one extending for more than a mile flank to flank.

An excited murmur ran up and down the Union line: "Here they come! Here they come! Here comes their infantry!" Most of the defenders were relieved to have the waiting over. They looked to their weapons, then lifted their heads and watched with a mix of admiration and incredulity as the rebel phalanx swept toward them. "Beautiful, gloriously beautiful, did that vast array appear," wrote an onlooker.

The beauty was short-lived. Union batteries that earlier had fallen silent abruptly roared back to life. Fire from half a dozen Parrott guns on Little Round Top, and from sixteen smoothbore Napoleons on Cemetery Hill, was especially deadly, killing and wounding as many as ten graybacks with each shot. A brigade of Virginians on the left could not stand the mauling and broke for the rear. The rest of the rebels pressed on, but their mile-long line kept contracting as units on the flanks crowded in toward the center, trying to escape the torrent of shells.

Like a tightly clenched fist, the Confederate formation crossed the Emmitsburg Road and started up the slope toward the clump of trees that was its objective. A low stone wall ran north to south along this portion of Cemetery Ridge, zigging outward to avoid hitting the grove, then zagging back to its original course. The salient it created had been dubbed "the Angle" by the Union defenders. It was here the attackers were going to strike. But first they had to cross another three hundred yards of open ground.

Blue regiments crouching behind the stone wall stood up and triggered their first volley. Artillery joined in, firing double charges of canister. The Confederate lines "underwent an instantaneous transformation," a Federal gunner recalled. "They were at once enveloped in a dense cloud of dust. Arms, heads, blankets, guns and knapsacks were tossed into the clear air. A moan went up from the field distinctly to be heard amid the storm of battle."

The parade-ground alignment the rebels had worked so hard to maintain was lost. Soldiers who had been marching erect, eyes forward, chests out, now stumbled up the incline in a half stoop, shoulders hunched and heads bowed as if walking into a driving rainstorm. "Steady, men! Close up!" the officers repeated over and over again. One sword-waving lieutenant cried out, "Home! Home, boys! Remember, home is over beyond those hills!"

The carnage was frightful but the rebels did not falter. Drawing to within a hundred yards of the stone wall, they stopped and discharged a volley of their own, the first they had fired since beginning the charge twenty minutes earlier. A Union battery was silenced, and the Pennsylvania regiment holding the apex of the Angle fled in panic.

General Armistead, his black-felt campaign hat perched on the point of his saber, exhorted the troops to make the final, supreme effort. "Come on, boys, give them the cold steel!" he roared. "Who will follow me?" Covering the last few yards at a run, he vaulted over the piled-up stones, laid his hand on the muzzle of one of the abandoned Union cannon, then crumpled to the ground, mortally wounded. His soldiers were right behind him. Shrilling triumphantly, they scaled the wall, advanced another seventy yards, and planted their battle flags in the shade of the trees.

For a moment—maybe a minute and a half—there was a gap in the Union line. Through this opening, devotees of the Lost Cause would later say, Confederate brigades could have poured, flooding into the Army of the Potomac's rear, winning the battle and perhaps the war. But it was all a pipe dream. The units that had stepped off from Seminary Ridge no longer existed as organized entities. Almost all of the senior field officers had been hit, leaving the enlisted men—the few who were still standing—leaderless. There were no reinforcements coming along behind, and only a handful of artillery batteries on hand to lend fire support. In short, the penetration of the Union center, achieved at such terrible cost, was strategically worthless. It could not be converted into a breakthrough. The gap was soon plugged, and the 300-odd soldiers who had heroically followed Armistead into the Angle were either shot or taken prisoner.

Those who had not entered the Angle and were still in one piece began the long, dangerous trek back toward Seminary Ridge. "For about a hundred yards I broke the lightning speed record," wrote June Kimball who, having upheld his oath to do his duty, now retreated as rapidly as he could, ducking and dodging the cannonballs that seemed to follow him every step of the way.

As Kimball and the other survivors staggered toward the shelter of their own lines, Lee rode forward to meet them. "All this will come right in the end," he called out reassuringly. "We'll talk it over afterwards. But in the meantime, all good men must rally. We want all good and true men just now."

Pickett appeared, tears streaming down his cheeks. Lee told him to prepare his division to receive a counterattack. The distraught Virginian shook his head. "General Lee, I have no division now," he sobbed.

"Come, General Pickett," said Lee. "Your men have done all that men could do. The fault is entirely my own."

Meade did not know that the rebels had been beaten back. When he finally rode forward and saw a mass of gray-clad prisoners coming down the east side of Cemetery Ridge, he mistook them for an attacking formation and nearly panicked. "How is it going here?" he anxiously asked a staff officer.

"I believe, General, the enemy's attack is repulsed," the officer replied.

"What!" exclaimed Meade. "Already repulsed?" Then he realized that the approaching Confederates carried no weapons. "Thank God," he muttered. He reached for his hat as if to doff it, thought better of it, and instead simply waved his hand and weakly cried, "Hurrah!"

When Lee returned to his headquarters tent around 1 A.M., the members of his staff were asleep. The only officer still awake was General John Imboden, whose cavalry brigade would escort the Confederate ambulance train when it headed south at daybreak.

Lee dismounted and rested his head against the flank of his horse. "The moon shone full upon his massive features and revealed an expression of sadness that I had never before seen on his face," Imboden wrote. To break the awkward silence, he ventured to say, "General, this has been a hard day on you."

Lee raised his head and wearily replied, "Yes, it has been a sad, sad day to us." He was quiet again for several minutes. Then suddenly he straightened up and spoke in a voice husky with emotion. "I never saw troops behave more magnificently than Pickett's Virginians did today."

His voice trailed off, his eyes glazed over, and his shoulders sagged. "Too bad!" he whispered, as if he were reliving the last moments of the attack. Then louder and more anguished: "*Too bad*. Oh! Too bad!"

Presently his customary reserve reasserted itself. He invited Imboden into his tent to look at the maps that were spread out there. "We must now return to Virginia," he said.

On board the CSS *Torpedo* in Hampton Roads, Alexander Stephens waited for a summons to Washington that would never come.

THIRTEEN

RETREAT, RAID, AND RIOT

July 4 dawned hot and hazy in Vicksburg. A preternatural hush hung over the city where for seven weeks shells had burst almost continuously. Unsure what to make of the sudden calm, the townspeople emerged from their caves and stumbled down debris-strewn streets, blinking at the unaccustomed daylight and reflexively scanning the sky for incoming mortar rounds. One man entered his demolished home, sat down in a rocking chair that stood miraculously untouched amid the ruins of the front parlor, and began to rock. "It seems to me I can hear the silence and feel it too," he said to his wife. "It wraps me like a soft garment; how else can I express this peace?"

In the forts surrounding the city it was strangely quiet too. Soldiers squatted on their heels, talking in low voices, trying not to betray the apprehension they felt. Officers cast furtive glances at their watches, willing the minute hands to move faster. Finally it was ten o'clock. For a moment the stillness seemed to deepen. Then a long, shuddering sigh, mingling sadness, relief, and joy, rose from the lines as white flags blossomed on the Confederate parapets. A few Federals cheered and tossed their caps into the air, but the vast majority remained silent, transfixed by the spectacle that now unfolded before them. All along the front, rebel troops emerged from their entrenchments, filed into no-man's-land, and stacked their arms. "The officers spoke the necessary words of command in a low tone, much like what we hear at funerals," wrote an eyewitness. "The men went through the scene with a downcast look, never uttering a word."

Several hundred Union soldiers marched into Vicksburg a short while later. They made straight for the Warren County Courthouse, formed into ranks, and stood at attention as a party of officers climbed to the top of the cupola to raise the Stars and Stripes. Noticing the name of a Cincinnati foundry molded into the cupola's cast-iron steps, a member of the flag detail damned the impudence of a people who thought they could win a war when they couldn't even make their own staircases. His comrades guffawed, then cut down the Confederate pennant and unfurled the national colors. A band below struck up "The Star-Spangled Banner," and out on the river Union gunboats fired a salute.

Later that afternoon, Yankee enlisted men were given leave to wander through the city. They engaged in a few acrimonious exchanges with defiant civilians, but by and large their behavior was quiet and courteous. "There is no jeering or tormenting from our men," a correspondent for the New York *Tribune* reported. "Nothing—absolutely nothing—has been done to add humiliation to the cup of sorrows which the rebels have been compelled to drink." Federals willingly shared their rations with hungry Confederates, and before long the two sides were fraternizing as if the struggle of the past nine weeks had never taken place.

Pemberton did not share in the bonhomie. His manner was cold to the point of rudeness when Grant paid a courtesy call on him at his headquarters. He declined to offer the Union commander a seat and told him if he wanted a glass of water, he could go fetch it for himself. Grant was unfazed by the frosty reception. He politely took his leave and rode down to the waterfront to greet Admiral Porter, whose flagship had just tied up at the city wharf. "That was a happy meeting," Porter recalled years later. "I opened all my wine lockers."

Under the watchful eye of Colonel Rawlins, Grant let others do the toasting while he contented himself with a cigar. "No one, to see him sitting there with that calm exterior amid all the jollity . . . would ever have taken him for the great general who had accomplished one of the most stupendous military feats on record," wrote Porter. "He behaved on that occasion as if nothing of importance had occurred."

In fact, the importance of what Grant had achieved could hardly be overstated. He had capped a nearly flawless campaign with a victory that permanently crippled the South's ability to make war. The Confederacy had lost the Mississippi River (the rebel commander at Port Hudson surrendered to Banks as soon as he learned of Pemberton's capitulation) and with it its links to all the territory to the west. It had also lost close to 45,000 troops—8,000 in the battles preceding the siege, 31,000 at Vicksburg, and 6,000 at Port Hudson—not to mention 172 cannons and 60,000 muskets. All this had been accomplished at modest cost. From April 30, the day of the Bruinsburg landing, to July 4, when Vicksburg fell, the Union army had suffered just 9,000 casualties.

Grant was not resting on his laurels. He had told Sherman to be ready to march on Jackson and Canton the moment Pemberton came to terms. Now he gave his subordinate the go-ahead, directing him to inflict all the punishment he could. Only then did he get around to sending a brief message to Washington announcing that Vicksburg had surrendered.

Nine hundred miles to the northeast, in a blood-spattered meadow beside the Chambersburg Pike, Confederate stretcher bearers were loading ambulances in preparation for the retreat from Gettysburg. It was an oppressive morning, hot and muggy under a slate-colored sky, and the smell of decaying flesh was overpowering.

Around one o'clock rain began to fall, a drizzle at first, then a blinding deluge, hampering the task of carrying the wounded from the field hospitals to the wagon park. Finally, at four, the job was finished. The teamsters whipped up their animals, and the caravan rumbled east toward Cashtown and Greenwood, buffeted by powerful wind gusts and rocked by peals of thunder. Once at Greenwood it would turn south and roll on through the night, making all possible speed for the Potomac River crossing at Williamsport, Maryland.

Lee watched the first wagons depart, then returned to his tent to complete arrangements for extricating the Army of Northern Virginia from its position on Seminary Ridge. It was a hazardous undertaking with the enemy poised less than a mile away. The rain would be helpful, however, keeping Federal patrolling to a minimum and muffling the sound of the Confederate departure. When darkness fell, he ordered Hill's corps to head down the Hagerstown Road, leaving its campfires burning to deceive the Yankees. Longstreet's command would follow, then Ewell's. Stuart's cavalry would screen the entire movement.

Everything went smoothly. By 2 A.M. on July 5, the last rebel unit was off Seminary Ridge and marching south. The gray columns passed through Fairfield, Pennsylvania, that afternoon, Hagerstown the next day, and arrived in Williamsport on the morning of the seventh. There was no sign of the enemy, and the troops breathed a sigh of relief. But the storm that had worked to their advantage during the withdrawal from Gettysburg now acted against them. Rainfall had swollen the Potomac until it was unfordable, and the Williamsport pontoon bridge had been destroyed. Further complicating matters was the wagon train, which had reached the river on the afternoon of the fifth. The wounded were suffering the torments of the damned in their waterlogged ambulances. "Scarcely one in a hundred had received adequate surgical aid," wrote the officer in charge. "From nearly every wagon . . . came such cries and shrieks as these: 'Oh, God!

Why can't I die?' 'My God, will no one have mercy and kill me?' 'Stop! Oh, for God's sake, stop!' 'I am dying! I am dying!' "

Appalled by this misery and by the high mortality rate it portended, Lee ordered the seizure of all ferryboats in the area. They would be used to carry the wounded to the Virginia shore, where they could resume their journey to Richmond without delay. But the rest of the army was stuck on the Maryland side. It would have to wait until the river subsided or a bridge was built. In the meantime food was running low, and there was barely enough ammunition left for a single day's fight. It was a dangerous situation, and Lee was visibly anxious as he deployed his battle-worn divisions in an arc around the Williamsport bridgehead and waited for the Federals to arrive.

Meade was in no hurry to assail him. The Army of the Potomac had suffered 23,049 casualties at Gettysburg. Some of its best units had been virtually wiped out. Other outfits were leaving for home because their enlistment periods had expired. Upward of 15,000 soldiers had deserted during the three-day battle. Provost marshals were scouring the countryside for them, but it would be several days before they could be rounded up and returned to their regiments. Roll call on the morning of July 4 revealed that only 51,414 men were present for duty—too few, in Meade's estimation, to conduct offensive operations. It was clear he thought the army had accomplished enough by forcing the enemy to fall back.

The Northern public was certainly satisfied with the Gettysburg victory, and when news of Vicksburg's surrender came, the rejoicing redoubled. Church bells rang, crowds cheered the names of Meade and Grant, and the price of gold tumbled, a sure sign that Union military fortunes were on the rise. In Washington a torchlight procession made its way down Pennsylvania Avenue to the White House to serenade the president. Lincoln stepped out onto the portico to tell the throng that it was entirely fitting that the rebellion had suffered a devastating double defeat on the anniversary of the Declaration of Independence. All Meade had to do now was pounce on Lee's crippled army, and the war would be over.

But Meade still had not set out after the Confederates. He was waiting for supplies and reinforcements, he said. In the meantime Union soldiers fanned out across the Gettysburg battlefield to retrieve the last of the wounded, bury the dead, and gather up weapons, cartridge boxes, shoes, and other gear. It was a gruesome task. The bodies of more than 5,500 men lay rotting in the summer sun. The stench was suffocating. "We would cover our faces with our hands and turn our backs toward the breeze and retch and gasp for breath," wrote Sergeant Thomas Meyer.

The wounded, numbering in the tens of thousands, were brought to the immense field hospital that had been established on the banks of Rock

Creek, east of the Baltimore Pike. There they were made as comfortable as circumstances would permit, which was none too comfortable given the lack of tents, blankets, food, and medicine. The dead were buried in shallow trenches, with a crude headboard erected at one end stating the number of bodies and the regiment they came from.

In addition to the human remains, a vast quantity of discarded weapons had to be disposed of. Some 27,000 muskets had been left behind. The ordnance officers overseeing the collection of these weapons took note of a peculiar phenomenon: close to a third were loaded with more than one charge, and some had as many as ten cartridges jammed into their barrels. In the bedlam of combat, the soldiers carrying them had failed to pull the trigger, reloading again and again without ever firing a shot.

On July 7 the Army of the Potomac finally headed south. The pace was slow, in part because of the wet weather but mostly because of Meade's wariness. A week later the bluecoats were finally in position to attack Lee, but by then it was too late. The Confederates had built a makeshift pontoon bridge, and on the night of July 13, they started filing across it. By eleven o'clock the next morning all but 500 of them were on Virginia soil. Lee ordered the pontoons cut loose, and the retreat resumed.

Lincoln was furious when he learned that the rebels had escaped. "We had them," he fumed. "We had only to stretch forth our hand, and they were ours." He considered relieving Meade, but decided against it. It would not do politically or militarily to sack the hero of Gettysburg less than two weeks after he had repelled the Confederate invasion. "He has made a great mistake, but we will try him further," he told Gideon Welles, reconciling himself to what had happened.

Word that the Army of Northern Virginia had fought a great battle in Pennsylvania reached Richmond on July fifth. "IMPORTANT FROM GETTYSBURG," a newspaper headline read. "ENEMY ROUTED . . . FORTY THOUSAND PRISONERS CAPTURED."

Rumors flew following this thrilling announcement: Washington was at the mercy of the rebel army; Lee would dictate terms of peace from Philadelphia; Baltimore had been burned to the ground; New York City was on the verge of revolt; Maine was going to secede and cast its lot with Canada. Adding to the excitement was a story in the *Dispatch* saying that Johnston had lifted the siege of Vicksburg.

Then, like a thunderclap, the truth came in the form of a detailed report from the front: Lee had suffered a bloody repulse at Gettysburg; the Army of Northern Virginia was retreating; the invasion had ended in failure. The tidings from the West were even worse: Vicksburg and Port Hudson had fallen; the Mississippi was under Yankee control from its headwaters to its mouth; Louisiana, Arkansas, and Texas were cut off from the rest of the Confederacy.

Astonished, indignant, sick with grief and suspicion, the public demanded an accounting. How could these disasters have happened? The belief that one Southern soldier could whip six Yankees was still strong; therefore, the thinking went, bungling generals must be to blame. The Northern-born Pemberton was an especially inviting target. He was pilloried as a Confederate Benedict Arnold, a traitorous wretch who had betrayed his army and handed Vicksburg to the enemy. Johnston also came in for harsh criticism, and even the sainted Lee was second-guessed. "Gettysburg has shaken my faith in [him] as a general," one armchair strategist wrote. "To fight an enemy superior in numbers at such terrible disadvantage of position . . . seems to have been a great military blunder."

Lee tendered his resignation, but Jefferson Davis refused to accept it. The country could not afford the loss of his services, he told Lee. The president sent a similarly supportive letter to Pemberton, telling him he had done right to sacrifice his army in an attempt to keep control of the Mississippi. For Johnston, however, Davis had nothing but scorn. When a War Department official remarked that Vicksburg had fallen for want of food, not spirit, the president's face darkened. "Yes," he snapped, "from want of provisions inside, and a general outside who wouldn't fight."

During the third week of July, it appeared that Johnston was going to get a fight whether he wanted one or not: Sherman's command was advancing east from the Big Black River, heading for the heart of Mississippi. Johnston had his small army entrenched on the outskirts of Jackson. He hoped Sherman would attack, but the Yankee general declined. He invested the city on three sides and opened fire with his artillery. Johnston withstood the bombardment for a few days, but the situation was hopeless. On July 16 he informed Richmond that retreat was his only option. That night he led his army across the Pearl River and away to the east, not stopping until he was nearly halfway to Alabama.

Federal troops entered Jackson the next morning and smashed and burned everything that had not been wrecked during the May occupation. When they were through, the Mississippi capital was a mass of charred

General William T. Sherman.
(National Archives)

ruins. "The inhabitants are subjugated. They cry aloud for mercy," Sherman boasted. With Grant's blessing, he decided not to follow Johnston. Instead, he headed back toward Vicksburg, razing everything in his path. Smoke-blackened chimneys, referred to as "Sherman tombstones," were all that was left after his army had passed. One of the properties destroyed was the residence of Dr. Owen Cox, a friend of Jefferson Davis and his brother Joseph. Earlier that summer, the president's personal belongings had been moved from Brierfield, his plantation near Vicksburg, to Cox's house for safekeeping. Sherman's men went wild when they discovered this cache. Crates full of "Old Jeff's" books were dragged into the yard, dumped on the ground, and trampled underfoot; his letters were taken as souvenirs or used as toilet paper; his draperies and Turkish rugs were cut into pieces and distributed as saddle blankets; his tables, chairs, desks, and cabinets were chopped into kindling; his wine cellar was drunk; his crystal and chinaware were used for target practice; and an oil portrait of him and his wife was bayoneted again and again until nothing was left but a few ragged strips of canvas.

Word of this vandalism stung Davis like salt sprinkled into an open wound. Mississippi had been his home; now it was a captured province, and his entire past, in the form of his furniture, books, and correspondence, had been obliterated. He held Johnston responsible. Seething, he removed the Virginia general as commander of the Department of the West and reduced the geographic area under his control to eastern Mississippi and southern Alabama. He would have drummed him out of the army if he dared, but Johnston had too many friends in the Confederate Congress. Davis reckoned that the drastic shrinking of the Virginian's command was rebuke enough. Grant's victory had turned Mississippi and Alabama into military backwaters. Johnston would have nothing to do in coming months except sit and shuffle papers; the focus of the war had shifted to Tennessee.

The Army of the Cumberland had been encamped at Murfreesboro for six months, recuperating from the Battle of Stones River and getting ready for further action. Its objective, Chattanooga, was only eighty miles away; but to get there it would have to go through or around the Army of Tennessee, which was dug in at Shelbyville and Wartrace in the Duck River Valley.

How to accomplish this feat was a strategic puzzle William Rosecrans was in no hurry to solve. The Stones River slugging match had convinced him that overwhelming logistical superiority was all-important, and so he concentrated on amassing supplies, putting off any move south until his preparations were complete. Slowly, methodically, he transformed Murfreesboro into a gigantic storehouse. "Forty thousand boxes of hard bread are stacked in one pile at the depot," an awestruck soldier recorded in his diary, "and greater quantities of flour, pork, vinegar, and molasses than I have ever seen before."

At first Rosecrans had only to ask to receive, but as time passed and his supply requests showed no sign of slacking off, patience began to wear thin at the War Department. Washington wanted him to make use of what he had and take Chattanooga. To get him moving, Halleck and Stanton tried a carrot-and-stick approach, the carrot being promotion, the stick the threat of removal. "There is a vacant major generalcy in the regular army, and I am authorized to say that it will be given to the general in the field who first wins an important and decisive victory," Halleck announced in a telegram sent to Rosecrans and Grant.

Rosecrans refused to bite. He and his troops stayed put for another twelve weeks. Then in the early morning hours of June 24, the long-awaited announcement arrived at the War Department: the Army of the Cumberland was on the move.

Murfreesboro was separated from the Duck River Valley by a ridge extending westward from central Tennessee's Cumberland Plateau. Several passes pierced this barrier. The three principal ones were Guy's Gap on the west, Bellbuckle Gap in the center, and Liberty Gap on the east. Bragg was counting on these defiles to funnel the Union attack into his defenses at Shelbyville and Wartrace. Rosecrans did not intend to do anything so obvious, however. He meant to outflank the rebels by sending the bulk of his force through Hoover's Gap, which lay five miles east of Liberty Gap. Bragg would not be expecting such a move because Hoover's Gap was steep and narrow—much more difficult for a large body of troops to traverse than the other passes—and because Rosecrans had devised an elaborate double feint to divert his attention elsewhere. This scheme involved sending a corps toward Guy's Gap to make Bragg think that Shelbyville was the offensive's main objective. Another corps would head east toward McMinnville, a movement Bragg was meant to recognize as a bluff aimed at distracting him from the Shelbyville thrust. It was a decoy in support of a decoy, a stratagem of which Rosecrans was particularly proud. If the plan worked, the rebel army would have to emerge from behind its earthworks to fight on open ground or fall back toward Chattanooga.

It was raining as the Army of the Cumberland broke camp in the predawn darkness of June 24, but the troops did not complain. They had not seen action for 170 days, and the sheer novelty of being on the move sustained them as they plodded south through the storm, putting their commander's program of deception into effect. Bragg was duped just as

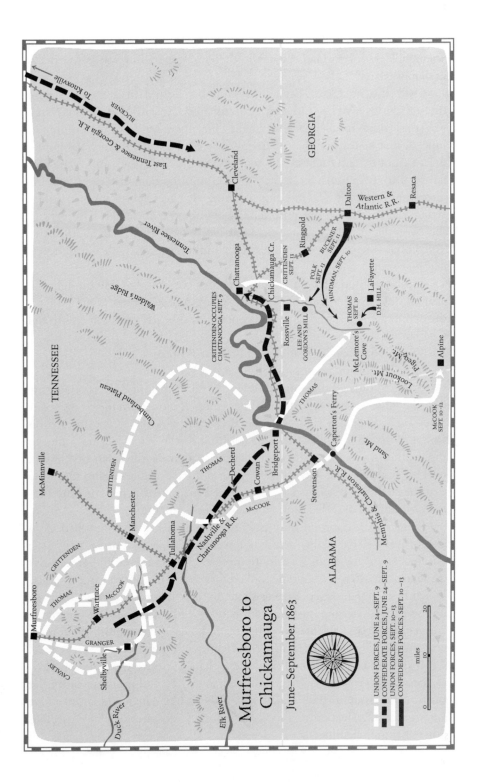

To Knoxville

BUCKNER

East Tennessee & Georgia R.R.

GEORGIA

Cleveland

Tennessee River

Chattanooga

Walden's Ridge

CRITTENDEN OCCUPIES CHATTANOOGA, SEPT. 9

Chickamauga Cr.

CRITTENDEN SEPT. 13

Ringgold

POLK SEPT. 13

BUCKNER SEPT. 11

HINDMAN, SEPT. 11

Dalton

Western & Atlantic R.R.

Resaca

Rossville

Lee and Gordon's Mill

THOMAS SEPT. 10

LaFayette

D.H. HILL

THOMAS

McLemor's Cove

Pigeon Mt.

Lookout Mt.

Alpine

Caperton's Ferry

Sand Mt.

McCOOK SEPT. 10–12

TENNESSEE

Cumberland Plateau

McMinnville

CRITTENDEN

THOMAS

Manchester

Dechert

Cowan

Bridgeport

Stevenson

Memphis & Charleston R.R.

ALABAMA

McCOOK

Nashville & Chattanooga R.R.

Tullahoma

CRITTENDEN

THOMAS

McCOOK

Wartrace

GRANGER

Shelbyville

CAVALRY

Murfreesboro

Duck River

Elk River

Murfreesboro to Chickamauga

June–September 1863

UNION FORCES, JUNE 24–SEPT. 9
CONFEDERATE FORCES, JUNE 24–SEPT. 9
UNION FORCES, SEPT. 10–13
CONFEDERATE FORCES, SEPT. 10–13

miles

0   10   20

Rosecrans had hoped. He thought the main blow was going to fall on Shelbyville. Hoover's Gap, the key to the entire operation, was left virtually undefended.

Over the next two days, blue columns flowed in a steady stream through Hoover's Gap and down the turnpike toward Manchester. Bragg was still waiting for an attack on Shelbyville; it was not until the evening of June 26 that he learned that a large portion of the Federal army was poised on his right flank. Dismayed, he sent urgent orders to Polk and Hardee to fall back to Tullahoma. Slowed by the unremitting rain, they did not complete their withdrawal until the morning of the twenty-ninth. By then Bragg had received more unsettling news: Yankee horsemen had torn up the Nashville & Chattanooga tracks at Decherd, fifteen miles southeast of Tullahoma. The Army of Tennessee's communications with Chattanooga had been cut.

That afternoon Bragg met with his corps commanders. He thought the army should make a stand at Tullahoma, but Polk disagreed, arguing that if the Confederates stayed put, the Federals would get between them and Chattanooga.

"Then you propose that we shall retreat?" Bragg asked.

"I do," Polk answered promptly.

Bragg adjourned the council of war without making a decision, but after receiving further reports of threatening Union movements, he concluded that Polk was right. On the afternoon of June 30, he ordered his troops to abandon Tullahoma and fall back to the Elk River ten miles to the southeast. On July 2, he deployed for battle near the town of Cowan, only to discover that the Yankees were outflanking him again. Deciding that the situation was hopeless, he resumed the retreat, across the Cumberland Mountains and the Tennessee River, to Chattanooga.

Rosecrans was proud of what his command had accomplished. At a cost of just 570 casualties, including fewer than 90 dead, it had expelled the Confederate army from middle Tennessee. He considered the eleven-day campaign a masterpiece, and he looked forward to the outpouring of praise he felt he richly deserved. But his strategic tour de force was overshadowed by the Federal victories at Gettysburg and Vicksburg. Instead of congratulations he received a snide note that made it clear Washington still considered him a sluggard. "Lee's army overthrown; Grant victorious," it read. "You and your noble army now have a chance to give the finishing blow to the rebellion. Will you neglect the chance?" To add insult to injury, the major generalship in the regulars that Halleck had dangled as an incentive went to Grant. Meade was also rewarded with a promotion. All Rosecrans got was more needling.

Ever since his late-April humiliation at McMinnville, John Hunt Morgan had been agitating to go on a foray deep behind enemy lines. What he had in mind was nothing less than a mini-invasion of the North—a thrust into Indiana and Ohio aimed at inciting an uprising among the region's Confederate sympathizers. Bragg rejected the plan, but Morgan, desperate for redemption, decided to execute it anyway. Without bothering to inform headquarters of his intentions, he set out during the third week of June, leading his division from its base at Alexandria, Tennessee, north toward Kentucky.

Riding at the general's side were his brothers Calvin, Richard, Charlton, and Thomas, and his brother-in-law, Colonel Basil Duke. Morgan was convinced that this would be a history-making raid, an exploit so astounding it would be celebrated in the Confederacy for years to come, and he wanted his kinsmen to share the glory. The risk of death or capture was high, but not intolerably so. Morgan intended to keep within a day's ride of the Ohio River so he could dash back into Kentucky if Federal pressure grew too great. In the event that proved impossible, he planned to press on to Pennsylvania and link up with Lee. It was heady stuff, and he was in high spirits as he splashed across the rain-swollen Cumberland River on July 2, followed by 2,460 troopers and a four-gun battery of field artillery.

The Union Army of the Ohio was preparing to march into Tennessee when Morgan's raid exploded in its rear. Ambrose Burnside hastily organized a mounted force to respond to the emergency, but he had no idea where to send it because of the misinformation he was receiving from Morgan. The Confederate general had a telegrapher on his staff who could tap into the wires at will. Bogus sighting reports giving false locations and exaggerating the size of the raiding party were transmitted to the bewildered Federals, and from Lexington to Louisville, Union commanders were convinced that the Confederate column was heading in their direction.

In fact, Morgan was about to enter In-

General John Hunt Morgan, C.S.A. (Library of Congress; photo courtesy of The Museum of the Confederacy, Richmond, Virginia)

diana. He had selected Brandenburg, Kentucky, forty miles downstream from Louisville, as his Ohio River crossing point. He sent an advance party to commandeer a pair of steamboats moored there, and on the afternoon of July 8, these two craft churned back and forth across the river, ferrying the division and its horses to Maukport, Indiana.

The southern third of the Hoosier State was Copperhead country, and Morgan anticipated a warm welcome. The rebel cavalry's reputation for indiscriminate pillaging had preceded it, however, and instead of turning out to greet the gray riders, the population either fled in terror or mobilized to defend its property. When the Confederates entered Corydon, Indiana, on the morning of July 9, they were ambushed by a mob of rifle-toting civilians. A saber charge scattered these would-be warriors, but not before they had killed eight troopers and wounded thirty-three.

Morgan received more bad news when he went to the Corydon Hotel for lunch. The proprietor informed him that Lee had been defeated at Gettysburg six days earlier. The contingency plan for joining the Army of Northern Virginia in Pennsylvania was no longer feasible. Morgan was not about to turn back, however. After finishing his meal, he led his command on to Salem, pausing to loot the towns of Greenville, Palmyra, and Paoli in retaliation for the losses suffered at Corydon.

When the division reached Salem on July 10, Morgan was faced with a difficult decision. Indianapolis, seventy-five miles to the north, was a tempting target. Six thousand Confederate prisoners of war were being held there; if they could be liberated, armed with weapons from the Indiana state arsenal, and marched back to Tennessee to join Bragg's army, it would be a remarkable coup. But it would also bring the raid to an early end, and Morgan didn't want that. Also giving him pause was up-to-the-minute intelligence furnished by his telegrapher. Thousands of militiamen were hastening to Indianapolis in response to Governor Morton's appeal for volunteers. Even more alarming was the news that 4,000 Federal cavalrymen had crossed the Ohio River and were only twenty-five miles away. That made up Morgan's mind. He led his men northeast toward the Ohio state line.

On the afternoon of July 13, the Confederate riders entered the Buckeye State twenty miles west of Cincinnati. This was one of the cities Morgan had dreamed of sacking when he conceived the raid eight weeks earlier. With his division dog tired, however, and reduced in size to fewer than 2,000 men, he dared not try it. He kept going, galloping through the Cincinnati suburbs under cover of darkness. The column did not halt until it reached Williamsburg just before sundown on July 14.

Morgan informed his staff that after a short rest the division would head for Buffington Ford, 120 miles to the east. There it would cross the

Ohio River and make for Kentucky by way of Huntington, West Virginia. The officers were skeptical; after riding ninety-five miles in thirty-five hours, men and mounts alike were spent. It seemed unlikely they could complete a forced march as long as the one Morgan was proposing.

But they had to try. The Yankee cavalry was only a few hours behind, and other Union forces were closing in as well. The hunters had become the hunted; their only hope was to keep moving in a last-ditch bid to escape.

Morgan's men had received no support from the inhabitants of the lower Midwest. To the contrary, they had run into fierce resistance in many of the rural communities just north of the Ohio River. But if the rebel raiders had failed to foment an antiwar uprising as they had hoped, it looked as though the impending Federal draft might do the trick, and not just in the Copperhead country of Indiana and Ohio. On June 8 Stanton had ordered War Department provost marshals to begin enrolling eligible men between the ages of twenty and forty-five. As soon as the lists were complete, a lottery would be held in those congressional districts that had failed to furnish their specified quota of volunteers.

The startup of the enrollment process caused an uproar all over the North. Thousands of draft-age men went into hiding or skedaddled to Canada; thousands of others lied about their age or gave false names and addresses; some fought back. In Indiana prospective draftees went from town to town confiscating enrollment books and threatening government agents. The Milwaukee city fathers had to call out the police when a mob beat up a draft official and threatened to riot. In Chicago brick-throwing protesters attacked and seriously injured a U.S. marshal who had arrested two men for refusing to give their names to an enrollment officer. In south-western Pennsylvania a coal company executive was murdered by gunmen who suspected him of giving information about his employees to the district provost marshal. Draft disturbances also broke out in Boston, Newark, and Albany. But the worst riot by far was the one that erupted in New York City during the second week of July.

With close to a half-million immigrants crammed into a few square miles of filthy, crime-ridden slums, New York in the summer of 1863 was a powder keg awaiting a spark. The city's Irish Catholics were especially restive, angry at the way wartime inflation had eaten into wages, resentful of the Protestant plutocracy that exploited their labor and disdained their religion, and bitterly opposed to conscription, which Democratic Party orators told them was part of a Republican plot to make them fight on behalf of Southern blacks.

It was in this volatile atmosphere that War Department officials began the draft on Saturday, July 11, drawing the first 1,236 names at Ninth District headquarters at Third Avenue and Forty-sixth Street. Their timing was atrocious. Casualty lists from Gettysburg had just been posted. To make matters worse, militia units that normally would have been on hand to help maintain order were in Pennsylvania with the Army of the Potomac.

The first day's lottery went peacefully, but on Sunday, Irish laborers congregated in bars all over the city and whipped themselves into an antidraft frenzy. "We are to give our lives while rich men pay three hundred dollars to stay at home," the patron of an Upper East Side saloon told a New York *Herald* reporter. He swore that there would be black eyes and bloody noses at the Ninth District draft office on Monday.

Sure enough, when the lottery resumed at 10 A.M. on July 13, hundreds of men and boys, many armed with axes and crowbars, were milling around the building that housed the draft office. It was miserably hot, the kind of weather that "makes you feel as if you had washed yourself in molasses and water," an eyewitness wrote. The odor of whiskey and unwashed bodies hung heavy in the air as the provost marshals, guarded by a cordon of police, began drawing names from a revolving drum. They had just conscripted the fifty-sixth man when a pistol shot rang out and the crowd surged forward. The police held the line long enough for the draft officials to scoop up their papers and escape, but they were powerless to save the office, which was smashed and set ablaze.

When police superintendent John Kennedy learned of the disturbance in the Ninth District, he left his office at 300 Mulberry Street and drove uptown to investigate. On Lexington Avenue, a few blocks from the burning draft building, he was recognized. "Here comes the son of a bitch Kennedy! Let's finish him!" someone screamed. With a bloodthirsty howl, a gang of ruffians hauled the superintendent from his buggy and beat him until he was nearly dead. A few minutes later they found a fresh batch of victims. Thirty-two members of the Invalid Corps, a group of disabled soldiers used for guard duty, had just gotten off the Third Avenue horsecar. The mob fell on them with sticks and paving stones, killing two and seriously injuring fifteen. A short while later forty-four policemen waded into the throng, cracking skulls with their billy clubs; the draft protesters fought back, and the outnumbered officers were swamped and savagely beaten.

With the soldiers and police vanquished, the mob was free to start destroying property. Shops were plundered, hotel lobbies demolished, and railroad tracks torn up. Lawyer George Templeton Strong, returning home from his Wall Street office, watched in disbelief as vandals set fire to a pair of Lexington Avenue townhouses.

In hopes of restoring order, the board of aldermen met in emergency session and proposed a $3.75-million bond issue, the proceeds of which were to be used to pay the $300 commutation fee for all draftees from New York City. The rioters were unaware of this and probably would not have cared if they had been aware. They were heading for the arsenal at Second Avenue and Twenty-first Street. Police commissioner Thomas Acton sent thirty-four members of the elite Broadway Squad to the scene of the trouble. The strapping six-footers, whose usual assignment was to direct traffic at the city's busiest intersections, barricaded themselves inside the armory. Moments later they were under attack. They opened fire with their revolvers, killing two and wounding six, but the onslaught continued. Realizing that they were going to be torn to pieces if they stayed any longer, they squeezed through a rear window and escaped. Baying triumphantly, the mob burst in, grabbed rifles and ammunition, and torched the building. Eight people who had been hiding on the upper floor burned to death; two died when they jumped to the street below.

As the afternoon wore on, the riot spread across the city and became increasingly racial in character. A British tourist out for a stroll was shocked to see a gang of whites chasing a black man down the street, screaming "Down with the bloody nigger! Kill all niggers!" Outside the Colored Orphan Asylum at Fifth Avenue and Forty-third Street, a crowd was chanting "Burn the niggers' nest! Burn the niggers' nest!" Authorities hustled 237 children out a back door moments before rioters battered down the main entrance and surged through the building. Clothing, carpets, crockery, and several hundred iron bedsteads were thrown out the windows. People immediately set off down the avenue loaded with loot, forming a procession that a New York *Times* reporter estimated was ten blocks long. A few minutes later the building was a mass of flames. When two engine companies arrived to fight the blaze, the frenzied crowd cut their hoses and disabled the hydrants.

In black neighborhoods along Sixth Avenue in the West Twenties and Thirties, white hooligans went from house to house terrorizing the inhabitants. Anyone who resisted risked death. There were several lynchings and numerous fatal or near-fatal beatings. Police precinct stations were jammed with Negro refugees. Thousands of others fled to Long Island, New Jersey, or sparsely settled upper Manhattan.

The hard-pressed police finally got some help Monday evening. Federal troops from forts in the harbor, several state militia units, and a detachment of marines from the Brooklyn Navy Yard arrived in the city. It was not enough. "New York is tonight at the mercy of the mob," an army officer telegraphed the War Department. As if to confirm this dire report, rioters descended on Printing House Square, intent on burning the offices of the city's pro-draft, pro-Republican newspapers. Henry J. Raymond, editor of the *Times,* had armed his staff with rifles and deployed three Gatling guns to keep the vandals at bay. But the building housing Horace Greeley's *Tribune* was undefended; the ground floor was gutted, and several fires were set.

Tuesday, July 14, dawned hot and hazy. Rioters returned to the streets to fight pitched battles with police and soldiers. Around 9:30 A.M., 300 officers marching up Second Avenue between Thirty-fourth and Thirty-fifth Streets were assaulted by an estimated 10,000 civilians hurling bricks, bottles, and paving stones. A 150-man detachment of the Eleventh New York Volunteers, led by Colonel Henry O'Brien, came to their aid. The infantry cleared the avenue by firing a volley into the air. Bullets hit two children standing at an upper-story window; eight-year-old John Mulhare was wounded, and two-year-old Ellen Kirk was killed. A few hours later O'Brien was dragged out of a neighborhood drugstore where he was seeking treatment for a cut. His assailants kicked, stoned, and burned him to death.

Thirteen blocks to the south, a crowd stormed the Union Steam Works, an armory where 3,000 carbines were stored. Two hundred policemen counterattacked, and a ferocious hand-to-hand fight erupted on Twenty-second Street between Second and First Avenues. Swinging their truncheons like tomahawks, the police finally secured the steam works, loaded the carbines into wagons, and took them to a nearby precinct station for safekeeping. Meanwhile, on Pitt Street, a platoon of troops was being harassed by a rock-throwing throng. The soldiers opened fire, killing eight of their tormentors and wounding four, then charged with their bayonets and routed the rest.

Hoping to forestall any more bloody clashes, New York governor Horatio Seymour gave a speech from the steps of City Hall. He told his listeners he was doing everything he could to stop the draft and pleaded with them to disperse in an orderly fashion.

His attempt at peacemaking failed; the riot roared on. By Tuesday afternoon there was an unmistakable whiff of class warfare in the air. Mansions on Lexington and Fifth Avenues were being ransacked, and it was no longer safe for well-dressed men to walk the streets. Those foolish enough to try it were set upon with shouts of "Down with the rich!" and "There goes a three-hundred-dollar man!"

In the financial district preparations were being made to defend against an all-out attack. A gunboat was cruising off the Battery, cannons loaded. Other ships carrying bullion, banknotes, and stock certificates were shuttling back and forth to Governor's Island. Inside the Sub-Treasury on Wall Street, artillery stood ready for action. At the Customs House, clerks armed with rifles and hand grenades were posted at every window. Employees of the Bank Note Company carried vats of sulfuric acid up to the roof and prepared to dump them on rioters. A few blocks uptown City Hall was ringed by troops and artillery. Greeley's *Tribune* building had been transformed into a citadel.

The burned-out ground floor was barricaded with bales of water-soaked newsprint, and a hose had been run up from a basement boiler so that intruders could be scalded with live steam. Upstairs, hand grenades sat on the windowsills. A stack of forty-pound bombshells furnished by the U.S. Navy stood beside a wooden chute, which would be used to launch them into Printing House Square if an assault appeared imminent.

The mob chose to attack more vulnerable targets instead. Brooks Brothers' store at the corner of Cherry and Catherine Streets was broken into and $50,000 worth of clothing carried away. On Worth Street Ann Derrickson, the wife of a black packinghouse worker, was kicked to death when she tried to save her son Alfred, who had been doused with kerosene preliminary to being set afire. On East Twenty-second Street the 18th Ward precinct house went up in smoke.

Earlier in the day, George Templeton Strong had sent a telegram to President Lincoln pleading for troops and a declaration of martial law. Five regiments from the Army of the Potomac were now on their way to the embattled city, but they would not arrive until Thursday, meaning that the riot would continue for at least another twenty-four hours.

Wednesday, July 15, was a day of unparalleled brutality. Drunken marauders roamed the streets, robbing, burning, and killing at will. "Three objects—the badge of a defender of the law, the uniform of the Union army, the skin of a helpless and outraged race—acted upon these madmen as water acts upon a rabid dog," wrote a witness. The hooligans' homicidal wrath was directed primarily at defenseless blacks. In one of the day's worst atrocities, a Negro coachman named Abraham Franklin was hanged from a lamppost on West Twenty-eighth Street while his sister was forced to look on. Later his body was cut down, stripped naked, and dragged by the genitals along Seventh Avenue as onlookers laughed and cheered.

Herman Melville spent the day watching the mayhem from a rooftop. He returned home that night and wrote a bitter poem:

> *The town is taken by its rats—ship-rats*
> *And rats of the wharves. All civil charms*
> *And priestly spells which late held hearts in awe—*
> *Fear-bound, subjected to a better sway*
> *Than sway of self; these like a dream dissolve,*
> *And man rebounds whole aeons back to nature.*

On July 17, in the morning, 4,000 Union infantrymen arrived in the city. "Houses were stormed at the point of the bayonet," a resident recalled.

Union infantrymen on riot duty in New York City.
(Courtesy Museum of the City of New York)

"Rioters were picked off by sharpshooters as they fired on the troops from the housetops; men were hurled, dying or dead, into the streets by the thoroughly enraged soldiery." By nightfall order was restored. Four days of violence had left 119 people dead and 306 injured and caused $1.5 million worth of property damage. The draft had been disrupted, but the War Department was determined to restart it as soon as possible. During the next five weeks an additional 16,000 troops were dispatched to New York, and on August 19 the lottery resumed. Governor Seymour pleaded for a suspension, warning that the city would once again erupt in violence, but Lincoln flatly refused. The Union needed more men to put down the rebellion. Conscription would continue, and the Federal government would use all the power at its disposal to enforce it.

Eight hundred miles south of the strife-torn streets of Manhattan, on a long, narrow sand spit called Morris Island, the black soldiers of the Fifty-fourth Massachusetts Regiment were getting ready to spearhead an attack on Battery Wagner, one of the Confederate forts guarding the entrance to Charleston Harbor.

After the repulse of the Union monitors back in April, the heads of the War and Navy Departments had devised a joint strategy for subduing Charleston. New commanders were appointed to carry it out. Stanton selected Major General Quincy Gillmore, an engineer and artillerist experienced in siege operations. Welles chose Rear Admiral John A. Dahlgren, chief of the Bureau of Ordnance and inventor of the bottle-shaped artillery piece that bore his name. It had been almost twenty years since Dahlgren had commanded ships at sea, but he was eager to see action. On July 6 he hoisted his flag on *New Ironsides,* and the combined operation against Charleston began.

The plan called for Gillmore's infantry, which had established a base on Folly Island, eight miles south of Charleston, to cross Lighthouse Inlet and land on the southern tip of Morris Island. The troops would then advance up the four-mile-long ribbon of sand, capture Battery Wagner and Battery Gregg at its northern end, and use rifled artillery to pulverize Fort Sumter, which lay less than a mile away. With its key defensive work knocked to pieces, Charleston would be at the mercy of Dahlgren's monitors.

At dawn on July 10, Union guns opened fire on Confederate positions at the southern end of Morris Island. After a two-hour bombardment, 3,000 troops hit the beach and drove swiftly northward. By 9 A.M. they were within sight of Battery Wagner, which was defended by 1,300 North and South Carolinians. Had the Federals rushed the fort at once, they might have taken it. Gillmore opted to wait until the next day, however. It was a decision that would prove deadly for a great many Union soldiers.

Although Battery Wagner was not much to look at, it was extremely well sited. Its palmetto-log parapet extended from the ocean on the east to an impassable tidewater swamp on the west. Battery Gregg guarded its rear. The only way to attack it was head-on, up the beach, which was barely a hundred feet wide.

Just before daybreak on July 11, Gillmore massed three regiments a few hundred yards south of the fort. As the sun rose from the blue-gray Atlantic swells, he sent them forward. The lead regiment made it as far as the moat in front of the parapet before being pinned down. The follow-on formations were hit by grapeshot and forced to fall back. The action was over in a matter of minutes. The attackers lost 339 men while the defenders suffered only 12 casualties.

Chastened by this repulse, Gillmore brought up forty-one big guns. He also made arrangements with Dahlgren to have a squadron of monitors blast Battery Wagner from the seaward flank. The bombardment was scheduled to begin at twelve o'clock on July 18 and last all afternoon. At 7:30 P.M., when the tide was out and the beach at its widest, three waves of Union infantrymen would storm the fort. Brigadier General George C. Strong, a fiery thirty-one-year-old Vermonter, was put in charge of the first wave. Given his choice of troops, he selected the Fifty-fourth Massachusetts to lead the attack.

Since their arrival in the Sea Islands in early June, the soldiers of the Fifty-fourth had seen almost no action. It was a state of affairs that irked their commander, Colonel Shaw. The colored troops should be given a chance to prove themselves in combat, he told his superiors. His lobbying paid off when the regiment was sent to raid Darien, Georgia, on June 10, but otherwise it remained in camp on remote St. Simon's Island, drilling and performing routine picket duty.

Life on St. Simon's had its charms. There was "a subtle languor in the hum of insects, the song of birds, the splash of warm green water upon the shore," wrote Captain Luis Emilio. However, a Deep South idyll was not what the regiment had had in mind when it shipped out from Boston. There was growing impatience in the ranks as the weeks slipped by with no indication that combat was imminent. The heat was "enough to make a fellow contemplate the place prepared for the ungodly," Sergeant Henry Gooding grumbled in one of his weekly letters to the New Bedford *Mercury,* adding, "our boys out on picket look sharper for snakes than they do rebels."

As if the boredom weren't bad enough, the regiment learned that the War Department had decided to pay black soldiers ten dollars per month— three dollars less than their white counterparts. It was a move bitterly resented by the men of the Fifty-fourth. "Are we *soldiers,* or are we *laborers?*" Gooding indignantly asked.

Thanks to General Strong, the regiment would soon have the opportunity to answer that question. During the first week of July, it was ferried up the coast to the Union staging area at Folly Island. On the afternoon of July 18, it crossed Lighthouse Inlet and landed on Morris Island. Up ahead Battery Wagner was being bombarded. Confederate gunners were not replying, and Federal observers concluded that the fort had been crippled by the avalanche of shot and shell.

The soldiers of the Fifty-fourth sat among the sand dunes, waiting for the call to move forward. Some tried to sleep; others took the opportunity to write letters. One of the latter was Sergeant R. J. Simmons of New York City. "God has protected me through this, my first fiery trial," he wrote his mother. "Goodbye! Likely we shall be engaged soon." Unbeknownst to him, the apartment house his mother lived in on East Twenty-eighth Street had been burned to the ground on July 15, and his seven-year-old nephew had been beaten to death by rioters.

Around 6 P.M. the cannonade stopped and the Fifty-fourth marched up the island to a point three-quarters of a mile south of Battery Wagner. The men were told to lie down with their bayonets fixed and their muskets loaded and wait for further orders. The sun set behind tall stands of marsh grass on the western horizon, and a cool breeze blew in off the sea. There was little talking; the hiss of waves washing across the hard-packed sand could be distinctly heard. Dusk deepened, stars began to twinkle overhead, and still the soldiers lay on the beach, hugging their weapons and waiting. Finally General Strong arrived and ordered the regiment to stand up. "Don't fire a musket," he called, "but go in and bayonet them at their guns!"

Shaw also addressed the troops. "I want you to prove yourselves," he said. "The eyes of thousands will look on what you do tonight." Taking his position in front, he unsheathed his sword, pointed it up the beach and called over his shoulder: "Move in quick time until within a hundred yards of the fort, then double quick and charge! Forward!"

The men stepped off in silence. The only sound was the crunch of their shoes and the sighing of the sea. Shaw marched just above the surf line, his eyes locked on the Confederate fort, which from this distance appeared to be nothing more than a giant sand dune glowing silvery white in the twilight. There was no sign of enemy activity, and for a moment the soldiers thought that the rebels had all been killed by the bombardment. But then came a sound like a sheet being ripped, and bullets from hundreds of rebel muskets slashed through the blue ranks.

Opponents of black enlistment had contended that Negroes were cowards who would flee the first time they encountered heavy fire. Over the next half hour that canard was forever laid to rest. Shaw led the way, waving his sword overhead. He plunged into the moat at the base of the fort, churned through the waist-deep water, and scrambled up the steep rampart. For a moment he stood atop the parapet, his figure silhouetted by muzzle flashes; then he pitched forward, shot through the heart. One hundred soldiers had followed him to the crest. They fought desperately to cling to a toehold there, but were soon forced to retreat.

As the remnants of the Fifty-fourth staggered back up the blood-soaked beach, other Union units charged and suffered the same fate. Bodies were piled three and four deep. Gillmore finally stopped the slaughter, but not before 1,515 of his soldiers had been killed, wounded, or captured. Confederate casualties came to 174.

Inside Battery Wagner on the morning of July 19, the Confederates dug a ditch and threw the dead of the Fifty-fourth Massachusetts into it. Later in the day, when a captured Union surgeon asked what had become of Shaw's corpse, the fort's commander sneered, "We have buried him in the trench with his niggers." This news caused great distress at Gillmore's headquarters, but Shaw's parents made it clear they wanted no special effort made to recover their son's remains. "We can imagine no holier place than that in which he is, among his brave and devoted followers," Francis Shaw told the press.

Although the Fifty-fourth had lost more than 40 percent of its strength, it had gained something invaluable, not only for itself, but for all American blacks: respect. "It is not too much to say that if this Massachusetts 54th had faltered when its trial came, 200,000 troops for whom it was a pioneer would never have been put into the field," the New York *Tribune* editorialized. "But it did not falter. It made Fort Wagner such a name for the colored race as Bunker Hill has been for ninety years to the white Yankees."

The sincerest compliment came from the Confederate side. Within days of the regiment's gallant charge, letters landed on Jefferson Davis's desk suggesting that the South mobilize its slaves for military service. Davis considered the idea but decided that arming blacks was too radical a step at this time. He agreed to let masters donate slaves to the army for employment as teamsters, cooks, and orderlies, however, and the fact that he did not reject the notion out of hand was indicative of just how swiftly and drastically the Fifty-fourth's performance under fire had altered white attitudes toward the colored race.

On the morning of July 16, the steamboat *Imperial* tied up at a New Orleans wharf and began off-loading cargo. This would not have been noteworthy under normal circumstances, but there was something special about this particular vessel: she had come downriver from St. Louis, the first merchant ship to do so in more than two years. Her arrival in the Crescent City was tangible proof that the Confederacy's grip on the Mississippi had finally been broken.

As the first crate came down the gangplank, a crowd of onlookers applauded. One of them, amateur poet Edna Dean Proctor, was moved to verse:

> *She comes from St. Louis! Who now will deny*
> *That Vicksburg and Port Hudson in ruins must lie?*
> *The good boat Imperial laughed them to scorn*
> *As bold to our levee she rounded at morn,*
> *And brought with her freedom and wealth from afar—*
> *She comes from St. Louis! Hurrah and hurrah!*

Abraham Lincoln's response to *Imperial's* safe voyage was only slightly less grandiloquent. "The Father of Waters," he said, "again goes unvexed to the sea."

John Morgan's raid is dying away eastward, and his force is melting away as it proceeds," the Chicago *Tribune* reported on July 16. "Their only care is escape, and their chances for that are very slight."

The newspaper's confidence was justified. Five thousand mounted men and 2,000 foot soldiers were chasing the rebels; navy gunboats had steamed up the Ohio River to prevent them from crossing into Kentucky or West Virginia; civilian volunteers were chopping down trees to obstruct their movements and sniping at them whenever possible.

Despite the panoply of forces arrayed against him, Morgan was determined to avoid capture. He kept moving east toward Buffington Ford, staying one step ahead of his pursuers. Late on the afternoon of July 18, the raiding party reached the ford, only to find it guarded by 300 Union infantrymen. Morgan let his worn-out command sleep through the night, then sent it forward at dawn. The Federals had fled, but as the gray column started across the shallows, a pair of gunboats came into view, cannon blazing. Moments later blue cavalry swooped in to attack. Outnumbered better than two to one, Morgan ordered Basil Duke's brigade to fight a rearguard action while he led the rest of the division north out of the trap the Yankees had sprung. Duke's troopers held off the bluecoats long enough for Morgan and 1,000 other men to escape, but the cost was high: 120 Confederates were killed, and 700 taken prisoner.

Later that afternoon Morgan tried again to ford the river, this time at Blennerhassett Island, a few miles downstream from Parkersburg, West Virginia. Once again Union gunboats were waiting. Three hundred raiders managed to swim across, but the remaining 700 had to stay on the Ohio shore. Morgan, who was midstream when the gunboats opened fire, returned to Ohio to lead the larger portion of his command.

For the next seven days the rebels rode north and east, twisting and turning to evade pursuit. Finally, on July 26, at the town of West Point, twenty-five miles south of Youngstown, Ohio, and less than fifty miles from Pittsburgh, they were surrounded and forced to surrender. Twenty-four days and eleven hundred miles after it had started, the great raid was over.

Morgan and his officers were brought back to Cincinnati, where Ambrose Burnside pronounced them ineligible for parole. Ohio governor David Tod did Burnside one better. He declared that the raiders were common criminals, not prisoners of war, and ordered their immediate transfer to the Ohio State Penitentiary. On July 30 the Confederate general and his followers were taken under heavy guard to the prison at Columbus. There they were stripped of their uniforms, shorn of their hair and beards, and forbidden to have visitors.

Morgan was downcast, especially after his mother, who had traveled all the way from Lexington to see him, was turned away by prison authorities. But he was not defeated, and as the summer wore on, his thoughts turned to escape.

The atmosphere at the Confederate War Department was positively stygian following the defeats at Gettysburg, Vicksburg, and Tullahoma. "Mr. Secretary Seddon . . . looks today like a galvanized corpse which has been buried two months," wrote John B. Jones. Department official Robert G. H. Kean characterized the month of July as "one of unexampled disaster," and confided in his diary: "We are *almost exhausted.* . . . God help this unhappy country!" Even Josiah Gorgas, the usually upbeat chief of the Confederate Ordnance Bureau, was despondent. "Events have succeeded one another with disastrous rapidity," he lamented. "It seems incredible that human power could effect such a change in so brief a space. Yesterday we rode on the pinnacle of success—today absolute ruin seems to be our portion. The Confederacy totters to its destruction."

Oddly enough, Jefferson Davis was not depressed by the July setbacks. Gettysburg had been a grievous defeat, he conceded, but Lee's army was intact, safely back in Virginia, and would soon be ready for renewed action. As for the loss of Mississippi and most of Tennessee, it was tragic but not completely catastrophic, he reasoned. By reducing the amount of territory to be defended, it would permit the Confederacy to concentrate its military resources more efficiently and allow for a greater degree of strategic flexibility. Most important, as Davis saw it, the Southern heartland, with its farms, foundries, mills, and transportation centers, was still unscathed. As long as that was so, the Confederacy could fight on indefinitely.

During the latter part of July, Davis signed off on several measures that showed he was willing to push the bounds of civilized warfare in an attempt to resuscitate the South's flagging military fortunes. The first involved the employment of a controversial new weapon developed by Brigadier General Gabriel J. Rains. Rains, an explosives expert, had developed a system for manufacturing land and underwater mines, which he called "torpedoes." These devices could be detonated in a variety of ways, and they promised to wreak havoc on both shipping and foot soldiers. Many in the Confederate army considered their use unethical, but after the reverses of the summer, Davis let it be known that "General Rains should now fully apply his invention."

Even more startling was his tacit support for a plot put forward by former Baltimore police superintendent George P. Kane. An ardent secessionist and habitual intriguer, Kane wanted to launch a raid from Canada against Union military installations at Chicago, Milwaukee, and Detroit. He also envisioned using captured gunboats to prey on Great Lakes shipping. Neither of these schemes ever got off the ground, but Davis's willingness to endorse them spoke volumes about his determination to prosecute the war as vigorously as possible.

He still drew the line at some things. Despite his bitterness about what had happened to his books, furniture, and personal papers in Mississippi, he would not countenance arson or the wanton destruction of civilian property, nor would he consider any of the memoranda that crossed his desk proposing the abduction or assassination of Lincoln and his cabinet. These he forwarded to Secretary Seddon without comment, his silence indicating his strong disapproval.

If Davis was unwilling to stoop to murder and arson, plenty of others in the Confederacy were eager to do so. One such man was twenty-six-year-old William Clarke Quantrill.

Quantrill had begun his wartime career as a Jayhawker—a pro-Union guerrilla engaged in irregular operations along the Missouri border. Then he had switched sides, received a captain's commission in the Confederate army, and become a Bushwacker—a pro-Southern partisan raiding into eastern Kansas. Five feet nine inches tall and slight of build, pale-complected with a thin black mustache and heavily hooded blue eyes, he looked more like a riverboat gambler than a guerrilla chieftain. His ruthlessness and mastery of hit-and-run tactics made him a natural leader among the Bushwackers, however. His band of followers included such desperadoes as Frank and Jesse James, Cole and Jim Younger, Bloody Bill Anderson, and Little Archie Clement.

The commander of Union forces in the region was Brigadier General Thomas Ewing, Jr., brother-in-law to William Tecumseh Sherman and like him a believer in total war. "There is a class of people, men, women, and children, who must be killed or banished before you can hope for peace and order," Sherman had admonished his relative-by-marriage. Ewing took this advice to heart as he launched an antiguerrilla campaign in July and August. Realizing that the elusive Bushwackers could not be suppressed by military means alone, he attacked their base of support—the family and friends who fed, clothed, and sheltered them. Federal troops swept through western Missouri, rounding up hundreds of suspected guerrilla sympathizers and taking them to Kansas City for deportation to Arkansas. Among those arrested were the mothers, wives, sisters, and sweethearts of Quantrill's men. Nine of them were imprisoned in a dilapidated brick building on the outskirts of Kansas City. This structure was so wobbly that wooden beams had been brought in to shore up its walls and ceilings. On the afternoon of August 13 the building collapsed, killing five of the women and leaving two others crippled for life.

News of the Kansas City tragedy enraged Quantrill's men. Convinced that Ewing had deliberately engineered the cave-in, they swore vengeance against him, his soldiers, and anyone allied with them. Particularly affected was Bloody Bill Anderson, whose sisters Josephine and Mary had been crushed to death. Prone to violence before the accident, he became a homicidal maniac afterward, his sole object to slaughter as many Yankees as possible. The other Bushwackers shared his bloodlust. When Quantrill proposed a retaliatory raid against the Unionist stronghold at Lawrence, Kansas, they eagerly agreed.

Quantrill and 300 men set out from Johnson County, Missouri, on August 19. Joined by another 150 guerrillas on the morning of the twentieth, they entered Kansas and rode toward their target forty miles to the west. Dawn on August 21 found them on a ridgetop overlooking Lawrence. Quantrill drew one of the four six-shooters strapped to his body and spurred his horse toward the sleeping city, screaming at the top of his lungs: "Kill! Kill! Kill!"

The first civilian to die was a man named Snyder, shot through the head as he milked a cow in his backyard. He was followed in short order by seventeen Union army recruits, slain in a tent camp on the edge of town. "Kill every man big enough to carry a gun!" Quantrill shouted to his followers as they thundered down Massachusetts Street, Lawrence's main thoroughfare. Over the next three hours, they did exactly that, going from house to house systematically murdering all the adult males. Bloody Bill Anderson, sobbing and foaming at the mouth, personally accounted for many of the victims, shooting them execution-style as they pleaded for mercy.

When they could find no more men to kill, the guerrillas turned to looting and arson; before they were through, close to two hundred structures would be consumed by flames. At 9 A.M. they reassembled and galloped out of Lawrence, leaving behind a fearsome scene of death and destruction. More than 150 bodies, many burned beyond recognition, lay in the smoldering rubble. Hysterical women, some carrying babies in their arms, ran through the streets crying and screaming for their menfolk. One wife was seen sitting next to the charred ruins of her house, hugging the fire-blackened skull of her husband to her breast. A man who had survived the bloodbath lifted his tear-streaked face to heaven and howled, "Oh God! Who shall avenge?"

Word of the Lawrence massacre spread swiftly across the Kansas plains. From outposts all over the eastern part of the state, Union cavalry columns converged on the shattered town, hoping to catch Quantrill and his men. The Bushwackers were long gone, however, racing south and east. They skirmished several times with small bands of pursuers, but were never in serious danger. In the early-morning hours of August 22, they crossed back into Missouri and scattered to all points of the compass, blending into the civilian population to escape detection.

Ewing's response to the Lawrence attack was swift and harsh. On August 25 he published General Orders No. 11, which required all persons residing in the border counties between the Missouri and Osage Rivers to pack up and leave by September 9; where and how they went was their problem. Nothing that might be of use to the Bushwackers was to be left behind. Food, forage, and shelter were all to be destroyed. Anyone still in the region after the deadline passed would be considered a rebel and was liable to be shot or taken prisoner.

Union soldiers enforced the order ruthlessly. Ten thousand Missourians were driven from their homes. After they had gone, swarms of vengeance-minded Kansans rampaged through the district, leaving vast stretches of territory completely desolate. Even pro-Union Missourians were appalled by the barbarity of the operation, but Ewing was unmoved. "This is war," he said.

Quantrill and his guerrillas were unharmed by the edict meant to destroy them. They had no trouble evading Union patrols and finding plenty to eat, and their depredations on the Missouri-Kansas border continued until early October, when they finally left the area to take up winter quarters in Texas.

Northerners were shocked and sickened by reports of what had happened in Lawrence. And yet the same people who decried the Bushwackers' atrocities had cheered Grant when he bombarded defenseless Vicksburg, and they cheered again, just a day after the Lawrence butchery, when Union gunners rained incendiary shells on Charleston. "What a wonderful retaliation," wrote one of them. "Frightened inhabitants fleeing from the wrath of a just avenger . . . ah indeed, but this is sweet!"

The Charleston barrage was the work of Quincy Gillmore, who had settled down to siege operations after the failure of the July 18 assault on Battery Wagner. By day his troops blazed away with muskets, mortars, and cannons, and by night they dug saps and parallels, burrowing their way up the beach toward the enemy earthworks. At the same time eighteen Parrott rifles hurled projectiles over Wagner and into Fort Sumter, punching gaping holes in its masonry walls.

Delighted by the destructiveness of this long-range fire and wanting to give Charleston a taste of the same, Gillmore ordered the construction of a battery in the marsh between Morris and James Islands. This emplacement would house an eight-inch Parrott capable of hurling two-hundred-pound shells four and a half miles into the Confederate city. Union engineers set to work at once. Floundering up to their waists in foul-smelling muck, they drove pilings into the marsh bottom, built a large wooden platform, and manhandled the monstrous gun, dubbed the "Swamp Angel," into position.

Everything was ready on the afternoon of August 21. Gillmore sent an ultimatum to Beauregard, demanding the immediate evacuation of Morris Island and Fort Sumter; otherwise he would raze Charleston. When no reply was received, he ordered the Swamp Angel into action. At 1:30 A.M. the gun roared, and a special shell filled with flammable liquid zoomed through the night sky, plunged into the heart of Charleston, and exploded. It was followed by fifteen others that also landed squarely on target.

The next morning Gillmore received a flag-of-truce message from Beauregard reproaching him for targeting civilians. Gillmore replied that Charleston had been given ample notice, and he ordered the cannonade continued. But much to his chagrin, the incendiaries failed to set the city ablaze. On August 23, after firing a total of thirty-six rounds, the Swamp Angel blew up.

No attempt was made to replace the shattered gun. Cummings Point, at the north end of Morris Island, was half a mile closer to the city, and

Outer wall of Fort Sumter.
(Library of Congress)

Gillmore expected to have possession of it soon. His sappers had pushed their trenches to within a hundred yards of Battery Wagner. On September 5 a forty-two-gun bombardment began preparatory to the launching of another infantry assault. Beauregard was one step ahead, however. He had concluded that Wagner and adjoining Battery Gregg had served their purpose, and he ordered their garrisons to withdraw to James Island. Thus when Federal foot soldiers advanced at dawn on September 7, they found nothing but abandoned ruins.

The same day that Battery Wagner fell, Admiral Dahlgren called for naval volunteers to make a small-boat landing on the tiny man-made island where Fort Sumter was situated. Gillmore's Parrott rifles had breached the fort's south-facing gorge wall. The admiral believed that a storming party attacking at night could overrun the place before its defenders knew what was happening. The officer he selected to lead the assault had his doubts, but Dahlgren brushed them aside. "You have only to go and take possession," he said. "You will find nothing but a corporal's guard."

On September 8, a moonless night, 400 sailors and marines climbed into thirty launches and were towed to within eight hundred yards of the fort. From there they proceeded toward their objective, rowing with muffled oars and taking great care to show no lights. Lookouts on Sumter's parapets spotted them anyway. When the first group of boats crunched onto the rocky beach, the Confederate garrison was lying in wait. Muskets blazed, hand grenades exploded, and batteries on nearby James and Sullivan's Islands lashed the waters around the fort with a deluge of metal. The sailors who had not landed yet rowed away as rapidly as possible. For the 124 men who had made it ashore, the battle was over in twenty minutes; they were all killed or taken prisoner. The Confederates suffered no losses.

This setback took all the fight out of Dahlgren. His health had been deteriorating since he arrived in South Carolina waters back in July, and now his spirits also began to decline. He found the summer heat intolerable, he was constantly seasick—a major embarrassment for an admiral—and the failure of the Sumter expedition weighed heavily on his mind. "My debility increases, so that it is an exertion to sit in a chair," he plaintively wrote. "How strange—no pain, but so feeble. It seems like gliding away to death. How easy it seems! Why not, to one whose race is run?" Given his depressed state of mind, it was not surprising that he decided against sending his fleet into Charleston's artillery-ringed, torpedo-infested inner harbor. To do so would be suicidal, and while that might suit him in his present condition, it would not be fair to the sailors under his command.

The sergeant was peculiar; everyone who knew him said so; and after spending a few minutes with the man, P.G.T. Beauregard could see why. Scrawny and slump-shouldered, with an ugly purplish-red scar puckering the top of his scalp, he stood before the general's desk compulsively clasping and unclasping his hands, chewing his lower lip, and looking around the room like a cornered animal.

Beauregard sighed, stroked his goatee, and glanced again at the sergeant's pencil sketches. War could be hard on men of artistic temperament, he thought, as he flipped through the pages of the portfolio. The illustrations were remarkably good. Beauregard had taken drawing classes at West Point, and he could appreciate the man's keen eye for detail, his extraordinary skill at conveying the effect of light and shadow. Anxiety aside, he was superbly qualified for the job the general had in mind. And perhaps the work would prove therapeutic.

Beauregard dictated the necessary order: Sergeant Conrad Wise Chapman was detached from his regiment and directed to make a pictorial record of the Charleston harbor defenses. Beauregard was extremely proud of these forts and batteries, several of which he had designed himself. Documenting them was an act of self-promotion on his part, a calculated attempt to win a place in history; but ironically it was the sergeant, not the general, whose reputation would benefit the most from this novel commission. The project was destined to produce some of the finest paintings of the Civil War—works that would establish Conrad Wise Chapman as the Confederacy's preeminent battlefield artist.

The twenty-two-year-old Chapman had learned to paint under the tutelage of his father, Virginia-born portrait and landscape artist John Gadsby Chapman. The elder Chapman's studio was in Rome, and as a consequence young Conrad had been raised in the Italian manner rather than in the American one. He retained strong ties to the Old Dominion, however, and when the war broke out, he sailed for New York, intending to make his way south and enlist in the Confederate army.

Chapman was an odd—some said eccentric—recruit. His quirky personality, thickly accented English, and fanatical devotion to art (he never went anywhere without his pencils, brushes, and drawing paper) amazed and amused his Southern comrades. "Old Rome" they called him, marveling at his European mannerisms and the deft way he dashed off sketches of people and things that interested him.

Chapman was a much better artist than a soldier. Six months after joining the army, he accidentally shot himself in the head while reloading his rifle. Evacuated to a hospital in Memphis, he recovered physically but not mentally. His brain had been traumatized, and for the rest of his life he would suffer from bouts of dementia. His aesthetic sense was unimpaired, however, and when Beauregard selected him for the Charleston assignment, he undertook it with enthusiasm.

Prowling the harbor fortifications day and night, Chapman filled sketchbook after sketchbook with pictures of soldiers, guns, and ships. "Often he sat under a heavy cannonade," one witness recalled; "he minded it no more than if he had been listening to the post band." The scenes he drew differed in substance and feel from those executed by his contemporaries. Other Confederate artists—landscapists like Edward Lamson Henry and William D.

Washington, portrait painters like Edward Caledon Bruce and L.M.D. Guillaume—remained studio-bound in Richmond, turning out conjectural works in the romantic antebellum style. Chapman, meanwhile, was working in a more realistic vein, limning a war-torn world whose strange, sinister beauty shaped and colored his distinctive artistic vision.

The scenes Chapman painted were haunting rather than heroic—"subtly ominous," an admiring critic called them—stark, ofttimes brooding studies of forlorn sentries standing atop wind-whipped parapets; of gun batteries disintegrating under enemy bombardment; of desolate beaches littered with the detritus of combat; of menacing machines of war, like ironclads, torpedo boats, and submarines.

Conspicuously missing from Chapman's work was the mythical quality his patron Beauregard doubtless had been hoping for. Although intensely loyal to the rebel cause, the artist-soldier was too acute an observer not to realize it was doomed. He hinted at this in one of his finest pieces, *Fort Sumter, Interior, Sunrise,* completed from a series of sketches made during the latter half of 1863. In the painting's foreground is a dark, debris-choked ruin that is barely recognizable as a fort. A few tiny figures cluster around campfires, but they are dwarfed by gigantic heaps of rubble. Atop a crumbling rampart a Confederate flag flaps defiantly in the breeze, while in the distance, ships of the Yankee blockading squadron cruise outside the harbor entrance. It is man against machine, individual bravery against industrial might, and the painting leaves little doubt as to which of these forces will prevail.

"A scene at sunrise," Chapman described this view, trying to suggest a hopeful interpretation. But the reddish-gold dawn looks suspiciously like a sunset—nightfall for Sumter, the once-proud symbol of secession, and for the Confederacy itself.

Conrad Wise Chapman.
(Courtesy The Museum of the
Confederacy, Richmond, Virginia)

The summer of 1863 was drawing to a close; the fall elections were less than two months away. Realizing that the balloting would be a referendum on his administration's conduct of the war, Abraham Lincoln addressed the people of the North in a long public letter.

He began his message by thanking those citizens whose support of the Union was unwavering. Then he lashed out at his Democratic critics. "You are dissatisfied with me about the Negro," he declared. "Quite likely there is a difference of opinion between you and myself on that subject. I certainly wish that all men could be free, while I suppose you do not. . . . You say you will not fight to free Negroes. Some of them seem willing to fight for you; but no matter. Fight you, then, exclusively to save the Union. I issued the [Emancipation] Proclamation on purpose to aid you in saving the Union . . . I thought that in your struggle for the Union, to whatever extent the Negroes should cease helping the enemy, to that extent it weakened the enemy in his resistance to you. Do you think differently? I thought that whatever Negroes can be got to do, as soldiers, leaves just so much less for white soldiers to do in saving the Union. Does it appear otherwise to you?

"The signs look better," he said in conclusion. "Peace does not appear as distant as it did. I hope it will come soon, and come to stay, and so come as to be worth the keeping in all future time. It will then have been proved that among free men there can be no successful appeal from the ballot to the bullet, and that they who take such appeal are sure to lose their case and pay the cost. And then there will be some black men who can remember that, with silent tongue and clenched teeth and steady eye and well-poised bayonet, they have helped mankind on to this great consummation, while I fear there will be some white ones unable to forget that, with malignant heart and deceitful speech, they have strove to hinder it."

PART FOUR

FALL

FOURTEEN

A MAD,
IRREGULAR BATTLE

William Rosecrans was incensed by the War Department's deprecatory response to his late-June offensive. Instead of congratulating him for capturing middle Tennessee, Stanton and Halleck complained about his failure to finish off Bragg's rebels. Their lack of gratitude galled him. It was wrong, he fumed, to slight the Army of the Cumberland's accomplishment simply because it had not been attended by great bloodshed. But if Rosecrans did not grasp the reasons for high-level dissatisfaction with his generalship, other officers did. "Brilliant campaigns without battles do not accomplish the destruction of an army," grumbled one of his aides. "A campaign like that of Tullahoma always means a battle at some other point."

Washington wanted a decisive battle fought soon. The Confederacy was on the brink of ruin after Gettysburg and Vicksburg; one more blow might finish it off. Of the three major Union forces, the Army of the Cumberland was in the best shape to mount an offensive, so Stanton and Halleck pressed Rosecrans to attack Chattanooga and open the way for a thrust deep into Georgia.

Situated near the Tennessee-Georgia border at the point where the Tennessee River cuts westward through the Cumberland Mountains, Chattanooga was a natural fortress, extremely hard to approach, much less capture. The Union army would have to scale a series of steep ridges on roads that were little more than cowpaths, cross a major waterway, then pry 30,000 Confederate troops out of entrenched positions in and around the city. The navy would be unable to help because its gunboats could not get past Muscle Shoals, two hundred miles downriver from Chattanooga. It shaped up as one of the most challenging campaigns of the war, and Rosecrans was determined to proceed with caution. He notified the War Department that as a first step he was going to repair the Nashville & Chattanooga Railroad between Tullahoma and the northern Alabama towns of Stevenson and Bridgeport, where he intended to establish forward supply depots. Not until this was done, and his quartermaster had stockpiled enough food and ammunition to sustain 66,000 soldiers for at least twenty days, would he begin an offensive. He also asked for reinforcements to protect his flanks and rear from enemy raids.

"He shall not have another damned man!" barked Stanton when he received Rosecrans's request. Halleck was also exasperated. He warned his subordinate that if he continued to procrastinate, a more aggressive general would be found to command the Army of the Cumberland. This was a familiar threat, and Rosecrans answered it in his usual way. "Whenever the Government can replace me by a commander in whom they have more confidence, they ought to do so, and take the responsibility for the result," he told the general in chief. Halleck lost his temper when he read this. He sent Rosecrans an ultimatum: Advance at once, or face the consequences.

Old Rosy realized he could stall no longer; he either had to move or submit his resignation. Deciding on the former, he issued marching orders to his corps commanders on August 15. The Army of the Cumberland would break camp the following morning and head south toward the Tennessee River.

While the Union soldiers were preparing for the action, Bragg's troops were marking time in Chattanooga. "It was the same drudge, drudge day by day," Private Sam Watkins wrote of the unvarying routine of drill, picket duty, and fortification building. "Occasionally, a Sunday would come; but when it did come, there came inspection. . . . Every soldier had to have his gun rubbed up as bright as a new silver dollar, have on clean clothes, and if he had lost any cartridges he was charged twenty-five cents each and had to stand extra duty. We always dreaded Sunday."

Adding to the army's woes was the infirmity of its commander. In addition to the dyspepsia, diarrhea, and migraine headaches that regularly plagued him, Bragg was suffering from an excruciating attack of boils. His wretched health, coupled with the pressures of his post, had brought him to the verge of physical and psychological collapse. "He was silent and reserved and seemed gloomy and despondent," wrote Major General Daniel Harvey Hill, who had recently arrived from Virginia to take over William Hardee's corps. "He had grown prematurely old since I saw him last, and showed much nervousness."

Hill's diagnosis of depression was accurate. Discouraged by the loss of middle Tennessee and disheartened by the unrelenting hostility of his subordinates, Bragg had succumbed to crippling pessimism. When Richmond proposed reinforcing him so that he could take back the territory surrendered earlier in the summer, he declined. His attitude toward holding Chattanooga was almost as bad. "It is said to be easy to defend a mountainous country," he whined to one of his corps commanders, "but mountains hide your foe from you, while they are full of gaps through which he can pounce upon you at any time." Convinced that he could not stop the Yankees from crossing the Cumberland Plateau, Bragg made no effort to track their movements. His lack of vigilance horrified Hill, who was used to the aggressive, wide-awake style of the Army of Northern Virginia. "The want of information at General Bragg's headquarters was in striking contrast with the minute knowledge General Lee always had of every operation in his front," he wrote. "I was most painfully impressed with the feeling that it was to be a haphazard campaign on our part."

W̲here Bragg was listless and apathetic, waiting with an air of weary resignation for his opponent to strike, Rosecrans was brisk and animated as he began the advance toward Chattanooga on August 16. The offensive would consist of three phases: first, the forward movement to the Tennessee River; second, the crossing; third, an assault on Chattanooga from the southwest. This last was something of a surprise. The obvious route of attack was from the northwest, across the Sequatchie Valley and Walden's Ridge toward the East Tennessee & Georgia Railroad between Chattanooga and Cleveland, Tennessee. It would have allowed Rosecrans to approach his objective over relatively flat ground, supported by Burnside's 24,000-man Army of the Ohio, which had recently entered east Tennessee and was threatening Knoxville. Rosecrans had rejected this strategy, however, because he believed it was what his opponent expected. Traversing the mountains and bridging the river southwest of Chattanooga was riskier, but it had the advantage of being unlooked for. Having befuddled Bragg during the Tullahoma campaign, he was confident he could do it again, and so he split his force into three columns and sent them forward across a sixty-mile front.

Crittenden's corps was on the left. Its mission was to cross the Cumberland Plateau, descend into the Sequatchie Valley, and make a show of preparing for an offensive. To embellish this feint, three infantry brigades were sent to the north bank of the Tennessee River to menace Chattanooga itself. Meanwhile, Thomas's corps in the center and McCook's corps on the right would march rapidly to the downstream crossing points, doing their utmost to keep their movements a secret.

The plan worked perfectly. The Confederates were unaware of the Federal advance until August 21. That morning several blue regiments appeared on Stringer's Ridge directly opposite Chattanooga and began shelling the city. Jefferson Davis had declared this a day of prayer and fasting throughout the South. Most of the Army of Tennessee's generals were in the local Presbyterian church, listening to Reverend B. M. Palmer plead for divine intervention on behalf of the Confederacy. When a projectile exploded on the street outside, Benjamin F. Cheatham assured the congregation that there was nothing to worry about. "It's our gunners practicing," he announced; "there's not a Yankee within fifty miles of here." Seconds later another shell whistled over the rooftop and burst with a loud bang. The panicky parishioners rushed for the exits, leaving the red-faced Cheatham behind to listen to the minister conclude what one observer later characterized as "the longest prayer I ever heard."

Union units continued to demonstrate on the riverbank across from Chattanooga for the next two weeks. They took potshots at the Confederate city, lit large numbers of campfires at night to create the illusion of an entire army going into bivouac, and pounded on empty barrels and tossed pieces of sawn lumber into the river to make the rebels think a flotilla of assault boats was being constructed. Falling for this ruse, Bragg positioned his forces to repel an attack from the northeast. He left the downstream crossings completely unguarded. By the night of September 4, the bulk of the blue army was over the river and heading into the mountains south of Chattanooga.

Two divisions, detached from Johnston's Mississippi command, arrived in Chattanooga during the last week of August, increasing the Army of Tennessee's strength by almost a third. Bragg still did not know where the Yankees were, however. It was not until August 30 that he learned from a civilian informant that a powerful Union column was crossing the river at Caperton's Ferry, thirty miles southwest of Chattanooga. In the days that followed, additional reports were received indicating that the Army of the Cumberland was swinging around the Confederate left, but Bragg refused to act on the basis of intelligence he considered unreliable. When he was finally presented with incontrovertible evidence that Rosecrans was in his rear, it was too late to do anything about it. His main supply line, the Western & Atlantic Railroad to Atlanta, was about to be cut. After much agonizing, he decided to abandon Chattanooga. Orders to that effect were issued, and on the night of September 7, the Army of Tennessee marched out of the sleeping city, heading south.

The bluecoats were in high spirits as they entered Georgia, passing through gaps in the lofty escarpments—Sand Mountain, Raccoon Mountain, Lookout Mountain, and Missionary Ridge—that extended like rocky fingers southwestward from Chattanooga. Most of the soldiers were Midwesterners accustomed to the flatlands of Ohio, Indiana, and Illinois. They were awed by the vistas that spread before them as they ascended the heights. "Far beyond mortal vision extended one vast panorama of mountains, forests, and rivers," one of them rhapsodized. "The broad Tennessee below us seemed like a ribbon of silver; beyond rose the Cumberlands, which we had crossed. The valley on both sides was alive with the moving armies of the Union, while almost the entire transportation of the army filled the roads and fields along the Tennessee."

Morale surged even higher when news of the rebel retreat circulated through the ranks. "Chattanooga is ours without a struggle, and East Tennessee is free," Rosecrans informed Washington on the evening of September 9. Intoxicated by his easy success, he resolved to keep moving and smash Bragg's retiring army, which Confederate deserters said was making for Rome, Georgia. Thomas urged him to concentrate his forces and establish a supply base at Chattanooga before taking up the pursuit, arguing that it was dangerous to plunge headlong into enemy country with the three Union corps widely dispersed and no solid line of communications established. Rosecrans disregarded this advice. He had the rebels on the run, and he was determined to catch them before they could reach Rome and dig in. He ordered Crittenden to occupy Chattanooga with a single brigade and follow the decamping graybacks with the remainder of his corps. McCook's command was instructed to march due south, cross Lookout Mountain via Winston Gap, then hurry east through Alpine and try to block the rebels' line of retreat in the vicinity of Summerville. Thomas's troops would take the middle route through Stevens and Dug Gaps to LaFayette and try to strike the Confederate force in its flank. The objective, Rosecrans announced, was to get the enemy "in our grip and strangle him, or perish in the attempt."

For the second time in as many months, Bragg had been forced to fall back to avoid being caught in a Federal trap. But despite being evicted from Chattanooga, he did not consider himself beaten. To the contrary, he was looking for an opportunity to counterattack. When he reached the town of Lee and Gordon's Mill, he ordered his troops to halt and prepare to fight the Union army as it emerged from behind the barrier of Lookout Mountain.

Fueling Bragg's newfound pugnacity was the prospect of additional reinforcements. His command had already been strengthened by the arrival of Major General Simon B. Buckner's 10,000-man corps, which had evacuated Knoxville during the first week of September, and more help was on the way in the form of two brigades from Mississippi and two divisions from Virginia. This rapid buildup reflected Jefferson Davis's conviction that Rosecrans had to be stopped before he did irreparable harm to the Confederacy's transportation network and industrial infrastructure. He told Johnston to bolster Bragg with as many troops as he could spare; then on September 5 he sent a large detachment from the Army of Northern Virginia to augment the Army of Tennessee. The president wanted Lee to accompany this contingent to Georgia and assume overall command there, but Lee begged off, expressing the belief that Bragg, who was already familiar with the terrain, would do a better job. Although Davis did not agree, he acquiesced. It was decided that Longstreet's corps, minus Pickett's division, which was still recuperating from its Gettysburg mauling, would be dispatched to reinforce Bragg. On September 6, Lee ordered his quartermaster to arrange for transportation. Two days later, Hood's and McLaws's divisions—12,000 troops in all—left their camps along the Rapidan River and set out for the railheads at Richmond and Orange Court House, where they would entrain for the long journey south and west.

Bragg was not waiting for their arrival to go over to the offensive. On the afternoon of September 9, he learned that the lead division of Thomas's corps had entered McLemore's Cove, a narrow valley situated between Lookout Mountain and its eastern spur, Pigeon Mountain. Here was an excellent opportunity to destroy an isolated fragment of the Union army. Bragg ordered Major General Thomas C. Hindman's division, which was at Lee and Gordon's Mill, to march south into McLemore's Cove and fall on the enemy's flank and rear. At the same time, Cleburne's division of Hill's corps was to move west from LaFayette through Dug Gap in Pigeon Mountain and join the attack.

Unfortunately for Bragg, nothing went right. Hindman advanced to within four miles of the unsuspecting Union division on the morning of September 10, then developed a bad case of nerves and stopped. Cleburne never budged from his bivouac at LaFayette because his immediate superior, D. H. Hill, declined to pass along Bragg's order. Frantic to get the attack under way before the bluecoats took alarm and withdrew, Bragg reinforced Hindman with one of Buckner's divisions and directed him to crush the enemy without delay. But Hindman continued to hesitate. Imagining all kinds of threats to his command, he did not advance in earnest until late on the afternoon of September 11. By then the Federals had gotten wind of what was going on and pulled back through Stevens Gap.

The Confederates got another chance on September 12 when one of Crittenden's divisions approached Lee and Gordon's Mill from the north. Bragg ordered Polk to gobble up this exposed unit, but like Hindman before him, Polk got cold feet in the presence of the enemy. Convinced that his corps was dangerously outnumbered, he decided against attacking. By midday on September 13 the Yankees were gone, and so too was the Army of Tennessee's second opportunity to score an easy victory.

Seething at the ineptitude of his subordinates, Bragg retired to LaFayette to ponder his options. Rosecrans, meanwhile, was rushing to reunite his army. He sent dispatches to McCook, Thomas, and Major General Gordon Granger, telling them to join Crittenden's corps near Lee and Gordon's Mill. It took several days, but by September 17 the Army of the Cumberland was concentrated in the valley of Chickamauga Creek. It was not a moment too soon. Observers on Lookout Mountain had spotted thick clouds of dust hanging over the roads leading from LaFayette to Lee and Gordon's Mill. Cavalry patrols confirmed that long columns of gray infantry were marching north toward the Union position.

On September 9 a train carrying the lead elements of Longstreet's corps chugged out of Richmond bound for Catoosa Station, the Western & Atlantic depot closest to Bragg's LaFayette headquarters. Because Knoxville had fallen to Burnside's army a few days before, the direct route across Virginia and eastern Tennessee was closed. Longstreet's veterans had had to make a circuitous journey down through the Carolinas and across the width of Georgia, using sixteen separate lines.

Despite being crowded like cattle, the men enjoyed the trip. Cheering crowds greeted them at every depot, and food and drink were plentiful. Lieutenant Augustus Dickert remembered how his fellow passengers remodeled the boxcars to improve the ventilation and get a better view. "The weather being warm, the troops cut all but the frame loose with knives and axes," he wrote. "They further wished to see outside and witness the fine country and delightful scenery that lay along the route; nor could those inside bear the idea of being shut up while their comrades on top were yelling themselves hoarse at the waving of handkerchiefs and flags in the hands of the pretty women along the roadside."

The sight of the derelict trains steaming past, loaded to overflowing with the cream of Lee's army, made an indelible impression on the civilians who witnessed it. "God bless the gallant fellows," a Kingsville, South Carolina, woman recorded in her diary. "Not one man intoxicated, not one rude word did I hear. It was a strange sight. What seemed miles of platform cars, and soldiers rolled in their blankets lying in rows with heads all covered, fast asleep. In their gray blankets packed in regular order, they looked like swathed mummies." This imagery distressed her: "A feeling of awful depression laid hold of me," she wrote. "All of these fine fellows going to kill or be killed."

From Kingsville, the trains rolled southwest to Augusta and then on to Atlanta, where they turned northwest and chugged the final 125 miles to Catoosa Station. The first units, three brigades of Hood's division, arrived on the afternoon of September 18. It had taken them nine days to complete the nine-hundred-mile journey from Virginia, and they were tired, stiff, and dirty. But they had reached their destination in time to play a key role in the battle that was about to begin along the densely forested banks of Chickamauga Creek.

Still brooding over the bungling of Hindman, Hill, and Polk, Bragg hatched a new plan for destroying the enemy. It called for the entire Confederate army to cross the Chickamauga north of Lee and Gordon's Mill, cut the Yankees off from Chattanooga, then drive them south into the cul-de-sac of McLemore's Cove. He marched his forces into position on September 17 and issued orders for the assault to begin at sunrise the following morning. Mindful of last week's foot-dragging, he closed his instructions with an admonitory sentence: "The above movements will be executed with the utmost promptness, vigor, and persistence."

He was destined to be bitterly disappointed. His subordinates seemed incapable of swift, decisive action. Brigadier General Bushrod Johnson's division, supported by Hood's brigades as they arrived on the field, was to advance across Reed's Bridge on the Confederate right, then wheel south and roll up the Union left. Johnson started off in the wrong direction, however, and when he finally got turned around, he moved at a crawl and did not reach the bridge until midday.

Meanwhile, Major General W.H.T. Walker's corps, which was to cross the Chickamauga at Alexander's Bridge, and Buckner's corps, which was to attack via Thedford's Ford, had become entangled on a narrow country road. Buckner managed to extricate his command from the traffic jam and get to the ford at 2 P.M., but there he stopped, afraid to press on because he had heard nothing from Walker and Johnson on his right. These two generals had run into Federal mounted units as they approached their respective bridges, and it had taken them the better part of the afternoon to vanquish them. So despite Bragg's call for promptness, only a small portion of the Army of Tennessee was across the Chickamauga by sunset—too late to launch the planned attack.

The gray columns continued to cross the creek during the night. At dawn on September 19 they were ready to strike. The Federal left was no longer in the same place, however. Rosecrans had shifted his army northward to meet the rebel assault. He accomplished this by leapfrogging Thomas's corps over Crittenden's and moving McCook's corps into the position vacated by Thomas. Thus, when Confederate skirmishers started forward on the morning of the nineteenth, they found Union troops standing squarely in their path.

For several hours the two sides surged back and forth over terrain so choked with scrub oak and pine saplings that opposing soldiers could not see each other until they were just a few yards apart. "A mad, irregular battle," was the way one officer described it, "very much resembling guerrilla warfare on a vast scale."

Hearing the sound of gunfire in the distance, Rosecrans decided to move his headquarters from Crawfish Springs, a mile and a half southwest of Lee and Gordon's Mill, to a spot nearer the action. The site he selected was a log cabin belonging to a war widow named Eliza Glenn. Perched on a knoll west of the LaFayette Road about two miles from where the combat was raging, the Glenn house offered as good a view of the surrounding countryside as could be had, which was not saying much given the thickness of the forest. "Although closer to the battle, we could see no more of it here than at Crawfish Springs," lamented Charles Dana, who had joined Rosecrans's staff eight days earlier.

Old Rosy stalked around the one-room cabin, waiting anxiously for dispatches to arrive. While he paced, his chief engineer unrolled a map of the area and plotted unit locations on it with only the sounds of gunfire and the Widow Glenn's observations to guide him. As New York *Herald* correspondent William Shanks described it, the engineer would wait for the battle noise to intensify, then look at the widow, who would cock her head, listen intently, and announce in a backwoods drawl that the racket came from "nigh out about Reed's Bridge somewhar," or "about a mile fornenst John Kelly's house." The newspaperman was contemptuous of this method of intelligence gathering: "Never was there anything so ridiculous," he snorted.

Rosecrans may not have known exactly what was transpiring in the woods to his front, but he was satisfied that his forces were holding their own. He continued to feed fresh units into the fight, while deploying others along the three-and-a-half-mile stretch of LaFayette Road that seemed to be the objective of the Confederate thrust. All went well until the early part of the afternoon, when he received unsettling news: rebel soldiers belonging to Hood's division had been captured—proof that Longstreet's corps was reinforcing the Army of Tennessee. Hoping to learn more, he went outside to interrogate one of the prisoners. The man he questioned, a captain from Texas, proved uncooperative. "General, it has cost me a great deal of trouble to find your lines," he said in reply to Rosecrans's inquiry about the Confederate dispositions. "If you take the same amount of trouble, you will find ours." Old Rosy kept pressing, but to no avail. The prisoner could not recall what division or corps he belonged to. "Captain," Rosecrans finally said in exasperation, "you don't seem to know much, for a man whose appearance seems to indicate so much intelligence."

"Well, General," the Texan drawled, "if you are not satisfied with my information, I will volunteer some. We are going to whip you most tremendously in this fight."

Shaking his head incredulously, Rosecrans ordered the prisoner taken to the rear.

Bragg had started the day confident of success, but when Yankees materialized on a part of the field where he had not expected them to be, the wind left his sails. He was unsure whether he should stick to his original plan or try something else. Ultimately he did neither. Instead he committed his troops piecemeal, sending them forward with vague instructions to pitch into the Federals wherever they found them.

D. H. Hill was appalled by Bragg's maladroit tactics. "There was no general advance, as there might have been," he wrote. "It was the sparring of an amateur boxer, and not the crushing blows of the trained pugilist." But even if Bragg had ordered a coordinated assault as Hill advocated, it is doubtful whether the rebel army could have pulled it off, given the jungle that lay between it and the blue line in front of the LaFayette Road. Advancing through heavy timber and clinging underbrush, enveloped by blinding clouds of powder smoke, units became separated and officers lost tactical control. "There was no generalship in it," remembered one of the combatants. "It was a soldier's fight purely."

For the rest of the afternoon and on into the evening, the frenzied struggle continued. Twice the Confederates broke through the Federals' LaFayette Road line and twice they were thrown back. Darkness finally put a stop to the bloodletting. The rebels flopped down on the ground and tried to fall asleep. The Yankees, sure that they would be attacked again tomorrow, worked with axes and shovels to build sturdy log-and-earth barricades.

At 8 P.M. Rosecrans called his corps and division commanders to a council of war. He was acutely aware that the Confederate assaults, as disorganized as they had been, had come very close to splintering his army. Even more disturbing to him was the knowledge that Longstreet's corps had reached the field. He feared that he was greatly outnumbered, and he was unsure how to proceed.

McCook had no advice to offer despite the fact that he had once taught tactics at West Point. Crittenden likewise had nothing to contribute. Thomas snored through the entire meeting, awakening only when Rosecrans addressed him directly. "Strengthen the left," he mumbled when asked what course of action he would recommend, then fell back asleep before he could be pressed for details.

At the conclusion of this discussion, Rosecrans announced that the army would stand on the defensive on Sunday the twentieth. Barring a retreat by the rebels—a possibility that could not be ruled out given Bragg's past history—the battle would be fought along the LaFayette Road line, just as it had been today. Thomas, who now had five divisions under his control, would hold his position on the left; McCook would move his two divisions north to connect with Thomas's right; Crittenden would wait in reserve, ready to plug any holes the enemy opened.

Neither exhaustion nor stress could dim Rosecrans's love of socializing. When the council was over, he asked his subordinates to stay and chat for a while. Orderlies brought in trays of bacon and hot coffee, and McCook entertained the gathering by singing a sentimental ballad entitled "The Hebrew Maiden's Lament." After this performance and a few minutes of desultory conversation, the generals took their leave.

Old Rosy was too overwrought to sleep. Filling his coat pockets with hardtack and fortifying himself with a canteen of cold tea, he went outside and paced back and forth in front of the cabin, not stopping until the eastern sky began to brighten. Then he asked an aide to wake Father Treacy so that he might hear mass before beginning the day's bloody work.

Like Rosecrans, Bragg convened a council of war on the night of the nineteenth. He informed his subordinates—all but D. H. Hill, who had been unable to find the command post in the darkness—that he was reorganizing the army. It would now be divided into two wings, the right commanded by Polk, with Hill and Walker serving under him, and the left commanded by Longstreet, who was rumored to have reached the battle-field, although he had not yet made an appearance at headquarters. The next day's plan was simple: Polk's divisions would attack *en echelon* beginning at dawn. Longstreet's wing would follow. The goal was to flank the Union army, then drive it south into McLemore's Cove.

As usual, Bragg's officers objected to his orders. Altering the chain of command in the middle of a battle was madness, they argued. It would lead to dangerous mix-ups, and it was bound to offend Hill, who was being forced to play second fiddle to Polk, even though both were lieutenant generals. Apprehensive about having to deal with a resentful subordinate, Polk tried to talk Bragg into splitting the army into three grand divisions so that Hill would have a command also, but to no avail. Nor would Bragg listen when Polk warned him that the bulk of the Union army was concentrated in front of the Confederate right, where the next day's assault was supposed to begin. As far as Bragg was concerned, Polk had more than enough troops to turn the Yankee flank. He sent him on his way without any written instructions, leaving it to him to communicate to Hill his diminished role in the new command structure and to make all the arrangements for the attack, which was scheduled to start in less than eight hours.

As unsettled as the situation was on the Confederate right, it was even worse on the left, where the man who was supposed to be in charge had not yet reached the front. Longstreet's train had pulled into Catoosa Station at 2 P.M. on the nineteenth. He and two high-ranking aides debarked, expecting to be met by a member of Bragg's staff. No guide was on hand to escort them to headquarters, however, nor was there anyone around who could brief them about the battle they heard raging off in the distance. After waiting on the platform for several hours, the three officers finally set out in the direction of Chickamauga Creek. The sun set, and still the trio wandered westward, blundering through the woods until they struck a Union picket line and had to beat a hasty retreat.

It was not until 11 P.M. that Longstreet and his companions found the Army of Tennessee's headquarters. Bragg had to be awakened to greet them. Puffy-eyed and groggy, he informed the startled Longstreet that he was to lead an attack just after daybreak tomorrow. He handed the Georgian a sketch map showing the main roads and

General James Longstreet, C.S.A.
(Courtesy U.S. Army Military
History Institute)

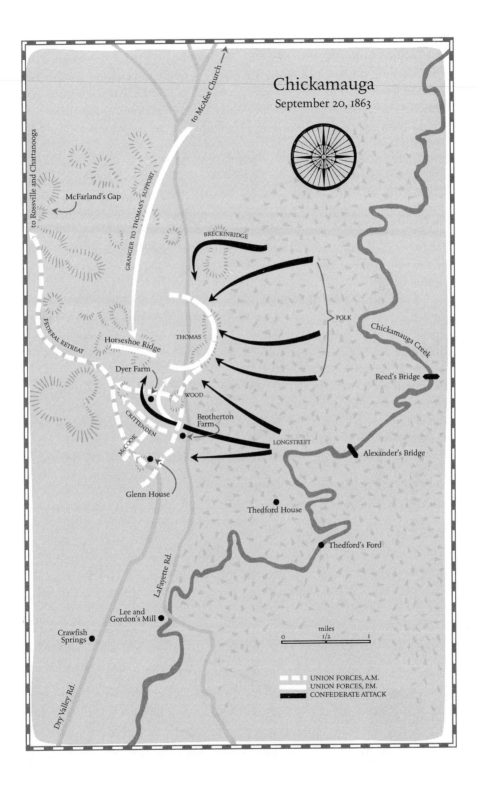

Chickamauga
September 20, 1863

to McAfee Church

to Rossville and Chattanooga

McFarland's Gap

GRANGER TO THOMAS'S SUPPORT

FEDERAL RETREAT

Horseshoe Ridge

Dyer Farm

CRITTENDEN

McCOOK

Glenn House

BRECKINRIDGE

THOMAS

WOOD

Brotherton
Farm

POLK

Chickamauga Creek

Reed's Bridge

LONGSTREET

Alexander's Bridge

Thedford House

Thedford's Ford

LaFayette Rd.

Lee and
Gordon's Mill

Crawfish
Springs

Dry Valley Rd.

miles
0   1/2   1

UNION FORCES, A.M.
UNION FORCES, P.M.
CONFEDERATE ATTACK

topographical features between Chickamauga Creek and Lookout Mountain, wished him well, then went back to bed.

Watching the stooped figure shuffle off, Longstreet wondered what he was getting into. He was too exhausted to worry for long. Without attempting to locate his command or communicate with his subordinates, he lay down where he was, scooped a blanket of leaves over himself, and fell sound asleep.

Sunday, September 20, dawned cold and misty. The ground was white with hoarfrost, the woods shrouded in smoke. Rosecrans's chief of staff, Brigadier General James Garfield, stepped out of the Glenn cabin, gestured at the crimson sky, and announced: "It is ominous. This will indeed be a day of blood!"

On the front lines, the rank and file were too busy griping about how cold and hungry they were to pay attention to such portents. It was a miserable morning, they all agreed. And yet, observed a Tennessee enlisted man, "the world never seemed half so attractive before, now that there was a good chance for leaving it soon."

Finishing with mass, Rosecrans hoisted himself into the saddle. Accompanied by his staff officers, he rode three-quarters of a mile north to the Dyer farm, where he established a hillside command post. Then he cantered east to confer with Thomas. Passing an Ohio regiment along the way, he waved and called out words of encouragement. His voice was weak and his face drawn and ashen, and the men could see that he was exhausted from lack of sleep. "I did not like the way he looked," recalled one of them, "but did not allow myself to think of any such thing as defeat."

Two miles to the south, near the Thedford house, Bragg was listening for the burst of gunfire that would signal the opening of the attack. Despite the foul-ups of the past two weeks, he expected his subordinates to begin the assault at dawn as scheduled. But it was not to be. The minutes ticked by, the sun climbed higher in the sky, and no musketry or artillery fire was heard.

The reason for the holdup was scandalous, even by the Army of Tennessee's sorry standards. D. H. Hill, who had become lost while searching for Bragg's headquarters on the night of the nineteenth, had also failed to get in touch with Polk, who in turn had made only a perfunctory effort to locate him before retiring. As a result, Hill did not know that his corps, consisting of Cleburne's and Breckinridge's divisions, was supposed to attack at first light. When Polk woke up on the morning of the twentieth and realized that Hill had not received his orders, he sent word directly to

Breckinridge and Cleburne to advance as soon as they were in position. The courier entrusted with this message found the two generals seated around a campfire, commiserating with Hill, who was in an ugly mood because Bragg had not chosen him to be a wing commander. After glancing at Polk's dispatch, Hill told the courier that the assault could wait until his troops had finished eating breakfast.

When Polk learned of this, he rode to Hill's headquarters to talk with him in person. What the two men said to each other was disputed after the battle. According to Hill's aides, Polk made no objection to the lengthy breakfast delay. Polk's partisans gave a different account. They had their man addressing Hill in an angry voice, saying: "Sir, this is not the time for eating; this is the time for fighting! Attack immediately!" Whatever the substance of the exchange, the paralysis on the Confederate right flank continued.

Bragg flew into a towering rage when he found out that Polk and Hill had made a hash of his plans. Spouting oaths, he galloped off to their sector to straighten things out. But even after he had berated the pair and demanded an immediate advance, the procrastinating continued. Confusion about assignments was widespread, and execution of orders spotty. It was not until 9:30 A.M. that the Confederate attack finally got started.

Breckinridge's division struck first, trying to turn the Union left and get astride the LaFayette Road. Thomas quickly shifted units to meet the threat and halted the rebel onslaught by the narrowest of margins. Then he sent a message to headquarters asking for help. Rosecrans had already ordered Major General James Negley's division to leave its position in the Union center and march north to bolster Thomas's corps. Negley's division did not move, however, because the unit that was to take its place in line, Brigadier General Thomas J. Wood's division, had not yet appeared. When he learned of Wood's tardiness, Rosecrans exploded. "What is the meaning of this, sir?" he screamed at the division commander when he found him chatting with his staff on a ridge west of the Dyer house. "You have disobeyed my specific orders! Move your division at once, as I have instructed, or the consequences will not be pleasant for yourself!" Wood did not deign to reply; he merely saluted and put his troops in motion, thereby freeing Negley's men to go to Thomas's aid. But he was seething inside, and his wounded pride would cost Rosecrans dearly in the hours to come.

Although Breckinridge's flank attack had been blunted, there was no respite for the bluecoats because three more rebel divisions were now going into action. Advancing in sequence, they hammered against the mile-long curve of Federal breastworks, applying pressure at all points so that Thomas could not concentrate his strength in any one area. Rosecrans was doing all that he could to help, throwing additional troops into the fray as fast as he could pull them out of the right and center of his line.

The frenetic flip-flopping of units as the entire army sidestepped north-ward was causing a great deal of confusion, however. It was only a matter of time before somebody made a serious mistake. Ironically, it was Rosecrans himself who committed the critical blunder, abetted by General Wood, the officer he had chewed out earlier in the morning.

At approximately 10:30 A.M. Rosecrans ordered John Brannan's divi-sion, which was posted in the center of the Union line between the com-mands of Wood and Major General Joseph Reynolds, to go to Thomas's aid. Then he turned to one of his aides and barked: "If Brannan goes out, Wood must fill his place. Write him that the commanding general directs him to close to the left on Reynolds and support him."

Wood received this dispatch at eleven o'clock. He was puzzled because Brannan's division had not gone anywhere. For him to close on Reynolds as ordered would leave a gap in the heart of the Union line. He was still smarting from Rosecrans's tongue-lashing, however, and he resolved to obey at once, even though he knew the consequences might prove cata-strophic. Tucking the piece of paper into his pocket, he put his command in motion, opening a hole a quarter mile wide that beckoned irresistibly to the rebel forces poised just three hundred yards to the east.

Longstreet had risen before daybreak and ridden west from Thedford's Ford to take charge of the left wing of the Army of Tennessee. Al-though four of the six divisions under his command were new to him, he approached his assignment with aplomb. Puffing placidly on a meerschaum pipe, he went from division to division, introducing himself to his subor-dinates and explaining what he wanted done. The memory of Gettysburg was still fresh in his mind, and he was intent on avoiding the mistakes that had been made there. Attacking piecemeal, as Lee had done in Pennsylva-nia and Bragg was doing here in Georgia, played into the hands of an en-trenched enemy by dispersing offensive strength over too wide a front. In boxing terms it was like slapping an opponent with an open palm rather than hitting him with a clenched fist. If he had to attack, Longstreet was determined to deliver a punch that was short, swift, and immensely pow-erful. Toward that end he formed his command into a column that was eight brigades deep, with another ten brigades massed in reserve. The blow would fall on the Union line where it crossed the seven-hundred-acre Brotherton farm, about three-quarters of a mile south of where Polk's di-visions were futilely battering against Thomas's breastworks.

An hour passed, and nothing was heard from headquarters. Growing impatient, Longstreet sent a messenger to Bragg requesting permission to advance, but he received no reply. Suddenly one of his divisions started forward on its own. Word came moments later that Bragg, infuriated by the dillydallying of Polk and Hill, was bypassing his senior generals and ordering division commanders to engage the enemy on their own initiative. Longstreet had to act fast, or the coordinated assault he had planned would go by the boards. He immediately called for his column of brigades to move out. At 11:10 A.M. the troops stepped off—11,000 men advancing on a front barely five hundred yards across.

As Longstreet's soldiers surged across the LaFayette Road and into the open fields of the Brotherton farm, they were hit by fire from the left and right, but none from straight ahead. Unsure what to make of this, they kept going past the house and barn until they struck a belt of timber on the farm's western boundary. There they saw a line of fortifications, unaccountably deserted, and beyond it, just visible through the tangle of trees, the tail end of Wood's division marching away in blind obedience to Rosecrans's order to support Reynolds. With perfect timing the Confederates burst through the quarter-mile gap in the blue line, tore the rear of Wood's formation to pieces, then plunged on until they reached the Dyer farm five hundred yards farther west.

After a brief pause to let his men catch their breath, Bushrod Johnson resumed the advance, penetrating another half a mile into the Union rear before halting to refill the division's cartridge boxes. He was concerned that the Federals might counterattack, but when he pulled out his field glasses and looked around, he realized that he had nothing to fear. To the west he could see Yankee wagons racing away toward McFarland's Gap, which led through Missionary Ridge to Rossville and Chattanooga beyond. Even more thrilling was the view to the south, in the direction of the Glenn house. There a blue-clad rabble was fleeing from a phalanx of bayonet-brandishing Confederates—clear indication that the attack was going well not just for his command but for all of Longstreet's left wing.

The rebel breakthrough caught Rosecrans completely by surprise. He and his staff were at the Dyer farm command post when Longstreet's assault began, and they barely had time to react before the battle engulfed them. "I was awakened by the most infernal noise I ever heard," wrote Charles Dana, who had been napping when the attack began. "I sat up on the grass, and the first thing I saw was General Rosecrans crossing himself. . . . 'Hello!' I said to myself, 'if the general is crossing himself, we are in a desperate situation.' I was on my horse in a moment. I had no sooner collected my thoughts and looked around toward the front where all this din came from, than I saw our lines break and melt away."

Harking back to Stones River, where he had rallied his troops under similar circumstances, Rosecrans galloped forward and tried to check the avalanche. He failed. The soldiers in blue were running for their lives; no one, not even their saber-waving commander, could stop them. Seeing that threats and exhortations were useless, Rosecrans jerked his mount about and tried to ride to Thomas's position on the left. His way was blocked by a sea of terrified humanity. When he looked east, in the direction the fugitives were coming from, he saw a wave of Confederates bearing down on him. With a start he realized that he and his aides were in mortal danger. "If you care to live any longer, get away from here!" he bawled, then headed for the rear as fast as his horse would carry him.

Rosecrans was not the only high-ranking Union general to flee; two of his three corps commanders and four of his ten division commanders bolted as well. But responsibility for the rout rested squarely on his shoulders, and as he rode northwest toward McFarland's Gap, he grew increasingly distraught. Forcing his way through the crush of men and vehicles clogging the narrow pass, he continued on to Rossville three miles to the north, where he stopped to rest his winded horse and to consider his next move. The road forked at Rossville, one branch leading to Chattanooga, the other back to the battlefield by an alternate route. He was not sure if his entire army had been obliterated, or if the left wing was still intact and in action. All signs pointed to the former, but he decided it was his duty to return to the front and find out for sure. He told his chief of staff what he intended to do and asked him to continue on to Chattanooga, round up as many stragglers as possible, and prepare to make a defensive stand. James Garfield objected strenuously. Rosecrans should go to Chattanooga, he said, while he, Garfield, rode back to the battlefield to determine what had happened to the Union left.

Too weary to argue, Rosecrans agreed. The two men went their separate ways, Garfield galloping east toward the sound of the guns, Rosecrans heading northwest to Chattanooga. In the weeks to come he would be harshly criticized for his decision. "Rosecrans should at once have gone to the front," averred one of his staff officers. "That was the turning point, and his hour had arrived."

But in truth Rosecrans's hour had passed. He was physically and emotionally spent. When he arrived in Chattanooga around 3:30 P.M, he was so tired, he could not dismount or walk without assistance. Once inside departmental headquarters, he sat with his head in his hands saying nothing. It was obvious to the officers who gathered around that he was in a state of shock, overcome by exhaustion and by the conviction that Chickamauga was the worst defeat sustained by the Union military since Chancellorsville.

Longstreet was elated by the collapse of the Federal right and center. Casualties were heavy among frontline Confederate units; his friend Hood had lost his right leg when a minié ball smashed the femur just below the hip socket; but half of the blue army had been pulverized, and Longstreet believed that the other half could be destroyed as well. His original intent had been to obey Bragg's orders and wheel to the left as the assault progressed. Such a move no longer made sense, however. A pivot to the right, followed by a northward drive toward Thomas's position, was clearly called for. Caught between the anvil of Polk's wing and the hammer of his own, the Federals would be crushed. He instructed his division commanders to sort out their intermingled brigades, draw a fresh supply of ammunition, and form a new line extending from the LaFayette Road a mile west to the Dry Valley Road. While this was being done, he conducted a quick reconnaissance, then returned to the Dyer house for a lunch of bacon and sweet potatoes.

Longstreet was eating with gusto—"we were not accustomed to potatoes of any kind in Virginia, and thought we had a luxury," he later wrote—when a courier galloped up and announced that Bragg wished to see him at once. Setting aside his meal, he rode off to confer with the army commander at his temporary headquarters a mile west of Reed's Bridge. It was not a successful meeting. Bragg listened in stony silence as Longstreet described the rout of the Federals in his sector and outlined his plan for clinching the victory. "There is not a man in the right wing who has any fight in him," Bragg snapped when the briefing was finished. He was still furious at Polk for failing to attack at dawn. Nor was he willing to believe that Longstreet had achieved success on another part of the field. The only thing he was certain of was that his strategy for herding the Yankees into McLemore's Cove had failed. He was so bitter about it that he was unwilling to consider alternative arrangements, and he rode away without issuing any orders.

Longstreet was flabbergasted. "From accounts of his former operations I was prepared for halting work," he wrote, "but this, when the battle was at its tide and in partial success, was a little surprising." He quickly regained his composure and resolved to carry out his plan for finishing off the crippled Union army, Bragg's rebuff notwithstanding.

General George H. Thomas.
(Library of Congress)

Standing six feet tall and weighing 250 pounds, with a grizzled beard and craggy countenance, George Thomas cut an imposing figure. He looked, wrote an admirer, like he had been "hewn out of a large block of the best-tempered material men are made of, not scrimped anywhere, and square everywhere—square face, square shoulders, square step." A Virginia-born West Pointer who had remained loyal to the Union, Thomas was renowned for his steadiness under fire; the hotter the combat was, the cooler he became. He would need every bit of that coolness now, for he and his troops were in for the fight of their lives.

When the rebels broke through at the Brotherton farm, then swung around to the north to take him in the flank and rear, Thomas reacted quickly. His original arc-shaped line faced east toward Chickamauga Creek. Extending westward from its southern end was a chain of hills collectively known as Horseshoe Ridge. It was on this elevation that he posted a scratch force consisting of fragments of units shattered by Longstreet's initial assault, as well as several brigades pulled from the north-south line facing Polk.

The Confederate attack hit the western end of Horseshoe Ridge around one o'clock. Federal bullets carpeted the ground with bodies, but still the rebels came on. If they broke through into the Federal rear, the line of retreat to McFarland's Gap would be cut, and what was left of the Army of the Cumberland would be crushed between the converging wings of Longstreet and Polk.

It was at this critical juncture that one of Thomas's aides spotted a dust cloud rising from a cornfield several miles north of the ridge. Immediately all eyes were fixed on the yellowish-brown haze, which was being churned up by a long column of soldiers. No one knew whether the approaching force was friend or foe. Thomas fumbled for his field glasses, but his capering mount made it impossible for him to focus. "Tell me what you see!" he shouted at the others, his celebrated self-control failing under the strain of the moment. A correspondent squinting through his own binoculars announced that the Stars and Stripes were flying above the forest of rifle barrels, and an audible sigh of relief went up from the assembled staff officers.

The blue troops coming to the rescue belonged to Gordon Granger's 5,400-man Reserve Corps, which had spent the nineteenth and a good part of the twentieth at McAfee Church, four miles north of the battlefield. Granger, a gruff, hard-bitten regular, had finally lost patience about 11 A.M. "Why the hell does Rosecrans keep me here?" he sputtered as he listened to the gunfire's unrelenting roar. "I am going to Thomas, orders or no orders!"

Thomas had pulled himself together by the time Granger joined him. He greeted the general with a handshake, pointed toward the fight at the far end of Horseshoe Ridge, and told him to pitch in at once. Granger obeyed without hesitation. The combat was hand to hand, and observers watching from a safe distance were amazed by its ferocity. Then by mutual consent the two sides separated and the firing died down. Granger's command had lost close to 700 men, but it had turned back the Confederate assault and solidified Union control of the ridge. Almost as important, it had brought 95,000 extra cartridges with it from McAfee Church. This ammunition would enable Thomas's Federals to hold on until nightfall.

The sun started to set at five o'clock. The fighting had slackened on Horseshoe Ridge, but to the east it was intensifying as Polk's wing resumed its onslaught after a lengthy respite. Thomas's pugnacity remained undimished, but he was realist enough to see that if he waited much longer, it might be too late to save his command. Reluctantly, he ordered a retreat. The eastward-facing divisions would leave the field first, each one pulling back and passing behind the unit to its left until all were on the road to McFarland's Gap and Rossville; then the divisions arrayed along Horseshoe Ridge would do the same.

The movement began at five thirty. One by one the Union divisions disengaged and marched off to the northwest. The remaining blue units fought on with desperate intensity, knowing that their chance to escape depended on keeping the Rossville Road open. In the end only a handful of Federals remained atop Horseshoe Ridge. As night fell, they were overrun. Screaming in exultation, the two wings of Bragg's army came together on the ground just abandoned by the Yankees. It was the "ugliest sound that any mortal ever heard," wrote Ambrose Bierce, who was part of the retreating Union column.

Dizzy with hunger, thirst, and fatigue, the Federals dragged themselves into Rossville around midnight. Thomas tried to form a defensive line, but it proved impossible. "At this hour of the night the army is simply a mob," John Beatty wrote in his diary. "There appears to be neither organization nor discipline. The various commands are mixed up in what seems to be inextricable confusion. Were a division of the enemy to pounce down upon us, I fear the Army of the Cumberland would be blotted out."

The Confederates were in no condition to pounce, however. They were just as disorganized as the Federals, and as the occupiers of the battlefield, they were burdened with tasks their Union counterparts did not have to worry about. "Everything had fallen into our hands," recalled Private Sam Watkins. "We had captured a great many prisoners and small arms, and many pieces of artillery and wagons and provisions. The dead, wounded, and dying were everywhere scattered."

While the enlisted men searched for fallen comrades, their commanders tried to figure out what to do next. Bragg was no help. He had gone to sleep while the battle was still in progress, and no one had bothered to wake him with the news that Thomas had retreated. "It did not occur to me on the night of the 20th to send Bragg word of our complete success," Longstreet wrote years later. "I thought that the loud huzzas that spread over the field just at dark were a sufficient assurance and notice to anyone within five miles."

Polk was likewise remiss. He went to sleep shortly after the fighting ended, and it was not until 1 A.M. that he awoke and made his way to army headquarters to brief Bragg. The Yankees had been routed, he told the bleary-eyed general. Bragg refused to believe it. A Confederate private who had been taken prisoner on the nineteenth, then escaped during the Union retreat on the twentieth, was brought before the army commander to describe the panic and disarray he had seen. Bragg would not credit the man's eyewitness account. "Do you know what a retreat looks like?" he asked, his voice dripping with sarcasm. The private's face darkened. "I ought to, General," he growled; "I've been with you during the whole campaign."

Bragg continued to harbor doubts about the battle's outcome the next morning. Defeat was such a habit with him that he found it hard to accept that his army had prevailed. Even after scouts reported that the enemy was in full flight, he remained skeptical. But when he rode across the field and saw the windrows of bodies stiffening in the September sun, the last trace of aggressiveness left him. The casualties were mind-boggling: 34,624 men had been killed, wounded, or captured in two days of fighting at Chickamauga—16,170 of them Federal, 18,454 Confederate. It would be several weeks before these exact figures were known, but the enormous dimensions of the slaughter were obvious to anyone who had eyes. As he made his way to Longstreet's command post, Bragg took in the grisly scene, noting not only the human toll but the loss in animals as well. It was enough to convince him that his army had been crippled. When Longstreet urged him to pursue the demoralized Union forces, he refused. "How can I?" he said. "Here is two-fifths of my army left on the field, and my artillery is without horses."

Another officer who disagreed with Bragg's decision was Nathan Bedford Forrest. Early that morning he had taken 400 troopers and ridden up the LaFayette Road to probe the Federal defenses at Rossville. Encountering a picket line a mile south of town, he ordered his men to charge. The Yankees fired a few shots, then ran for their lives. One of the bullets hit

Forrest's horse in the neck, severing the main artery; the general thrust a finger into the wound and galloped onward. When the charge ended and the finger was withdrawn, the stricken beast collapsed and bled to death. Forrest paid no heed; he was shinnying up a tall tree that afforded an excellent view to the north and west. What he saw thrilled him. He hastily scrawled a dispatch to his immediate superior, Polk: "Genl: We are [with]in a mile of Rossville. . . . Can see Chattanooga and everything around. The enemy's trains are leaving. . . . I think they are evacuating as hard as they can go. . . . [W]e ought to press forward as rapidly as possible."

When no reply came, he sent a second message directly to Bragg. A single brigade could capture Chattanooga if it moved quickly, he wrote. Still there was no response. Finally Forrest rode back to the battlefield to talk to Bragg in person. The army commander insisted that an advance was impossible, citing lack of supplies. "We can get all the supplies our army needs in Chattanooga!" Forrest pleaded, but Bragg's mind was made up.

Disgusted, the cavalryman stomped out of army headquarters. "What does he fight battles for?" he shouted, incensed that an extraordinary opportunity, purchased with the blood of more than 18,000 Confederate soldiers, was being squandered. There was nothing he or anyone else in the Army of Tennessee could do about it, however. By daybreak on September 22, Rosecrans had all his forces back in Chattanooga. The rebels continued to rest near the Chickamauga battlefield, and it was not until September 23 that Bragg finally sent them north to besiege the city.

FIFTEEN

STARVATION CAMP

As swiftly as it had arisen, the panic gripping the Army of the Cumberland subsided. The mob of stragglers streaming into Chattanooga stopped and sorted itself out. The chain of command was reestablished, and military discipline, which had dissolved completely during the retreat from Chickamauga, was restored. Officers and men rejoined their regiments, regiments re-formed into brigades, brigades coalesced into divisions, and the reconstituted divisions were deployed in a defensive line guarding the southern and eastern approaches to the town. The soldiers burrowed into the alluvial soil of the Chattanooga Valley with picks and shovels, and when they were snug behind sturdy fortifications, they realized that their situation was nowhere near as desperate as they had first thought. True, they had been driven from the battlefield, but before they fled, they had inflicted terrible punishment on the enemy, and it stood to reason that the Confederates were as debilitated in victory as the Federals were in defeat. There was enough food and ammunition on hand to hold out for several weeks, and reinforcements were reported to be on the way. Now that they had regained their composure, the Union troops could see that there was ample reason to feel hopeful, and morale rose accordingly.

Almost alone, William Rosecrans failed to recover from the Chickamauga defeat. The humiliation of his flight from the battlefield had plunged him into a deep depression. Subordinates found him anxious and irresolute, agonizing over decisions he would have made easily in the past. Captain Alfred L. Hough witnessed a particularly troubling scene: Rosecrans kneeling in his office, tears rolling down his cheeks, pleading with Father Treacy for spiritual solace. Such overt displays of anguish were rare, but it was obvious to all during the last week of September that the army commander was desolate and leaning heavily on the crutch of religion.

Rosecrans derived great comfort from his faith, but its effect on his generalship was decidedly negative. Passivity is an undesirable characteristic in a military leader, and that was precisely the quality the post-Chickamauga crisis called forth in him. "Our fate is in the hands of God, in whom I hope," he informed Washington on September 22. Then he made a dreadful decision based on this submissive line of thinking. Following the retreat from Chickamauga, a brigade of Federals had dug in on the northernmost promontory of Lookout Mountain, an eighteen-hundred-foot-high eminence commanding the rail and wagon routes running into Chattanooga from the west. As long as they held this point, the Army of the Cumberland's communications with the rest of Tennessee would be secure. Rosecrans panicked when the rebels approached the city on September 24, however. He ordered Lookout Mountain abandoned. His staff officers objected strenuously, asserting that control of the summit was vital to the defense of Chattanooga, but Rosecrans rejected their counsel and the brigade was withdrawn. Bragg promptly took advantage, posting troops and artillery not only atop Lookout Mountain but on Missionary Ridge as well. As a result, the Army of the Cumberland found itself penned in and facing serious logistical problems.

Union soldiers in besieged Chattanooga. (Courtesy Massachusetts Commandery Military Order of the Loyal Legion and U.S. Army Military History Institute)

The bulk of the Federals' supplies had been arriving by rail from depots at Nashville and Murfreesboro. The trains had run southeast to Stevenson, Alabama, then northeast along the Tennessee River to Bridgeport and Chattanooga, passing beneath the brow of Lookout Mountain. Bragg's high-sited batteries, and the infantry he had patrolling in the valleys below, rendered this stretch of track unusable. An alternate route had to be pressed into service. From Bridgeport a narrow wagon road wound its way up the Sequatchie Valley to the town of Anderson's Crossroads, then zigzagged south over rugged Walden's Ridge before descending to the north bank of the Tennessee across from Chattanooga. Depending on the weather, it took anywhere from eight to twenty days for loaded wagons to complete this sixty-mile journey, and the toll on draft animals as they dragged heavily laden vehicles through boulder fields, gullies, and quagmires was enormous.

Recognizing the vulnerability of this makeshift supply line, Bragg ordered his cavalry to attack it. Joseph Wheeler and 5,000 troopers splashed across the Tennessee River on the morning of October 1, then galloped northeast to the town of Jasper. There the raiding party split up. One division headed for McMinnville, while Wheeler led the other into the Sequatchie Valley. At Anderson's Crossroads on October 2, Wheeler's command intercepted a Yankee caravan that was about to ascend Walden's Ridge. Four hundred vehicles were seized, their cargoes burned, and their mule teams sabered or shot. Much to the raiders' delight, the haul included dozens of sutlers' wagons; a river of wine and whiskey was soon being quaffed. The revelry ended abruptly when a division of Union cavalry arrived on the scene. There was a clash, and Wheeler's besotted horsemen suffered close to 300 casualties before they were able to disengage and ride north to rejoin their comrades.

The combined force destroyed the Union supply dump at McMinnville on the morning of October 3, but was unable to push on to Murfreesboro because a large contingent of Yankees was blocking the way. With enemy forces converging on his raiding party from three directions, Wheeler decided to turn back. He sacked Shelbyville on October 6, then raced south toward the Tennessee River, hounded by Union cavalry. A running fight ensued, and by October 9, the day the raiders returned to Alabama, they had lost upward of 700 killed or wounded.

Wheeler's command had destroyed an enormous quantity of Federal supplies during its nine-day foray. Even better from the Confederate perspective were the torrential rains that fell throughout the first week of October, wreaking havoc on the mountain road that the Union wagon trains were using. Washouts, sinkholes, and rock slides caused massive traffic jams, and there were days when the entire operation ground to a standstill.

On October 2 Rosecrans ordered his army to cut its food consumption in half. Hunger pangs intensified, and spirits plummeted. "This is a starvation camp," wrote Sergeant Isaac Doan. By mid-October famished enlisted men were taunting their officers with cries of "Crackers! Crackers!" William Shanks reported that whenever a supply wagon rolled into town, a pack of soldiers would follow close behind, fighting over the bits of bread, rice, and corn that fell from the boxes and sacks.

Close attention to logistical matters had always been a hallmark of Rosecrans's leadership, but now he seemed indifferent to the worsening supply situation. He "dawdles with trifles in a manner which scarcely can be imagined," wrote Charles Dana. He "cannot perceive the catastrophe that is upon us, nor fix his mind upon the means of preventing it. I [have] never seen anything so lamentable and hopeless." Worried that Chattanooga would have to be abandoned, the War Department urged immediate action. Old Rosy continued to languish, however. He had no plan for lifting the siege, preferring to wait for an act of divine intervention. "We must put our trust in God, who never fails those who truly trust," he announced. He spent the bulk of his time either talking theology with Father Treacy or working on a lengthy report aimed at shifting blame for the Chickamauga defeat to shoulders other than his own.

The Union soldiers trapped in Chattanooga felt they were in a terrible fix, and if anyone had suggested to them that their besiegers were equally bad off, they would have responded with disbelief and indignation. But the fact was the rebels were also wet, cold, and hungry, and the rumblings of discontent rising from the mountains overlooking the town were virtually identical to those emanating from the trenches below. "I cannot remember of more privations and hardships than we went through at Missionary Ridge," wrote Private Sam Watkins. "The soldiers were starved and almost naked, and were covered all over with lice and camp itch and filth and dirt. The men looked sick, hollow-eyed, and heart-broken, living principally upon parched corn, which had been picked out of the mud and dirt under the feet of officers' horses."

While his unhappy troops huddled on the heights around Chattanooga, praying that the Yankees would succumb to exposure and lack of food before they did, Bragg was busy purging his staff of disloyal and incompetent generals. On September 28, he relieved Polk and banished him to Atlanta. Hindman was also sacked. D. H. Hill escaped dismissal for the time being, but he was censured for his insubordinate attitude, clear indication that his head was on the chopping block too.

Bragg's dissatisfaction with his generals was matched by their disapproval of him. "Our chief has done but one thing that he ought to have done," Longstreet complained to Secretary of War Seddon on September 26. "That was to order the attack upon the 20th. All other things that he has done he ought not to have done." Polk likewise lashed out at his superior, branding him a failure for not finishing off the Union army and declaring it imperative that he be replaced at once.

The command crisis worsened during the first week of October. Bragg's disgruntled subordinates drafted a petition urging his removal on the grounds that he was physically and mentally unfit for field service. Twelve generals, including Longstreet and Hill, signed this document. Meanwhile, in Atlanta, Polk was loudly proclaiming his innocence and demanding that a court of inquiry be convened to investigate Bragg's questionable actions.

As if he did not have enough enemies already, Bragg made another in early October. He named Wheeler commander of the army's cavalry corps, a move that infuriated Nathan Bedford Forrest. Accompanied by his staff surgeon, Dr. J. B. Cowan, Forrest burst into Bragg's tent and unleashed a blistering tirade, which he punctuated by repeatedly jabbing his index finger into the army commander's face. "You have played the part of a damned scoundrel, and are a coward, and if you were any part of man I would slap your jaws and force you to resent it," he raged. "You have threatened to arrest me for not obeying your orders promptly. I dare you to do it, and I say to you that if you ever again try to interfere with me or cross my path it will be at the peril of your life."

Cowan was appalled. "Now you are in for it!" he exclaimed as he and Forrest left Bragg's tent, but Forrest disagreed. "No," he muttered, "he'll never say a word about it, and mark my word, he'll take no action in the matter. I will ask to be transferred to a different field, and he will not oppose it."

This prediction proved accurate. Bragg made no attempt to punish Forrest, and he approved his request for a transfer when it was submitted a short time later. "The man is ignorant and does not know anything of cooperation," Bragg sniffed. He was shaken by the episode, however. It, along with Polk's noisy attacks and the petition gotten up by his discontented generals, made him realize that he was losing control of the army. In the past Jefferson Davis had always backed him in his disputes with subordinates, and he hoped that he

General Nathan Bedford Forrest, C.S.A. (Courtesy U.S. Army Military History Institute)

would do so again. On October 5 he sent a message to the president asking him to come to Georgia.

Davis, who had been monitoring the strife in the Army of Tennessee's
high command with growing alarm, had already decided to pay a visit to
Bragg's headquarters. Accompanied by his private secretary, two military
aides, and John Pemberton, he left Richmond on the morning of October 6 and reached Atlanta two days later. There he met briefly with Polk.
He pleaded with the general to return to his corps and let bygones be bygones, but Polk refused: he wanted a court of inquiry or a transfer to another department. Davis reluctantly agreed to the latter, then traveled on to
Marietta, where Bragg was waiting for him.

The two men talked at length on October 9. The president assured
Bragg that he had come not to ask for his resignation but rather to heal the
rift between him and his subordinates. Toward that end he called the army's
senior generals to a parley on the evening of the tenth. The meeting was
polite until Davis asked the assembled officers if they had any suggestions
to make. Longstreet promptly launched into an anti-Bragg diatribe, declaring him incompetent to manage an army. The other generals concurred:
Bragg had lost the confidence of officers and men and should be relieved
at once.

The president was startled by this blunt advice, but he was not swayed
by it. He had made up his mind to retain Bragg even before he left Richmond. His sense of loyalty would not permit him to fire an old friend, and
besides, there was no one better available to take his place. Lee had declined
the post, Beauregard and Johnston he could not abide, and Longstreet was
out of the running because to promote him would give the appearance of
rewarding insubordination. Despite all the evidence to the contrary, Davis
thought the feuding generals could be cajoled into working together. He
spent the remainder of his visit trying to do just that.

Bragg was not in a conciliatory mood, however. He would not tolerate
disobedience or disrespect from any officer, he told Davis, and he moved at
once to crush his detractors. Hill was dismissed and his corps turned over
to John Breckinridge. Buckner was demoted from corps commander to division commander. Polk was replaced by William J. Hardee, and Longstreet
was stripped of several divisions. The president acquiesced in this punitive
reorganization and asked only one thing in return: that a job be found for
Pemberton. Bragg was willing, but Pemberton proved so unpopular with
the rank and file that the idea of giving him a division had to be dropped
for fear it would spark a mutiny.

Davis wound up his visit by touring the siege lines and issuing a proclamation, which was read aloud to the troops at a parade on October 17. He
praised the men for all they had done and urged them to rally behind their

commander. "He who sows the seeds of discontent and distrust prepares for the harvest of slaughter and defeat," he declared, speaking with more prescience than he knew.

News of the Chickamauga defeat dismayed Abraham Lincoln. "Well, Rosecrans has been whipped, as I feared," he sighed after reading the battle dispatches on the evening of September 20.

His spirits soon revived. The Army of the Cumberland still held Chattanooga, and as long as it did so, the Confederacy would be denied the use of one of its most important rail hubs. All Rosecrans had to do was maintain his position, observed the president, and "the rebellion can only eke out a short and feeble existence, as an animal sometimes may with a thorn in its vitals."

To make sure the thorn stayed firmly embedded, Lincoln undertook to rush reinforcements to Chattanooga. Four divisions under Sherman were ordered east from Memphis. They had 250 miles to march, however, so it would be several weeks before they arrived. Closer at hand was Burnside's Army of the Ohio, now based in Knoxville. The president directed it to go to Rosecrans's aid, but its commander objected: he was about to attack the rebel-held town of Jonesboro in Tennessee's far northeastern corner. "Damn Jonesboro!" Lincoln swore, and reiterated his order. Burnside continued to demur, and the exasperated president finally gave up and told him to stay where he was. Rosecrans would have to be reinforced from some other quarter.

It was Stanton who ultimately solved the problem. At an emergency cabinet meeting on the night of September 23, he proposed that a sizable portion of the Army of the Potomac be sent to Tennessee by rail. Lincoln was skeptical; he doubted that a large body of troops could be delivered to Chattanooga in a week or less as Stanton claimed. Still, he knew that the attempt had to be made. It was agreed that two corps, Slocum's and Howard's, would be detached from the Army of the Potomac, placed under the command of Fighting Joe Hooker, and transferred to the western theater as rapidly as possible.

Stanton summoned railroad company executives to the War Department and made the necessary arrangements. On the afternoon of September 25 the first load of troops left Culpeper, Virginia, passed through Washington, and headed for Bridgeport by way of Wheeling, Indianapolis, Louisville, and Nashville. At 10:30 P.M. on September 30, the lead train reached its destination. Dozens of others followed in rapid succession. By October 2 the transfer was complete: 23,000 men had been delivered to the depot thirty miles west of Chattanooga, along with 3,000 horses and mules, ten batteries of field artillery, and a hundred carloads of ammunition and supplies.

It was an outstanding logistical feat, but it failed to yield decisive results. The relief force was too small to dislodge Bragg's army by itself. Nor did it make sense for it to march into Chattanooga when there were not enough rations to feed the men already there. All that Hooker could do was guard the train tracks and river crossings around Bridgeport and wait for Rosecrans to figure out a way to break the enemy's stranglehold.

Old Rosy remained in a daze, however, and in Washington confidence in his leadership evaporated. The general was acting "confused and stunned, like a duck hit on the head," the president told John Hay, his derogatory figure of speech indicating that Rosecrans's days were numbered. In fact by mid-October the question was no longer whether Rosecrans should stay or go, but rather who would take his place. George Thomas was one possibility; Ulysses S. Grant was another. Lincoln decided that the best arrangement would utilize the talents of both men. On October 16 he devised a plan that did exactly that.

Ever since his retreat from Gettysburg, Robert E. Lee had been looking forward to the day when he could once again attack the Army of the Potomac. In early October, when his scouts reported that two of Meade's corps had been sent west to reinforce Rosecrans, he decided the time was ripe. Orders were issued, and on October 9 Ewell's Second Corps and A. P. Hill's Third Corps set out from the Confederate camps around Orange Court House. They marched west up the Rapidan, crossed the river in the vicinity of Liberty Mills, then headed northeast toward Culpeper, their advance screened by a division of Stuart's cavalry. Federal forces had been concentrated around Culpeper for the past several weeks, but when Lee's soldiers entered the town on the afternoon of October 11, the Yankees were gone. Jubilant civilians reported that Meade and his men had pulled out the previous day; they were falling back toward Washington, following the line of the Orange & Alexandria Railroad.

This was exactly what Lee had hoped for. If his troops pursued rapidly, they would catch the Army of the Potomac strung out and vulnerable somewhere between Culpeper and Manassas. Early the next morning Ewell's and Hill's corps resumed the northeastward march on roads paralleling Meade's route of retreat. At Warrenton on the afternoon of the thirteenth they received word from Stuart that the bluecoats were at Catlett's Station, ten miles to the east. A hard push tomorrow, and the Confederates would overtake them.

Hill's troops took the lead on the fourteenth, tramping north and east through the towns of New Baltimore and Greenwich, bound for Bristoe Station, the projected interception point on the Orange & Alexandria line. Excitement mounted as the morning wore on. Knapsacks, blanket rolls, and other pieces of equipment left lying by the roadside showed that the Yankees were fleeing in haste. "We were convinced that Meade was unwilling to face us," remembered a South Carolina captain, "and we therefore anticipated a pleasant affair if we should succeed in catching him." The pace of the march quickened until the men were almost jogging. Word flashed up and down the column that Hill had donned the red hunting shirt he always wore in combat.

As the Third Corps approached Bristoe Station, Hill galloped ahead to a knoll affording a clear view of the surrounding countryside. A Federal corps was crossing Broad Run, a meandering stream some eight hundred yards northeast of Bristoe Station. Half of the corps had already forded the creek and was moving up the railway toward Manassas Junction four miles distant. The other half was still milling around on the southwestern bank.

Salivating at the sight, Hill ordered Heth's division to deploy for an attack. Heth rushed to obey, but as he was about to swoop down upon the unsuspecting Federals, he caught sight of another large body of blue troops massing behind the Orange & Alexandria embankment to his right front. He asked Hill whether he should investigate this menacing formation before making the assault. No, came the reply, attack at once before the enemy gets away. Heth did so and stumbled straight into one of the deadliest ambushes of the war.

The troops behind the railroad embankment belonged to the Union Second Corps. Approaching Broad Run from the south at the same time the Confederates were coming in from the west, they had spotted Heth's division preparing to advance. They immediately occupied a position from which they could enfilade the rebels as they approached the stream. "It was as fine a trap as could have been devised by a month's engineering," a student of the battle later averred, and indeed, all the Federals had to do was lay their musket barrels diagonally across the train tracks, take aim, and squeeze the trigger as the gray ranks drew abreast of them. The volley shredded Heth's exposed formation. The survivors recoiled in shock, then wheeled right and lunged toward the embankment in a desperate bid to drive the Union soldiers from cover. The attempt failed, and the slaughter continued. In a matter of minutes, upwards of 1,400 Confederates were killed or wounded, and another 450 captured.

By early afternoon the lopsided contest was over. The Federals crossed Broad Run unmolested, while Hill's mangled corps pulled back toward Greenwich. "A worse managed affair than this . . . did not take place during the war," a rebel officer said of the Bristoe Station fiasco. Even Hill admitted that he had blundered. "I made the attack too hastily," he conceded in his after-action report.

Lee refrained from criticizing his subordinate for fear of making a bad situation worse. "Well, well, General," he said to Hill after touring the battlefield on the morning of the fifteenth, "bury these poor men and let us say no more about it." He was anxious to move on and engage Meade at Manassas. Meade refused to stop and fight, however. He kept retreating until he reached Centreville, where he placed his army behind a long line of earthworks.

After studying the situation, Lee concluded that an assault was out of the question: the Centreville fortifications were too strong. He could draw Meade into the open by crossing into Maryland, but he did not think his troops were up to another invasion of the North. Although it pained him to admit it, the Army of Northern Virginia was a pale shadow of the crack fighting force he had led into Pennsylvania four months earlier. It was smaller, less robust, and even more poorly clothed and shod than it had been back in June.

Unable to advance and lacking the logistical wherewithal to stay where he was, Lee's only choice was to retreat. On October 17 the Confederate army headed south. By the end of the month it was below the Rappahannock near Brandy Station. Although nobody realized it at the time (except perhaps Lee), October 1863 marked a turning point in the history of the Army of Northern Virginia. Henceforward it would fight strictly on the defensive; never again would it carry the war to the enemy.

On October 10, the day that Lee was advancing toward Culpeper and Davis was meeting with Bragg outside Chattanooga, Ulysses S. Grant received a mysterious message from Henry Halleck. It ordered him to travel to Cairo, Illinois, then report by telegraph to the War Department for further instructions. Although Halleck gave no explanation for the summons, Grant surmised that it was related to Rosecrans's troubles in Tennessee. He left his headquarters at once, impatient to learn what his new assignment would be.

Grant's eagerness to be off was understandable in light of the frustration he had endured since the fall of Vicksburg three months earlier. A few days after accepting Pemberton's surrender, he had proposed to Washington that he and Nathaniel Banks join forces to capture Mobile, then move northeast through Selma, Montgomery, and Talladega, Alabama, to menace

Bragg's rear in Tennessee. Halleck had rejected the plan and ordered Grant to conduct mopping-up operations in Mississippi and western Louisiana. Then, at the beginning of August, the conqueror of Vicksburg suffered the further indignity of having a large portion of his army taken away from him and given to Banks so that the latter could invade Texas.

The Texas expedition was to be "of a diplomatic rather than of a military character," Halleck cryptically announced, "and resulted from some European complications." What he was referring to was the recent occupation of Mexico City by a French army. Emperor Napoleon III was taking advantage of the war between North and South to violate the Monroe Doctrine and establish a French colony in the Americas. His troops had overthrown Mexico's elected leader, Benito Juárez, and were preparing to install Napoleon's puppet, the Austrian archduke Ferdinand Maximilian, in his place. Washington had decided it was imperative to get Federal forces into position along the Rio Grande to deter further French adventurism and to signal Napoleon that the United States intended to deal with him once the rebellion was over.

Grant was unaware of the geopolitical ramifications of Banks's assignment. All he knew was that a large number of his troops had been placed under someone else's command. With nothing to do but supervise the building of new defensive works around Vicksburg, he grew bored. Boredom begat drinking, and drinking begat trouble. Matters came to a head during a trip to New Orleans in early September. After attending a dinner at which wine flowed freely, Grant went for a ride on a borrowed horse. The animal was spirited, Grant was tipsy, and the inevitable happened: The horse ran out of control, then reared and fell, pinning Grant to the ground and knocking him unconscious. When he came to, he found himself in a room at the St. Charles Hotel being worked on by a team of worried doctors. The left side of his body between the knee and the armpit was grotesquely swollen; the pain was so severe, he found it difficult to breathe.

Banks, who had been Grant's host at the fateful dinner, was deeply distressed. "I am frightened when I think that he is a drunkard," he wrote his wife. "His accident was caused by this, which was too manifest to all who saw him." He did not let his concern about Grant's condition interfere with the opening of the Texas campaign, however. On September 4 he sent 4,000 troops to assault Sabine Pass on the Louisiana-Texas border. Capture of the port was to be the prelude to an overland march on Beaumont, Houston, and Galveston, followed by a move south to the Rio Grande.

The ships carrying the Union infantry arrived on schedule, but the operation fizzled when the naval flotilla assigned to neutralize a Confederate fort at the mouth of the pass failed to execute its mission. Two of the four gunboats involved were disabled by rebel shell fire, and the expedition commander, deciding that discretion was the better part of valor, brought the attack force back to New Orleans without attempting a landing. Upset by the unraveling of his plan, Banks did what any self-respecting army officer would do: he blamed the navy. Then he went back to the drawing board to come up with a new scheme for securing a lodgment on the Texas coast.

Grant, meanwhile, had recovered sufficiently to return to Vicksburg, where he continued to mend under the watchful eye of his wife. By September 25 he was able to get out of bed and move around with the aid of crutches. Although he was still very weak and his left hip and thigh were a mass of purplish-blue bruises, he informed the War Department that he was fit for duty. By then it was clear that something big was afoot in Tennessee. Sherman and his four divisions were heading east to reinforce Rosecrans, and rumors were flying that a change of leadership was imminent. Grant's hopes soared, and when he got Halleck's dispatch calling him to Cairo, he was off like a shot.

Reaching the Illinois town on October 16, he contacted the War Department as instructed and received another mysterious telegram, this one directing him to travel to the Galt House hotel in Louisville, where an officer would be waiting with further orders. Accompanied by his staff, Grant promptly boarded an eastbound train. It rolled into Indianapolis early on the morning of the eighteenth, arriving just a few minutes ahead of a special train from Washington. The War Department agent who was responsible for arranging the Louisville rendezvous was on this train. Much to Grant's surprise, it turned out to be Edwin Stanton, a man he had corresponded with frequently but had never met in person.

The secretary of war entered Grant's car, handed him two sets of orders dated October 16, and told him that he was to choose between them. Both sets contained the same opening paragraph: "By direction of the President of the United States, the Departments of the Ohio, of the Cumberland, and of the Tennessee, will constitute the Military Division of the Mississippi. Major General U. S. Grant, United States Army, is placed in command of the Military Division of the Mississippi, with his headquarters in the field." The difference was that the first set left Rosecrans in charge of the Army of the Cumberland, while the second put George Thomas in his place. Grant was not fond of Thomas, but he liked Rosecrans even less. He unhesitatingly chose the second set of orders. Stanton nodded, and that was that. Rosecrans was out and Thomas was in. Sherman would succeed Grant as commander of the Army of the Tennessee. Burnside would continue as head of the Army of the Ohio.

The secretary and the general spent most of October 19 talking strategy. That evening Grant and his wife went out on the town while Stanton, exhausted by the long journey from Washington, retired to his bedchamber at the Galt House. He had been asleep only a few minutes when an aide shook him awake. An alarming dispatch had just come in from Chattanooga: Rosecrans was preparing to evacuate the city. Highly agitated, Stanton sent bellhops and staff officers all over the city, searching for Grant. No one could find him. Finally, at about eleven, the general and Julia returned to the hotel. Limping upstairs on a cane, Grant found Stanton fluttering about in his nightclothes, waving the telegram overhead. Something had to be done to prevent the loss of Chattanooga, he babbled. Grant agreed and immediately dashed off two dispatches of his own, one telling Rosecrans that he was relieved of command, the other advising Thomas that he was now in charge of the Army of the Cumberland. "Hold Chattanooga at all hazards," he wrote. "I will be there as soon as possible."

While the uncertain military situation was Abraham Lincoln's primary concern during the first half of October, he also had to pay close attention to the upcoming elections. Most observers expected Republican candidates to do well in light of the Union victories at Gettysburg and Vicksburg. The president remained apprehensive, however, fearful that if the Peace Democrats won any important contests, the South would seize on the results as a sign it could still gain independence at the negotiating table. The state he was watching most closely was Ohio, where Clement Vallandigham was running for the governorship. Privately, Lincoln was incredulous that "one genuine American would or could be induced to vote for such a man." But he knew that Vallandigham's election could not be ruled out.

The Ohio gubernatorial campaign was unusual in that Vallandigham never set foot in the state. He stayed in exile in Windsor, Ontario, while a team of surrogates traveled the hustings on his behalf. The Republicans ran an unconventional race too. To attract bipartisan support they chose a prowar Democrat, John Brough, as their nominee. They campaigned under the banner of the National Union Party—tacit admission that the word *Republican,* to which the adjective *Black* or *Radical* was usually affixed, had bad connotations in many sections of the Buckeye State.

The military triumphs of the summer had robbed the Peace Democrats of their main issue. They could no longer argue that the war was a complete failure. Curtailment of civil liberties and antipathy toward abolitionism were potent topics on which to run, however, and Vallandigham's backers hammered away at them. The president was excoriated as a bloody tyrant who was conspiring with Brough to let Ohio be overrun by freed slaves. To make sure voters understood the consequences of this heinous policy, young women dressed in white and carrying placards reading, FATHERS, SAVE US FROM NEGRO EQUALITY, appeared at every Democratic gathering.

The Republican strategy for winning the election was to brand Vallandigham a traitor. Brough spearheaded the attack, accusing his opponent of treason, hinting that he had instigated the New York City riot, and suggesting that if he became governor, he would try to take Ohio out of the Union. Republican editors, clergymen, and elected officials followed Brough's lead, denouncing the Democratic candidate as a Confederate sympathizer who belonged in jail, not the governor's mansion.

Election day was October 13. The weather was warm and dry, and Ohioans flocked to the polls in record numbers. The suspense was keen; both parties were predicting victory. In Washington Lincoln spent the day at the War Department waiting for the results to come in. He felt more anxious about this election than he had about the 1860 presidential contest, he told Gideon Welles. Late that evening word came that Brough had trounced Vallandigham by more than 100,000 votes. Lincoln was jubilant. "Glory to God in the highest," he wired the victorious candidate; "Ohio has saved the Nation."

Republicans also scored solid gains in Iowa, Illinois, Minnesota, Wisconsin, Pennsylvania, New York, and Maryland. The overall victory was a decisive repudiation of the peace movement, a ringing endorsement of the administration's war policy, and Lincoln felt liberated by it. The "fire in the rear" he had been fretting about for months had been extinguished. The danger of Democratic governors interfering with the draft or pulling their state's regiments out of the army had been dispelled. With Vallandigham and others of his ilk consigned to the political wilderness, he could now get on with the business of defeating the rebels. With that objective in mind, he issued a proclamation on October 17 calling for 300,000 more troops "to reinforce our victorious armies in the field and bring our needful military operations to a prosperous end."

Hopeful that his efforts to foster harmony in the Army of Tennessee would soon bear fruit, Jefferson Davis bade Braxton Bragg adieu on October 17 and headed to Selma, Alabama, to tour the arsenal there. Then he traveled west through Demopolis to Meridian, where he huddled with Joe Johnston and William Hardee. At the conclusion of the conference, he made a personnel change that he had been contemplating for several weeks: Hardee was sent back to Georgia to command a corps under Bragg, while Polk was brought out to Mississippi to serve under Johnston. With that flip-flop accomplished, Davis rode to the nearby town of Lauderdale to visit his older brother, Joseph, who had taken up residence there after being driven from his Vicksburg-area plantation by marauding Federals. The refugee existence Joseph and his wife were living dismayed the Confederate president. He feared it was a glimpse of what lay in store for all the members of the South's planter class if the war should be lost, and he left his brother's ramshackle house more determined than ever to defeat the foe that had inflicted this hardship on his family.

At Mobile on October 24, Davis inspected coastal defenses and gave a speech calling on the locals to do everything in their power to resist the Yankees. Two days later he was in Montgomery, where he met with Polk and Forrest. Then it was back to Atlanta for a brief stopover, followed by a 260-mile train trip to Savannah. He arrived in that city on Halloween and was feted with a torchlight procession and a gala party at the Masonic Hall. A young woman who passed through the receiving line was impressed with his appearance. "He has a good, mild, pleasant face," she wrote, "and, altogether, looks like a president of our struggling country *should* look—careworn and thoughtful, and firm, and quiet."

Davis would soon look even more careworn, for from Savannah his tour took him to Charleston, where two of his harshest critics, General P.G.T.

Shell damage in Charleston. (Courtesy U.S. Army Military History Institute)

Beauregard and newspaper editor Robert Barnwell Rhett, held sway. The pair were on hand to welcome him when his train pulled into the depot on November 2. After an awkward exchange of greetings, the president and the general climbed into an open carriage to drive to city hall.

Their route led past buildings damaged by Yankee shelling. Davis noted with pride that Confederate and South Carolina state flags still flew from their smoke-blackened facades. The cheers of the people lining the streets further lifted his spirits, and he was surprised and touched when he saw garlands of laurel festooning city hall and an immense banner bidding him welcome hanging from the courthouse portico.

A speech was called for, and the president did not disappoint, though in view of the offense his remarks gave Beauregard, it probably would have been better if he had kept his mouth shut. He congratulated the townspeople for their courage under fire and praised Fort Sumter's commander, Major Stephen Elliott, for the skill he had displayed in repelling the enemy's small-boat assault in September. But he said not a word about the pivotal role Beauregard had played in organizing and directing the city's defense. In fact, he failed to mention Beauregard by name at all, a snub that infuriated the hypersensitive Creole. "He has done more than if he had thrust a fratricidal dagger into my heart!" Beauregard raged afterward. "He has killed my enthusiasm for our holy cause!" Asked to attend a dinner in Davis's honor that evening, he declined, stating that henceforward he would observe only official relations with the president and would not participate "in any act of politeness which might make him suppose otherwise."

Davis did not miss Beauregard's company, either at the dinner party that night or at subsequent social functions held at the home of former governor William Aiken, whose guest he was for the next week. He thoroughly enjoyed his stay—"Mr. Aiken's perfect old-Carolina style of living delighted him," observed diarist Mary Chesnut; "those grey-haired darkies and their automatic noiseless perfection of training"—and he was pleased with what he saw and heard of Charleston's determination to resist the invaders.

The latest manifestation of this defiant spirit was the sortie of *David,* a cigar-shaped torpedo boat powered by a small steam engine and armed with an explosive charge attached to a ten-foot spar protruding from the bow. On the night of October 5, the low-slung craft had ventured out of the harbor in search of a Yankee goliath. Passing through a tiny gap in the antiship net strung between Fort Sumter and Sullivan's Island, it headed toward the largest enemy vessel in sight, the 3,500-ton *New Ironsides.* Lookouts aboard the steam frigate did not spot the Confederate boat until it was a few yards away. Voices cried out in warning and muskets blazed along the big ship's rail, but it was too late: *David's* submerged spar struck the bow of *New Ironsides* six feet below the waterline, and the copper-encased black-powder torpedo detonated with a muffled roar. A column of water shot high into the air, flooding *David's* cuddy and dousing the fire under her boiler. As she drifted helplessly, marksmen aboard *New Ironsides* riddled her superstructure, forcing the four crewmen to leap over the side. Two of them were later fished out by the Federals. The other two returned to *David* once the shooting stopped, relighted the boiler, and slipped back into the harbor before dawn.

Damage to *New Ironsides* was limited to a broken inner bulkhead and a leak in the hull, both of which were easily repaired. Not so easily mended was the morale of the bluejackets. Their sense of security, built up over six months of uneventful duty, had been shattered by *David's* surprise attack. Henceforward they would always be on edge, quick to sound the alarm and fire at any unidentified floating object that approached their ship. Admiral Dahlgren shared his sailors' unease. "Among the many inventions with which I have been familiar, I have seen none which have acted so perfectly at first trial," he informed Secretary Welles. "The secrecy, rapidity of movement, control of direction, and precise explosion indicated, I think, the introduction of the torpedo element as a means of certain warfare. It can be ignored no longer. If sixty pounds of powder, why not six hundred pounds?"

Jefferson Davis felt the same way, and he left Charleston in an upbeat mood, hopeful that pluck and ingenuity would be enough to offset the material superiority of the North. The acclaim he received when he returned to Richmond on the evening of November 7 brightened his disposition even more. John B. Jones noted in his diary that "the press, a portion rather, praises the president for his carefulness in making a tour of the armies and forts south of us; but as he retained Bragg in command, how soon the tune would change if Bragg should meet with disaster!"

Jones's words were prophetic. Disaster was already heading Bragg's way in the unprepossessing form of Ulysses S. Grant. The commander of the newly created Division of the Mississippi left Louisville by rail on the morning of October 20, stayed overnight in Nashville, then continued on the following day to Stevenson, Alabama. As his train crept through Murfreesboro, curious soldiers trotted alongside his car, craning their necks to get a look at him. "He was seated entirely alone," one of them later wrote. "He had on an old blue overcoat, and wore a common white wool hat drawn down over his eyes, and looked so much like a private soldier, that but for the resemblance to the photographs that can be seen on every corner of this town, it would have been impossible to have recognized him. . . . He was either tired with riding all night, or had something on his mind, for he appeared almost sad as he looked vacantly without seeming to see anything that he was passing."

At Stevenson, Grant met briefly with Rosecrans, who was on his way home to Cincinnati. Their conversation was as cordial as the circumstances would allow. Rosecrans described the situation in Chattanooga and talked about how it could be improved. Grant allowed that his suggestions were excellent. "My only wonder was that he had not carried them out," he afterward remarked. Later that night Grant traveled to Bridgeport, where he bunked with Oliver O. Howard in the latter's tent. Early the next morning the corps commander noticed Grant sitting on the edge of his cot, gazing longingly at a whiskey flask hanging from a tent pole. "I never drink," Howard stammered in embarrassment, explaining that the flask belonged to a staff officer. "Neither do I," deadpanned Grant, then rose from the cot and limped out to mount his horse for the journey to Chattanooga.

Rain was falling in torrents as Grant and his escort rode up the Sequatchie Valley and over Walden's Ridge. John Rawlins wrote that it was the worst road he had ever been on, adding that if he had not witnessed it with his own eyes, he would never have believed that vehicles could successfully negotiate it. What struck Grant most forcefully was the sight of hundreds of dead horses and mules piled by the wayside. At one point his own mount came perilously close to having a fatal accident; it slipped and fell on a mud-slicked rock, sending Grant tumbling head over heels.

Bedraggled and saddle-sore, the traveling party finally got to Chattanooga at nightfall on October 23. Grant went straight to Thomas's headquarters for a briefing. The news was not good. The soldiers' daily ration had been reduced to almost nothing, but even so there was less than a week's worth of food on hand. Grant slumped in an armchair by the fireplace, a cigar clenched between his teeth, clouds of steam rising from his rain-soaked clothing. He was "immovable as a rock and as silent as a sphinx," wrote one of the officers present. It was not until Thomas's chief engineer, William F. "Baldy" Smith, began to speak, that he showed any signs of life. Smith had been studying the terrain around Chattanooga and had come up with a plan for opening a new, shorter supply route back to the railhead at Bridgeport. He talked for several minutes, outlining his idea, and when he had finished, Grant straightened up in his chair, pulled the cigar from his mouth, and began asking questions.

The answers impressed everyone present. Smith's scheme was risky but eminently feasible. Just beyond Chattanooga the Tennessee River made a sharp southward turn toward the foot of Lookout Mountain, then swung back to the northwest, enclosing a two-mile-wide tongue of land called Moccasin Point. From the pontoon bridge already in place north of town, a road led west across Moccasin Point to Brown's Ferry. Significantly, this road was out of range of the rebel artillery atop Lookout Mountain. From Brown's Ferry the river flowed northwest for five miles to the base of Walden's Ridge, then looped south around the northern brow of Raccoon Mountain, creating a second peninsula across whose neck ran a road connecting Brown's Ferry to Kelley's Ferry. Kelley's Ferry could be reached either by road or by steamboat from Bridgeport, approximately twenty-five miles to the west. Thus a direct supply line, half as long as the one over Walden's Ridge and nowhere near as treacherous, could be established. The key was wresting control of Brown's Ferry and the road linking it to Kelley's Ferry from the brigade of Confederates that had been detailed to hold it.

Smith's plan for accomplishing this was inspired. Two Union brigades would attack Brown's Ferry. The first would transit the Tennessee via the Chattanooga bridge and march across Moccasin Point to the objective. The second would float downriver in pontoon boats under cover of darkness and land on the Raccoon Mountain side of Brown's Ferry. Once the rebel pickets had been driven off, the combined brigades would build a bridge out of the pontoon boats, then head west to seize control of the Kelley's Ferry Road. Meanwhile, Hooker would bring three of his four divisions across the Tennessee at Bridgeport and march them east along the Nashville & Chattanooga Railroad to Wauhatchie in Lookout Valley. There they would be in position to support the two brigades operating on the Raccoon Mountain peninsula, and to prevent the Confederate forces around Chattanooga from interdicting the wagon and steamboat traffic that would soon be traveling back and forth between Bridgeport and Kelley's Ferry.

Grant set out early the next morning to reconnoiter the area around Brown's Ferry. Everything was as Smith had described it. On the way back to Chattanooga, the engineer showed Grant a makeshift sawmill his men had built the previous week. Fifty pontoon boats had already been built from lumber cut by the mill, and a crew of carpenters was busy making repairs to a small steamboat, *Paint Rock,* which would be used to haul supplies upriver once the ferries had been secured.

Satisfied that Smith had thought of everything, Grant approved the operation. Hooker was ordered to move out on October 26, timing his arrival at Wauhatchie to coincide with the assault on Brown's Ferry. General John B. Turchin's brigade, numbering about 3,500 soldiers, was selected to make the march across Moccasin Point beginning at 3 A.M. on October 27. At the same time 1,600 handpicked men led by William B. Hazen would embark in the fleet of pontoon boats and drift downriver to execute the amphibious part of the attack.

Patchy fog was drifting above the surface of the Tennessee River during the early-morning hours of October 27 when Hazen's detachment arrived at the Chattanooga waterfront to board the oblong, flat-bottomed scows that would carry them down to Brown's Ferry. One by one the boats cast off and were swept downstream by the strong current. Confederate picket fires were burning along the south shore, and from time to time the Union soldiers could hear sentinels talking and singing to stay awake. The armada floated on. About 5 A.M. it came abreast of a series of signal fires lit by Turchin's detachment, which had earlier moved into position on the Moccasin Point side of Brown's Ferry. "Pull in! Pull in!" bellowed Hazen, and the oarsmen rowed for all they were worth toward the west bank.

The bluecoats swarmed ashore and secured the beachhead. Unloaded boats brought Turchin's soldiers across from the opposite bank. Then the engineers set to work building the all-important bridge while the assault force moved inland along the Kelley's Ferry Road, searching for the rebel brigade that occupied the Raccoon Mountain peninsula. It did not take long to find it. Colonel William C. Oates, the Alabamian who had almost captured Little Round Top on July 2, was the commander at Raccoon Mountain. When he learned that the Yankees had landed at Brown's Ferry, he immediately ordered his troops to attack. They did so, pushing Hazen's men back toward the river. But as reinforcements from Turchin's command joined the fight, the tide turned, and the outnumbered Confederates were forced to retreat. When Oates galloped forward to rally his men, his right hip was smashed by a minié ball. "God da—!" he screamed as he went down, cutting off the "damn" in midword because he did not want his dying utterance to be a blasphemous one. He survived, as it turned out, but with his wounding the defense of Raccoon Mountain and the Kelley's Ferry Road collapsed. The Federals were in control of the peninsula by sunup. The Brown's Ferry pontoon bridge was finished by midafternoon, and before darkness fell, additional troops and artillery had arrived from Chattanooga to consolidate the lodgment.

"It was as fine a thing as was ever done," an officer on Grant's staff said of the operation, which had been accomplished at a cost of thirty-eight Union casualties, only six of whom were fatalities. Hazen was even more exultant: "We've knocked the cover off the cracker box!" he shouted to his men as he walked along their lines that evening. Thereafter the new supply route into Chattanooga would be known as the "Cracker Line."

James Longstreet had been in a sullen mood ever since Jefferson Davis's mid-October visit. His bid to supplant Bragg as head of the Army of Tennessee had failed, and now he found himself frozen out of headquarters deliberations, his strategic advice ignored, his requests for supplies and reinforcements rebuffed. He tended to behave insubordinately whenever he was not getting his way; that was exactly what he did on October 27, when Bragg ordered him to retake Brown's Ferry. Asserting that the enemy's seizure of the ferry was a feint designed to draw attention away from a move against the southern end of Lookout Mountain, he refused to do as he was told. Bragg repeated the order later that night. Again Longstreet disregarded the instructions and did nothing. When dawn passed with no sign of an attack on Brown's Ferry, Bragg rode to the top of Lookout Mountain to talk with his recalcitrant corps commander. Longstreet was nowhere to be found. For over an hour staff officers searched high and low for him, but with no success. Finally, around 9 A.M., he was located, eating a leisurely breakfast at a camp several miles from the front line. It took another hour for him to finish and make his way to the spot where Bragg was waiting.

The two generals were exchanging sharp words when a signalman interrupted to announce that a column of Yankees had been spotted marching north along the base of Lookout Mountain. Bragg dismissed the report as nonsense. But when he looked down into the valley, he saw that it was true. Hooker's three divisions had arrived from Bridgeport. One of them, under the command of Brigadier General John W. Geary, was moving into position near Wauhatchie, while the other two continued up the Raccoon Mountain peninsula to link up with Hazen's force. Angry and alarmed in equal measure, Bragg ordered Longstreet to attack Brown's Ferry at once, then stalked off muttering about the Georgian's sloth and stupidity.

Longstreet's subsequent actions indicated that he was more interested in spiting Bragg than assailing the enemy. He continued to stall, and it was not until late afternoon that he got an attack organized—a thrust that was not what Bragg wanted or expected. Instead of advancing toward Brown's Ferry in daylight with his entire corps, he sent a single division to make a night assault on Geary's position near Wauhatchie.

This ill-conceived operation got under way shortly after sunset. Hood's old division, now commanded by Brigadier General Micah Jenkins, hiked down from Lookout Mountain and deployed on the Wauhatchie–Brown's Ferry Road. Two brigades faced north to prevent Hooker's main force from reinforcing Geary, while the other two marched south toward the Union bivouac on the outskirts of Wauhatchie. The night was dark, the route unfamiliar, and it was well past midnight before the attack column found the Federal camp. Roused from sleep by the sound of gunshots, Geary's troops spilled from their tents, formed an L-shaped battle line, and fired into the shadowy mass of Confederates. Jenkins's men advanced, halted, then advanced again. For the next hour the two sides traded volleys at close range, aiming at each other's muzzle flashes.

The din coming from the direction of Wauhatchie alerted Hooker that Geary was under assault. He promptly ordered Carl Schurz's division to double-quick toward the sound of the guns, with the troops of Adolph von Steinwehr following close behind. Schurz's soldiers had covered about half the distance to Wauhatchie when they ran into the two brigades Jenkins had left behind. The Federals charged, and another chaotic night action ensued. The Confederates were dug in on a two-hundred-foot-high hill, and even though they were badly outnumbered, they managed to repel several Yankee onslaughts. Finally, around 3:30 A.M., two of von Steinwehr's regiments swept the rebels aside and opened the way to Wauhatchie. By then Geary no longer needed help; the Confederates who had been attacking his camp had given up and retired across Lookout Creek.

When the sun came up on October 29, the Federals were still in control of the Raccoon Mountain peninsula. Grant told Thomas to get *Paint Rock* down to Bridgeport as quickly as possible. The steamboat made the trip that night, and on the thirtieth it hauled the first load of provisions upriver to Kelley's Ferry. Signal rockets streaked skyward as the heavily laden vessel nosed in to the landing at Kelley's, and the hungry soldiers cheered as if they had won a great victory.

Grant certainly considered it such. "The question of supplies may now be regarded as settled," he wired Washington. "If the rebels give us one week more time I think all danger of losing territory now held by us will have passed away, and preparations may commence for offensive operations."

Although food would remain scarce for several more weeks, the Union troops in Chattanooga knew that it was only a matter of time before full rations were restored. The Confederates outside the city were not as fortunate. The dilapidated railroad running between their position and Atlanta had not been repaired, and their stocks of bacon and hardtack dwindled away to nothing as October turned to November. "I was hungrier day before yesterday than I ever have been in my life," Lewis Poates of the

Sixty-third Tennessee wrote his wife on November 15. "Great God! how earnestly I pray that this war may cease. I am tired of it, tired, tired, tired!"

Zach Jackson, a soldier in the Eighth Georgia, was so famished that he sent word to his wife, who was living on a farm in Snake Creek Gap forty miles to the southeast, to bring him some food before he starved. Twenty-eight-year-old Fannie Jackson left her children with her mother-in-law, loaded a wagon, and set out for Chattanooga. Her two-day trip took her across the Chickamauga battlefield, which was still strewn with human remains. When she arrived at the Eighth Georgia's bivouac, the revulsion she felt at the sight of the moldering corpses was replaced by dismay at how emaciated her husband and his comrades were. "The living were but little better than the dead," she wrote in her diary. Morale was abysmally low. "There is no confidence in the Confederate cause," Fannie observed, noting that the talk around the campfire was of ending the war and going home. Zach was closemouthed in the presence of his messmates, "but when alone with me he said that he hated the Confederacy and that if I and the children could get away we should all go north. He felt condemned when he thought that he was fighting for slavery, when he detested it."

Such sentiments were rife in the Army of Tennessee, and hostility toward the planter class, the officer corps, and the government intensified with each passing day. "There is not a particle of meat in any of the regiments—yet the brigade commanders, aides, etc., have as much bacon as they desire," wrote Sergeant Washington Ives. He was also angry at the politicians who called for greater sacrifice from the men at the front while they lived in comparative luxury in Richmond. "There is really a great deal of romance and affectation yet in the South, which I wish would give way to something like the realities of life," he grumbled. "A person at home has no idea of the suffering and hardships endured by the soldiers. . . . Enough has been endured to end any war."

Just when it seemed that conditions could get no worse, a mid-November cold snap made life even more miserable. "We need blankets," lamented Texan Isaiah Harlan. "I could do well enough if [only] I could get a pair of pants, an overcoat, a blanket, and a few pairs of socks." He resolved to stick it out even though he was freezing. Hundreds of others had had enough, however; they either deserted or surrendered to the Federals.

The Army of Tennessee was disintegrating, but Bragg paid little heed. He was preoccupied with reassigning the command of regiments, brigades, and divisions to reward his supporters and punish his detractors. He also stepped up his criticism of Longstreet in the aftermath of the Wauhatchie affair. The Georgian was guilty of flagrant insubordination, he informed Jefferson Davis, hinting broadly that some kind of disciplinary action should be taken. The president was not about to censure Longstreet. He did, however, suggest that Bragg consider detaching Longstreet's corps and sending it, along with Wheeler's cavalry, to Knoxville to attack Burnside's army. This move made no sense strategically; Chattanooga, not Knoxville, was the key to controlling Tennessee. But it had the advantage of separating two generals who were incapable of working together, and it would put Longstreet in position to rejoin Lee in Virginia once he had vanquished Burnside.

Bragg eagerly embraced the idea. Even though it would cost his command two divisions, getting rid of Longstreet was his top priority. The fact that he would be left with barely 40,000 troops to face a Federal force that would soon number 70,000 did not faze him. The order dispatching Longstreet to Knoxville was issued on November 4.

Abraham Lincoln felt immensely relieved as October came to a close. Meade was moving south again, pushing Lee back toward Richmond. In Charleston harbor, Union gunners were subjecting Fort Sumter to one of the heaviest bombardments of the war. In the Far West, Banks had finally gained a foothold in Texas, putting a division ashore at Brazos Island off the mouth of the Rio Grande. Best of all was the news from Chattanooga. After Rosecrans's agonizing paralysis, Grant's burst of activity was breathtaking. The president was once again struck by the fact that here was a general who got things done, quickly and decisively, without fussing or making unreasonable demands.

Looking ahead, Lincoln could foresee an end to the fighting, and he began to give thought to explaining what that end would mean, to talking about the war's broader significance so as to provide the country "a chart and compass for the days and years ahead." The success of his late-August public letter encouraged him to do this. That message had been hailed as a masterpiece, a "true and noble" document whose eloquent defense of emancipation and black enlistment had done much to change the electorate's attitude toward the Negro. Now, with the conflict entering its final phase, he wanted to address the public again, to make the case that the North was fighting not just to restore the Union, but to save democracy and sanctify the principles of liberty and equality.

Since his inauguration two and a half years ago, Lincoln had made speeches by proxy only, and had traveled away from Washington just four times. He had turned down numerous requests to speak on the grounds that he couldn't spare the time. But on November 2, when he received an invitation to attend the dedication of a new military cemetery at Gettysburg, he accepted. The letter from the event's organizers made it clear that his role in the ceremonies would be limited; he was being asked to make "a few appropriate remarks" at the conclusion of the program—nothing more. That was good enough, however. This was the opportunity he had been seeking, and the setting was perfect. He would speak at Gettysburg.

SIXTEEN

OF NAMELESS GRAVES
ON BATTLE-PLAINS

Like the boom of breakers beating on a distant reef, the sound of Yankee siege guns grinding Fort Sumter to dust reverberated through the streets of Charleston. By day, two-hundred-pound Parrott projectiles smashed into the fort's right-flank and gorge walls, pulverizing the masonry with sledgehammer force. By night, giant mortar shells burst above the rubble-strewn parade ground, sending fiery chunks of shrapnel flying in all directions. This around-the-clock bombardment had begun on October 26. It would continue through November and into December, waxing and waning in intensity but never stopping. To Charleston poet Henry Timrod, its grim relentlessness, indicative of unbridled malice and an inexhaustible supply of ammunition, augured ill for the fate of the Confederacy.

Two and a half years earlier, Timrod had rocketed to prominence with the publication of "Ethnogenesis." The poem's opening stanza:

> *Hath not the morning dawned with added light?*
> *And shall not evening call another star*
> *Out of the infinite regions of the night,*
> *To mark this day in Heaven? At last, we are*
> *A nation among nations; and the world*
> *Shall soon behold in many a distant port*
>   *Another flag unfurled!*

Henry Timrod. (Courtesy The
South Carolina Library)

had thrilled Southern secessionists and won for the thirty-three-year-old Timrod the unofficial title "Laureate of the Confederacy." He had cemented his popularity with "The Cotton Boll," a paean to the economic and political power of cotton; "Carolina," a clarion call to arms; and "Carmen Triumphale," a song celebrating the rebel victory at Chancellorsville.

Timrod's own attempts to serve in the ranks were unavailing. He was small, frail, and afflicted with tuberculosis. Twice he enlisted and twice he was discharged after suffering near-fatal lung hemorrhages. His tenure as a combat correspondent for the Charleston *Mercury* was likewise cut short, and he returned to South Carolina ill and dispirited.

Friends assured him that the bugler was as important as the rifleman; the poet's role was to rally the nation with words, not deeds. But Timrod thought it hypocritical to sound the charge while remaining safely in the rear. To make matters worse, he had become profoundly disillusioned with the conflict. During his brief stint as a reporter, he had seen enough death and dismemberment to cure him forever of his romantic notions about war. He could no longer bring himself to exhort the South's young men to "feed your country's sacred dust / With floods of crimson rain."

The damage done to Charleston dismayed Timrod too. Historic buildings disfigured by fire and explosions, the downtown business district evacuated because of indiscriminate shelling, once-bustling marketplaces left empty and lifeless by the enemy blockade—all this he saw, and with sinking heart he wondered what further degradation lay in store for the proud city.

A tragic tone pervaded his writing now, a sense of loss and bitter regret. To the public he was still the ultrapatriotic "Harp of the South," but in his own mind he had become a threnodist, singing songs of lamentation for the "ten times ten thousand" who had fallen fighting for a lost cause. Dark, drizzly November depressed him further, and with the ceaseless rumble of the bombardment droning in his ear, he sadly chanted his ode to "The Unknown Dead":

> *The rain is plashing on my sill,*
> *But all the winds of Heaven are still;*

And so it falls with that dull sound
Which thrills us in the church-yard ground,
When the first spadeful drops like lead
Upon the coffin of the dead. . . .
What strange and unsuspected link
Of feeling touched, has made me think—
While with a vacant soul and eye
   I watch that gray and stony sky—
   Of nameless graves on battle-plains
   Washed by a single winter's rains,
   Where, some beneath Virginian hills,
   And some by green Atlantic rills,
   Some by the waters of the West,
   A myriad unknown heroes rest.

By the second week of November, 3,512 plots had been readied in the new Soldiers' National Cemetery at Gettysburg, and the process of retrieving, identifying, and reburying corpses was well under way.

The need for such an enterprise had become apparent soon after the fighting ended. Before they left for Maryland, Union soldiers spaded dirt over all the bodies they could find, but heavy rains washed away this thin covering, leaving arms, legs, and heads protruding from the soil. Hundreds of additional bodies, hidden behind rocks or concealed beneath underbrush, had not been buried at all. The stench was so nauseating that the townspeople were forced to tie rags around their noses and mouths and tuck camphor sticks or vials of peppermint oil in their shirt pockets. The battlefield required a thorough cleansing, and when Pennsylvania governor Andrew Curtin arrived in Gettysburg a few days after the battle, he asked local attorney David Wills to arrange for the systematic disposal of the remains.

Rather than shipping corpses to cities and towns all over the North, Wills proposed that a permanent burial place be established at Gettysburg. The Union dead would be interred there, while the Confederate slain were consigned to mass graves dug on the battlefield. His plan was approved by the Northern governors. Each state would pay a share of the costs based on the size of its population.

In mid-August Wills purchased seventeen acres on Cemetery Hill and engaged landscape architect William Saunders to lay out the grounds. Then he solicited bids for the job of recovering the bodies. Thirty-four entre-

Burial of Confederate dead on the Gettysburg battlefield.
(Courtesy U.S. Army Military History Institute)

preneurs sought the contract, submitting bids ranging from $8 to $1.59 per body. The winner promptly hired a crew of black laborers and set to work digging up decomposed cadavers. Every effort was made to identify the dead by name and state. If no headboard was present, personal effects such as Bibles, rings, wallets, and diaries were studied for clues to the owner's identity. The items were then cataloged and set aside in case family members wanted them.

The task of determining who was who was complicated by the intermingling of body parts and by the fact that many Southern soldiers had been wearing captured Union uniforms when they were killed. Ultimately 1,664 sets of remains would be placed in the cemetery's "Unknown" section. The contractor who was responsible for the reburials swore that no rebel bodies polluted the sacred resting place of Union martyrs, but the truth was that a number of Confederate dead were inadvertently mixed in.

With corpses being brought to the cemetery at a rate of sixty per day, Wills's thoughts turned to organizing a dedication ceremony. A lengthy funeral oration would be the centerpiece of the event, and he hoped to prevail on Boston's Edward Everett, the preeminent public speaker of the day, to deliver it.

Everett had been an editor, clergyman, politician, and diplomat during his distinguished fifty-year career, but his real love was lecturing on classical and patriotic themes. His carefully crafted declamations, recited in a deep, ringing voice and augmented by dramatic gestures, never failed to thrill his audiences.

Wills invited the seventy-year-old Bostonian to be the principal orator at the cemetery consecration, which was scheduled to take place on October 23. Everett accepted, provided he was given more time to prepare. Wills agreed, and the dedication was pushed back to November 19.

It was not until the second week of November that Lincoln began thinking about the short speech he would deliver at Gettysburg. He knew that the organizing committee was afraid he would not take the event seriously. His penchant for quips and uncouth stories was well known. Rumor had it that during a tour of the Antietam battlefield in October 1862, he had laughed and sung ribald songs. It was this episode Wills had in mind when he informed the president that the consecration would be "imposing and solemnly impressive" and instructed him to keep his speech brief and dignified. Lincoln was not offended by this presumptuousness. He accepted the Pennsylvania attorney's offer of dinner and lodging the night before the ceremony and asked the War Department to arrange for a train to take him to Gettysburg.

The four-coach special, its locomotive decorated with red-white-and-blue bunting, pulled into the Gettysburg depot just before sunset on November 18. The sight of coffins piled high on the platform made the president wince, but he perked up when the reception committee handed him a telegram from Washington reporting that his son Tad, who had been running a high fever earlier in the day, was feeling better.

After breakfast on the morning of the nineteenth, Lincoln slipped out of the Wills house to visit some of the battle sites. Returning around 10 A.M., he donned a new black suit, silk top hat, and white gloves and joined the long, slow-moving procession that was making its way to the burial ground. Close to 20,000 people had turned out for the dedication, and the raised speakers' platform looked like a tiny raft floating on a sea of humanity.

Reverend Thomas H. Stockton, chaplain of the House of Representatives, opened the ceremony with an invocation; the Marine band played "Old Hundred"; then Everett ascended the platform and launched into his two-hour address. In a throbbing voice that carried to the farthest reaches of the crowd, he described the funeral rites of ancient Athens, summarized

*Procession en route to the Gettysburg National Cemetery, November 19, 1863.
(Courtesy Adams County Historical Society)*

the history of the present war, reviewed the three-day battle fought at Gettysburg, and paid tribute to the Union dead. It was a magnificent speech, all the more remarkable for the fact it was recited entirely from memory. The audience was enthralled.

When the ovation for Everett's performance had subsided, the Baltimore Glee Club sang a hymn composed especially for the occasion. This was Lincoln's cue that his turn to speak was near. He straightened up, put on his steel-rimmed spectacles, drew his manuscript from his coat pocket, and reviewed it one last time.

"The President of the United States," intoned the master of ceremonies. Lincoln rose, stiff after hours of slouching in a too-small chair, stepped up to the lectern, and read in his high tenor voice the "few appropriate remarks" that lawyer Wills had requested of him.

He was astonishingly brief, and yet in ten sentences he changed forever the way Americans viewed their nation's past and thought about its future. He spoke not of the battle or the cemetery, but of liberty and equality, and rather than eulogizing the dead, he called on the living to rededicate themselves to the ideals enunciated in the Declaration of Independence so that the nation might know a new birth of freedom.

Caught off guard by the president's brevity, the crowd hesitated a moment before breaking into a polite round of applause. It was a tepid response, and Lincoln professed to be disappointed by it: "That speech won't scour," he mut-

Address delivered at the dedication of the Cemetery at Gettysburg.

Four score and seven years ago our fathers brought forth on this continent, a new nation, conceived in Liberty, and dedicated to the proposition that all men are created equal.

Now we are engaged in a great civil war, testing whether that nation, or any nation so conceived and so dedicated, can long endure. We are met on a great battle-field of that war. We have come to dedicate a portion of that field, as a final resting place for those who here gave their lives that that nation might live. It is altogether fitting and proper that we should do this.

But, in a larger sense, we can not dedicate— we can not consecrate— we can not hallow— this ground. The brave men, living and dead, who struggled here have consecrated it, far above our poor power to add or detract. The world will little note, nor long remember what we say here, but it can never forget what they did here. It is for us the living, rather, to be dedicated here to the unfinished work which they who fought here have thus far so nobly advanced. It is rather for us to be here dedicated to the great task remaining before us— that from these honored dead we take increased devotion to that cause for which they gave the last full measure of devotion— that we here highly resolve that these dead shall not have died in vain— that this nation, under God, shall have a new birth of freedom— and that government of the people, by the people, for the people, shall not perish from the earth.

Abraham Lincoln.

November 19. 1863.

The Gettysburg Address. (Corbis-Bettmann)

tered as he took his seat. "It is a flat failure." But he had accomplished what he had set out to do. With 272 carefully chosen words he had transformed the Gettysburg butchery into a sublime act of sacrifice. He had invested the slaughter with a transcendent significance that would shine down the years like an inextinguishable beacon, illuminating for succeeding generations the meaning of this battle and of the entire war. As a future historian would write: "That speech did indeed scour, even in dark and bloody ground."

Jefferson Davis arrived at his office on November 9, eager to resume the day-to-day duties of the presidency after more than a month on the road. But the pleasure afforded him by familiar faces and a return to the accustomed routine proved short-lived. Problems pressed in from all sides, and the optimism that had sustained him during his trip through the Deep South was supplanted by feelings of anxiety and disappointment.

Politics was one source of worry. In the recent congressional elections, Southern voters had registered their displeasure with taxation, inflation, impressment, and conscription by sending a raft of anti-Davis candidates to Richmond. It was a decisive repudiation of the status quo, and the president knew that his administration was in for some rough handling when the House and Senate reconvened in December.

Even as he was reconciling himself to that unpleasant prospect, Secretary of the Navy Stephen Mallory informed him that the Confederacy had suffered a devastating diplomatic defeat at the hands of the British foreign office. In the summer of 1862, the navy's purchasing agent in Europe had contracted with the Laird shipyard in Birkenhead, England, to build two powerful ironclads for blockade-breaking duty. The "Laird rams," as these state-of-the-art warships were called, were bigger, faster, and more heavily armed than the Federal monitors. It was thought they would have no difficulty dispersing the Yankee fleets cruising off Wilmington, Charleston, and Mobile. Delivery of the ships had been expected sometime this fall. But now, Mallory reported, Prime Minister Palmerston had succumbed to Union pressure and dispatched a gunboat and a detachment of marines to Birkenhead to make sure the rams did not leave port. The South's last best hope for lifting the blockade had been dashed.

The president did not brood for long about British perfidy because other matters demanded his attention. The Chattanooga situation was particularly worrisome. It was obvious that Grant's army was going to attack as soon as it was strong enough, and Davis sent Bragg a note urging him to make a preemptive strike. Bragg ignored this advice. Convinced that his

Missionary Ridge position was impregnable, he made no effort to interfere with the Yankee buildup in the valley below.

Davis was also distressed by Longstreet's poor showing. It had taken him nearly two weeks to move his corps from Chattanooga to Knoxville—more than enough time for Burnside's Yankees to occupy earthworks ringing the city. Faced with these fortifications, Longstreet was at a loss what to do. He hunkered down and started calling for reinforcements.

Even Lee, the one general the president trusted completely, was struggling this month. Following the retreat from Centreville in mid-October, he had deployed the Army of Northern Virginia near Brandy Station on the south side of the Rappahannock River. The Confederate soldiers built log huts in anticipation of spending the winter there, but Lee was not ready to suspend operations. He left pontoons in place at Rappahannock Station and fortified a bridgehead on the river's north bank so he could move the army across rapidly if an opportunity to attack presented itself.

While the Confederates were settling into their bivouacs, Meade's Federals were advancing southwest. On November 6 rebel outposts reported that the Union host was approaching Rappahannock Station. Lee was not alarmed. The commander of the bridgehead garrison had said he could fend off the entire Yankee army if need be. Meade had a surprise up his sleeve, however. After sunset on November 7 he launched a night attack. Seven rebel regiments were obliterated, and the pontoon bridge fell into Federal hands.

Loss of the bridge rendered Lee's position untenable. The Army of Northern Virginia had to abandon its encampment and fall back in great haste. The situation was so perilous that Lee decided against traveling to Richmond for a meeting he had scheduled with the president. Instead he asked the chief executive to visit him at the front. On the twenty-first Davis obliged. By then Meade's cautious nature had reasserted itself; the threat of a Union follow-up attack had subsided.

Davis spent three days at Lee's headquarters near Orange Court House, discussing strategy and inspecting the troops. They were in good spirits, which was more than could be said for their commander, who was concerned about gathering enough supplies to get through the winter.

Davis returned to Richmond on the afternoon of November 24. That evening he was handed a telegram from Bragg's headquarters. The Army of Tennessee was under attack and had "sustained considerable loss." Davis's heart sank when he read this ominous phrase. The dispatch did not say which side had prevailed, but from the way it was worded, he suspected that the Confederates had suffered a serious defeat on the heights south of Chattanooga.

Grant had been itching to assail Bragg since learning of Longstreet's departure for east Tennessee on November 5. He was compelled to bide his time, however, until his army's logistical situation improved and Sherman's four divisions completed their 250-mile march from Memphis.

The waiting was difficult. Lincoln, Stanton, and Halleck were badgering him to help Burnside before Knoxville was lost. Grant, who was in constant communication with Burnside, knew that the Knoxville garrison was in no immediate danger. Still the nagging telegrams kept coming, and the strain became so great that he started drinking again. Fearful that this relapse would prove fatal, John Rawlins wrote a letter to Grant, pleading with him to give up whiskey before it was too late. "Two more nights like the last will find you prostrated on a sick bed unfit for duty," he warned. The letter was never delivered. On November 14 Sherman rode into Chattanooga. Cheered by his friend's arrival and by the prospect of action, Grant stopped drinking and started girding for battle.

Early on the morning of November 15, the Union brass rode up the Tennessee River to reconnoiter Bragg's right flank. Grant told Sherman to bring his troops east from Bridgeport via Lookout Valley, cross the river at Brown's Ferry, march through the hills north of Chattanooga, then return to the river three miles above town. Meanwhile, Baldy Smith would assemble a fleet of pontoon boats and, when all was in readiness, float an infantry brigade downstream to a secure landing site just below the mouth of Chickamauga Creek. The pontoons would be used to bridge the Tennessee, allowing Sherman's divisions to move across and occupy the northern end of Missionary Ridge as far as Tunnel Hill, the portion of the bluff through which the Western & Atlantic Railroad tracks passed. To keep Bragg from reinforcing his right, Thomas was to demonstrate against the Confederate center with the Army of the Cumberland. Once Tunnel Hill was in Union hands, he would link up with Sherman, and the combined forces would drive the enemy off Missionary Ridge. Hooker was to place Howard's corps in reserve on the north side of the river, then sit tight with the rest of his soldiers, menacing but not attacking the rebel left flank on Lookout Mountain.

These assignments reflected Grant's opinion of his generals and the troops they led. He had complete confidence in Sherman and his veteran divisions. He was not so keen on Thomas, considering him sluggish and unaggressive, and he feared that the Army of the Cumberland would fight poorly after its collapse at Chickamauga. Hooker and his men he trusted hardly at all, viewing them as castoffs from the Army of the Potomac. Thus

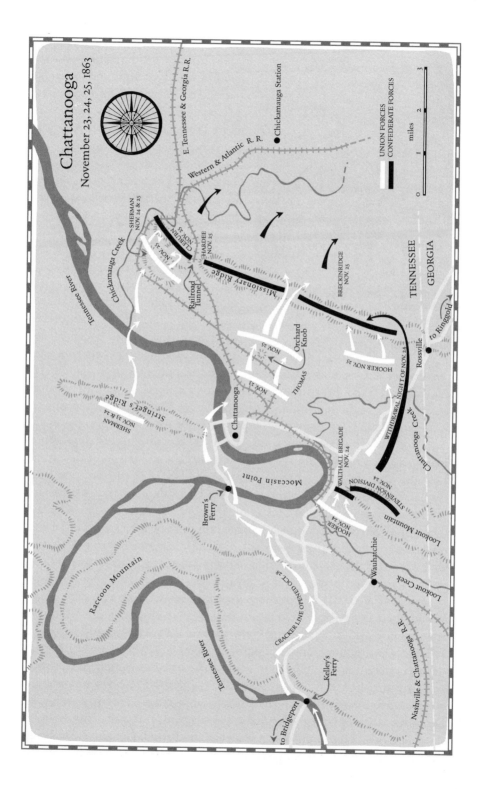

Chattanooga
November 23, 24, 25, 1863

UNION FORCES
CONFEDERATE FORCES

miles
0   1   2   3

E. Tennessee & Georgia R. R.

Western & Atlantic R. R.

Chickamauga Station

TENNESSEE
GEORGIA

to Ringgold

Rossville

Chickamauga Creek

SHERMAN
NOV. 24 & 25

Tennessee River

Railroad Tunnel

Missionary Ridge

CLIFTON
NOV. 25

HARDEE
NOV. 25

BRECKINRIDGE
NOV. 25

NOV. 25

NOV. 25

Orchard Knob

THOMAS

NOV. 23

HOOKER NOV. 25

WITHDRAWAL NIGHT OF NOV. 24

Chattanooga Creek

Stringer's Ridge

SHERMAN
NOV. 23 & 24

Chattanooga

Moccasin Point

WALTHALL BRIGADE
NOV. 24

STEVENSON DIVISION
NOV. 24

Brown's Ferry

HOOKER
NOV. 24

Lookout Mountain

Raccoon Mountain

CRACKER LINE OPENED OCT. 28

Wauhatchie

Lookout Creek

Tennessee River

Kelley's Ferry

to Bridgeport

Nashville & Chattanooga R. R.

General William T. Sherman.
(Library of Congress)

Sherman was awarded the lead role in the offensive even though he was unfamiliar with the terrain and his troops were weary from their long trek from Memphis. The Ohioan eagerly embraced the challenge: "I can do it," he announced after studying Missionary Ridge through a pair of field glasses. That was all Grant needed to hear. Orders were drafted and distributed; the attack would commence at dawn on November 21.

Returning to Bridgeport, Sherman started his command toward Chattanooga on the morning of the seventeenth. He thought his soldiers would have no trouble completing the twenty-seven-mile march in the time allotted, but he failed to take Tennessee's atrocious late-fall weather into account. It began raining on November 18, the dirt road from Bridgeport to Brown's Ferry turned into a quagmire, and the blue column bogged down. As if the ankle-deep mud weren't hindrance enough, the Tennessee River rose, threatening to wash away the Brown's Ferry pontoon bridge. Three of Sherman's divisions managed to cross the flood-buffeted span, but the fourth, commanded by Brigadier General Peter J. Osterhaus, was stranded when the structure gave way on November 23. Repairs could not be made until the floodwaters subsided, so Osterhaus was sent south to join Hooker in Lookout Valley. The rest of Sherman's command slogged on to the east, moving at a snail's pace. It was not until the evening of November 23, more than sixty hours after the attack was scheduled to have begun, that they finally reached their jump-off position northeast of Chattanooga.

Grant chafed at the unexpected delay. He was worried that Bragg would figure out what the Union forces were up to and either reinforce his right in anticipation of Sherman's thrust or withdraw his army altogether. His concern mounted on the night of November 22 when a pair of rebel deserters came into the blue lines and reported that the Confederate army was retreating from Missionary Ridge.

The deserters were mistaken. The troop movements they had seen earlier in the day were not the beginning of an armywide evacuation; rather, they were the divisions of Simon Buckner and Patrick Cleburne departing for Knoxville by way of Chickamauga Station. After watching Sherman's column toil across Moccasin Point and disappear into the hills above Chattanooga, Bragg had concluded that it was heading northeast to bolster Burnside. He responded by sending reinforcements to Longstreet. Grant did not know this, however. He had received other reports on the twenty-second indicating that the rebel army was pulling back, and the deserters' story seemed to confirm them. He needed to find out for sure, so on the morning of November 23 he directed Thomas to advance toward Missionary Ridge and determine if the Confederates still occupied defensive positions at its base. If Bragg was found to be retreating, the entire Union army would pursue at once; if he was holding his ground, the original plan would remain in effect, with Sherman making his flank attack on the twenty-fourth.

Recognizing that this was an audition of sorts, Thomas marshaled his forces with care. "It was an inspiring sight," a spectator wrote. "The sharp commands of hundreds of company officers, the sound of drums, the ringing notes of the bugle, companies wheeling and countermarching and regiments getting into line, the bright sun lighting up 10,000 polished bayonets till they glistened and flashed like a flying shower of electric sparks—all looked like preparations for a peaceful pageant rather than for the bloody work of death."

The rebels thought so too. They believed, they later said, that the Yankees were staging a review. They were disabused of that notion at 1:50 P.M. when the blue ranks began to march across the open plain that extended from Chattanooga to the foot of Missionary Ridge. Their objective was Orchard Knob, a tree-covered hillock that anchored a line of Confederate rifle pits, located about three-quarters of a mile west of the ridge.

Back at the attack's starting point, Grant and Thomas waited anxiously to see if the rebels would offer any resistance. The Federal formations advanced unopposed until they were within a few hundred yards of the enemy position. Then there was a crackle of fire from the rifle pits in front of Orchard Knob, followed by a tremendous roar of artillery from Missionary Ridge—clear indication that Bragg's army was still in place and ready to fight. Once this determination was made, Thomas's troops were supposed to return to their fortifications on the outskirts of Chattanooga. But eager to prove their mettle, they kept going, up and over the summit of Orchard Knob, shooting or bayoneting those defenders who had not already fled.

The fight was over in a matter of minutes. A loud cheer went up, informing the watchers in Chattanooga that the hill had been captured. Thomas, bursting with pride, signaled his division commanders: "You have gained too much to withdraw. Hold your position, and I will support you." Then he hurried forward with additional troops and artillery. Grant was delighted too. The Army of the Cumberland had performed much better than he had expected; its élan boded well for the success of the main assault. It would stay where it was until daylight, waiting for Sherman's divisions to get into position at the mouth of Chickamauga Creek.

The loss of Orchard Knob stunned Bragg. He had assumed the enemy would not dare attack rugged Missionary Ridge. Now he realized he was mistaken, and as the sun set on November 23, he hastened to adjust his troop dispositions to meet the new threat. Cleburne's division was recalled from Chickamauga Station and placed in reserve behind the Confederate center. W.H.T. Walker's division was pulled off Lookout Mountain and sent to shore up the right flank near Tunnel Hill. Finally all units were ordered to strengthen their fortifications.

While Bragg's soldiers deepened their rifle pits at the base of Missionary Ridge and constructed breastworks on the crest five hundred feet above, Sherman's command got ready to cross the Tennessee River northeast of Chattanooga. Baldy Smith's engineers had hidden 116 pontoon boats in a creek four hundred yards above its juncture with the Tennessee, and around one o'clock on the morning of November 24, the soldiers of the Eighth Missouri and 116th Illinois regiments climbed aboard and cast off. "Not a word was spoken," recalled one of the Illinoisans. "We hushed our very whispers, and the oars were carefully muffled." The bulky craft drifted silently down the creek, swirled out into the fog-shrouded river, and floated south toward the landing site three miles distant. The Confederate pickets standing watch on the eastern bank did not spot the passing flotilla. At 1:30 A.M. the first wave of Union infantrymen scrambled ashore, disarmed a squad of enemy sentries, and fanned out to form a defensive perimeter around the beachhead.

For the next four hours boats shuttled back and forth, ferrying more troops across the river. By daybreak two divisions were over and construction of the pontoon bridge was under way. The 1,350-foot span was finished at 12:30 P.M.; Sherman immediately brought a third division across, then sent his troops to seize the northern end of Missionary Ridge.

The Federal columns advanced across the swampy flatland between the river and the ridge and began ascending the steep slope, meeting surprisingly little resistance. When they reached the summit around 4 P.M. they halted and dug in. Sherman informed Grant that he had secured a lodgment on Tunnel Hill and would renew his assault early the next morning.

There was just one problem with this promise: Sherman was not where he thought he was. His maps, which showed Missionary Ridge to be a continuous elevation, were inaccurate, and he had not bothered to examine the terrain in person before nightfall. If he had, he would have seen that the high ground his troops were ensconced on was not Tunnel Hill, but an isolated eminence separated from the northern end of Missionary Ridge by a heavily wooded ravine. He was a half mile short of his objective. What was more, he had forfeited the element of surprise. Cleburne's division had occupied Tunnel Hill and the bluffs north and east of it.

Sherman was oblivious to this; it would be another twelve hours before he discovered his error. By then the area in front of him would be crawling with rebels. He would have to fight a terrific battle just to reach the spot from which he was supposed to start his flank attack.

While Sherman was bridging the Tennessee River, Hooker was going into action southwest of Chattanooga. His original assignment had been strictly defensive, but when Osterhaus's division was added to his command, giving him a total of 10,000 troops, Grant decided that he should play a more aggressive role and directed him to attack Lookout Mountain.

To conduct this operation, Hooker had Osterhaus's division of Sherman's Fifteenth Corps, Brigadier General Charles Cruft's division of Thomas's Fourth Corps, and Brigadier General John Geary's division of his own Twelfth Corps—three units that had never fought together before. Further complicating matters was the terrain confronting the Federals. From the valley floor, Lookout Mountain's timber-covered slopes rose to a height of eight hundred feet, leveled off to form a plateau upon which stood the house of farmer Robert Cravens, then soared upward another six hundred feet to the palisades, a line of limestone cliffs crowning the summit. Lookout Creek meandered around the western base and emptied into the Tennessee not far from the mountain's northernmost point. A brigade of Mississippians commanded by Brigadier General Edward C. Walthall manned a curving two-mile-long picket line running along the east bank of the creek and up the west side of the mountain as far as the palisades. Another Confederate brigade, led by Brigadier General John C. Moore, occupied a defensive position on the northeastern slope, extending from the riverbank up to the Cravens house plateau. Two more brigades under Brigadier Generals Edmund W. Pettus and John C. Brown were dug in on the mountaintop.

Despite these obstacles, Hooker was determined to capture the peak, a feat he hoped would erase the stigma of Chancellorsville. On the dark, drizzly morning of November 24, he put his plan into effect. Geary's division, supported by one of Cruft's brigades, marched south from Wauhatchie, crossed

Lookout Creek, formed into a column, and started up the mountainside, its movements concealed from the enemy by dense fog. When the head of the column reached the base of the palisades, the soldiers all wheeled to the left, forming a line about nine hundred yards long. Then they started north toward the Tennessee River, sweeping around the side of the mountain, grabbing at bushes, tree limbs, and boulders to keep their balance on the forty-five-degree slope.

At 10:30 A.M. the bluecoats struck Walthall's picket line, where it extended from Lookout Creek up the western side of the mountain. The rebels had been expecting an attack from below, not from the flank. They fired a few wild shots, then retreated in the direction of the Cravens house half a mile distant.

While Geary's command was rolling up the gray picket line on the mountainside, Osterhaus's division, augmented by Cruft's other brigade, was crossing Lookout Creek near its junction with the Tennessee River. Climbing the northwestern shoulder of the mountain, Osterhaus's troops linked up with Geary's men. Supported by artillery fire from Federal batteries in Lookout Valley and on Moccasin Point, the combined force continued its relentless advance. "The rebels broke and ran and we ran after them," remembered Lieutenant Albert Greene. "Into holes, over rocks and stumps and logs, through a camp of hut and shelter tents, and over fires where rebel breakfasts were cooking, on, capturing squads of the fleeing enemy, till the dense fog shut in again over and around us, and we must stop and feel our way."

Around 1:30 P.M. Walthall's crumbling command was reinforced by the brigades of Moore and Pettus. A fierce fight erupted on the plateau east of the Cravens house. The Yankees attacked again and again but could not drive off the Confederates. Half an hour later the rain clouds that had obscured the summit all day settled over the entire mountain. The drizzle became heavier; visibility, which had been poor to start with, was reduced to almost nothing. This factor, plus fatigue and a shortage of ammunition, prompted Hooker to suspend the assault. He consolidated his position and appealed to Grant and Thomas for support. Thomas responded by sending one of his brigades, laden with extra cartridges, up the mountainside. These troops reached the Cravens house at 7 P.M. and joined Hooker's units, which were huddled on the cold, wet plateau waiting for the night to pass and the fighting to resume.

Unbeknownst to the Federals, the battle for Lookout Mountain was over. Bragg had ordered its defenders to withdraw under cover of darkness, cross Chattanooga Valley, and march up Missionary Ridge to reinforce Cleburne's division at Tunnel Hill. The retreat began shortly after midnight.

The sky had cleared an hour or so earlier, and the moon was shining brightly as the tired Confederates stumbled down the east side of the mountain. By 3 A.M. on November 25 the evacuation was complete; after sixty-three days of Confederate occupation, Lookout Mountain was back in Yankee hands.

Just before daybreak, six Union soldiers scaled the palisades and discovered that the summit was deserted. They had brought a large United States flag with them, and as the sun's first rays struck the mountaintop, they planted the banner on a jutting limestone outcrop, where it could be seen for miles around. For a minute or two, there was no reaction; then the bluecoats in the valley below caught sight of the rippling colors and broke into jubilant cheers. "I did not stop with waving my hat, but yelled and clapped my hands, jumped up and down, laughed and cried for joy," an Indiana captain wrote. "In fact, the whole army in front of Chattanooga was simply wild with excitement."

The "Battle Above the Clouds," as Northern newspapers called the fight for Lookout Mountain, was destined to become one of the war's most celebrated actions. This delighted the publicity-hungry Hooker but irked Grant, who considered the affair little more than a glorified skirmish. "It is all poetry," he grumbled after reading romanticized press accounts of the engagement. Still, he had to admit that capture of the mountain helped the Federals immensely. It meant that supplies could be brought into Chattanooga by rail instead of over the Cracker Line. It also meant that Hooker's troops were available for action on another part of the field. He promptly ordered them to march to Rossville Gap in Missionary Ridge and assail the enemy's left.

On the night of November 24, Bragg summoned Breckinridge and Hardee to his headquarters. With Hooker atop Lookout Mountain and Sherman poised to attack Tunnel Hill, both of his flanks were in grave danger. If either one gave way tomorrow, the Army of Tennessee would be threatened with annihilation.

Hardee favored an immediate withdrawal. The Confederate army should either form a new defensive line east of Chickamauga Creek or retire into Georgia, he said. Breckinridge disagreed. It was too late to organize a retreat tonight, he insisted; if the army tried such a move, it would end up scattered all over the countryside. Besides, if Southern troops could not make a stand on Missionary Ridge, they could not make one anywhere.

Heartened by Breckinridge's bellicosity, Bragg decided to stay and fight.

The troops that had been stationed on Lookout Mountain would be sent to shore up the right flank. This meant that Hardee would have four divisions with which to defend the northern third of the ridge, while Breckinridge would have just three to hold the remaining two-thirds. It was a calculated risk; the line would be very thin in Breckinridge's sector; but Bragg was counting on the rugged terrain to keep the Federals at bay on that front. Grant's main attack, he was convinced, would come against Tunnel Hill.

Before sunrise on November 25, Sherman set out to examine the ground his command would advance over later that morning. It was during this ride that he discovered his soldiers were not deployed on the northern terminus of Missionary Ridge as he had originally thought, but on a detached knoll separated from the main ridge by a deep valley. Shocked at the magnitude of his blunder, he wavered. Instead of attacking at dawn as planned, he spent the next two hours stalling. Finally, at 7 A.M., he could procrastinate no longer. He glumly ordered a single division to advance. He did not commit more troops, he later said, because the narrow front leading to the apex of Tunnel Hill could accommodate only a brigade at a time. But the truth was that he had no stomach for the assault and would have preferred not to try it at all.

The delay worked to the Confederates' advantage. Reinforcements had been arriving since first light. Cleburne used them to form a defensive line that ran from the railroad tunnel northward for several hundred yards along the spine of Tunnel Hill to its summit, then doglegged to the east atop a steep, tree-covered spur. Artillery batteries were sited at key locations, and most of the rebel infantrymen had breastworks to shelter behind.

For the next nine hours Union troops swarmed up the north and west faces of Tunnel Hill, trying to dislodge Cleburne's rebels. "Still they advance, and still we shoot them down," wrote Captain Samuel Foster. "To see them bluecoats fall is glorious. . . . [We] lie here and shoot them down and we don't get hurt—we are behind these logs. We give them fits." Several times the Yankees got to within a hundred feet of the barricades, only to be pinned down by withering fire. At 4 P.M. a fierce Confederate counterattack brought the fight for Tunnel Hill to an abrupt end.

It had been one of the worst days of Sherman's military career. With over 20,000 troops at his disposal, he had failed to take an objective defended by a single division. "The general was in an unhappy frame of mind," a fellow officer wrote with considerable understatement. "He gave vent to his feeling in language of astonishing vivacity."

Sherman was not angry enough to lose his head, however. Having suffered close to 2,000 casualties, he was not about to authorize any more ad hoc attacks against the rebel stronghold. If Missionary Ridge was to be carried, some other Union general would have to do it.

For a time it appeared that Fighting Joe Hooker might be the man. Upon receiving Grant's order to strike Bragg's left flank, Hooker detailed two regiments to hold Lookout Mountain and set out with the rest of his command. The column moved fast, and by 1:30 P.M. it had reached Chattanooga Creek, one and a half miles from Rossville. There it came to an abrupt halt. Retreating rebels had burned the bridge over the stream, and there were no suitable fords nearby. Engineers began making repairs while the rest of the soldiers sat down by the roadside to wait. Hooker informed headquarters that he would be delayed about an hour. High water and a paucity of building materials hampered the engineers, however, and the span was not fixed until three thirty. It took another hour to get all the troops across, and by the time they reached Rossville, the sun was setting behind Lookout Mountain.

Although the hour was late, Hooker pressed on. He got his three divisions into assault formation as fast as he could and started them north with instructions to drive the enemy before them.

The Confederate left flank was anchored by a brigade of Alabamians. Unlike Cleburne's command, which had taken advantage of steep terrain to nullify Sherman's numerical superiority, these soldiers were poorly positioned. When Hooker's battle line smashed into them, they collapsed. Breckinridge, who had ridden down from Bragg's headquarters to check on the situation, barely escaped with his life. "Boys, get away the best you can!" he screamed as he galloped for the rear. A few of the Alabamians took his advice, but most did not. Hemmed in by Union units, 679 of them dropped their rifles and surrendered.

Hooker was exhilarated. He was doing to Bragg what Stonewall Jackson had done to him seven months ago. But like Jackson, he had started his assault too late in the afternoon. Darkness forced him to stop his divisions before they could sweep the entire length of the ridge. Had he not been detained for three hours at the bridge, he might have crumpled the Confederate line like an accordion and expunged forever the blot of Chancellorsville. His chance at glory, however, had slipped through his fingers. Victory, and the accompanying honors, would go to another general today.

Grant's anxiety mounted steadily during the morning and early after-noon of November 25. He was counting on Sherman to push the rebels down Missionary Ridge so that he could send Thomas forward to deliver the coup de grâce. But from his observation post on Orchard Knob, he could see that Sherman was making no headway. News that Hooker had stalled a mile and a half short of Rossville added to his discomfort.

At 2:30 P.M. Grant finally admitted that his strategy wasn't working. Peering at Missionary Ridge through his binoculars, he saw columns of gray troops marching north along the crest. It looked like Bragg was preparing to counterattack at Tunnel Hill. Afraid that Sherman would be swamped, he directed Thomas to seize the rifle pits at the base of Missionary Ridge.

The order did not sit well with the Army of the Cumberland commander. It had been his understanding that he would not advance until one or both of the Union flank attacks had succeeded. Sending his troops across a mile of open ground in full view of every rebel gunner on the ridge struck him as suicidal. Grant was adamant, however: the movement had to be made. "Now is your time," he said to Thomas in a tone of voice that brooked no argument. The burly Virginian nodded and told his corps commanders to get their divisions ready. The signal to attack would be six cannon shots fired in rapid succession.

The troops deployed quickly. Absalom Baird's division was on the left, Thomas Wood's and Phil Sheridan's in the center, and Richard Johnson's on the right. At 3:40 P.M. the signal guns boomed, and the two-and-a-half-mile line of battle stepped off.

The Confederates on the ridge were thunderstruck. "The sight was imposing in the extreme," wrote Brigadier General Arthur Manigault. "I noticed some nervousness amongst my men." Rebel artillerists raced to their cannons. The Federals cringed in expectation of a bloodbath, but it quickly became clear that little damage was going to be done. Salvo after salvo passed overhead and exploded harmlessly in the rear. The Confederates could not depress their gun tubes enough to achieve the proper range. A loud cheer of relief went up from the Union soldiers, and many units spontaneously broke into a run, eager to cross the exposed flat as quickly as possible.

The rebels occupying the rifle pits at the base of the ridge were dismayed by their artillery's failure to stop the blue juggernaut. From where they stood, it looked like all the Yankees in creation were bearing down on them. They opened fire when the range fell below three hundred yards, but their fusillades seemed to have no effect. The Union host kept coming. It was too much for the Confederates to stand. They threw their weapons aside and sprinted for the rear. "All order was lost," General Manigault wrote, "as each, striving to save himself, took the shortest direction for the summit."

Now Thomas's Federals had to make a decision. The Confederates on the crest were pouring volleys down into their midst, and the rifle pits they had just captured provided no protection. There were only two options: retreat, or continue the charge. They unhesitatingly chose the latter. Retreating across the plain would give the enemy cannoneers another chance to find the range. It would also entail more disgrace for an army still suffering from the humiliation of Chickamauga. First one regiment, then another, and another climbed out of the rifle pits and started forward. There was no carefully drawn line of battle this time, just long files of men scrambling up the hillside, taking advantage of whatever cover rocks, ravines, and fallen logs afforded them.

Back on Orchard Knob, Grant was shocked when he saw what was happening. Lowering his binoculars, he turned on Thomas and barked: "Who ordered those men up the ridge?"

"I don't know; I didn't," the tight-lipped Virginian answered.

Grant was determined to find the culprit. "Did you order them up, Granger?"

"No," the Fourth Corps commander replied in a voice quivering with excitement, "they started without orders. When those fellows get started all hell can't stop them!"

Grant scowled fiercely. Someone was going to be court-martialed if the attack failed, he growled; then he went back to watching the action. It was a riveting spectacle. Clusters of tiny blue figures were swarming all over the side of Missionary Ridge, speeding up and slowing down depending on the difficulty of the terrain, but always climbing higher. "At times their movements were in a shape like the flight of migratory birds—sometimes in line, sometimes in mass, mostly in V-shaped groups with the points toward the enemy," observed Lieutenant Colonel Joseph Fullerton. "At these points regimental flags were flying, sometimes dropping as the bearers were shot, but never reaching the ground, for other brave hands were there to seize them. Sixty flags were advancing up the hill."

That was the way the action looked from a mile off—antiseptic and slightly unreal. Seen up close, it was messy and chaotic. Thousands of panting, perspiration-soaked soldiers were frantically clawing their way upward. The clatter of gunfire was deafening, the clouds of powder smoke blinding. Some parts of the slope were so steep, the troops had to crawl on their hands and knees. But they kept going, unnerving the enemy with their grim perseverance. "Those defending the heights became more and more desperate as our men approached the top," an Illinois captain recalled. "They shouted 'Chickamauga' as though the word itself were a weapon; they thrust cartridges into guns by the handfuls, they lighted the fuses of shells and rolled them down, they seized huge stones and threw them, but nothing could stop the force of the desperate charge."

Too late the Confederates discovered that the bulk of their breastworks were in the wrong place. Most had been erected on the ridge's topographical crest—the highest elevation—rather than on the military crest, the portion of the forward slope providing the best field of fire. This faulty layout created blind spots that permitted large numbers of attackers to approach in relative safety. By 4:50 P.M. approximately half a dozen intermingled Union regiments had gathered below the lip of the ridge where the Confederates could not see them. They rested there for a few minutes, then fixed bayonets and stormed over the crest. A few yards in front of them was a fortification occupied by a brigade of Mississippians. Before these soldiers could pull the trigger, the bluecoats were on top of them. "Such a confused mass I never saw," wrote one of the Federals. "Here were officers trying to rally their men, and everywhere running rebels—fellows 'lighting out' for dear life—and our men popping them over as if they were quails."

The panic gripping the Mississippians proved contagious. As more Yankee units came over the crest, hundreds and then thousands of Confederates abandoned their defenses and scampered down the back side of the ridge. Braxton Bragg tried to stem the tide. Clutching a flag, he rode back and forth, imploring the fear-crazed troops to stand and fight. They would not listen. Most rushed by without even looking at him. Others jeered or swore as they dashed past. Dismounting, Bragg tried to shame a group of fugitives into rejoining the battle. "Stop," he shouted, "don't disgrace yourselves. Fight for your country! Here is your commander!"

"And here's your mule!" roared a husky private, grabbing the general around the waist and throwing him aside. Bragg picked himself up and resumed his harangue, but being manhandled by one of his own soldiers had shaken him in a way that the Federal breakthrough had not. "[He] looked so scared," Sam Watkins remembered, "so hacked and whipped and mortified and chagrined."

After a few minutes Bragg stopped trying to check the stampede and started thinking about his own safety. Dispirited as he was, he did not want to be killed or captured. After sending messengers to tell Breckinridge and Hardee to get their troops away as best they could, he mounted his horse and rode east toward Chickamauga Station, surrounded by the flotsam of his shattered army.

Grant was astounded by the abrupt collapse of the Confederate center. One moment he was steeling himself for a catastrophe, the next he was being congratulated by jubilant staff officers as Union battle flags fluttered all along the crest of Missionary Ridge.

When it was confirmed that the rebels had been routed, Grant, Thomas, and Granger left Orchard Knob and rode out to the ridge, where a wild victory celebration was under way. Some soldiers were dancing for joy; others were throwing their hats, haversacks, and canteens into the air; still others were gathered around groups of enemy prisoners, taunting them with cries of "Chickamauga! Chickamauga, God damn you!" Thomas cracked a rare smile as he steered his horse through the delirious mob. Granger gleefully yelled, "I am going to have you all court-martialed! You were ordered to take the works at the foot of the hill, and you have taken those on top! You have disobeyed orders, all of you!" Grant rode back and forth, doffing his hat and thanking the men for what they had done even as they cheered him to the skies.

Hardly anyone on the captured heights gave serious thought to pursuing the Confederates that night. The adrenaline that had propelled the Union soldiers up the slope had worn off. All they wanted to do was rest, eat a hot meal, and savor their triumph. Their leaders were of a like mind. They felt the army had done enough for one day.

Phil Sheridan was the only general intent on harrying the retreating rebels. Acting on his own initiative, he led his division down the hill in the direction of Chickamauga Station. Advancing through the dusk, Sheridan's troops captured nine pieces of Confederate artillery and several hundred dazed stragglers. A half mile east of Missionary Ridge, they ran into organized resistance. Fifteen hundred Southern troops had occupied a blocking position on the road leading to Chickamauga Station. The Federals swooped down on this detachment and dislodged it. The way was now open for an attack on Bragg's supply depot, a stroke Sheridan believed would finish off the Confederate army. He did not think his division could do the job by itself, however, so around 8 P.M. he galloped back to Missionary Ridge to get help.

When he reached the ridge, he discovered that Grant and Thomas had returned to Chattanooga. Granger was the ranking officer present, and he had gone to sleep. Sheridan woke him and explained the situation, but the Fourth Corps commander refused to take action without clearing it first with his superiors. Sheridan kept agitating, and Granger finally told him to go forward on his own; reinforcements would be sent if he ran into serious trouble. Sheridan returned to his division at midnight and resumed the advance. Two hours later his troops reached Chickamauga Creek. The pugnacious Irishman wanted to cross the stream and attack the enemy, but again his lack of numbers gave him pause. Hoping to trick Granger into sending help, he ordered two of his regiments to simulate an engagement by firing volleys into the woods on the other side of the stream. The ruse failed. Granger did not respond, and Sheridan was forced to bivouac where he was. "I was much disappointed that my pursuit had not been supported, for I felt that great results were in store," he wrote years later. "Had the troops under Granger's command been pushed out with mine when Missionary Ridge was gained, we could have reached Chickamauga Station by 12 o'clock the night of the 25th . . . and worked incalculable danger to the Confederates."

As it was, Federal forces did not enter Chickamauga Station until noon on November 26. By then the graybacks had departed for Dalton, Georgia, twenty-five miles to the southeast. After rummaging through a mess of broken-down wagons, spiked cannons, and burning foodstuffs, the bluecoats also set out for Dalton, skirmishing with Cleburne's division, which was acting as the rear guard for Bragg's retreating army.

On the morning of the twenty-seventh, the lead elements of Hooker's corps entered Ringgold Gap, a narrow pass between White Oak Mountain and Taylor's Ridge, twelve miles northwest of Dalton. Several hours earlier, Cleburne had placed his infantrymen in well-concealed positions on either side of the gorge. Now they sprang an ambush, catching the unwary Yankees in a deadly crossfire. The survivors fell back, regrouped, came on again, and a ferocious battle erupted. For five hours the rebel division stood its ground, beating back repeated attacks by the much larger Federal force. When Cleburne was satisfied he had delayed Hooker long enough for the rest of the rebel army to reach Dalton, he signaled for his command to withdraw. Hooker made no effort to follow. After losing 509 soldiers, he was not interested in further combat.

Grant had had enough, too; on November 28 he abandoned the chase. "Had it not been for the imperative necessity of relieving Burnside, I would have pursued the broken and demoralized retreating enemy," he explained in his report on the Chattanooga campaign. "But my advices were that Burnside's supplies would only last until the 3rd of December. It was already getting late to afford the necessary relief."

Sherman took six divisions and departed for Knoxville posthaste, while Thomas and Hooker brought the rest of the Union army back to Chattanooga. Five days later word came that the Knoxville siege was over. Longstreet had assaulted Fort Sanders, the strongest of the Federal earthworks, and suffered a bloody repulse. Disheartened by this defeat and alarmed by news of Sherman's approach, he had ordered his men to retreat into the mountains along the Tennessee-Virginia border.

Sherman entered Knoxville on December 6. He was annoyed to discover that Burnside's soldiers were in better shape than his own. Contrary to the War Department's alarmist reports, they had never been in danger of starving. Unionists in the region had furnished them with enough beef, bacon, and cornmeal to ward off serious hunger. Leaving two divisions at Knoxville, Sherman returned to Chattanooga with the remaining four. "My troops are in excellent heart, ready for Atlanta or anywhere," he informed Grant.

Grant considered a campaign against Atlanta impractical at present. Northern Georgia was mountainous, the roads there were terrible this time of year, and the countryside was too impoverished to support an invading army. An advance would have to wait until the weather improved and enough supplies had been accumulated to sustain the army for at least six months.

Delighted with what Grant had already accomplished, Washington accepted his decision to forgo a winter offensive without complaint. "Understanding that your lodgment at Chattanooga and Knoxville is now secure," Lincoln wrote him on December 8, "I wish to tender you and all under your command my more than thanks, my profoundest gratitude for the skill, courage, and perseverance with which you and they, over so great difficulties, have effected that important object. God bless you all."

Northern newspapers were even more effusive. "Gen. Grant is one of the great soldiers of the age," gushed the New York *Herald,* while the New York *World* hailed his "wondrous" tactics, which had produced that rarity of rarities, a victory "not coupled with news of a great and terrible slaughter."

Grant knew that these accolades were undeserved. The contest had not gone according to his plan. ("Damn the battle; I had nothing to do with it," he purportedly said after the successful storming of Missionary Ridge.) But whether his generalship had contributed anything to the final outcome or not, the fact remained that forces under his command had triumphed in one of the most important engagements of the war. At a cost of just 5,824 casualties, they had smashed the Army of Tennessee, cemented Union control of the Volunteer State, and opened the door for a war-ending invasion of the Southern heartland.

General Ulysses S. Grant.
(Library of Congress)

The fruits of defeat were bitter for Braxton Bragg. The number of Confederates killed and wounded at Orchard Knob, Lookout Mountain, Missionary Ridge, and Ringgold Gap was 2,521, a comparatively modest total. But the number taken prisoner, 4,146, was huge. Given the manpower shortage in the Confederacy, these losses would be almost impossible to make up. The same was true of artillery and small arms. Forty cannons and more than 7,000 rifles had been left behind when the Army of Tennessee retreated, weapons that the South's overburdened arsenals would be hard-pressed to replace.

Then there was the matter of morale. "For the first time during our struggle for national independence our defeat is chargeable to the troops themselves and not to the blunders and incompetency of their leaders," lamented the Richmond *Daily Dispatch*. This was stretching things a bit. With a few notable exceptions, Confederate leadership at Chattanooga had been extremely poor. But there was no getting around the fact that thousands of veteran soldiers had fled from perfectly defensible positions, quitting a contest they easily could have won.

Bragg tried to account for this and found he could not. "No satisfactory excuse can possibly be given for the shameful conduct of our troops," he wrote in his report of the battle. "The position was one which ought to have been held by a line of skirmishers against any assaulting column."

As he continued to brood about the Missionary Ridge debacle, Bragg came to the realization that he had to shoulder the responsibility himself. In a private letter to President Davis, he referred to the rout as "my shameful discomfiture" and declared: "The disaster admits of no palliation and is justly disparaging to me. . . . I fear we both erred in the conclusion for me to retain command here after the clamor raised against me."

Davis agreed. When Bragg submitted his resignation on November 29, the president accepted it. After eleven months of defeat, retreat, and lost opportunities, the Army of Tennessee was finally going to get a new leader. Officers and men rejoiced, hoping for better days under a different general. But many in the ranks knew the change was coming too late. At Chattanooga they had lost more than a battle: they had lost the war.

SEVENTEEN

THE NEW RECKONING

The people of the North had barely had time to read the headlines proclaiming victory at Missionary Ridge, when startling news arrived from Virginia: the Army of the Potomac, thought to have gone into hibernation following its early-November push across the Rappahannock, was on the move again, trying to crush Lee's force before the arrival of winter precluded further campaigning.

Meade's decision to attack had been precipitated by intelligence reports putting enemy troop strength at less than half his total, and by a newfound aggressiveness spawned by his recent successes at Bristoe Station and Kelly's Ford. On November 25, after a week of intensive planning, he alerted his five corps commanders to be ready for action at six o'clock the following morning. The Army of the Potomac would cross the Rapidan River at Jacob's, Germanna, and Ely's Fords, advance west along the Orange Turnpike, and pounce on Lee's right flank. Speed was essential, so Meade ordered the Union columns to travel light; only ammunition and ambulance wagons would accompany the troops on the march.

To Meade's intense irritation, the operation bogged down at the outset. Major General William H. French, who had succeeded Daniel Sickles as head of the Third Corps, was two hours late leaving his assembly area. When he finally arrived at Jacob's Ford, he discovered that the opposite bank was too steep for artillery to ascend. He sent his batteries downstream to Germanna Ford, causing a traffic jam there. His infantry did not get across the river until nightfall, throwing the offensive badly off schedule.

Anxious to make amends, French started out bright and early on November 27. But his column took a wrong turn, got lost, and had to backtrack, snarling traffic once again. It was early afternoon before the mess was

General George G. Meade (third from left) and staff. (Library of Congress)

straightened out. By then Lee had discovered what was afoot and deployed his army for battle. The position he selected was a wooded ridge on the west bank of Mine Run, a creek flowing north into the Rapidan. He ordered his troops to dig rifle pits, build breastworks, and clear fields of fire on this commanding elevation.

Although his battle plan had been ruined by French's bungling, Meade decided to engage the enemy anyway, counting on his two-to-one numerical advantage to carry the day. He massed the Army of the Potomac's fifteen divisions along the east bank of Mine Run and began searching for a chink in the rebel defenses.

It was not until the night of November 29 that a weak spot was found and a course of action settled upon. The Second Corps under Gouverneur Warren was to attack the Confederate right flank at 8 A.M. on November 30. Once its assault got rolling, the Sixth Corps, led by John Sedgwick, would strike the Confederate left.

Lee anticipated the Union commander's gambit, and daybreak on the thirtieth revealed a formidable new line of entrenchments directly in front of the Second Corps. Warren looked at these fortifications through a spyglass, then sent word to headquarters that the attack should be canceled. Meade was irate when he received this message, but after riding to Warren's position and studying the situation himself, he agreed with his subordinate and directed the troops to stand down.

Lee kept his soldiers behind their breastworks for another twenty-four hours, hoping Meade would change his mind and try a frontal assault after all. When it became apparent he would not, Lee decided to go over to the offensive. Cavalry patrols reported that the Union left was in the air, so two of A. P. Hill's divisions were pulled out of the Mine Run line and sent southeast with orders to fall on the exposed flank at dawn on December 2. A second Chancellorsville was what Lee had in mind, except that this time the bluecoats would not be saved by darkness as they had been back in May.

It was not to be. When Hill's soldiers started forward at first light on the second, they discovered that the Army of the Potomac was gone; it had slipped away unnoticed during the night. Lee ordered an immediate pursuit, but Meade's columns had a twelve-hour head start. They were safely across the Rapidan before the rebels could overtake them.

So ended the Mine Run campaign, the last major military operation of 1863. The opposing armies went into winter quarters, while their commanders pondered the might-have-beens. Meade blamed French for the failure of his strategy, but he harbored no illusions about whom Washington would call to task. "I am conscious that my head is off," he glumly told a friend. "There will be a great howl." The howl came, but contrary to his prediction, he was not forced to relinquish his post. Lincoln thought about making a change, then decided against it. "I do not think it would do to bring Grant away from the West," he wrote a few days after the Mine Run standoff. The other two candidates he had in mind—Sherman and Baldy Smith—were not compelling enough to warrant Meade's ouster. The status quo would prevail at Army of the Potomac headquarters, at least until next spring.

Lee was frustrated by the lack of vigilance that had allowed the Yankees to escape on the night of December 1. His staff was critical of Hill and Early, intimating that Jackson and Longstreet would have done better. Lee refused to fault his subordinates, however. He held himself accountable instead. "I am too old to command this army," he said sadly. "We should never have permitted those people to get away."

News of another escape electrified both North and South during the last week of November: John Hunt Morgan, confined to a cell in the Ohio State Penitentiary at Columbus for the past four months, had made a daring break for freedom on the night of the twenty-seventh.

It was one of Morgan's subordinates, Captain Thomas Hines, who had come up with the idea of digging a tunnel. During a conversation with a guard, he had learned that a ventilation shaft ran beneath the floor of the cell block where the Confederate general and sixty-seven of his followers were confined. The next day he smuggled two table knives out of the dining hall, and after lights out he and his cellmates started chipping away at the concrete slab. Powdered debris was placed inside the firebox of a stove, while larger chunks were hidden in the prisoners' mattresses. The hole was covered with personal belongings during the daytime, and as inspections were infrequent and perfunctory, the opening went undiscovered.

It took three nights to break through the six-inch-thick floor and gain entry to the air shaft below. The knives were then replaced with a shovel stolen from the prison coal pile, and the excavating began in earnest. The tunnel would surface in an exercise yard lying between the cell block and the prison's twenty-five-foot-high outer wall. To surmount this barrier, Calvin Morgan, the general's brother, braided a thirty-foot-long rope from strips of bedding and attached a hook fashioned from a piece of stove iron to one end. When the time came, the hook would be tossed over the top of the wall and pulled taut against the coping, permitting the men to climb over.

The tunnel was completed on November 20, and the final details of the escape plan were worked out. To minimize the chances of detection, it was decided that no more than six men would accompany General Morgan, and that once outside the prison they would head for Kentucky. A discarded newspaper provided information about rail service to Cincinnati. A train departed Columbus every morning at one o'clock and arrived in the Queen City before dawn. It was agreed that Morgan and Captain Hines would catch this train while the other fugitives headed southwest on foot or horseback, following different routes to throw off pursuers.

The night of November 27 was chosen for the attempt. After the turnkey had finished his midnight bed check, the seven escapees entered the tunnel, burrowed through the last few feet of soil at its end, and emerged into the exercise yard. Much to their delight, they discovered that the sentries who normally patrolled the prison perimeter were inside seeking shelter from a rainstorm. The rope and hook worked perfectly, and in a matter of minutes the men were over the wall and dispersing into the streets of Columbus.

Morgan and Hines went straight to the railroad station. Arriving in Cincinnati a few hours later, they crossed the Ohio River in a skiff, obtained horses from a friend, and galloped south into the Bluegrass State. By the time the authorities in Columbus discovered they were missing, the pair were in Boone County, Kentucky, more than 120 miles from the penitentiary. In the days that followed, they continued to put more distance between themselves and the Union cavalry patrols that were hunting them. Two of their comrades were recaptured in Louisville, but the general and the captain managed to evade detection. Riding steadily southward, they crossed the Cumberland River near Burkesville, Kentucky, pushed on as far as Livingston, Tennessee, then headed east, not stopping until they reached the safe haven of North Carolina.

Word that Morgan would rejoin the Confederate army after spending Christmas with his wife was cause for rejoicing in the South. But the hoopla surrounding his getaway could not disguise the fact that the year was drawing to a dismal close. A quick look at a map revealed how dire the military situation had become. The Mississippi Valley was gone, eliminating Texas, Louisiana, and Arkansas from the strategic equation. Tennessee had been lost for good, and Grant's Yankees were poised to drive toward Atlanta and the sea. In Virginia the battle lines had shifted hardly at all, but the lack of movement was misleading. Bled white in the epic struggles of the spring and summer, Lee's army was no longer capable of offensive warfare; safeguarding Richmond was all it could do. It was a far cry from the early days of 1863, when victory had seemed within the South's grasp. Now the best that could be hoped for was to stave off defeat, and with the Confederate economy a shambles, foreign intervention doubtful, and the North stronger and more determined than ever, that looked like a futile objective.

"I have never actually despaired of the cause, priceless, holy as it is, but my faith in [it] is daily weakened," Robert G. H. Kean confessed in his diary. "Steadfastness is yielding to a sense of hopelessness. The country has lost all confidence . . . and the prospect grows more and more gloomy."

In the North in the waning days of 1863, there was a growing sense that the war's outcome was no longer in doubt. Grant, Sherman, and Thomas were names spoken with immense pride—they were the killer generals who would administer the death blow to the rebellion. Another name was being spoken as well: Abraham Lincoln. Little by little the country was awakening to the fact that he was a great president. James Russell Lowell, poet, professor of modern languages at Harvard, and sometime critic of the man in the White House, expressed this sentiment in an article he was writing for the January 1864 issue of the *North American Review*. The Union was going to be saved, he declared, "mainly due to the good sense, the good humor, the sagacity, the large-mindedness, and the unselfish honesty of the unknown man whom a blind fortune, as it seems, has lifted from the crowd to the most dangerous and difficult eminence of modern times. . . . If we wish to appreciate him, we have only to conceive the inevitable chaos in which we should now be weltering, had a weak man or an unwise one been chosen in his stead."

The recipient of this compliment was in no condition to enjoy it. Within twenty-four hours of his return from Gettysburg, Lincoln had been stricken with what doctors at first thought was a cold. Then a rash appeared on his body, a high fever set in, and it was announced that he was ill with varioloid, a mild form of smallpox. Although his life was not in danger, he would be quarantined in the White House for the next three weeks, under physician's orders to conduct as little public business as possible.

Once the worst of the symptoms subsided, the president found that he rather enjoyed being an invalid. For the first time in two and a half years he was spared the ceaseless importuning of office-seekers. They had fled the Executive Mansion upon learning of his malady, which was too bad, he joked, because he finally had something he could give everybody. Heeding his doctor's advice, he rested as much as possible, but the best medicine, he found, was reading the dispatches describing Grant's victory at Chattanooga and the subsequent lifting of the Knoxville siege. "This is one of the most important gains of the war," he told John Nicolay as he sat propped up with pillows, studying a military map. Of the three great strategic objectives he had set at the beginning of the year, two—opening the Mississippi and liberating east Tennessee—had been achieved. The third—destruction of the Army of Northern Virginia and capture of Richmond—was well on its way to being realized.

He could foresee the collapse of the Confederacy, and that eventuality had him thinking about what would happen when the fighting was over. Bringing the South back into the Union would involve a host of complicated, politically explosive issues. Among the questions to be answered, three were particularly thorny: Had the rebellious states, in a strictly legal sense, remained in the Union all along, or by engaging in the treasonable act of secession, had they reverted to the condition of territories? Would Congress or the Executive have jurisdiction over reconstruction? Should freed slaves be granted citizenship and the right to vote?

Radical and conservative Republicans were already debating these points. In a piece published in the October issue of the *Atlantic Monthly,* Senator Charles Sumner had staked out the radical position, contending that the Confederate states had ceased to exist when they rebelled and should therefore be ruled by Congress under its constitutional authority to govern territories. He advocated enfranchisement of emancipated Negroes and distribution of confiscated land to Union soldiers, poor Southern whites, and black freedmen.

The conservative response came from Postmaster General Montgomery Blair in a speech delivered at Rockville, Maryland, on October 3. The reconstruction program favored by Sumner and his fellow abolitionists would lead to intermingling of the races, Blair warned. Loyal white Southerners should be permitted to form new state governments; each seceded state would then be restored to its place in the councils of the nation with all its former attributes and rights intact. Blair also argued that the president, not a legislative committee, should set the terms under which this process went forward.

The intraparty squabble over reconstruction did not worry Lincoln. He was confident that conservative Republicans, for all their insistence that Southern whites be permitted to direct their own affairs, did not wish to see the secessionist element brought back into the national government. Nor did he think the radicals really wanted to rule the Southern states as conquered provinces, their vengeful rhetoric notwithstanding. Keeping former rebels from outvoting the loyal minority was the most important thing, he believed; otherwise the Confederate oligarchy would remain in power, and the war would have been fought in vain. On that point he was sure there would be no disagreement among his Republican colleagues.

During the quiet, distraction-free days of his convalescence, Lincoln began drafting a Proclamation of Amnesty and Reconstruction. In it he spelled out his plan for bringing the South back into the nation. The linchpin was an offer of full pardon to all rebels (excluding Confederate government officials, high-ranking army and navy officers, former U.S. congressmen and judges, and individuals found guilty of mistreating Union prisoners of war) who took an oath of loyalty to the United States and pledged to obey its laws and proclamations regarding slavery. This would avert any attempt at re-enslaving the newly freed blacks, he explained. Once 10 percent of the electorate in a seceded state had taken the loyalty oath, it could establish a state government, which would be recognized as legitimate by his administration. It would be up to the legislative branch to decide whether to seat the senators and representatives elected from those states.

Lincoln appended the Proclamation of Amnesty and Reconstruction to his Annual Message to Congress, which was to convene on Monday, December 7. As he worked on the document in the sanctuary of his sickroom, he found himself harking back to last year's message and reflecting on the remarkable transformation the past twelve months had wrought. The war, which many in the North had given up as lost, was now almost won. The Copperheads had been vanquished at the polls. Emancipation

Abraham Lincoln, November 8, 1863.
(Chicago Historical Society)

and black enlistment were now a reality, accepted, if not embraced, by a majority of the Northern public. "Thus we have the new reckoning," he wrote. "The crisis which threatened to divide the friends of the Union is past."

In conclusion, he urged Congress and the country to remain focused on the task at hand. "In the midst of other cares," he declared, "we must not lose sight of the fact that the war power is still our main reliance. To that power alone can we look yet for a time."

On December 8 Lincoln sent his message and the appended amnesty proclamation up to Capitol Hill. The response was overwhelmingly positive. Radical and conservative Republicans alike declared his reconstruction plan highly satisfactory. "We only wanted a leader to speak the bold word; it is done, and all can follow," enthused one listener. John Hay, taking the pulse of the House and Senate immediately after the reading of the address, could scarcely believe the effect it had produced. "Men talked as if the millennium had come," he reported. "All day the tide of congratulation ran on." Outside of Washington reaction was also favorable. A few antiwar newspapers attacked the message, but most of the press applauded it.

Lincoln savored the praise. It was intensely satisfying after the strident criticism he had been subjected to most of the year, and he felt no small measure of pride in what he had accomplished, militarily and politically. "I am very glad, that I have not, by native depravity, or under evil influences, done anything bad enough to prevent the good result," he wrote a Republican senator. Renomination and re-election to a second term, events that had seemed unthinkable a few months ago, now looked like distinct possibilities.

Jefferson Davis's annual message to the Confederate Congress, which like its Northern counterpart reconvened on December 7, was published concurrently with Lincoln's. The contrast between the two documents was stark. Where Lincoln was emboldened by Union victories to begin plan-

ning for the postwar period, Davis was impelled by Confederate defeats to
do everything in his power to prolong the struggle. Hence the truculent
tone of his message, in which he accused the Yankees of perpetrating
ghastly atrocities in their effort to subjugate the South. "Having begun the
war in direct violation of their Constitution . . . they have been hardened
by crime until they no longer attempt to veil their purpose to destroy the
institutions and subvert the sovereignty and independence of these States,"
he railed. "We know now that the only hope for peace is in the vigor of
our resistance."

Violent as Davis's words were, they drew scant notice in the rebel press.
The editors were more interested in excoriating Lincoln's amnesty proclamation. "We who have committed no offense, need no forgiveness," spat
the Richmond *Sentinel*. "How impudent it is to come, with our brothers'
blood upon his accursed hands, and ask us to accept his forgiveness!" The
Confederate Congress considered a resolution denouncing "the imbecile
and unprincipled usurper," but tabled it on the grounds that "the true and
only treatment which that miserable and contemptible despot . . . should
receive at the hands of this House is silent and unmitigated contempt."

Silence was something the legislators were incapable of, however. They
continued to spew vituperation at the Yankee president, and the shrillness
of their oratory showed that his proclamation had cut them to the quick.
They were excluded from his offer of amnesty and could expect personal
ruin, or worse, if the plan ever went into effect. It was rumored that public officials would be hanged for treason if the North triumphed. With this
grim specter haunting their deliberations, the congressmen lashed out not
only at Lincoln but at Davis, whom they blamed for the loss of Mississippi
and Tennessee. The Confederate president was guilty of "gross misconduct
in retaining his favorites in office, and with partialities and prejudices
which, if persisted in longer, will prove fatal to our cause," charged Tennessee representative Henry S. Foote. He called for an investigation of the
Vicksburg and Chattanooga defeats and demanded to know who Bragg's
successor would be.

Davis was trying to repair the damage done by the Chattanooga
calamity, but it was difficult given his limited options. Hardee had declined
to take command of the Army of Tennessee on a permanent basis, and
Lee, who now, as before, was the president's first choice for the post, refused
to leave Virginia. That left Beauregard and Johnston, generals Davis detested. Unable to stomach the idea of promoting either one, he summoned
Lee to Richmond on December 8 and spent the next week trying to convince him to go to Georgia. Lee resisted, however, holding to his belief that
someone else should head the Army of Tennessee. He urged the appointment of Johnston, as did a majority of the president's cabinet. On Decem-

ber 16 Davis reluctantly agreed. With misgiving to the end, he gave the command to a soldier whose specialty was retreat. It was yet another sign of the Confederacy's rapid slide toward the abyss.

Christmas in Richmond. For the fortunate few who were very wealthy, the holiday provided an occasion for entertaining in a style reminiscent of antebellum times. At the home of Colonel and Mrs. John Preston, the menu included oyster soup, boiled mutton, ham, boned turkey, wild duck, partridge, and plum pudding. Sauterne and burgundy were the dinner wines, with sherry and Madeira served afterward. The guest of honor was John Bell Hood, still convalescing from his Gettysburg and Chickamauga wounds. With his left arm in a sling and his right trouser leg flapping empty, the tall, blond-bearded general was carried into the drawing room and placed on a settee with an afghan draped over his stump. Young ladies fluttered around him, some looking "as if it would be a luxury to pull out their handkerchiefs and have a good cry," others plying him with orange slices. "The money value of friendship is easily counted now," a cynical onlooker remarked. "Oranges are five dollars apiece." Reflecting on this party and others she had attended during the holiday period, diarist Mary Chesnut was appalled by the heedless frivolity. "God help my country!" she exclaimed. "I think we are like the sailors who break into the spirits closet when they find out the ship must sink. There seems to be for the first time a resolute determination to enjoy the brief hour, and never look beyond the day."

The vast majority of Richmonders could only dream of a Christmas dinner as sumptuous as the one served by the Prestons. Even the old holiday standby, eggnog, was prohibitively expensive, with milk costing twenty dollars a gallon and brandy thirty dollars a quart. "It is a sad Christmas," sighed John B. Jones. "I shall have no turkey today, and do not covet one. It is no time for feasting."

At St. Paul's Episcopal Church, a visiting bishop preached the homily, telling the congregation that "He who was a man of sorrows and acquainted with grief, who had not where to lay his head, and was hated without a cause, knew how to sympathize with us, who have not a friend or ally on earth." Parishioner Jefferson Davis was comforted by these words. Robert E. Lee, who was also a member of St. Paul's, was not. He had returned to his field headquarters near Orange Court House on December 21. With no action imminent he could have spent Christmas in Richmond with his wife, but his sense of duty would not permit it. If his soldiers had to celebrate the holiday without their loved ones, then so must he.

On Belle Isle, a windswept speck of land in the middle of the James River, a mile southwest of Richmond's Capitol Square, 6,300 Union prisoners of war passed the day shivering in their dirty, overcrowded tent camp. "We did not get anything to eat until eight o'clock at night," Iowan John Whitten recorded in his diary, "and then nothing but turnips."

The patients at Chimborazo Military Hospital on the city's eastern outskirts fared considerably better. Matron Phoebe Yates Pember had solicited donations from the community and was able to serve a dozen turkeys, seven gallons of oysters, and twenty-four gallons of eggnog to her delighted charges.

At the Executive Mansion on East Clay Street, the president and his family dined frugally. The Davises bought their own food and thus felt the pinch of inflation just as ordinary folk did. When the meal was finished, the children played hide-and-seek while their parents sat before the fire. For the president the pleasure of being in the bosom of his family was not enough to banish his melancholy. Critics in Congress and the press were hounding him unmercifully, and their savage rhetoric seemed to be resonating with the public. A few days earlier a bullet had whistled past his head while he took his customary late-afternoon horseback ride. Was it an assassination attempt or merely a random shooting? Davis professed not to know or care, but the incident had upset him more than he let on. He no longer felt safe in his own capital, and henceforward he would be accompanied by bodyguards whenever he went riding.

Christmas Day at Mount Pisgah Church, Virginia. "Ground covered with snow, and very cold," wrote Henry Berkeley, an artilleryman in the Army of Northern Virginia. "Camp very quiet. Our dinner consisted of some soldier-bread and black rice and a piece of salted beef about two inches square. The beef not being worth dividing, we cast lots for it. John Lewis Berkeley won and ate it. The rest of us, five in number, ate our rice and bread. The Hardy boys and George Bray got merry about dark. A little applejack had gotten into camp."

It was a cold, dreary Christmas at the Confederate hospital in Newnan, Georgia. "Just at peep of dawn," wrote nurse Kate Cumming, "the little gallery in front of our house was crowded with wounded. The scene was worthy of a picture; many of them without a leg or an arm. . . . I constantly hear the unmarried ones wondering if the girls will marry them

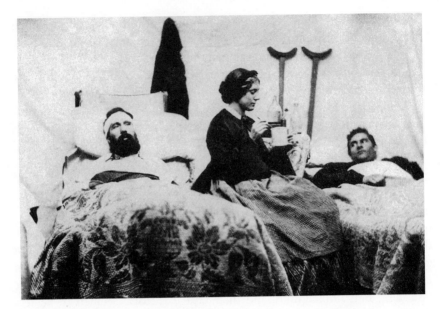

*A military hospital. (Courtesy Massachusetts Commandery Military
Order of the Loyal Legion and U.S. Army Military History Institute)*

now. Dr. Hughes did his best to have a nice dinner for the convalescents and nurses. . . . I only wish the men in the army could have fared as well."

Christmas night in Lamar County, Texas. "The day has passed most quietly, not a cake, not a visitor," Kate Stone recorded in her journal. "We did have an eggnog, but only the servants enjoyed it. Made of mean whiskey, it smacked of Texas. . . . [This] morning when dear little Beverly raised up in bed and saw only some homemade toys in her stocking, she hid her head, sobbing. . . . Aunt Laura told her how bad that was, and that poor Santa Claus had done his best, but he could not pass through the Yankee lines."

Santa had no trouble finding his way to Cincinnati. A newspaperman strolling through the shopping district was amazed by the cornucopia of merchandise for sale. "The catalogue includes books splendidly bound in morocco and gold, jewelry costlier than ever before witnessed in this city, furs from the polar regions, silks, velvets, and articles that would augur badly for the children's monopoly of the holiday, were it not for the endless variety of toys that everywhere meet the eye," he wrote.

The only hint that the nation was at war was the ubiquity of military miniatures. Batteries of tin artillery, regiments of tin infantry, and squadrons of tin cavalry fought bloodless battles on counters and in display cases. No one thought it in poor taste. "If young America does not rejoice this year as never before, it will not be the fault of our storekeepers," the reporter declared, consigning to journalistic oblivion the tens of thousands of orphans the year's fighting had created.

In New York, too, Christmas was an occasion for conspicuous consumption. Shoppers flush with cash crowded into Macy's and Alexander Stewart's. A forest of evergreen trees lined the sidewalks of Barclay, Vesey, and Fulton Streets; turkeys, geese, oysters, and venison filled the marketplaces. "Everything is twice as dear as it was last year, and as twice as much of everything is bought, some idea may be formed of the abundance of money," an observer wrote.

Entertainments of all kinds drew overflow crowds. Productions of *Faust, Ione,* and *Don Giovanni* were sold out, as were Christmas concerts by the New York Philharmonic and performances of the hit play *Ticket-of-Leave Man.* For those with less-refined tastes, Van Amburg's Menagerie, the Broadway Circus, and Barnum's Museum filled the bill.

On Christmas Day an estimated 100,000 New Yorkers went ice skating on the frozen ponds of Central Park. "For a war-ridden people, for a tax-burdened people, for a calamity-stricken people, we are the lightest-hearted, the most thoughtless, reckless people in the world," bragged the editor of *Frank Leslie's Illustrated Newspaper.* "These holiday times have proved a perfect carnival of pleasure."

Christmas week, Camp Sedgwick, Virginia. "We are quiet in our winter quarters," wrote Elisha Rhodes of the Second Rhode Island. "The men have built huts of logs, and we are very comfortable. . . . Tonight we have had a meeting of the officers to decide whether we are willing to remain in service after [our enlistments expire]. . . . I decided without hesitation. I am young and in good health, and I feel that I owe a duty to my country. I entered the army as a private, expecting that the war would end in a few months. It has dragged along, and no one can tell when the end will come. But when it does come, I want to see it, and so I am going to stay."

Christmas Day, Charleston. Beginning at 1 A.M., Union shells slammed into the city at the rate of one every ten minutes. The pealing of church bells calling worshipers to Christmas services was drowned out by the crash of explosions and the clanging of fire alarms. At midnight, when the bombardment finally ceased, one civilian was dead, eight were wounded, and ten buildings had burned to the ground.

In Washington the only projectiles people had to duck were popping champagne corks. "Gayety has become as epidemic this winter as gloom was last winter," marveled Frederick Seward, the secretary of state's son. "A year ago [father] was 'heartless' or 'unpatriotic' because he gave dinners; now the only complaint of him is that he don't have dancing."

Adding zest to the holiday social whirl was the arrival in the capital of a large delegation of Russian naval officers. Czar Alexander had sent his fleet across the Atlantic on a goodwill mission, and the major cities of the Northeast were competing to see which could offer the most extravagant reception. In mid-November New York had feted the visitors with a parade down Broadway and a ball at the Academy of Music—a dazzling affair at which the guests consumed 12,000 oysters, 1,200 game birds, 250 turkeys, 400 chickens, 1,000 pounds of tenderloin, 100 pyramids of pastry, 1,000 loaves of bread, and 3,500 bottles of wine. Now it was Washington's turn to host the Russians, and the round of parties, receptions, and dinners given in their honor was lavish even by the capital's sybaritic standards. For those not fortunate enough to be invited to one of these soirees, there were daily sightseeing tours of the fleet, which was anchored in the Potomac near Alexandria. Most evenings groups of Russian sailors—"fiendishly ugly" and possessed of "vast absorbent powers," wrote John Hay—could be seen drinking in the bars on Pennsylvania Avenue.

Washington society hoped that a ball, bigger and more brilliant than the one given in New York, would be held at the White House before the Russians departed. But the Lincolns did not cooperate. The president was still recovering from his bout with varioloid, and the first lady was busy caring for her half sister, Emilie Todd Helm, whose husband, Confederate general Benjamin Hardin Helm, had been killed at Chickamauga.

"Little Sister," as the Lincolns called Emilie, was welcomed at the White

House with open arms, but her loyalty to the South soon became a source of friction. The president tried to keep her visit a secret, fearing an uproar if the public learned that the widow of a high-ranking rebel was a guest at the Executive Mansion. Word leaked out anyway, and Dan Sickles, who had been on leave in Washington since his maiming at Gettysburg, confronted Lincoln. "You should not have that woman in your house!" he shouted, pounding a table in anger. Lincoln froze him with an icy glare. "Excuse me, General," he said, "my wife and I are in the habit of choosing our own guests. We do not need from our friends either advice or assistance in the manner."

Realizing that she was an embarrassment to her brother-in-law, Emilie left for Kentucky soon thereafter. Before she departed, the president took her aside and with tears in his eyes said he hoped she did not blame him for the loss of her husband.

No, she replied, it was the fortunes of war. Lincoln embraced her, and they both wept.

Two days after Christmas Joseph Johnston arrived in Dalton, Georgia, to take command of the Army of Tennessee. He had been pleasantly surprised when he received the telegram informing him of his new assignment, but after inspecting the wreck of an army Bragg had left him, his enthusiasm evaporated. When he read the letter of instructions Jefferson Davis had sent on December 23, he was even more discomfited: The commander in chief wanted an offensive launched as soon as possible. It was a preposterous order, one that suggested the president was losing touch with reality. The Army of Tennessee was too weak to attack the Federals at Chattanooga, and it could not be reinforced without drawing troops from Virginia or South Carolina, thereby hazarding the loss of Richmond or Charleston. Nor could conscription be counted on to replenish the ranks. There simply were not enough able-bodied men left in the South.

"Your Excellency well impresses upon me the importance of recovering the territory we have lost," Johnston wrote to Davis, his pen dripping sarcasm, "but difficulties appear to me in the way."

No one better understood the consequences of the South's manpower woes than the frontline combat commanders. One such officer was Patrick Cleburne. On December 31 he wrote a memorandum proposing a startling solution to the problem of insufficient troops. Why not, he asked, enlist the South's male slaves, promising freedom to them and their families in exchange for their service? This action would not only rejuvenate the armies of the Confederacy, it "would remove forever all selfish taint from our cause and place independence above every question of property. The very magnitude of the sacrifice itself, such as no nation has ever voluntarily made before, would appall our enemies . . . and fill our hearts with a pride and singleness of purpose which would clothe us with new strength in battle."

He intended to present his paper at a meeting of the Army of Tennessee's general staff the day after New Year's. He knew his suggestion would be controversial, but he believed his colleagues could be persuaded to support it. "As between the loss of independence and the loss of slavery," he wrote in conclusion, "I assume that every patriot will freely give up the latter—give up the negro slave rather than be a slave himself."

He would soon find out just how wrong he was.

In the encampment of the Fifty-fourth Massachusetts on Morris Island, preparations were under way to commemorate the one-year anniversary of the Emancipation Proclamation. Sergeant William Gray, who would be the featured speaker at the New Year's Day ceremony, sat by his tent, composing his remarks. "It is something to deck the pages of history, that on South Carolina soil the race that her laws have been studiously framed to oppress . . . stand upright as living men, with irresistible arguments in their hands, to make their liberty permanent," he wrote. "Yes, we have cause to rejoice . . . for the steps we have taken can never be retraced, the mite we have gained can never be snatched from our tenacious grasp."

It was a cold, dismal New Year's Eve in the Confederate camp at Mount Pisgah Church, Virginia. Artilleryman Henry Berkeley squatted in his musty hut, writing in his diary by candlelight. "It rained hard toward evening," he scrawled. "We drew some coffee, sugar, and peaches today. Have not had any of these for a long time. The old year will soon die. Let it die, with its bloody record of battles, deaths, devastated homes, and vacant chairs!"

New Year's Eve, New York City. John Templeton Strong sat beside a crackling fire in the study of his Gramercy Park townhouse, sipping brandy and reflecting on the events of the past twelve months. "Eighteen sixty-three is now *in extremis,*" he wrote. "It has proved a far better year for the country than it promised at its birth. If its nascent successor proves half as propitious to the national cause, it will witness the downfall of rebellion."

At Hascosea Plantation in Halifax County, North Carolina, Catherine Edmonston spent December 31 in her work room, listening to the wind howl and the rain beat on the roof. "It seems as though the year is going out in tears for the sorrow and misery which it has brought us," she remarked in her journal. "So dies 1863!—a year of calamity and distress the like of which God grant may never fall to our lot either as individuals or members of the community to see again. We look back to it as to a time of horror, but nevertheless God has sustained us through it all, and in its fullness have we tasted the fulfillment of His promise: 'As thy days, so shall thy strength be.' "

In Washington a cold rain also fell. It drenched Pennsylvania Avenue, formed deep puddles on the muddy expanse of the Mall, and sluiced off the plates of the Capitol's new cast-iron dome.

Several weeks earlier thousands of citizens had congregated to witness

The Capitol dome under construction, 1863. (Library of Congress)

the completion of this spectacular structure, which had been under construction for ten years. The president had been criticized for pushing ahead with the project when men and money were needed for the war effort, but he had insisted it was the proper thing to do. "If the people see the Capitol going on," he said, "it is a sign we intend the Union shall go on."

And so the work had continued. Northern military fortunes had waxed and waned, and Washington had weathered political crises too numerous to count, but all the while the dazzling white dome had risen higher. Finally, on a raw December day in 1863, all that remained to be done was to hoist the crowning statue, Thomas Crawford's *Freedom Triumphant in War and Peace,* to the top of the cupola. No formal ceremony was planned, but a large crowd gathered anyway, drawn by the potent symbolism of the occasion. The Capitol—"the ark of the American covenant"—was about to be made whole again. If it could be torn apart and rebuilt, bigger, stronger, and more magnificent than ever, then so too could the nation.

One after another the sections of the sixteen-and-a-half-foot-high statue were drawn skyward, swung into position, and bolted together. Crawford had depicted Freedom as a helmeted goddess, carrying a shield in one hand and a sword in the other, and as her majestic figure took shape inside the cage of scaffolding, the crowd grew more and more excited. At last there was only one piece left. At noon precisely a pulley whined, a wire cable snapped taut, and the great bronze head rose, hung suspended for a moment, then settled into place on the gleaming torso. Three sledgehammer strokes, and the job was done.

The Stars and Stripes ran up a flagstaff, the spectators cheered long and loud, and in the park east of the Capitol, a battery of artillery fired a salute of thirty-five guns, one for each state in the Union.

SOURCE NOTES

ABBREVIATED TITLES

BG   Henry Steele Commager, ed., *The Blue and the Gray: The Story of the Civil War as Told by the Participants,* 2 vols. (Indianapolis: 1950)

BL   Clarence C. Buell and Robert U. Johnson, eds., *Battles and Leaders of the Civil War,* 4 vols. (New York: 1888)

CH   Sam R. Watkins, *"Co. Aytch": A Sideshow of the Big Show* (Collier Civil War Classics edition, New York: 1962)

CWL   Abraham Lincoln (Roy P. Basler, ed.), *The Collected Works of Abraham Lincoln,* 9 vols. (New Brunswick, N.J.: 1952–55)

DGW   Gideon Welles, *Diary of Gideon Welles,* 3 vols. (New York: 1960)

DJH   John Hay (Tyler Dennett, ed.), *Lincoln and the Civil War in the Diaries and Letters of John Hay* (New York: 1939)

EG   William M. Lamers, *The Edge of Glory: A Biography of General William S. Rosecrans* (New York: 1961)

GMS   Bruce Catton, *Grant Moves South* (Boston: 1960)

GTC   Bruce Catton, *Grant Takes Command* (Boston: 1969)

ICW   David D. Porter, *Incidents and Anecdotes of the Civil War* (New York: 1885)

JD   William C. Davis, *Jefferson Davis: The Man and His Hour* (New York: 1991)

JDC   Jefferson Davis (Dunbar Rowland, ed.), *Jefferson Davis, Constitutionalist, His Letters, Papers and Speeches,* 10 vols. (Jackson, Miss.: 1923)

LL   Douglas Southall Freeman, *Lee's Lieutenants: A Study in Command,* 3 vols. (New York: 1942–44)

LWY   Carl Sandburg, *Abraham Lincoln: The War Years,* 4 vols. (New York: 1936–39)

MTWF   Wiley Sword, *Mountains Touched with Fire: Chattanooga Beseiged, 1863* (New York: 1995)

NCR   Bruce Catton, *Never Call Retreat* (Garden City, New York: 1965)

OR   *The War of the Rebellion: A Compilation of the Official Records of the Union and Confederate Armies,* 128 vols. (Washington: 1880–1900)

ORN   *Official Records of the Union and Confederate Navies in the War of the Rebellion,* 30 vols. (Washington: 1894–1922)

PMG   Ulysses S. Grant, *Personal Memoirs of U.S. Grant* (Bison Books edition, Lincoln, Neb.: 1996)

RCW   Charles A. Dana, *Recollections of the Civil War* (Collier Civil War Classics edition, New York: 1963)

REL   Douglas Southall Freeman, *R. E. Lee: A Biography*, 4 vols. (New York: 1934–35)

RR   Frank Moore, ed., *The Rebellion Record: A Diary of American Events*, 12 vols. (New York: 1864–68)

RWC   John B. Jones (Henry Swiggett, ed.), *A Rebel War Clerk's Diary at the Confederate States Capitol*, 2 vols. (New York: 1935)

TAW   *The Annals of the War Written by Leading Participants*, 3 vols. (Philadelphia: 1879)

TCW   Shelby Foote, *The Civil War: A Narrative*, 3 vols. (New York: 1958, 1963, 1974)

TFD   Arthur James Lyon Fremantle (Walter Lord, ed.), *The Fremantle Diary: Being the Journal of Lieutenant Colonel Arthur James Lyon Fremantle, Coldstream Guards, on His Three Months in the Southern States* (New York: 1954)

I. WE CANNOT ESCAPE HISTORY

p. 3   "Well, I guess," David Homer Bates, *Lincoln in the Telegraph Office* (New York: 1907), 41.

p. 5   "Would you shake," *LWY*-2:175.

p. 6   "The central idea," *DJH*:19.

p. 6   "The will of," *CWL*-5:403–404.

p. 7   "great eagle-scream," Jane Stuart Woolsey, "One Great Eagle Scream," *BG*-1:44.

p. 7   "The people," Wood Gray, *The Hidden Civil War: The Story of the Copperheads* (New York: 1942), 110.

p. 8   "I can't spare," Alexander K. McClure, *Lincoln and Men of War-Times* (Philadelphia: 1892), 193.

p. 9   "some time," Margaret Leech, *Reveille in Washington, 1861–1865* (New York: 1941), 220.

p. 11   "I certainly have," *CWL*-5:509–510.

p. 11   "His hair," Noah Brooks (P. J. Staudenraus, ed.), *Mr. Lincoln's Washington: Selections from Writings of Noah Brooks, Civil War Correspondent* (New York: 1967), 29.

p. 11   "I know," Salmon P. Chase, *Diary of S. P. Chase*, Vol. 2 (Washington: 1903), 87.

p. 12   "destroyed and replaced," Allan Nevins, *The War for the Union*, Vol. 2 (New York: 1960), 241.

p. 12   "The part assigned," *LWY*-2:306.

p. 13   " 'One generation,' " *CWL*-5:518–537.

II. A FAITHFUL SENTINEL

p. 15   "After an absence," *RR*-6:294–301.

p. 17   "At this critical," *TCW*-2:5.

p. 17   "The present alarming," *OR*-1-17-2:788.

p. 18   "Real Rio," Gilbert E. Govan and James W. Livingood, *A Different Valor: The Story of General Joseph E. Johnston* (Indianapolis: 1956), 169.

p. 18   "bleedings," Craig L. Symonds, *Joseph E. Johnston: A Civil War Biography* (New York: 1992), 174.

p. 19   "My God," *PMG*:388.

p. 19   "not a single," *CH*:49.

p. 20   "If the necessity," *TCW*-2:9.

p. 20   "What luck," Govan and Livingood, *A Different Valor,* 170.

p. 21   "a place," Lucy McCrae Bell, "A Girl's Experience in the Siege of Vicksburg,"
         Harper's Weekly, Vol. 56, June 8, 1912, 12.

p. 21   "We may take," *LWY*-2:106.

p. 22   "wanting in polish," *TCW*-1:776.

p. 22   "His want," *OR*-1-17-2:788.

p. 22   "He did not know," Varina Davis, *Jefferson Davis, Ex-President of the Confederate
         States. A Memoir by His Wife,* Vol. 2 (New York: 1890), 12.

p. 23   "Davis has fettered," Clifford Dowdey, *The Land They Fought For* (New York:
         1955), 157.

p. 23   "The issue," *RR*-6:294–301.

p. 24   "great truth," Thomas E. Schott, *Alexander Stephens of Georgia: A Biography* (Baton
         Rouge: 1988), 334.

                    CHAPTER 1. BLOW YE THE TRUMPET, BLOW

p. 29   "each and all," Washington, D.C. *National Intelligencer,* 1-2-63.

p. 31   "My gosh!" Brooks (Staudenraus, ed.), *Mr. Lincoln's Washington,* 59.

p. 31   "the breaking up," Kenneth W. Leish, *The White House* (New York: 1972), 50.

p. 31   "flub dubs," Benjamin B. French (Donald B. Cole and John J. McDonough, eds.),
         Witness to the Young Republic (Hanover, N.H.: 1989), 382.

p. 31   "To say," Herbert Mitgang, ed., *Lincoln as They Saw Him* (New York: 1956), 297.

p. 31   "like a man," Amy L. Jensen, *The White House and Its Thirty-five Families* (New
         York: 1970), 91.

p. 32   "By the President," *CWL*-6:28–30.

p. 32   "had all," Richard Hofstadter, *The American Political Tradition and the Men Who
         Made It* (New York: 1948), 131.

p. 32   "If my name," Charles M. Segal, ed., *Conversations with Lincoln* (New York: 1961),
         234–235.

p. 32   "like so many," *CWL*-1:260.

p. 33   "republican example," *CWL*-2:255.

p. 34   "Must a government," *CWL*-4:426.

p. 35   "I never," Segal, *Conversations with Lincoln,* 234–235.

p. 35   "That will do," F. B. Carpenter, *The Inner Life of Abraham Lincoln* (New York:
         1866), 21.

p. 35   "The word," Ralph Waldo Emerson, *Emerson's Works: Poems* (Boston: 1904),
         203–204.

p. 36   "It is far easier," Frank Donovan, *Mr. Lincoln's Proclamation* (New York: 1964),
         116.

p. 36   "Eight, nine," Frederick Douglass, *The Life and Times of Frederick Douglass*
         (Cleveland: 1883), 389.

p. 37   "Sound the loud," Benjamin Quarles, *Lincoln and the Negro* (New York: 1962), 145.

p. 37   "I look upon it," Robert Manson Myers, ed., *The Children of Pride: A True Story of
         Georgia and the Civil War* (New Haven: 1992), 967–968.

p. 40   "so simple," Thomas Wentworth Higginson, *Army Life in a Black Regiment*
         (Boston: 1870), 39–41.

p. 40   "some of their," James M. McPherson, *The Negro's Civil War* (New York: 1965),
         64–65.

p. 40   "They do not perceive," Randall C. Jimerson, *The Private Civil War: Popular Thought During the Sectional Conflict* (Baton Rouge: 1988), 62.

p. 41   "Freedom are," Quarles, *Lincoln and the Negro*, 148.

p. 41   "I used to think," John R. McClure (Nancy N. Baxter, ed.), *Hoosier Farm Boy in Lincoln's Army: The Civil War Letters of Pvt. John R. McClure* (N.p.: 1971), 44.

p. 41   "The first sheet," McPherson, *The Negro's Civil War*, 49–50.

p. 42   "Once the time," *The Liberator*, 1-16-63.

p. 42   "if he would," McPherson, *The Negro's Civil War*, 50.

CHAPTER 2. OLD ROSY IS THE MAN

p. 43   "intensified Roman," *TCW*-2:80.

p. 44   "sandy-haired fellows," Edmund Kirke, *Down in Tennessee and Back by Way of Richmond* (New York: 1864), 215.

p. 44   "debating," *TCW*-2:80.

p. 44   "Boys," *EG*:187.

p. 44   "go to your," *NCR*:37.

p. 44   "Old Rosy," James Lee McDonough, *Stone River: Bloody Winter in Tennessee* (Knoxville: 1980), 41.

p. 45   "We move," *EG*:201.

p. 46   "John Barleycorn," *CH*:76.

p. 46   "Home," McDonough, *Stones River*, 78.

p. 47   "Our way," Robert Stewart, "The Battle of Stones River, as Seen By One Who Was There," *Blue and Gray*, Vol. 5, 1895, 12.

p. 49   "The noise," Peter Cozzens, *No Better Place to Die: The Battle of Stones River* (Urbana, Ill.: 1990), 128.

p. 49   "The right wing," *EG*:219.

p. 49   "Never mind," *Cincinnati Commercial*, 1-3-63.

p. 49   "All right," *ibid.*

p. 50   "Mount," *EG*:224.

p. 50   "This battle," McDonough, *Stones River*, 115.

p. 50   "We raised," *CH*:78.

p. 50   "His left arm," *CH*:79.

p. 50   "Watch your language," *EG*:227.

p. 51   "Never mind," *EG*:225.

p. 51   "I am very sorry," *EG*:233.

p. 53   "Be a little," *EG*:233.

p. 53   "Men, do you," *NCR*:44.

p. 53   "The battle had," *OR*-1-20-1:545.

p. 53   "It got so hot," McDonough, *Stones River*, 144–145.

p. 53   "I saw," Dr. Homer Pittard, "The Strange Death of Peter Garesche," *Civil War Times Illustrated*, October, 1962, 25.

p. 54   "It was stiff," McDonough, *Stones River*, 154.

p. 54   "For a long time," *ibid.*, 154.

p. 54   "this army," Richard O'Connor, *Thomas: Rock of Chickamauga* (New York: 1948), 214.

p. 55   "They have got," Thomas L. Crittenden, "The Union Left at Stones River," *BL*-3:634.

p. 55 "Go to your commands," Philip H. Sheridan, *Personal Memoirs of P. H. Sheridan* (New York: 1904), Vol. 1, 236–237.

p. 55 "The enemy," OR-1-52-2:402.

p. 55 "This gloomy," Edwin Porter Thompson, *History of the Orphan Brigade* (Louisville: 1898), 175–176.

p. 56 "Sir, my information," William C. Davis, *The Orphan Brigade: The Kentucky Confederates Who Couldn't Go Home* (Baton Rouge: 1983), 155.

p. 56 "General Preston," Thompson, *History of the Orphan Brigade,* 177.

p. 56 "impractical madness," Davis, *The Orphan Brigade,* 155.

p. 56 "absolutely murderous," *ibid.*

p. 57 "Our intrepidity," Gervis D. Grainger, *Four Years with the Boys in Gray* (Dayton: 1972), 14.

p. 57 "opened the door," James Street, Jr., *The Struggle for Tennessee: Tupelo to Stones River* (Alexandria, Va.: 1985), 154.

p. 57 "I have never," Cozzens, *No Better Place to Die,* 194.

p. 57 "He was raging," Davis, *The Orphan Brigade,* 160.

p. 57 "My poor Orphan," *ibid.*

p. 57 "The contest," OR-1-20-1:668.

p. 58 "Say," *ibid.*

p. 58 "Common prudence," OR-1-20-1:669.

p. 58 "Who are you?" Colonel David Urquhart, "Bragg's Advance and Retreat," BL-3:609, and McDonough, *Stones River,* 218.

p. 59 "God bless," CWL-6:424.

p. 59 "The victory," OR-1-20-1:187.

CHAPTER 3. MIST, MUDDLE, AND FOG

p. 62 "the President," Richmond *Daily Dispatch,* 1-7-63.

p. 62 "I am proud," JDC-5:390–395.

p. 62 "peculiar," JD:489.

p. 63 "Boomerang Bragg," JD:490.

p. 63 "So far," Richmond *Daily Examiner,* 1-6-63.

p. 63 "Bragg is said," Robert G. H. Kean (Edward Younger, ed.), *Inside the Confederate Government: The Diary of Robert Garlick Hill Kean* (New York: 1957), 38.

p. 64 "Unanimous," OR-1-20-1:699.

p. 65 "revolutions develop," JDC:312.

p. 65 "Our government," JDC:460–462.

p. 66 "When everything," TCW-1:395.

p. 66 "the principle," JD:454.

p. 66 "Jeems," Varina Davis, *Jefferson Davis,* Vol. 2, 326.

p. 66 "They've come!" Louisa May Alcott (Bessie Z. Jones, ed.), *Hospital Sketches by Louisa May Alcott* (Cambridge, Mass: 1960), 27–38.

p. 67 "Having a taste," *ibid.*

p. 67 " 'Round," *ibid.*

p. 67 "If she had," *ibid.*

p. 67 "like any tidy," *ibid.*

p. 68 "very much," *ibid.*

p. 68 "broken only," *ibid.*

p. 68 "plain almost," Leech, *Reveille in Washington,* 210.

p. 68   "I long," Louisa May Alcott (Joel Myerson, Daniel Shealy, and Madeleine B. Stern, eds.), *The Journals of Louisa May Alcott* (Boston: 1989), 105.

p. 68   "like a massive," Alcott (Jones, ed.), *Hospital Sketches,* 43.

p. 69   "Though often," Alcott (Myerson, et al., eds.), *Journals,* 113–116.

p. 69   "a noble," *ibid.*

p. 69   "A pleasant," *ibid.*

p. 70   "the conviction," *ibid.*

p. 70   "all blowzed," *ibid.*

p. 70   "a ghost," Madeleine B. Stern, *Louisa May Alcott* (New York: 1996), 130.

p. 70   "graphically drawn," Marjorie Worthington, *Miss Alcott of Concord* (New York: 1958), 143.

p. 70   "touches," Stern, *Louisa May Alcott,* 136.

p. 70   "Let no one," Alcott (Jones, ed.), *Hospital Sketches,* 75–76.

p. 70   "Once I went," Alcott (Myerson, et al., eds.), *Journals,* 117.

p. 71   "could see," Orville H. Browning, *The Diary of Orville Hickman Browning* (Springfield, Ill.: 1925), Vol. 1, 613.

p. 71   "has done," Worthington Chauncy Ford, ed., *A Cycle of Adams Letters* (Boston: 1920), Vol. 1, 243–245.

p. 71   "I do not," Bell I. Wiley, *The Life of Billy Yank: The Common Soldier of the Union* (Indianapolis: 1952), 41–42.

p. 72   "behind," James A. Garfield (Theodore Clark Smith, ed.), *The Life and Letters of James Abram Garfield* (New Haven: 1925), Vol. 1, 373.

p. 72   "putting away," James M. McPherson, *Battle Cry of Freedom: The Civil War Era* (New York: 1988), 559.

p. 72   " 'the fire,' " Edward L. Pierce, ed., *Memoirs and Letters of Charles Sumner* (Boston: 1887), Vol. 4, 114.

p. 72   "terrible," Frank L. Klement, *The Limits of Dissent: Clement L. Vallandigham and the Civil War* (Lexington, KY: 1970), 74.

p. 72   "It is the desire," *ibid.,* 79.

p. 73   "Stop fighting," Clement L. Vallandigham, "The Great Civil War in America," in Frank Freidel, ed., *Union Pamphlets of the Civil War* (Cambridge, Mass.: 1967), Vol. 2, 697–738.

p. 73   "forever impossible," *JDC*-5:396–415.

p. 73   "nerves," Klement, *The Limits of Dissent,* 131.

p. 74   "It is contemplated," *OR*-3-3:4.

p. 74   "If the cause," Albert Gallatin Riddle, *Recollections of War Times: Reminiscences of Men and Events in Washington, 1860–1865* (New York: 1895), 321.

p. 75   "The lack," Charles Francis Adams, *Richard Henry Dana: A Biography* (Boston: 1890), Vol. 2, 264–265.

p. 75   "What ship," Raphael Semmes (Philip Van Doren Stern, ed.), *The Confederate Raider* Alabama (Bloomington, Ind.: 1962), 165–166.

p. 76   "I am grieved," *DGW*-1:220.

p. 77   "Abram Lincoln," *TCW*-2:117.

p. 77   "no human intelligence," *NCR:*66.

p. 77   "There is much," *OR*-1-21:944–945.

p. 78   "I do not ask," *OR*-1-21:945.

p. 78   "I do not yet see," *CWL*-6:46.

p. 78   "the great object," *OR*-1-21:954.

p. 78 "The auspicious moment," *OR*-1-21:127.

p. 79 "our eyes," Daniel G. Crotty, *Four Years Campaigning in the Army of the Potomac* (Grand Rapids, Mich.: 1874), 80.

p. 79 "were completely," Robert G. Carter, *Four Brothers in Blue or Sunshine and Shadow of the War of the Rebellion: A Story of the Great Civil War from Bull Run to Appomattox* (Austin: 1978), 225.

p. 80 "They would flounder," New York *Times*, 1-26-63.

p. 80 "might as well," Carter, *Four Brothers in Blue*, 225.

p. 80 "Nothing was heard," William K. Goolrick, *Rebels Resurgent: Fredericksburg to Chancellorsville* (Alexandria, Va.: 1985), 95.

p. 80 "An indescribable chaos," New York *Times*, 1-26-63.

p. 81 "General," Rufus Dawes, (Alan T. Nolan, ed.), *Service with the Sixth Wisconsin Volunteers* (Madison, Wisc.: 1962), 116.

p. 81 "until," Walter H. Hebert, *Fighting Joe Hooker* (Indianapolis: 1944), 164.

p. 81 "General Joseph Hooker," *OR*-1-21:998.

p. 82 "I have prepared," *ibid.*

p. 83 "at his own," *OR*-1-21:1004.

CHAPTER 4. THE RIGHT ROAD

p. 85 "Oh, this long," Kate Stone Holmes (John Q. Anderson, ed.), *Brokenburn: The Journal of Kate Stone, 1861–1868* (Baton Rouge: 1955), 133.

p. 85 "Silk," *ibid.*, 147.

p. 85 "After experimenting," *ibid.*, 181.

p. 85 "In proportion," *ibid.*, 110.

p. 86 "In some way," *ibid.*, 37.

p. 86 "runaways," *ibid.*, 28.

p. 86 "the house servants," *ibid.*, 33.

p. 86 "What will be," *ibid.*, 145–146.

p. 86 "nearly six feet," *ibid.*, 171.

p. 87 "The life," *ibid.*, 185.

p. 87 "We have been," *ibid.*, 179.

p. 87 "A great many," *ibid.*, 184.

p. 87 "I think," *ibid.*, 183.

p. 87 "I was never," *ibid.*, 196.

p. 88 "behaved," *ibid.*, 198.

p. 88 "So passes," *ibid.*, 203.

p. 88 "Tears," *ibid.*, 268.

p. 89 "The sight," *ibid.*, 200–201.

p. 90 "It was just thrown," *ibid.*, 191.

p. 90 "dark corner," *ibid.*, 237.

p. 90 "the earth," *ibid.*, 227.

p. 90 "Conquered," *ibid.*, 339–340.

p. 91 "No proper," New York *Times*, 2-23-63.

p. 91 "No stranger," *GMS*:3

p. 91 "an altogether," *GMS*:172.

p. 92 "without scarf," New York *Times*, 6-21-63.

p. 94 "at this time," *PMG*:262.

p. 94   "One of my superstitions," *PMG*:35.

p. 94   "a series," *PMG*:264.

p. 95   "Direct your attention," OR-1-24-1:10.

p. 95   "water above," James M. Merrill, *William Tecumseh Sherman* (Chicago: 1971), 219.

p. 95   "This little affair," OR-1-24-3:32.

p. 95   "by a little digging," OR-1-24-3:33.

p. 96   "I let," *PMG*:266.

p. 97   "like nothing else," OR-1-24-1:373.

p. 97   "like a toy skiff," Jerry Korn, *War on the Mississippi: Grant's Vicksburg Campaign* (Alexandria, Va.: 1985), 76.

p. 97   "Seeing such," James H. Wilson, *Under the Old Flag* (New York: 1912), Vol. 1, 151–152.

p. 97   "I am confirmed," OR-1-24-1:376.

p. 99   "Great forests," *ICW*:137.

p. 100 "all would be," *ICW*:158.

p. 100 "a large green," *ICW*:159.

p. 100 "That's nothin'," *ibid*.

p. 100 "Dear Sherman," *ICW*:161.

p. 101 "The night," William T. Sherman, *Memoirs of Gen. William T. Sherman* (New York: 1891), Vol. 1, 337–338.

p. 101 "I doubt," *ibid*.

p. 101 "Thank you, no," *ICW*:169.

p. 101 "as people," *ICW*:172.

p. 101 "hardest cruise," *ibid*.

p. 101 "inured," David D. Porter, *The Naval History of the Civil War* (New York: 1886), 307.

p. 101 "Some men," *ICW*:173.

p. 101 "His energy," *GMS*:390.

p. 102 "The soldiers," *ibid*.

CHAPTER 5. THE DICTATES OF WAR

p. 105 "a morbid passion," Riddle, *Recollections,* 219–221.

p. 107 "the accursed heresy," Bray Hammond, *Sovereignty and an Empty Purse: Banks and Politics in the Civil War* (Princeton: 1970), 333–334.

p. 108 "$300 exemption," Frank L. Klement, *The Copperheads in the Middle West* (Chicago: 1960), 77–78.

p. 109 "The sooner," Klement, *The Limits of Dissent,* 153–154.

p. 109 "I am a Democrat," *ibid.,* 163.

p. 110 "determine," Cincinnati *Daily Enquirer,* 5-23-63.

p. 110 "with my opinions," Cincinnati *Daily Enquirer,* 7-20-63.

p. 112 "Once let," Quarles, *Lincoln and the Negro,* 184.

p. 112 "Our people," James Henry Gooding (Virginia M. Adams, ed.), *On the Altar of Freedom: A Black Soldier's Civil War Letters from the Front* (Amherst, Mass: 1991), 4.

p. 112 "gentlemen," Luis F. Emilio, *A Brave Black Regiment: History of the Fifty-fourth Regiment of Massachusetts Volunteer Infantry, 1863–1865* (New York: 1894), 3.

p. 113 "We can get," New York *Times,* 3-8-63.

p. 113 "In Ohio," Norwood P. Hallowell, *Selected Letters and Papers of N. P. Hallowell* (Peterborough, N.H.: 1963), 30–35.

p. 114   "They are not," Robert Gould Shaw (Russell Duncan, ed.), *Blue-eyed Child of Fortune: The Civil War Letters of Colonel Robert Gould Shaw* (Athens, Ga.: 1992), 300.

p. 114   "I am perfectly," *ibid.*, 313.

p. 114   "The skeptics," *ibid.*, 316.

p. 115   "Most of," *ibid.*, 14–15.

p. 115   "so long as," Emilio, *A Brave Black Regiment*, 29.

p. 115   "The 54th Massachusetts," Shaw (Duncan, ed.), *Blue-eyed Child*, 332.

p. 116   "lest I should," John Greenleaf Whittier (John B. Pickard, ed.), *Letters of John Greenleaf Whittier* (Cambridge, Mass.: 1975), Vol. 3, 362.

p. 116   "Saw the first," Stephen B. Oates, *With Malice Toward None: The Life of Abraham Lincoln* (New York: 1978), 341.

p. 116   "The more I think," Shaw (Duncan, ed.), *Blue-eyed Child*, 335.

p. 116   "There is not a man," Gooding (Adams, ed.), *On the Altar of Freedom*, 24.

p. 117   "some great mechanic," William Douglass O'Connor, "The Good Gray Poet, A Vindication," reprinted in Jerome Loving, *Walt Whitman's Champion: William Douglass O'Connor* (College Station, Tex.: 1978), 157–203.

p. 117   "Old and young," Walt Whitman, "Song of Myself," *Leaves of Grass*.

p. 117   "with the sunlight," O'Connor, "The Good Gray Poet," in Loving, *Walt Whitman's Champion*, 157.

p. 117   "reckless," Justin Kaplan, *Walt Whitman: A Life* (New York: 1980), 205.

p. 117   "mass," Milton Hindus, ed., *Walt Whitman: The Critical Heritage* (New York: 1971), 32–33.

p. 118   "Why, how can I," Walt Whitman (Edwin H. Miller, ed.), *The Collected Works of Walt Whitman: The Correspondence* (New York: 1961–77), Vol. 1, 74.

p. 118   "very bad book," James Thomson, *Walt Whitman the Man* (New York: 1971), 156.

p. 118   "distraction," Walt Whitman (Floyd Stovall, ed.), *Walt Whitman: Prose Works 1892* (New York: 1963), Vol. 1, 112.

p. 118   "Breaking up," Whitman (Miller, ed.), *Collected Works: The Correspondence*, Vol. 1, 61.

p. 118   "by far," *ibid.*, 75.

p. 118   "saw Chief Justice," Walt Whitman (Walter Lowenfels, ed.), *Walt Whitman's Civil War* (New York: 1960), 63.

p. 118   "much gab," Whitman (Miller, ed.), *Collected Works: The Correspondence*, Vol. 1, 82.

p. 118   "a hoosier," *ibid.*

p. 118   "A new world," *ibid.*, 69.

p. 118   "curious and stirring," *ibid.*, 114.

p. 118   "never did I feel," *ibid.*, 103.

p. 118   "a most noble," *ibid.*, 84.

p. 118   "This is the greatest place," *ibid.*, 63.

p. 119   "To any one dying," Whitman, "Song of Myself," *Leaves of Grass*.

p. 119   "O what a sweet," Whitman (Miller, ed.), *Collected Works: The Correspondence*, Vol. 1, 122.

p. 119   "There comes," Kaplan, *Walt Whitman: A Life*, 276.

p. 119   "I know," Whitman (Miller, ed.), *Collected Works: The Correspondence*, Vol. 1, 162.

p. 120   "Many a soldier's arms," Whitman, "The Wound-Dresser," (Maurice Bucke et al, ed.), *The Complete Writings of Walt Whitman*, Vol. 2 (New York: 1902).

p. 120   "masculine young manhood," Whitman (Miller, ed.), *Collected Works: The Correspondence*, Vol. 1, 69–70.

p. 120   "healthy, handsome," *ibid.*, 114.

p. 120 "O eyes," Walt Whitman (Emory Holloway, ed.), *The Uncollected Poetry and Prose of Walt Whitman* (Garden City, N.Y.: 1921), Vol. 2, 93.

p. 120 "I never before," Whitman (Miller, ed.), *Collected Works: The Correspondence*, Vol. 1, 77.

p. 120 "It may well," *Scientific American*, 1-17-63.

p. 120 "Our hired man," Wayne D. Rasmussen, "The Civil War: A Catalyst of Agricultural Revolution," *Agricultural History*, October, 1965, 187–196.

p. 121 "Our sailors," Colonel Henry S. Olcott, "The War's Carnival of Fraud," *TAW*:706–707.

p. 121 "The mania," *RCW*:39.

p. 121 "I never despaired," NCR: 71.

p. 122 "This war," New York *Herald*, 10-6-63.

p. 123 "There is no clap-trap," Nicolai Cikovsky, Jr., *Winslow Homer* (New York: 1990), 16.

p. 123 "It is a work," Gordon Hendricks, *The Life and Work of Winslow Homer* (New York: 1974), 50.

p. 123 "If this is the work," Harold Holzer and Mark E. Neely, Jr., *Mine Eyes Have Seen the Glory: The Civil War in Art* (New York: 1993), 297.

p. 123 "In no period," "Literature and Literary Progress in 1863," *The American Cyclopaedia and Register of Important Events of the Year 1863* (New York: 1864), 573.

p. 123 "I had hoped," Harvey O'Connor, *Mellon's Millions: The Life and Times of Andrew W. Mellon* (New York: 1933), 23–24.

p. 124 "A little side issue," Jules Abels, *The Rockefeller Billions* (New York: 1965), 38–40.

p. 125 "They were talking," *ibid*.

p. 125 "I wanted," Allan Nevins, *John D. Rockefeller: The Heroic Age of American Enterprise* (New York: 1940), Vol. 1, 139.

p. 125 "Along with," Matthew Josephson, *The Robber Barons: The Great American Capitalists, 1861–1901* (New York: 1962), 59.

p. 125 "Do not let," Andrew Sinclair, *Corsair: The Life of J. Pierpont Morgan* (Boston: 1981), 16.

p. 126 "pressing necessities," *Report and Testimony of the Select House Committee Appointed to Inquire into Government Contracts*, 37th Cong., 2d Sess. (1861), Vol. 2, 515.

p. 126 "The honest people," Josephson, *The Robber Barons*, 19.

p. 126 "rat pit," Maury Klein, *The Life and Legend of Jay Gould* (Baltimore: 1986), 69.

p. 126 "den," James K. Medbery, *Men and Mysteries of Wall Street* (Boston: 1877), 241.

p. 126 "The chaos," *ibid*.

p. 128 "I shall remember," Andrew Carnegie, *Autobiography of Andrew Carnegie* (New York: 1920), 80.

p. 128 "Days would elapse," *ibid.*, 103.

p. 129 "I am determined," Joseph Frazer Wall, *Andrew Carnegie* (New York: 1970), 191.

CHAPTER 6. BREAD OR BLOOD

p. 130 "The gaunt form," *RWC*-1:282–283.

p. 131 "there is now," John K. Bettersworth, ed., *Mississippi in the Confederacy: As They Saw It* (Baton Rouge: 1961), 287–288.

p. 131 "on the principle," H. E. Sterkx, *Partners in Rebellion: Alabama Women in the Civil War* (Rutherford, N.J.: 1970), 142.

p. 132 "love of lucre," Jefferson Davis (James D. Richardson, ed.), *The Messages and Papers of Jefferson Davis and the Confederacy* (Washington: 1905), Vol. 1, 328.

p. 132   "Can it be possible," Paul D. Escott, *After Secession: Jefferson Davis and the Failure of Confederate Nationalism* (Baton Rouge: 1978), 123–124.

p. 132   "the lawn," Mary Elizabeth Massey, *Ersatz in the Confederacy* (Columbia, S.C.: 1952), 20.

p. 133   "All shame," *OR*-1-17-2:790.

p. 133   "Never did a law," *ibid.*

p. 133   "I wish to fill," James Lusk Alcorn (P. L. Rainwater, ed.), "Letters of James Lusk Alcorn," *Journal of Southern History,* May, 1937, 202–203.

p. 134   "We often hear," Escott, *After Secession,* 111.

p. 135   "For God's sake," George C. Rable, *The Confederate Republic: A Revolution Against Politics* (Chapel Hill, N.C.: 1994), 190.

p. 136   "Fasting," *RWC*-1:280.

p. 136   "persuaders," Douglas O. Tice, "Bread or Blood! The Richmond Bread Riot," *Civil War Times Illustrated,* February, 1974, 12.

p. 137   "a tall, daring," Varina Davis, *Jefferson Davis,* Vol. 2, 373.

p. 137   "You say," *ibid.,* 374–375.

p. 138   "a handful," Richmond *Daily Examiner,* 4-4-63.

p. 139   "cradle," *TCW*-2:221.

p. 139   "Carolinians and Georgians!" *OR*-1-14:782.

p. 139   "If the country," T. Harry Williams, *P.G.T. Beauregard: Napoleon in Gray* (Baton Rouge: 1955), 161.

p. 143   "Like a sledgehammer," Henry Villard, *Memoirs* (Boston: 1904), Vol. 2, 41.

p. 143   "as if," *TCW*-2:229.

p. 143   "riddled," C.R.P. Rodgers, "Du Pont's Attack at Charleston," *BL*-4:40.

p. 143   "Charleston cannot be taken," *ORN*-14-1:3.

p. 143   "These monitors," Samuel F. Du Pont (John D. Hayes, ed.), *Samuel Francis Du Pont: A Selection from His Letters* (Ithaca, N.Y.: 1969), Vol. 3, 10.

p. 144   "My expectations," *OR*-1-14-1:242.

p. 145   " 'Get up,' " *TFD*:23.

p. 145   "all looked," *TFD*:8.

p. 145   "He had been," *TFD*:9.

p. 145   "the shooting-down," *TFD*:17–18.

p. 145   "a damned sight," *TFD*:61.

p. 145   "we received," *TFD*:65.

p. 146   "They are," *TFD*:64.

p. 146   "place reminded," *TFD*:79.

p. 146   "They examined," *TFD*:85–86.

p. 147   "The news," *TFD*:101–102.

p. 147   "people are," *TFD*:102.

p. 147   "It is," *TFD*:103.

p. 147   "In consequence," *TFD*:107.

p. 147   "all state capitals," *TFD*:139.

p. 147   "war-worn," *ibid.*

p. 148   "This officer," *TFD*:115.

p. 148   "If the appointment," Symonds, *Joseph E. Johnston,* 197.

p. 148   "Order General Bragg," *OR*-1-23-2:674.

p. 149   "February 15: Rained," Larry J. Daniel, *Soldiering in the Army of Tennessee: A Portrait of Life in a Confederate Army* (Chapel Hill: 1991), 87.

p. 150   "I don't make," *ibid.,* 85.

p. 150   "my bowels," *ibid.,* 73.
p. 150   "I know," *ibid.,* 90.
p. 151   "seems to," Nashville *Daily Union,* 4-14-63.
p. 151   "I fear," *OR*-1-23-2:656.
p. 152   "degraded," Nashville *Dispatch,* 5-24-63.
p. 152   "a rake," Fayetteville *Observer,* 6-4-63.
p. 152   "the atmosphere," *OR*-1-17-2:789.
p. 152   "I am weary," Robert G. Hartje, *Van Dorn: The Life and Times of a Confederate General* (Nashville: 1967), 248.
p. 152   "I *am,*" *ibid.,* 290.
p. 153   "The more," *TFD*:247.

CHAPTER 7. IN MOTION IN ALL DIRECTIONS

p. 154   "arose," *RCW*:48.
p. 155   "We all knew," Sherman, *Memoirs,* Vol. 1, 343.
p. 155   "You have asked," *GMS*:395.
p. 155   "The truth," Nevins, *The War for the Union,* Vol. 2, 388.
p. 155   "at every phrase," *RCW*:73.
p. 155   "[He] was an uncommon fellow," *RCW*:82.
p. 156   "I will be," *ICW*:174.
p. 157   "Vicksburg is daily," *OR*-1-17-2:828.
p. 157   "In General Pemberton," John C. Pemberton, *Pemberton: Defender of Vicksburg* (Chapel Hill: 1942), 44–45.
p. 157   "it is but," *ibid.*
p. 158   "Those bridges," Wilson, *Under the Old Flag,* Vol. 1, 168–169.
p. 158   "[T]he ingenuity," *PMG*:275–276.
p. 159   "A shapeless mass," Richard Wheeler, *The Siege of Vicksburg* (New York: 1978), 107.
p. 159   "It disappeared," Franc B. Wilkie, *Pen and Powder* (Boston: 1888), 315.
p. 160   "We will slip," *ICW*:175.
p. 160   "Magnificent, but terrible," *PMG*:274.
p. 160   "Our men," Wheeler, *The Siege of Vicksburg,* 111.
p. 160   "she had," *ICW*:176.
p. 160   "A perfect tornado," Wheeler, *The Siege of Vicksburg,* 111.
p. 161   "Enemy is constantly," *OR*-1-24-3:730.
p. 161   "The most brilliant," D. Alexander Brown, *Grierson's Raid: A Cavalry Adventure of the Civil War* (Urbana, Ill.: 1954), 223.
p. 162   "It seems," *OR*-1-24-3:50.
p. 163   "Oats," *OR*-1-24-3:197.
p. 163   "As usual," Brown, *Grierson's Raid,* 32–33.
p. 164   "marching by fours," *OR*-1-24-1:521–522.
p. 165   "The Yankees," Brown, *Grierson's Raid,* 145.
p. 166   "Hearing nothing," *OR*-1-24-1:527.
p. 166   "A straight line," Richard W. Surby, *Grierson Raids* (Chicago: 1865), 106.
p. 167   "Men by the score," Brown, *Grierson's Raid,* 210.
p. 167   "Feeling confident," *ibid.,* 215.
p. 167   "The most successful," *OR*-1-24-1:33.
p. 168   "brilliant," *OR*-1-24-1:58.
p. 168   "This fellow," Vicksburg *Daily Whig,* 5-2-63.

p. 168   "My dear Alice," Brown, *Grierson's Raid*, 230.

p. 168   "I presume," *ibid.*, 230–232.

p. 168   "Commence immediately," *OR*-1-24-3:237.

p. 168   "especial favorite," *OR*-1-24-1:74.

p. 169   "Not a single," *RCW*:57.

p. 170   "push right along," S.H.M Byers, "Some Recollections of Grant," *TAW*:342–343.

p. 170   "When [the crossing]," *PMG*:284.

p. 171   "If Grant's army," *ibid.*

p. 171   "Unless very large," *OR*-1-24-3:814–815.

p. 171   "The battle," *ibid.*

p. 171   "Unite," *ibid.*

CHAPTER 8. HIS NAME MIGHT BE AUDACITY

p. 172   "I have seen," Ernest B. Furgurson, *Chancellorsville 1863* (New York: 1992), 30.

p. 172   "All know," Crotty, *Four Years Campaigning*, 80–81.

p. 173   "desecrated vegetables," Charles E. Davis, "Life with the Thirteenth Massachu-setts," *BG-1*:275.

p. 173   "It is wonderful," James I. Robertson, Jr., *Soldiers Blue and Gray* (Columbia, S.C.: 1988), 79.

p. 173   "For God," Survivors' Association, *History of the Corn Exchange Regiment 118th Pennsylvania Volunteers* (Philadelphia: 1888), 166–167.

p. 174   "rather too rosy," Bruce Catton, *Glory Road* (Garden City, N.Y.: 1952), 146.

p. 174   "nervous verve," Furgurson, *Chancellorsville*, 30.

p. 174   "a man," Carl Schurz (Frederick Bancroft, ed.), *Speeches, Correspondence, and Public Papers of Carl Schurz* (New York: 1913), Vol. 1, 251.

p. 174   "open to temptation," George G. Meade, *Life and Letters of George Gordon Meade* (New York: 1913), Vol. 1, 351.

p. 174   "blemished character," Charles Francis Adams, *Charles Francis Adams, 1835–1916, an Autobiography* (Boston: 1916), 161.

p. 174   "Don't call me," Hebert, *Fighting Joe Hooker*, 91.

p. 174   "If the enemy," New York *Tribune*, 3-21-63.

p. 174   "I have the finest," Hebert, *Fighting Joe Hooker*, 183.

p. 175   "The men," *OR*-1-25-2:687.

p. 175   "tents were wrecked," Robertson, *Soldiers Blue and Gray*, 89.

p. 176   "the best looking man," Harry W. Pfanz, *Gettysburg: The Second Day* (Chapel Hill: 1987), 105.

p. 176   "cold and quiet," Mary B. Chesnut (Ben Ames Williams, ed.), *A Diary from Dixie* (Boston: 1949), 95.

p. 176   "If there is," E. P. Alexander, *Military Memoirs of a Confederate* (New York: 1907), 110–111.

p. 177   "would have presented," Carter, *Four Brothers in Blue*, 236.

p. 177   "What do you suppose," Darius N. Couch, "Sumner's Right Grand Division," *BL*-3:120.

p. 177   "it struck me," *ibid.*

p. 177   "Beware of rashness," *OR*-1-25-2:4.

p. 178   "When I get," Noah Brooks (Herbert Mitgang, ed.), *Washington in Lincoln's Time* (New York: 1958), 56.

p. 178   "*If* you get," Noah Brooks, "Personal Reminiscences of Lincoln," *Scribner's Monthly*, March, 1878, 673.

p. 178   "Excuse me," *ibid.*

p. 178   "about the worst," *ibid.*

p. 178   "our prime object," *CWL*-6:164.

p. 178   "had got a leader," Catton, *Glory Road,* 163.

p. 179   "This is splendid," John Bigelow, Jr., *The Campaign of Chancellorsville* (New Haven: 1910), 221.

p. 179   "I have Lee," Joseph P. Cullen, "The Battle of Chancellorsville," *Civil War Times Illustrated,* May, 1968, 11.

p. 179   "The rebel army," William Swinton, *Campaigns of the Army of the Potomac* (New York: 1866), 275.

p. 180   "It is with," *OR*-1-25-1:171.

p. 181   "Make arrangements," *OR*-1-25-2:762.

p. 182   "You are," Furgurson, *Chancellorsville,* 129–130.

p. 182   "It is," Couch, "The Chancellorsville Campaign," *BL*-3:159.

p. 182   "[To] hear," *ibid.,* 161.

p. 182   "in the air," *LL*-2:539.

p. 183   "How can we," *LL*-2:540.

p. 183   "You know best," *ibid.*

p. 183   "General Stuart," *LL*-2:541.

p. 183   "My troops," *ibid.*

p. 183   "General Jackson," *LL*-2:546.

p. 184   "Tell Old Jack," James P. Smith, "Stonewall Jackson's Last Battle," *BL*-3:205–206.

p. 184   "See that," *LL*-2:550.

p. 184   "How strong," Oliver O. Howard, "The Eleventh Corps at Chancellorsville," *BL*-3:195.

p. 186   "We know," *OR*-1-25-2:363.

p. 186   "We had heard," John L. Collins, "When Stonewall Jackson Turned Our Right," *BL*-3:183.

p. 186   "Unharness those horses," Furgurson, *Chancellorsville,* 172.

p. 187   "Are you ready?" Smith, "Stonewall Jackson's Last Battle," *BL*-3:208.

p. 187   "So sudden," Furgurson, *Chancellorsville,* 179.

p. 188   "a fresh mass," Collins, "When Stonewall Jackson Turned Our Right," *BL*-3:184.

p. 188   "General," *TCW*-2:296–297.

p. 188   "My God," Bigelow, *The Campaign of Chancellorsville,* 301.

p. 188   "a confused," Furgurson, *Chancellorsville,* 184.

p. 188   "Receive the enemy," Bigelow, *The Campaign of Chancellorsville,* 307.

p. 189   "General, don't you," *LL*-2:565–567.

p. 189   "The danger," *ibid.*

p. 189   "Cease firing," *ibid.*

p. 189   "Who gave," *ibid.*

p. 189   "His hands," *LL*-2:578.

p. 189   "For a moment," *LL*-2:582.

p. 190   "It only required," Couch, "The Chancellorsville Campaign," *BL*-3:164.

p. 190   "I think that," *ibid.*

p. 190   "I have always," *ibid.,* 170.

p. 191   "rose high," Charles Marshal, *An Aide-de-Camp of Lee* (Boston: 1927), 173.

p. 192   "A tremendous roar," Joseph E. Stevens, *America's National Battlefield Parks: A Guide* (Norman, Okla.: 1990), 69.

p. 192   "Look to the," *OR*-1-25-2:410.

p. 192 "[He] stated," Couch, "The Chancellorsville Campaign," *BL*-3:171.

p. 193 "What was," *ibid.*

p. 193 "The commander," Furgurson, *Chancellorsville,* 333.

p. 193 "Had a thunderbolt," Brooks (Staudenraus, ed.), *Mr. Lincoln's Washington,* 179.

p. 193 "He held," Brooks (Mitgang, ed.), *Washington in Lincoln's Time,* 60–61.

p. 193 "praise to God," *OR*-1-25-1:805.

p. 194 "Surely, General Jackson," *LL*-2:674.

p. 194 "Doctor, Anna informs," Lenoir Chambers, *Stonewall Jackson* (New York: 1959), Vol. 2, 445.

p. 194 "Very good," *ibid.*

p. 194 "it is," *ibid.*

p. 194 "A few moments," *ibid., pp.* 446–447.

CHAPTER 9. TO THE GATES OF VICKSBURG

p. 196 "receives no intelligence," *OR*-1-23-2:761.

p. 196 "The enemy," *OR*-1-24-3:269.

p. 197 "To wait," *PMG*:290–291.

p. 197 "Stop all troops," *ibid.*

p. 199 "Since leaving," *OR*-1-24-1:33.

p. 200 "Is it not," *OR*-1-24-3:849.

p. 200 "I must stand," *OR*-1-24-3:846.

p. 200 "plump," *GMS*:431.

p. 201 "I prayed," Peter F. Walker, *Vicksburg: A People at War, 1860–1865* (Chapel Hill: 1960), 159.

p. 201 "All the enemy's," *PMG*:294.

p. 201 "as nearly perfect," Stephen E. Ambrose, "Struggle for Vicksburg," *Civil War Times Illustrated,* July, 1967, 21.

p. 201 "Proceed at once," *OR*-1-24-1:215.

p. 202 "I am too late," *ibid.*

p. 202 "Foundries," Sylvanus Cadwallader (Benjamin P. Thomas, ed.), *Three Years with Grant* (New York: 1955), 75.

p. 203 "The object," *OR*-1-24-3:876.

p. 203 "The order," *OR*-1-24-1:241.

p. 203 "He looked," Edwin C. Bearrs, *The Vicksburg Campaign* (Dayton: 1986), Vol. 2, 583.

p. 204 "that most trying," Byers, "Some Recollections of Grant," *TAW*:343.

p. 204 "mental promises," Charles Longley, *War Sketches and Incidents* (Des Moines: 1898), 208–214.

p. 204 "On and upward," *ibid.*

p. 205 "Tell General Grant," *RR*-6:619.

p. 205 "tell him," Ulysses S. Grant, "The Vicksburg Campaign," *BL*-3:511.

p. 206 "degree of hatred," Bearrs, *The Vicksburg Campaign,* Vol. 2, 620.

p. 206 "willing for Pemberton," *ibid.*

p. 206 "ill-tempered jests," *ibid.*

p. 206 "the courier," *ibid.*

p. 206 "We ran," Byers, "Some Recollections of Grant," *TAW*:346.

p. 206 "Where is Loring?" Pemberton, *Pemberton,* 161.

p. 206 "even this," *OR*-1-24-2:126.

p. 207 "Had the movement," *OR*-1-24-1:264–265.

p. 207   "All around us," Wilbur F. Crummer, *With Grant at Fort Donelson, Shiloh and Vicksburg* (Oak Park, Ill.: 1915), 104–106.

p. 207   "when suddenly," *RCW*:68.

p. 207   "stood up," *ibid.*

p. 209   "We are sold," Michael B. Ballard, *Pemberton: A Biography* (Jackson, M.S.: 1991), 167.

p. 209   "Just thirty years ago," Samuel H. Lockett, "The Defense of Vicksburg," *BL*-3:488.

p. 210   "so steep," *OR*-1-24-2:169.

p. 211   "were busy divesting," Osborn H. Oldroyd, *A Soldier's Story of the Siege of Vicksburg* (Springfield, Ill.: 1885), 31–32.

p. 211   "Up the hill," Korn, *War on the Mississippi,* 130.

p. 211   "I don't believe," Sherman, *Memoirs,* Vol. 1, 327.

p. 212   "General McClernand's dispatches," *OR*-1-24-1:37.

p. 212   "resulted in," *ibid.,* 56.

p. 212   "We'll have to," Korn, *War on the Mississippi,* 132.

CHAPTER 10. INVASION

p. 215   "it becomes," *OR*-1-25-2:790.

p. 217   "There never were," Robert E. Lee (Clifford Dowdey and Louis H. Manarin, eds.), *The Wartime Papers of R. E. Lee* (Boston: 1961), 490.

p. 217   "It is horrible," *TCW*-2:315.

p. 217   "The country is not lost," Richard Wheeler, *Lee's Terrible Swift Sword* (New York: 1992), 406.

p. 218   "Hooker's career," Furgurson, *Chancellorsville,* 333.

p. 218   "the events," *OR*-1-25-1:171.

p. 218   "I shall not complain," *CWL*-6:217.

p. 218   "entangled upon," *CWL*-6:249.

p. 218   "disperse and destroy," *OR*-1-27-3:27.

p. 220   "Wouldn't we," Fairfax Downey, *Clash of Cavalry: The Battle of Brandy Station, June 9, 1863* (New York: 1959), 81.

p. 220   "It was a," Lee (Dowdey and Manarin, eds.), *The Wartime Papers,* 507.

p. 221   "Tell General Jones," *LL*-3:9.

p. 221   "Ride back there," *ibid.*

p. 221   "*made* the federal," Henry B. McClellan, *The Life and Campaigns of Major General J.E.B. Stuart* (Boston: 1885), 294.

p. 221   "puffed-up," Richmond *Examiner,* 6-12-63.

p. 221   "rollicking," *LL*-3:51.

p. 221   "a tournament," Richmond *Examiner,* 6-12-63.

p. 222   "vigilance," Richmond *Sentinel,* 6-12-63.

p. 222   "Hurrah," *LL*-3:23.

p. 223   "Your progress," *OR*-1-27-3:914.

p. 224   "the most exciting," Marguerite Merington, ed., *The Custer Story: The Life and Intimate Letters of General Custer and His Wife Elizabeth* (New York: 1950), 33.

p. 225   "I was surrounded," Frederick Whitaker, *A Complete Life of Gen. A. Custer* (New York: 1876), 155–159.

p. 226   "golden-haired apotheosis," Gregory J. W. Urwin, *Custer Victorious: The Civil War Battles of General George Armstrong Custer* (Rutherford, N.J.: 1983), 29.

p. 226   "To promotion," Jay Monaghan, *Custer: The Life of General George Armstrong Custer* (Boston: 1959), 131.

p. 226   "He acts," Marsena R. Patrick (David S. Sparks, ed.), *Inside Lincoln's Army: The Diary of Marsena R. Patrick* (New York: 1964), 260.

p. 226   "He has declared," *ibid.*, 261.

p. 227   "It did not," *CWL*-6: 297.

p. 227   "I don't know," *TCW*-2:449.

p. 228   "positively," *TCW*-2:443.

p. 228   "Dere ain't no," Pfanz, *Gettysburg: The Second Day,* 11.

p. 228   "Here's your played-out," *TCW*-2:443.

p. 228   "We might get," *LL*-3:76–77.

p. 229   "Free every slave," T. Harry Williams, *Lincoln and the Radicals* (Madison, Wisc.: 1941), 12.

p. 229   "The cherry crop," Richard Wheeler, *Witness to Gettysburg* (New York: 1987), 82.

p. 229   "band-box boys," *ibid.*

p. 230   "ripe for rudeness," Charles F. Benjamin, "Hooker's Appointment and Removal," *BL*-3:242.

p. 230   "He will fight," T. Harry Williams, *Lincoln and His Generals* (New York: 1952), 260.

p. 230   "Well, I've been," Benjamin, "Hooker's Appointment and Removal," *BL*-3:243.

p. 231   "had enough," Meade, *Life and Letters,* Vol. 2, 11.

p. 231   "dividing and weakening," Lee (Dowdey and Manarin, eds.), *The Wartime Papers,* 508.

p. 231   "I am not," Alexander H. Stephens, *A Constitutional View of the Late War Between the States* (Philadelphia: 1868), Vol. 2, 558.

p. 232   "Gentlemen," Whitaker, *A Complete Life of Gen. George A. Custer,* 161–162.

p. 232   "How are you," *ibid.*

p. 232   "Hello," *ibid.*

p. 232   "Look," *ibid.*

p. 233   "I don't," *REL*-3:60.

p. 233   "General Meade," *ibid.*, 64.

p. 234   "[We] scare them," *LL*-3:75.

p. 234   "a damned old," Warren Hassler, *Commanders of the Army of the Potomac* (Baton Rouge: 1962), 161.

p. 234   "smooth bore," *DGW*-1:349.

p. 234   "What has Meade," Freeman Cleaves, *Meade of Gettysburg* (Norman, Okla.: 1960), 128.

p. 234   "take him," *ibid.*

p. 235   "I must move," *OR*-1-27-1:61.

p. 236   "having this 'boy,' " Whitaker, *A Complete Life of Gen. George A. Custer,* 170.

p. 236   "1863 Spring Styles," Gettysburg *Compiler,* 6-29-63.

p. 237   "If there is," *LL*-3:78.

p. 237   "None," *ibid.*

CHAPTER 11. SIEGE

p. 238   "Out-camping," *PMG*:312.

p. 238   "these could not," *ibid.*

p. 239   "The enemy," *OR*-1-24-1:37.

p. 239   "An army," *OR*-1-24-3:899.

p. 239   "The utmost," Vicksburg *Daily Citizen,* 6-13-63.

p. 239   "Vicksburg is," *OR*-1-24-1:272.

p. 240   "I am trying," *OR*-1-24-3:892.

p. 240   "Bragg is sending," *OR*-1-24-3:917.

p. 240   "When may I," *ibid.*

p. 240   "Whether a battery," *OR*-1-24-2:177.

p. 241   "whizzing and zipping," Cadwallader (Thomas, ed.), *Three Years with Grant,* 101.

p. 241   "Rats," Walker, *Vicksburg,* 166.

p. 242   "I snatched," Dora Miller Richards, "A Woman's Diary of the Siege of Vicksburg," *Century Magazine,* September, 1885, 767–775.

p. 243   "squalling infants," William Lord, Jr., "A Child at the Siege of Vicksburg," *Harper's Monthly,* December, 1908, 44–53.

p. 243   "like sardines," Lida Lord, "A Woman's Experiences During the Siege of Vicksburg," *Century Magazine,* April, 1901, 922–928.

p. 243   "Not the slightest," A. A. Hoehling, *Vicksburg: 47 Days of Siege* (Englewood Cliffs, N.J.: 1969), 92.

p. 243   "Our situation," *OR*-1-26-1:525-526.

p. 244   "You say," *GMS*:460.

p. 244   "You God-damn idiot," Samuel Carter, *The Final Fortress: The Campaign for Vicksburg, 1862–1863* (New York: 1980), 245.

p. 244   "Tonight," *GMS*:463.

p. 245   "He made several," Cadwallader (Thomas, ed.), *Three Years with Grant,* 103–104.

p. 245   "I enticed," *ibid.*

p. 246   "fresh as a rose," *RCW*:91.

p. 246   "If we had," Cadwallader (Thomas, ed.), *Three Years with Grant,* 106.

p. 246   "The road," *ibid.,* 107.

p. 246   "We reached," *ibid.,* 109.

p. 246   "I turned," *ibid.*

p. 247   "I have sent," *OR*-1-24-3:953.

p. 247   "I am waiting," *OR*-1-24-3:958.

p. 247   "No information," *OR*-1-24-3:963.

p. 247   "I think," *OR*-1-24-3:964.

p. 247   "My men," *OR*-1-24-3:967.

p. 248   "Ho!" Vicksburg *Daily Citizen,* 6-18-63.

p. 248   "such reinforcements," Steven E. Woodworth, *Jefferson Davis and His Generals* (Lawrence, Kan.: 1990), 213.

p. 248   "We cannot hope," *OR*-1-24-1:224.

p. 248   "You must rely," *ibid.*

p. 249   "Vicksburg must not," *OR*-1-24-1:227.

p. 249   "The eyes," *OR*-1-24-1:228.

p. 249   "As foreseen," Richard Taylor, *Destruction and Reconstruction* (New York: 1879), 139.

p. 249   "All is going," *GMS*:466.

p. 249   "one of the," *CWL*-6:230.

p. 249   "an atrocious act," Williams, *Lincoln and His Generals,* 231.

p. 250   "For me," *CWL*-6:383.

p. 250   "Why has," New York *Times,* 5-26-63.

p. 250   "Without the stimulus," *OR*-1-24-2:177.

p. 250   "two picking," Andrew Hickenlooper, "The Vicksburg Mine," *BL*-3:541–542.

p. 251   "swollen ankles," *OR*-1-24-3:392.

p. 251   "indifference," *OR*-1-24-3:175.

p. 251   "Oh, that don't," *GMS*:458.

p. 251 "It is a difficult," Carter, *The Final Fortress*, 272.

p. 251 "If I cut," *OR*-1-24-3:974.

p. 252 "Don't be uneasy," Symonds, *Joseph E. Johnston*, 214–215.

p. 252 "Negotiations," *OR*-1-24-3:980.

p. 252 "and thus enable," *OR*-1-24-3:987.

p. 252 "I have," *OR*-1-24-1:283.

p. 253 "The useless effusion," *ibid.*

p. 253 "Those terms stated," Earl Schenk Miers, *The Web of Victory: Grant at Vicksburg* (New York: 1955), 290–291.

p. 253 "The conference," *PMG*:329.

p. 253 "I can assure," John C. Pemberton, "The Terms of Surrender," *BL*-3:544.

p. 253 "Very well," *PMG*:329–330.

p. 253 "Had I insisted," *ibid.*

p. 254 "in the main," *OR*-1-24-1:284–285.

p. 254 "The terms proposed," *ibid.*

CHAPTER 12. THE LAST FULL MEASURE OF DEVOTION

p. 257 "The enemy is advancing," Warren W. Hassler, Jr., *Crisis at the Crossroads: The First Day at Gettysburg* (Tuscaloosa: 1970), 37.

p. 257 "Forward, men," Edwin B. Coddington, *The Gettysburg Campaign: A Study in Command* (New York: 1968), 269.

p. 258 "There are those," Hassler, *Crisis at the Crossroads*, 52.

p. 258 "Throw down," Wheeler, *Witness to Gettysburg*, 131.

p. 259 "I am not prepared," *LL*-3:86.

p. 260 "foaming," Champ Clark, *Gettysburg: The Confederate High Tide* (Alexandria, Va.: 1985), 62.

p. 261 "grew hot," Hassler, *Crisis at the Crossroads*, 122.

p. 262 "I think," E. P. Halstead, "Incidents of the First Day at Gettysburg," *BL*-3:285.

p. 263 "You see," *LL*-3:93.

p. 263 "if practicable," *OR*-1-27-2:318.

p. 263 "Can't you," *REL*-3:79–80.

p. 263 "Then perhaps," *ibid.*

p. 264 "Well, Longstreet," *ibid.*

p. 264 "Oh, my God," Tillie Pierce Alleman, *At Gettysburg: Or What a Girl Saw and Heard of the Battle, A True Narrative* (New York: 1889).

p. 265 "Help me, doctor," Joseph Persico, *My Enemy, My Brother: Men and Days of Gettysburg* (New York: 1977), 119.

p. 265 "We thought," Albertus McCreary, "Gettysburg: A Boy's Experience of the Battle," *McClure's Magazine*, July, 1909.

p. 267 "No," James Longstreet, "Lee's Right Wing at Gettysburg," *BL*-3:339–340.

p. 268 "Oh, generals," *OR*-1-27-1:130.

p. 268 "Certainly," Daniel E. Sickles, "The Meade-Sickles Controversy," *BL*-3:419.

p. 269 "Wait," John Gibbon, *Personal Recollections of the Civil War* (New York: 1928), 136.

p. 269 "stuck out," *TCW*-2:496.

p. 269 "Warren!" Pfanz, *Gettysburg: The Second Day*, 201.

p. 269 "General!" Cleaves, *Meade of Gettysburg*, 148.

p. 269 "I will withdraw," W. A. Swanberg, *Sickles the Incredible* (New York: 1956), 212.

p. 270 "I wish," Coddington, *The Gettysburg Campaign*, 346.

p. 270   "General," Burke Davis, *Jeb Stuart: The Last Cavalier* (New York: 1957), 334.

p. 270   "I have brought," *ibid.*

p. 271   "as though," Editors of Time-Life Books, *Voices of the Civil War: Gettysburg* (Alexandria, Va.: 1995), 105.

p. 271   "We'll be putting," Pierce Alleman, *At Gettysburg.*

p. 272   "Fix bayonets," Pfanz, *Gettysburg: The Second Day,* 167.

p. 272   "with the noise," Wheeler, *Witness to Gettysburg,* 187.

p. 274   "By this time," Time-Life Books, *Voices of the Civil War: Gettysburg,* 81.

p. 275   "As we reached," Porter Farley, "General Warren Seizes Little Round Top," *BG-2*:612–613.

p. 275   "I saw that," Glenn Tucker, *Hancock the Superb* (Indianapolis: 1960), 144.

p. 276   "My God!" Pfanz, *Gettysburg: The Second Day,* 410–411.

p. 276   "Every man realized," Clark, *Gettysburg,* 109.

p. 277   "We have not," *REL-3*:105 n70.

p. 278   "was one solid," Clark, *Gettysburg,* 116.

p. 278   "Such then," John Gibbon, "The Council of War on the Second Day," *BL-3*:314.

p. 278   "General, I have," *LL-3*:144.

p. 278   "No, I am," Longstreet, "Lee's Right Wing at Gettysburg," *BL-3*:342.

p. 278   "General, it is," *LL-3*:144–145.

p. 278   "[T]hese poor boys," George R. Stewart, *Pickett's Charge: A Microhistory of the Final Attack at Gettysburg* (Boston: 1959), 108.

p. 278   "With my knowledge," Longstreet, "Lee's Right Wing at Gettysburg," *BL-3*:343.

p. 278   "Never was I," *REL-3*:109.

p. 281   "You craven fool!" Cleaves, *Meade of Gettysburg,* 160.

p. 282   "as still," Stewart, *Pickett's Charge,* 100.

p. 283   "All we had," *ibid.,* 141.

p. 283   "For God's sake," Alexander, *Military Memoirs of a Confederate,* 423.

p. 283   "General, shall I," *LL-3*:155.

p. 283   "My feelings," *ibid.*

p. 283   "I shall lead," *ibid.*

p. 284   "You'ns load," Urwin, *Custer Victorious,* 76.

p. 284   "Great heavens!" *ibid.,* 79.

p. 284   "Come on," *ibid.,* 80.

p. 285   "The two columns," *ibid.,* 79.

p. 285   "For a moment," *ibid.,* 81.

p. 285   "Advance slowly," Stewart, *Pickett's Charge,* 170.

p. 285   "Don't forget," *LL-3*:157.

p. 285   "remember your wives," Stewart, *Pickett's Charge,* 170.

p. 285   "Forward!" *ibid.*

p. 285   "A passage," *TCW-2*:537.

p. 285   "June Kimball," Stewart, *Pickett's Charge,* 96.

p. 286   "Here they come!" Edmund Rice, "Repelling Lee's Last Blow at Gettysburg," *BL-3*:387.

p. 286   "Beautiful," Stewart, *Pickett's Charge,* 182.

p. 286   "underwent," Clark, *Gettysburg,* 139.

p. 286   "Steady," Stewart, *Pickett's Charge,* 198.

p. 286   "Home!" *ibid.,* 199.

p. 287   "Come on," Time-Life Books, *Voices of the Civil War: Gettysburg,* 108.

p. 287   "For about," Stewart, *Pickett's Charge,* 248.

p. 287   "All this," *TFD*:214–215.

p. 287   "General Lee," *REL*-3:129–130.

p. 287   "Come, General Pickett," *ibid.*

p. 288   "How is it," Cleaves, *Meade of Gettysburg,* 165.

p. 288   "I believe, General," *ibid.*

p. 288   "What!" *ibid.,* 166.

p. 288   "General, this has," John D. Imboden, "The Confederate Retreat from Gettysburg," *BL*-3:421–422.

CHAPTER 13. RETREAT, RAID, AND RIOT

p. 289   "It seems," Richards, "A Woman's Diary of the Siege of Vicksburg," *Century Magazine,* September, 1885, 774.

p. 289   "The officers spoke," Wheeler, *The Siege of Vicksburg,* 233.

p. 290   "There is no," New York *Tribune,* 7-15-63.

p. 290   "That was a happy," *ICW*:200–201.

p. 291   "Scarcely one," Imboden, "The Confederate Retreat from Gettysburg," *BL*-3:423–424.

p. 292   "We would cover," Time-Life Books, *Voices of the Civil War: Gettysburg,* 142.

p. 293   "We had them," *DJH*:66–67.

p. 293   "He has made," *DGW*-1:374.

p. 293   "Important from Gettysburg," Richmond *Sentinel,* 7-7-63.

p. 294   "Gettysburg has shaken," *ICW*:84.

p. 294   "Yes, from want," Josiah Gorgas (Frank Vandiver, ed.), *The Civil War Diary of Josiah Gorgas* (Tuscaloosa: 1947), 50.

p. 295   "The inhabitants," *OR*-1-24-2:529.

p. 296   "Forty thousand boxes," John Beatty, *Memoirs of a Volunteer* (New York: 1946), 182.

p. 296   "There is a," *OR*-1-23-2:95.

p. 298   "Then you propose," *OR*-1-23-1:621–622.

p. 298   "I do," *ibid.*

p. 298   "Lee's army overthrown," *OR*-1-23-2:518.

p. 302   "We are to give," New York *Herald,* 7-12-63.

p. 302   "makes you feel," Adrian Cook, *The Armies of the Street: The New York City Draft Riots of 1863* (Lexington: 1974), 59.

p. 302   "Here comes," *ibid.,* 63.

p. 303   "Down with," *TFD*:240.

p. 303   "Burn," Cook, *Armies of the Street,* 77.

p. 303   "New York is," *OR*-1-27-2:887.

p. 304   "Down with," Cook, *Armies of the Street,* 117.

p. 305   "Three objects," *TCW*-2:636.

p. 305   "The town," Herman Melville, "The House-top. A Night Piece," in Hennig Cohen, ed., *The Battle Pieces of Herman Melville* (New York: 1963), 89–90.

p. 305   "Houses," *TCW*-2:637.

p. 308   "a subtle languor," Emilio, *A Brave Black Regiment,* 49.

p. 308   "enough," Gooding (Adams, ed.), *On the Altar of Freedom,* 27.

p. 308   "our boys," *ibid.,* 30.

p. 308   "Are we *soldiers,*" *ibid.,* 119.

p. 308   "God has protected," Peter Burchard, *One Gallant Rush: Robert Gould Shaw and His Brave Black Regiment* (New York: 1965), 130.

p. 309   "Don't fire," Emilio, *A Brave Black Regiment*, 77.

p. 309   "I want you," *ibid.*, 78.

p. 309   "We have buried," Peter M. Chaitin, *The Coastal War: Chesapeake Bay to Rio Grande* (Alexandria, Va.: 1984), 128.

p. 309   "We can imagine," Geoffrey C. Ward, *The Civil War: An Illustrated History* (New York: 1990), 248.

p. 310   "It is not," New York *Tribune*, 9-8-63.

p. 310   "She comes from," *RR*-7:100.

p. 310   "The Father," *CWL*-6:409.

p. 311   "John Morgan's raid," Chicago *Tribune*, 7-16-63.

p. 312   "Mr. Secretary," *RWC*-1:380–381.

p. 312   "one of unexampled," Kean (Younger, ed.), *Inside the Confederate Government*, 79.

p. 312   "Events," Gorgas (Vandiver, ed.), *Diary*, 55.

p. 312   "General Rains," *OR*-1-24-1:200.

p. 313   "There is," Thomas Goodrich, *Bloody Dawn: The Story of the Lawrence Massacre* (Kent, Ohio.: 1991), 23.

p. 314   "Kill!" Albert Castel, *William Clarke Quantrill: His Life and Times* (New York: 1962), 126–128.

p. 314   "Oh God!" Goodrich, *Bloody Dawn*, 131.

p. 315   "What a wonderful," *NCR*:226.

p. 317   "You have only," *TCW*-2:700.

p. 317   "My debility," *ibid*.

p. 318   "Often he sat," Edward D.C. Campbell, Jr., "The Eccentric Genius of Conrad Wise Chapman," *Virginia Cavalcade*, Spring 1988, 175.

p. 318   "subtly ominous," Harold Holzer and Mark E. Neely, Jr., "Portrait of a City Under Siege," *Military History Quarterly*, Autumn 1995, 102.

p. 320   "A scene at sunrise," Holzer and Neely, Jr., *Mine Eyes Have Seen the Glory*, 39.

p. 320   "You are dissatisfied," *CWL*-6:406–410.

CHAPTER 14. A MAD, IRREGULAR BATTLE

p. 323   "Brilliant campaigns," Henry Cist, *The Army of The Cumberland* (New York: 1882), 170.

p. 324   "He shall not," *EG*:295.

p. 324   "Whenever," *OR*-1-23-2:585.

p. 324   "It was the same," *CH*:93.

p. 324   "He was silent," Daniel H. Hill, "Chickamauga—The Great Battle of the West," *BL*-3:639.

p. 325   "It is said," *ibid.*, 641.

p. 325   "The want," *ibid.*, 640.

p. 326   "It's our gunners," Peter Cozzens, *This Terrible Sound* (Urbana, Ill.: 1992), 36.

p. 326   "the longest prayer," *ibid*.

p. 327   "Far beyond," *TCW*-2:688.

p. 327   "Chattanooga is ours," *OR*-1-30-3:407.

p. 327   "in our grip," *ibid.*, 479.

p. 329   "The weather," *LL*-3:228.

p. 329   "God bless," Mary B. Chesnut (C. Vann Woodward, ed.), *Mary Chesnut's Civil War* (New Haven: 1981), 469–470.

p. 330   "The above movements," *OR*-1-30-2:31.

p. 331 "A mad, irregular," *NCR*:246.
p. 331 "Although closer," *RCW*:112–113.
p. 331 "nigh out about," W.F.G. Shanks, *Personal Recollections of Distinguished Generals* (New York: 1866), 266.
p. 332 "General, it has," Frank Moore, ed., *The Civil War in Song and Story* (New York: 1889), 343.
p. 332 "There was no," Hill, "Chickamauga—The Great Battle of the West," *BL*-3:650–651.
p. 332 "There was no generalship," *TCW*-2:717.
p. 333 "Strengthen the left," *RCW*:112.
p. 336 "It is ominous," Glenn Tucker, *Chickamauga: Bloody Battle in the West* (Indianapolis: 1961), 203.
p. 336 "the world never," Cozzens, *This Terrible Sound,* 305.
p. 336 "I did not," Tucker, *Chickamauga,* 204.
p. 337 "Sir, this is," Cozzens, *This Terrible Sound,* 309.
p. 337 "What is," Tucker, *Chickamauga,* 207.
p. 338 "If Brannan goes," *EG*:343.
p. 339 "I was awakened," *RCW*:115.
p. 340 "If you care," Tucker, *Chickamauga,* 307.
p. 340 "Rosecrans should," Cist, *The Army of The Cumberland,* 225.
p. 341 "we were not," James Longstreet, *From Manassas to Appomattox* (Philadelphia: 1896), 451.
p. 341 "There is not," *ibid.,* 452.
p. 341 "From accounts," Longstreet, *From Manassas to Appomattox,* p. 452.
p. 342 "hewn," Freeman Cleaves, *Rock of Chickamauga: The Life of General George H. Thomas* (Norman, Okla.: 1948), 179.
p. 342 "Tell me," Tucker, *Chickamauga,* 345.
p. 342 "Why the hell," J. S. Fullerton, "Reinforcing Thomas at Chickamauga," *BL*-3:666.
p. 343 "ugliest sound," Ambrose Bierce (William McCann, ed.), *Ambrose Bierce's Civil War* (Gateway editions, Chicago: 1956), 37.
p. 343 "At this hour," Beatty, *Memoirs,* 252–254.
p. 343 "Everything had fallen," *CH*:109–110.
p. 344 "It did not occur," Hill, "Chickamauga—The Great Battle of the West," *BL*-3:659n.
p. 344 "Do you know," James Lee McDonough, *Chattanooga—A Death Grip on the Confederacy* (Knoxville: 1984), 23.
p. 344 "How can I?" Tucker, *Chickamauga,* 392.
p. 345 "Genl: We are," Brian Steel Wills, *A Battle from the Start: The Life of Nathan Bedford Forrest* (New York: 1992), 142.
p. 345 "We can get," *ibid.*
p. 345 "What does he fight," *ibid.*

CHAPTER 15. STARVATION CAMP
p. 347 "Our fate," *OR*-1-30-1:161.
p. 349 "This is starvation camp," *MTWF*:101.
p. 349 "Crackers!" *OR*-1-30-1:221.
p. 349 "dawdles," *OR*-1-30-1:218–219.
p. 349 "We must put our trust," *OR*-1-30-4:307.
p. 349 "I cannot remember," *CH*:113–114.

p. 350   "Our chief," *OR*-1-30-4:706.

p. 350   "You have played," Wills, *A Battle from the Start,* 146–147.

p. 350   "Now you are in for it!" *ibid.*

p. 350   "The man is ignorant," McDonough, *Chattanooga,* 32.

p. 352   "He who sows," *OR*-30-1-4:744.

p. 352   "Well, Rosecrans," *DJH:*92.

p. 352   "the rebellion," *OR*-30-1-1:148.

p. 352   "Damn Jonesboro," Bates, *Lincoln in the Telegraph Office,* 202.

p. 353   "confused and stunned," *DJH:*106.

p. 354   "We were convinced," *LL*-3:241.

p. 354   "It was as fine," *REL*-3:182–183.

p. 354   "A worse managed," *ibid.*

p. 355   "I made the attack," *OR*-1-29-1:427.

p. 355   "Well, well, General," *LL*-3:247.

p. 356   "of a diplomatic," *OR*-1-26-1:673.

p. 356   "I am frightened," *GTC:*26.

p. 357   "By direction," *OR*-1-30-4:404.

p. 357   "Hold Chattanooga," *OR*-1-30-4:479.

p. 357   "one genuine American," David H. Donald, *Lincoln* (New York: 1995) 455.

p. 359   "Fathers, save us," Gray, *The Hidden Civil War,* 150.

p. 359   "Glory to God," Benjamin P. Thomas, *Abraham Lincoln* (New York: 1952), 399.

p. 359   "to reinforce," *CWL*-6:424.

p. 360   "He has a good," Hudson Strode, *Jefferson Davis, Confederate President* (New York: 1952), 489.

p. 361   "He has done more," Williams, *Napoleon in Gray,* 199.

p. 361   "in any act," *ibid.*

p. 361   "Mr. Aiken's," Chesnut (Williams, ed.), *Diary from Dixie,* 322.

p. 362   "Among the many," *ORN*-1-15:13.

p. 362   "the press," *RWC*-2:90–91.

p. 362   "He was seated," William S. McFeely, *Grant: A Biography* (New York: 1981), 143.

p. 363   "My only wonder," *PMG:*354.

p. 363   "I never drink," *GTC:*37.

p. 363   "Neither do I," *ibid.*

p. 363   "immovable as a rock," Horace Porter, *Campaigning with Grant* (New York: 1897), 4–5.

p. 365   "Pull in!" *GTC:*52.

p. 365   "God da—!" *MTWF:*121.

p. 365   "It was as fine," Alfred L. Hough (Robert G. Athearn, ed.), *Soldier in the West: The Civil War Letters of Alfred Lacey Hough* (Philadelphia: 1957), 162.

p. 365   "We've knocked," *GTC:*53.

p. 367   "The question," *OR*-1-31-1:56.

p. 367   "I was hungrier," *MTWF:*164.

p. 368   "The living," Fannie Oslin Jackson (Joan F. Curran and Rudena K. Mallory, eds.), *On Both Sides of the Line* (Kansas City: 1989), 33–39.

p. 368   "There is not," *MTWF:*164–166.

p. 368   "We need," *MTWF:*166.

p. 369   "a chart and compass," Thomas, *Abraham Lincoln,* 403.

p. 369   "true and noble," Oates, *With Malice Toward None,* 360.

CHAPTER 16. OF NAMELESS GRAVES ON BATTLE-PLAINS

p. 371 "Hath not the morning," Henry Timrod, "Ethnogenesis," in Ed Winfield Parks and Aileen Wells Parks, eds., *The Collected Poems of Henry Timrod* (Athens, Ga.: 1965), 92.

p. 372 "feed your country's," Timrod, "A Cry to Arms," *ibid.*, 108.

p. 372 "ten times ten," Timrod, "Carolina," *ibid.*, 111.

p. 372 "The rain is plashing," Timrod, "The Unknown Dead," *ibid.*, 126–127.

p. 375 "imposing," *LWY*-2:455.

p. 376 "That speech," Ward Hill Lamon (Dorothy Lamon Teillard, ed.), *Recollections of Abraham Lincoln, 1847–1865* (Washington: 1911), 169–179.

p. 378 "That speech did indeed," *TCW*-2:833.

p. 379 "sustained considerable loss," *OR*-1-31-2:677.

p. 380 "Two more nights," *GTC*:65.

p. 382 "I can do it," *MTWF*:157.

p. 383 "It was an inspiring," Joseph S. Fullerton, "The Army of the Cumberland at Chattanooga," *BL*-3:721.

p. 383 "You have gained," Cleaves, *Rock of Chickamauga,* 195.

p. 384 "Not a word," *MTWF*:193.

p. 386 "The rebels broke," Peter Cozzens, *The Shipwreck of Their Hopes* (Urbana, Ill.: 1994), 177.

p. 387 "I did not stop," *MTWF*:228.

p. 387 "It is all poetry," *MTWF*:230.

p. 388 "Still they advance," Samuel T. Foster (Norman D. Brown, ed.), *One of Cleburne's Command: The Civil War Reminiscences and Diary of Capt. Samuel T. Foster, Granbury's Texas Brigade, CSA* (Austin, Tx.: 1980), 62–63.

p. 388 "The general was in," Carl S. Schurz, *Reminiscences,* Vol. 3 (New York: 1907), 75.

p. 389 "Boys, get away," William C. Davis, *Breckinridge: Statesman, Soldier, Symbol* (Baton Rouge: 1973), 390.

p. 390 "Now is your time," Cleaves, *Rock of Chickamauga,* 197.

p. 390 "I noticed," Arthur M. Manigault, *A Carolinian Goes to War* (Columbia, S.C.: 1983), 138.

p. 391 "All order," *ibid.*, 137.

p. 391 "Who ordered," Fullerton, "The Army of the Cumberland at Chattanooga," *BL*-3:725.

p. 391 "At times," *ibid.*

p. 392 "Those defending," Cleaves, *Rock of Chickamauga,* 199.

p. 392 "Such a confused mass," Cozzens, *The Shipwreck of Their Hopes,* 294.

p. 392 "Stop, don't disgrace," *MTWF*:312.

p. 392 "Here is your commander!" *CH*:117.

p. 392 "And here's," Judith Hallock, *Braxton Bragg and Confederate Defeat* (Tuscaloosa: 1991), Vol. 2, 141.

p. 392 "[He] looked," *CH*:118.

p. 393 "I am going," Fullerton, "The Army of the Cumberland at Chattanooga," *BL*-3:726.

p. 394 "I was much disappointed," Sheridan, *Personal Memoirs,* Vol. 1, 316–318.

p. 394 "Had it not," *OR*-1-31-2:35.

p. 395 "My troops," *TCW*-2:866.

p. 395 "Understanding," *OR*-1-31-2:51.

p. 395 "Damn the battle," *OR*-1-31-2:340.

p. 396 "For the first time," Richmond *Daily Dispatch,* 12-3-63.

p. 396 "No satisfactory excuse," *OR*-1-31-2:666.

p. 396 "my shameful," *OR*-1-52-2:745.

CHAPTER 17. THE NEW RECKONING

p. 399   "I am conscious," Cleaves, *Meade of Gettysburg*, 212.

p. 399   "I do not think," Williams, *Lincoln and His Generals*, 290.

p. 399   "I am too old," Charles S. Venable, "General Lee in the Wilderness Campaign," *BL*-4:240.

p. 401   "I have never," Kean (Younger, ed.), *Inside the Confederate Government*, 119.

p. 401   "mainly due," *LWY*-2:496–497.

p. 402   "This is one," Oates, *With Malice Toward None*, 367.

p. 404   "Thus we have," *CWL*-7:50.

p. 404   "In the midst," *CWL*-7:52-53.

p. 404   "We only wanted," *DJH*:131–132;

p. 404   "Men talked," *ibid*.

p. 404   "I am very glad," *CWL*-7:24.

p. 405   "Having begun," *RR*-8:264-279.

p. 405   "We who have," *LWY*-2:489.

p. 405   "the imbecile," *LWY*-2:488.

p. 405   "gross misconduct," *JD*:529–530.

p. 406   "as if," Chesnut (Williams, ed.), *Diary from Dixie*, 332.

p. 406   "The money value," *ibid*.

p. 406   "God help," *ibid.*, 342.

p. 406   "It is," *RWC*-2:119–120.

p. 406   "He who was a man of sorrows," Ernest B. Furgurson, *Ashes of Glory: Richmond at War* (New York: 1996), 238.

p. 407   "We did not get," *ibid.*, 238.

p. 407   "Ground covered," Henry Robinson Berkeley (William H. Runge, ed.), *Four Years in the Confederate Artillery: The Diary of Henry Robinson Berkeley* (Chapel Hill: 1961), 64.

p. 407   "Just at peep," Kate Cumming (Richard B. Harwell, ed.), *Kate: The Journal of a Confederate Nurse* (Baton Rouge: 1959), 181.

p. 408   "The day has passed," Holmes (Anderson, ed.), *Brokenburn*, 269.

p. 408   "The catalogue includes," Cincinnati *Daily Enquirer*, 12-25-63.

p. 409   "Everything is twice," *Frank Leslie's Illustrated Newspaper*, 1-9-64.

p. 409   "For a war-ridden," *ibid*.

p. 409   "We are quiet," Elisha Hunt Rhodes (Robert Hunt Rhodes, ed.), *All For the Union: The Civil War Diary and Letters of Elisha Hunt Rhodes* (New York: 1991), 135–136.

p. 410   "Gayety," Leech, *Reveille in Washington*, 284.

p. 410   "fiendishly ugly," *DJH*:134.

p. 411   "You should not," Katherine Helm, *The True Story of Mary, Wife of Lincoln* (New York: 1928), 230–231.

p. 411   "Excuse me," *ibid*.

p. 411   "Your Excellency," *OR*-1-32-2:510.

p. 412   "would remove forever," *OR*-1-52-2:586–592.

p. 412   "It is something," Gooding (Adams, ed.), *On the Altar of Freedom*, 97.

p. 412   "It rained," Berkeley (Runge, ed.), *Four Years in the Confederate Artillery*, 64.

p. 412   "Eighteen sixty-three," George Templeton Strong (Allan Nevins and Milton H. Thomas, eds.), *Diary of George Templeton Strong* (New York: 1952), Vol. 3, 387.

p. 413   "It seems" Catherine Ann Devereux Edmonston (Beth G. Crabtree and James W. Patton, eds.), *Journal of a Secesh Lady: The Diary of Catherine Ann Devereux Edmonston, 1860–1866* (Raleigh: 1979), 513.

p. 414   "If the people," Leech, *Reveille in Washington*, 279.

p. 414   "the ark," Henry James, *The American Scene* (New York: 1907), 359.

INDEX

About the Author

Joseph E. Stevens, a graduate of Princeton University, lives in Santa Fe, New Mexico. His first book, *Hoover Dam: An American Adventure*, received the Western Writers of America Spur Award, the John H. Dunning Prize of the American Historical Association, and the W. Turrentine Jackson Prize of the Western History Association. He is also the author of *America's National Battlefield Parks: A Guide*.